Advanced

Financial

Accounting

**Fourth
Edition**

Advanced

Financial
Accounting

**Fourth
Edition**

Thomas H. Beechy
Schulich School of Business, York University

Elizabeth Farrell
Schulich School of Business, York University

Toronto

Canadian Cataloguing in Publication Data

Beechy, Thomas H., 1937–
    Advanced financial accounting

4th Canadian ed.
Previously published under title: Canadian advanced financial accounting.
Includes index.
ISBN 0-13-090626-3

1. Accounting.   I. Farrell, Elizabeth.   II. Title   III. Title: Canadian advanced financial accounting.

HF5635.B465   2002   657'.48   C00-933011-9

0-13-090626-3

Vice President, Editorial Director: Michael Young
Senior Acquisitions Editor: Samantha Scully
Marketing Manager: James Buchanan
Developmental Editor: Anita Smale
Production Editor: Marisa D'Andrea
Copy Editor: Gail Marsden
Production Coordinator: Deborah Starks
Page Layout: Nelson Gonzalez
Permissions Research: Susan Wallace-Cox
Art Director: Julia Hall
Interior Design: David Cheung
Cover Design: David Cheung
Cover Image: PhotoDisc

1 2 3 4 5   05 04 03 02 01

Printed and bound in Canada.

Materials from the Canadian Institute of Chartered Accountants, The Society of Management Accountants of Canada, and Institute of Chartered Accountants of Ontario are reprinted with permission.

Extract from *Financial Accounting 4 Exam* published by the Certified General Accountants Association of Canada © CGA-Canada, 2000, reprinted with permission.

Brief Contents

Preface		xv
Chapter 1	Setting the Stage	1
Chapter 2	Intercorporate Investments: An Introduction	32
Chapter 3	Business Combinations	77
Chapter 4	Wholly-Owned Subsidiaries: Reporting Subsequent to Acquisition	128
Chapter 5	Consolidation of Non-Wholly-Owned Subsidiaries	183
Chapter 6	Subsequent-Year Consolidations: General Approach	238
Chapter 7	Strategic Investments: Additional Aspects of Share Capital	317
Chapter 8	Segmented and Interim Reporting	358
Chapter 9	Foreign Currency Transactions	389
Chapter 10	Reporting Foreign Operations	429
Chapter 11	Financial Reporting for Non-Profit Organizations	491
Chapter 12	Public Sector Financial Reporting	545
Solutions to Self-Study Problems		562
Index		589

Contents

Preface   xv

Chapter 1

Setting the Stage   1

Introduction   1

The Context—Overview   2

Professional Judgement   2

Professional Judgement in Advanced
Accounting Topics   3

Applicability of GAAP   4

Form of Business Organization   5
Public vs. Private Corporations   5
Disclosed Basis of Accounting   7

Financial Reporting Objectives   9
User Objectives   9
Preparer Objectives   12
Other Objectives   16
Matrix of Objectives   17
Resolving Conflicts Among Objectives   17

Summary of Key Points   18

Weblinks   19

Review Questions   20

Cases   22

Chapter 2

**Intercorporate Investments:
An Introduction**   32

Introduction   32

Branch Accounting   33

Definition of Intercorporate Investments   33

Portfolio Investments—A Quick Review   34

Strategic Intercorporate Investments   35
Controlled Subsidiaries   35
Significantly Influenced Affiliates   40
Joint Ventures   41

Reporting Investments in Affiliates and
Subsidiaries   42
Cost-Basis Reporting   42
Equity-Basis Reporting   42
Consolidation   43
Reporting versus Recording Methods   44

Example of Accounting for Strategic
Investments   45
Consolidation When the Cost Method Is Used 46
The Equity Method   52

Unconsolidated Statements   57

Limitations of Consolidated Statements   57

Summary of Accounting for Intercorporate
Investments   59

Summary of Key Points   60

Weblinks   61

Self-Study Problem   62

Review Questions   63

Cases   65

Problems   69

Chapter 3

Business Combinations   77

Introduction   77

Definition of a Business Combination   77

Accounting for Business Combinations—
General Approach   78
Measuring the Cost   78
Determining Fair Values   79
Allocating the Cost   80

Illustration of a Direct Purchase of Net Assets 81

Purchase of Shares   83
Reasons for Purchasing Shares   83
Share Exchanges   85
Illustration of a Share Exchange   87

Alternative Approaches to Reporting
Business Combinations   88

Overview	88
Pooling of Interests	89
Purchase Method	91
New-Entity Method	91
Other Approaches	92
Purchase vs. Pooling	92
Current Canadian Practice	93
Corporate Restructurings—Non-Arm's-Length Pooling	94
International Practices for Business Combinations	94
Consolidation Procedures	96
Direct Method	96
Worksheet Method	97
Negative Goodwill	99
Disclosure	101
Recording Fair Values: Push-Down Accounting	102
Summary of Key Points	104
Weblinks	105
Self-Study Problem	106
Appendix: Income Tax Allocation	107
Introduction	107
Temporary Differences in Business Combinations	108
Unrecognized Tax Loss Carryforwards	110
Equity-Basis Reporting	111
Review Questions	111
Cases	114
Problems	120

Equity-Basis Reporting of Non-Consolidated Subsidiaries	140
Comparison of Consolidation vs. Equity Reporting	142
Discontinued Operations and Extraordinary Items	144
Consolidation in Second Subsequent Year	145
Basic Information	145
Direct Method	145
Worksheet Approach	150
Completed Consolidated Financial Statements	153
Alternative Presentation of Goodwill Amortization	153
Note Disclosure	155
Consolidating Parent-Founded Subsidiaries	156
Indirect Holdings	157
Summary of Key Points	157
Weblinks	158
Self-Study Problems	159
Appendix: Income Tax Allocation Subsequent to Acquisition	162
Introduction and Review	162
Post-Acquisition Tax Accounting for Fair Value Increments	162
Unrealized Profit	164
Summary	165
Review Questions	165
Cases	166
Problems	170

Contents

viii

Chapter 4

Wholly-Owned Subsidiaries: Reporting Subsequent to Acquisition	**128**
Introduction	128
Consolidation One Year After Acquisition	128
Basic Information	129
Amortization of Fair Value Increments	131
Unrealized Profits	132
Direct Method	133
Worksheet Approach	137

Chapter 5

Consolidation of Non-Wholly-Owned Subsidiaries	**183**
Introduction	183
Conceptual Alternatives	183
Illustration of the Alternative Approaches	185
Summary of Consolidation Approaches	190
Consolidation at Date of Acquisition	190
Direct Method	190
Worksheet Approach	192
Consolidation One Year after Acquisition	193

Basic Information 193
Direct Method 194
Worksheet Approach 200

Consolidation in Second Subsequent Year 202
Direct Method 204
Worksheet Approach 207

The Next Steps 210

Summary of Key Points 210

Weblinks 210

Self-Study Problems 211

Review Questions 216

Cases 217

Problems 223

Chapter 6

**Subsequent-Year Consolidations:
General Approach** **238**

Introduction 238

Intercompany Sale of Long-Term Assets 239
General Concept 239
Downstream Sales of Amortizable Assets 240
Upstream Sales of Amortizable Assets 242
Direct Amortization 243
Subsequent Sale of Capital Assets Acquired
Intercompany 245

Subsequent-Year Consolidations—General
Approach 245
Basic Conceptual Approach 246
Basic Information 247
A Caveat for Students 250
Direct Approach 250
Worksheet Approach 256

Equity-Basis Reporting 261

Consolidation with Equity-Basis Recording 263

Extraordinary Items and Discontinued
Operations 265

Summary of Key Points 265

Weblinks 266

Self-Study Problems 267

Appendix: Intercompany Bond Holdings 268

Intercompany Bond Transactions 268
Indirect Acquisitions of Bonds 269
Non-Wholly-Owned Subsidiaries 271
Subsidiary Purchase of Parent's Bonds 273
Summary 274
Self-Study Problem (Appendix) 275
Review Questions 275
Cases 276
Problems 284

Chapter 7

**Strategic Investments: Additional
Aspects of Share Capital** **317**

Introduction 317

Preferred and Restricted Shares of Investee
Corporations 318
Introduction 318
Effect of Preferred Shares on Investor's
Ownership Interest 318
Investment in Preferred Shares 320
Restricted Shares 320

Changes in Ownership Interest 322
Step Purchases 322
Increases in Equity-Basis Investments 327
Acquisition of Significant Influence 327

Decreases in Ownership Interest 328
Sale of Part of an Investment 328
Issuance of Shares by Subsidiary 330
Summary of Key Points 332

Weblinks 333

Self-Study Problems 333

Review Questions 335

Cases 336

Problems 342

Chapter 8

Segmented and Interim Reporting **358**
Introduction 358

Segmented Reporting 358

Introduction   358
Applicability   359
Operating Segments   360
Enterprise-Wide Disclosures   363
Examples of Segmented Reporting   365

Interim Reporting   366
Introduction   366
General Principles of Application   368
The Periodicity Problem   370
Discrete Approach   371
Integral Approach   371
Application in Practice   372
Illustrative Interim Statement   374
Summary of Key Points   380
Weblinks   381
Review Questions   382
Cases   383
Problems   384

Chapter 9

Foreign Currency Transactions   **389**
Introduction   389

Foreign Currency Transactions   389
Causes of Exchange Rate Changes   390
Transactions and Current Balances   391
Long-Term Balances   396

Accounting for Hedges   400
Nature of Hedging   400
Hedge Accounting Recommendations—
Old versus Proposed   402
Hedging a Monetary Position   402
Hedging a Commitment   410
Implicit Hedges   412
Imperfect Hedges   414
Summary of Key Points   415
Weblinks   416
Self-Study Problems   417
Review Questions   418
Cases   420
Problems   422

Chapter 10

Reporting Foreign Operations   **429**
Introduction   429

Translation Methods   429
Temporal Method   430
Monetary/Nonmonetary Method   433
Relationship of Temporal Method to
Transaction Accounting   433
Current-Rate Method   435
Current/Noncurrent Method   436
Summary of Translation Methods   437

Accounting Exposure vs.
Economic Exposure   438

Alternatives for Reporting Translation
Gains and Losses   440
Immediate Recognition   440
Disaggregation   442
Deferral   442

The Two Solitudes: Integrated vs.
Self-Sustaining Operations   443
Integrated Foreign Operations   444
Self-Sustaining Foreign Operations   445
Operations in Hyper-Inflationary Economies   446

Application of Section 1650
Recommendations   446
Integrated Operations   446
Self-Sustaining Operations   447
Extending the Example   447

Comparison of Accounting Implications   454
Summary of Key Points   455
Weblinks   456
Self-Study Problems   456
Review Questions   458
Cases   460
Problems   473

Chapter 11

**Financial Reporting for Non-Profit
Organizations**   **491**
Introduction   491

Overview of Non-Business Organizations 491

Characteristics of Non-Profit Organizations 492
No Owners 493
A Different "Bottom Line" 493
Relationship Between Revenue and Costs 494

Objectives of Financial Reporting 495

Primary Reporting Issues 496
Expense versus Expenditure Reporting 496
Capital Assets 498
Segregation of Resources 499
Donated Goods and Services 500
Accounting for Pledges 501
Accounting for a Collection 501
Defining the Reporting Entity 502
Consolidated or Combined Statements 503

GAAP for Non-Profit Organizations 504

Types of Financial Statements 505

Reporting Options 505
Traditional Method 505
CICA Handbook Methods 506

Illustration of Reporting Methods 512
Deferral Method 512
Restricted Fund Method 513

The Chore of Users: Unravelling GAAP 514

Budgetary Control and Encumbrance
Accounting 515
Budgetary Control Accounts 516
The Encumbrance System 516

A Final Example 517

Summary of Key Points 521

Appendix: Fund Accounting 524
Introduction 524
Purpose of Fund Accounting 525
Types of Funds 525

Account Groups 527
Fund Accounting and the Segregation
of Funds 528
Interfund Transfers 528

Summary of Key Points 529

Weblinks 530

Review Questions 530

Cases 532

Chapter 12

Public Sector Financial Reporting **545**

Introduction 545

Contrast Between NPOs and Governments 545

Public Sector Reporting Standards 546
The Compliance Issue 548

Objectives of Governmental Reporting 549

Qualitative Characteristics 550

Types of Financial Statements 551

Major Reporting Issues 553
Cash vs. Accrual 553
Expense vs. Expenditure Basis 554
Capital Assets 555
Consolidation and the Reporting Entity 556
Restricted Assets and Revenues 557
Liability Measurement 558
Other Issues 558

Summary of Key Points 559

Weblinks 560

Review Questions 560

Cases 561

Solutions to Self-Study Problems 562

Index 589

About the Authors

Thomas H. Beechy, DBA, CPA (Illinois)

Thomas H. Beechy (Tom) is Professor Emeritus of Accounting at the Schulich School of Business, York University. He has been an active accounting textbook author since the early 1980s, when he wrote the first edition of *Canadian Advanced Financial Accounting*, the first completely Canadian textbook above the introductory level. Tom was born, raised, and educated in the USA, but came to Canada in 1971. He holds degrees from The George Washington University (BA), Northwestern University (MBA), and Washington University (DBA). He also is a Certified Public Accountant in the state of Illinois. Prior to migrating to Canada, he taught at Northwestern University, Illinois Institute of Technology, and Washington University. At the Schulich School of Business, Professor Beechy was Associate Dean for 12 years and has served in a variety of other capacities including BBA Program Director, Executive Director of International Relations, and Executive Director of the York-CGA International Business Research Program. Tom loves to travel, and often can be found in Asia or Europe. He is a classical music fanatic, but he also likes piano jazz and live theatre.

Elizabeth Farrell, CA

Elizabeth Farrell is Adjunct Professor of Accounting at the Schulich School of Business, York University. In recognition of her excellence in teaching, she was selected as the winner of the 1999 Seymour Schulich Award for Teaching Excellence. Professor Farrell holds degrees from Queen's University (BA/BPHE) and York University (MBA). Elizabeth is actively involved in professional accounting education. She has served as a member of the Education, Program, Administration and Examination Committee for the Institute of Chartered Accountants of Ontario. In addition, she was their representative for the Ontario government mathematics expert panel for secondary curriculum reform. Her other publications include an accounting case analysis software package, study guide, professional development courses, a variety of case material, and other publications. She also enjoys snowboarding.

Preface

Welcome to *Advanced Financial Accounting, Fourth Edition*! Since the first edition was published in 1984, many tens of thousands of students have learned about business combinations, consolidations, international operations, and non-business accounting through this text. The fourth edition has been eagerly anticipated by many past users of the book, not the least of whom are the authors themselves!

Users of the earlier editions will immediately see that this book is more than just a revision—it is a complete rewrite. The book has been dramatically shortened and reorganized to fit more comfortably into the standard one-semester framework of an advanced accounting course.

Instead of 18 chapters in the previous edition, there now are 12. The early chapters have been condensed into a single large chapter; consolidations and business combinations have been reduced from seven chapters to six and brought forward in the book; international operations has been reduced from three chapters to two; and non-business organizations has been condensed into two chapters.

Despite the dramatic shortening of the book, the essential characteristics that have distinguished the earlier editions have been retained:

- a balanced, critical analysis of alternatives rather than a cookbook approach,

- extensive emphasis on the crucial role of judgement in accounting,

- in procedural discussions, an emphasis on the way companies *really* do their accounting,

- a balance between preparers' and users' viewpoints and concerns,

- self-study problems to help students understand the technical material, and

- a broad range of assignment materials, from highly judgemental cases to very practical problems and exercises with varying levels of challenge.

Chapter 1 presents the framework for accounting decisions. This is not the usual brief introductory chapter, but instead is the foundation for all that follows. It should not be ignored, because later chapters build on the base of Chapter 1. For some students, the material in this chapter will be familiar. But many others will not have encountered the basic structure of criteria and objectives that form the context for all accounting decisions in financial reporting. The objectives of financial reporting are especially important. All preparers and users of financial information should have a sophisticated understanding of the various objectives and of the potential conflicts between different objectives.

Although the primary emphasis in Chapter 1 is on corporate reporting, partnership accounting and the applicability of a disclosed basis of accounting are also discussed.

Chapters 2 through 7 comprise the core of the book—the topic of business combinations and consolidations that is the principal topic of all advanced financial accounting courses. There are some major revisions in these chapters that should make the book even more user-friendly than it already was.

Probably the most far-reaching of the changes is the methodology for consolidation. In response to many requests, we have used the *direct approach*, in addition to a worksheet (or *spreadsheet*) approach. Every example is illustrated first by the direct approach and then by a spreadsheet approach. Some readers will find the more intuitive direct approach to be more to their liking, while others will prefer the discipline of the spreadsheet approach. Using two approaches does introduce redundancy into each example, illustrating the consolidation process from two different viewpoints.

However, it is quite possible to study the material by focusing solely on one of the two methods. If a student finds the direct approach more understandable, then he or she may skip over the spreadsheet approach and work only with the direct approach. The reverse also is true—the direct approach can be skipped and only the spreadsheet approach used.

We also have simplified the worksheet or spreadsheet technique, compared to the previous edition. We have retained the three-column separation of eliminating and adjusting entries in order to retain the distinction among the time frames to which the adjustments pertain. However, the spreadsheets now use a trial balance format rather than the mock financial statement approach used in the third edition. The trial balance format coincides with the technique used in professional practice (whether manual or computerized). The debit-credit format of the adjustments also will be more familiar to any student who has used worksheets in previous courses.

Accounting for business combinations reflects the new harmonized reporting recommendations that are being finalized cooperatively by the U.S. Financial Accounting Standards Board and the CICA Accounting Standards Board. As we go to press, the new standard as it will appear in the *CICA Handbook* has not been finalized, and therefore all detailed cross-references are to the *Business Combinations Exposure Draft*. But the new principles and recommendations are all thoroughly incorporated into the text material.

The income tax aspects of consolidation have been removed from the main text and placed in two chapter appendices. In the "old days," the only income tax impact was to recognize the deferred tax effect of unrealized intercompany profits. Under the new balance sheet approach to income tax allocation, the tax aspects become much more complicated. Many students have a lot of trouble coping with income tax allocation. Therefore, we thought it best not to superimpose those complexities on top of the challenge of learning consolidations. Still, the material is in the appendices for those who wish to examine the tax allocation implications of consolidating business combinations.

Throughout the consolidations chapters, we have based our examples on the assumption that the parent corporation uses the cost method of *recording* its investment in subsidiaries. This is the practical reality. We see little point in spending a lot of time examining the techniques of consolidation when the equity method of recording is used by the parent, because it just doesn't happen in practice. There is no *reporting* implication of using the cost vs. equity basis for *recording*. Therefore we have only a brief discussion of the consequences of consolidating equity-basis accounts in the unlikely event that a parent actually uses that method of recording. *Reporting* on the equity method is, of course, fully discussed.

There also has been some reorganization of material within the consolidations chapters. Pooling of interests is of decreasing importance on the world stage. The discussion of pooling has been retained in Chapter 3 as one of the alternative approaches to business combinations, but there no longer is a separate chapter on pooling.

The illustration of proportionate consolidation for joint ventures also has been reduced. Canada's approach to joint venture reporting is unique, but it is an approach that almost certainly will be harmonized out of existence in the near future.

Other aspects of the consolidations chapters have been rewritten and clarified. In some instances (e.g., step acquisitions), the amount of detail has been reduced. In others (e.g., intercompany sales of amortizable assets), the coverage has been expanded and clarified. Illustrative journal entries have been simplified by avoiding "compound" entries. Throughout the book, we have clarified the sources and calculations underlying numbers used in journal entries and in financial statements.

The chapter on segmented and interim reporting has been updated for the recent revisions in segmented and interim reporting recommendations. As well, a new example has been added that illustrates segment reporting in interim statements.

Reporting for international activities is presented in two chapters. Chapter 9 focuses on foreign-currency-denominated transactions, while Chapter 10 deals with foreign operations.

As we go to press, the Accounting Standards Board is about to issue an Exposure Draft that will eliminate the defer-and-amortize method for accounting for unrealized currency exchanges and losses on long-term monetary items. We anticipated this change, and therefore it is easy to skip over the sections relating to defer-and-amortize in Chapters 9 and 10.

Chapter 10 retains a discussion of the several alternatives for translating foreign operations, including the much-maligned current/non-current approach. Current accounting standards for translation and consolidation of foreign subsidiaries is far from fully satisfactory. Of course, the two currently recommended approaches are clearly explained and fully illustrated.

The book ends with two chapters devoted to accounting for non-business organizations. Chapter 11 discusses non-profit organizations, and Chapter 12 presents the accounting issues of governments. In this edition, an overview of fund accounting is provided in an appendix to Chapter 11 rather than in a separate chapter. The appendix is purely textual, not numerical. The bookkeeping aspect of fund accounting is readily available from many other sources, and our focus in this book is on preparing professional accountants, not high-class bookkeepers. For Public Sector Accounting, we have included the new proposed standards in the CICA's *Senior Government Reporting Model*—these recommendations had not been finalized as we go to press.

Supplements

There are many changes underway in accounting standards. As events unfold, we will post updates on the book's Web site: **www.pearsoned.ca/beechyfarrell**. In addition to this new Web site, we are offering to instructors a comprehensive Instructor's Resource Manual including Solutions, as well as a new Test Item File containing additional material for tests and extra student practice.

Acknowledgements

As in previous editions, much of the assignment material has been drawn from the professional examinations of Canada's three professional accounting bodies:

CGA-Canada, CICA, and SMA-Canada. A few cases have also been included by the kind permission of the Institute of Chartered Accountants of Ontario. We are deeply indebted to all of these organizations for their cooperation and support in permitting us to use their copyrighted material. An acknowledgement appears at the end of each case or problem that was obtained from one of these four professional sources.

We also are deeply indebted to the individuals who reviewed the revision plan and the manuscript and who provided valuable suggestions. The following individuals provided comments on the proposed revision plan:

- Margaret Kelly, University of Manitoba

- Patsy Marsh, University of Calgary

- Neville Ralph, Mount Allison University

- Scott Sinclair, British Columbia Institute of Technology

- Deirdre Taylor, Ryerson Polytechnic University

The experienced instructors who provided comments on the draft manuscript are as follows:

- Joan Conrod, Dalhousie University

- Valorie Leonard, Laurentian University

- Philippe Levy, McGill University

- Neville Ralph, Mount Allison University

- James Moore, Ryerson Polytechnic University

We are grateful for the enthusiastic support and encouragement of the people at Pearson Education Canada for bringing this project to a rapid and successful conclusion. In particular, we would like to thank Patrick Ferrier, former Editorial Director, for bringing the book to Pearson Education Canada from its previous publisher and Samantha Scully, Senior Acquisitions Editor, for getting the overdue fourth edition underway. We also are deeply indebted to Anita Smale, Developmental Editor, for her unflagging enthusiasm and support. Gail Marsden was the copy editor who understood what we were doing and helped to clarify our writing. Marisa D'Andrea was the unflappable production editor who guided the book through an unusually rapid production cycle, so that Canadian instructors could have the book on their desks well in advance of the 2001–2002 academic year.

On a personal level, we would like to thank our friends and family for their support and encouragement throughout the lengthy process of bringing this book to a close. From the Farrell end of things, we'd like especially to thank Ed, Catherine, Michael, and Megan Farrell. In the Beechy contingent, kudos for patience and forbearance go to Brian McBurney and Calvin Luong.

Despite the efforts of many people and many sets of eyes, errors have a nasty habit of creeping into all books. Of course, we authors bear the responsibility for any errors that you may find. We would greatly appreciate your bringing any and all errors to our attention, no matter how minor. We will forward these corrections to other students and instructors. We also will then be able to correct errors before the next printing of the book.

Please report any errors by e-mail to **tbeechy@schulich.yorku.ca**.
Thank you for using *Advanced Financial Accounting, Fourth Edition.* We hope that you find it an enjoyable book to use.

Thomas H. Beechy
Elizabeth Farrell

Setting the Stage

Introduction

What is *advanced financial accounting*? Basically, "advanced" accounting is simply the study of certain rather specialized technical areas of accounting. You may have studied some of these topics at a more general, conceptual level in an intermediate accounting course. Intermediate accounting courses contain the core of financial accounting knowledge and are intended to provide a strong background both to future accountants and to others who work (or expect to work) in financial areas, such as corporate financial management or securities analysis.

In contrast, advanced accounting courses are intended almost exclusively for students who plan to become professional accountants. As such, they concentrate on a smaller number of highly technical subjects. These are subjects that are not too difficult to grasp in general, but that lead to a lot of technical difficulties in practice. In most advanced accounting courses, there are three major topics.

First, the core of almost all advanced accounting courses is the study of the complex accounting issues that arise from intercorporate investments, especially from strategic investments in other companies, including *business combinations*.

Second, advanced accounting courses almost always include a discussion of the accounting approaches for foreign currency transactions and international operations. This topic is particularly important for Canadian students, because the Canadian economy is highly dependent on exports. Exports often are priced in foreign currency, and therefore *foreign currency transactions* become an everyday fact of life for Canadian companies. In addition, many companies obtain part or all of their financing in foreign currencies, most commonly in U.S. dollars.

As well, any Canadian company that hopes to take its place among the world's international companies must establish operations outside of Canada; Canada's small population and economic base limits opportunities for domestic growth. Therefore, another aspect of international activities is the financial reporting of subsidiaries that are located in other countries, known as *foreign operations*.

A third topic commonly included in advanced accounting courses is accounting for non-business organizations. The financial reporting objectives and measurement issues that arise in non-profit organizations and governments are quite different from business enterprises, and therefore a somewhat extended look at accounting for non-business organizations is necessary for any well-rounded professional accountant.

This book deals with the three topics described above. Most of its length is devoted to intercorporate investments—six chapters are devoted to this topic, which is not exhaustive even at that length! Two chapters deal with international activities, and another two cover non-profit organizations and governmental reporting.

The Context—Overview

Accounting is not a matter of simply following rules; a professional accountant must continuously exercise professional judgement in the exercise of her or his responsibilities.

Judgement depends on context. A professional accountant must understand the context within which judgemental issues arise; otherwise, there is no difference between professional judgement and non-professional judgement—anyone's guess would be as valid as the accountant's! Therefore, this chapter will deal first with the meaning of professional judgement and how it comes into play in the topics covered in this book.

Next, the chapter briefly reviews the applicability of generally accepted accounting principles, or GAAP. GAAP is not *always* the appropriate basis of reporting, and every accountant must be capable of recognizing the situations in which some elements of GAAP may not be appropriate. Sometimes, a *disclosed basis of accounting* should be used. We will discuss the disclosed basis of accounting a little later in the chapter.

The chapter ends with a review of financial reporting objectives. Many judgements affecting accounting numbers are shaped by management's financial reporting objectives. Is management seeking to satisfy users' needs, such as facilitating cash flow prediction or performance evaluation, or do they want to maximize reported earnings, minimize current income taxes, or meet debt covenants? Understanding management's financial reporting objectives (which often are implicit rather than explicitly stated) is crucial to the exercise of professional judgement.

Much of what follows in this chapter may already be familiar to you. Nevertheless, it may well be useful to review this material. It never hurts to refresh one's awareness of the factors that affect the exercise of professional judgement.

Professional Judgement

In the practise of her or his profession, the accountant functions in a world of conflicting demands and multiple alternatives. Professional judgement is essential in choosing from among alternative valid approaches to solving a problem. But the exercise of judgement requires the availability of benchmarks or explicit criteria by which to evaluate alternative approaches and alternative results. The use of professional judgement is not an application of arbitrariness. If choices were purely arbitrary, then there would be no difference between professional judgement and non-professional judgement; the professional would be in no better position to make a decision than would someone with no accounting background.

Judgement is required whenever there are choices to be made. There are three types of choices that are pervasive in accounting:

1. Accounting policy choices

2. Accounting estimates

3. Disclosure decisions

Accounting policy choices arise whenever there is more than one acceptable accounting policy that can be used in a particular situation. An obvious example is the choice of depreciation method. Several different policies are equally acceptable under GAAP—which one to choose?

Accounting policies such as inventory valuation, revenue recognition, intangible asset recognition and amortization, tangible capital asset depreciation, and various other types of expense recognition policies all have a significant impact on both the balance sheet and the income statement. Some also affect the way in which transactions are reported on the cash flow statement. Accounting policy choices have a more or less permanent impact on financial reporting because they cannot easily be changed.

The use of *accounting estimates* is at least as important as the choice of accounting policy. Significant accounting policies should be disclosed, but accounting estimates very rarely are disclosed. Accounting estimates are the unseen factor that management can use to shape reported accounting numbers.

For example, accounting policies for inventory valuation (e.g., first-in first-out, average cost, lower of cost or market) usually are disclosed, but companies never disclose the methods used to estimate these amounts. What cost components are included in acquisition cost? How much overhead is included in inventory cost? What measures of "market" are used in LCM valuation? How long does it take for a company to decide that inventory should be written down? All of these decisions affect reported results, but we will look in vain for any description of these estimates in the financial statements or the notes thereto.

Disclosure decisions is the third area in which accounting judgements must be made. What should be disclosed, and in how much detail? The *CICA Handbook* suggests quite a lot of disclosure, but much of it is "advisable" rather than obligatory. Even the "recommended" disclosures are subject to a great deal of judgement about the extent of clarity and detail.

Disclosures beyond the *CICA Handbook*'s specific disclosure recommendations are purely judgemental. Many companies are quite vague (in their financial statement notes) about the extent of non-arm's-length transactions, about their relationships with other companies, about who controls the company, or about how significant accounting policies (such as revenue recognition) are applied. Some companies seem to prefer favourable disclosures to unfavourable disclosures—it is common for the sources and nature of unusual losses to be disclosed, but unusual gains often seem to end up in income without being separately disclosed!

It is management's responsibility to make decisions about accounting policies, accounting estimates, and disclosure. However, a professional accountant must be able to advise management on acceptable accounting practices—on the range of feasible and ethical alternatives. As well, an auditor must use her or his professional judgement to determine whether management's choices are suitable within the context of the company—the company's form of organization, the applicability of GAAP, the financial reporting objectives, and the reasonableness of business estimates and measurements.

Professional Judgement in Advanced Accounting Topics

As we go through the topics in this book, it may appear that the *CICA Handbook* severely constrains the possible accounting alternatives. In particular, the accounting choices related to intercorporate investments may seem to be sharply limited. However, there are a number of choices that still exist, some of which are quite significant. These are summarized in Exhibit 1-1.

Notice that there is not a lot of policy choice in some areas, particularly those connected with business combinations and consolidations, but there can be sub-

EXHIBIT 1–1 ACCOUNTING POLICY CHOICES AND ACCOUNTING ESTIMATES—EXAMPLES WITHIN GAAP

	Extent of choice	
	Policy	**Estimates**
Consolidations:		
Which subsidiaries to consolidate	None	None
Amount of unrealized profit	None	Large
Joint ventures	None	Medium
Business combinations:		
Cost of acquisition—cash purchase	None	Small
Cost of acquisition—share exchange	Small	Large
Method of consolidation	None	N/A
Allocation of purchase price	None	Large
Amortization of fair value increments/decrements	None	Medium
Amortization of goodwill	Small	Large
Foreign operations:		
Foreign-currency denominated transactions	None	Small
Designation of implicit hedges	Medium	Some
Designation of each foreign operation (integrated vs. self-sustaining)	Large	Medium
Non-business organizations:		
Non-profit organizations	Large	Large
Governments	Large	Large

stantial measurement issues that require many accounting estimates. The detail in this table may not mean much at first, but you should refer to it as you make your way through the book. The table will be a useful reminder of the importance of professional judgement in the areas of financial reporting that are discussed in this book.

Applicability of GAAP

You undoubtedly will have studied the origins and meaning of GAAP in your earlier accounting courses. We will not belabour the issue here. But it is worth remembering that GAAP is defined partially by the *CICA Handbook* and partially by existing (and therefore "generally accepted") practices. For the topics covered in this book, the *CICA Handbook* is particularly important.

Who must comply with GAAP? The easy answer is "everyone." But the easy answer is seldom the correct answer. There are important exceptions to the GAAP requirement. If GAAP is not necessarily applicable to a specific reporting entity, a broader range of possible accounting options is available. Any entity is likely to conform to GAAP for the vast majority of its accounting practices, simply because GAAP is derived largely from existing practices (rather than from the *CICA Handbook*) and existing practices evolved to satisfy reporting needs.

When management of a reporting entity chooses to deviate from GAAP, they do not throw the entire structure of GAAP out the window. Instead, deviation from GAAP usually is on one or two specific accounting issues. A small business may decide, for example, to account for income taxes on a "taxes payable" or flow-through basis rather than using the complex tax allocation procedures recommended in Section 3650 of the *CICA Handbook*. A private company may decide not to capitalize its lease obligations, in order to clarify the cash flow aspects of its operations in the income statement.

When a company decides to deviate from GAAP, two approaches are possible. One approach is for the company to point out in its accounting policy note the aspects of the company's accounting that deviate from GAAP. If the financial statements are audited or reviewed, the auditor will also point out the non-GAAP aspects in the audit report.

The second approach is for the company to use a **disclosed basis of accounting** (**DBA**). Under this approach, the company's specific accounting policies are described in the accounting policy note and the auditor's review of the financial statements (if any) will refer to the DBA rather than to GAAP. The circumstances under which DBA can be used are described a little later in this chapter.

There are two circumstances that affect whether GAAP is accepted as a constraint: (1) the form of business organization, and (2) the relevant financial reporting objectives. The following sections of this chapter will discuss these two issues.

Form of Business Organization

Public vs. private corporations

Whether a corporation is *public* or *private* is an important determinant of whether GAAP is a binding constraint. A private corporation is one that does not have its shares approved for trading by the provincial securities commission(s).

Public companies are subject to scrutiny by the securities commissions, and questionable accounting practices can lead to a suspension of trading. The securities commissions therefore have an effective tool by which they can force compliance with the GAAP reporting requirements. Companies with securities traded on major exchanges will almost always restrict their accounting policies to GAAP.

Even public companies, however, may depart from *CICA Handbook* recommendations if the company and its auditors concur that a particular recommendation is not appropriate for the company under its specific circumstances. The *CICA Handbook*'s "Introduction to Accounting Recommendations" states quite explicitly that

> …no rule of general application can be phrased to suit all circumstances or combination of circumstances that may arise, nor is there any substitute for the exercise of professional judgement in the determination of what constitutes fair presentation or good practice in a particular case. [p. 9]

The reporting issue for private companies is less clear. The *Canadian Business Corporations Act* (*CBCA*) and the securities and corporations acts of the various provinces normally state that financial statements of a corporation shall be submitted annually to the appropriate provincial or federal minister and, in the case of public companies, to the appropriate securities commission.

On the surface, therefore, it would appear that virtually all corporations in Canada are constrained to use GAAP. In practice, such is not the case. If all companies complied with the statutory requirements, there would be no such thing as a qualified audit opinion, and yet we know that such opinions are used.

The corporations acts generally state that each company will submit audited financial statements to its shareholders at the general annual meeting. However, the shareholders of a private company can waive the audit by unanimous consent. For example, the *British Columbia Company Act* states "if all the members of a company that is not a reporting company [i.e., a public company] consent in writing to a resolution waiving the appointment of an auditor, the company is not required to appoint an auditor" [sec. 203(1)].

Some of the acts limit the availability of a waiver to companies that are below certain size thresholds. The thresholds under the *CBCA* are gross revenues of $10 million *or* total assets of $5 million. The provincial limits are less—for example, Ontario limits are half of the *CBCA* amounts. In provinces where size tests exist, companies that are larger than these size limits should, in theory, submit their financial statements to audit and should comply with GAAP.

In fact, private companies may have little concern about the statutory requirements. Quite a few corporations that exceed the size tests do not have an audit, and many of those that do have an audit do not comply strictly with GAAP. The reason for the apparent non-compliance is that there is little basis for enforcing the statutory provisions on private companies of limited ownership. Since a waiver of an audit is done by consent of the shareholders, the shareholders have little basis for complaint if it turns out later that the financial statements were incorrect or the system of internal control was not operating properly.

The vast majority of corporations in Canada are private corporations. Many are quite small. But even among large companies, very many are private. In the annual *Financial Post* listing of Canada's largest 500 corporations, 40% are private. Many of those are subsidiaries of foreign parents, and Canadian GAAP is largely irrelevant for those subsidiaries. At least half of the economic activity in Canada is through private companies.[1]

Private companies obtain external financing through bank loans or through private placements of securities.[2] Bankers and the purchasers of private placements are assumed to be sophisticated users of financial information. If they rely on unaudited statements or on non-GAAP statements, they are presumed to know what they are doing and to have implicitly consented to receive such statements.

Even when a private company's financial statements are audited, the company's managers may choose to use accounting policies that are outside of GAAP if they feel that non-GAAP policies best serve the reporting needs of the enterprise. The auditors will, of course, qualify the audit opinion and insist on disclosure of the nature and impact of any non-GAAP policies, but the existence of non-GAAP policies need not cause external users of the statements undue concern.

In summary, GAAP is a broad set of accounting alternatives that constitute a framework for financial reporting. Public companies are usually limited to using GAAP alternatives, and professional judgement is required for selecting from among the many available alternatives. Private companies use GAAP as a frame of reference, but they have little need to stick strictly to GAAP as long as the

---

1. Relatively few public companies in Canada are widely held. Most have a control block held by an individual, a family, or another corporation. In the *Financial Post 2000* listing, only about 11% of the 500 largest companies are designated as being "widely held" by the investing public.

2. Any issuance of securities over a specified lower limit is exempt from the securities acts' reporting requirements. The minimum amount is $97,000 or $150,000, depending on the province.

shareholders and major lenders have no objection to specific deviations that suit (or at least do not hamper) their needs. Only for public companies is GAAP a real constraint, due to the power of the securities commissions to suspend trading.

Disclosed basis of accounting

Occasionally, it is necessary or desirable for a reporting organization to use specific accounting policies that are outside the body of generally accepted accounting policies. The notes to financial statements normally include an accounting policy note that explains the choices made by the reporting entity when there are alternatives available. The *CICA Handbook* recommends that:

> A clear and concise description of the significant accounting policies of an enterprise should be included as an integral part of the financial statements. [CICA 1505.04]

For example, the accounting policy note should describe the entity's revenue recognition policy, depreciation policies, policies relating to inventory valuation, and so forth.

When the policies described in the policy note are outside GAAP, the organization is then using a *disclosed basis of accounting* (*DBA*) in lieu of GAAP. In the "Financial Accounting Concepts" section, the *CICA Handbook* suggests that the use of DBA would be appropriate for general purpose financial statements prepared in accordance with regulatory requirements or contractual requirements.[3]

Reporting in accordance with regulatory requirements is normal for banks and regulated public utilities. For banks, financial reporting is governed by the *Bank Act.*

For regulated public utilities, rates usually are set on the basis of *revenue requirements.* **Revenue requirements** are the revenue that the company must generate in order to recover its costs of providing service *plus* a fair return on the assets employed. In some jurisdictions, certain expenses that arise through interperiod cost allocations must be excluded when establishing the corporation's revenue requirements and the rates charged to customers. The costs are excluded even though they may be a normal part of GAAP, such as the future (i.e., deferred) tax portion of income tax expense.

Allocated expenses that the regulatory agency excludes from the revenue requirement calculation should also be excluded from the general purpose financial statements. Otherwise, financial statement users would be evaluating management on a basis that does not reflect the operating realities of the company. Therefore the financial reporting follows the regulatory requirements rather than GAAP.

An open question seems to be the use of DBA for enterprises that are not regulated. As mentioned above, the *CICA Handbook* suggests that DBA may be used when the statements are prepared in accordance with contractual requirements. Examples of such contractual requirements include borrowing contracts and buy/sell agreements in shareholders' agreements. If the contractual requirements are those of a *public* company, then statements prepared in accordance with the contract would seem to be **special purpose reports** rather than general purpose reports, and the *CICA Handbook* addresses only the policies used in general purpose reports.[4]

---

3. *CICA Handbook*, paragraph 1000.59.

4. Donald J. Cockburn discusses the issue of when to use a disclosed basis of accounting in his article, "GAAP vs. AADBA" in *CA Magazine*, January 1992, pp. 35 ff.

In *private* corporations, however, the external contracting parties may well be the only significant external users of the entity's financial statements, and the special purpose report in effect becomes the general purpose report. In such cases, there is no reason to prepare separate general purpose statements in addition to those prepared in accordance with the contractual requirements.

Disclosed basis of accounting (DBA) is sometimes given other names that more clearly identify the reason behind the departure from GAAP. These include **regulatory accounting policies** (**RAP**) for regulated entities (including banks) and **tailored accounting policies** (**TAP**) to describe accounting policies that are "tailored" to satisfy the needs of contractual arrangements.[5] However, DBA remains the broader term.

Partnerships

The disclosed basis of accounting is widely used for reporting by partnerships. The accounting policies used by partnerships vary widely due to the nature of the partnership agreement, the services provided, the asset base, and the funding sources. For that reason GAAP is often not an appropriate basis of accounting for their specific needs.

The basic accounting for partnerships is relatively easy and is covered in most introductory financial accounting textbooks. However, the reporting issue can be explored in the context of the disclosed basis of reporting. Using an example, we will explore this issue a little further.

The partnership agreement is often the driving force behind the accounting policies chosen by a partnership. One dilemma that needs to be addressed in the partnership agreement is how partners enter and leave the partnership. The financial issue is (1) how much capital a new partner should invest and (2) how much capital a partner who is leaving the partnership should receive.

One alternative is for the partnership to use market values for its asset and liability valuation, and to accrue earnings on a performance basis (rather than on a completion basis). GAAP does not generally embrace market values, and therefore market values can be used only under a disclosed basis of accounting. Of course, the partnership agreement (and the DBA) needs to further define *market* to avoid future disagreements.

Another alternative is to use historical cost. If GAAP historical cost accounting is used, problems result—e.g., the appreciation in the value of assets over time and the value of work in progress will not be shown. This will result in partners entering the partnership paying too little and partners leaving not receiving their fair share. Of course, there are other valid reasons why a partner entering would pay below market. For example, a partnership may need their unique talents or services. Or an exiting partner may receive a lower amount to be able to get cash out quickly. Using historical cost as the reporting basis will require an annual valuation of the assets and liabilities to bring assets to market value. This annual valuation will then be the DBA.

Therefore, partnerships usually declare their financial reporting policies in a note and the auditor's opinion (if any) states that "the financial statements have been prepared in accordance with the accounting policies described in Note 1," or some similar wording.

A DBA is particularly useful in this type of situation where there are a limited group of users (the partners) who have a specific need (determining the amount to enter or exit the partnership).

---

5. For example, Professors Daniel B. Thornton and Murray J. Bryant studied the use of TAP relating to lease accounting for debt covenants in lending agreements: *GAAP vs. TAP in Lending Agreements: Canadian Evidence* (Toronto: Canadian Academic Accounting Association, 1986).

Financial Reporting Objectives

The most fundamental set of criteria governing the application of professional judgement is the **financial reporting objectives** that are being used by the reporting enterprise. Accounting policy choices, accounting measurements and estimates, and disclosure policies are all affected by the specific reporting objectives of management. *Reporting objectives* does not mean something vague and unmeasurable like "to serve the general reader" or "to provide fair presentation"; general objectives like these are no help at all to the practising professional accountant. If there are several choices available within GAAP (or alternate framework, if appropriate), how can an objective like *fair presentation* provide any guidance? Obviously, fair presentation is much better than unfair presentation, but unfair presentation basically is unethical and/or fraudulent reporting.

The *CICA Handbook* is not much help for setting objectives. The *CICA Handbook* states that the general financial reporting objective "is to communicate information that is useful"—not, to be sure, information that is useless—for the purpose of making the users' "resource allocation decisions and/or assessing management stewardship." [6] What users? What types of resource allocation decisions? How is management performance to be assessed? Not only is the meaning unclear, but also there is conflict between the various types of decisions implied by this broadly stated objective.

We will not discuss financial reporting objectives at length, you will be glad to hear. But we will make a quick review. The importance of financial reporting objectives will become apparent in subsequent chapters when we discuss circumstances in which there is a choice of accounting policies or accounting estimates.

User objectives

Financial-statement readers are using the statements as a basis for decisions. Users often want information that will help them to:

1. predict cash flows,

2. ascertain whether the company has complied with contractual requirements, and

3. evaluate the performance of management.

Cash flow prediction

Investors and creditors often are concerned about the cash flow of a company. On a continuing basis, they are particularly interested in the cash flow from operations, because it is the operating cash flow that provides the cash for paying bills, for paying dividends, and for expansion. Users, therefore, often want accounting decisions made in a way that facilitates their *cash flow prediction*.

The objective of a cash flow prediction objective is that the financial statements should convey information to users that will help them to predict future cash flows of the company based on past and current data. The statements should describe the current pattern of cash flows, and should indicate any expected alteration of those flows.

One important aspect of this objective is that the phrase "cash flow" should not be taken too literally. Cash flow from operations does not really mean just the net cash received for a specific period of time. The concept is really more of a

---

6. *CICA Handbook*, paragraph 1000.15.

longer-term view of how much cash will be returned to the enterprise as the result of current operations. Thus cash flow should be viewed within the context of accrual accounting to include prepaid and accrued items:

> [Users'] interest in an enterprise's future cash flows. . . leads primarily to an interest in information about its earnings rather than information directly about its cash flows. . . . Information about enterprise earnings and its components measured by accrual accounting generally provides a better indication of enterprise performance than information about current cash receipts and payments.[7]

There are two principal accounting impacts when a cash flow prediction objective is adopted as the primary reporting objective:

1. net income will tend to be measured in a way that indicates long-run cash flow from operations, and

2. notes will be used to describe future cash flows not indicated in the body of the statements themselves, including expected changes in those flows that are reported.

The dominant impact of the cash flow prediction objective is that accounting choices will measure revenue and expenses in a way that most closely corresponds to accrual-basis cash flows. If a company uses many interperiod allocations of past costs and estimates of future costs in measuring earnings, the relationship between earnings and cash flow is unclear. When earnings relate closely to cash flows, prediction of future cash flows is easier than when earnings do not relate closely to cash flows.

Accountants are accustomed to the fact that periodic earnings measurement is different from cash flow measurement. Cash flow and net income are two different measures. In the long run, however, they are equal. An enterprise's lifetime net income is the net cash return on the investment. There is a clear relationship between cash flow and earnings, and earnings cannot be measured without direct reference to past, present, and future cash flows.

Financial analysts refer to earnings that correspond closely to cash flows as **high-quality earnings**. *Low-quality* earnings, on the other hand, are those that are not reflected in cash flows from operations. Since investors tend to be interested in cash flows, high-quality earnings are preferred to low-quality earnings, and this preference may show up in the market as higher share prices or a greater willingness by a bank to lend money.

Under the cash flow prediction objective, then, companies will opt for immediate recognition of costs rather than deferral and amortization. For example, retail chains regularly open and close stores as they adjust to changing markets. The costs of opening new stores can either be expensed immediately or deferred and amortized. Using a cash flow prediction objective, the costs would be expensed immediately because that treatment reflects the fact that the cash has been spent on an activity that is a normal, recurring business activity in the industry. Similarly, interest costs incurred on new development activities would be expensed rather than being capitalized as part of the costs of the project.

A secondary impact of the cash flow prediction objective is that the notes to the financial statements may be used to disclose supplementary information about future cash flows. Some of the disclosures that are currently recommended in the *CICA Handbook* reflect the need for information about future flows.

---

7. *Statement of Financial Accounting Concepts No. 1: Objectives of Financial Reporting by Business Enterprises* (Stamford, Connecticut: Financial Accounting Standards Board, 1978), paragraphs 43–44.

Examples include the detailed information on amounts due for debt repayments and lease payments over the next five years. In addition, however, a company could also disclose information such as major expected changes in cost structure, the size of the order backlog, or the current value of inventories.

Contract compliance

Both *shareholders' agreements* and *loan agreements* (including bond indentures) usually contain specific requirements that involve accounting measurements. A **shareholders' agreement** is a contract among the shareholders. Shareholders' agreements are normal in a private company, but sometimes exist in a public company (primarily to limit voting power).

Shareholders' agreements in private corporations often contain provisions such as dividend entitlements, limitations on cash withdrawals, and valuation. Valuation is a particularly important issue in private companies because valuation provisions govern the way shares are valued if an investor wishes to buy additional shares or sell her or his shares. Valuation is determined on the basis of accounting measurements, usually book value per share, since there is no public market for the shares of private companies. Asset valuation and income measurement policies obviously have a significant impact on book values.

A **loan agreement** is the contract between a borrower and a lender. Lenders usually include **covenants** or **maintenance tests** in loan agreements, which are requirements that the borrower must meet in order to keep the loan in good standing. Examples of covenants or maintenance tests are:

- a minimum level of the current ratio

- a maximum age of receivables

- a minimum turnover of inventory

- a maximum debt:equity ratio

- a minimum times-interest-earned ratio

- a maximum dividend payout ratio

Failure to meet the requirements of the loan agreement could result in the lender's calling the loan or refusing to renew or extend loans. A lender will use the financial statements of the borrower to determine whether or not the maintenance tests have been met. The level of the maintenance tests is (or should be) determined by the lender after taking into consideration the accounting policies used by the borrower. Therefore, the lender is concerned not only with the level of the ratios but also whether consistent accounting policies have been used as the basis for their calculation.

Performance evaluation

Frequently, financial statement readers want to know how well management is running the business. Indeed, managers themselves usually need a report card to see how they are doing. In a small business, the managers may have a good idea of the success of their management, but may need the financial statements in order to show creditors or silent partners how the business is going. On the other hand, managers may think they are doing all right, but need the statements in order to verify their perceptions.

In larger businesses, financial statements are essential for determining how well the company is managed. Investors and creditors are concerned, as are the directors and the managers themselves. In a diversified corporation, the separate-entity financial statements of the individual operating companies may form the primary basis by which the corporation's top management evaluates the performance of the component companies and their managers.

It is very difficult to separate good management from the benefits of a good economy or simply from good luck. Nevertheless, financial statements can be of some assistance in performance appraisal, especially when used in conjunction with the statements of similar businesses and with more general economic information.

When performance appraisal is the primary objective of the financial statements, the accounting policies should, as much as possible, reflect the way in which decisions are made. For example, suppose that the management of a chain of hotels wants to issue financial statements that show investors how well they are managing. The chain opens new hotels fairly regularly, and it has a policy of renovating older hotels.

Suppose that management decides to build a new hotel based on an analysis of the future market in the area, and on the potential net cash flow and present value of the project. Start-up costs will be substantial, but management believes that future revenues will recover these costs. Since the decision was made by offsetting the start-up costs against revenues in future periods, the performance evaluation objective would call for capitalizing the costs and amortizing them against the future revenues.

The treatment of hotel start-up costs would be quite different under the cash flow prediction alternative. For cash flow prediction, it would be better to expense the costs immediately because the cash outflow occurred immediately and because start-up costs are a routine part of doing business and opening new hotels.

One problem with the performance evaluation objective is that it sometimes is indistinguishable from an approach that seeks simply to maximize reported earnings. Statement users who are close to the company, such as managers, directors, owners of private corporations, or controlling shareholders of public companies, are frequently in a position to tell which objective is being followed. But for an external user, it is sometimes hard to tell the two apart. Clues may be gained by closely scrutinizing the accounting policies relating to revenue and expense recognition in the notes to the financial statements.

Preparer objectives

The preceding objectives relate to users' decision needs. The preparers of the statements are likely to have their own set of priorities when they select accounting policies. **Preparers** refers to the *managers*, not to their accounting staff. Remember that the financial statements are the responsibility of management. The accountant provides the expertise to assist the managers in meeting their reporting objectives, but the statements are management's.

The policies that management chooses will have an impact on the reported results and therefore may affect users' perceptions. The policies may also have a more direct impact on the managers themselves—compensation levels often are tied to accounting measurements, and the managers' future job prospects may be enhanced by reporting the "right" results.

In the following sections, we will discuss four major reporting objectives of the preparers. These are:

1. Income tax deferral

2. Net income maximization or minimization

3. Income smoothing

4. Minimum disclosure and contract compliance

Some accountants would prefer to refer to these preparer reporting objectives as preparer **motivations** rather than as objectives, reserving the term objectives to relate to the legitimate decision needs of the users.

Income tax deferral

One of the responsibilities of management is to maximize the discounted net present value of the enterprise's future cash flow. One way of doing this is to delay the liability for income taxes. There is a time value of money, and a dollar of taxes paid in the future has a smaller present value than a dollar of taxes paid currently. Thus the deferral of tax payments will increase the present value of the company.

To some extent, adopting accounting policies and accounting measures that reduce revenue and/or increase current expense recognition can reduce current income taxes. In particular, revenue recognition policies can have a significant impact on the amount of taxes due. If tax deferral is the objective, revenue recognition is delayed as long as feasible. In contrast, a performance evaluation objective often leads to early revenue recognition. Some companies may have little flexibility in this regard. A retail business with a high proportion of cash sales, for instance, has little option in revenue recognition.

Expense recognition also offers some flexibility for tax deferral, particularly in inventory valuation—minimizing the amount of overhead included in inventory has the effect of recognizing overhead expenses as soon as possible. However, interperiod cost allocations seldom have much impact on income taxes. Development costs, for example, are tax-deductible when incurred, regardless of whether the company chooses to defer and amortize those expenditures.

Bear in mind that shifting relatively small amounts of revenue or expense from one period to another can have a substantial impact on *net* income. If net income is 10% of revenue, delaying recognition of 2% of revenue will have an impact of up to 20% of net income.

In general, an objective of tax deferral (sometimes cited as *tax minimization*) leads to accounting policies that delay revenue recognition and speed up expense recognition. The result reduces net income to a level that is lower than would be reported under alternative acceptable accounting policies. The policies must be long-term in scope; the accounting treatment cannot be changed from year to year.

For some companies, particularly small private corporations, tax deferral may be the dominant (or only) objective of financial reporting. The managers know that net income is on the low side of the permissible range of accounting net income figures, and they can explain the situation to bankers or other major creditors who might be using the statements. Since tax deferral reduces the current cash flow drain on the company, bankers may welcome the astute tax management and may evaluate the company's reported performance more favourably.

Tax deferral might seem to be a desirable objective for all companies. But for many enterprises, the low net income that would be reported is incompatible with other objectives of the financial statements. If the company is trying to attract investors, for example, a low reported net income will not help. Bear in mind that the company cannot say in its annual report that the accounting figures should be taken with a grain of salt because they are tax-influenced amounts. The company must live with the results of its accounting policy decisions because they are chosen from an array of acceptable alternatives. Therefore, many companies choose not to emphasize tax deferral as an objective of financial reporting, but rather adopt other objectives that are more important to the overall corporate goals.

Maximization or minimization of earnings

Sometimes management's objective of financial reporting is simply to *maximize* or *minimize* the enterprise's reported net income. Management may wish to maximize earnings in order to attract new investors or to allay the fears of present investors.

Companies that are having a difficult time have been known to adopt accounting policies that increase earnings by recognizing revenue earlier or expenses later. If bond indentures or loan agreements contain covenants concerning dividend payout ratios, times-interest-earned ratios, etc., a high level of earnings will make it easier to comply with the restrictions. Other companies may be in satisfactory financial health, but wish to look even better in order to be well perceived in a competitive financial and business market. In addition, management bonuses or salaries may be tied to reported earnings, so that the managers benefit directly by maximizing reported earnings.

On the other hand, management may wish to minimize reported earnings (for reasons other than tax deferral). Management may feel that the company's earnings are embarrassingly high and may wish to discourage the entry of new competitors or to avoid attracting public or political attention, or higher wage demands by employees. Management may hope to discourage takeover bids if control is not firmly held by friendly shareholders. Earnings can be minimized by delaying revenue recognition as long as possible and to expense (rather than defer) as many costs as possible.

Such tactics should not fool an efficient market. Indeed, research suggests that the stock market reacts adversely to changes in accounting policies that would tend to increase earnings, because the change is interpreted as a signal that management expects real earnings to decline.

Similarly, minimization of earnings may not be expected to mislead an efficient market. There is ample empirical evidence that the stock market will adjust for different accounting policies in assigning a value to shares. And understated earnings surely would not lead astray any acquisition-minded managers of another company. If anything, reduced reported earnings would only depress the potential price that the acquiree's shareholders would receive.

But management may not be trying to influence the reactions of the market as a whole. They may be more concerned with the perceptions of individual shareholders or outsiders, and individual users are not necessarily efficient and unbiased processors of information. Indeed, managers may believe that it is more important to cater to the biases and perceptions of a single large shareholder or shareholder group (such as a controlling family) than to recognize the efficiency of the public securities markets.

Earnings maximization—the "big bath"

One aspect of earnings management that merits special mention is the practice of taking a "big bath" or "big hit" in a loss year. This is an observed tendency of companies to load all possible losses and write-downs into a year that is going to be a low-earnings or loss year anyway. Management's view is that if they're going to report a loss, they may as well report a large one and "clean up the balance sheet."

Companies often take the opportunity offered by a loss year to write down assets of doubtful future benefit, especially intangible assets. Sometimes, the write-down is very substantial, and there have been cases in which the auditors have objected that the company is writing its assets down to an amount that is well below recoverable cost. Another strategy is to make substantial provisions for future costs related to current decisions and actions, such as restructuring costs or reclamation costs.

The earnings-management objective of the big bath is that, by writing down assets, the company has less amortization in future years. Hence, future earnings are enhanced. This is why the big bath strategy is a part of an earnings maximization objective. Similarly, when a company makes provisions for future costs that are at the high end of the feasible range of estimates, the current provision reduces the amount of expense that is charged in future years. Indeed, if the current charge turns out to be excessive, the company can recognize a gain in future years when they reduce the recorded liability.

The big bath approach is an aggressive use of accounting estimates. Not only can estimates be used to write down assets and to charge large future cost provisions against current earnings, the estimates relating to routine accounting measurements can be adjusted. For example, pension cost estimates are subject to a wide range of very future-oriented estimates. A relatively minor adjustment to an estimate (such as the future earnings rate of the pension plan) can contribute significantly to the big bath.

The big bath philosophy treads very close to the line of ethical reporting. The intent, either conscious or unconscious, is to increase future earnings by stretching the limits of accounting estimates. Taken far enough, a big bath can result in deliberate misstatement of accounting results, in both the current and future periods. If all of the charges in a big bath are legitimate, then one wonders whether the prior years' financial statements were misstated because they included assets that had no future benefit.

Income smoothing

Investors and creditors are concerned not only with the level of earnings, but also with the business risk of a company. The level of risk is equated with the volatility of earnings and cash flows. In attempting to influence users' perceptions about the company, managers may wish to select accounting policies that not only increase the apparent *level* of earnings but also decrease the apparent *volatility* of earnings. Accounting policies can have the effect of smoothing earnings.

Smoothing may be accomplished through either revenue or expense recognition policies, or both. Revenue can be smoothed by spreading its recognition over an earnings cycle, such as by using percentage-of-completion rather than completed contract, or by timing the recognition of irregular lumps of revenue to fall into periods of low economic activity. Expenses can be smoothed by amortizing costs over a period of years rather than by recognizing them at inception; examples include development costs and start-up costs.

Smoothing can also be accomplished through the recognition of significant future-oriented cost estimates. A great deal of flexibility pervades such estimates as the future restructuring costs, reclamation costs, costs/benefits of discontinued operations, and so forth. Indeed, accounting pronouncements in recent years have tended to increase the ability of management to "manage" the recognition of major future-related cost estimates.

The smoothing of expenses is most effective if the expenses can be related to levels of revenue, since smoothing of expenses will not in itself necessarily lead to the smoothing of net income. For example, if net revenue fluctuates substantially, the smoothing of an expense will tend to lower the entire level of earnings over a period of years but will not decrease the fluctuation. Indeed, if the same volatility exists but at a lower overall level of earnings, the relative risk will appear to increase rather than to decrease.

As with the maximization or minimization of earnings, one might assume that smoothing tendencies would not fool an efficient market. Discerning the impacts of interperiod allocations is easier said than done, however, since smoothing is often accomplished through the adroit use of accounting estimates.

Minimum compliance and contract compliance

Sometimes management wishes to report the least possible amount of information to external stakeholders. This practice is known as **minimum compliance**.

In a public company, minimum compliance takes the form of compliance with all of the reporting requirements of the securities and corporations acts and with the "required" recommendations of the *CICA Handbook*; the reporting company provides none of the "desirable" disclosures recommended by the *CICA Handbook*. Managers may be motivated to use minimum disclosure because they do not wish to reveal what they consider to be confidential information to competitors, labour unions, etc. Often, the practice of minimum compliance derives from a somewhat secretive attitude on the part of managers—the "it's none of your business" approach to financial reporting.

The managers of private companies commonly adhere to the practice of minimum compliance. As the number of external stakeholders is limited, the managers need only provide the minimum information required to satisfy their external reporting requirements.

Related to the practice of minimum compliance (especially, but not exclusively, in a private company) is financial reporting that is based on the goal of optimizing compliance with the terms of contracts. This objective of **contract compliance** may be observed when managers choose accounting policies that will most readily enable the company to meet covenants imposed by major lenders in loan agreements. Often, the desire to meet (or, when the provisions are restrictive, to avoid) contract provisions translates to other reporting objectives such as income maximization or smoothing. The real motivation may be the contract provisions, however.

Other objectives

The user and preparer objectives discussed above are only some of the most common objectives. There can be a wide array of other objectives, depending on the nature of the enterprise and its reporting environment.

Regulated companies, for example, normally are permitted to earn a maximum percentage return on their invested capital. As a result, a regulated company will tend to use accounting policies that maximize the book value of the asset base in order to maximize the permitted dollar return on investment (and, after financial leverage, on the shareholders' equity).

Similarly, a company that is subsidized by some level of government is apt to use accounting policies that maximize the amount of subsidy to which the company is legally and ethically entitled.

Canadian companies that are wholly-owned subsidiaries of foreign parents usually must comply with the accounting mandates of their parents. Generally, that means complying with U.S. GAAP or with International Accounting Standards (IAS). About 65% of the wholly-owned foreign subsidiaries in the *Financial Post 500* have U.S. parents, and U.S. GAAP will prevail in those subsidiaries.

For subsidiaries of non-U.S. parent companies, IAS usually is used. IAS is accepted as the reporting standard on the vast majority of stock exchanges worldwide. Even in Europe, where separate-entity reporting must comply with local law, consolidated statements usually are prepared in accordance with IAS. For the topics covered in this book, there is little difference between IAS and the *CICA Handbook* recommendations, but in a broader accounting context there are significant differences.

In addition to ignoring Canadian GAAP, however, a wholly-owned subsidiary of a foreign parent derives its reporting objectives from its parent, and the parent's reporting objectives may be driven by factors that are quite different from anything encountered in Canada. Therefore, an accountant who is working for such a subsidiary must be sensitive to and familiar with its different reporting context.

Matrix of objectives

The various financial reporting objectives can be classified into three general categories on the basis of a time dimension. The categories are:

1. Retrospective uses, to comprehend and learn from past actions and events of the entity;

2. Contractual uses, to provide for current monitoring and execution of contracts with parties both internal and external to the entity; and

3. Predictive uses, to reduce uncertainty for managers and investors.

Among the user objectives, the primary retrospective use is performance evaluation and the primary predictive use is cash flow prediction. The contractual uses include income tax determination and compliance with a variety of contracts, including debt agreements, shareholder agreements, and compensation agreements.

The time dimension can be applied to preparer objectives also. There is a subtle distinction between management's retrospective objective on performance evaluation depending on whether they are *using* the financial statements for evaluating their own performance or attempting to *influence other users' perceptions* as to the performance of the company and its management. When management is actually using the statements for evaluation, they are acting as users and the objectives are users' objectives, but when they are trying to affect other users' evaluations (e.g., by maximizing and/or smoothing net income) they then are exercising preparer objectives.

Similarly, management may select accounting policies and make accounting estimates that they hope will influence contractual arrangements; they are then acting as preparers. Income tax deferral is an example of a preparer objective, while assessing income tax is a user (i.e., Canada Customs and Revenue Agency, formerly known as Revenue Canada) objective. Exhibit 1-2 summarizes some of the user and preparer objectives in a matrix, with the time category as the second dimension.

Resolving conflicts among objectives

In any financial reporting situation, there is a potential conflict between user objectives and preparer motivations. Since the managers are preparing the statements, it would appear that preparer motivations would dominate the selection of objectives.

EXHIBIT 1–2 SOME OBJECTIVES OF FINANCIAL REPORTING

Type	Users (uses)	Preparers (motivations)
Retrospective	Performance evaluation	Optimize performance measures
Contractual	Income tax assessment	Income tax deferral
	Determine profit sharing and/or bonuses	Optimize management compensation
	Compliance, such as with:	Optimize contractual measures
	Debt agreement covenants	Minimize disclosure
	Shareholders' agreements	
Predictive	Current liquidity/solvency	Maximize operating earnings
	Cash flow prediction	Minimize "ability to pay"

However, users are not without power. Canada Customs and Revenue Agency clearly has the power to assess taxes on taxable income determined independently of reported accounting income. Major shareholders can, through the board of directors and its audit committee, have an influence on reporting objectives. Public shareholders have little direct influence, but security analysts and the financial press can put pressure on corporations to provide financial information that is most useful to outsiders rather than self-serving to managers. Major lenders certainly have more direct power to demand attention to their reporting needs, although competitive forces temper this power—banks sometimes worry that if they are too insistent, the customer will go to another bank.

All financial reporting situations therefore involve a trade-off between users and preparers in determining the reporting objectives. The relative strength of the two groups will influence the selection of accounting policies.

In some companies, there may be only one significant reporting objective, be it a user objective or a preparer objective. In most cases, however, there will be several objectives, and the objectives may not be compatible with each other. For example, a corporation's management (1) may need to satisfy covenants in a loan agreement, (2) may wish to defer income taxes, and (3) may want to maximize reported earnings in order to maximize executive compensation.

When choosing from amongst alternative accounting policies, management will not be able to select policies that satisfy all of these objectives simultaneously. Therefore it is necessary to prioritize the objectives by deciding which is the most important, which is the next most important, and so forth.

The prioritizing of reporting objectives is called a **hierarchy** of objectives. A hierarchy of objectives must be tailored to each reporting enterprise; there is no generalized hierarchy. When there is a conflict in the accounting policies indicated by the various objectives, the objective(s) at the top of the hierarchy will win out over those further down.

Summary of Key Points

1. *Advanced accounting* is the in-depth study of selected topics that are primarily of interest to students who intend to become professional accountants. Usually, the topics will have been studied in a more general way in intermediate accounting.

2. The primary topics in almost all advanced accounting courses are (1) inter-corporate investments—primarily consolidations, (2) accounting for foreign currency transactions and foreign operations, and (3) accounting for non-business organizations. These are the topics of this book.

3. *Professional judgement* is the use of criteria for deciding from among acceptable accounting policies, accounting estimates, and disclosures. Professional judgement is what distinguishes an accountant from a bookkeeper.

4. Accounting choices are the responsibility of management. The accountant's role is to advise management on acceptable and ethical alternatives, or, as an auditor, to verify that management's choices are appropriate within the company's reporting context. Many aspects of the topics covered within this book are highly constrained by the recommendations of the *CICA Handbook*. However, choices still remain, especially in the broad area of *accounting estimates*.

5. Public companies must comply with generally accepted accounting principles, or GAAP.

   Private companies may obtain exemption from the general rule in corporations acts that every company must have an audit. An exemption can be obtained if the shareholders unanimously agree to waive the audit requirement. Private companies may choose to deviate from GAAP in selected treatments, such as in income tax accounting or lease accounting. But deviating from GAAP does not imply that the entire generally accepted framework of financial accounting is discarded.

   An alternative to GAAP is DBA, a *disclosed basis of accounting*. DBA is sometimes known as *tailored accounting policies* (TAP). DBA is widely used by private companies and by partnerships.

6. The most important single set of criteria by which accounting judgements are made is that of *financial reporting objectives*. Financial reporting objectives must be determined for each enterprise individually. There are two general types of objectives: (1) user objectives and (2) preparer (i.e., management's) objectives. Common user objectives are cash flow prediction, contract compliance, and management performance evaluation. Common preparer objectives are income tax deferral, earnings maximization, income smoothing, and influencing contract compliance criteria.

   There usually are several relevant objectives for a single enterprise. The objectives often conflict with each other. In order for the accountant (and management) to choose from among alternative accounting policies and estimates, conflicting objectives must be prioritized. The objectives at the top of the hierarchy (with higher priority) take precedence over those further down the list.

Weblinks

CICA (Canadian Institute of Chartered Accountants)
www.cica.ca

The Canadian Institute of Chartered Accountants has a membership of over 66,000 professional accountants and 8,500 students. Refer to this bilingual site to find accounting standards, CICA products, conferences and courses, and related sites.

Canada Customs and Revenue Agency
www.ccra-adrc.gc.ca/

Available in French and English, the CCRA's Web site provides information on child and family benefits, tax credit programs, and taxes for businesses, individuals, registered plans, and charities. You can also view or download publications.

Financial Post
www.nationalpost.com/financialpost/
The Globe and Mail
www.globeandmail.com

Updated daily, these online newspapers list recent articles and provide access to their archives of articles. You can also follow the progress of your stocks with the portfolio tracker.

Review Questions

1-1 What distinguishes *professional judgement* from non-professional judgement?

1-2 When is professional judgement required? What are three types of choices in accounting that require the use of professional judgement?

1-3 When would the use of GAAP not be appropriate?

1-4 How much of the body of generally accepted accounting principles in Canada is contained in the *CICA Handbook*?

1-5 What is the largest single source of GAAP?

1-6 What are the authoritative sources of GAAP other than the *CICA Handbook*?

1-7 How does the form of the business organization and financial reporting objectives affect whether GAAP is a constraint?

1-8 In general, why might accounting principles that have been developed in some industries not be appropriate for use in other industries?

1-9 When is GAAP most likely to be an effective constraint on a corporation's financial reporting?

1-10 Why are departures from GAAP more common for private companies than for public companies?

1-11 What is meant by a *size threshold*?

1-12 What is a *disclosed basis of accounting*? When is it appropriate?

1-13 Explain the difference between a *special purpose report* and a *general purpose report*.

1-14 Provide a specific example of why a partnership may want to use a disclosed basis of accounting instead of GAAP?

1-15 Does the existence of a *CICA Handbook* recommendation on a particular accounting issue eliminate the need for professional judgement on that issue? Explain.

1-16 How can a company tailor its accounting policies?

1-17 Why is it necessary for the accountant to define the objectives of financial reporting for the enterprise for which he or she is preparing financial statements?

1-18 Since most externally reported financial statements are required to be in accordance with GAAP, how can the existence of specific objectives of financial reporting affect the preparation of the statements?

1-19 If externally reported financial statements are *general purpose* statements, how can specific objectives influence their content?

1-20 What is the long-term relationship between cash flow and earnings?

1-21 How does the accrual method of accounting fit into the concept of a cash flow prediction emphasis for financial reporting?

1-22 Explain what is meant by *high-quality earnings*.

1-23 In what general ways would a *cash flow prediction* objective influence the selection of accounting policies?

1-24 What is a *covenant*? Give five examples.

1-25 What is a *shareholders' agreement*?

1-26 Why is it usually difficult to separate the results of good management from good luck?

1-27 In what general way will the adoption of a *performance evaluation* objective influence the selection of accounting policies?

1-28 How can the accounting policies adopted for financial reporting affect the assessment of income tax?

1-29 Do companies maintain "two sets of books," one for financial reporting and one for income tax purposes? Explain.

1-30 In what general ways would an objective of *income tax deferral* affect the financial statements?

1-31 Why would management adopt an *earnings maximization* objective?

1-32 Why would management adopt an *earnings minimization* objective?

1-33 What is a "big bath" and when would a company have this objective?

1-34 Why would managers be users of their company's general purpose external financial statements?

1-35 What users are served by each of the following objectives of financial reporting?
   a. Contract compliance
   b. Cash flow prediction
   c. Performance appraisal

1-36 Explain the difference between user objectives and preparer objectives.

1-37 How can a manager be both a *preparer* and a *user* of financial statements?

1-38 Why might a manager be tempted to adopt *income smoothing* as a financial reporting objective?

Cases

Case 1-1

Provincial Hydro

Provincial Hydro is a Crown corporation that generates, supplies, and delivers electricity to industrial and retail customers throughout the province. Its accounting policies have been prepared in accordance with those for rate-regulated industries. The general principle is that costs should relate to the period that will provide benefit to the customers.

In 2001, the government passed legislation to privatize Provincial Hydro. The utility will now be operating in the open marketplace. To facilitate this process the utility is considering the segregation of its company into separate companies to handle different aspects of its business. Then one or more of these companies could be sold to raise cash. Another alternative being considered is to sell shares or have a bond issue for each of these companies.

To protect the customer, a committee approves all increases in electricity rates. To facilitate this process the utility must provide audited financial statements to the committee on an annual basis. With privatization there will now be open competition and prices will be established based on the marketplace. However, all companies will only be allowed to earn a fixed rate of return each year.

Two specific examples of accounting policies for 2000 based on rate regulation for Provincial Hydro are:

1) Gains and losses on U.S.-dollar short-term financing that replaces long-term financing are deferred and amortized over the period of the original debt.

2) Costs to rehabilitate (bring in to operation after being shut down for a period of time) are deferred and amortized over the next 10 years.

Required:

Mr. Bright, the controller of Provincial Hydro, has requested a report from you discussing whether the accounting policies for the utility should change with privatization. Provide a general discussion, then address the two specific accounting policies identified for 2000.

Case 1-2

Green Tree Farm

The Green Tree Farm is a small Ontario Christmas tree nursery with about 25,000 trees on 20 hectares. Although the average consumer may be unaware of it, the grower determines the value of a white pine Christmas tree based exclusively on height. Since shape and thickness can be controlled by pruning, and colour is determined by spray dyes, these characteristics are not relevant when setting the wholesale price. When planted, seedlings are about one foot tall. Stages of "production" are measured according to the height of the tree to the nearest foot. No tree is ever allowed to grow beyond 10 feet tall. (Metric measurements have not yet been reflected in this industry.)

The Christmas tree market is an almost classic example of pure competition. No supplier is able to affect the wholesale price for the product. Each year, a grower is faced with the decision of how many trees to harvest. The price is known and, as indicated, varies with height only. The decision may be based on the grower's expectations of prices in future years, but is generally determined by cash flow requirements: how much of the crop the grower wishes to cash in this year, as opposed to letting the crop grow more and cashing in later at a higher amount per tree.

The cost of growing the trees is quite predictable. The grower knows the cost of seedlings and the cost of tending the trees as they get older. Trees that are damaged or misshapen are scrapped as soon as their unsuitability becomes apparent. The normal scrappage rate is fairly predictable, barring natural calamities such as hurricanes.

Required:

Dean Greene, president of the Green Tree Farm, has hired you to write a report to him detailing the various ways in which he might value inventories and measure annual income for the farm. He would like your report to be divided into two sections: (1) methods of inventory valuation and income measurement that adhere to traditional measurement of historical cost, realization, and matching; and (2) methods that may deviate from the principle of historical cost for asset valuation, but still make some economic sense regarding realization and matching. He wants you to provide logical support for each of the methods you suggest, but he does not want you to make any recommendations. If measurement problems arise with any of the methods, be sure to point out the nature of the problem. Mr. Greene has specifically asked that the report be succinct and to the point.

Case 1-3

Miltonics Potions Ltd.

Miltonics Potions Ltd. (MPL) is a privately held Ontario corporation engaged in the development and marketing of patent medicines. In early 1996, the company's research chemists began working on a project to develop a patent remedy for colitis (a disease that causes inflammation of the bowel). During the year, $200,000 was spent in research on this project without developing a useful product.

Work continued in 1997, with an additional $100,000 spent. By the end of 1997, an apparently feasible product had been developed and was being considered by MPL's top management for further development and exploitation. On February 14, 1998 (prior to completion and issuance of the 1997 financial statements), the managers reached the decision to proceed with further development, production, and marketing of the product, barring adverse medical results (i.e., unacceptable side effects) from tests then underway. Such adverse results were possible, but were considered unlikely since nothing untoward had occurred to date in the testing program.

During 1998, the product was refined and the mass production formulation was developed (at a cost of $150,000). Production facilities were prepared (at a cost of $300,000), and Patent Number 381-1003-86 was obtained on the product. Legal expenses totalled $32,000.

In early 1999, production and distribution began. Sales in the first year were modest, totalling only $450,000. However, $500,000 was spent on promotion, mainly in print media advertising and in sending free samples to doctors and clinics. Only in 2000 did the sales reach forecast levels, thereby indicating that MPL had a successful product.

However, the success of the product spawned an imitator and, in 2000, MPL sued a competitor for patent infringement. MPL demanded that the competitor cease production and marketing of the competing product and requested

$2,000,000 in damages. Legal costs of $50,000 were incurred in this action in 2000; the case was still pending at the end of the year.

In July 2001, after MPL had spent an additional $20,000 in legal fees, the case was dismissed in court, thereby rendering MPL's patent indefensible. Since the competitor was a well-known pharmaceutical firm, MPL's sales suffered considerably from the competition.

Required:

a. On a year-by-year basis, describe the alternative accounting methods that MPL could use for the costs incurred in developing, patenting, and defending the new product. Do not use hindsight in arriving at your alternatives.

b. Explain what additional information you would need and what criteria you would use to make a decision on the alternative to adopt for each year.

Case 1-4

Smith and Stewart

Smith and Stewart (Stewart) is a partnership of lawyers. It was recently formed from a merger of Becker and Brackman (Becker) and Copp and Copp (Copp). Stewart has 38 partners, which include 6 from Becker and 32 from Copp. In addition, there are 75 employees. At the date of the merger, Stewart purchased land and an office building for $2 million, and fully computerized its offices. The partners have agreed to have the annual financial statements audited even though this was not done in the past.

The partnership agreement requires an annual valuation of the assets and liabilities of the firm. This valuation will be used to determine the amount an existing partner will receive from the partnership when exiting the partnership, and the amount a new partner will pay to enter the partnership.

The partners have been busy getting the new partnership up and running and have paid little attention to accounting policies.

Prior to the merger, Becker recorded revenue when it invoiced the client. Daily time reports were used to keep track of the number of hours worked for each client. This information was not recorded in the accounting system and in general the accounting records were not kept up-to-date.

Copp also recorded revenue at the time the client was invoiced. This was based on partner hours, which was determined based on work in progress. This was recorded for employees at their regular billing rate, based on the hours worked. At year-end, an adjustment was made to reduce work in progress to reflect the actual costs incurred by Copp.

The new partnership agreement requires a valuation of work in progress at the merger date. This amount, which has yet to be determined, will be recorded as goodwill.

Stewart has arranged a line of credit with a bank that allows the partnership to borrow up to 75% of the carrying value of accounts receivables and 40% of the carrying value of work in progress based on the partnership's monthly financial statements. The bank has also provided mortgage financing of $950,000 for Stewart's land and building. The bank requires unaudited monthly financial statements as well as the annual audited financial statements.

As at the date of the merger, fixed assets owned by the predecessor firm were transferred to the new partnership.

Each partner receives a monthly "draw" payment, which is an advance on his or her share of annual profit.

Your auditing firm has been hired by Stewart to prepare a report advising the partnership on accounting policies. They would like alternatives identified as well as specific supported recommendations. A partner in your auditing firm has asked you to prepare the report.

Required:

Prepare the requested report.
[CICA]

Case 1-5

Time-Lice Books, Ltd.

Time-Lice Books, Ltd. (TLBL) is a well-established company that publishes a wide variety of general interest nonfiction books. The company is incorporated under the *Canada Business Corporations Act*, and the heirs of Harold Lice, the firm's founder, hold 30% of the shares. The heirs do not take any active interest in the affairs of the company, but rely on the advice of their professional financial advisor, Mr. Hornblower Weeks, in voting their shares. The remaining 70% of the shares are widely distributed and are traded on the Montreal Exchange.

TLBL distributes some of its books (about 25%) through retail bookstores, but the bulk of the sales (75%) are made directly to customers by direct mail advertising. About half of the direct mail sales are for series of books, and the company has decided to review its accounting policy for this segment of the business. TLBL is also exploring the alternative of selling its books through the Internet in the future.

A book series is a set of books on a particular topic. Rather than publish all of the books at once, the approach is to issue one book at a time, at two- to four-month intervals. Topics of some series that have recently begun are Great Impressionist Artists, Time-Lice Guides to Home Maintenance, and Lives of Great Accountants (a particularly popular series).

When TLBL decides to begin a new series, the first step is to design an elaborate and expensive full-colour advertising brochure for the series, in which the first book is offered free of charge to those who return a postage-free postal card. This brochure is then mailed to about two million homes in Canada, using TLBL's own mailing list plus purchased mailing lists. While the mail campaign is going on, TLBL contracts writers to prepare the text of the first book in the series, and begins design of the book. However, actual production of the book does not occur until the mail campaign has ended and the number of copies needed has been determined from the returned postal cards.

The second book is produced about two months after the first has been mailed out, and it is sent to all those customers who received the first (free) volume. However, customers are then asked either to subscribe to the entire series at a fixed price or to return the second volume without charge. Company experience has been that, on average, 80% of the customers elect to subscribe and about 15% return the second book. The other 5% neither subscribe nor return the book, and TLBL takes no action against these subscribers except to send them a letter and to delete their names from its mailing lists. While 80% is the average subscription rate, the rate for specific series may vary anywhere from 70% to 85%.

Customers who do subscribe have a choice of paying for the entire series all at once, or of paying for each book (at a higher price) as it is sent. Roughly half of the customers elect each alternative, although there has been a trend towards advance payment since TLBL began accepting Visa and MasterCard (for advance payments only) two years ago.

The advertising brochure and direct mail campaign is the largest single cost incurred. The writers of the books are under a fixed-fee contract with TLBL and do not receive royalties. The layout and design work on each volume is performed by TLBL's salaried designers. Although printing costs have been escalating sharply, the cost to print and bind each book has been about $5.00 lately. The books are sold to customers at about $30.00 per copy. All customers may cancel their subscriptions at any time. The advance-payment subscribers must send a letter of cancellation, but few do so. The instalment subscribers may cancel simply by returning one of the volumes within fifteen days of receipt, whereupon they are sent no more volumes in the series. At some point before the conclusion of the series, 20 to 30% of instalment subscribers cancel.

Required:

Evaluate the revenue and expense recognition alternatives for TLBL for the book series.

Case 1-6

Bay and Eastern Corp.; Harbinger Ltd.

Helen Hook is president and chief executive officer of Bay and Eastern Corp. Bay and Eastern is a large, diversified corporation with its head office in Halifax and its executive offices in Toronto. The corporation controls 27 other corporations, mainly in North America, but also in Europe. Bay and Eastern's common shares are traded on both the Toronto Stock Exchange and on the New York Stock Exchange. Its preferred shares are held exclusively by a group of life insurance companies that purchased the shares in a private offering several years ago. The same insurance companies hold about half of Bay and Eastern's bonds, while the rest are publicly traded.

Helen's brother, Harvey, is president of Harbinger Ltd., a small chain of employment offices operating in and around Vancouver. The company was founded by Harvey Hook in 1981, when he left the personnel services division of a national consulting firm. Harvey owns 67% of the shares of Harbinger. His father, Henry, owns the other 33%. Henry was an important source of capital for Harvey when he started the business. Henry lent Harbinger $175,000 at its inception, and in 1986 accepted a 33% ownership interest in lieu of repayment of the debt. Harbinger has no other major creditors, although a line of credit has just been negotiated with a branch of the Royal Bank.

Required:

Explain how the objectives of financial reporting would differ between Bay and Eastern Corp. and Harbinger Ltd. Be as specific as possible.

Case 1-7

Wraps Inc.

Wraps Inc. is a franchiser of fast-food restaurants that specialize in providing a variety of wraps filled with healthy food. The most popular wrap is the sun-dried tomato wrap filled with fresh vegetables and a special California sauce. The restaurants all do business under the name of Wraps, but all are owned and operated by independent entrepreneurs; the original Wraps outlets are separately owned by the founding shareholders of Wraps Inc., and not by the franchiser corporation itself.

Wraps Inc. sells franchises for $400,000. Of the total amount, $50,000 is due when the franchise agreement is signed; another $60,000 is due when the outlet opens; and the remainder is due 18 months after the opening. Each payment is non-refundable. Wraps Inc. also receives a royalty of 3% of the invoice cost of the special supplies that the outlets are required to use (such as the special California sauce and the paper goods and other supplies that are imprinted with the Wraps logo). Wraps Inc. does not produce any of these goods; special arrangements are made with suppliers in each region of the country, and the royalties are forwarded to Wraps directly by the suppliers rather than by the franchisees.

Before the franchise agreement is signed, there is a period of discussion and exploration that can last from one to six months. During this time, the general feasibility of establishing a new outlet is examined. Market surveys are conducted to determine whether the local market could support another fast-food outlet, and the financial strength and backing of the prospective franchisee are examined. The costs incurred during the pre-signing stage are borne by Wraps Inc.

Once the franchise agreement is signed, Wraps Inc. actively assists the franchiser in selecting a site, planning the restaurant, gaining building permits, equipping the restaurant, and selecting and training the staff. All of the direct costs of establishing the outlet are paid by the franchisee, but Wraps Inc. contributes substantial assistance in the form of legal, architectural, planning, and management experts. The experts are retained by Wraps Inc. as regular staff consultants, and they are paid a fixed fee retainer each month, regardless of the amount of service that they provide to Wraps or its franchisees in that month. A supporting staff is employed directly by the franchiser.

Some of the expert assistance is delivered on-site, with Wraps Inc. paying the travel and other incidental costs. Head office provides other assistance, such as drafting of construction blueprints (based on master plans kept at Wraps Inc. head office) and preparation of supporting documents for city council site-zoning bylaws; and Wraps Inc. absorbs those costs as well. The period of time between the signing of the franchise agreement and the opening of the outlet can vary from six months to two years. On average, though, it takes about one year.

The direct involvement of Wraps Inc. largely ends when the outlet opens. Some additional management and employee training assistance is sometimes offered, but any significant additional services must be paid for by the franchisee.

Required:

Assume that you are an accounting advisor to Wraps Inc. Recommend an accounting and reporting policy for revenue and expense recognition for Wraps Inc. under each of the three following separate cases. Be sure to evaluate all of the alternative policies in light of the objectives of financial reporting in each case.

Case A: Wraps Inc. is a well-established franchiser that has franchised hundreds of successful outlets throughout North America. The corporation is controlled by the original founders, who own 54% of the outstanding common shares. The remaining shares are publicly traded on the Montreal Exchange. The success rate is very high for the franchisees; only 3% of the licensed franchisees have failed to open during the history of Wraps Inc., and only 8% have failed before payment of the final instalment of the franchise fee.

Case B: Wraps Inc. is privately owned by its three founders; each owns one-third of the common shares. There is no long-term debt, and few current liabilities.

The company is well established, and has a good record of successful openings, similar to the success rate described in Case A, above.

Case C: Wraps Inc. is a relatively new company, having been founded only three years previously. Only five franchised restaurants have been opened (in addition to the three owned by Wraps Inc.'s founders) and all have been successful. Eight more franchise agreements have been signed and good progress is being made towards opening all of the new outlets. Wraps Inc. is planning to offer shares to the public in the near future. In the meantime, the corporation has been borrowing substantial sums from the bank in order to meet the upfront costs of opening new franchises.

Case 1-8

Capreol Carpet Corporation

Capreol Carpet Corporation (CCC) is a manufacturer of broadloom carpeting located in Winnipeg, Manitoba. The company enjoys a good reputation for its product, but unfortunately has not been very profitable in recent years, owing to increasing imports of cheaper carpeting. In order to combat this threat, CCC invested substantial sums of money in new equipment to upgrade efficiency. Although efficiency picked up as a result, the improvement seemed only to keep the profit picture from getting any worse, rather than actually increasing net income.

CCC is a public company, but control was held by Bay and Eastern Corporation, a large conglomerate. Three months ago, Bay and Eastern sold its 70% interest in CCC to Upper Lip Enterprises Ltd., a British carpet manufacturer. Upper Lip planned to integrate CCC into its own operations, such that CCC would be the manufacturer of certain carpets sold by all of Upper Lip's distributors and would be the North American distributor of Upper Lip's British-made carpets.

Last week, the financial vice-president of Upper Lip sent a letter to David Blase, the controller of CCC, in which he detailed certain changes in accounting policy that CCC should institute in order to make its reporting practices consistent with those of Upper Lip, for purposes of consolidation and divisional performance appraisal. Included in the letter were the following:

1. Inventories, both of raw materials and finished goods, should be valued on the LIFO basis rather than on the average-cost basis previously used by CCC.

2. Carpeting sold to Upper Lip and its other subsidiaries should be billed at standard cost plus 10%, rather than at full list price less 15%, as is now the case. In effect, the gross margin on the intercompany transfers would be reduced from 35% of cost to 10% of cost. Carpet purchased by CCC from the Upper Lip group of companies would also be invoiced to CCC at cost plus 10%.

3. Depreciation on the new equipment should be increased from 8% per year (straight-line) to 12.5% per year. Standard costs would be adjusted to reflect the higher rate.

The financial vice-president, in his letter to David, has asked for a report identifying any problems in implementing the suggested changes in accounting policies. He has asked for specific comments on what the problem is for CCC in implementing the change and solutions to any problems that exist.

Required:

Assume that you are David Blase. Draft the report for the vice-president on the suggested changes to the accounting policies.

Case 1-9

Madayag Development Corporation

Madayag Development Corporation (MDC) is a real estate development company that is 60% owned by Thomas Madayag. Seaton's Inc., a privately-owned Canadian department store chain, owns 30%, and 10% is owned by a Canadian bank. MDC engages in two types of development: residential land sites and commercial retail space.

Mr. Madayag has been considering issuing a new class of MDC non-voting common shares to a small group of private investors. The purpose would be to provide a larger equity base so that MDC could be more aggressive in its commercial division. Like all real estate development companies, MDC is very highly leveraged; about 90% of the assets are financed by debt, most of which is provided by or through the shareholder bank. The issue price of the new share would be determined on the basis of the net market-value equity of the company's properties (that is, the total appraised values minus the company's outstanding debt). Since the company will continue to be private, a shareholders' agreement will govern the company's buy-back of the new shares should any investor decide in the future to sell his or her shares. The buy-back price of the non-voting shares is to be determined as the original issue price of the shares plus a proportionate share in the increase in the net book value of the common share equity from the date of issue to the date of repurchase, based on the most recent audited financial statements.

The shareholders' agreement places no restrictions on the potential resale price of the voting shares held by Mr. Madayag, Seaton's Inc., and the bank; should any of these shares be sold, they would be sold at their fair market value (which, for real estate developments, is normally based on the present value of future cash flows).

Mr. Madayag is interested in the implications of the proposed non-voting share issue for financial reporting. Therefore he has engaged an accounting advisor to offer advice on the most desirable accounting policies. A description of the business of the company follows.

Residential development In the residential division, MDC buys large tracts of land near major Canadian cities and holds the land for a few years until the growth of the city makes the land attractive for residential development. The purchase of the land is financed at least 90% by bank loans, and the loans provide for a line of credit to enable the company to borrow from the bank to pay the interest on the loans for up to five years after the land purchase; this holding period is considered by the bank to be the development period. When the time seems right (but usually within five years), MDC develops the land by providing services (e.g., sewer, water, electrical, and telephone mains and connections), laying out roads, and subdividing the land into home sites. The development process takes less than a year.

The sites are then advertised and sold to customers; about 25% of the sales are for cash, but most often they are for a 10–20% down payment with MDC accepting a mortgage for the remainder. The mortgages are usually for a 5-year term and a 20-year amortization and bear interest at a fixed rate that is one or two percentage points below the market rate of mortgage interest (but above the cost of MDC's borrowing). The prices charged to customers for the land vary within an individual tract. Some locations are considered more desirable than others and may therefore carry a price that is as much as double that of the less desirable locations within the same development.

MDC does no residential building; the company only sells the sites. Purchasers must arrange for construction of the houses themselves. Usually, however, MDC enters into an exclusive contract with one (or sometimes two) house builder(s) to perform the construction on the sites. The builder(s) erect model homes on the front sites (i.e., on the major access road), and then negotiate separately with the customers for construction of their homes. MDC charges the builders rent for the properties occupied by the model homes. When sale of the sites is complete, MDC sells the sites that the model homes are on to the purchasers of the model homes or to the builder.

MDC has been quite successful in its residential land development business. However, there is one land tract outside of Calgary that it has been unable to sell as quickly as desired. Purchased eight years ago and developed three years ago, only about 30% of the tract has been sold. Defaults by purchasers have been high, and the proceeds from the land sales have not been sufficient to pay the interest on the bank loan; the company has had to use cash from other developments to service the loan.

Commercial development The commercial division builds and leases retail developments in urban and suburban locations. Sometimes the shopping centres are built on a part of the residential development areas described above, but usually the sites are completely independent of the residential division. There is little lag between acquisition and development of a retail site, although the project can take up to six years from land assembly to final grand opening. The acquisition and development costs are financed by the bank, although in very large developments the bank will syndicate its participation (that is, bring in other banks to share the cost and the risk). Syndicate members demand audited financial statements from MDC.

MDC's general policy is to hold and operate the properties, although the company will sell if the price is right. Each property usually has a Seaton's store as an 'anchor' store; an anchor store is a major retailer that occupies a large space and provides much of the attractiveness of the development to shoppers and thereby to smaller retail lessees. There is a long-term lease agreement between the Seaton's store and MDC that locks the store into the development for at least 30 years. Similar leases bind other major anchor stores, but smaller retailers usually sign 5-year leases that are cancellable by either party at the end of the lease term.

The long-term leases are for fixed lease payments, with provision for increases due to inflation and due to increases in operating costs. Shorter-term (e.g., 5-year) leases are for a minimum monthly amount plus a percentage of the gross sales of the store. Smaller lessees also pay a large amount, equivalent to 50% of one year's minimum lease payments, at the inception of the lease; this payment is not repeated for lease renewals. MDC's cash flow from the lease payments is used to operate the developments and to service the bank debt that financed them. MDC has not had to pay any income taxes in the commercial division because capital cost allowance on the properties is more than enough to offset lease income. Excess CCA from the commercial division cannot be used to offset profits in the residential division, however, for income tax purposes.

Most of the retail developments have been very successful; the insurable value of the properties is, in aggregate, four times the depreciated historical cost of the properties. There are three recently built shopping centres that have not yet reached their full potential but are expected to do so within the next two years. Four other developments were built in the late 1990s in parts of the country that were hit hard by the economic recession in those years and they have never fully recovered; these properties are unable to recover their full operating and carrying costs.

Required:

Outline the accounting policies that would seem to best serve the reporting objectives of MDC, assuming that the new share issue is to occur. Your recommendations should include (but not be limited to) recognition of the revenues for each division, treatment of costs (including development costs and interest), and valuation of properties under development and after development.
[ICAO]

Intercorporate Investments:

An Introduction

Introduction

Much of Canada's economic activity is carried out not by corporations function-ing as independent units, but rather by groups of corporations that together form a single economic entity. One corporation will ordinarily own many other cor-porations. Of the 100 largest Canadian corporations, 37 are subsidiaries of another company, often of a foreign parent.[1] Each of those subsidiary corpora-tions operates through an extensive series of subsidiaries of its own, often num-bering in the dozens. The Canadian political, legal, and tax structures make it convenient to carry out operations through several corporate entities rather than just one. Differing provincial income taxes, for example, render it most practical to have business conducted by a separate corporation in each province.

Even small businesses frequently use more than one corporate entity to con-duct business. A small chain of restaurants may incorporate each restaurant indi-vidually in an attempt to isolate the business risk of each restaurant; the failure of one will not necessarily bring down the whole group.

Each of the various corporate entities that comprise an operating group will prepare its own financial statements for income tax and certain other purposes. The statements for an individual company are known as **separate-entity** finan-cial statements. For some users of the statements, however, such a fragmented view of the overall economic entity may be of limited usefulness. In fact, the high level of intercorporate (and non-arm's-length) transactions that take place between related companies may well make it almost impossible to get a clear view of the combined entity's overall operations solely by looking at the financial statements of the individual companies. Therefore, a broad set of reporting prin-ciples has developed over time, requiring related enterprises to report in ways that enable financial statement users to understand more clearly the overall financial position and operating results of a group of related companies. This set of prin-ciples is known simply as *reporting for intercorporate investments*. We will discuss and illustrate these principles in Chapters 2 through 7.

In this chapter, we review the types of intercorporate investments, the con-cepts of control and of significant influence, and the basic approach to the prepa-ration of consolidated financial statements. Chapter 3 discusses business combinations and the alternative approaches to achieving and reporting business combinations. Chapters 4 through 7 then discuss and illustrate various facets of preparing consolidated financial statements.

---

1. Compiled from *The Financial Post 500*, May 2000. Of the 37, 26 are subsidiaries of non-Canadian compa-nies; of the 26 with non-Canadian parents, 22 are private companies 100%-owned by their foreign parents.

Branch Accounting

Before plunging into our discussion of intercorporate investments, we should point out the difference between branch accounting and consolidated financial statements. Branch accounting is an application of control account procedures for keeping track of operating results of individual branches that are *not* separate corporations. When operations are carried out through separate corporations that are controlled by the parent, a parent-subsidiary relationship exists. Subsidiaries may function like branches of the parent corporation in a substantive sense, but they are not branches in an accounting sense.

In traditional practice, each branch has its own set of operating accounts. These are supporting accounts to a general ledger control account at head office. The extent of the branch account structure depends on whether the branch is a cost centre, revenue centre, profit centre, or investment centre. When the head office prepares financial statements for the company as a whole, the control account for each branch must be disaggregated—the revenues and expenses for the branch are included in the company's overall revenues and expenses rather than being reported as a single, net amount. The process of disaggregation has much in common with the process of preparing consolidated financial statements, which is the focus of Chapters 2 to 7, but without the completeness and much of the complexity of consolidation.

In modern, computerized accounting systems, branch accounts are usually integrated into the head office reporting structure rather than being tied into a control account. The account numbering system classifies each account by both branch and type (and perhaps by other dimensions, such as by product line), thereby permitting a matrix approach to reporting. The operating results of each branch can easily be drawn from the system, and the combined results can equally easily be reported. Since the branch and head office account systems are integrated, there is no need for control accounts and there is no need for quasi-consolidation procedures to disaggregate the control accounts.

In contrast, "branches" that are separate legal corporations *must* have separate accounts and separate financial statements for legal and tax reasons. The parent keeps track of the subsidiaries through a single investment account for each subsidiary. In modern practice, therefore, there is a fundamental procedural difference between accounting for a branch (as a responsibility centre) and accounting for a corporate subsidiary. Management accounting systems are designed to report on responsibility centres, including branches. In this book, our focus is on financial reporting, whether internal or external, of corporate entities.

Definition of Intercorporate Investments

An **intercorporate investment** is any purchase by one corporation of the securities of another corporation. Broadly speaking, the investment may be in bonds, preferred shares, or common shares.

Many intercorporate investments are made simply as uses of excess cash or as investments to yield interest, dividend income, or capital gains. These investments do not give the investor any ability to control or influence the operations of the investee corporation, and are accounted for as *temporary investments* (for short-term investments) or as *portfolio investments* (for long-term investments).

A substantively different type of intercorporate investment is an investor corporation's purchase of enough of the voting shares of an investee corporation to give the investor the ability to control or *significantly influence* the affairs of the investee corporation. The reporting practices used for portfolio investments are not adequate for share investments that give the investor the ability to affect the investee's operations. Therefore, entirely different reporting procedures are usually necessary. The reporting and accounting practices for intercorporate investments will be surveyed in subsequent sections of this chapter. But first, we will take a brief look at the accounting for portfolio investments.

Portfolio Investments—A Quick Review

Portfolio investments are reported on the *cost basis*. Under the **cost basis**:

- investments are carried on the balance sheet at their historical cost,

- dividends are reported as revenue when declared, and

- interest is recognized as revenue as it accrues.

The only departure from the cost basis for long-term portfolio investments occurs when the market value drops below the historical cost. The carrying value of the investment may be written down if the decline is judged to be "other than a temporary decline" [CICA 3050.20]—that is, if the decline in value is more long-lived than simply a short-term fluctuation in market price. The decision to write down an investment is highly judgemental; accounting history is littered with disputes between managements and auditors as to whether specific investments should be written down.

Carrying value may also be reduced when dividends received are in excess of the investor's proportionate share of the investee's net earnings. When dividends are in excess of earnings, the excess amount can be viewed as a liquidating dividend and credited to the investment account as a return of capital [CICA 3050.02(c)]. For some types of investments, a liquidating dividend approach is quite appropriate, such as in investment companies, mining companies with an expiring resource base, and companies that are intentionally downsizing their operations.

In other situations, however, the dividend-paying company may simply be maintaining a constant dividend policy through a period of temporarily depressed earnings. In these cases, it is more common practice to recognize the dividends fully as revenue instead of treating the excess portion as a liquidating dividend; the excess is viewed essentially as an advance against future earnings.

Accounting for bonds purchased as portfolio investments normally entails amortization of the discount or premium *if* the intent of management is to hold the bonds as a long-term investment and if the amount of discount or premium is material. The amortization is not on the discount or premium from the original issue of the bonds (unless the investor purchased the original issue). Instead, amortization is based on the spread between the price paid by the investor and the face value of the bonds. Original issue discount/premium is usually quite small, but subsequent discount/premium can be substantial; the market value of bonds can fluctuate widely, in response to fluctuations in the market rates of interest.

The discount/premium amortization is credited/charged to interest revenue and the carrying value of the bonds is adjusted accordingly [CICA 3050.19]. Amortization can be either straight-line or "scientific" (i.e., on an effective yield basis); the choice is essentially arbitrary, and thus management should choose the method that is most consistent with the financial reporting objectives of the investor company.

When bonds are purchased as a short-term or "temporary" investment, however, there is no point to amortizing discount or premium because long-term interest yield is not the objective of the investment and because the change in market price between purchase and resale can readily overwhelm any amount of amortization.

The market value of all portfolio investments should be disclosed. It sometimes is argued that the market value of a large block of securities (especially shares) will not be the same as the value of the small trades that may set the market price. While that may be the case, quoted market values will be a far better indicator of economic value than the carrying value, and therefore quoted market values as of the balance sheet date should be disclosed.

Accounting for portfolio investments is a topic that is discussed extensively in intermediate accounting textbooks and is not examined further here. A brief review of portfolio investment accounting was presented as a refresher and to clarify the distinction between portfolio investments and those investments that are used to control or significantly influence the investee corporation. The remainder of this chapter examines intercorporate share investments that are *not* portfolio investments, beginning with a discussion of the meaning of control.

Strategic Intercorporate Investments

The previous section discussed the accounting for "passive" investments, those wherein the investor invests in the securities of another corporation simply in order to earn a return on the investment. In contrast, many intercorporate investments are made for the explicit purpose of controlling or significantly influencing the operations of the investee corporation.

When the effect of an intercorporate investment is to enable the investor to affect the operations of the investee, the cost basis of reporting is not appropriate because it does not reflect the substance of the relationship between the two corporations. Instead, other financial reporting approaches must be used.

Controlled subsidiaries

The meaning of control

The term *control* is commonly used in its dictionary sense of one company's ability to exercise authority over another company. Often, control in this loose sense can be exercised by a company that holds only a relatively small proportion of the shares of another. While it is tempting to use the term in this broader sense, *control* in fact has a much more precise meaning in financial reporting and in law.

The *CICA Handbook* defines *control* as follows:

> **Control** of an enterprise is the continuing power to determine its strategic operating, investing and financing policies without the co-operation of others. [CICA 1590.03(b)]

When one corporation controls another, the controlled corporation is a *subsidiary* of the investor or *parent* corporation. The *CICA Handbook* defines this relationship as follows:

> A **subsidiary** is an enterprise controlled by another enterprise (the **parent**) that has the right and ability to obtain future economic benefits from the resources of the enterprise and is exposed to the related risks. [CICA 1590.03(a)]

In the *CICA Handbook* definitions, the fact of control defines a subsidiary; an investee that is not controlled by the investor is not a subsidiary of the investor.

Normally, control exists when one corporation has the ability to elect a majority of the board of directors of another corporation. Such control is usually obtained by owning sufficient voting shares (or "equity interest," in *CICA Handbook* terminology[2]) to ensure a majority of the votes for the board of directors of the controlled corporation.

Some corporations have more than one class of voting shares, with different voting rights. Canadian Tire, for example, has two classes of shares that participate equally in dividends but that vary significantly in voting rights; Class A has one vote per share while Class B has 10 votes per share. Control then depends on having a majority of the *votes* rather than a majority of the shares outstanding.

In some cases, one corporation may control another without owning a sufficient equity interest to have a majority of the votes. Examples include the following:

- the parent corporation holds convertible securities or stock options that, if converted or exercised, would give the parent a majority of the seats on the board of directors.

- in a private corporation, a *shareholders' agreement* gives control to a shareholder who owns 50% or less of the shares.

- a major creditor (who also has an equity interest in the debtor) has the right to select a majority of the board of directors as a result of a debt agreement.

Regardless of the means by which control is obtained, control can exist only if there is an existing or attainable right to elect a majority of the board of directors *without the co-operation of other shareholders.*

Control is presumed to exist as long as the parent corporation has the ability to determine the subsidiary's strategic policies, and it ceases to exist when the parent loses that power. A parent can lose control voluntarily, (1) by selling enough of its interest to lose its vote majority or (2) by permitting the subsidiary to issue sufficient voting shares to reduce the parent's interest to a non-controlling interest.[3]

A parent can also lose control involuntarily, such as when a subsidiary enters receivership and control passes to a trustee. Similarly, some loan agreements may give a major creditor voting shares as collateral, or non-voting common or preferred shares may automatically become voting shares in specified circumstances of financial distress. A foreign country may restrict a parent's control of a subsidiary. In these cases, the investee corporation ceases to be a subsidiary once control has passed from the parent. Until control ceases, however, the investee remains a subsidiary. The *possibility* of losing control does not affect the parent-subsidiary relationship (or the financial reporting thereof). Only when control is lost *in fact* does the parent-subsidiary relationship cease to exist.

A key phrase in the *CICA Handbook* definition of control is "without the co-operation of others." One corporation may appear to control another because it owns a relatively small block of shares and the remainder of the shares are widely held. In this case the corporation relies on the co-operation of the other shareholders, either by their active allegiance or by their passive disinterest, to exert control. However, the other shareholders may at any time decide not to co-operate or may rebel, and thus control does not truly exist. When the investor corporation owns a small block of shares but nevertheless can influence the

---

2. "A parent's control over a subsidiary . . . [is] normally acquired through an equity interest in the subsidiary" [CICA 1590.06].

3. Reduction of the parent's ownership interest is discussed in Chapter 7.

strategic policies of the investee, the investor is said to have **significant influence** over the affairs of the investee, *but not control.* Significant influence is discussed more fully later in this chapter.

Indirect control

Control need not be direct. **Indirect control** exists when a subsidiary is controlled by another subsidiary rather than by the parent company. Exhibit 2-1 shows three examples of indirect control.

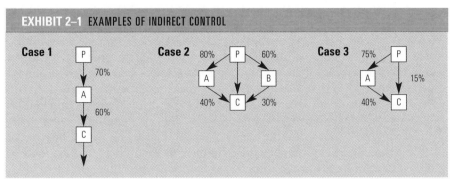

EXHIBIT 2–1 EXAMPLES OF INDIRECT CONTROL

In Case 1, the parent (**P**) controls subsidiary **A** by owning 70% of **A**'s voting shares, and **A** controls **C** by owning 60% of **C**'s voting shares. Since **P** controls **A**, **P** can control **A**'s votes for **C**'s board of directors. Therefore, **P** has indirect control of **C**. **C** is a subsidiary of **A**, and both **C** and **A** are subsidiaries of **P**.

Voting control is a yes–no matter, not multiplicative. **P** controls 60% of the votes for **C**'s board of directors, not just 42% (70% × 60%). **P** controls **A**, and **A** controls **C**; therefore **P** controls **C**. Ownership of 60%, whether direct or indirect, gives **P** virtually complete control over the strategic policies of **C**.

In Case 2, control of **P** over **C** is achieved indirectly through two direct subsidiaries of **P**: **A** and **B**. Neither **A** nor **B** has control of **C** because each has less than a majority of **C**'s voting shares. However, **P** can control **C** because **P** controls 70% of the votes in **C** through its control of **A** and **B** (40% + 30%). In this example, **A**, **B**, and **C** are all subsidiaries of **P**, but **C** is *not* a subsidiary of either **A** or **B**.

In Case 3, **P** has both direct and indirect ownership interests in **C**. Control is achieved only by virtue of the shares of **C** that are owned by both **P** and **A**, and thus **P**'s control of **C** is still indirect, despite **P**'s direct ownership of 15% of **C**'s voting shares. The sum of one corporation's direct and indirect interest in another corporation is known as the **beneficial interest**. **P** has a 55% beneficial interest in **C**. **A** and **C** are subsidiaries of **P**; **C** is *not* a subsidiary of **A**.

Other types of ownership arrangements can exist; these three examples are merely illustrative. Some intercorporate ownerships are very complex, and require careful analysis in order to determine who controls whom.

Limitations on control

The ownership of a majority of votes of another corporation gives the parent control over the strategic policies of the subsidiary, but not necessarily *absolute* control. Legislation generally requires that *special resolutions* be approved by at least two-thirds of the votes of the shareholders. **Special resolutions** include proposals to change a corporation's charter or bylaws, including any changes to the structure of the share ownership. Thus a parent cannot be completely assured of the ability to restructure a subsidiary, to amalgamate it, or to change the broad business purposes stated in its charter (which is called the **letters patent**) unless the parent owns at least two-thirds of the voting shares.

While two-thirds ownership can guarantee the approval of special resolutions, it still does not give absolute control. As long as there are outside shareholders, the parent corporation cannot require the subsidiary to follow any policies that are detrimental to the interests of the non-controlling shareholders. Parent action that is detrimental to the interests of non-controlling shareholders is called **oppression of minority shareholders**.

For example, assume that ParentCorp owns controlling interest in SubLtd, and that SubLtd is the major source of supply for the primary raw material that is used by ParentCorp. The board of directors of ParentCorp may want SubLtd to sell the raw material to ParentCorp at less than market value. If ParentCorp owns 100% of SubLtd, then SubLtd can do so without harming any shareholders. The reduced profit in SubLtd is offset by increased profit in ParentCorp. But if ParentCorp owns only 70% of SubLtd, then the shifting of profits from SubLtd to ParentCorp will harm the 30% minority shareholders in SubLtd. Their equity, their potential dividends, and the market value of their shares will all be reduced.

Therefore, many corporations prefer to own 100% of their subsidiaries. One hundred percent ownership is particularly common when there is a close working relationship between the parent and the subsidiary, or among the various subsidiaries.

Because of the relatively unfettered ability of a parent to control the affairs of a wholly-owned subsidiary, creditors of such a subsidiary frequently take steps to protect their own interests. Creditors may insist that the parent guarantee the subsidiary's debts, may require fairly liquid collateral (such as assignment of accounts receivable), or may include restrictive covenants in bond indentures.

A parent corporation can acquire a subsidiary in either of two ways: (1) by founding (or creating) a new corporation, or (2) by buying a controlling interest in an existing corporation.

Parent-founded subsidiaries

Most subsidiaries are founded by the parent corporation in order to carry out some segment of the parent's business. Subsidiaries are formed for a variety of legal, regulatory, and tax reasons. For example, if a corporation is subject to taxation in several countries or provinces, it usually simplifies tax reporting if there is a separate legal entity in each taxation jurisdiction.

Similarly, lines of business that are subject to regulation are usually carried out in separate legal entities. The intercorporate organization of BCE is an example of a regulatory-inspired organization—Bell Canada and certain other subsidiaries are subject to regulation, while other subsidiaries are not. Maintaining distinct legal separation between regulated and non-regulated lines of business prevents the non-regulated businesses from unnecessarily falling under regulation.

Financing arrangements may also be facilitated by having subsidiaries rather than a single legal entity conduct all the corporation's business. A separate corporation is frequently established to conduct customer financing activities. Finance companies have quite different financial structures than do product or service organizations. It may be easier to arrange the secondary financing of customers' instalment debt or leases if the receivables from customers are assets of a distinct corporate finance company. Also, there can be tax advantages to creating a separate legal entity to carry out specialized finance services such as leasing.

The vast majority of parent-founded subsidiaries are wholly owned by the parent. Sometimes the parent will reduce its ownership below 100% once the subsidiary is established. There are two ways by which the parent can dilute its ownership interest. One is by selling part of its holding of the subsidiary shares to the public or to a private buyer. The other is by having the subsidiary issue new shares to public or private buyers. Both approaches reduce the parent's ownership share, but the first approach also reduces the parent's investment in the subsidiary. The second approach maintains the parent's share investment and raises new capital for the subsidiary.[4] The sale of Air Canada shares to the public illustrates both approaches. The initial public share offer, in 1988, was an issuance of new shares by the corporation, while the second share offer in 1989 was a sale of the government's shares. The 1988 proceeds went to Air Canada, while the 1989 proceeds went to the federal government.

When a parent establishes a subsidiary in a foreign country, the parent may decide not to own 100% of the subsidiary's shares. The decision may be to include host-country shareholders for business reasons. In some countries, the parent has little choice. The host country may encourage or require local participation in the ownership of subsidiaries of foreign-owned parents in order to improve the subsidiary's responsiveness to economic conditions in the host country and in order to establish a basis for accountability to the host country's citizens or government.

Despite the exceptions, most subsidiaries are wholly owned. This fact greatly simplifies the preparation of consolidated statements, as we shall see when we get into the actual process of consolidation.

Purchasing a subsidiary

Instead of founding a subsidiary, a corporation can purchase a controlling interest in an existing corporation as a going concern. There are many reasons for acquiring a going concern instead of starting up a new subsidiary. For example:

- The acquired subsidiary may effectively remove a competitor from the marketplace.

- The acquired company may provide a product or service that fills a void in the purchaser's existing product line.

- The acquired company may have licences or geographic rights that complement those of the purchaser.

- The new subsidiary may enable the acquirer to pursue a new strategic direction without having to start from scratch in a highly competitive environment.

- The new subsidiary may ensure sources of supply or provide direct access to the industrial, retail, or Internet market.

- The newly acquired company may have a business that is counter-cyclical to the parent's, thereby increasing the parent's overall stability and reducing investors' and creditors' perceptions of the financial risk of the total entity.

- The subsidiary may generate a large cash flow that is needed by the parent to fund its operations or product development.

Whenever one corporation buys a controlling interest in another, and thereby obtains control over the net assets of the acquired company, a **business combination** has occurred. A business combination can be accomplished in a variety of

---

4. The accounting and reporting implications of changes in the parent's ownership share are discussed in Chapter 7.

ways, and the accounting problem is to report the substance of the combination regardless of the legal form of the transaction. This topic is discussed at length in Chapter 3.

Non-controlling and minority interests: a terminology note

Prior to the introduction of Section 1590 in 1992, the *CICA Handbook* used the phrase "minority interest" to designate the interest of those shareholders who did not have a controlling interest. Section 1590 explicitly recognized that it may be possible to have a controlling interest while owning less than 50% of the investee's shares, and thus a controlling interest could also be a minority interest. As a result, the terminology in the *CICA Handbook* was altered; "minority interest" was consistently replaced by "non-controlling interest."

Non-controlling interest is the broader, all-inclusive phrase. In practice, however, the vast majority of non-controlling interests really are minority interests. Indeed, it will be very rare for a *majority* non-controlling interest to exist (although it is possible). As a result, consolidated financial statements continue to use the phrase minority interest. Just because the phrase has disappeared from the *CICA Handbook* does not mean it will disappear from financial statements.

Significantly influenced affiliates

Frequently, one corporation will purchase less than a controlling equity interest in another corporation. However, the investor may nevertheless be able to have a substantial impact on the strategic operating, investing, and financing policies of the investee. Such substantial impact is known as **significant influence**.

Significant influence can be achieved if the investee corporation's shares are widely distributed and there is no effective opposition to the investor's active involvement. However, *control* does not exist in such situations. It is possible for another investor or group of investors to acquire control over a majority of the shares of the investee, and then to wrest influence from the hands of the minority investee. When such a change in control takes place against the wishes of the previously dominant shareholder (and, usually, against the wishes of the board of directors), the change is known as a **hostile takeover**.

It usually is clear when control exists. The investor either can elect a majority of the board of directors (without the co-operation of other shareholders) or it cannot. In contrast, the presence of significant influence is not so clearly determinable. The general numerical guideline cited in the *CICA Handbook* [CICA 3050.04] is that significant influence is presumed to exist if the investor corporation owns 20% or more of the voting shares of the investee (but does not have a controlling interest).

The percentage of ownership is only a guideline; it is the *substance* of the relationship between the two companies that must be examined. The issue is important because investments in significantly influenced companies are reported on a different basis than are subsidiaries or portfolio investments. Subsidiaries are consolidated, while portfolio investments are reported on the cost basis.

Income from portfolio investments is recorded only when dividends are declared by the investee. If the investor has the ability to influence significantly the strategic policies of the investee, then reporting the investment as a portfolio investment gives the investor the ability to manipulate its own income by influencing the affiliate's dividend policy. If the investor wanted to smooth its reported net income, the affiliate could be "influenced" to declare small dividends in years in which the investor had high operating income, and to declare large dividends in years of low investor operating income.

When an investor has significant influence, then the investor plays a part in the earnings process of the investee. It is logical in such instances for the investor to report its proportionate share of the investee's earnings, regardless of whether the earnings have been passed on to the investor in the form of dividends.

Several factors must be examined in order to determine whether significant influence exists. The composition of the board of directors is one important factor. If the board contains representatives of the investor, these representatives may be able to influence corporate policies significantly in the boardroom. This is particularly true when the investor's non-controlling shareholding is the largest single block of shares. In that case, a majority of the investee's board may be representatives of the investor. Significant influence may exist, however, when other investors also have significant influence over the investee corporation and even when another investor holds controlling interest in the investee.

The existence of significant influence is determined by more than just the extent of share ownership. A voting interest of less than 20% can carry significant influence if there are other important relationships between the two companies, or if the affiliate's shares are widely held and all other owners are passive, or if the investor corporation has the active support of other shareholders. Conversely, a voting interest of up to 50% may not give significant influence if the management and controlling shareholders of the investee corporation are hostile to the investor corporation, and will not accede to the investor's demands or permit the investor's nominees to sit on the investee's board.

Significant influence may also be indicated by the extent of intercorporate transactions. If the investor is a major supplier or major customer of the investee, significant influence can be exercised not only by the ownership of shares but also by means of the supplier-customer relationship. Other indications of significant influence include substantial debt financing provided by the investor, the investor's ownership of patents, trademarks or processes upon which the affiliate's business depends, and the provision of managerial or technical assistance to the affiliate.

Obviously, there is a larger grey area for the existence of significant influence than there is for the existence of control. Nevertheless, it is reasonably clear in most real situations whether or not significant influence does exist. If there is doubt, then significant influence probably does not exist. But the doubt must arise as a result of examining the substance of the operating situation, and not merely by looking at the percentage of ownership of the voting shares.

Joint ventures

A particular instance in which significant influence is a matter of contractual right is when the investor corporation is part-owner of a *joint venture*. A **joint venture** is "an arrangement whereby two or more parties jointly control a specific business undertaking and contribute resources towards its accomplishment" [CICA 3055.06]. Joint ventures are common in certain industries (such as resource exploration), and are common in global competition when two otherwise competing companies join forces to establish operations in another country or when one company joins with the host country's government in establishing a new venture. For example, Nortel established joint ventures with Motorola in the U.S. and the Matra Group in France to jointly develop the market for cordless digital telephones by shared technologies.

An essential and distinguishing characteristic of a joint venture is that the investors or *co-venturers* enter into an agreement that governs each co-venturer's involvement in the joint venture, including its capital contribution, its representation on the board of directors, and its involvement in management. No one investor can make major strategic decisions unilaterally; major decisions require the consent of all of the co-venturers. This is known as **joint control**.

Joint ventures are always established by a very limited number of co-venturers. Joint ventures are always private companies. The joint venture agreement is similar to the **shareholders' agreement** in private corporations that clarifies the rights and responsibilities of the various shareholders. The difference is that, in private corporations, a single shareholder or a small group may exercise control. In a joint venture, in contrast, no one investor (or subgroup of investors) can control the joint venture even though that investor may contribute a majority of the capital. Joint ventures require agreement amongst the co-venturers, not voting power.

Joint control should not be confused with *profit sharing*. Control is joint, but profit sharing is not necessarily equal. The joint venture stipulates how the risks and benefits of the venture will be shared, including the distribution of profits and dividends.

Since each investor in a joint venture has participation rights, each investor has significant influence in the joint venture. Significant influence in a joint venture is a matter of fact, not professional judgement.

Reporting Investments in Affiliates and Subsidiaries

When an investor corporation prepares its financial statements, there are three basic ways in which investments in the voting shares of other corporations can be reported: (1) the *cost method*, (2) the *equity method*, and (3) *consolidation*.

Cost-basis reporting

The **cost method** or **cost basis** is the approach that is used for portfolio investments; that is, for investments in the shares of companies over which the investor does not have significant influence. The investment is shown in the balance sheet at cost, and dividends are reported in the investor's income when declared by the investee. The cost method is also used for all investments in fixed-income securities, including preferred shares, regardless of whether the investee corporation is significantly influenced or not.

The cost method is used for subsidiaries and significantly influenced affiliates only if the parent is prevented from exercising its control or influence. The exercise of control or significant influence can be blocked by foreign governments (for affiliates in foreign countries). If the affiliate enters receivership, control or influence also is lost, at least temporarily. Loss of control or significant influence may be an indication that the investment has been impaired. A write-down of the investment may be advisable if there is a decline in value "that is other than a temporary decline" [CICA 3050.20].

Equity-basis reporting

Significantly influenced subsidiaries

The **equity method** or **equity basis** is the method that is used for reporting investments in income-participating shares of significantly influenced investee corporations. Income-participating shares include all unrestricted and restricted common shares and cumulative participating preferred shares, regardless of whether the shares are voting or non-voting. Since the investor has the ability to significantly influence the operations of the investee, the investee's economic performance is closely bound to that of the investor.

To give the investor's stakeholders a fair presentation of the corporation's overall economic performance, it is necessary to include in the investor's earnings its proportionate share of (or equity in) the *investee's earnings*, rather than just the dividends declared. The financial reporting objective of performance evaluation is thereby better served. The cash flow prediction objective is also better served—since the investor can control the dividend policy of the investee, the equity method requires that the full amount of earnings available as dividends (and thus hypothetically transferable in cash) be reported in the investor's income statement.

Historically, the manipulative possibilities inherent in reporting income on a dividend-only basis from controlled or significantly influenced investee corporations led to accounting standards that recommend the equity method. Section 3050, "Long-Term Investments," of the *CICA Handbook* is a good example of an accounting standard that gives precedence to user objectives over preparer objectives; it removes the ability of the investor to manipulate its own net income by regulating the dividend flow from the affiliate.

On the balance sheet, the investment account is reported at cost, plus the investor's share of the affiliate's net income (or minus the investor's share of losses), less dividends received.[5] The net result is that at any point in time, the investment account reflects the historical cost of the shares to the investor plus the investor's proportionate share of the increase (or decrease) in the investee's net asset value since the date of the initial investment.

Joint ventures

Equity-basis reporting is the method that is used in most countries for reporting investments in joint ventures. Prior to 1995, Canadian co-venturers could use either equity reporting or a technique known as *proportionate consolidation*. We will discuss proportionate consolidation later in this chapter.

The AcSB changed its recommendations effective 1 January 1995 to require the use of proportionate consolidation only [CICA 3055.17]. This uniquely Canadian requirement has put Canada out of step with the rest of the world, which does not use proportionate consolidation. It is quite possible that the AcSB's objective of harmonizing Canadian standards with International Accounting Standards will lead to another change, back to equity-basis reporting *only*. At the time of writing this, however, equity reporting is not permitted for joint ventures by the *CICA Handbook* recommendations.

Consolidation

Subsidiaries

Consolidation is the process of reporting the full amount of assets, liabilities, revenues, and expenses of an economic entity comprised of a parent corporation and its subsidiaries on a single set of financial statements. Because the parent corporation can control the activities of its subsidiaries, financial statements for each individual company in the group are potentially misleading if relied upon exclusively. Consolidated statements will show the *total* economic activity of the parent and all of its subsidiaries. All of the resources and obligations under the control of the parent corporation are reported on consolidated statements.

---

5. In many situations, it is necessary to make adjustments to the reported earnings of the affiliate before the investor's share is reported on the investor's income statements. These adjustments and the reasons for them will be explained later, beginning in Chapter 4.

Canadian practice calls for consolidation of *all* of a parent company's subsidiaries [CICA 1590.16]. Non-consolidated reporting is permitted in certain reporting situations; these will be discussed toward the end of this chapter.

Consolidated statements are prepared from the point of view of the shareholders of the parent company. Consolidation is accomplished by adding the elements in the financial statements of subsidiaries with those of the parent. On the balance sheet, there will be no investment account for the consolidated subsidiaries. Instead, the assets and liabilities of the subsidiaries will be added to those of the parent in order to show the economic resources of the entire economic entity comprising the parent and its subsidiaries. On the income statement, the revenues and expenses will be the totals for each item for the parent plus the subsidiaries. The effects of any intercompany transactions will be eliminated in order to avoid double-counting.

When there are several layers of subsidiaries, consolidated statements will normally be prepared at each level, particularly when there are non-controlling shareholders in the intermediate layers. For example, assume that Corporation **A** owns 70% of Corporation **B**, and Corporation **B** owns 60% of **C**. The following financial statements will be prepared:

- **C** will prepare its own separate-entity financial statements, which will be used by **C**'s minority shareholders.

- **B** will prepare separate-entity (i.e., non-consolidated) statements for tax purposes, internal purposes, and perhaps for specific users, such as the bank. In the non-consolidated statements, the investment in **C** will be shown as an asset.

- For issuance to the general public, **B** will also prepare consolidated statements that include the assets, liabilities, revenue, expenses, and cash flows of **C**. These statements are relevant for **B**'s non-controlling shareholders.

- **A** will prepare consolidated statements that include all of the assets, liabilities, revenues, expenses, and cash flows of the consolidated statements of **B**, which includes **C**. **A**'s consolidated statements are relevant to the shareholders of **A**, and of **A** *only*. **A** will also prepare non-consolidated statements for tax purposes.

Non-controlling or minority shareholders are interested only in the statements of the company in which they own shares. **B**'s non-controlling shareholders are not interested in the statements of **A**, even though **B** is controlled by **A**, because they are not shareholders of **A**.

Joint ventures

A special case of consolidation arises for joint ventures. We noted above that equity-basis reporting is widely used around the world for investments in joint ventures. However, Canadian practice currently (in 2001) requires another approach to reporting investments in joint ventures—*proportionate consolidation*. Instead of consolidating *all* of the assets, liabilities, revenues, and expenses of the investee, **proportionate consolidation** combines only the *investor's share* of the joint venture balances in the consolidated statements.

Reporting versus *recording* methods

The next section gives an introductory illustration of consolidation. Before turning our attention to the preparation of consolidated statements, however, it is important to point out that the *reporting* of intercorporate investments often is not the same as the *recording* of the investments in the books of the investor.

Investments in significantly influenced affiliates are normally *reported* in the investor's financial statements on the equity basis, but the investment account on the books of the investor corporation may be *recorded in the investor's books* on the cost basis. The necessary adjustments to convert from the cost to the equity basis for reporting purposes are then made on working papers and are not necessarily recorded on the books of the investor. Therefore, the reporting method for the investment in significantly influenced affiliates *may* be different from the recording method used in the investor's books.

Consolidation is a different story. Consolidated statements are prepared by means of a series of adjustments and eliminations that are *always* made only on working papers and are *never* recorded on the books of the parent company. An investor corporation's recording procedures for investments in affiliates and subsidiaries is frequently based on ease of record keeping. The reported amounts on the investor's consolidated financial statements are derived from schedules and worksheets that are prepared only for reporting purposes. The adjustments are not recorded on anyone's books, because there is no legal or bookkeeping entity that corresponds to the consolidated statements. Consolidated statements are reports intended to reflect an economic concept, rather than a practical or legal reality.

Remember the rules:

- Investments in significantly influenced affiliates *may* be recorded in the investor's books on the cost basis, even when reporting is on the equity basis. In that case, adjustments to convert from cost to equity for reporting purposes are on worksheets and working papers only.

- Consolidations *must* occur on worksheets only. The adjustments made for consolidation are *never* recorded on any company's books. There are no journal entries recorded anywhere except on the accountant's working papers.

Example of Accounting for Strategic Investments

We will begin our illustration by preparing consolidated statements under the assumption that the cost method of recording is used on the parent's books. We will then use the same example to illustrate the use of the equity basis of reporting in unconsolidated statements. Finally, we will prepare consolidated statements assuming that the equity method of recording is used on the parent's books.

EXHIBIT 2–2 SEPARATE-ENTITY TRIAL BALANCES

December 31, 2005

	Parco Dr	Parco Cr	Subco Dr	Subco Cr
Cash	$ 70,000		$ 40,000	
Accounts receivable	200,000		110,000	
Receivable from Subco	60,000		—	
Inventories	150,000		120,000	
Land	100,000		—	
Buildings and equipment	1,000,000		450,000	
Accumulated depreciation		$ 300,000		$ 100,000
Investment in Subco (at cost)	80,000			
Accounts payable		120,000		80,000
Due to Parco		—		60,000
Long-term notes payable		—		300,000
Future income taxes		140,000		30,000
Common shares		300,000		80,000
Dividends declared	30,000		20,000	
Retained earnings, December 31, 2004		762,000		60,000
Sales revenue		800,000		400,000
Dividend income		20,000		—
Cost of sales	480,000		280,000	
Depreciation expense	130,000		30,000	
Income tax expense	32,000		20,000	
Other expenses	110,000		40,000	
	$ 2,442,000	$ 2,442,000	$ 1,110,000	$ 1,110,000

Consolidation when the cost method is used

To illustrate the process of consolidation (and, thereafter, the equity method of accounting), assume that Parco established a subsidiary in 2000 by creating a new corporation named Subco. Subco issued 100 common shares to Parco in return for $80,000 cash paid by Parco for the shares. Parco has remained the sole shareholder of Subco in succeeding years.

On December 31, 2005, several years after the incorporation of Subco, the trial balances for the two companies are as shown in Exhibit 2-2. The 2005 separate-entity financial statements of the two companies (derived from the trial balances) are presented in Exhibit 2-3, prior to any adjustments related to Parco's investment in Subco. We have highlighted in colour those elements that are of particular interest for consolidation purposes.

In order to prepare the consolidated statements, we first need to know the nature and extent of financial interactions between the two. Important facts relating to the 2005 statements are as follows:

1. Parco's investment in Subco is carried on Parco's books at cost ($80,000).

2. The two balance sheets include $60,000 that is owed by Subco to Parco. The amount is a current asset for Parco and a current liability for Subco.

EXHIBIT 2–3 SEPARATE-ENTITY FINANCIAL STATEMENTS

Balance Sheets
December 31, 2005

	Parco	Subco
Assets		
Current assets:		
Cash	$ 70,000	$ 40,000
Accounts receivable	200,000	110,000
Receivable from Subco	**60,000**	—
Inventories	150,000	120,000
	480,000	270,000
Property, plant, and equipment:		
Land	100,000	—
Buildings and equipment	1,000,000	450,000
Accumulated depreciation	(300,000)	(100,000)
	800,000	350,000
Other assets:		
Investment in Subco (at cost)	**80,000**	—
Total assets	$ 1,360,000	$ 620,000
Liabilities and shareholders' equity		
Current liabilities:		
Accounts payable	$ 120,000	$ 80,000
Due to Parco	—	**60,000**
	120,000	140,000
Long-term notes payable	—	300,000
Future income taxes	140,000	30,000
Total liabilities	260,000	470,000
Shareholders' equity:		
Common shares	300,000	**80,000**
Retained earnings	800,000	70,000
Total shareholders' equity	1,100,000	150,000
Total liabilities and shareholders' equity	$ 1,360,000	$ 620,000

Statements of Income and Retained Earnings
Year Ended December 31, 2005

	Parco	Subco
Sales revenue	$ 800,000	$ 400,000
Dividend income	**20,000**	—
	820,000	400,000
Operating expenses:		
Cost of sales	480,000	280,000
Depreciation expense	130,000	30,000
Income tax expense	32,000	20,000
Other expenses	110,000	40,000
	752,000	370,000
Net income	68,000	30,000
Retained earnings, December 31, 2004	762,000	60,000
Dividends declared	(30,000)	**(20,000)**
Retained earnings, December 31, 2005	$ 800,000	$ 70,000

3. Dividends received from Subco during the year are shown as dividend income on Parco's income statement.

4. The sales of Parco include $100,000 of merchandise sold to Subco, all of which was sold by Subco to outside customers during the year.

When a subsidiary's financial statements are consolidated with those of the parent, the parent and the subsidiary are viewed as a single economic entity. The objective of consolidation is to show on the consolidated statements of the parent all of the assets, liabilities, revenues, and expenses over which the parent company has control.

To prepare its consolidated financial statements, Parco will add together the financial statement amounts for Parco and Subco. In the process, however, some changes to the pre-consolidation reported balances must be made. There are two types of changes that are made when statements are consolidated: (1) *eliminations* and (2) *adjustments*.

- **Eliminations** are changes that prevent certain amounts on the separate-entity statements from appearing on the consolidated statements. Eliminations are necessary to avoid double-counting (such as intercompany sales) and to cancel out offsetting balances (such as intercompany receivables and payables).

- **Adjustments**, on the other hand, are made to alter reported amounts in order to reflect the economic substance of transactions rather than their nominal amount.

There are two general approaches to preparing consolidated financial statements. One is called the *direct approach*. The **direct approach** prepares the consolidated statements by setting up the balance sheet and income statement formats and computing each consolidated balance directly. Each asset, liability, revenue, and expense is separately calculated and entered into the consolidated statement. The direct approach works from the separate-entity financial statements (that is, by using Exhibit 2-3).

The alternative method is the *worksheet approach*. The **worksheet** (or **spreadsheet**) **approach** uses a multi-columnar worksheet to enter the trial balances of the parent and each subsidiary. Then, eliminations and adjustments are entered onto the worksheet, and the accounts are cross-added to determine the consolidated balances. The finished consolidated statements are then prepared from the consolidated trial balance.

The direct approach is intuitively appealing because we are working directly with the statements and can see clearly what is happening to the consolidated statements as we make eliminations and adjustments.

The worksheet approach is more methodical and is the technique that is used in practice (usually computerized). A worksheet is less intuitive, but its use enables us to keep better track of the eliminations and adjustments, some of which get very complicated.

In this book, we will illustrate both approaches. The direct approach will be presented first, and the worksheet approach second. Both approaches yield the same result. It doesn't matter which approach is used—what is important is the result, not the method used to derive the result.

Direct approach to consolidation

The Parco consolidated financial statements for 2005 are shown in Exhibit 2-4. In this exhibit the statements have been prepared by using the direct method. The

EXHIBIT 2–4 PARCO CONSOLIDATED FINANCIAL STATEMENTS

Balance Sheet
December 31, 2005

Assets

Current assets:

Cash [70,000 + 40,000]	$ 110,000
Accounts receivable [200,000 + 110,000]	310,000
Receivable from Subco [60,000 + 0 – **60,000**]	—
Inventories [150,000 + 120,000]	270,000
	690,000

Property, plant, and equipment:

Land [100,000 + 0]	100,000
Buildings and equipment [1,000,000 + 450,000]	1,450,000
Accumulated depreciation [300,000 + 100,000]	(400,000)
	1,150,000

Other assets:

Investment in Subco, at cost [80,000 + 0 – **80,000**]	—
Total assets	$ 1,840,000

Liabilities and shareholders' equity

Current liabilities:

Accounts payable [120,000 + 80,000]	$ 200,000
Due to Parco [0 + 60,000 – **60,000**]	—
	200,000

Long-term notes payable [0 + 300,000]	300,000
Future income taxes [140,000 + 30,000]	170,000
	670,000

Shareholders' equity:

Common shares [300,000 + 80,000 – **80,000**]	300,000
Retained earnings [800,000 + 70,000]	870,000
	1,170,000

Total liabilities and shareholders' equity	$ 1,840,000

Consolidated Statement of Income and Retained Earnings
Year Ended December 31, 2005

Revenue:

Sales revenue [800,000 + 400,000 – **100,000**]	$ 1,100,000
Dividend income [20,000 + 0 – **20,000**]	—
	1,100,000

Operating expenses:

Cost of sales [480,000 + 280,000 – **100,000**]	60,000
Depreciation expense [130,000 + 30,000]	160,000
Income tax expense [32,000 + 20,000]	52,000
Other expenses [110,000 + 40,000]	150,000
	1,022,000
Net income	$78,000
Retained earnings, December 31, 2004 [762,000 + 60,000]	822,000
Dividends declared [30,000 + 20,000 – **20,000**]	(30,000)
Retained earnings, December 31, 2005	$ 870,000

consolidated financial statements are obtained by: (1) adding together the individual amounts on the parent and subsidiaries' financial statements and (2) subtracting amounts as necessary for adjustments and eliminations, and then (3) entering the resulting amounts *directly* into consolidated financial statements.

An important point is that the consolidated statements are being prepared by Parco for submission to its shareholders. The net assets and shareholders' equity that will be shown in Parco's consolidated balance sheet will be *the net assets* (= shareholders' equity) *from the point of view of the Parco shareholders*. The common shares that are outstanding for Parco are the $300,000 shown in Parco's balance sheet, not the total of $300,000 + $80,000 that would be obtained by adding the two separate-entity balances together.

Therefore, the first elimination in preparing the consolidated balance sheet is the $80,000 common share amount for Subco. The common share line in Exhibit 2-4 shows $300,000 + $80,000 − **$80,000**, the amount in bold colour being the elimination of Subco's share equity.

Since a credit balance of $80,000 is being eliminated, there must be an offsetting elimination in order to preserve the equality of debits and credits on the balance sheet. The offset is the $80,000 debit shown as "Investment in Subco" on the Parco balance sheet. The investment account is really just an aggregate that represents the net assets of the subsidiary; instead of showing the *net* investment in the subsidiary as an asset, the consolidated statements show all of the assets and liabilities of the subsidiary that underlie the investment. Thus neither the $80,000 debit for Parco's investment nor the $80,000 credit for the common shares of Subco will appear on the consolidated balance sheet; both amounts are eliminated.

Notice that Subco's accumulated retained earnings is *not* eliminated. Since Subco is a wholly-owned, parent-founded subsidiary, the amount of retained earnings shown by Subco represents Parco's earnings on its investment that have not been distributed to Parco in the form of dividends. In other scenarios later in the book, some or all of the subsidiary's retained earnings may be eliminated, depending on (1) the degree of ownership and (2) whether the subsidiary was purchased or parent-founded. Stay tuned for further developments!

Second, the amount owed by Subco to Parco must be eliminated. The current assets of Parco ("Receivable from Subco") are reduced by $60,000 and the current liabilities of Subco ("Due to Parco") are reduced by an equal amount.

Third, the intercompany sales of $100,000 have to be eliminated. Sales are reduced by $100,000 to eliminate the amount from consolidated sales. On Subco's books, the cost of the merchandise purchased from Parco was recorded as $100,000. When Subco subsequently sold the merchandise to outsiders, the cost of sales would be recorded as $100,000. Therefore, the offsetting account for elimination of the sales amount is the cost of sales.

Similarly, an elimination must be made to offset the dividends paid by Subco against the dividend income recorded by Parco. The consolidated statements must only reflect the results of transactions between the consolidated entity and outsiders. Since the payment of dividends by a subsidiary to its parent is an intercompany transaction, the dividend flow must not be reported on the consolidated statements.

Worksheet approach to consolidation

When the statements to be consolidated are fairly simple, it is quite feasible to compile the consolidated statements by the direct method. In more complex situations, it becomes difficult to keep track of the many adjustments, with the frustrating result that the financial statements won't balance! In complex situations, therefore, accountants usually find it easier to use a worksheet to summarize the necessary eliminations and adjustments. The worksheet also provides the management trail (or audit trail) that explains how the consolidated statements were derived.

Exhibit 2-5 illustrates a worksheet based on the separate-entity trial balances for each company. The trial balances of the parent and the subsidiary (or subsidiaries) are listed in the first columns of the worksheet, and the eliminations and adjustments are inserted in the next column. Cross-adding the rows yields the amounts that will be used to prepare the consolidated statements.

EXHIBIT 2–5 PARCO CONSOLIDATION WORKSHEET—COST BASIS OF RECORDING

December 31, 2005

| | Trial balances | | | Parco |
	Parco Dr/(Cr)	Subco Dr/(Cr)	Adjustments Dr/(Cr)	consolidated trial balance
Cash	$ 70,000	$ 40,000		$ 110,000
Accounts receivable	200,000	110,000		310,000
Receivable from Subco	60,000	—	$ (60,000) **b**	—
Inventories	150,000	120,000		270,000
Land	100,000	—		100,000
Buildings and equipment	1,000,000	450,000		1,450,000
Accumulated depreciation	(300,000)	(100,000)		(400,000)
Investment in Subco (at cost)	80,000	—	(80,000) **a**	—
				—
Accounts payable	(120,000)	(80,000)		(200,000)
Due to Parco	—	(60,000)	60,000 **b**	—
Long-term notes payable	—	(300,000)		(300,000)
Future income taxes	(140,000)	(30,000)		(170,000)
Common shares	(300,000)	(80,000)	80,000 **a**	(300,000)
Dividends declared	30,000	20,000	(20,000) **d**	30,000
Retained earnings, December 31, 2004	(762,000)	(60,000)		(822,000)
Sales revenue	(800,000)	(400,000)	100,000 **c**	(1,100,000)
Dividend income	(20,000)		20,000 **d**	—
Cost of sales	480,000	280,000	(100,000) **c**	660,000
Depreciation expense	130,000	30,000		160,000
Income tax expense	32,000	20,000		52,000
Other expenses	110,000	40,000		150,000
	$ —	$ —	$ —	$ —

The eliminations that were made in preparing Parco's consolidated statements can be summarized as follows, in general journal format. The parentheses indicate the company on whose statements the accounts being adjusted appear:

(a) Common shares (of *Subco*)	80,000	
Investment in Subco (by *Parco*)		80,000
(b) Due to Parco (*Subco*)	60,000	
Receivable from Subco (*Parco*)		60,000

(c) Sales (*Parco*)	100,000	
Cost of sales (*Subco*)		100,000
(d) Dividend income (*Parco*)	20,000	
Dividends declared (*Subco*)		20,000

In each of the eliminations, one side eliminates an amount on Subco's financial statements, while the other side of the entry eliminates an amount on Parco's statements. It therefore should be obvious that there is no way that these entries can or should be recorded on either company's books. Consolidation elimination "entries" are entered only on working papers in order to prepare the consolidated statements, and they are never entered on the formal books of account of either the parent or the subsidiary.

The equity method

Separate-entity financial statements

The preparation of consolidated financial statements does not eliminate the need for each separate legal entity to prepare its own financial statements. Each corporation is taxed individually, and unconsolidated statements are necessary for income tax reporting if for no other purpose.

Consolidated statements may not be adequate for the needs of creditors or other users of financial statements. Creditors have claims on the resources of specific corporations, not on the resources of other corporations within a consolidated group of companies. Therefore it may be of little benefit to a creditor to see the consolidated assets and liabilities when the credit risk is associated with the financial position of a single company.

When separate-entity statements are prepared for the parent corporation, the investment in the unconsolidated subsidiaries often is reported on the equity basis. This is especially true when the separate-entity statements are for an external user, such as a bank or other major lender, who is interested in the net assets, earnings, and cash flow of the individual corporation. The equity basis permits the financial statement user to discern the full economic impact of the operations of the overall economic entity (i.e., the parent corporation and its subsidiaries) and yet still see the assets, liabilities, results of operations, and cash flows for the parent company alone.

On Parco's books, the investment in Subco is being carried at cost. Therefore, preparation of Parco's equity-basis financial statements requires the conversion of the accounts relating to the investment in Subco to the equity basis for external reporting purposes.

The adjustments to convert the investment account from the cost to the equity basis *can* be formally recorded on Parco's books, but do not need to be. Indeed, it is likely that Parco will not record the adjustments, but will continue to carry the investment account on the cost basis for ease of bookkeeping. In that case, the adjustments will appear only on the working papers used to prepare the equity-basis unconsolidated financial statements for Parco as a separate entity.

We explained earlier that, under the equity method, the parent's share of the earnings of the subsidiary or affiliate is reported on the parent's income statement. On Parco's 2005 unconsolidated income statement, the dividend income is eliminated and is replaced by a line for *equity in earnings of subsidiary.*

Since Parco is the sole owner of Subco, 100% of Subco's 2005 earnings will be reported on Parco's income statement. The increase of $10,000 in Parco's earnings that results from deleting the $20,000 dividend income and replacing it with

Subco's $30,000 net income is treated as an increase in Parco's investment in Subco. The debit/credit effect of the adjustment is as follows:

Investment in Subco	10,000	
Dividend income	20,000	
Equity in earnings of subsidiary (1/S)		30,000

In addition to the **unremitted earnings** (i.e., net income less dividends) of $10,000 for Subco for 2005, the investment account should also include the unremitted earnings for the years between the creation of Subco by Parco and the beginning of the 2005 fiscal year. The amount of unremitted earnings from prior years is equal to the amount of the retained earnings of Subco at the beginning of 2005, $60,000. Therefore, the investment account and Parco's prior years' earnings must be adjusted before the unconsolidated statements for Parco are prepared:

Investment in Subco	60,000	
Retained earnings		60,000

These two adjustments increase the balance of the investment account from $80,000 under the cost method to $150,000 under the equity method of reporting. The offsetting credits are a net increase of $10,000 in 2005 income and an increase of $60,000 in retained earnings for prior years' income.

Note that under the equity method, it is *not* necessary to eliminate intercompany transactions such as the $100,000 sales by Parco to Subco. The necessary adjustments are only for items that affect net income—the intercompany transaction washes out in its effect on net income.[6]

Exhibit 2-6 provides a comparison of the financial statements of Parco under the three different policies for reporting the investment in Subco. The first column shows Parco's separate-entity financial statements with the investment in Subco reported on the cost basis. These financial statements are derived from the first column of Exhibit 2-3.

The second column shows Parco's separate entity financial statements prepared on the equity basis. Note that the first two columns are identical except for the investment in Subco and reported earnings from Subco. As a result, the reported net income and retained earnings of Parco differ significantly between the first and second columns.

The third column of Exhibit 2-6 shows Parco's consolidated financial statements. Almost all of the amounts in the third column are different from those in the first two columns. The assets, liabilities, revenues, and expenses include those of both Parco and Subco, while the investment account and the related earnings accounts have disappeared.

It is impossible to tell from the third column which of the assets and liabilities are those of Parco, since the two corporations are reported as a single economic entity. If a lender were to extend a line of credit to Parco based on (for example) 75% of Parco's accounts receivable, the lender would not be able to tell from the consolidated statements just how much of the $310,000 reported accounts receivable is an asset of Parco.

While most of the consolidated amounts differ from those in the first two columns of Exhibit 2-6, two items are the same in the second and third columns but different from the first column: *Retained Earnings* and *Net Income*. A basic and important attribute of the equity method is that the parent's reported net

---

6. If some of the intercompany merchandise remains in inventory at year-end, an additional complication arises. We will deal with the necessary adjustment in later chapters. But there never is a need to eliminate the intercompany sale transaction itself for equity-basis reporting.

EXHIBIT 2–6 PARCO FINANCIAL STATEMENTS USING DIFFERENT REPORTING PRACTICES

Balance Sheet, December 31, 2005

	Cost basis	Equity basis	Consolidated
Assets			
Current assets:			
Cash	$ 70,000	$ 70,000	$ 110,000
Accounts receivable	200,000	200,000	310,000
Receivable from Subco	60,000	60,000	—
Inventories	150,000	150,000	270,000
	480,000	480,000	690,000
Property, plant, and equipment:			
Land	100,000	100,000	100,000
Buildings and equipment	1,000,000	1,000,000	1,450,000
Accumulated depreciation	(300,000)	(300,000)	(400,000)
	800,000	800,000	1,150,000
Other assets:			
Investment in Subco	80,000	150,000	—
Total assets	$1,360,000	$1,430,000	$1,840,000
Liabilities and shareholders' equity			
Liabilities:			
Current accounts payable	$ 120,000	$ 120,000	$ 200,000
Long-term notes payable	—	—	300,000
Future income taxes	140,000	140,000	170,000
	260,000	260,000	670,000
Shareholders' equity:			
Common shares	300,000	300,000	300,000
Retained earnings	800,000	870,000	870,000
	1,100,000	1,170,000	1,170,000
Total liabilities and shareholders' equity	$1,360,000	$1,430,000	$1,840,000

Statement of Income and Retained Earnings
Year Ended December 31, 2005

	Cost basis	Equity basis	Consolidated
Sales revenue	$ 800,000	$ 800,000	$1,100,000
Operating expenses:			
Cost of sales	480,000	480,000	660,000
Depreciation expense	130,000	130,000	160,000
Income tax expense	32,000	32,000	52,000
Other expenses	110,000	110,000	150,000
	752,000	752,000	1,022,000
Net income from operations	48,000	48,000	78,000
Dividend income	20,000		
Equity in earnings of Subco		30,000	
Net income	$ 68,000	$ 78,000	$ 78,000
Retained earnings, December 31, 2004	762,000	822,000	822,000
Dividends declared	(30,000)	(30,000)	(30,000)
Retained earnings, December 31, 2005	$ 800,000	$ 870,000	$ 870,000

MUST BE THE SAME.

income and net assets (shareholders' equity) will be the same as when the subsidiaries are consolidated. The effect of consolidation is to disaggregate the net investment in the subsidiary into the component assets and liabilities, and to disaggregate the parent's equity in the earnings of the subsidiary into its components of revenue and expense.

The equity method is frequently referred to as **one-line consolidation** because the equity method and consolidation both result in the same net income and shareholders' equity for the parent. There is one line on the balance sheet that shows the net asset value of the subsidiary, and one line on the income statement that shows the net earnings derived from the subsidiary.[7]

The one-line adjustment to the parent's earnings is commonly known as the **equity pick-up** of the subsidiary's earnings.

Consolidation: equity *recording*

In our earlier illustration of direct consolidation and of the consolidation worksheet, we assumed that the parent company carried the investment in Subco at cost. While the cost method is most commonly used for internal record keeping, the equity method may also be used.

If Parco had been using the equity method, then the investment account would be $150,000 at the end of 2005, Parco's opening retained earnings would be $822,000 instead of $762,000, and the income statement accounts would include the $30,000 equity in the earnings of Subco rather than dividend income of $20,000. All of these amounts are explained in the immediately preceding section.

The first column of Exhibit 2-7 shows the condensed financial statements for Parco, assuming that the investment has been recorded by use of the equity method. The accounts and amounts that are affected by using the equity method rather than the cost method are highlighted in bold colour. When the eliminating entries are prepared, the two entries to eliminate the balance of the investment account differ from those shown in Exhibit 2-4 because the composition of the balance in the investment account is different.

Under the cost method, only the original cost of the investment is included in the investment account, and the only elimination necessary is one to offset the cost of the investment against the common share account of the subsidiary.

Under the equity method, however, the investment account includes both the original cost of the investment and the unremitted earnings of the subsidiary. Both of these amounts must be eliminated. The parent's retained earnings also include the earnings of the subsidiary, since the subsidiary's earnings are taken into the parent's income each year. If the retained earnings of Subco were added to the retained earnings of Parco, as we did in deriving the consolidated retained earnings under the cost method, we would be double-counting Subco's retained earnings. Therefore, the worksheet entries to eliminate the investment account are shown as follows when the equity method of recording the investment has been used:

(a) Common shares (*Subco*)	80,000	
Retained earnings (*Subco*)	60,000	
Investment in Subco *(Parco)*		140,000
(b) Equity in earnings of subsidiary *(Parco)*	30,000	
Dividends declared (*Subco*)		20,000
Investment in Subco *(Parco)*		10,000

---

7. An exception arises for the investor's share of any discontinued operations or extraordinary items of the investee. The investor's proportionate share of discontinued operations and extraordinary items will be reported net of related taxes on the investor's income statement after net income from continuing operations.

EXHIBIT 2–7 PARCO CONSOLIDATION WORKSHEET—EQUITY BASIS OF RECORDING

December 31, 2005

	Trial balances		Elimination & adjustments	Parco consolidated
	Parco Dr/(Cr)	Subco Dr/(Cr)	Dr/(Cr)	trial balance
Cash	$ 70,000	$ 40,000		$ 110,000
Accounts receivable	200,000	110,000		310,000
Receivable from Subco	60,000	—	$ (60,000) c	—
Inventories	150,000	120,000		270,000
Land	100,000	—		100,000
Buildings and equipment	1,000,000	450,000		1,450,000
Accumulated depreciation	(300,000)	(100,000)		(400,000)
Investment in Subco (at equity)	150,000	0	(140,000) a (10,000) b	
Accounts payable	(120,000)	(80,000)		(200,000)
Due to Parco	—	(60,000)	60,000 c	—
Long-term notes payable	—	(300,000)		(300,000)
Future income taxes	(140,000)	(30,000)		(170,000)
Common shares	(300,000)	(80,000)	80,000 a	(300,000)
Dividends declared	30,000	20,000	(20,000) b	30,000
Retained earnings, December 31, 2004	(822,000)	(60,000)	60,000 a	(822,000)
Sales revenue	(800,000)	(400,000)	100,000 d	(1,100,000)
Equity in earnings of Subco	(30,000)		30,000 b	—
Cost of sales	480,000	280,000	(100,000) d	660,000
Depreciation expense	130,000	30,000		160,000
Income tax expense	32,000	20,000		52,000
Other expenses	110,000	40,000		150,000
	$ —	$ —	$ —	$ —

Worksheet entry **a** eliminates the original investment and the accumulated retained (and unremitted) earnings of Subco of prior years. Entry **b** eliminates the dividends and the double-counting of Subco's earnings for the current year. In effect, the two adjustments reverse the entries that were originally made by Parco to record its interest in the earnings of Subco and to record the original investment.

The process of consolidation cancels out entries made for the equity pick-up of the subsidiaries' earnings. Since the process of consolidation eliminates the equity adjustments, most companies simply record the investment on the cost basis instead of the equity basis. It is simpler *not* to use the equity method for *recording* the investment.

The remaining two eliminations, for the intercompany debt and the intercompany sales, are unaffected by the method of recording the investment.

The net effect of the eliminations to the statement of income and retained earnings is to reduce the combined ending retained earnings by $70,000, thereby preventing the double-counting of Subco's ending retained earnings. This net change of $70,000 is transferred to the balance sheet to complete the worksheet.

Unconsolidated Statements

Limitations of consolidated statements

The theory underlying consolidated financial statements is that financial statements should disclose the resources and obligations of the entire economic entity. This is a straightforward application of the entity concept in accounting. When one corporation can control the resources of another, the economic entity includes the combined assets of both companies over which the directors of the parent corporation have control. Since the parent is assumed to be able to control the resources of the subsidiary, unconsolidated statements are frequently viewed as potentially misleading because they do not reflect the total economic resources that are at the disposal of the parent.

For example, a parent company may have little cash available within its own accounts, but a subsidiary may have surplus cash balances. The parent can obtain access to the subsidiary's cash, such as by instructing the subsidiary to declare dividends, by charging management fees to the subsidiary, or by borrowing. Since the parent controls the subsidiary, a loan need not be repaid at any specific date, if ever.

Similarly, a parent corporation has the ability to control the operations of a subsidiary, particularly if there are substantial intercompany transactions. For example, the parent could improve its apparent sales level by requiring the subsidiary to purchase unneeded quantities of goods from the parent, or it could generate other revenue by charging high management fees or royalties to the subsidiary. Consolidated statements eliminate the potential benefit of such intercompany activities.

But there also are problems with relying only on consolidated statements. While it is true that the parent and its subsidiaries are an *economic* entity, they are still separate *legal* entities. The title to assets and the obligation for liabilities attaches to the legal entity and not to the economic entity. A parent can go bankrupt while the subsidiaries remain healthy (or vice versa). Consolidated statements may hide the precarious financial position of a parent corporation because the stronger net asset position of the subsidiaries cloaks the shaky structure of the parent.

Creditors of the parent have no claim on the assets of the subsidiaries, unless the parent has deliberately been transferring assets to the subsidiaries in order to get them out of reach of the creditors in anticipation of bankruptcy. The share investment in the subsidiaries is, of course, an asset of the parent that can be sold in order to satisfy creditors' claims. But the assets of the subsidiaries are beyond the reach of the parent's creditors.

For example, PLC Industries Ltd. was delisted from the Toronto Stock Exchange and was in very precarious financial health. However, its major operating subsidiaries remained healthy. One wholly-owned subsidiary, PLC Plastics, turned its back totally on its parent company, keeping its cash and other resources to itself and pledging its own assets for bank credit. Anyone reading consolidated statements of PLC Industries (the parent) would be led to believe that the parent was healthy because of the consolidated cash flows and net assets of its subsidiaries, and yet the parent itself was in bad shape.

It is an unwise lender who relies exclusively on consolidated financial statements.

Circumstances when unconsolidated statements are permissible

The *CICA Handbook* explicitly recognizes that there are times when non-consolidated financial statements may be appropriate. Paragraph 3050.43 states:

Non-consolidated financial statements that do not conform to the requirements of Subsidiaries, Section 1590, but otherwise conform to generally accepted accounting principles may be prepared when:

(a) a reporting enterprise is itself a wholly-owned subsidiary, and the sole owner has access to all pertinent information concerning the resources and results of operations of the group;

(b) a reporting enterprise that prepares consolidated financial statements also prepares non-consolidated financial statements for income tax or other special purposes; or

(c) the owners of the reporting enterprise have access to all pertinent information concerning the resources and results of operation of the group; and the owners, including those not otherwise entitled to vote, unanimously consent to the preparation of non-consolidated financial statements.

The first circumstance applies to parent companies that themselves are wholly-owned subsidiaries of another parent company. Since there are no external investors, and since bankers, creditors, and managers may all have need for separate-entity statements in preference to consolidated statements, non-consolidated statements are permitted.

The second circumstance simply states that separate-entity statements may be useful even when consolidated statements are also prepared. This provision is especially useful for reporting to banks and other creditors who want separate-entity statements but who also want an auditor's assurance that the statements are otherwise in accordance with GAAP.

The third circumstance is the private company provision. Where there are no external shareholders and the existing shareholders all agree, then non-consolidated statements can be prepared. Note that consent is needed not only from voting shareholders, but also from holders of restricted, non-voting shares (including preferred shares).

When non-consolidated statements are prepared, the investments in unconsolidated subsidiaries can be reported on either the cost or equity basis. While the equity basis would ordinarily be more appropriate, the objective of non-consolidated statements is not to portray the operations and financial position of the larger economic entity but rather to portray the separate earnings, cash flows, and financial position of the separate legal entity. For such purposes, equity reporting would not enhance the statements. Therefore the *CICA Handbook* states that when non-consolidated financial statements are prepared in the circumstances described above, "the cost method may be used to account for an investment that would otherwise be accounted for by the equity method" [CICA 3050.46].

The permission to use the cost method applies not only to unconsolidated subsidiaries, but also to investments in significantly influenced investees. When the cost method is used, it would be desirable to disclose the amount of unrealized intercompany profit [CICA 3050.47] so that readers are aware of separate-entity balances (such as inventories) that are being reported at values that are above their arm's-length cost to the economic entity.

When non-consolidated financial statements are prepared under one of the circumstances discussed above, the *CICA Handbook* recommends an explanation (by note disclosure) of:

- the reason for preparing non-consolidated statements,

- the fact that further information may be needed by the user,

- a reference to consolidated statements if they exist, and

- the method of accounting for subsidiaries in the non-consolidated statements [CICA 3050.39].

On the face of the separate-entity statements, the investments in and income from the unconsolidated subsidiaries should be shown separately [CICA 3050.40 and .41]. If any of the shares of the reporting legal entity are owned by its subsidiaries, details should be disclosed [CICA 3050.42] because "their disclosure enables outside interests in the reporting enterprise to be distinguished from the interests of other companies in the group" [CICA 3050.44].

In summary, the *CICA Handbook* recommends consolidation of all subsidiaries. Nevertheless, the recommendations also recognize that there are circumstances in which the needs of users are better served by non-consolidated statements than by consolidated statements. When non-consolidated statements are prepared, the audit opinion (if any) will state that "the financial statements are in accordance with generally accepted accounting principles except that they are prepared on a non-consolidated basis" [CICA 3050.39(d)], thereby giving audit assurance without tying such assurance exclusively to consolidated statements.

Summary of Accounting for Intercorporate Investments

Exhibit 2-8 presents a broad summary of the appropriate accounting approaches for intercorporate investments. In general, (1) significantly-influenced affiliates are reported by the equity method, while (2) subsidiaries are consolidated. Joint ventures are not included in the chart; they (at the time of writing) are reported by proportionate consolidation—a unique Canadian approach!

The appropriate reporting method for an investment may vary over time. An investment may start out as a portfolio investment (reported on the cost basis), and then become a significant-influence investment (reported on the equity basis) as a larger proportion of shares is acquired. If control is eventually acquired, consolidation will be required for general purpose financial statements.

Similarly, an investment may go from a consolidated subsidiary to being a signficantly-influenced affiliate, and finally becoming just a portfolio investment.

Non-consolidated statements may be prepared for specific users, and may also be prepared by private corporations if the shareholders all agree.

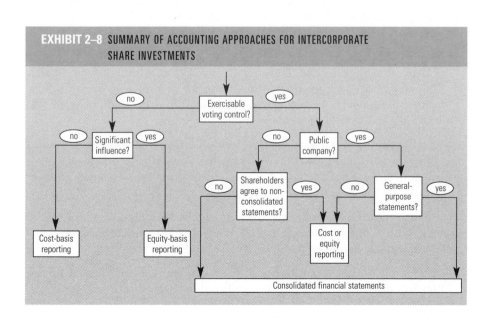

EXHIBIT 2–8 SUMMARY OF ACCOUNTING APPROACHES FOR INTERCORPORATE SHARE INVESTMENTS

A basic assumption underlying Exhibit 2-8 is that the investment is in voting shares. Investments in non-voting shares are reported on the cost basis, unless the investor holds enough non-voting common shares in conjunction with voting shares to gain significant influence or control. Investments in debt securities are always reported as portfolio investments—there is no alternative.

Summary of Key Points

1. It is very common for Canadian businesses to operate through a multi-corporate structure, with a parent company controlling several subsidiaries. Each legal corporate entity must prepare its own separate-entity financial statements for tax and other special purposes. Corporations that issue general purpose financial statements are required to issue only consolidated financial statements to the general public.

2. Branch accounting is not the same as consolidation. Branch accounting is simply the use of control accounts or an account matrix to monitor and control the finances of branches.

3. An intercorporate investment is any investment by one corporation in the debt or equity securities of another.

4. A portfolio investment is an intercorporate investment in debt, non-voting shares, or a relatively small number of voting shares in another corporation. Portfolio investments do not carry the ability to influence the strategies of the investee corporation. Portfolio investments are accounted for on the cost basis.

5. A strategic intercorporate investment is intended to enable the investor to control or significantly influence the strategic financing, operating, and investment policies of the investee. If the investor has the ability to determine the strategic policies of the investee *without the co-operation of others*, the investor controls the investee. The controlled company is deemed to be a subsidiary of the investor, or parent, corporation.

   Control can be either direct or indirect. Indirect control exists when the parent company controls an intermediate company that controls another company. *Control* does not imply *absolute* control. Only 100% ownership gives the parent company complete control over the subsidiary.

6. Most subsidiaries are created by the parent company to carry on some aspect of the company's business. These are known as parent-founded subsidiaries. Other subsidiaries are acquired by buying voting control from the subsidiary's former shareholders. When a parent controls a subsidiary by owning less than 100% of the shares, a non-controlling interest exists.

7. Significant influence may exist if the investor holds less than voting control, but more than a nominal amount. The general guideline is that ownership of between 20% and 50% of the voting shares gives the investor significant influence.

8. A joint venture is a co-operative venture undertaken in concert with one or more other investors. No one investor controls a joint venture. All of the co-venturers must agree on strategic policies.

9. Cost-basis reporting is used for portfolio investments, when the investor corporation neither controls nor has significant influence over the investee cor-

poration. Equity-basis reporting is normally used to report investments in significantly-influenced companies and in joint ventures. Equity-basis reporting is sometimes called one-line consolidation.

10. Parent companies should prepare consolidated statements that report on the total economic entity that is controlled by the parent. All subsidiaries should be consolidated. Joint ventures are reported by proportionate consolidation, wherein only the investor's share of the joint venture's revenues, expenses, assets, and liabilities are included in the consolidated statements.

11. The recording and reporting of strategic intercorporate investments are two different things. Intercorporate investments are usually recorded on the books of the investor on the cost basis. If the equity basis is used for reporting, the adjustments from cost to equity are entered on working papers and are not recorded in the investee's books.

Consolidated financial statements are always prepared on working papers. The working papers may use either a direct approach or a spreadsheet approach. It is not possible to record the adjustments needed for consolidation, because there is no set of books that corresponds to the consolidated economic entity.

12. Exceptions to the consolidation policy can occur when the reporting enterprise is a private corporation and all of the shareholders agree to waive the requirement for consolidated statements. Parent corporations that are themselves wholly owned by other corporations also need not prepare consolidated statements.

Weblinks

Air Canada
www.aircanada.ca

Use Air Canada's Web site to make online reservations, view flight schedule information, register for Websaver specials, peruse details about vacation packages, or read articles about the latest Air Canada news.

Nortel
www.nortelnetworks.com/

Nortel Networks has a comprehensive portfolio of products and services designed to address today's and tomorrow's needs of any networking environment, from the smallest SOHO user to the largest global enterprise network. This extensive Web site outlines the many products, services, and customer support channels available to users.

Motorola
www.motorola.com

Motorola is a global leader in providing integrated communications solutions and embedded electronic solutions, including software-enhanced wireless telephone systems, messaging and satellite communications products and systems, embedded semiconductor solutions, embedded electronic systems, and set-top terminals for broadband cable television operators.

PLC Industries
www.plc.com.sg/abtus.html

Based in Singapore, PLC Industries develops optical and aerospace products, and machines complex milling requests. Their Web site outlines their capabilities, products, and how to contact PLC Industries.

Self-Study Problem 2-1[8]

Bunker Ltd. is a wholly-owned subsidiary of Archie Corp. Bunker was formed by Archie with an initial investment of $1,000,000. Bunker produces some of the merchandise sold by Archie in its retail stores. Bunker also sells some of its output to other unrelated companies. The December 31, 2003 trial balances for Archie and Bunker are shown in Exhibit 2-9. The condensed balance sheets and income statements for both companies are shown in Exhibit 2-10. Additional information is as follows:

1. During 2003, Bunker sold goods with a production cost of $2,600,000 to Archie for $4,000,000. Archie subsequently sold the goods to its customers for $7,000,000.

2. Included in Archie's current receivables is $80,000 in dividends receivable from Bunker.

3. Included in Bunker's current receivables is $200,000 due from Archie for merchandise purchases.

4. During 2003, Archie declared dividends of $2,000,000 and Bunker declared dividends of $500,000.

Required:

Prepare a consolidated balance sheet and a consolidated statement of income and retained earnings for Bunker Ltd. for the year ended December 31, 2003. Use either the direct method or the worksheet method (or both!).

EXHIBIT 2–9 SEPARATE-ENTITY TRIAL BALANCES				
December 31, 2003				
	Archie Corp.		**Bunker Ltd.**	
	Dr	**Cr**	**Dr**	**Cr**
Cash and current receivables	$ 200,000		$ 400,000	
Inventories	900,000		500,000	
Furniture, fixtures, and equipment (net)	2,000,000		1,700,000	
Buildings under capital leases (net)	6,000,000		3,000,000	
Investment in Bunker Ltd. (at cost)	1,000,000			
Current liabilities		1,500,000		400,000
Long-term liabilities		4,000,000		2,000,000
Common shares		1,500,000		1,000,000
Retained earnings, December 31, 2002		2,100,000		1,600,000
Dividends declared	2,000,000		500,000	
Sales revenue		13,000,000		5,000,000
Dividend income		500,000		—
Cost of sales	7,000,000		3,200,000	
Other expenses	3,500,000		700,000	
	$22,600,000	$22,600,000	$10,000,000	$10,000,000

8. The solutions to all the Self-Study Problems are at the end of the book, following Chapter 12.

EXHIBIT 2–10 SEPARATE-ENTITY FINANCIAL STATEMENTS

Balance Sheets
December 31, 2003

	Archie Corp.	Bunker Ltd.
Assets		
Cash and current receivables	$ 200,000	$ 400,000
Inventories	900,000	500,000
Furniture, fixtures, and equipment		
(net of accumulated depreciation)	2,000,000	1,700,000
Buildings under capital lease		
(net of related amortization)	6,000,000	3,000,000
Investment in Bunker Ltd. (at cost)	1,000,000	—
	$10,100,000	$5,600,000
Liabilities and shareholders' equity		
Current liabilities	$ 1,500,000	$ 400,000
Long-term liabilities	4,000,000	2,000,000
Common shares	1,500,000	1,000,000
Retained earnings	3,100,000	2,200,000
	$10,100,000	$5,600,000

Statements of Income and Retained Earnings
Year Ended December 31, 2003

	Archie Corp.	Bunker Ltd.
Revenue		
Sales	$13,000,000	$5,000,000
Dividend income	500,000	—
	13,500,000	5,000,000
Expenses		
Cost of sales	7,000,000	3,200,000
Other operating expenses	3,500,000	700,000
	10,500,000	3,900,000
Net income	$ 3,000,000	$1,100,000
Retained earnings, December 31, 2002	2,100,000	1,600,000
Dividends declared	(2,000,000)	(500,000)
Retained earnings, December 31, 2003	$ 3,100,000	$2,200,000

Review Questions

2-1 Define the following terms:
   a. Intercorporate investment
   b. Subsidiary
   c. Significant influence
   d. Control
   e. Indirect control
   f. Joint control

g. Non-controlling interest

h. Minority interest

i. Business combination

j. Consolidated statements

k. Equity method

l. Temporary investment

m. Portfolio investment

2-2 What distinguishes a *branch* from a *subsidiary*?

2-3 What is the difference between a *portfolio* and a *temporary investment*?

2-4 P Corporation owns 75% of S Corporation, and S Corporation owns 55% of T Corporation. Is T a subsidiary of P?

2-5 P Corporation owns 55% of Q Corp. and 58% of R Corp. Q and R each own 30% of W Ltd. Is W a subsidiary of one or more of the other three companies? If so, which one(s)?

2-6 Why do many parent corporations prefer to own 100% of the shares of their subsidiaries, rather than smaller proportions?

2-7 What advantages are there to a parent in owning *less* than 100% of its subsidiaries?

2-8 "The extent of share ownership does not necessarily coincide with the extent of control exercised." Explain.

2-9 Under what circumstance can one corporation control another without owning a majority of the controlled corporation's voting shares?

2-10 Why do many corporations carry out their operations through multiple subsidiaries?

2-11 Why would a company purchase a subsidiary rather than simply establish a new subsidiary of its own?

2-12 Why would a corporation want to continue a purchased subsidiary as a separate legal entity?

2-13 When should an investor corporation report its investment in the shares of another corporation on the equity basis?

2-14 ABC Corporation owns 12% of XYZ's common shares. Is the cost method of reporting the investment necessarily appropriate?

2-15 What factors should be examined to determine whether significant influence exists?

2-16 What is a *joint venture*?

2-17 Is profit sharing equal in a joint venture?

2-18 What method of accounting is used for a joint venture?

2-19 Distinguish between the *recording* and the *reporting* of intercorporate investments.

2-20 Why might a corporation use the cost method of recording while using the equity method or consolidation for reporting?

2-21 How are dividends received from an investee corporation reported by an investor corporation if the investor is using the equity method?

2-22 What is the objective of preparing consolidated financial statements?

2-23 Explain the purpose of consolidation eliminating entries.

2-24 Explain the purpose of consolidation adjusting entries.

2-25 What are the two general approaches to preparing consolidated financial statements? Do the different approaches provide different results?

2-26 When intercompany sales are eliminated, why is cost of sales reduced by the amount of intercompany sales?

2-27 Are consolidation eliminating and adjusting entries entered on the books of the parent or of the subsidiary?

2-28 Why is the equity method often referred to as *one-line consolidation*?

2-29 Why might it be necessary for a parent company to prepare *unconsolidated* financial statements as well as consolidated statements?

2-30 How does the process of consolidation differ when the parent company has used the equity method of recording its investment in a subsidiary, as compared to consolidation when the cost method of recording has been used?

2-31 Under what circumstances does the *CICA Handbook* consider it acceptable to prepare non-consolidated statements?

2-32 What is the essential or necessary condition for consolidating a subsidiary?

2-33 When might consolidated statements be misleading?

2-34 Is it possible for a parent company to go bankrupt while its operating subsidiaries stay healthy?

2-35 To what extent do the creditors of a subsidiary have a claim on the assets of the parent company?

Cases

Case 2-1

Holding Corp.

Holding Corp. (HC) is an Ontario corporation that is 54% owned by Michael Smith. The rest of the shares are owned by other wealthy individuals, many of whom were schoolmates of Mr. Smith. HC does not engage in direct operations, but holds investments in a number of other companies. Part of the financing for these investments has been provided by the Great Canadian Bank.

One of HC's principal investments is its 73% voting interest in Operating Corporation (OC). A smaller investment is that in United States, Inc. (USI), in which HC has a 16% interest. USI is the U.S. producer and distributor of OC's principal product; this product accounts for 75% of USI's total revenue. USI operates autonomously, but makes substantial per-unit royalty payments to OC, as well as payment of annual licence fees to OC. OC can cancel the licensing arrangements upon six months' notice to USI.

OC owns 41% of the common shares of Associated Corporation (AC), which, like OC, is incorporated under the *Canada Business Corporations Act.* Another 21% of the shares of AC is owned by Michael Smith.

Required:

a. What accounting and reporting policies should be followed by HC and OC for the various share holdings? How will the direct and indirect ownerships be reflected in the various companies' financial statements?

b. Assume that AC acquires 35% of USI's common shares. Has a business combination occurred? Explain.

Case 2-2

Multi-Corporation

Multi-Corporation has been on a growth and diversification strategy for the last two years. To accomplish this goal they have been making a series of strategic investments. This growth has been financed through the bank and private investors. Next year the company is going to issue shares to the public.

You have just finished a meeting with Catherine, the controller of Multi-Corporation. She has asked you to provide recommendations on how to report the following investments that were made in 2000:

1) Multi-Corporation purchased all of the 100,000 outstanding B shares of Suds Limited. Each share has one vote. The previous owner, Megan, retained all of the 80,000 outstanding A shares of Suds Limited. Each share also has one vote. In order to avoid sudden changes to the business, Megan stipulated in the sales agreement that she was to retain the right to refuse the appointment of management for Suds Limited and to approve any significant transactions of Suds Limited.

2) Multi-Corporation owns 37% of the voting common shares of Berry Corporation. The remaining 63% of the shares are held by members of the family of the company founder. To date, the family has elected all members of the board of directors, and Multi-Corporation has not been able to obtain a seat on the Board. Multi-Corporation is hoping eventually to buy a block of shares from an elderly family member and eventually own 60% of the shares.

Required:

Provide a report to Catherine outlining the appropriate method of accounting for these investments.

[CICA, adapted]

Case 2-3

Salieri Ltd.

Salieri Ltd. is a manufacturer of musical instruments that is controlled by Tony Antonio. Salieri Ltd. was originally a private company, but it became public in 1969 when a substantial public share issue occurred. The Antonio family now holds 68% of the shares of Salieri; the remaining 32% are widely distributed throughout Canada.

Although Salieri is an operating company, it also has substantial investments in a number of other Canadian corporations. One such investment is its ownership of 80% of the shares of Bach Burgers, Inc., a chain of fast-food outlets. Salieri acquired its shares in Bach from the original founder of the company, John Sebastian, in 1978. Bach Burgers is run completely independently; Teresa Antonio (Tony's wife) is one of the members of Bach Burgers' twelve-person board of directors, but otherwise Salieri exercises no direction over the operations of Bach Burgers.

Another investment of Salieri Ltd. is its 45% interest in Pits Mining Corporation. This investment was the outcome of a takeover attempt by Salieri two years ago. Salieri was frustrated in its attempt by a coalition of other companies in the extraction industry, which effectively blocked Salieri's bid for control. Salieri was left with the 45% interest that it had managed to acquire. Although Salieri's block of Pits shares is by far the largest single block, Salieri has not been able to gain representation on the Pits board of directors. Salieri Ltd. has instituted court action against Pits Mining in order to force the other shareholders to admit Salieri nominees to the board.

Mozart Piano Corporation is a piano manufacturer that is 20% owned by Salieri Ltd. Although Salieri does manufacture musical instruments, it does not produce pianos, and Salieri and Mozart frequently conduct joint marketing efforts since their products are complementary and not competitive. Mozart is a private company; all of the other shares are held by the Amadeus family. Mozart has an 80%-owned subsidiary, Leopold Klaviers, Inc., which manufactures harpsichords and clavichords to be sold domestically through Mozart and internationally through other agents.

Salieri Ltd. also owns 15% of Frix Flutes, Ltd. The 15% share was acquired several years ago to provide Frix with some new financing at a time when the company was experiencing financial difficulties. Salieri also assisted Frix by licensing to Frix the rights to use patents owned by Salieri. The licensing agreement can be cancelled by Salieri upon six months' written notice.

The only other corporate share investment held by Salieri is its 100% ownership of Salieri Acceptance Corporation (SAC). SAC was formed by Salieri to aid its customers in purchasing Salieri instruments on an instalment basis. Six of the nine SAC directors are also directors of Salieri Ltd. The other three are representatives of the financial institutions that finance SAC's operations.

Required:

Discuss the manner in which Salieri should account for its various investments when issuing its annual financial statements. Specify what additional information you would like to have, if any. Recommend an accounting approach for each investment, stating any assumptions that you make in arriving at your recommendations.

Case 2-4

Happy Family Drugs Inc.

Happy Family Drugs Inc. (HFD) is the franchisor of 15 family pharmacies, all operating under the name Happy Family Drugs. HFD's franchise agreement with all its franchisees contains the following selected provisions:

1. The name Happy Family Drugs is the property of HFD and is issued under licence only. The franchisee will operate the business of a drugstore under the

trade name "Happy Family Drugs," in accordance with the policies of the franchisor as set out in the franchise manual from time to time.

2. Each franchisee must be a limited company and can have only one shareholder (other than HFD) who must be a licensed pharmacist, hereinafter referred to as the "franchisee pharmacist." This shareholder must work a minimum of 40 hours in the drugstore each week and is to manage the day-to-day operations of the drugstore in accordance with the provisions contained in the franchise manual. HFD shall determine the amount of salary or dividend that may be withdrawn from the company by the franchisee.

3. The franchisee pharmacist shall hold 70% of the common shares and HFD shall hold the remaining 30% of the common shares of the franchisee corporation. All shares shall be issued for the nominal sum of $1.00 each. The franchisee corporation shall not issue any further voting shares.

4. No initial franchise fee shall be payable to HFD.

5. HFD shall rent the premises from which the franchisee operates. The franchisee shall reimburse HFD for rental costs incurred for said premises.

6. HFD shall guarantee the bank loans of the franchisee to a maximum amount equivalent to the franchisee's inventory, calculated at the lower of cost or fair market value.

7. HFD shall determine the appropriate level of inventory for the store and shall require the franchisee to purchase inventory from approved suppliers. The franchisee cannot buy inventory from unapproved suppliers.

8. The franchise agreement can be terminated by either the franchisee or HFD on 30 days' notice and without cause or reason. If the agreement is terminated, HFD shall purchase the assets used in the business at the franchisee's cost or fair market value, whichever is lower. No profit can be recognized by the franchisee as a consequence of the termination.

9. The franchisee shall pay a monthly franchise fee to HFD; the monthly fee shall be a fair amount as determined by HFD from time to time.

The following events occurred during HFD's fiscal year ended October 31, 2001:

1. A franchisee terminated his franchise agreement with HFD. As required by the franchise agreement, HFD purchased the franchisee's assets and continued to operate the store as a franchisor store. HFD's agreements with its major suppliers require HFD to pay a franchisee's debts if the franchisee is not able to do so. In this case, the franchisee declared bankruptcy and HFD paid $750,000 to suppliers.

2. A new franchisee was found to operate the above-noted store. It is HFD's policy not to permanently operate any stores as franchisor stores.

3. HFD negotiated a very favourable arrangement with a large supplier of its franchisees. The agreement requires that all orders to the supplier be placed by HFD and not the franchisees. Payment is to be made directly to the supplier by each individual franchisee. As part of the agreement, HFD guarantees the debts of its franchisees to the supplier. HFD will receive a volume rebate of 5% of each franchisee's purchases. Franchisees are not informed of this rebate and the rebate is income to HFD.

4. HFD terminated its franchise agreement with a very profitable franchisee and sold the assets of this franchisee to another drugstore chain, realizing a profit of $1,000,000. This has greatly enhanced HFD's income statement for the 2001 fiscal year.

The majority of HFD's franchisees are of the opinion that they have been fairly treated and have been instrumental in promoting the chain to new pharmacists. Accordingly, HFD has not had any difficulty attracting new franchisees.

For the year ended October 31, 2001, HFD recorded gross franchise fee revenue of $1,800,000 and volume rebates from suppliers of $650,000. Net income was $800,000, including the $1,000,000 gain on the sale of the one store.

HFD's decline in profitability and its rapid expansion over the past few years have caused its bankers some concern and they now require audited financial statements in accordance with generally accepted accounting principles.

Required:

a. Discuss the appropriateness of consolidating each HFD franchisee with HFD. Present your conclusion.

b. Ignore the issue of appropriateness and *assume* that you *would* consolidate the HFD franchisees with HFD. What are the minimum financial statement and note disclosures, as recommended by the *CICA Handbook*, that HFD must make in its consolidated financial statements for the year ended October 31, 2001 pertaining to the issues in this question?

[ICAO]

Problems

P2-1

On April 30, 1998, Large Inc. established a subsidiary known as Small Inc. Large invested $250,000 in the shares of Small. Small has no other shares outstanding. Since its establishment, Small has had the following earnings and paid the following dividends:

Year	Net income (loss)	Dividends
1998	$(25,000)	—
1999	30,000	$ 8,000
2000	28,000	19,000
2001	52,000	22,000

Required:

a. Determine the amount of Small Inc.'s earnings that will be reported as investment income by Large Inc. in 2001, under the equity method.

b. Calculate the balance of the investment in the Small Inc. account on Large Inc.'s books at December 31, 2001, assuming that Large Inc. maintains the investment account on the equity basis.

P2-2

Max Corporation has a wholly-owned subsidiary, Min Ltd., which was formed several years ago. Min's initial capital was provided by Max, which purchased all of Min's shares for $500,000. At December 31, 2001, the balance sheet accounts of Max and Min appeared as follows:

	Max	Min
Cash	$ 90,000	$ 30,000
Accounts receivable	200,000	130,000
Receivable from Min	80,000	—
Property, plant, and equipment	2,500,000	1,400,000
Accumulated depreciation	(670,000)	(360,000)
Investment in Min	500,000	—
Total assets	$2,700,000	$1,200,000
Accounts payable	$ 300,000	$ 200,000
Payable to Max	—	80,000
Bonds payable	1,000,000	—
Future income taxes	100,000	50,000
Common shares	400,000	500,000
Retained earnings	900,000	370,000
Total equities	$2,700,000	$1,200,000

During 2001, Min paid dividends of $80,000 to Max, and purchased goods from Caldwell at a total price of $1,200,000. All of the purchases from Max were subsequently sold to third parties during the year.

Required:

Prepare a consolidated balance sheet for Max Corporation at December 31, 2001.

P2-3

Hook Corp. is a wholly-owned, parent-founded subsidiary of Chappell Inc. The unconsolidated statements of income and retained earnings for the two companies for the year ended December 31, 2001, are as follows:

	Chappell	Hook
Revenues:		
Sales	$6,500,000	$2,100,000
Interest	200,000	60,000
Dividends	100,000	—
	6,800,000	2,160,000
Expenses:		
Cost of goods sold	3,300,000	1,300,000
Depreciation expense	600,000	160,000
Administrative expense	900,000	300,000
Income tax expense	780,000	170,000
Other expenses	290,000	40,000
	5,870,000	1,970,000
Net income	930,000	190,000
Retained earnings, January 1, 2001	1,920,000	520,000
Dividends declared	(330,000)	(100,000)
Retained earnings, December 31, 2001	$2,520,000	$ 610,000

Additional Information:

1. During the year, Hook acquired merchandise from Chappell at a total sale price of $900,000. None of the merchandise was in Hook's inventory at year-end.

2. At the beginning of the year, Hook borrowed $800,000 from Chappell at 10% interest per annum. The loan (and accrued interest) was still outstanding at the end of the year.

3. Chappell carries its investment in Hook at the cost basis in its accounts.

Required:

Prepare a consolidated statement of income and retained earnings for Chappell Inc., for the year ended December 31, 2001.

P2-4

Colin Corporation owns 100% of Heather Ltd. During 2001, Colin sold $4 million of goods to Heather at cost. At the end of 2001, Heather still had $800,000 of these goods in inventory. The total inventory of Heather at year-end was $1.4 million and the total inventory of Colin was $2.1 million. Partial income statements (unconsolidated) for the two companies were as follows:

	Colin	Heather
Sales	$15,000,000	$9,000,000
Cost of goods sold	9,000,000	6,000,000
Gross margin	$ 6,000,000	$3,000,000

Required:

Compute the amounts that would be shown on Colin's consolidated financial statements for 2001 for:

a. Inventory

b. Sales

c. Cost of goods sold

d. Gross margin

[CGA, adapted]

P2-5

Thorne Ltd. is a wholly-owned subsidiary of Fellows Corporation. The balance sheets and statements of retained earnings for each company are shown below. Additional information is as follows:

1. Thorne sells most of its output to Fellows. During 2001, intercompany sales amounted to $3,500,000. Fellows has accounts payable to Thorne for $200,000.

2. Fellows owns the land on which Thorne's building is situated. Fellows leases the land to Thorne for $30,000 per month.

3. The long-term note payable on Thorne's books represents a loan from Fellows. The note bears interest at 10% per annum.

4. Both companies declare dividends quarterly. The last quarter's dividends were declared on December 31, 2001, payable on January 10, 2002.

Required:

Prepare a consolidated balance sheet and a consolidated statement of income and retained earnings for Fellows Corporation.

Separate Entity Financial Statements
Statements of Income and Retained Earnings

	Fellows	Thorne
Revenues:		
Sales	$5,600,000	$4,700,000
Interest, dividend and lease	650,000	15,000
Equity in earnings Thorne	350,000	—
	6,600,000	4,715,000
Expenses:		
Cost of goods sold	4,400,000	2,500,000
Interest expense	—	70,000
Other expenses	1,300,000	1,795,000
	5,700,000	4,365,000
Net income	900,000	350,000
Retained earnings, January 1, 2001	1,430,000	100,000
Dividends declared	(700,000)	(200,000)
Retained earnings, December 31, 2001	$1,630,000	$ 250,000

Balance Sheets
December 31, 2001

	Fellows	Thorne
Assets		
Current assets:		
Cash	$ 180,000	$ 25,000
Accounts receivable	700,000	135,000
Temporary investments and		
accrued investment income	360,000	90,000
Inventories		330,000
	1,240,000	580,000
Property, plant, and equipment		
Land	900,000	—
Buildings and equipment	—	1,500,000
Accumulated depreciation	—	(500,000)
	900,000	1,000,000
Long-term note receivable	700,000	—
Investment in Thorne	750,000	—
Total assets	$3,590,000	$1,580,000
Equities		
Current liabilities:		
Accounts payable and accrued liabilities	$ 240,000	$ 80,000
Dividends payable	120,000	50,000
	360,000	130,000
Long-term note payable	—	700,000
Total liabilities	360,000	830,000
Shareholders' equity		
Common shares	1,600,000	500,000
Retained earnings	1,630,000	250,000
Total liabilities and shareholders' equity	$3,590,000	$1,580,000

P2-6

Empire Optical Co., Ltd. is a chain of eyeglass outlets. Empire owns 100% of Class Glass Ltd., a competing chain that Empire established in order to serve a different market segment. To obtain the best deal from suppliers, Empire buys most of the materials and frames for both chains, and resells to Class whatever that chain needs.

During 2001, Empire sold materials costing $3,500,000 to Class at cost. At the end of the year, Class still owed Empire $180,000 for purchases of the materials.

Empire records its investment in Class on the equity basis. During 2001, Class declared and paid dividends totalling $200,000. Empire has not yet recorded its equity in the earnings of Class for 2001. The pre-consolidation trial balances for the two companies are as shown below.

Required:

Prepare a consolidated balance sheet and income statement for Empire Optical Co., Ltd. for 2001.

	Trial balances Dr (Cr)	
	Empire	**Class**
Cash	$ 400,000	$ 50,000
Accounts receivable	300,000	150,000
Inventory	1,200,000	600,000
Fixtures and equipment (net)	5,000,000	1,400,000
Investment in Class Glass Ltd.	2,100,000	
Other investments	500,000	—
Accounts payable	(700,000)	(500,000)
Common shares	(1,600,000)	(1,000,000)
Retained earnings	(5,700,000)	(1,300,000)
Dividends paid	600,000	200,000
Sales	(16,000,000)	(7,100,000)
Cost of goods sold	11,000,000	5,000,000
Other operating expenses	3,000,000	2,500,000
Dividend and interest income	(100,000)	—
	$ 0	$ 0

P2-7

The Selby Hotel Corporation of Vancouver held 100% of the shares of Lotus Hotel, Inc. of Toronto. Lotus was established by Selby in 1995 with an investment of $2,000,000. Selby provides management services to Lotus for a fee, and also provides financing when needed. During 2001, relations between the two hotels included the following:

1. Selby charged Lotus $80,000 for management services. At year-end, $50,000 of this amount had not yet been paid by Lotus.

2. Lotus was engaged in extensive room renovations. During the year, the amount of financing provided by Selby increased from $2,100,000 to $3,300,000. Interest of $400,000 accrued during the year, and was recorded by both companies, but none of the interest had yet been paid at year-end.

3. Lotus declared dividends of $240,000. One-fourth of the dividends (for the final quarter) were not paid until January 6, 2002. Selby recorded the dividends as dividend income.

The unconsolidated trial balances of the two companies are shown below.

Required:

a. Prepare a consolidated balance sheet and a consolidated income statement for 2001 for Selby.

b. Determine Selby's 2001 net income and the balance of Selby's retained earnings at December 31, 2001, assuming that Selby did not consolidate Lotus but instead reported Lotus on the equity basis.

Balance Sheets
December 31, 2001

	Selby	Lotus
Assets		
Current assets:		
Cash	$ 300,000	$ 250,000
Accounts receivable	1,200,000	300,000
Accrued revenue	500,000	150,000
Advances to Lotus Hotel Inc.	3,700,000	—
	5,700,000	700,000
Buildings and furnishings:		
Building	15,000,000	8,000,000
Furnishings	13,000,000	7,000,000
Accumulated depreciation	(9,750,000)	(2,600,000)
	18,250,000	12,400,000
Investments:		
Investment in Lotus Hotel Inc.	2,000,000	—
Total assets	$25,950,000	$13,100,000
Liabilities		
Current liabilities:		
Accounts payable	$ 350,000	$ 190,000
Accrued liabilities	100,000	400,000
Dividends payable	—	60,000
	450,000	650,000
Long-term liabilities:		
Mortgage notes payable	10,000,000	5,900,000
Due to Selby Hotel Corporation	—	3,300,000
	10,000,000	9,200,000
Total liabilities	10,450,000	9,850,000
Shareholders' equity		
Common shares	8,000,000	2,000,000
Retained earnings	7,500,000	1,250,000
	15,500,000	3,250,000
Total liabilities and shareholders' equity	$25,950,000	$13,100,000

Statements of Income and Retained Earnings
Year Ended December 31, 2001

	Selby	Lotus
Revenue:		
Hotel revenue	$5,500,000	$3,000,000
Investment income and interest	500,000	—
Other revenues	800,000	400,000
	6,800,000	3,400,000
Expenses:		
Salaries and wages	1,900,000	700,000
Maintenance and repairs	900,000	400,000
Supplies	200,000	100,000
Depreciation	600,000	400,000
Interest	1,400,000	1,000,000
Income taxes	600,000	200,000
Other expenses	300,000	350,000
	5,900,000	3,150,000
Net income	900,000	250,000
Retained earnings, December 31, 2000	7,300,000	1,240,000
Dividends declared	(700,000)	(240,000)
Retained earnings, December 31, 2001	$7,500,000	$1,250,000

Business
Combinations

Introduction

In the previous chapter, we pointed out that a corporation can obtain a subsidiary either by establishing a new corporation (a *parent-founded subsidiary*) or by buying an existing corporation (through a *business combination*). We also demonstrated the preparation of consolidated financial statements for a parent-founded subsidiary.

When a subsidiary is purchased in a business combination, the consolidation process becomes significantly more complicated. The purpose of this chapter is to explore the meaning and the broad accounting implications of business combinations. First, we will examine the general meaning of *business combination*, which can mean a purchase of assets as well as a purchase of a subsidiary. Next, we will look more closely at the issues surrounding purchase of a subsidiary and at consolidation at the date of acquisition. The procedures for consolidating a purchased subsidiary subsequent to acquisition are the primary focus of Chapters 4 to 7.

Definition of a Business Combination

A **business combination** occurs when one corporation obtains *control* of a group of *net assets* that constitutes a *going concern*. A key word is *control*—**control** can be obtained either by:

1. buying the assets themselves (which automatically gives control to the buyer), or

2. buying *control* over the corporation that owns the assets (which makes the purchased corporation a subsidiary).

A second key aspect of the definition of a business combination is that the purchaser acquires control over "net assets that constitute a business" [ED 1980.03][1]—i.e., a going concern. Purchasing a group of idle assets is not a business combination.

A third aspect is the phrase *net assets*—**net assets** means assets minus liabilities. Business combinations often (but not always) require the buyer to assume some or all of the seller's liabilities. When the purchase is accomplished by buying control over another corporation, liabilities are automatically part of the package. But when the purchaser buys a group of assets separately, there may or may not be liabilities attached, such as when one corporation sells an operating division to another company. In any discussion of business combinations, remember that *net assets* includes any related liabilities.

---

1. "ED" refers to the September 1999 CICA Exposure Draft on business combinations.

Finally, observe that *business combination* is not synonymous with *consolidation*. As we discussed in the previous chapter, consolidated financial statements are prepared for a parent and its subsidiaries. The subsidiaries may be either parent-founded or purchased. A purchased subsidiary *usually* is the result of a business combination. But sometimes one corporation will buy control over a shell corporation or a defunct corporation. Since the acquired company is not an operating business, no business combination has occurred.

As well, not all business combinations result in a parent-subsidiary relationship. When a business combination is a direct purchase of net assets, the acquired assets and liabilities are recorded directly on the books of the acquirer, as we shall discuss shortly.

Accounting for Business Combinations—General Approach

The general approach to accounting for business combinations, whether (1) a direct purchase of net assets or (2) a purchase of control, is a three-step process:

1. Measure the cost of the purchase

2. Determine the fair values of the assets and liabilities acquired

3. Allocate the cost on the basis of the fair values

The *mechanics* of accounting for the acquisition will depend on the nature of the purchase, particularly on whether the purchase was of the *net assets* directly or of *control* over the net assets through acquisition of shares of the company that owns the assets. Let's look at the general features that apply to all business combinations before we worry about the acquisition method used.

Measuring the cost

The acquirer may pay for the assets (1) in cash or other assets, (2) by issuing its own shares as consideration for the net assets acquired, or (3) by using a combination of cash and shares.

When the purchase is by cash, it is not difficult to determine the total cost of the net assets acquired. When the purchase is paid for with other assets, the cost is measured by the fair value of the assets surrendered in exchange.

One of the most common methods of acquiring the net assets of another company is for the acquirer to issue its own shares in full or partial payment for the net assets acquired. When shares are issued as consideration for the purchase, the cost of the purchase is the value of the shares issued. If the acquirer is a public company, then the valuation of the shares issued is based on the market value of the existing shares.

Note that although the valuation of the shares issued is *based* on the market value, the value assigned to the newly issued shares may not actually *be* the market price on the date of acquisition. The value assigned to the issued shares is more likely to reflect an average price for a period (e.g., 60 days) surrounding the public announcement of the business combination. The *CICA Handbook* suggests, for example, that the value of shares issued should be "based on the market price of the shares over a reasonable period of time before and after the date the terms of the acquisition are agreed to and announced" [ED 1580.18]. Notice the use of the words *based* and *reasonable*, both of which are subject to professional judgement.

The assigned value may be further decreased to allow for the under-pricing that is necessary for a new issue of shares. Nevertheless, the value eventually assigned to shares issued by a public company normally will bear a proximate relationship to the value of the shares in the public marketplace.

Exceptions to the use of market values do still arise, even when a public market value exists. The *CICA Handbook* suggests that the fair value of the net assets acquired could be used instead of the value of the shares issued if "the quoted market price is not indicative of the fair value of the shares issued, or the fair value of the shares issued is not otherwise clearly evident" [ED 1580.18]. Again, notice the use of the judgemental words *not indicative* and *clearly evident.*

A business combination, whether paid for by assets or by shares, may include a provision for **contingent consideration**. Contingent consideration is an add-on to the base price that is determined some time after the deal is finalized. The amount of contingent consideration can be based on a number of factors, such as:

- a fuller assessment of the finances and operations of the acquired company,

- the outcome of renegotiating agreements with debt holders,

- achievement of stated earnings objectives in accounting periods *following* the change of control, or

- achievement of a target market price for the acquirer's shares by a specified future date.

Contingent consideration that is paid in future periods usually is considered to be additional compensation. The treatment of additional compensation varies:

- If the additional future amount can be estimated at the time that the business combination takes place, the estimate is included in the original calculation of the cost of the purchase [ED 1580.20].

- If the amount cannot be estimated at the date of the combination but additional compensation is paid in the future, the fair value of the net assets is adjusted (usually by increasing the amount of goodwill attributed to the purchase) [ED 1580.23].

- If additional shares are issued because the market price of the issued shares falls below a target price (or fails to reach a target price in the future), the additional shares do *not* represent an additional cost, but simply the issuance of more shares to maintain the same purchase price [ED 1580.24].

Valuation of shares issued by a private company is even more judgemental. If it is not feasible to place a reliable value on the shares issued, it will instead be necessary to rely upon the fair value of the net assets acquired in order to measure the cost of the purchase. In practice, the fair values assigned to the acquired assets and liabilities in a purchase by a private corporation often are remarkably similar to their recorded book values on the books of the acquiree.

There is a lot of room for the exercise of professional judgement in determining the cost of an acquisition.

Determining fair values

Guidelines for determining fair values of net assets are outlined in the *CICA Handbook* [ED 1580.38]. In general, the recommended approaches are:

1. Net realizable value for assets held for sale or conversion into cash

2. Replacement cost for productive assets such as raw materials and tangible capital assets

3. Appraisal values for intangible capital assets, land, natural resources, and non-marketable securities

4. Market value for liabilities, discounted at the current market rate of interest

These guidelines are completely consistent with International Accounting Standards and the newly issued standard in the U.S.A. However, they are only guidelines. Furthermore, it should be apparent that fair value measurements are *accounting estimates*. The fair values are judgemental combinations of different methods of valuation—a bit of a hodgepodge, really. There is a great deal of latitude for management to exercise judgement in determining these values. As we shall explain in the next chapter, such judgement can have significant consequences for reporting in future periods.

Fair values should be determined for all identifiable assets (and liabilities) acquired, whether or not they appear on the balance sheet of the selling company. The basket of acquired assets may include valuable trademarks, patents, or copyrights, none of which may be reflected on the seller's books. Similarly, unrealized tax benefits (that is, the benefits from tax loss carryforwards) may also accrue to the purchaser; these too should be valued.

One type of asset and/or liability that is not given a fair value is any future income tax amounts that appear on the selling company's balance sheet.[2] These are not assets and liabilities from the standpoint of the buyer, since they relate solely to the differences between tax bases and accounting carrying values on the books of the *acquired company*.

We don't escape the complications of income tax allocation, however. Future income tax accounting is a factor in the purchaser's financial reporting for purchased subsidiaries. Acquiring companies must determine their own future income tax balances based on the difference between the asset and liability values they show on their consolidated financial statements and the tax bases. Future income tax considerations tend to confuse students who are trying to understand the sufficiently complex issues in business combinations and consolidations. Therefore, we have decided to treat future income tax aspects separately in an appendix to this chapter (as well as in an appendix to Chapter 4).

Allocating the cost

The third step in accounting for a business combination is to allocate the cost. It is a generally accepted principle of accounting that when a company acquires a group of assets for a single price, the total cost of the assets acquired is allocated to the individual assets on the basis of their fair market values. If a company buys land and a building for a lump sum, for example, the land and building are recorded at their proportionate cost, as determined by estimates of their fair values.

The same general principle applies to assets and liabilities acquired in a business combination. The total cost of the purchase is allocated on the basis of the fair market values of the assets and liabilities acquired.

However, the price paid for the operating unit will be determined in part by its earnings ability. The acquirer may or may not choose to continue to operate the unit in the same manner; but regardless of the acquirer's plans, the price to be paid will take into account the acquired unit's estimated future net revenue stream.

2. This refers to the results of the interperiod income tax allocation process, sometimes known as deferred income tax accounting. Any *current* taxes receivable or payable are assigned a fair value.

If the unit has been successful and has demonstrated an ability to generate above-average earnings, then the acquirer will have to pay a price that is higher than the aggregate fair value of the net assets. On the other hand, if the unit has not been successful, the price may be less than the fair value of the net assets (but not normally less than the liquidating value of the net assets including tax effects).

The difference between the fair value of the net assets (assets less liabilities assumed) and the acquisition cost is known as **goodwill** when the acquisition cost is higher than the fair value of the net assets, and as **negative goodwill** when the cost is less.

Goodwill acquired in a purchase of net assets is recorded on the acquirer's books, along with the fair values of the other assets and liabilities acquired. It is important to understand that goodwill *is* a purchased asset. The purchaser paid good money (or shares) for the goodwill just as surely as for buildings and inventory. In some circles (and in some countries), goodwill is called a "nothing," which derives from the fact that it does not represent any specific asset, either tangible or intangible. But the fact that we can't point at an object (for a tangible asset) or a specific right (for an intangible or financial asset) does not make its cost any less real.

Negative goodwill, however, is not recorded as such. Instead, the costs assigned to the *non-financial* assets are reduced until the total of the costs allocated to the individual assets and liabilities is equal to the total purchase price of the acquired net assets. If there still is negative goodwill left over after the fair value of the non-financial assets has been written down to zero, the excess is reported as an extraordinary item.[3]

The allocation process, therefore, is essentially a two-step process:

1. acquisition cost is allocated to the fair values of the net assets acquired, and

2. any excess of acquisition cost over the aggregate fair value is viewed as goodwill.

Illustration of Direct Purchase of Net Assets

To illustrate the accounting for a direct purchase of net assets, assume that on December 31, 2001, Purchase Ltd. (Purchase) acquires all of the assets and liabilities of Target Ltd. (Target) by issuing 40,000 Purchase common shares to Target. Before the transaction, Purchase had 160,000 common shares outstanding. After the transaction, 200,000 Purchase shares are outstanding, of which Target owns 20%. The pre-transaction balance sheets of both companies are shown in Exhibit 3-1.

The estimated fair values of Target's assets and liabilities are shown at the bottom of Exhibit 3-1. Their aggregate fair value is $1,100,000. If we assume that the market value of Purchase's shares is $30 each, then the total cost of the acquisition is $1,200,000. The transaction will be recorded *on the books of Purchase* as follows:

Cash and receivables	200,000	
Inventory	50,000	
Land	400,000	
Buildings and equipment	550,000	
Goodwill	100,000	
Accounts payable		100,000
Common shares		1,200,000

---

3. Negative goodwill is discussed more fully at the end of this chapter.

EXHIBIT 3–1 PRE-TRANSACTION BALANCE SHEETS

December 31, 2001

	Purchase Ltd.	Target Ltd.
Cash	$1,000,000	$50,000
Accounts receivable	2,000,000	150,000
Inventory	200,000	50,000
Land	1,000,000	300,000
Buildings and equipment	3,000,000	500,000
Accumulated depreciation	(1,200,000)	(150,000)
Total assets	$6,000,000	$900,000
Accounts payable	$1,000,000	$100,000
Long-term notes payable	400,000	—
Common shares*	2,600,000	200,000
Retained earnings	2,000,000	600,000
Total liabilities and shareholders' equity	$6,000,000	$900,000

* for Purchase Ltd.—160,000 shares outstanding

Fair values of Target Ltd.'s net assets:

Cash	$50,000
Accounts receivable	150,000
Inventory	50,000
Land	400,000
Buildings and equipment	550,000
Accounts payable	(100,000)
Total	$1,100,000

The selling company, Target, will record the transaction by writing off all of its assets and liabilities and entering the new asset of Purchase's shares, recognizing a gain of $400,000 on the transaction.

The post-transaction balance sheets for the two companies will appear as shown in Exhibit 3-2. Purchase's assets and liabilities increase by the amount of the fair values of the acquired assets and by the purchased goodwill, while Target's previous net assets have been replaced by its sole remaining asset, the shares in Purchase. If the transaction had been for cash instead of Purchase shares, Target's sole remaining asset would have been the cash received.

The purchase of Target's net assets by Purchase is a business combination, but it is not an intercorporate investment by Purchase because Purchase is not investing in the *shares* of Target. Since Purchase is acquiring the assets and liabilities directly instead of indirectly through the purchase of Target shares, Purchase records the assets and liabilities directly on its books and there is no need for consolidated statements; Target is not a subsidiary of Purchase.

After the net asset purchase has been recorded, Purchase Ltd. will account for the assets as they would any new assets. There is no special treatment required.

EXHIBIT 3–2 POST-TRANSACTION BALANCE SHEETS

December 31, 2001

	Purchase Ltd.	Target Ltd.
Cash	$1,050,000	$ —
Accounts receivable	2,150,000	—
Inventory	250,000	—
Land	1,400,000	—
Buildings and equipment	3,550,000	—
Accumulated depreciation	(1,200,000)	—
Goodwill	100,000	
Investment in Purchase Ltd. shares	—	1,200,000
Total assets	$7,300,000	$1,200,000
Accounts payable	$1,100,000	$ —
Long-term notes payable	400,000	—
Common shares*	3,800,000	200,000
Retained earnings	2,000,000	1,000,000
Total liabilities and shareholders' equity	$7,300,000	$1,200,000

* for Purchase Ltd.—200,000 shares outstanding

Purchase of Shares

Reasons for purchasing shares

Buying the *assets* (or *net assets*) of another company is one way to accomplish a business combination. However, a much more common method of acquiring control over the assets of another company is to buy the *voting shares* of the other business. If one company buys a controlling block of the shares of another company, then control over the assets has been achieved, and the acquirer has a new subsidiary.

An acquirer can obtain a controlling share interest by any one or a combination of three methods:

- buying sufficient shares on the open market,

- entering into private sale agreements with major shareholders, or

- issuing a public tender offer to buy the shares.

Regardless of the purchase method used, the acquirer purchases shares already outstanding. The transaction is with the existing shareholders, not with the target company. The buyer does not need the co-operation of the acquired company itself. Sometimes the target company's board of directors opposes a takeover attempt and tries to persuade the shareholders not to sell their shares to the acquirer—this is known as a **hostile takeover**. Nevertheless, if the purchaser can convince enough of the target company's shareholders to sell their shares, a business combination will occur.

Unlike a direct purchase of assets, a business combination that is achieved by an acquisition of shares does not have any impact on the asset and equity structure of the acquired company.[4] The acquired company continues to carry its assets and liabilities on its own books. The purchaser has acquired *control* over the assets, but has not acquired the assets themselves.

Purchase of shares rather than assets has the obvious advantage that control can be obtained by buying considerably less than 100% of the shares. Control can be obtained at substantially less cost than would be the case if the acquirer purchased the assets directly.

There are several other advantages to buying shares rather than the net assets themselves:

- The shares may be selling at a price on the market that is less than the fair value per share (or even book value per share) of the net assets. The acquirer can therefore obtain control over the assets at a lower price than could be negotiated for the assets themselves.

- By buying shares rather than assets, the acquirer ends up with an asset that is more easily saleable than the assets themselves, in case the acquirer later decides to divest itself of the acquired business, or a portion thereof.

- The acquirer may prefer to retain the newly acquired business as a separate entity for legal, tax, and business reasons. The acquired business's liabilities need not be assumed directly, and there is no interruption of the business relationships built up by the acquired corporation.

- Income tax impacts can be a major factor in the choice between purchasing assets and purchasing shares. A purchase of shares may benefit the seller because any gain to the seller on a sale of shares will be taxed as a capital gain. However, if the assets are sold, gains may be subject to tax at full rates, such as (1) CCA (capital cost allowance) recapture, (2) a sale of inventory, or (3) a sale of intangibles that were fully deducted for tax purposes when paid for initially. Also, the acquired company may have substantial tax loss carryforwards, the benefits of which are unlikely to be realized. The purchaser may be able to take advantage of these carryforwards.

For the buyer, however, a purchase of assets may be more desirable than a purchase of shares from a tax viewpoint. When the assets are purchased directly, their cost to the acquiring company becomes the basis for their tax treatment. For example, depreciable assets are recorded on the acquiring company's books at fair values, and CCA will be based on those fair values. Similarly, goodwill purchased is treated as *eligible capital property* for tax purposes and 75% of the goodwill is subject to CCA (the other 25% is not deductible).

If control over the assets is obtained via a share purchase, on the other hand, there is no change in the tax basis for the assets because there is no change in the assets' ownership. Thus the buyer cannot take advantage of any increased tax shields if net assets are purchased at fair values that are greater than book values.

Another advantage of buying control over another company is that the acquirer does not automatically assume the contingent liabilities of the target company, such as lawsuits or environmental liabilities. If large unexpected liabilities arise, the controlling company can let the subsidiary go bankrupt—the parent loses its investment, but that's better than being pulled down by overwhelming liabilities.

---

4. An exception occurs when "push-down" accounting is used. We will discuss this concept towards the end of the chapter.

Obviously, the decision on acquisition method is subject to many variables. In a friendly takeover, the method of purchase and the purchase price are subject to negotiation, taking into account the various factors affecting both parties, including income tax. If the takeover is hostile, then a purchase of shares is the only alternative.

The share acquisition can be accomplished by paying cash or other assets, or by issuing new shares of the acquirer, or by some combination thereof. When the acquirer issues new shares as consideration for the shares of an acquired business, the transaction is frequently called an **exchange of shares**. When there is an exchange of shares, it is important to keep track of who owns which shares, in order to determine who exercises control over whom.

Share exchanges

There are many different ways in which shares can be exchanged in order to accomplish a business combination. Some of the more common and straightforward methods include the following:

- The acquirer issues new shares to the shareholders of the acquired company in exchange for the shares of the target company (the acquiree).

- *Subsidiaries* of the acquirer issue shares in exchange for the acquiree's shares.

- A new corporation is formed; the new corporation issues shares to the shareholders of both the acquirer and the acquiree in exchange for the outstanding shares of both companies.

- The shareholders of the two corporations agree to a statutory amalgamation.

- The acquiree issues new shares to the shareholders of the acquirer in exchange for the acquirer's outstanding shares.

The first method listed above is the most common approach. The acquirer ends up having more shares outstanding in the hands of shareholders, while the acquiree's shares that were previously held by external shareholders are now held by the acquirer. Both corporations continue to exist as separate legal entities, but the acquirer's shareholder base has been expanded to include shareholders who had previously been shareholders of the acquiree. The acquiree does not hold any shares in the acquirer; it is the former *shareholders* of the acquiree who hold the newly issued acquirer shares.

The second approach is similar to the first, except that the acquirer does not issue its own shares to acquire the company directly. Instead, the acquirer obtains indirect control by having its subsidiaries issue new shares to acquire the company. This approach is useful when the acquirer does not want to alter the ownership percentages of the existing shareholders by issuance of additional shares. For example, if the controlling shareholder of the acquirer owns 51% of the acquirer's shares, the issuance of additional shares would decrease the controlling shareholder's interest to below 50%, and control could be lost. But if the acquirer has a subsidiary that is, say, 70% owned, quite a number of additional shares could be issued by the subsidiary without jeopardizing the parent's control.

Under the third method, a new company is created that will hold the shares of both the other combining companies. The holding company issues its new shares in exchange for the shares of both of the acquiree and the acquirer. After the exchange, the shares of both operating companies are held by the holding company, while the shares of the holding company are held by the former shareholders of both the acquiree and the acquirer.

In a **statutory amalgamation**, the shareholders of the two corporations approve the combination or amalgamation of the two companies into a single surviving corporation. Statutory amalgamations are governed by the provincial or federal corporations acts under which the companies are incorporated. For two corporations to amalgamate, they must be incorporated under the same act. The shareholders of the combined company are the former shareholders of the two combining companies.

Statutory amalgamation is the only method of combination wherein the combining companies cease to exist as separate legal entities. It is also the only method of share exchange in which the assets of both companies end up being recorded on the books of one company, similar to the recording of assets in a direct purchase of net assets. In all other forms of share exchange, there is no transfer of assets and thus no recording of the acquiree's assets on the acquirer's books—the results of the combination are reported by means of consolidated financial statements, as we discussed in the previous chapter. In contrast, consolidated statements are not needed for the combined companies after a statutory amalgamation because only one company survives. Of course, if either amalgamating company had subsidiaries, it would still be necessary to prepare consolidated statements that include those subsidiaries.

The foregoing four methods of combination all specify one corporation as the acquirer. The acquirer is defined as the corporation "that obtains control over the other entity" [ED 1580.10]. It is possible to arrange the combination in such a way that the company that legally appears to be the acquirer is, in substance, the acquiree (the fifth method).

For example, suppose that LesserLimited has 100,000 shares outstanding before the combination, and issues 200,000 new shares to acquire all of GreaterCorp's shares. LesserLimited will own all of the shares of GreaterCorp and thus will legally control GreaterCorp. However, two-thirds of the shares of LesserLimited will be owned by the former shareholders of GreaterCorp, and the former shareholders of GreaterCorp will have voting control of LesserLimited after the combination. The substance of the combination is that control resides with GreaterCorp's shareholders even though the legal form of the combination is that LesserLimited acquired GreaterCorp. This form of business combination is called a **reverse takeover**.

After a reverse takeover occurs, the consolidated financial statements will be issued under the name of the legal parent (in this example, LesserLimited) but should reflect the substance of the combination as a continuation of the financial statements of the legal subsidiary (i.e., GreaterCorp). Pre-combination comparative statements and historical data should be those of the legal subsidiary (and in-substance acquirer) rather than of the legal parent (and in-substance acquiree). Because of the potential confusion from reporting the substance of the activities of the legal subsidiary under the name of the legal parent, it is common for reverse takeovers to be accompanied by a company name change so that the name of the legal parent becomes almost indistinguishable from that of the legal subsidiary.

An example of a reverse takeover is the 1999 acquisition of Allied Hotel Properties by King George Development Corporation. King George acquired 100% of the shares of Allied by issuing King George shares. After the share exchange, the former shareholders of Allied owned a majority of the shares of King George. In the 1999 annual report, the consolidated financial statements after the acquisition reflect the fair values of King George and the book values of Allied. After the combination, the name of King George Development Corporation was changed to Allied Hotel Properties Inc.[5]

5. For additional details, the post-consolidation financial statements of Allied Hotel Properties Inc. (i.e., the new name) can be accessed through SEDAR.com.

One of the main reasons for a reverse takeover is to acquire a stock exchange listing. If LesserLimited had a Toronto Stock Exchange (TSE) listing and GreaterCorp wanted one, a reverse takeover can be arranged instead of going to the trouble and expense of applying to the Ontario Securities Commission (OSC) and the TSE for a listing. In some instances, the legal acquirer (and in-substance acquiree) is just a shell company that has an exchange listing but no assets.

The accounting problem in any business combination is to report in accordance with the *substance* of the combination, and not to be misled by its legal form. Accountants must be sensitive to the objectives of managers and owners in arranging business combinations, and must examine the end result in order to determine who purchased what and for how much.[6]

Illustration of a share exchange

To illustrate the acquirer's accounting for a purchase of shares, assume that on December 31, 2001, Purchase Ltd. acquires all of the outstanding shares of Target Ltd. by issuing 40,000 Purchase shares with a market value of $30, or $1,200,000 total, in exchange.[7] After the exchange of shares, all of the Target shares will be held by the corporate entity of Purchase, while the newly issued shares of Purchase will be held by the former shareholders of Target and *not* by Target as a corporate entity. Target will have no shareholders external to the combined entity, while the shareholder base and the number of shares outstanding for Purchase have increased.

When Purchase acquires the shares, the entry to record the purchase on the books of Purchase will be as follows:

Investment in Target	1,200,000	
Common shares		1,200,000

There will be no entry on Target's books, because Target is not a party to the transaction; the transaction is with the shareholders of Target and not with the company itself. After the original purchase is recorded, the investment is accounted for on Purchase's books by either the cost or equity method, as discussed in Chapter 2.

Exhibit 3-3 shows the balance sheets of Purchase and Target on December 31, 2001, both before and after the purchase of Target's shares by Purchase. The pre-transaction amounts are the same as were shown in Exhibit 3-1, when Purchase purchased the net assets of Target.

The post-transaction amounts on Purchase's separate-entity balance sheet differ from the pre-transaction amounts only in one respect—Purchase now has an account, "Investment in Target Ltd.," that reflects the cost of buying Target's shares, offset by an equal increase in Purchase's common share account. The purchase price was $1,200,000, determined by the value of the 40,000 Purchase common shares given to Target's shareholders in exchange for their shares in Target.

Target's balance sheet is completely unaffected by the exchange of shares. Target's *owner* has changed, but nothing has changed in the company's accounts. Target's net asset book value was $800,000 prior to the change of ownership, and remains $800,000 after the change of ownership.

---

6. A detailed description of reverse takeover accounting is beyond the scope of this book. The Emerging Issues Committee issued abstract EIC-10 in January 1990, "Reverse Takeover Accounting," which deals with many of the issues that arise when attempting to account for reverse takeovers.

7. This transaction has the same value as the illustration used earlier in the chapter for a direct purchase of net assets.

EXHIBIT 3–3 BALANCE SHEETS, DECEMBER 31, 2001

	Before the exchange of shares		After the exchange of shares	
	Purchase Ltd.	Target Ltd.	Purchase Ltd.	Target Ltd.
Cash	$1,000,000	$ 50,000	$1,000,000	$ 50,000
Accounts receivable	2,000,000	150,000	2,000,000	150,000
Inventory	200,000	50,000	200,000	50,000
Land	1,000,000	300,000	1,000,000	300,000
Buildings and equipment	3,000,000	500,000	3,000,000	500,000
Accumulated depreciation	(1,200,000)	(150,000)	(1,200,000)	(150,000)
Investment in Target Ltd.	—	—	1,200,000	—
Total assets	$6,000,000	$900,000	$7,200,000	$900,000
Accounts payable	$1,000,000	$100,000	$1,000,000	$100,000
Long-term notes payable	400,000	—	400,000	—
Common shares*	2,600,000	200,000	3,800,000	200,000
Retained earnings	2,000,000	600,000	2,000,000	600,000
Total liabilities and share equity	$6,000,000	$900,000	$7,200,000	$900,000

*For Purchase Ltd., 160,000 shares before the exchange; 200,000 shares after the exchange.

Target is now a subsidiary of Purchase, and therefore Purchase will prepare consolidated financial statements for public reporting purposes. The preparation of consolidated statements for a purchased subsidiary is somewhat more complex than for parent-founded subsidiaries, and involves choices from among several optional approaches. Consolidation of a purchased subsidiary at the date of acquisition will be illustrated shortly.

Alternative Approaches to Reporting Business Combinations

Overview

In Chapter 2, we demonstrated the preparation of consolidated statements for Parco. To obtain the Parco consolidated balance sheet, we simply added the balances of Subco's assets and liabilities to those of Parco, after eliminating the intercompany balances. It might seem logical to use the same procedure to prepare Purchase's consolidated balance sheet, adding the book values of the two companies' assets and liabilities together to get the consolidated amounts.

However, in Chapter 2 we were demonstrating consolidation of a *parent-founded* subsidiary. In wholly-owned parent-founded subsidiaries, the carrying values of the subsidiary's net assets represent the cost of the assets to the consolidated economic entity, because it was the parent's initial investment (and subsequent non-withdrawal of earnings) that provided the equity to purchase the assets. When a subsidiary is purchased, however, the purchase price of the net assets acquired will almost certainly be different from the carrying value of those assets on the subsidiary's books.

Target has net assets with a book value of $800,000. Purchase issued shares worth $1,200,000 to acquire control over Target's net assets. The $400,000 difference between the purchase price and the book value of the net assets acquired is known as the **purchase price discrepancy**. Any method of combining the balance sheets of the two companies must find a way of disposing of the $400,000 difference.

Three general alternative approaches are available for combining the balance sheets of Purchase and Target in order to obtain a consolidated balance sheet for Purchase. These alternatives are:

1. Add together the book values of the assets and liabilities of the two companies (the **pooling-of-interests** method).

2. Add the fair values of Target's assets and liabilities at the date of acquisition to the book values of Purchase's assets and liabilities (the **purchase** method).

3. Add the fair values of Target's assets and liabilities to the fair values of Purchase's assets and liabilities (the **new-entity** method).

The two variables that determine the results are (1) the valuation of the parent's net assets and (2) the valuation of the subsidiary's net assets. The alternatives can be summarized as follows:

Method	Net assets of parent company	Net assets of subsidiary
Pooling of interests	Book value	Book value
Purchase	Book value	Fair value
New entity	Fair value	Fair value

To demonstrate the alternatives, we need to know the fair values of the two companies' net assets. Exhibit 3-4 compares each company's book values with its assumed fair values. To keep this example simple, we assume that only the capital assets have fair values that are different from book values. The capital assets are highlighted in Exhibit 3-4.

Pooling of interests

Pooling of interests certainly is the simplest method of consolidating a purchased subsidiary. Under this method, the book values of the parent and the subsidiary are added together and reported on the parent's consolidated balance sheet.

EXHIBIT 3–4 BOOK VALUES AND FAIR VALUES, DECEMBER 31, 2001

[Dr/(Cr)]

	Purchase Ltd.		Target Ltd.	
	Book value	**Fair value**	**Book value**	**Fair value**
Cash	$ 1,000,000	$ 1,000,000	$ 50,000	$ 50,000
Accounts receivable	2,000,000	2,000,000	150,000	150,000
Inventory	200,000	200,000	50,000	50,000
Land	**1,000,000**	**2,000,000**	**300,000**	**400,000**
Buildings and equipment	**3,000,000**	**2,300,000**	**500,000**	**550,000**
Accumulated depreciation	**(1,200,000)**	**—**	**(150,000)**	**—**
Accounts payable	(1,000,000)	(1,000,000)	(100,000)	(100,000)
Long-term notes payable	(400,000)	(400,000)	—	—
Net assets	$ 4,600,000	$ 6,100,000	$ 800,000	$1,100,000

The assumption underlying the pooling method is that the combined economic entity is a continuation under common ownership of two previously separate going concerns, and that the operations of both companies will continue without substantial change. If the companies continue to function as separate entities—although now under common ownership—then it is presumed that there should be no change in the basis of accountability for the assets and liabilities as a result of the combination.

If we consolidate the net assets of the two companies at book values, then a problem remains: what should we do with the $400,000 purchase price discrepancy (i.e., $1,200,000 purchase price minus Target's $800,000 net asset book value)?

The theoretically correct approach in pooling is to carry forward on the consolidated statements the pre-acquisition combined shareholders' equity of the two companies. That means we add Target's common shares and retained earnings to those of Purchase *prior* to the purchase—the amounts shown in the first two columns of Exhibit 3-3. The first column of Exhibit 3-5 shows the result.

The consolidated (pooled) shareholders' equity is $5,400,000, as compared to Purchase's unconsolidated shareholders' equity of $5,800,000 after the combination. The $400,000 difference is offset against the investment account upon consolidation, thereby completely eliminating the $1,200,000 investment account.

The difficulty with applying this approach is that corporations acts in Canada generally state that corporations must record and report issued shares at their *current cash equivalent* at the date of issue. For example, Article 25 of the *Canada Business Corporations Act* provides that "a share shall not be issued until the consideration for the share is fully paid in money or in property or past service that is *not less in value than the fair equivalent of the money that the corporation would have received if the share had been issued for money*" (emphasis added). Article 26 states that "a corporation shall add to the appropriate stated capital account the

EXHIBIT 3–5 ALTERNATIVE APPROACHES TO CONSOLIDATED STATEMENTS FOR A BUSINESS COMBINATION

Purchase Ltd.
Consolidated Balance Sheet
December 31, 2001

	Pooling	Purchase	New Entity
Cash	$ 1,050,000	$ 1,050,000	$1,050,000
Accounts receivable	2,150,000	2,150,000	2,150,000
Inventory	250,000	250,000	250,000
Land	1,300,000	1,400,000	2,400,000
Buildings and equipment	3,500,000	3,550,000	2,850,000
Accumulated depreciation	(1,350,000)	(1,200,000)	—
Goodwill	—	100,000	100,000
Total assets	$ 6,900,000	$ 7,300,000	$8,800,000
Accounts payable	$ 1,100,000	$ 1,100,000	$1,100,000
Long-term notes payable	400,000	400,000	400,000
Common shares*	2,800,000	3,800,000	3,800,000
Add'l paid-in capital: Reappraisal surplus	—	—	1,500,000
Retained earnings	2,600,000	2,000,000	2,000,000
Total liabilities and share equity	$ 6,900,000	$ 7,300,000	$8,800,000

*200,000 shares issued and outstanding

full amount of any consideration it receives for any shares it issues." If the Purchase shares were worth $1,200,000 at the date of their issue, then it would be in contravention of the *Act* to report the shares at only $800,000 on the consolidated financial statements. Therefore, the Purchase shareholders' equity cannot legally be reduced to $5,400,000 for consolidated reporting; the full $5,800,000 must be reported.

While there is a technical legal impediment to application of the pooling-of-interests approach in many instances of corporate combination, there can be combinations that would satisfy the legal requirements, as when shares are issued whose market value approximates the book value of the shares acquired. Also, pooling is easily applied to private companies, where there is no market value for the shares and therefore no readily measurable current cash equivalent. Finally, the fact is that there is no effective enforcement mechanism in the corporations acts short of the extreme remedy of withdrawing the corporation's legal charter.

Purchase method

The purpose of Purchase's purchase of Target's common shares was to obtain control over the net assets and the operations of Target. The control obtained by a purchase of shares is essentially the same as by purchasing Target's net assets directly. If Purchase had purchased the net assets, Purchase clearly would have recorded the acquired net assets at their fair values. If the price paid exceeded the total fair value, the excess would be assigned to goodwill.

The purchase of shares achieves the same result, as does the direct purchase of assets. Therefore, the objective of the purchase method of consolidation is to report the results of the purchase of shares as though the assets had been acquired directly. The fair values of the subsidiary's assets and liabilities are added to those of the parent (at book value), because the fair value is considered to be the cost of the assets and liabilities to the acquirer. Any excess of the purchase price over the aggregate fair value is assigned to goodwill.

The allocation of the purchase price discrepancy was illustrated earlier, when we assumed that Purchase bought Target's net assets directly. The same calculation applies when the method of combining is an exchange of shares. The fair value of Target's net assets is $1,100,000. The purchase price was $1,200,000. The difference of $100,000 between the purchase price and the net asset fair value is attributed to Goodwill.

The second column of Exhibit 3-5 shows Purchase's consolidated balance sheet under the purchase method. Note that the purchase-method consolidated balance sheet is exactly the same as the post-transaction balance sheet for direct purchase of the assets as shown in Exhibit 3-2.

New-entity method

The purchase method has been criticized because the consolidated balance sheet contains a mixture of old book values (for Purchase's assets) and date-of-acquisition fair values (for Target's assets). One can argue that when a business combination occurs, a new economic entity is formed, and that a new basis of accountability should be established for *all* of the assets.

Under the new-entity approach, the assets and liabilities of Purchase are revalued to fair value, so that the consolidated balance sheet will disclose the current fair values (on the date of the combination) of all of the assets for the combined entity. The third column of Exhibit 3-5 shows Purchase's consolidated balance sheet under the new-entity method.

Notice that a new account has appeared in the new-entity column: "reappraisal surplus." We have written up the carrying values of Purchase Ltd.'s assets, and we need an offsetting account to credit. Any upward asset revaluation is reflected in shareholders' equity, as a part of paid-in capital. This is true any time that an asset is written up, whether as a part of a business combination or because assets are carried at fair value instead of cost.

Under certain circumstances, there is merit in the arguments for the new-entity method. If the combining enterprises are of roughly comparable size, and if the operations of the newly combined enterprises are going to be substantially different from the predecessor operations, then a case can be made for establishing a new basis of accountability.

However, there are significant practical problems in implementing the method. Obtaining fair values for all of the assets is likely to be an expensive and time-consuming project, unless the acquiring company already uses current values for internal reporting purposes. In addition, a substantial degree of subjectivity would inevitably exist in the fair-value determination.

While subjective estimates are required to assign the purchase price of a subsidiary to the subsidiary's specific assets and liabilities, the total of the fair values assigned is limited by the total purchase price paid by the parent. But in revaluing the parent's assets for application of the new-entity method, there is no verifiable upper limit for the fair values because no transaction has occurred. In addition, the measurement of goodwill for the parent corporation would be highly subjective. Since it is not clear how the new-entity method would improve the decisions of users of the consolidated financial statements, it has not been accepted in practice.

Other approaches

In the past, approaches to consolidation other than the three discussed above have been used in practice. One of the more common was to value the transaction at the fair value of the consideration given, as in a purchase, but to consolidate the subsidiary's assets and liabilities at their book values, as under pooling. The difference between the book value and the purchase price would be assigned to goodwill on the consolidated statements.

This approach, sometimes called the *carrying-value purchase method*, has the same net impact on the acquirer's net assets as the fair-value purchase method. However, the assignment of the entire excess of the purchase price over net book value to goodwill can have a significant impact on consolidated earnings subsequent to the acquisition, because amortization of goodwill will most likely be different in impact than would subsequent reporting of the fair values of specific assets and liabilities.

Purchase vs. pooling

Before leaving our discussion of the alternative methods of consolidation, we should consider further the use of the purchase method as opposed to the pooling-of-interests method.

In most business combinations, one company clearly is acquiring the other. The acquirer is the company whose pre-combination shareholders have a majority of the voting shares in the combined enterprise, regardless of which company is legally acquiring the shares of the other. If one company can be identified as the acquirer, then there is widespread agreement that the purchase method should be used.

An acquirer can *always* be identified when the purchase of shares is for cash, notes, or other assets of the acquirer. In such an acquisition, the former shareholders of the acquiree have no stake in the combined venture, and clearly they are not pooling their interests with those of the acquirer's shareholders. An exchange of shares must occur for the possibility of pooling even to arise.

Consolidated financial statements can be drastically affected by the choice of pooling or purchase accounting. The consolidated asset values usually will differ considerably, especially for tangible and intangible capital assets. Goodwill that is reported under the purchase method is not shown under pooling. The difference in the asset values will have a consequent impact on earnings measurement because the amounts of amortization will be different.

Another important difference between purchase and pooling is that pooling is applied retroactively, while the purchase method is applied only from the date of the purchase. Under pooling, the two enterprises are reported as though they had always been combined. The comparative financial statements and other financial information (such as earnings per share, total assets, total sales, and so forth) are restated for the periods prior to the combination in order to reflect the operations of both companies. Under the purchase method, however, there is no restatement of prior years' results. The business combination is viewed as any other investment by the acquiring company, and the acquired company's operating results are reflected in the acquirer's operating results only from the date of acquisition.

The difference in reporting can have an impact not only on the *size* of earnings, but also the comparative *direction* over time. Pooling could cause post-combination earnings per share (EPS) to increase, relative to pre-combination earnings, while purchase accounting could cause EPS to decrease. The reverse situation could also occur.

The difference in results is not something that external financial statement users can adjust for. If pooling is used, there is no way to know what the reported results would have been under purchase accounting—there is no information available to the public about the fair values of the net assets acquired. When information on measurements under different accounting methods does not exist, the market cannot adjust for the differences.

Due to the significant differences between reported results under the two methods, there has long been a controversy about the use of pooling versus purchase. This controversy has now been resolved firmly in favour of purchase, as we shall discuss in the next section.

Current Canadian practice

Purchase method

The recommendation of the Business Combinations exposure draft is clear: "The purchase method should be used to account for all business combinations" [ED 1580.08]. This recommendation is intended to slam the door on the use of pooling by public companies.

Pooling was never widespread in Canada. Indeed, around the world, pooling was in widespread use only in the United States. Other countries either prohibited pooling or restricted its use to very narrow circumstances. The *CICA Handbook*, for example, previously stated that pooling could be used only *when an acquirer could not be identified.* As we will discuss more fully in a later section, the change in Canada to prohibit pooling was basically part of a multi-country strategy to help the Financial Accounting Standards Board (FASB) to prohibit pooling in the United States.

Identifying the acquirer

The acquirer in a business combination is the corporation whose shareholders control the combined economic entity. When the purchase is for cash (or other assets), it is obvious that the acquirer is the company that pays to acquire the other (or the assets of the other). When the combination is effected by an exchange of shares, the acquirer may not be so obvious.

The corporation that issues the shares is usually, but not always, the acquirer. Earlier in this chapter, we discussed the issue of *control* and the fact that some business combinations are reverse takeovers. Therefore, it is necessary to examine which shareholder group has control of the combined economic entity in order to determine who is the acquirer.

Voting control may appear to be evenly split between the shareholders of the two combining companies. If that is the case, other factors must be examined to determine who is the acquirer [ED 1580.12]. Examples of other factors include:

- the existence of major voting blocks,

- special voting rights for some shareholders, or voting restrictions on others,

- holdings of convertible debt securities and other options or derivatives,

- the composition of the board of directors, and

- the composition of the senior management team.

Corporate restructurings—non-arm's-length pooling

The AcSB's purchase method recommendation does not apply to combinations of companies under common control [ED 1580.02]. The *CICA Handbook* cites three examples that relate to transfers between subsidiaries or between a parent and its existing or newly-formed subsidiaries. The exemption of transfers between entities under common control also would apply to corporations that are not in a parent-subsidiary relationship, but that have a common controlling shareholder.

A shifting of assets among companies under common control is often called a **corporate restructuring**. A parent company (or its owners) may decide to rearrange the intercorporate ownerships of the economic entity comprised of the parent and its several subsidiaries. New subsidiaries may be formed, or parts of the economic entity may be combined or otherwise regrouped or redefined. When a corporate restructuring takes place, there is no arm's-length transaction because all of the legal corporations are ultimately controlled by the same shareholders. Since there is no arm's-length transaction, the assets cannot be revalued for reporting on either the separate-entity or the consolidated financial statements.

Voluntary restructurings of corporate ownerships are quite common in both public and private companies in Canada. Since corporate ownership restructurings are accounted for as though they were poolings of interest, it is necessary to understand the pooling method even though it is not widely used for business combinations reported by public companies.[8]

International Practices for Business Combinations

In general, countries around the world have required that the purchase method be used for business combinations. Pooling has been permitted in many coun-

---

8. The relevance of pooling for combinations by private companies is another matter, however. These will be discussed in a later section of this chapter, "Acquisitions by private companies."

tries, such as Canada and the U.K., if an acquirer cannot be determined. The one big exception to the general application of the purchase method has been, throughout the last half of the twentieth century, the United States. The U.S.A. has been the most enthusiastic pooler in the world, by far.

In contrast, Australia and New Zealand banned the use of pooling altogether; only purchase accounting has been permitted. Although it may, in some instances, be difficult to establish which company among equals is the acquirer, "experience with the Australian standard suggests that any difficulties in identifying the acquirer are not insurmountable."[9]

Originally, there were absolutely no restrictions on the use of pooling in the United States. Pooling could be used for *any* business combination, regardless of the relative size and power of the combining companies. Pooling could even be used when the purchase was for cash, with no continuing share ownership by the previous shareholders of the target company.

In 1970, the AICPA's Accounting Principles Board tried to rein in the use of pooling by imposing a set of 12 criteria that would govern whether the transaction should be accounted for as a purchase or by pooling.[10] Given the radically different reported results that can be obtained under pooling, it was hardly surprising that many U.S. acquirers structured their purchase transactions in a way that would then require them to use their preferred method of accounting.[11]

The result of the use of pooling was that "two economically similar business combinations can be accounted for using different accounting methods that produce dramatically different financial results."[12] A further consequence was that companies that could not use pooling (such as Canadian companies that were competing for acquisitions) felt that they were severely disadvantaged by lower reported earnings that may be caused by their inability to use pooling. Some observers felt that companies that could use pooling were able to pay more for a target acquisition than a company that could not use pooling. Therefore, "having two accounting methods that produce dramatically different results affect competition in markets for mergers and acquisitions."[13]

In 1999, the standard setters of Canada, Australia, New Zealand, the U.K., and the U.S. (i.e., the "G4" countries) co-operated on the issuance of new standards to eliminate the use of pooling. Effectively, the only country whose standards were seriously changed by the new proposals was the U.S.A. The new standards will achieve international harmonization on a major issue in accounting.

International Accounting Standard 22, *Business Combinations*, is in agreement with the new harmonized standard of the G4. However, it does still permit the pooling of interests method, known as "uniting of interests." It is quite possible that the IASC will eliminate this alternative in a future amendment of the standard.

9. *Methods of Accounting for Business Combinations: Recommendations of the G4+1 for Achieving Convergence*, paragraph 75. Published simultaneously by the standard setting bodies of Canada, U.S.A., U.K., Australia and New Zealand, December 1998.

10. *APB Opinion 16*, issued in 1970. The Accounting Principles Board, or APB, was the standard-setting body in the U.S. prior to establishment of the FASB in 1971.

11. This should be a familiar scenario. It is similar to companies' approach to lease transactions—decide how they want the lease to be reported (i.e., capital or operating), and then structure the lease contract accordingly.

12. Edmund L. Jenkins, FASB Chairman, in testimony before the U.S. Senate Committee on Banking, Housing, and Urban Affairs, March 2, 2000; quoted in the FASB *Status Report* of March 24, 2000.

13. *Ibid.*

Consolidation Procedures

Exhibit 3-5 illustrated the purchase-method consolidated statements in the second column. We explained that the amounts in that column were obtained by adding the book value of each of Purchase's assets and liabilities to the fair values of Target's.

Before plunging into the greater complexities of consolidation in the following chapters, we will more carefully illustrate the general procedure for consolidating subsidiaries that were acquired through a business combination. The key factor that differentiates the procedure is that, for business combinations, consolidation mechanics must adjust for fair values. Fair values are not an issue for parent-founded subsidiaries.

Direct method

After one company acquires control over another, each company will still continue to prepare its own separate-entity financial statements. Remember that each company is still a legal and operating entity. Consolidated statements are an artificial construct of the accounting profession—*artificial* in that there is no legal entity that corresponds to the economic entity of the parent and its subsidiaries. But the reporting objective is *substance over form*. Although the parent and its subsidiaries are separate *legal* entities and prepare separate, individual financial statements, the overall *economic* entity is the group of companies. For that reason, consolidated statements are called **group accounts** in most parts of the world, even though there are no formal group accounts—just consolidation working papers and statements.

In theory, purchase accounting combines the book values of the parent with the fair values (*at date of acquisition*) of the purchased subsidiaries. In practice, consolidation actually begins with *book values* of both companies. At date of acquisition, it is clear that the book values and the fair values relate to the same assets and liabilities. As time moves on, however, assets will enter and leave the balance sheet of each purchased subsidiary, and the asset base will change.

Therefore, consolidation takes the book values of both companies and adds the *fair value increments* relating to the assets of Target that existed when Target was acquired. The fair value increments (or decrements) are the differences between Target's book values and fair values at the date of acquisition.

An analysis of the purchase price is illustrated in Exhibit 3-6. Of the $1,200,000 purchase price, $800,000 is attributed to the book value of the net assets acquired, $300,000 is the total of the fair value increments, and the residual $100,000 is attributed to goodwill. On a continuing basis, consolidated net assets will be computed as:

- book value of each asset and liability,

- plus any fair value increments (or minus any fair value decrements) relating to assets still on Target's books from the date of consolidation,

- plus goodwill, if any.

Exhibit 3-7 (page 98) shows the derivation of Purchase's consolidated balance sheet at December 31, 2001, using the direct method. For each item on the balance sheet, we take the book value for Purchase, add the book value of Target, and add the fair value increment. The fair value increment (and goodwill) adjustments are indicated with a "**b**." Also, we must eliminate Purchase's investment account and Target's shareholders' equity accounts (indicated with an "**a**"). The

EXHIBIT 3–6 ALLOCATION OF PURCHASE PRICE

100% Purchase of Target Ltd., December 31, 2001

Purchase price						$1,200,000
	Book value	Fair value	Fair value increment	% share	FVI acquired	
Cash	$50,000	$50,000	—			
Accounts receivable	150,000	150,000	—			
Inventory	50,000	50,000	—			
Land	300,000	400,000	$100,000 × 100% =		$100,000	
Buildings and equipment	500,000	550,000	50,000 × 100% =		50,000	
Accumulated depreciation	(150,000)	—	150,000 × 100% =		150,000	
Accounts payable	(100,000)	(100,000)	—		_____	
Total fair value increment					300,000	
Net asset book value	$ 800,000			× 100% =	800,000	
Fair value of assets acquired					$1,100,000	
Goodwill					$ 100,000	

resulting balance amounts are identical to those shown in the second column of Exhibit 3-5.

There is one aspect of Exhibit 3-7 that merits explanation. You'll notice that *accumulated depreciation* is calculated by adding the two companies' amounts together, and then *subtracting Target's accumulated depreciation at the date of acquisition.* We subtract Target's accumulated depreciation because we want to show the fair value of Target's depreciable assets at the date of acquisition. This amount is included in the capital asset account itself. If we carried Target's accumulated depreciation forward, we would be reducing the fair value. In effect, we would be combining fair value in the asset account with written-off cost in the accumulated depreciation. To emphasize the point, the *CICA Handbook* explicitly points out that "the accumulated depreciation of the acquired entity is not carried forward" in the consolidated statements [ED 1580.38(d)].

Although we have indicated which adjustments on Exhibit 3-7 are for fair value increments and which are eliminations, bear in mind that these purchase adjustments and eliminations are not independent. Essentially, all of the adjustments shown in Exhibit 3-7 are allocations of the $1,200,000 purchase price. In future years, all of the components of this purchase adjustment must be made simultaneously, as we will illustrate in the following chapters.

Worksheet method

Exhibit 3-8 shows the trial balance-based spreadsheet for Purchase's consolidated balance sheet. The separate-entity columns for the individual companies correspond to the post-transaction balance sheets shown in the last two columns of Exhibit 3-3.

The eliminations and adjustments that are necessary in order to prepare the consolidated trial balance are composed of two elements. First, it is necessary to eliminate the shareholders' equity accounts of Target Ltd. by offsetting the balances of these accounts against the investment account:

EXHIBIT 3–7 PURCHASE LTD. CONSOLIDATED BALANCE SHEET

Balance Sheet
December 31, 2001

Assets

Current assets:

Cash [1,000,000 + 50,000]	$ 1,050,000
Accounts receivable [2,000,000 + 150,000]	2,150,000
Inventory [200,000 + 50,000]	250,000
	3,450,000

Property, plant, and equipment:

Land [1,000,000 + 300,000 **+ 100,000b**]	1,400,000
Buildings and equipment [3,000,000 + 500,000 **+ 50,000b**]	3,550,000
Accumulated depreciation [1,200,000 + 150,000 – **150,000b**]	(1,200,000)
	3,750,000

Other assets:

Investment in Target Ltd. [1,200,000 – **800,000a** – **400,000b**]	—
Goodwill [**+ 100,000b**]	100,000
Total assets	$ 7,300,000

Liabilities and shareholders' equity

Liabilities:

Current accounts payable [1,000,000 + 100,000]	$ 1,100,000
Long-term notes payable [400,000 + 0]	400,000
	1,500,000

Shareholders' equity:

Common shares [3,800,000 + 200,000 – **200,000a**]	3,800,000
Retained earnings [2,000,000 + 600,000 – **600,000a**]	2,000,000
	5,800,000
Total liabilities and shareholders' equity	$ 7,300,000

a	Common shares (Target)	200,000	
	Retained earnings (Target)	600,000	
	Investment in Target Ltd. (Purchase)		800,000

The names in parentheses indicate the company trial balance to which that particular elimination element refers. Again, we must emphasize that there is no actual journal entry on either company's books—this is purely a worksheet entry.

The second entry adjusts the asset accounts of the subsidiary from their carrying values on the subsidiary's books to the fair values at the date of acquisition:

b	Land (Target)	100,000	
	Buildings and equipment (Target)	50,000	
	Accumulated depreciation (Target)	150,000	
	Goodwill	100,000	
	Investment in Target Ltd. (Purchase)		400,000

EXHIBIT 3–8 PURCHASE LTD. CONSOLIDATION WORKSHEET AT DATE OF ACQUISITION

December 31, 2001

| | Trial balances | | | Purchase |
	Purchase Dr/(Cr)	Target Dr/(Cr)	Adjustments Dr/(Cr)	consolidated trial balance
Cash	$ 1,000,000	$ 50,000		$ 1,050,000
Accounts receivable	2,000,000	150,000		2,150,000
Inventories	200,000	50,000		250,000
Land	1,000,000	300,000	100,000 **b**	1,400,000
Buildings and equipment	3,000,000	500,000	50,000 **b**	3,550,000
Accumulated depreciation	(1,200,000)	(150,000)	150,000 **b**	(1,200,000)
Investment in Target Ltd.	1,200,000	—	{ (800,000) **a** (400,000) **b** }	—
Goodwill			100,000 **b**	100,000
Accounts payable	(1,000,000)	(100,000)		(1,100,000)
Long-term notes payable	(400,000)	—		(400,000)
Common shares	(3,800,000)	(200,000)	200,000 **a**	(3,800,000)
Retained earnings	(2,000,000)	(600,000)	600,000 **a**	(2,000,000)
	$ —	$ —	$ —	$ —

The net result of these two adjustments is to eliminate the investment account, eliminate the subsidiary's share equity accounts at the date of acquisition, and establish the fair values of the assets and liabilities acquired by Purchase through purchase of Target's shares. These two adjustments will be made in every subsequent period when the consolidated statements are prepared.

Negative Goodwill

In the example of a business combination used earlier in this chapter, control over net assets with a fair value of $1,100,000 was acquired for $1,200,000. The difference between the purchase price and the fair value of the acquired net assets is treated as goodwill.

It is not unusual, however, for the total fair value of the assets and liabilities to be *greater* than the purchase price. This excess of fair values over the purchase price is commonly known as **negative goodwill**, although the title is not particularly indicative of the accounting treatment of the amount. The total of the net debits (to record the fair values) is greater than the credits (to record the consideration paid), and therefore there are more debits than credits in the consolidated statements—not a tolerable situation in a double-entry system. The task is to correct the balance by either increasing the credits or decreasing the debits.

Once upon a time, it was common practice to increase the credits by establishing an account to credit for the amount of negative goodwill. It was not normally called "negative goodwill," of course. Usually a more opaque title was chosen, such as "excess of fair value over cost of assets acquired." This is now a prohibited practice in Canada, and in most countries. Instead of creating a credit for negative goodwill, the balance of debits and credits must be achieved by reducing the total amount allocated to the net assets.

Negative goodwill is, in essence, an indication that the acquirer achieved a bargain purchase. A bargain purchase is possible for a variety of reasons. If the acquisition is by a purchase of shares, then the market price of the acquiree's shares may be well below the net asset value per share. Or if the acquiree is a private company, a bargain purchase may be possible if the present owners are anxious to sell because of the death of the founder-manager, divorce, changed family financial position, or simply an inability to manage effectively.

Regardless of the reason, negative goodwill should be viewed as a discount on the purchase and not as a special credit to be created and amortized. When any company buys an asset at a bargain price, the asset is recorded at its cost to the purchaser, and not at any list price or other fair value. For example, suppose that a company buys a large computer from a financially troubled distributor for only $80,000. The price of the computer from any other source would be $120,000. On the buyer's books, the computer obviously would be recorded at $80,000, not at $120,000 with an offsetting credit for $40,000.

The same general principle applies to bargain purchases in business combinations. The purchase price is allocated to the acquired assets and liabilities on the basis of fair values, but not necessarily *at* fair values if the total fair value exceeds the purchase price. A problem does arise, however, in deciding to which assets and liabilities the bargain prices or negative goodwill should be assigned.

A business combination involves the assets and liabilities of a going concern. The net assets acquired usually comprise a mixture of financial and non-financial, current and long-term assets and liabilities. Because the various assets and liabilities have varying impacts on reported earnings, the allocation of negative goodwill will affect the amount of future revenues and expenses.

For example, suppose that Purchase acquired all of the shares of Target, as above, but at a cost of only $1,050,000. Since the fair value of Target's net assets is $1,100,000, negative goodwill of $50,000 exists. Target's assets and liabilities will be reported on Purchase's consolidated balance sheet at a total amount of $1,050,000, $50,000 less than their fair values. At least one of the Target assets must be reported at an amount that is less than its fair value.

If the negative goodwill were assigned to inventory, Target's inventory would be consolidated at zero value, since the fair value of Target's inventory was assumed to be $50,000 (Exhibit 3-4). Reduction in the cost assigned to inventory will flow through to the income statement in the following year as a reduction in cost of goods sold and an increase in net income. If, on the other hand, the negative goodwill were assigned to buildings and equipment, then the effect of the bargain purchase would be recognized over several years in the form of reduced depreciation on the lower cost allocated to buildings and equipment. Allocation of the negative goodwill to land would result in no impact on earnings until the land was sold; allocation to monetary receivables would result in a gain when the receivables were collected.

The choice of assets to report at less than fair values is essentially arbitrary. The AcSB [ED 1580.32] recommends that negative goodwill should be allocated in the following order:

1. pro rata to any intangible assets that do not have an observable market value, and then

2. pro rata to depreciable *non-financial* assets (both tangible and intangible).

If the purchase price allocations to the non-financial assets have all been reduced to zero and there still is negative goodwill remaining, the remaining amount is recognized as an extraordinary gain, even though the normal conditions for recognizing an extraordinary gain have not been met.

Disclosure

Business combinations are significant events. They often change the nature of operations of a company and thus change the components of the earnings stream. All users' financial reporting objectives are affected by substantial business combinations. At a minimum, the asset and liability structure of the reporting enterprise is changed. Disclosure of business combinations therefore is quite important.

The AcSB recommends a long list of disclosures for business combinations completed during the period [ED 1580.65-1580.68]. We will not reproduce the list here, but the acquirer should disclose essential aspects such as:

- a description of the acquired subsidiary, its business, the date of purchase, and the nature of the purchase transaction,

- the cost of the acquisition and the nature and value of the consideration given,

- a summary of the major classes of asset and liability acquired,

- the amount of the purchase price that is attributed to goodwill, and

- the nature of any contingent consideration.

For acquisitions that are individually immaterial, similar information should be disclosed in the aggregate [ED 1580.66].

Also, the acquirer should disclose significant intangible assets that have been acquired as part of the business combination. The nature of the assets and the amortization basis should be described.

Exhibit 3-9 shows the 1999 disclosure note of Geac Computer Corporation Limited. This disclosure has several interesting aspects:

- Geac acquired seven businesses during fiscal 1999.

- Three of the business combinations were purchases of assets; the other four were purchases of shares. One of the asset purchases (Cruickshank Technology) included the shares of a subsidiary.

- In all seven acquisitions, Geac paid cash.

- The purchase price for News Holdings Corp. was $25,808,000. Of the purchase price, $45,842,000 was allocated to goodwill, 178% of the purchase price. The reason that goodwill is higher than the purchase price is that the acquired company had a negative net asset value (i.e., more liabilities than assets).

- In aggregate, the other acquired businesses also had negative net assets— goodwill amounted to 186% of the total purchase prices.

Exhibit 3-10 (page 103) illustrates disclosure of another purchase. In this case, the acquisition was of significant influence, and therefore is not a business combination. Corel will report this investment by the equity method, as the note states. An unusual aspect of Corel's purchase of 25% of Rebel.com is that the consideration was neither cash nor shares—the purchase was paid for by exchanging the assets shown in the note, described as follows in Corel's MD&A (Management's Discussion and Analysis):

On February 17, 1999, the Company transferred all of the assets of Corel Computer supporting the NetWinder family of Linux-based thin client/thin server computers and $1.6 million cash in exchange for a 25% equity stake in Rebel.com.

Recording Fair Values: Push-Down Accounting

We have emphasized that the fair values of the net assets of the acquiree are never recorded in the books of the acquirer; the full purchase price is simply recorded in an investment account on the acquirer's books. We have also stated that when a business combination is accomplished by a purchase of shares (rather than by a direct purchase of assets), the acquiree continues to exist as a separate legal and reporting entity. The carrying values of the acquiree's net assets are not affected by the acquisition or by the fair values attributed to the assets by the acquirer.

EXHIBIT 3–9 DISCLOSURE OF ACQUISITIONS

Geac Computer Corporation

13. ACQUISITIONS

Year ended April 30, 1999

During the year ended April 30, 1999, the Company acquired for cash the businesses shown in the table below. Cruickshank Technology Pty Limited, Stowe Computing Australia, Stowe Computing Finance Pty Limited, Stowe Computing (NZ) Limited, and Phoenix Systems Limited were asset purchases. The Company acquired the remaining 75% interest in its former joint venture Soluzioni Gestionali. In each of the remaining acquisitions, the Company acquired all of the issued and outstanding shares. Acquisitions are accounted for by the purchase method with the results of operations of each business included in the financial statements from the respective dates of acquisition. Geac accrues or reserves for known or anticipated customer, supplier, or other problems at the time of acquisition just as it would in ongoing businesses.

The total purchase price of News Holdings Corp. and its subsidiary Interealty Corp. was $25,808. The acquired business included, at fair value, $13,685 of current assets, $11,654 of fixed assets, and $45,373 of current liabilities. The difference between the total purchase price and the net fair value of all identifiable assets and liabilities acquired was $45,842 and is accounted for as goodwill.

The total purchase price of the remaining acquired business was $15,088. These businesses included, at fair value, $979 of cash, $10,833 of other current assets, $1,191 of fixed assets, and $26,032 of current liabilities. The difference between the total purchase price and the net fair value of all identifiable assets and liabilities acquired was $28,117 and is accounted for as goodwill.

Acquisition	Effective date
Remanco International, Inc. and its subsidiary Remanco Systems, Ltd.	May 31, 1998
Assets of Cruickshank Technology Pty Limited and all of the issued and outstanding shares of its subsidiary Mainpac Limited	June 1, 1998
News Holdings Corp. and its subsidiary Interealty Corp.	September 7, 1998
Soluzioni Gestionali SrL	October 15, 1998
TWG Technologies Inc.	December 1, 1998
Assets of Stowe Computing Australia Pty Ltd., Stowe Computing Finance Pty Limited and Stowe Computing (NZ) Limited	December 3, 1998
Assets of Phoenix Systems Limited	April 30, 1999

EXHIBIT 3–10 PURCHASE OF SIGNIFICANT INFLUENCE

Corel Corporation

3. Investments

(a) Rebel.com

On February 17, 1999, the Company purchased a 25% interest in Rebel.com for $3,351,000. The Company's share of the net book value of the underlying assets was $1,299,000. The remaining balance of the purchase price of $2,052,000 has been allocated to goodwill and is being amortized on a straight-line basis over three years. The fair value of the assets used to purchase the Company's share of Rebel.com was as follows (in thousands of US$):

Cash	$ 1,561
Capital assets	1,341
Inventory	381
Accounts receivable	68
Total purchase price	$ 3,351

The Company is accounting for this investment using the equity method. In 1999, $342,000 of goodwill was amortized and the Company's share of Rebel.com's net loss of $136,000 was deducted from the value of the investment.

An exception to the general rule that the acquiree's carrying values are unaffected by the purchase may arise when substantially all of the acquiree's shares are purchased by the acquirer. In that case, the acquirer may direct the acquiree to revalue its assets in accordance with the fair values attributed thereto by the acquirer. This practice is known as **push-down accounting**, because the fair values are "pushed down" to the acquiree's books. The net effect is the same as if the acquirer had formed a new subsidiary, which then purchased all of the assets and liabilities of the acquiree.

There are two advantages to push-down accounting. The first is that the financial position and results of operations of the acquiree will be reported on the same economic basis in both the consolidated statements and its own separate-entity statements. Without push-down accounting, for example, it would be possible for the subsidiary to report a profit on its own and yet contribute an operating loss to the parent's consolidated results, if the consolidation adjustments are sufficient to tip the balance between profit and loss.

The second advantage is that the process of consolidation will be greatly simplified for the parent. Since the carrying values will be the same as the acquisition fair values, there will be no need for many of the consolidation adjustments that otherwise will be required every time consolidated statements are prepared.

Although push-down accounting is used in Canada, the practice is more prevalent in the United States, where the Securities and Exchange Commission *requires* its registrants to use the practice when an acquired subsidiary is "substantially" wholly owned and there is no publicly held debt or senior shares.

In 1992, the CICA Accounting Standards Board issued *CICA Handbook* section 1625, "Comprehensive Revaluation of Assets and Liabilities." Push-down accounting *may* be used when:

All or virtually all of the equity interests in the enterprise have been acquired, in one or more transactions between non-related parties, by an acquirer who controls the enterprise after the transaction or transactions. [CICA 1625.04(a)]

A guideline of 90% ownership is provided for the phrase "virtually all of the equity interests" [CICA 1625.10]. Note that the recommendation provides for acquisitions that are accomplished by a series of smaller share purchases rather than by one large transaction—substantially complete ownership need not be achieved all at once.

Despite the permissibility of applying push-down accounting, acquirers may choose not to apply push-down accounting to subsidiaries that have outstanding public debt. The reason is that the basis for assessing contract compliance is disturbed by an asset revaluation. Reported results (e.g., earnings per share) will be discontinuous, and debt covenants may be violated or rendered less suitable if the reporting basis is changed. Indeed, debt agreements with banks may be based on accounting principles in effect on the date of the agreement, and thereby effectively constrain the application of push-down accounting.

A special case of push-down accounting arises in a reverse takeover. In a reverse takeover, it is the legal acquirer that is really the in-substance acquiree—the fair values reported on the consolidated statements will be those of the company issuing the statements (the legal parent but in-substance subsidiary). In that case, it makes little sense for the in-substance acquiree to be carrying its assets and liabilities at book values that will never be reported in its own financial statements. It is more logical simply to put the fair values on the books of the in-substance acquiree.

Summary of Key Points

1. A business combination is the acquisition of net assets or *control* over net assets that constitute a functioning business. Control over net assets is usually obtained by buying a majority of the shares in the operating company that owns the assets. When control is acquired, the acquired net assets remain the property of the controlled subsidiary. Therefore, consolidated financial statements are necessary.

2. Accounting for a business combination requires three steps: (1) determine the cost of the acquisition, or purchase price, (2) determine the fair values of the acquired assets and liabilities, and (3) allocate the purchase price to the identifiable assets and liabilities, with any excess attributed to goodwill.

   The basis for the allocation of purchase price is the fair values of the acquired assets and liabilities. If the purchase price is less than the aggregate fair value of the net assets, negative goodwill arises. The value assigned to non-financial assets, starting with intangible assets with no observable market value, must be reduced until the total allocated amount equals the purchase price.

   If the purchase price is less than the fair value of the non-financial assets, the excess of fair value over the purchase price is recognized as an extraordinary item.

   A purchase of net assets may be accomplished (1) by paying cash or other assets or (2) by issuing shares. A combination of cash and shares may be used.

   When shares are issued, the purchase price is based on the market value of the shares, if determinable. If the market value of issued shares is not determinable, the fair value of the net assets acquired may be used as the measure of the purchase price. Fair values are determined on various bases, depending on the type of asset or liability. Generally, fair values of assets are based on net realizable values, replacement costs, and appraised values. Liabilities are measured at their discounted present value, using the market rate of interest at the time of the combination.

If the net assets are purchased directly, the fair values of the acquired assets and liabilities are recorded on the books of the acquirer. There is no parent-subsidiary relationship because the acquirer did not buy another corporation—it bought the net assets instead.

3. Acquisition of majority control over another company enables the investor to obtain control over the assets without having to pay the full fair value of the assets. Shares can be purchased for cash or other assets. Alternatively, the purchaser can issue its own shares in exchange for the shares of the acquiree. If there is an exchange of shares, the acquirer does not have to give up any cash. The previous holders of the acquiree's shares now hold shares in the acquirer instead.

4. Theoretically, there are three approaches to reporting consolidated financial statements following purchase of control over another corporation: pooling, purchase, and new entity.

Under the pooling method, the book values of the parent and the subsidiary are simply added together and reported as the consolidated amounts.

Under purchase accounting, the date-of-acquisition fair values of the subsidiary are added to the parent's book values. The purchase method of consolidation gives the same results as if the net assets had been purchased directly.

With the new-entity method, the fair values of the parent and the subsidiary are added together to form a new basis of accountability for the ongoing economic entity.

5. Pooling has been in widespread use only in the U.S.A. Other countries, including Canada, have sharply limited pooling to those rare instances in which an acquirer cannot be identified. Effective in 2001, the pooling method is not permitted for arm's-length business combinations by the *CICA Handbook*, by FASB standards in the U.S.A., or by International Accounting Standards. However, the pooling method is applied to non-arm's-length corporate restructurings, including the combination of companies under common control.

6. Normally, fair values are not recorded on the books of the acquiree; adjustments are made solely on working papers to prepare consolidated financial statements. However, fair values may be recorded on the books of the acquired company if the investor corporation has acquired substantially all of the shares of the subsidiary. This practice is known as *push-down accounting*.

Weblinks

Ontario Securities Commission
www.osc.gov.on.ca/

The Ontario Securities Commission administers and enforces securities legislation in the Province of Ontario. Their mandate is to protect investors from unfair improper and fraudulent practices, foster fair and efficient capital markets, and maintain public and investor confidence in the integrity of those markets. Learn about the rules and regulations, market participants, and investor resources from this comprehensive Web site.

Allied Hotel Properties
www.alliedhotels.com/

Allied Hotel Properties is a Canadian hotel company focused on the ownership of first class business hotels in major Canadian urban centres. Properties include the Crowne Plaza Hotel Georgia and Delta Pacific Resort & Conference Centre in Vancouver, Crowne Plaza Chateau Lacombe in Edmonton, and Crowne Plaza Toronto Don Valley Hotel in Toronto. Read news releases and stock quotes at their Web site.

Corel
www.corel.com

From its early years as a pioneer in the graphics software field to its current innovations in business and Internet software for a variety of platforms, Corel has consistently developed products that respond to evolving consumer needs. Current products include CorelDraw, WordPerfect, and Corel Painter. Find out more about these programs or order them online at their Web site.

Self-Study Problem 3-1

Ace Corporation acquired Blue Corporation on August 31, 2004. Both corporations have fiscal years ending on August 31. Exhibit 3-11 shows the balance sheet for each corporation as of August 31, 2004, immediately *prior* to the combination, and net income amounts for each corporation for the fiscal year ended August 31, 2004.

The fair values of the assets and liabilities of the two companies at the date of acquisition are shown in Exhibit 3-12. The deferred development costs represent the unamortized amount of the companies' leading-edge products. There is no observable market value for this identifiable intangible asset, but Ace expects to fully recover the costs in future years.

Before the combination, Ace had 1,200,000 common shares issued and outstanding. Blue had 750,000 common shares issued and outstanding.

EXHIBIT 3–11 PRE-COMBINATION BALANCE SHEETS, AUGUST 31, 2004		
	Ace	**Blue**
Cash and cash equivalents	$ 2,350,000	$ 1,200,000
Accounts receivable	2,000,000	1,800,000
Land	5,000,000	—
Machinery and equipment, net	13,500,000	8,400,000
Deferred development costs	600,000	3,100,000
	$23,450,000	$14,500,000
Accounts payable	$ 650,000	$ 1,100,000
Notes payable, long-term	2,000,000	1,000,000
Common shares	15,000,000	6,950,000
Retained earnings	5,800,000	5,450,000
	$23,450,000	$14,500,000
Net income, year ended August 31, 2004	2,450,000	1,300,000

EXHIBIT 3–12 FAIR VALUES, AUGUST 31, 2004		
	Ace	**Blue**
Cash and cash equivalents	$ 2,350,000	$ 1,200,000
Accounts receivable	2,000,000	1,800,000
Land	8,500,000	—
Machinery and equipment, net	11,000,000	11,000,000
Deferred development costs	750,000	4,000,000
Accounts payable	(650,000)	(1,100,000)
Notes payable, long-term	(2,000,000)	(900,000)
Net asset fair value	$21,950,000	$16,000,000

Required:

Prepare the Ace Corporation post-combination balance sheet under each of the following *independent* situations:

1. Ace Corporation purchased the assets and assumed the liabilities of Blue Corporation by paying $2,000,000 cash and issuing long-term instalment notes payable of $18,000,000.

2. Ace issued 400,000 common shares for all of the outstanding common shares of Blue. The market value of Ace's shares was $50 per share.

3. Ace purchased 100% of Blue's outstanding common shares from Blue's previous shareholders. As consideration, Ace issued 270,000 common shares and paid $1,000,000 in cash. The market value of Ace's shares was $50 per share.

Appendix

Income Tax Allocation

Introduction

In your intermediate accounting course, you undoubtedly studied the topic of income tax allocation. The effects of income tax allocation show up as "future income taxes" on almost all balance sheets, as well as being a component of income tax expense. Future income taxes arise from two causes:

1. temporary differences between accounting income and taxable income, and

2. unrealized tax loss carryforwards.

In the main body of Chapter 3, we avoided any discussion of future income taxes as they relate to business combinations. However, they do play a part in the allocation of the purchase price and the calculation of goodwill. We have left this topic to an Appendix because we did not want to obscure the principal issues of accounting for business combinations. Income taxes are not irrelevant, but they are not central to an understanding of business combinations and the reporting of strategic investments.

Temporary differences in business combinations

In general, temporary differences arise because the carrying values of assets (and liabilities) differ from their tax bases. The most common type of temporary difference relates to depreciable capital assets—book depreciation methods *(accounting method)* are usually different from CCA *(tax method)*, and therefore an asset's carrying value is different from its tax basis.

A similar situation arises in business combinations. The cost allocated to an asset in a business combination is based on the asset's fair value. The fair value then becomes its carrying value. However, Canada Customs and Revenue Agency doesn't care about an asset's fair value—only its tax basis matters. Therefore, a temporary difference arises and must be dealt with.

For the purpose of consolidated statements, an asset's temporary difference is measured as the difference between its tax basis and the carrying value on the *parent's* consolidated financial statements—which is based on the asset's fair value at the date of acquisition. The relevant carrying value is **not** *its carrying value on the books of the* **subsidiary**.

Exhibit 3-13 attempts to clarify the situation. Suppose that a newly acquired subsidiary, S, has an asset with a tax basis of $70 and a carrying value *on S's books* of $100. The temporary difference is $30. If S's tax rate is 40%, the future income tax liability pertaining to that asset is $30 × 40% = $12 on *S's separate-entity balance sheet.*

However, the fair value of that asset is $150. P, the parent company, will show the asset on P's *consolidated* balance sheet at $150. For P's consolidated statements, the temporary difference is $150 − $70 = $80. At a 40% tax rate, the future income tax liability pertaining to that asset is $80 × 40% = $32 *on P's consolidated balance sheet.*

The amount shown as the future income tax liability on P's consolidated balance sheet does not affect the tax status of S. S and P are each taxed as a separate corporate entity.

Now, let's apply income tax allocation to the example in the main body of this chapter.

- Purchase acquired 100% of the shares of Target for $1,200,000.

- The carrying value of Target's net assets *on Target's books* was $800,000.

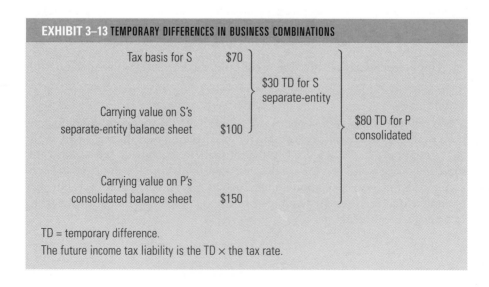

EXHIBIT 3–13 TEMPORARY DIFFERENCES IN BUSINESS COMBINATIONS

Tax basis for S	$70	
		$30 TD for S separate-entity
Carrying value on S's separate-entity balance sheet	$100	$80 TD for P consolidated
Carrying value on P's consolidated balance sheet	$150	

TD = temporary difference.
The future income tax liability is the TD × the tax rate.

- Fair value increments totalled $300,000: $100,000 for land plus $200,000 for buildings and equipment.

- Goodwill was $100,000.

Let's make some additional assumptions:

- The tax basis for the land is equal to its carrying value on Target's books of $300,000.

- The tax basis of Target's buildings and equipment is $250,000.

- The tax basis for all other Target Ltd. assets and liabilities is equal to their carrying values.

- The tax rate for both Target and Purchase is 40%.

The relevant amounts can be summarized as follows.

	Land	Buildings & Equipment	Total
Tax basis	$300,000	$250,000	$550,000
Target Ltd.'s carrying value	300,000	350,000	650,000
Fair value to Purchase Ltd.	400,000	550,000	950,000

For Target Ltd., the total temporary difference is $650,000 − $550,000 = $100,000. The future income tax liability is $100,000 × 40% = $40,000. For simplicity's sake, we did not include this amount among the net assets shown in the main body of the chapter.

For Purchase Ltd.'s consolidated statements, the temporary difference is $400,000, and the future income tax liability (at 40%) is $160,000. Exhibit 3-14 shows the allocation of the purchase price with the future income tax liability included. We have fudged the original amounts a bit by subdividing accounts payable and shifting $40,000 to a future income tax liability account,

EXHIBIT 3–14 ALLOCATION OF PURCHASE PRICE, INCLUDING FUTURE INCOME TAXES

100% purchase of Target Ltd., December 31, 2001

Purchase price						$1,200,000
	Book value	Fair value	Fair value increment	% share	FVI acquired	
Cash	$ 50,000	$ 50,000	—			
Accounts receivable	150,000	150,000	—			
Inventory	50,000	50,000	—			
Land	300,000	400,000	$ 100,000 × 100% =	$ 100,000		
Buildings and equipment	500,000	550,000	50,000 × 100% =	50,000		
Accumulated depreciation	(150,000)	—	150,000 × 100% =	150,000		
Accounts payable	(60,000)	(60,000)	—			
Future income tax liability	**(40,000)**	**(160,000)**	**(120,000) × 100% =**	**(120,000)**		
Total fair value increment					180,000	
Net asset book value	$ 800,000			× 100% =	800,000	
Fair value of assets acquired		$980,000			$ 980,000	
Goodwill					**$ 220,000**	

to be consistent with our calculation of Target's temporary differences. This slight adjustment to the original numbers maintains the total amount of Target's net assets at $800,000. Thus we can clearly see what impact future income taxes have on the allocation of the purchase price.

Notice what happens to goodwill. Because we now are recognizing a liability that we did not recognize in Exhibit 3-6, the amount of the purchase price that is allocated to the net assets goes down. This forces the difference between the purchase price and the net book value to go up, thereby increasing the residual. The residual is goodwill. Therefore, the net result of recognizing the future income taxes is to increase liabilities with an offsetting increase in goodwill.

The current recognition of future income taxes based on consolidation fair values has been subject to some criticism. Prior to the effective date of Section 3465 (in 2000), fair value increments were viewed as permanent differences because the fair value increments never flow through to the income tax return. Fair value increments are purely an accounting construct and are irrelevant for tax purposes.

Now, however, temporary differences are recognized in this situation because the current approach to income tax accounting requires a future tax liability to be recognized on the assumption that assets are sold *at their carrying values,* thereby attracting taxation.[1] Since the carrying values for a purchased subsidiary are the fair values at date of acquisition, strict application of the concept results in the recognition of future income tax liabilities for what are sometimes called "phantom" values.

What happens to these amounts? We shall see in the following chapters that the fair value increments must be amortized (except for land). As the fair values are amortized, the temporary difference goes down and the future income tax liability is comparably reduced. As well, goodwill (at its heightened amount) is either amortized or subjected to the impairment test. Therefore, the recognition of future income tax liabilities based on fair values triggers three types of interperiod allocation in following years. Such complexity is the reason that we have chosen to put income tax allocation factors in Appendices rather than in the main body of each chapter.

Unrecognized tax loss carryforwards

One valuable asset that some companies have is tax loss carryforwards. Sometimes, this is a target company's most attractive asset. When substantial amounts of unused tax loss carryforwards exist, a purchaser may be willing to pay quite a lot for those benefits even if the target company appears to be a real loser. To obtain the benefit of tax loss carryforwards, the business combination must be accomplished through an exchange of shares, not by paying cash (or other assets).

The target company may or may not have already recognized those benefits on their balance sheet. Recognition depends on the "more likely than not" criterion prior to acquisition. If the company has serious financial difficulties, the probability criterion won't have been met and therefore their tax losses would not be recorded as a future income tax asset. However, the acquisition may change the probabilities, so that the "more likely than not" criterion may have now been met. Therefore these losses now have value to the parent company. The losses will be recognized at their fair value in the purchase price allocation and be identified as a future income tax asset in the purchaser's consolidated balance sheet.

Using the following data we will consider what will happen in a business combination under two scenarios. XYZ Corporation purchased 100% of the

---

1. CICA 3465.02.

shares of ABC Corporation for $2,000,000 and the fair value of the net assets (excluding tax losses) totalled $1,400,000. In addition, unused tax loss carryforwards that the target company had not recorded on the books have a fair value of $200,000.

If it is more than 50% likely that the benefit will occur, then the purchase price will be allocated as follows:

Purchase price		$2,000,000
Fair value of net assets acquired (excluding tax loss benefits)	$1,400,000	
Future income tax asset	200,000	1,600,000
Goodwill		$ 400,000

If the "more likely than not" criterion has *not* been met, the purchase price will be recorded as:

Purchase price		$2,000,000
Fair value of net assets acquired (excluding tax loss benefits)	$1,400,000	
Future income tax asset	0	1,400,000
Goodwill		$ 600,000

Note the difference in the goodwill amount depending on whether the "more likely than not" criterion has been met. This difference will have an impact on future financial statements through increased amortization expense when goodwill is recognized at a higher amount. If the future income tax asset is recognized this will be considered a temporary difference.

Equity-basis reporting

The preceding brief discussion focused on business combinations. However, exactly the same process is followed for all investments that are reported on the equity basis, whether they are unconsolidated subsidiaries or significantly influenced affiliates. Temporary differences and future tax loss carryforward benefits must enter the allocation of the purchase price exactly as illustrated above.

Review Questions

3-1 Define the following terms:
   a. Business combination
   b. Net assets
   c. Goodwill
   d. Negative goodwill
   e. Hostile takeover
   f. Statutory amalgamation
   g. Reverse takeover
   h. Purchase price discrepancy
   i. Exchange of shares
   j. Corporate restructuring
   k. Push-down accounting

3-2 Describe the two basic types of acquisitions that can result in a business combination.

3-3 What are the three steps in accounting for a business combination?

3-4 What are the forms of consideration that can be used in a business combination?

3-5 When one corporation buys the assets or assets and liabilities of another company, at what values are the acquired assets recorded on the buyer's books?

3-6 Does a direct purchase of assets constitute an intercorporate investment by the buying company?

3-7 P Ltd. has just purchased all of the assets of S Corp.'s automobile parts division. S Corp. had shut down the division the year before. Has a business combination occurred? Explain.

3-8 In general, how would fair values be determined for productive assets?

3-9 In general, how would fair values be determined for liabilities?

3-10 When an acquirer buys the net assets of another company by issuing shares, what is the relationship between the two companies after the transaction has taken place?

3-11 On what basis is the cost of a purchase of assets allocated?

3-12 What are the advantages for the acquirer of obtaining control over assets by a purchase of shares rather than by a direct purchase of assets?

3-13 What are the disadvantages for the acquirer of obtaining control by a purchase of shares?

3-14 For the acquirer, what is the difference in income tax treatment of goodwill acquired in a direct purchase of assets as compared to goodwill acquired in a purchase of shares?

3-15 How can an acquirer obtain control if the management of the acquiree is hostile to the business combination?

3-16 If an acquirer issues a tender offer, is it necessary for the offering company to buy all of the shares tendered?

3-17 From an income tax standpoint, what may be the disadvantages for an acquirer in obtaining control through a purchase of shares rather than by a direct purchase of net assets?

3-18 Company P issues its shares in exchange for the shares of Company S. After the exchange, who owns the newly issued shares of P?

3-19 In an exchange of shares, how can the acquirer be identified?

3-20 What is the most common reason for a combination of a public company and a private company accomplished by means of a reverse take-over?

3-21 In consolidated statements following a reverse take-over, which company's net assets are reported at fair values: the legal acquirer or the legal subsidiary?

3-22 Why is a reverse take-over often immediately followed by a name change of the legal parent corporation?

3-23 In what form(s) of business combination do the combining companies cease to exist as separate legal entities?

3-24 When a business combination is executed via a purchase of shares, at what values are the assets and liabilities of the acquiree recorded on the books of the acquirer?

3-25 Briefly explain the difference between these three approaches to preparing consolidated financial statements:
a. Pooling-of-interests method
b. New-entity method
c. Purchase method

3-26 What is the purchase price discrepancy?

3-27 What is the logic underlying the use of pooling-of-interests reporting for a business combination?

3-28 How prevalent is pooling-of-interests reporting in Canada?

3-29 What is the essential characteristic that must be present in a business combination in order for it to be reported as a pooling of interests?

3-30 How does the treatment of pre-combination financial data differ under pooling-of-interests reporting as compared to purchase reporting for a business combination?

3-31 What is a corporate restructuring? How are restructurings accounted for?

3-32 Why has the new-entity method not found acceptance in practice?

3-33 What is the recommended treatment of negative goodwill, according to the *CICA Handbook*?

3-34 Company P has 800,000 common shares outstanding. The shares are traded on the Montreal Exchange. The founders and managers of Company P hold 200,000 shares, and another 250,000 are held by institutional investors as long-term investments. P's board of directors has approved issuance of an additional 300,000 shares to acquire the net assets of Company S. What difficulties may arise in attempting to set a value on the newly issued shares in order to determine the cost of the acquisition?

3-35 Under what circumstances would a corporation be able to obtain control over the net assets of another corporation for less than the fair value of those net assets?

3-36 Define *push-down accounting*.

3-37 Under what circumstances is push-down accounting most likely to be used?

Cases

Case 3-1

XYZ Ltd.

During 2001, XYZ Ltd. purchased for cash all of the 100,000 Class B shares of Sub Limited. Each share carries one vote. The previous owner, Mr. Bill, retained all 20,000 outstanding Class A shares of Sub Limited, each carrying four votes. In order to avoid sudden changes, Mr. Bill stipulated in the sale agreement that he was to retain the right to refuse the appointment of management for Sub Limited and to approve any significant transactions of Sub Limited.

Required:

Should XYZ Ltd. consolidate the operations of Sub Limited in its 2001 financial statements, which are to be issued in accordance with generally accepted accounting principles? Provide support for your recommendation.

[CICA]

Case 3-2

Boatsman Boats Limited

Boatsman Boats Limited (BBL) is a dealer in pleasure boats located in Kingston, Ontario. The company is incorporated under the *Ontario Business Corporations Act* and is wholly owned by its founder and president, Jim Boatsman. In 2000, BBL had revenues of $2,500,000 with total assets of about $1,000,000 at year-end.

Late in 2001, Jim Boatsman reached an agreement with Clyde Stickney for the combination of BBL and Stickney Skate Corporation (SSC). SSC is a manufacturer of ice skates and is located in Ottawa, Ontario. SSC's 2000 revenue totalled $2,000,000 and year-end assets totalled $1,500,000. Clyde Stickney is president and general manager of SSC, and he owns 65% of the SSC shares. The other 35% is owned by Clyde's former partner, who left the business several years previously because of a policy disagreement with Clyde.

Clyde and Jim decided to combine the two businesses because their seasonal business cycles were complementary. Common ownership would permit working capital to be shifted from one company to the other, and the larger asset base and more stable financial performance of the combined company would probably increase the total debt capacity.

Under the terms of the agreement, BBL would issue common shares to Clyde Stickney in exchange for Clyde's shares in SSC. As a result of the exchange, Jim's share of BBL would drop to 60% of the outstanding BBL shares, and Clyde would hold the remaining 40%. Clyde and Jim signed a shareholders' agreement that gave each of them equal representation on the BBL board of directors.

As the end of 2001 approached, Jim, Clyde, and CA (the BBL auditor) were discussing the appropriate treatment of the business combination on BBL's 2001 financial statements. Clyde was of the opinion that CA should simply add together the assets and liabilities of the two companies at their book values (after eliminating intercompany balances and transactions, of course). Jim, on the other hand, thought that the combination had resulted in a new, stronger entity, and that the financial statements should reflect that fact by revaluing the net assets of both BBL and SSC to reflect fair values at the date of the combination. CA, however, insisted that only SSC's net assets should be revalued, and then only to the extent of the 65% of the assets that were represented by BBL's shareholdings in SSC.

While Jim and Clyde disagreed with each other on the appropriate valuation of the assets, both disagreed with CA's proposal. Jim and Clyde clearly controlled SSC through BBL, they argued; that was the whole point of the combination. In their opinion it would be inappropriate to value the same assets on two different bases, 65% current value and 35% book value. If only SSC's assets were to be revalued, then they reasoned that the assets at least should be valued consistently, at 100% of fair value.

In an effort to resolve the impasse that was developing, Jim and Clyde hired an independent consultant to advise them. The consultant was asked (1) to advise the shareholders on the pros and cons of each alternative in BBL's specific case, and (2) to make a recommendation on a preferred approach. The consultant was supplied with the condensed balance sheets of BBL and SSC as shown in Exhibit 1, and with CA's estimate of fair values (Exhibit 2).

Required:

Prepare the consultant's report. Assume that the business combination took place on December 31, 2001.

EXHIBIT 1

Condensed Balance Sheets
December 31, 2001

	Boatsman Boats Ltd.	Stickney Skate Corp.
Current assets	$ 600,000	$ 350,000
Land	—	250,000
Buildings and equipment	—	2,500,000
Accumulated depreciation	—	(1,500,000)
Furniture and fixtures	800,000	300,000
Accumulated depreciation	(330,000)	(100,000)
Investment in Stickney Skate Corp.	1,300,000	—
Total assets	$2,370,000	$ 1,800,000
Current liabilities	$ 370,000	$ 400,000
Long-term liabilities	300,000	900,000
Common shares	1,500,000	200,000
Retained earnings	200,000	300,000
Total equities	$2,370,000	$ 1,800,000

EXHIBIT 2

Net Asset Fair Values
December 31, 2001

	Boatsman Boats Ltd.	Stickney Skate Corp.
Current assets	$ 600,000	$ 350,000
Land	—	700,000
Buildings and equipment:		
estimated replacement cost new	—	5,000,000
less depreciation	—	(3,000,000)
Furniture and fixtures:		
estimated replacement cost new	1,300,000	500,000
less depreciation	(520,000)	(240,000)
Current liabilities	(370,000)	(400,000)
Long-term liabilities*	(270,000)	(930,000)
Net asset fair value	$ 740,000	$ 1,980,000

* Discounted at current long-term interest rates.

[ICAO]

Case 3-3

Ames Brothers Ltd.

Ames Brothers, Ltd. (ABL) is a relatively small producer of petrochemicals located in Sarnia. The common shares of the firm are publicly traded on the Brampton stock exchange, while the non-voting preferred shares are traded on the over-the-counter market. Because of the strategic competitive position of the firm, there was considerable recent interest in the shares of the company. During 2001, much active trading occurred, pushing the price of the common shares from less than eight dollars to more than twenty dollars by the end of the year. Similarly, the trading interest in the preferred shares pushed the dividend yield from 12% to only 9%.

Shortly after the end of 2001, three other firms made public announcements about the extent of their holdings in ABL shares. Silverman Mines announced that they had acquired, on the open market, 32% of the common shares of ABL; Hislop Industries announced that it had acquired 24% of ABL's common shares in a private transaction with an individual who had previously been ABL's major shareholder; and Render Resources announced that it had accumulated a total of 58% of ABL's preferred shares.

However, Silverman Mines and Hislop Industries are related. The Patterson Power Corporation owns 72% of the voting shares of Hislop Mines and 38% of the voting shares of Silverman Mines. There are no other large holdings of stock of either Silverman or Hislop. Render Resources is not related to Silverman, Hislop, or Patterson.

Required:

a. Has a business combination occurred in 2001, with respect to ABL, as the term "business combination" is used in the context of the *CICA Handbook* recommendations? Explain fully.

b. What implications do the various accumulations of ABL shares have for the financial reporting (for 2001 and following years) for:

1. Silverman Mines

2. Hislop Industries

3. Render Resources

4. Patterson Power Corporation

Case 3-4

Pool Inc. and Spartin Ltd.

Pool Inc. and Spartin Ltd. are both public companies incorporated under the *Canada Business Corporations Act*. The common shares of Pool have been selling in a range of $30 to $43 per share over the past year, with recent prices in the area of $33. Spartin's common shares have been selling at between $18 and $23; recently the price has been hovering around $20.

The two companies are in related lines of business. In view of the increasing exposure of the companies to world competition arising from the reduction in tariff barriers, the boards of directors have approved an agreement in principle to combine the two businesses. The boards have also agreed that the combination should take the form of a share exchange, with one share of Pool equivalent to two shares of Spartin in the exchange.

The manner of executing the combination has not yet been decided. Three possibilities are under consideration:

1. Pool could issue one new share in exchange for two of Spartin's shares.

2. Spartin could issue two new shares in exchange for each of Pool's shares.

3. A new corporation could be formed, PS Enterprise Inc., which would issue one share in exchange for each share of Spartin and two shares in exchange for each share of Pool.

The directors are uncertain as to the accounting implications of the three alternatives. They believe that the fair values of the assets and liabilities of both companies are approximately equal to their book values. They have asked you to prepare a report in which you explain how the accounting results would differ under the three share exchange alternatives. They have provided you with the condensed balance sheets of both companies. Pool Inc. presently has 1,600,000 common shares outstanding, and Spartin Ltd. has 1,200,000 shares outstanding.

Required:

Prepare the report requested by the boards of directors.

Condensed Balance Sheets

	Pool Inc.	Spartin Ltd.
Current assets	$ 7,000,000	$ 4,500,000
Capital assets	63,000,000	22,500,000
	$70,000,000	$27,000,000
Current liabilities	$ 6,000,000	$ 1,500,000
Long-term debt	14,000,000	5,500,000
Common shares	17,000,000	16,000,000
Retained earnings	33,000,000	4,000,000
	$70,000,000	$27,000,000

Case 3-5

Growth Inc.

Growth Inc. has just acquired control of Minor Ltd. by buying 100% of Minor's outstanding shares for $6,500,000 cash. The condensed balance sheet for Minor on the date of acquisition is shown below.

Growth is a public company. Currently, it has two bank covenants. The first requires Growth to maintain a specific debt-to-equity ratio and the second requires a specific current ratio. If these covenants are violated, the bank loan will be payable on demand. Growth is in a very competitive business. To encourage its employees to stay, it has adopted a new business plan. This plan provides managers a bonus based on a percentage of net income.

The president of Growth Inc., Teresa, has hired you, CA, to assist her with the accounting for Minor.

In order to account for the acquisition, Growth's management has had all of Minor's capital assets appraised by two separate, independent engineering consultants. One consultant appraised the capital assets at $7,800,000 in their present state. The other consultant arrived at a lower figure of $7,100,000, based on the assumption that imminent technological changes would soon decrease the value-in-use of Minor's capital assets by about 10%.

The asset amount for the leased building is the discounted present value of the remaining lease payments on a warehouse that Minor leased to Growth Inc. five years ago. The lease is noncancellable and title to the building will transfer to Growth at the end of the lease term. The lease has fifteen years yet to run, and the annual lease payments are $500,000 per year. The interest rate implicit in the lease was 9%.

Minor's debentures are thinly traded on the open market. Recent sales have indicated that these bonds are currently yielding about 14%. The bonds mature in 10 years.

The future income tax balance is the accumulated balance of CCA/depreciation temporary differences. The management of Minor sees no likelihood of the balance being reduced in the foreseeable future, because projected capital expenditures will enter the CCA classes in amounts that will more than offset the amount of depreciation for the older assets.

The book value of Minor's inventory appears to approximate replacement cost. However, an overstock of some items of finished goods may require temporary price reductions of about 10% in order to reduce inventory to more manageable levels.

Required:

Provide a report for Teresa outlining how the assets of Minor Ltd. should be valued for purposes of preparing consolidated financial statements. She wants you to identify alternatives and support your decision.

Minor Ltd.
Condensed Balance Sheet

Cash	$ 200,000
Accounts receivable	770,000
Inventories	1,000,000
Capital assets (net)	5,000,000
Leased building	4,030,000
	$11,000,000
Accounts payable	$ 300,000
8% debentures payable	7,000,000
Future income taxes	700,000
Common shares	1,000,000
Retained earnings	2,000,000
	$11,000,000

Case 3-6

Greymac Credit Corp.

Greymac Credit Corporation purchased 54% of the shares of Crown Trust Co. from Canwest Capital Corporation at $62 per share. Greymac Credit was a private investment company controlled by Leonard Rosenberg, a Toronto mortgage broker. Greymac also negotiated a purchase of another 32% of Crown Trust shares from BNA Realty Ltd. at a somewhat lower price. BNA Realty had purchased its block of Crown Trust shares only a few weeks earlier, but BNA's ownership was being challenged by the Ontario Securities Commission because "the regulators had alleged that Mr. Burnett [who controlled BNA Realty] was unfit to hold what amounted to veto control over the affairs of Crown." The two purchases of blocks of Crown Trust shares, in addition to other shares already held by Greymac, gave Greymac 97% of the shares of Crown Trust. Greymac was expected to make an offer for the remaining minority shares.

A little earlier in the same year, Greymac Credit Corporation had arranged a deal to purchase most of Cadillac Fairview Corporation's Toronto-area apartment buildings. The purchase involved some 10,931 apartments in 68 buildings, and was in line with Cadillac-Fairview's intention of leaving the residential housing market.

Required:

a. Had business combinations occurred with respect to Greymac's purchase of (1) the Crown Trust shares and (2) the Cadillac-Fairview apartments?

b. How could the OSC view a 32% minority interest as having "veto control"?

Case 3-7

Sudair Ltd.

On February 7, 2001, Sudair Ltd. and Albertair Ltd. jointly announced a merger of the two regional airlines. Sudair had assets totalling $500 million and had 1,000,000 common shares outstanding. Albertair had assets amounting to $400 million and 600,000 shares outstanding. Under the terms of the merger, Sudair will issue two new Sudair shares for each share of Albertair outstanding. The two companies will then merge their administrative and operating structures and will coordinate their routes and schedules to improve interchange between the two lines and to enable the combined fleet of nine jet aircraft to be more efficiently used. Both companies are publicly owned.

Required:

How should the merger of Sudair and Albertair be reported?

Problems

P3-1

Company L and Company E have reached agreement in principle to combine their operations. However, the boards of directors are undecided as to the best way to accomplish the combination. Several alternatives are under consideration:

1. L acquires the net assets of E (including the liabilities) for $1,000,000 cash.

2. L acquires all of the assets of E (but not the liabilities) for $1,400,000 cash.

3. L acquires the net assets of E by issuing 60,000 shares in L, valued at $1,000,000.

4. L acquires all of the shares of E by exchanging them for 60,000 newly issued shares in L.

The current, condensed balance sheets of L and of E are shown below. Prior to the combination, L has 240,000 shares outstanding and E has 30,000 shares outstanding.

Required:

a. In a comparative, columnar format, show how the consolidated balance sheet of L would appear immediately after the combination under each of the four alternatives using the purchase method.

b. For each of the four alternatives, briefly state who owns the shares of each corporation and whether L and E are related companies.

Condensed Balance Sheets
(thousands of dollars)

	L Co.		E Co.	
	Balance sheet	**Fair values**	**Balance sheet**	**Fair values**
Current assets	$ 4,000	$ 4,000	$ 300	$300
Capital assets	6,000	8,000	400	700
Investments	—	—	300	200
	$10,000		$1,000	
Current liabilities	$ 2,000	3,000	100	100
Long-term liabilities	3,000	3,000	400	300
Future income taxes	1,000	1,000	100	—
Common shares	1,000	10,000	200	900
Retained earnings	3,000		200	
	$10,000		$1,000	

P3-2

North Ltd. acquired 100% of the voting shares of South Ltd. In exchange, North Ltd. issued 50,000 common shares, with a market value of $10 per share to the common shareholders of South Ltd. Both companies have a December 31 year-end, and this transaction occurred on December 31, 2001. The outstanding preferred shares of South Ltd. did not change hands. The call price of the South Ltd. preferred shares is equal to their book value.

Following are the balance sheets of the two companies at December 31, 2001, before the transactions took place:

Balance Sheets
As at December 31, 2001

	North Ltd.		South Ltd.	
	Book value	**Fair value**	**Book value**	**Fair value**
Current assets	$ 150,000	$200,000	$210,000	$260,000
Capital assets, net	950,000	820,000	780,000	860,000
Goodwill	110,000		—	
Total	$1,210,000		$990,000	
Current liabilities	$ 100,000	$ 90,000	$165,000	185,000
Long-term liabilities	500,000	520,000	200,000	230,000
Preferred shares	—		270,000	270,000
Common shares	300,000		100,000	
Retained earnings	310,000		255,000	
Total	$1,210,000		$990,000	

Required:

Prepare the consolidated balance sheet for the date of acquisition, December 31, 2001, under each of the following methods:

a. Pooling of interests

b. Purchase

c. New entity

[CGA–Canada, adapted]

P3-3

On December 31, 2001, the balance sheets of the Bee Company and the See Company are as follows:

	Bee Company	See Company
Cash	$ 400,000	$ 700,000
Accounts receivable	1,600,000	1,800,000
Inventories	1,000,000	500,000
Plant and equipment (net)	3,500,000	5,000,000
Total assets	$6,500,000	$8,000,000
Current liabilities	$ 600,000	$ 300,000
Long-term liabilities	900,000	600,000
Common shares	2,500,000	1,000,000
Retained earnings	2,500,000	6,100,000
Total equities	$6,500,000	$8,000,000

Bee Company has 100,000 common shares outstanding, and See Company has 45,000 shares outstanding. On January 1, 2001, Bee Company issues an additional 90,000 common shares to See Company at $90 per share in return for all of the assets and liabilities of that company. See Company distributes Bee Company's common shares to its shareholders in return for their outstanding common shares, and ceases to exist as a separate legal entity. At the time of this transaction the cash, accounts receivable, inventories, and current liabilities of both companies have fair values equal to their carrying values. The plant and equipment and long-term liabilities have fair values as follows:

	Bee Company	See Company
Plant and equipment (net)	$3,900,000	$5,300,000
Long-term liabilities	600,000	500,000

The plant and equipment of both companies has a remaining useful life of nine years on December 31, 2001, and the long-term liabilities of both companies mature on December 31, 2001. Goodwill, if any, is to be amortized over 20 years.

For the year ending December 31, 2001, Bee Company, as a separate company, has a net income of $980,000. The corresponding figure for See Company is $720,000.

Required:

Assume that this business combination is to be accounted for by the purchase method of accounting for business combinations. Prepare the balance sheet at January 1, 2002, for Bee Company after the purchase.

[SMA, adapted]

P3-4

On December 31, 2001, Retail Ltd. purchased 100% of the outstanding shares of Supply Corporation by issuing Retail Ltd. shares worth $960,000 at current market prices. Supply Corporation was a supplier of merchandise to Retail Ltd.; Retail had purchased over 80% of Supply's total output in 2001. Supply had experienced declining profitability for many years, and in 1999 began experiencing losses. By December 31, 2001, Supply had accumulated tax-loss carry-forwards amounting to $280,000. In contrast, Retail Ltd. was quite profitable, and analysts predicted that Retail's positioning in the retail market was well suited to weather economic downturns without undue deterioration in profit levels.

The balance sheet for Supply Corporation at the date of acquisition is shown below, together with estimates of the fair values of Supply's recorded assets and liabilities. In addition, Supply held exclusive Canadian rights to certain Swedish production processes; the fair value of these rights was estimated to be $200,000.

Required:

Explain what values should be assigned to Supply Corporation's assets and liabilities when Retail Ltd. prepares its consolidated financial statements (including goodwill, if any).

Supply Corporation

	Balance Sheet December 31, 2001		Fair values
Current assets:			
Cash	$ 20,000		$ 20,000
Accounts receivable (net)	40,000		40,000
Inventories	210,000		200,000
		$ 270,000	
Plant, property, and equipment:			
Buildings	$ 600,000		500,000
Machinery and equipment	500,000		370,000
Accumulated depreciation	(450,000)		
	$ 650,000		
Land	200,000		360,000
		850,000	
Investments in shares		100,000	110,000
Total assets		$1,220,000	
Current liabilities:			
Accounts payable	$ 60,000		60,000
Unearned revenue	170,000		150,000
Current portion of long-term debt	100,000		100,000
		$ 330,000	
Bonds payable		400,000	380,000
Shareholders' equity:			
Common shares	$ 150,000		
Retained earnings	340,000		
		490,000	
Total liabilities and shareholders' equity		$1,220,000	

Askill Corporation (Askill), a corporation continued under the *Canada Business Corporations Act*, has concluded negotiations with Basket Corporation (Basket) for the purchase of all of Basket's assets at fair market value, effective January 1, 2001. An examination at that date by independent experts disclosed that the fair market value of Basket's inventories was $150,000; the fair market value of its machinery and equipment was $160,000. The original cost of the machinery and equipment was $140,000 and its undepreciated capital cost for tax purposes at December 31, 2000, was $110,000. It was determined that accounts receivable were fairly valued at book value.

Basket held 1,000 common shares of Askill and the fair market value of these shares was $62,000. This value corresponds to the value of Askill's common shares in the open market and is deemed to hold for transactions involving a substantially large number of shares.

The purchase agreement provides that the total purchase price of all assets will be $490,000, payable as follows:

1. The current liabilities of Basket would be assumed at their book value.

2. The Basket debenture debt would be settled at its current value in a form acceptable to Basket debenture holders.

3. Askill shares held by Basket and acquired by Askill as a result of the transaction would be subsequently returned to Basket at fair market value as part of the consideration.

4. Askill holds 1,000 shares of Basket and these would be returned to Basket. The value to be ascribed to these shares is 1/10 of the difference between the total purchase price of all assets stated above ($490,000) less the current value of its liabilities.

5. The balance of the purchase consideration is to be entirely in Askill common shares, except for a possible fractional share element that would be paid in cash.

The Basket debenture holders, who are neither shareholders of Askill nor Basket, have agreed to accept face value of newly issued Askill bonds equal to the current value of the Basket bonds. The Basket debentures are currently yielding 10%. The Askill bonds carry a 10% coupon and trade at par.

Basket, upon conclusion of the agreement, would be wound up. The balance sheets of both corporations, as at the date of implementation of the purchase agreement (January 1, 2001), are as follows:

	Askill Corp.	Basket Corp.
Cash	$ 100,000	$ —
Accounts receivable	288,000	112,000
Inventories at cost	250,000	124,000
Investment in Basket (1,000 shares)	20,000	—
Investment in Askill (1,000 shares)	—	40,000
Machinery and equipment—net	412,000	100,000
Total assets	$1,070,000	$376,000
Current liabilities	$ 60,000	$ 35,000
7% debentures due Dec. 31, 2005 (Note 1)	—	100,000
10% bonds due Dec. 31, 2005 (Note 1)	500,000	—
Premium on bonds	20,000	—
Capital–common shares (Note 2)	200,000	100,000
Retained earnings	290,000	141,000
Total liabilities and shareholders' equity	$1,070,000	$376,000

Note 1—Interest is paid annually.
Note 2—Each company has issued 10,000 shares.

Both corporations have fiscal years that are identical to the calendar year.

Required:

a. Prepare Askill's pro-forma balance sheet at January 1, 2001.

b. Draft a note to the 2001 Askill financial statements disclosing the purchase of Basket's net assets.
   [CICA, adapted]

P3-6

Par Ltd. purchased 100% of the voting shares of Sub Ltd. for $1,400,000 on October 1, 2001. The balance sheet of Sub Ltd. at that date was:

Sub Ltd.
Balance Sheet
October 1, 2001

	Net book value	Fair market value
Cash	$ 300,000	$300,000
Receivables	410,000	370,000
Inventory	560,000	750,000
Capital assets, net	1,220,000	920,000
	$2,490,000	
Current liabilities	$ 340,000	370,000
Preferred shares (Note 1)	800,000	
Common shares	400,000	
Retained earnings	950,000	
	$2,490,000	

Note 1:

The preferred shares are cumulative, pay dividends of $4 per year ($1 per quarter at the end of each calendar quarter) and have a call (redemption) premium of $1 per share. There are 100,000 preferred shares outstanding and they are non-participating.

Required:

Prepare the eliminating entry(ies) required *at the date of acquisition* that would be necessary to consolidate the financial statements of Sub Ltd. with those of Par Ltd.

[CGA–Canada, adapted]

P3-7

On December 31, 2001, Prager Limited acquired 100% of the outstanding voting shares of Sabre Limited for $2 million in cash; 75% of the cash was obtained by issuing a five-year note payable. The balance sheets of Prager and Sabre and the fair values of Sabre's identifiable assets and liabilities immediately before the acquisition transaction were as follows:

	Prager Limited	Sabre Limited Book value	Sabre Limited Fair value
Assets:			
Cash	$ 800,000	$ 100,000	$ 100,000
Accounts receivable	500,000	300,000	300,000
Inventory	600,000	600,000	662,500
Land	900,000	800,000	900,000
Buildings and equipment	6,000,000	1,400,000	1,200,000
Accumulated depreciation	(2,950,000)	(400,000)	
Patents	—	200,000	150,000
	$5,850,000	$3,000,000	
Liabilities and shareholders' equity:			
Accounts payable	$1,000,000	$ 500,000	500,000
Long-term debt	2,000,000	1,000,000	900,000
Common shares	1,500,000	950,000	
Retained earnings	1,350,000	550,000	
	$5,850,000	$3,000,000	

Required:

Prepare the consolidated balance sheet for Prager Limited immediately following the acquisition of Sabre Limited.

[SMA, adapted]

P3-8

On January 4, 2001, Practical Corp. acquired 100% of the outstanding common shares of Silly Inc. by a share-for-share exchange of its own shares valued at $1,000,000. The balance sheets of both companies just prior to the share exchange are shown below. Silly has patents that are not shown on the balance sheet, but that have an estimated fair value of $200,000 and an estimated remaining productive life of four years. Silly's buildings and equipment have an estimated fair value that is $300,000 in excess of book value, and the deferred charges are assumed to have a fair value of zero. Silly's building and equipment are being depreciated on the straight-line basis and have a remaining useful life of 10 years. The deferred charges are being amortized over the following three years.

Balance Sheets
December 31, 2001

	Practical	Silly
Cash	$ 110,000	$ 85,000
Accounts and other receivables	140,000	80,000
Inventories	110,000	55,000
Buildings and equipment	1,500,000	800,000
Accumulated depreciation	(700,000)	(400,000)
Deferred charges	—	120,000
	$1,160,000	$740,000
Accounts and other payables	$ 200,000	$100,000
Bonds payable	—	200,000
Future income taxes	60,000	40,000
Common shares*	600,000	150,000
Retained earnings	300,000	250,000
	$1,160,000	$740,000

*Practical = 300,000 shares; Silly = 150,000 shares.

Required:

Prepare a consolidated balance sheet for Practical Corp., immediately following the share exchange.

Wholly-Owned Subsidiaries: Reporting Subsequent to Acquisition

Introduction

The previous chapter discussed the conceptual foundations underlying the accounting and financial reporting for business communications. We saw that control can be acquired either by a direct purchase of the assets or by buying voting control in the corporation that owns the assets. The purchase of voting control is the more common method. It also is the more challenging for the accountant.

In Chapter 3 we discussed the alternative approaches to the preparation of consolidated financial statements for an acquired subsidiary. We focused on consolidation at the date of acquisition in order to illustrate the essential characteristics of the different approaches.

The date of acquisition is the easiest date upon which to perform a consolidation, since we need to deal only with the balance sheet. However, the date of acquisition occurs only once, and consolidated statements are seldom prepared on that date for external reporting.

After that one-time event, consolidated financial statements must be prepared on every subsequent reporting date. Subsequent reporting must adjust not only for fair value increments and goodwill, but also for any intercompany transactions that occurred during the reporting period.

This chapter focuses on the preparation of financial statements for periods subsequent to the parent's acquisition of 100% of the shares of a subsidiary, or after the formation of a parent-founded subsidiary. In this chapter, we deal only with wholly-owned subsidiaries. Subsequent chapters will relax that simplifying assumption, thereby introducing further complexities.

Now, sit back, pay attention, and enjoy the ride!

Consolidation One Year After Acquisition

Before we begin to talk about consolidated financial statements, we must point out that each corporation, the parent and each of its subsidiaries, will prepare its own financial statements. These separate-entity financial statements will have no fair values, and will include any intercompany transactions that occur between the related companies.

When we talk about *consolidated* statements, we are referring to the set of statements that a parent company prepares for distribution to its shareholders in accordance with GAAP. These statements are based on the concept of the *economic entity*—there is no corresponding legal entity. We don't mean to belabour the point, but it is important to remember that consolidated statements comprise only one set of financial statements, intended for a specific purpose—every corporation still prepares its own individual statements for the tax authorities, for its bankers, for its own performance evaluation, and so forth.

Chapter 3 used an example of Purchase Ltd.'s acquisition of 100% of the shares of Target Ltd. To prepare Purchase's consolidated financial statements *after* the date of acquisition, we will need four types of information:

Wholly-Owned
Subsidiaries:
Reporting
Subsequent to
Acquisition

129

1. the details of the purchase transaction,

2. the amortization or depreciation policy for capital assets,

3. the nature and extent of intercompany transactions between the two companies, including intercompany receivables and payables, and

4. the disposition of assets that were sold intercompany (including the assets in the original acquisition).

Over the next three chapters, we will add various types of transactions to our basic example of Purchase and Target. We will not attempt to be exhaustive—this is an accounting textbook, not an all-inclusive consolidation handbook. By the time you finish with Chapter 6, however, you should have a thorough understanding of the consolidation process and of the types of interactions that must be accounted for.

Basic information

Assume that on December 31, 2001, Purchase Ltd. purchased all of the outstanding shares of Target Ltd. by issuing 40,000 new shares of Purchase in exchange for the shares of Target. The newly issued Purchase shares had a market value of $30 per share—a total purchase cost of $1,200,000. The total cost was apportioned to the fair values of Target's assets and liabilities and to goodwill *at the date of acquisition* as shown in Exhibit 4-1.[1] These fair values and goodwill are the same amounts used in the illustration in the previous chapter.

At every balance sheet date after December 31, 2001, Purchase will have to include the fair value increments (and/or decrements) and goodwill in its *consolidated* net assets. However:

- The carrying values of most fair valued assets flow to income, either directly through cost of sales (for current assets such as inventories) or indirectly, through amortization or depreciation for tangible and intangible capital assets (including goodwill).

- Assets included in the purchase transaction may be sold or retired.

When either of these events happens, we have to make periodic adjustments to the initial fair value increments (as well as to goodwill).

---

1. Exhibit 4-1 is identical to Exhibit 3-6. The same example is used throughout Chapters 3 to 6 in order to help readers with comparisons and to make it easier to see the impact of additional complexities.

EXHIBIT 4–1 ALLOCATION OF PURCHASE PRICE

100% Purchase of Target Ltd., December 31, 2001

Purchase price						$1,200,000
	Book value	Fair value	Fair value increment	% share	FVI acquired	
Cash	$50,000	$50,000	—			
Accounts receivable	150,000	150,000	—			
Inventory	50,000	50,000	—			
Land	300,000	400,000	$100,000 × 100% =		$100,000	
Buildings and equipment	500,000	550,000	50,000 × 100% =		50,000	
Accumulated depreciation	(150,000)	—	150,000 × 100% =		150,000	
Accounts payable	(100,000)	(100,000)	—			
Total fair value increment						300,000
Net asset book value	$800,000			× 100% =		800,000
Fair value of assets acquired						$1,100,000
Goodwill						$ 100,000

Other adjustments are needed to eliminate or "back out" intercompany transactions. In Chapter 2, we illustrated the elimination of intercompany sales and of offsetting receivables and payables. In addition, we also need to find out what happened to any assets that were sold from one company to another. For the year ended December 31, 2002, we will assume the following:

1. Target's buildings and equipment will be depreciated over 10 years after the date of acquisition, using straight-line depreciation.

2. Purchase Ltd. will amortize goodwill over 20 years.

3. During 2002, Target sold goods of $55,000 to Purchase. Target's gross margin is 40% of sales.

4. On December 31, 2002, $20,000 of the goods acquired by Purchase Ltd. from Target Ltd. are still in Purchase's inventory.

5. During 2002, Target Ltd. paid dividends totalling $30,000 to Purchase Ltd., Target's sole shareholder. Purchase maintains its Investment in Target account on the cost basis, and therefore the dividends received were recorded as Dividend Income.

Chapter 2 illustrated the basic approach to eliminating intercompany transactions and balances. Chapter 3 explained the eliminations that are required when a subsidiary is purchased. The example in this chapter will combine these two types of adjustments, and will add two more issues that are essential to understanding consolidations:

1. amortization of fair value increments and goodwill, and

2. elimination of unrealized profit on intercompany sales.

The next three sections will discuss these issues.

Amortization of fair value increments

A large part of the purchase price in a business combination may be allocated to fair value increments. A study of 756 U.S. business combinations revealed that the purchase price discrepancy—fair value increments and goodwill—equalled, on average, almost 200% of book value. The aggregate purchase price was $404 billion, comprised of $137 billion in book value and $267 billion in purchase price discrepancy.[2]

Therefore, fair value increments (or decrements) and goodwill most likely will significantly impact consolidated earnings subsequent to the purchase. Each of the major categories of asset is discussed below.

Wholly-Owned
Subsidiaries:
Reporting
Subsequent to
Acquisition

131

Inventory

Fair value increments for inventory will flow through cost of sales to decrease net income when the inventory is sold to third parties. In the period in which the inventory is sold, the fair value increment is added to cost of sales instead of to inventory on the consolidation working papers.

Tangible capital assets

Tangible capital assets are reported in accordance with the recommendations of Section 3060 of the *CICA Handbook*, "Capital Assets." The recommendations apply to fair value increments as well as to the carrying values shown on the subsidiary's books.

A purchased subsidiary will continue to amortize the depreciable capital assets that are recorded on its books. However, the subsidiary's depreciation will be based on the carrying value of the assets on its books. Unless push-down accounting is used, the depreciation on the *subsidiary's separate-entity* financial statements will not reflect the higher prices paid by the parent in the business combination.

When the *parent's consolidated statements* are prepared, the fair value increments on depreciable assets must be amortized in accordance with the depreciation policy being used by the subsidiary. If, for example, a building has a 20-year estimated remaining useful life from the date of the business combination, the fair value increment must be amortized over the 20-year remaining period. The maximum amortization period for property, plant, and equipment is 40 years, unless a longer life is clearly demonstrable [ED 3060.37].

Intangible capital assets and goodwill

Intangible assets are assumed to have a maximum useful life of 20 years, unless clearly identifiable cash flows are expected to continue for a longer period [ED 3060.39]. The fair value increments that are allocated to intangible assets must be amortized over the remaining useful life of the assets. Amortization must occur, whether or not the assets are recorded on the books of the subsidiary.

A 20-year life should not be an automatic assumption. Intangible assets usually contribute to cash flows over a relatively short period of time. The IASC and the standard-setters of Australia, Canada, New Zealand, the U.K., and the U.S.A. had initially proposed that the normal amortization period should be assumed to be no more than 10 years. This limit was relaxed to 20 years in the 1999 FASB and CICA business combination exposure drafts.

---

2. Benjamin C. Ayers, Craig E. Lefanowicz, and John R. Robinson, "The Financial Statement Effects of Eliminating the Pooling-of-Interest Method of Acquisition Accounting," *Accounting Horizons*, March 2000, pp. 1–19.

Goodwill is treated differently. The long-standing Canadian requirement was that goodwill should be amortized over not more than 40 years. In the 1999 Business Combinations exposure draft, the maximum period was reduced to 20 years in order to harmonize with international standards. However, in late 2000, the FASB decided to eliminate any requirement for goodwill amortization, but instead to permit companies to keep goodwill on the balance sheet until its value could be shown to be impaired.

In Canada, the AcSB decided to follow the FASB and eliminate the requirement for goodwill amortization, because the whole point of changing Section 1580 of the *CICA Handbook* was to harmonize with the U.S. The FASB action was taken in order to quell unrest with the proposed elimination of pooling and to head off possible legislation in the U.S. Congress. Therefore, Canadian standards have been changed for U.S. political expediency.

Unrealized profits

One of the more challenging aspects of consolidated statements is the need to keep track of assets that were sold by one company in the group to another. In Chapter 2, we described intercompany sales of inventory, and we explained that sales from a parent to a subsidiary are **downstream** sales, while sales from a subsidiary to a parent are called **upstream** sales. Sales between subsidiaries also are treated as upstream sales.

In Chapter 2, all of the inventory that was sold downstream was sold to third parties before the fiscal year-end. That is the easy scenario. A more difficult situation arises when some or all of the inventory is still on the receiving corporation's books at the balance sheet date. In that situation, we must deal with the problem of **unrealized profit**.

In the facts for Purchase and Target listed above, there are three points relating to the intercompany sales:

- Target had sales to Purchase (i.e., *upstream* sales) of $55,000,

- $20,000 of those goods are still in Purchase's inventory at year-end, and

- Target's gross margin on sales is 40%.

The $20,000 of goods in Purchase's inventory are stated at their acquisition price to Purchase. However, they cost Target less than that to produce. Target's gross margin is 40%, which means that the $20,000 inventory contains a gross profit margin of $20,000 \times 40\% = \$8,000$; the goods cost $12,000 to produce.

Consolidated statements must show only the results of transactions between the consolidated entity and those companies and individuals outside the combined economic entity. In substance, the $8,000 gross profit is only an internal transaction, not external. Therefore, consolidated inventory must be reduced by eliminating the $8,000 *unrealized profit* on intercompany sales.

Obviously, the consolidated inventory must be reduced by $8,000, but what happens to the offset? When we compute cost of sales, beginning inventory and purchases are added together, and ending inventory is subtracted. The income statement effect of an *overstated ending inventory* is to *understate cost of sales*. Therefore, we must not only reduce consolidated inventory by $8,000, but also we must increase cost of sales by $8,000. If this seems confusing, just remember that *increasing* a cost will *reduce* net income, thereby eliminating the unrealized profit.

In summary, two adjustments are necessary: one to eliminate the intercompany sale transaction, and another to eliminate the unrealized profit. We will illustrate these adjustments shortly.

Unrealized profit arises any time that one corporation sells assets to another, and those assets remain within the consolidated economic entity instead of being sold externally. Inventory is the most common type of intercompany sale, but capital assets or investments may also be sold. The same principles apply, regardless of the nature of the asset(s) involved.

Direct method

The unconsolidated financial statements for Purchase and Target are shown in Exhibit 4-2. We have assumed that Purchase *records* its investment in Target on the cost basis in its accounts, as is usually the case. Therefore, the separate-entity financial statements show (1) the investment at the purchase price of $1,200,000 and (2) the dividends of $30,000 received by Purchase from Target as dividend income.

Wholly-Owned
Subsidiaries:
Reporting
Subsequent to
Acquisition

133

When using the direct method, we can go down the income statement and balance sheet and insert the correct amounts on a line-by-line basis. In Exhibit 4-3, we have added together the separate-entity amounts. For some items, we will make additional adjustments and eliminations. The necessary adjustments and eliminations are as shown below, starting with the income statement.

Statement of income and retained earnings

- *Sales revenue.* The combined sales total $2,700,000. We must eliminate the upstream intercompany sales of $55,000. The result is consolidated sales of $2,645,000.

- *Dividend income.* Since this income is Target's dividends paid to Purchase, the entire $30,000 must be eliminated.

- *Cost of sales.* The combined cost of sales is $1,750,000 + $180,000 = $1,930,000. This amount must be decreased by the full amount of the intercompany sales ($55,000) and increased by the unrealized profit of $8,000 that is in Purchase's ending inventory.

- *Depreciation expense.* The net book value of Target's buildings and equipment *at the date of acquisition* was $350,000 (net of depreciation: $500,000 – $150,000). The fair value was $550,000. The fair value increment is $200,000. This fair value increment must be amortized. The facts presented above state that the remaining useful life is 10 years. Therefore, we must add 1/10 of the fair value increment to the depreciation account, or $20,000.

- *Goodwill amortization expense.* Purchase's policy is to amortize goodwill over its expected life. Assuming a 20-year amortization period, the additional amortization expense is $100,000 ÷ 20 = $5,000 per year. For greater clarity, we have kept the tangible capital asset depreciation separate from goodwill amortization. The consolidated financial statements should show the amount of goodwill amortization.

The combined, unadjusted, net incomes of the two companies is $330,000 + $65,000 = $395,000. After adjustments for amortization of fair value increments and goodwill, and after eliminating unrealized profit, consolidated net income drops to $332,000. The total reduction is $63,000. Remember this number—you will see it again shortly!

EXHIBIT 4–2 SEPARATE-ENTITY FINANCIAL STATEMENTS FOR 2002

Income Statements
Year Ended December 31, 2002

	Purchase Ltd.	Target Ltd.
Revenue:		
Sales	$2,400,000	$ 300,000
Dividend income	30,000	—
	2,430,000	300,000
Expenses:		
Cost of sales	1,750,000	180,000
Depreciation expense	100,000	35,000
Other operating expenses	250,000	20,000
	2,100,000	235,000
Net income	$ 330,000	$ 65,000
Retained earnings, December 31, 2001	2,000,000	600,000
Dividends declared	—	(30,000)
Retained earnings, December 31, 2002	$2,330,000	$ 635,000

Balance Sheets
December 31, 2002

	Purchase Ltd.	Target Ltd.
Assets		
Current assets:		
Cash	$ 980,000	$ 100,000
Accounts receivable	2,200,000	250,000
Inventory	250,000	70,000
	3,430,000	420,000
Property, plant, and equipment:		
Land	1,000,000	300,000
Buildings and equipment	3,000,000	500,000
Accumulated depreciation	(1,300,000)	(185,000)
	2,700,000	615,000
Other assets:		
Investments (at cost)	1,200,000	—
Total assets	$7,330,000	$1,035,000
Liabilities and shareholders' equity		
Liabilities:		
Accounts payable	$800,000	$200,000
Long-term notes payable	400,000	—
	1,200,000	200,000
Shareholders' equity:		
Common shares	3,800,000	200,000
Retained earnings	2,330,000	635,000
	6,130,000	835,000
Total liabilities and shareholders' equity	$7,330,000	$1,035,000

Statement of Income and Retained Earnings
Year Ended December 31, 2002

Sales revenue [2,400,000 + 300,000 – **55,000**]	$2,645,000
Dividend income [30,000 + 0 – **30,000**]	—
Operating expenses:	
Cost of sales [1,750,000 + 180,000 – **55,000 + 8,000**]	1,883,000
Depreciation expense [100,000 + 35,000 **+ 20,000**]	155,000
Goodwill amortization [**+ 5,000**]	5,000
Other expenses [250,000 + 20,000]	270,000
	2,313,000
Net income	$ 332,000
Retained earnings, December 31, 2001 [2,000,000 + 600,000 – **600,000**]	2,000,000
Dividends declared [0 + 30,000 – **30,000**]	—
Retained earnings, December 31, 2002	$2,332,000

Balance Sheet
December 31, 2002

Assets

Current assets:	
Cash [980,000 + 100,000]	$1,080,000
Accounts receivable [2,200,000 + 250,000]	2,450,000
Inventory [250,000 + 70,000 – **8,000**]	312,000
	3,842,000
Property, plant, and equipment:	
Land [1,000,000 + 300,000 **+ 100,000**]	1,400,000
Buildings and equipment [3,000,000 + 500,000 **+ 50,000**]	3,550,000
Accumulated depreciation [1,300,000 + 185,000 – **150,000 + 20,000**]	(1,355,000)
	3,595,000
Other assets:	
Investments [1,200,000 + 0 – **1,200,000**]	—
Goodwill [**100,000** × **19/20**]	95,000
Total assets	$7,532,000

Liabilities and shareholders' equity

Liabilities:	
Current accounts payable [800,000 + 200,000]	$1,000,000
Long-term notes payable [400,000 + 0]	400,000
	1,400,000
Shareholders' equity:	
Common shares [**Purchase Ltd. shares only**]	3,800,000
Retained earnings	
[2,330,000 + 635,000 – **600,000 – 8,000 – 20,000 – 5,000**]	2,332,000
	6,132,000
Total liabilities and shareholders' equity	$7,532,000

Balance sheet

- *Inventory.* Combined inventories must be reduced by the unrealized profit of $8,000.

- *Land.* The fair value increment of $100,000 must be added.

- *Buildings and equipment.* The total fair value increment for Target's buildings and equipment is $200,000. The increase is recognized in the consolidated statements by (1) eliminating Target's date-of-acquisition accumulated depreciation of $150,000, and (2) increasing the buildings and equipment asset account by $50,000. Therefore, only $50,000 is added to the asset account.

- *Accumulated depreciation.* Target's accumulated depreciation at December 31, 2002, is $185,000. This amount includes the $150,000 accumulated at the date of acquisition plus $35,000 additional depreciation expense for 2002. The $150,000 must be eliminated—the acquired company's accumulated depreciation at the date of acquisition should not be carried forward. The $35,000 is permitted to remain, because it represents depreciation *after* the date of acquisition. But the $35,000 represents depreciation on Target's *book* value. To reflect depreciation on the *fair* value, the $20,000 amortization of the fair value increment must be added.

- *Investments.* The investment account must be reduced by the cost of Purchase's investment in Target.[3] In this example, there are no other investments—we simply could have ignored the investment account when we started work on the balance sheet. In many situations, however, there will be other investments that will not be eliminated. It generally is best to start with all accounts, including the investment account.

- *Goodwill.* Goodwill has been amortized for one year of its assumed 20-year life. The unamortized goodwill at the end of 2002 is 19/20ths of the original amount, or $95,000.

- *Common shares.* Only Purchase Ltd.'s common shares are included.

- *Retained earnings* (at year-end). This is the challenging one! We start by adding the two companies' retained earnings together. Next, we must eliminate Target's date-of-acquisition retained earnings ($600,000). Then we make the adjustments that were necessary for the consolidated income statement:

  - eliminate the unrealized profit of $8,000,

  - reduce retained earnings by the amount of additional fair value amortization—$20,000, and

  - reduce retained earnings by the amount of goodwill amortization, $5,000.

There is one income statement adjustment that is missing from this little list: dividend income. The reason that it doesn't show up among our adjustments on the retained earnings line of the balance sheet is that the amount has already washed out. Dividend income has *increased* Purchase's net income and retained earnings, while dividends paid has *reduced* Target's retained earnings. When the retained earnings amounts for the two companies are added together, the reduc-

3. If the investment account has been *recorded* on the equity basis, Purchase's equity in Target will be eliminated, with offsetting eliminations in retained earnings. In Chapter 6, we will discuss the consolidation adjustments when equity-basis recording has been used.

tion in Target's offsets the increase in Purchase's, and there is no need for an adjustment.

Remember the $63,000 decrease in net income from separate-entity to consolidated net income? That consists of two amounts: $30,000 dividend income shown as revenue to Purchase but *not as an expense to Target*, plus the $33,000 (i.e., $8,000 + $20,000 + $5,000) in other adjustments to consolidated net income. *When deriving consolidated retained earnings, all adjustments to consolidated net income are made* except *for intercompany dividends.*

You might ask why we simply don't take the consolidated retained earnings amount from the bottom of the statement of income and retained earnings and put that in the balance sheet. The answer is that we must be able to derive the retained earnings independently, to make sure that the statements balance and that we haven't overlooked anything.[4]

Wholly-Owned

Subsidiaries:

Reporting

Subsequent to

Acquisition

137

Worksheet approach

The general approach is to (1) start with the *pre-closing* separate-entity trial balances of the parent and its subsidiaries, (2) make the necessary eliminations and adjustments, and finally (3) cross-add the rows to determine the consolidated trial balance. The amounts in the consolidated trial balance are used to construct the income statement, statement of retained earnings, and the balance sheet. The final column of the worksheet does not, in itself, constitute consolidated financial statements. It does include all of the consolidated financial statement *elements* (assets, liabilities, revenues, and expenses), however.

Exhibit 4-4 shows a worksheet with the trial balances of the two companies in the first two numerical columns. These trial balances yield exactly the same amounts that are shown in the separate-entity financial statements in Exhibit 4-2.

To conserve space, our worksheets will have only one column for both debit and credit amounts. Double columns could be used just as well. An advantage of a single column (in addition to avoiding over-sized worksheets) is that, in a computer spreadsheet, we can constantly see whether we are maintaining the zero total of each column as we make adjustments and eliminations (i.e., that the debits equal the credits!).

An additional convention that we will follow is that we will strive for greater clarity by putting the eliminations and adjustments that arise from the acquisition adjustment in one column, while we enter post-combination adjustments in another. There is no need to follow this practice—one column can easily be used for all adjustments.

Acquisition adjustment

The starting point of any consolidation must be to adjust the accounts to reflect the economic substance of the purchase transaction. As we already have stated several times, we (1) eliminate Target's shareholders' equity accounts at the date of acquisition, and (2) adjust the net assets for FVI and goodwill. The offset for both of these adjustments is to eliminate Purchase's investment account. We are indicating this set of adjustments with the letter **a**—it helps to keep track of which additions and subtractions on the financial statements belong to which others, in case we don't balance at the end and have to embark on a diagnostic investigation. In general journal form, the acquisition adjustments (**a**) are:

---

4. From a very practical student standpoint, it also is very useful to be able to derive consolidated retained earnings without having to work through a consolidated income statement. That is a favourite examination question, both in coursework and in professional examinations!

EXHIBIT 4–4 PURCHASE LTD. CONSOLIDATION WORKSHEET—COST BASIS OF RECORDING

December 31, 2001

	Trial balances		Adjustments		Purchase
	Purchase Dr/(Cr)	Target Dr/(Cr)	Adjustments Dr/(Cr) - a	Operations Dr/(Cr) - c	consolidated trial balance
Cash	$ 980,000	$ 100,000			$1,080,000
Accounts receivable	2,200,000	250,000			2,450,000
Inventories	250,000	70,000		(8,000) c2	312,000
Land	1,000,000	300,000	100,000 a2		1,400,000
Buildings and equipment	3,000,000	500,000	50,000 a2		3,550,000
Accumulated depreciation	(1,300,000)	(185,000)	150,000 a2	(20,000) c4	(1,355,000)
Investments (at cost)	1,200,000	—	{ (800,000) a1	}	—
			(400,000) a2		
Goodwill			100,000 a2	(5,000) c5	95,000
					—
Accounts payable	(800,000)	(200,000)			(1,000,000)
Long-term notes payable	(400,000)	—			(400,000)
Common shares	(3,800,000)	(200,000)	200,000 a1		(3,800,000)
Dividends declared	—	30,000		(30,000) c3	—
Retained earnings, December 31, 2001	(2,000,000)	(600,000)	600,000 a1		(2,000,000)
					—
Sales	(2,400,000)	(300,000)		55,000 c1	(2,645,000)
Dividend income	(30,000)	—		30,000 c3	—
Cost of sales	1,750,000	180,000		(55,000) c1	
				8,000 c2	1,883,000
Depreciation expense	100,000	35,000		20,000 c4	155,000
Goodwill amortization expense				5,000 c5	5,000
Other expenses	250,000	20,000			270,000
	$ —	$ —	$ —	$ —	$ —

a1	Common shares	200,000	
	Retained earnings	600,000	
	Investments		800,000
a2	Land	100,000	
	Buildings and equipment	50,000	
	Accumulated depreciation	150,000	
	Goodwill	100,000	
	Investments		400,000

An important aspect of this adjustment is the debit to retained earnings. We add Target's year-end 2002 retained earnings of $650,000 to Purchase's, but we eliminate only $600,000. The goal is not to eliminate Target's retained earnings at the balance sheet date. Instead, the objective is to eliminate Target's retained earnings *as of the date of acquisition*.

The reason for eliminating only Target's date-of-acquisition retained earnings is that we are eliminating the shareholders' equity accounts that offset the acquired net assets. Additional earnings that accumulate in Target's retained earnings after acquisition represent part of consolidated retained earnings.

Operations adjustments

We will label the adjustments and eliminations for post-acquisition activities and events the *operations adjustments,* just to keep them distinct from the acquisition adjustment. We will label all of the operations adjustments as **c**. (We will add another column for **b** later in the chapter.) The operations adjustments are as follows:

Wholly-Owned
Subsidiaries:
Reporting
Subsequent to
Acquisition

139

Intercompany sales: Target sold $55,000 of goods to Purchase during 2002, an *upstream* sale. If the entire inventory had been sold by Purchase to third parties outside the consolidated enterprise for $80,000, the books of Target and Purchase would show the following (recall that Target sold the goods to Purchase at a 40% gross margin on sales):

	Target Ltd.	Purchase Ltd.	Total
Sales	**$55,000**	$80,000	$135,000
Cost of sales	33,000	**55,000**	88,000
Gross margin	$22,000	$25,000	$ 47,000

In this example, we are assuming that $20,000 of the goods remain in Purchase's ending inventory. Goods sold by Target to Purchase for $20,000 would include a gross profit to Target of 40% of that amount, or $8,000. Therefore, Purchase's ending inventory includes goods that cost $20,000 to Purchase as a separate entity, but that cost only $12,000 to the consolidated entity. Unrealized profit of $8,000 must be eliminated from the consolidated ending inventory.

Since cost of goods sold is determined by subtracting the ending inventory from purchases plus beginning inventory, including $8,000 of unrealized profit in the ending inventory causes the cost of goods sold to be *understated* by $8,000. Therefore, in Exhibit 4-4, we have two steps: (1) eliminate the $55,000 intercompany sale, and (2) eliminate the unrealized profit by debiting cost of sales and crediting inventory by $8,000:

c1 Sales		55,000	
Cost of sales			55,000
c2 Cost of sales		8,000	
Inventory			8,000

Other intercompany transactions: The adjustment eliminates the intercompany payment of dividends. We eliminate $30,000 from both dividends declared and dividend income:

c3 Dividend income		30,000	
Dividends declared			30,000

This adjustment is based on the fact that, in our example, Purchase is recording its investment in Target on the cost basis; the dividends received by Purchase have been credited to dividend income and must be eliminated. Similarly, the credit to dividends declared is based on a scrutiny of the Target accounts in Exhibit 4-4, which reveals that Target debits that account when dividends are declared. If Target's debit had been directly to retained earnings, then the credit in the elimination entry would be to retained earnings.

If there had been any other intercompany transactions during the period, they would also have to be eliminated. For example, intercompany interest payments or accruals, lease payments, management fees, or royalty fees would be eliminated, along with any outstanding intercompany receivables and payables.

Fair value increments and goodwill: Target's depreciation expense is $35,000. This amount represents 2002 depreciation on Target's buildings and equipment. The depreciation is based on the $350,000 net book value (that is, $500,000 cost – $150,000 accumulated depreciation) and the 10-year remaining life of Target's assets beginning in 2002.

Consolidated depreciation expense must reflect depreciation on the *fair value* of Target's capital assets. The fair value was $550,000 at the beginning of 2002. Therefore, depreciation expense must be increased to $55,000, an increase of $20,000:

c4	Depreciation expense	20,000	
	Accumulated depreciation		20,000

The acquisition of Target included goodwill of $100,000. The goodwill is being amortized. Assuming a 20-year useful life, the adjustment is:

c5	Amortization expense	5,000	
	Goodwill		5,000

Completing the worksheet

When all of the eliminations and adjustments have been entered on the worksheet (or computer spreadsheet), the rows can be added across. The final column shows the consolidated trial balance, from which the consolidated financial statements can be prepared. For Purchase Ltd., the consolidated statements will be the same as those shown in Exhibit 4-3.

Two important reminders:

1. Either the direct method or the worksheet method can be used to derive the consolidated amounts. The approach used is a matter of personal preference. It's only the result that matters.

2. The eliminations and adjustments shown in the worksheet (or in the direct approach financial statements) are *never* entered in any formal set of accounts. These are working paper adjustments only.

Equity-Basis Reporting of Non-Consolidated Subsidiaries

A parent company that is also a public company will issue only consolidated statements as its general purpose financial statements. A private company may or may not choose to issue consolidated statements.

In addition to the consolidated statements, every parent company will also prepare non-consolidated statements. Non-consolidated statements are used for income tax reporting, for a bank's credit analysis, and for the shareholders of a private company when the shareholders agree to waive the normal requirement for consolidated statements.

In non-consolidated statements, the subsidiaries can be reported on either the cost or equity basis. When the equity method of reporting is used, the parent corporation includes in its net income the parent's share of the subsidiary's earnings. Target's 2002 separate-entity net income is $65,000, as shown in Exhibit 4-2. Using the equity method, Target's net income (after adjustment) will be reported in Purchase's income statement as a single amount.

The Target net income cannot be reported by Purchase simply as $65,000, because to do so would ignore the substance of the purchase transaction. Since Purchase has acquired control over the assets and liabilities of Target, the earnings of Target must be reported in Purchase's statements *as though the net assets of Target had been purchased directly by Purchase.*

If the assets and liabilities had been purchased directly, then they would have been recorded at their fair values, and goodwill of $100,000 would have been recorded. The fair values and the goodwill are amortized and any transactions between the Target division and the rest of the company will not appear on the financial statements of Purchase. In other words, it is necessary to adjust the earnings of Target to reflect *all of the same adjustments that would be made if Target were consolidated.*

Part A of Exhibit 4-5 shows the computation of Target's adjusted earnings. Starting with the Target reported net income of $65,000, deductions are made for (1) depreciation of the fair-value increment on buildings and equipment, (2) amortization of goodwill, and (3) elimination of the unrealized profit on intercompany sales.

The adjusted Target earnings amount to $32,000. Purchase owns 100% of the shares of Target—Purchase will report this entire amount on Purchase's income statement as equity in the earnings of Target Ltd. (the *equity pick-up*).

EXHIBIT 4–5 EQUITY BASIS OF REPORTING PURCHASE'S INVESTMENT IN TARGET LTD.

Year Ended December 31, 2002

A. Equity in earnings of Target Ltd.:

Earnings as reported by Target	$ 65,000
Adjustments:	
1 Amortization of fair value increment on buildings & equipment: $200,000/10 years	(20,000)
2 Amortization of goodwill: $100,000/20 years	(5,000)
3 Elimination of unrealized profit on upstream sales: $20,000 x 40% gross margin	(8,000)
Adjusted Target Ltd. earnings, equity basis	$ 32,000

B. Investment in Target Ltd.:

Balance, December 31, 2001	$1,200,000
Plus Purchase's share of Target's equity basis earnings: $32,000 × 100%	32,000
Less dividends received from Target	(30,000)
Balance, December 31, 2002	$1,202,000

Part B of Exhibit 4-5 summarizes the impact of the equity method on the investment account. The year-end balance of $1,202,000 will be reported on Purchase's unconsolidated balance sheet. The investment account reflects (1) the cost of the investment plus (2) the cumulative amount of unremitted adjusted earnings since the date of acquisition.

The adjustments made to Target's net income are made only for *reporting* on Purchase's statements. Target will report net income of $65,000 on its own separate-entity financial statements, even though Purchase's equity-basis income statement will report the lesser amount of $32,000 in earnings from Target.

Purchase may choose to *record* the equity-basis earnings of Target in its accounts, in which case the adjustment will appear as follows:

Investment in Target	32,000	
Equity in earnings of Target		32,000

The credit to the income statement account is offset by a debit to increase the investment account. When Target declares dividends, the declaration will be recorded as follows:

Dividends receivable	30,000	
Investment in Target		30,000

When the dividends are paid, Purchase will debit cash and credit the dividends receivable account.

It is not necessary for Purchase to *record* its investment in Target on the equity basis, even though it may *report* the investment on the equity basis. As a bookkeeping convenience, it is most common for the investor to maintain the investment account on the cost basis.

Comparison of consolidation vs. equity reporting

Exhibit 4-6 shows the balance sheet and income statement for Purchase for the year ended December 31, 2002. The first column shows the results of reporting Target on the equity basis, while the second column shows consolidated statements.

In the unconsolidated statements, the assets and liabilities are only those of Purchase, and the revenues and expenses are also only those generated or incurred by Purchase. One of the assets of Purchase is the investment in Target, which appears as a non-current asset on the balance sheet. Similarly, the income statement shows Purchase's equity in the earnings of Target as a separate item.

When we consolidate Purchase and Target, however, we eliminate the investment in the Target account on the balance sheet and instead show all of the individual assets and liabilities of Target that the investment represents. The shareholders' equity accounts are exactly the same in both columns. The total net asset value of Purchase is not altered by the process of consolidation; all that happens is that the investment account is disaggregated so that the readers of Purchase's financial statements can see the total resources (of both Purchase and Target) that are under the control of the management of Purchase.

The unconsolidated income statement includes the net equity-basis earnings of Target on a single line. Upon consolidation, that line disappears and the net amount thereof ($32,000) is disaggregated by including the revenues and expenses of Target in the main body of the statement, along with those of Purchase. The consolidated net income is exactly the same as the unconsolidated net income of Purchase, since the investment in Target has been reported on the equity basis.

EXHIBIT 4–6 COMPARING EQUITY-BASIS REPORTING AND CONSOLIDATION

Purchase Ltd.
Statement of Income and Retained Earnings
Year Ended December 31, 2002

	Equity Basis	Consolidated
Sales revenue	$2,400,000	$2,645,000
Equity in earnings of Target Ltd.	32,000	—
	2,432,000	2,645,000
Operating expenses:		
Cost of sales	1,750,000	1,883,000
Depreciation expense	100,000	155,000
Goodwill amortization	—	5,000
Other expenses	250,000	270,000
	2,100,000	2,313,000
Net income	$ 332,000	$ 332,000
Retained earnings, December 31, 2001	2,000,000	2,000,000
Dividends declared	—	—
Retained earnings, December 31, 2002	$2,332,000	$2,332,000

Purchase Ltd.
Balance Sheet, December 31, 2002

	Equity Basis	Consolidated
Assets		
Current assets:		
Cash	$ 980,000	$1,080,000
Accounts receivable	2,200,000	2,450,000
Inventory	250,000	312,000
	3,430,000	3,842,000
Property, plant, and equipment:		
Land	1,000,000	1,400,000
Buildings and equipment	3,000,000	3,550,000
Accumulated depreciation	(1,300,000)	(1,355,000)
	2,700,000	3,595,000
Other assets:		
Investments	1,202,000	—
Goodwill	—	95,000
Total assets	$7,332,000	$7,532,000
Liabilities and shareholders' equity		
Liabilities:		
Current accounts payable	$ 800,000	$1,000,000
Long-term notes payable	400,000	400,000
	1,200,000	1,400,000
Shareholders' equity:		
Common shares	3,800,000	3,800,000
Retained earnings	2,332,000	2,332,000
	6,132,000	6,132,000
Total liabilities and shareholders' equity	$7,332,000	$7,532,000

Wholly-Owned
Subsidiaries:
Reporting
Subsequent to
Acquisition

143

The equity-basis investment account is increased by the $32,000 equity pick-up of Target's earnings, minus the $30,000 dividends received from Target. As a result, the investment account is shown at $1,202,000 in the equity basis column.

Because the equity-basis investment account and equity-in-earnings account summarize the investor's interest in the net assets and earnings from operations of the investee corporation in a single line on the financial statements of the investor, the equity method is sometimes referred to as **one-line consolidation**. Because the investor's equity in the earnings of the investee is computed by making the same adjustments as would be made for consolidation, this approach to equity-basis accounting is sometimes called the **consolidation method** of equity reporting. The net income and the shareholders' equity on the equity-basis unconsolidated statements are the same as they are on the consolidated statements.

Discontinued Operations and Extraordinary Items

As a general rule, gains and losses from extraordinary items and discontinued operations that are shown on the income statement of an investee corporation retain their classification when that investee's financial results are consolidated or are reported on the equity basis.[5]

For example, if A owns 40% of B, and if A reports its investment in B on the equity basis, then A would normally show as an extraordinary item 40% of any extraordinary item reported by B.

Similarly, discontinued operations and extraordinary items of a subsidiary should be reported separately, net of non-controlling interest, *if the items represent discontinued operations or are extraordinary to the parent* [CICA 1600.66].

A subsidiary may discontinue a line of business or sell a division and therefore report a gain or loss from the discontinuance in its own financial statements. But if there are other, similar operations within the consolidated economic entity, shutting down that operation in the subsidiary just represents a realignment of the activity, not its discontinuance. Therefore, a gain or loss reported as a discontinued operation in a subsidiary's separate-entity income statement may be reported as an operating gain or loss in the parent's consolidated income statement.

Similar reasoning applies to extraordinary items. There are three necessary conditions that gains or losses must satisfy in order to be classified as extraordinary [CICA 3480.02]:

1. They are not expected to occur frequently over several years.

2. They do not typify the normal business activities of the entity.

3. They do not depend primarily on decisions or determinations by management or owners.

To these three we can add the implicit fourth requirement that they must be material in amount.

A transaction in a subsidiary or a significantly influenced company may meet these criteria and be properly classified as extraordinary. But when the transaction is considered from the viewpoint of the parent or investor corporation, it may fail to meet one or more of the criteria. The most obvious potential failing is on the

---

5. The AcSB's recommendations relating to equity-basis reporting can be found in CICA 3050.09. The recommendations for reporting subsidiaries' discontinued operations and extraordinary items on consolidated statements are in CICA 1600.66 and 1600.67.

dimension of materiality—what is material to a subsidiary may not be material to a much larger consolidated entity. An extraordinary item may fail to satisfy one of the other criteria instead of, or in addition to, the materiality criterion. In particular, transactions that are nonrecurring in an individual company may actually be recurring in the consolidated entity.

Thus the general rule of maintaining the status of an extraordinary item is, like many other recommendations in accounting, one that must be applied with professional judgement.

Wholly-Owned
Subsidiaries:
Reporting
Subsequent to
Acquisition

145

Consolidation in Second Subsequent Year

Basic information

Before we generalize the approach to preparing consolidated financial statements (which we do in Chapter 6), we will extend this example for one more year. The two companies' financial statements for the year ended December 31, 2003 are shown in Exhibit 4-7. Additional information is as follows:

1. Target had sales of $60,000 to Purchase (i.e., upstream); Target's 2003 gross margin was 45%; $10,000 (sales price) of the goods are in Purchase's inventory on December 31, 2003. Unrealized upstream profit therefore is $10,000 × 45% = $4,500.

2. Purchase had sales of $20,000 to Target (i.e., downstream); Purchase's 2003 gross margin was 30%; $6,000 (sales price) of the goods sold to Target are in Target's 2003 ending inventory. Unrealized downstream profit is $6,000 × 30% = $1,800.

3. Purchase borrowed $500,000 from Target on December 29, 2003. Both companies have reported this as a current item on their individual separate-entity balance sheets.

4. Target sold its land to Purchase for $450,000. The land originally cost Target $300,000, and its fair value at the date of Purchase's acquisition of Target was $400,000. The gain on the sale ($150,000) is separately disclosed on Target's income statement as an unusual item.

Direct method

Statement of income and retained earnings

The consolidated statement of income and retained earnings is shown in Exhibit 4-8. The amounts that require adjustment are as follows:

- *Sales.* The two companies' combined sales of $3,400,000 must be adjusted for the intercompany sales. In 2003, there were upstream sales (Target to Purchase) of $60,000 and downstream sales (Purchase to Target) of $20,000. The sum of these amounts must be removed from sales revenue: $60,000 + $20,000 = $80,000.

- *Dividend income.* All of the dividend income shown on Purchase's income statement was received from Target. The intercompany dividends must be eliminated.

- *Gain on sale of land.* Target sold its land to Purchase during 2003 and recognized a gain of $150,000 on the transaction. However, the land is still owned

EXHIBIT 4–7 SEPARATE-ENTITY FINANCIAL STATEMENTS FOR 2003

Income Statements
Year Ended December 31, 2003

	Purchase Ltd.	Target Ltd.
Revenue:		
Sales	$3,000,000	$ 400,000
Dividend income	20,000	—
Gain on sale of land	—	150,000
	3,020,000	550,000
Expenses:		
Cost of sales	2,100,000	220,000
Depreciation expense	100,000	35,000
Other operating expenses	440,000	75,000
	2,640,000	330,000
Net income	$ 380,000	$ 220,000
Retained earnings, December 31, 2002	2,330,000	635,000
Dividends declared	(135,000)	(20,000)
Retained earnings, December 31, 2003	$2,575,000	$ 835,000

Balance Sheets
December 31, 2003

	Purchase Ltd.	Target Ltd.
Assets		
Current assets:		
Cash	$ 490,000	$ 70,000
Accounts receivable	1,900,000	775,000
Inventory	300,000	60,000
	2,690,000	905,000
Property, plant, and equipment:		
Land	1,450,000	—
Buildings and equipment	3,800,000	500,000
Accumulated depreciation	(1,400,000)	(220,000)
	3,850,000	280,000
Other assets:		
Investments (at cost)	1,200,000	—
Total assets	$7,740,000	$1,185,000
Liabilities and shareholders' equity		
Liabilities:		
Accounts payable	$ 865,000	$ 150,000
Long-term notes payable	500,000	—
	1,365,000	150,000
Shareholders' equity:		
Common shares	3,800,000	200,000
Retained earnings	2,575,000	835,000
	6,375,000	1,035,000
Total liabilities and shareholders' equity	$7,740,000	$1,185,000

Wholly-Owned

Subsidiaries:

Reporting

Subsequent to

Acquisition

147

EXHIBIT 4–8 PURCHASE LTD. CONSOLIDATED INCOME STATEMENT (DIRECT METHOD)

Statement of Income and Retained Earnings
Year Ended December 31, 2003

Revenue:

Sales revenue [3,000,000 + 400,000 – **60,000 – 20,000**]	$3,320,000
Dividend income [20,000 + 0 – **20,000**]	—
Gain on sale of land [0 + 150,000 – **150,000**]	—
	3,320,000

Operating expenses:

Cost of sales	
[2,100,000 + 220,000 – **60,000 – 20,000** + 4,500 + 1,800 – **8,000**]	2,238,300
Depreciation expense [100,000 + 35,000 **+ 20,000**]	155,000
Goodwill amortization [**+ 5,000**]	5,000
Other expenses [440,000 + 75,000]	515,000
	2,913,300
Net income	$ 406,700
Retained earnings, December 31, 2002	2,332,000
[2,330,000 + 635,000 – **600,000 – 20,000 – 5,000 – 8,000**]	
Dividends declared [135,000 + 20,000 – **20,000**]	(135,000)
Retained earnings, December 31, 2003	$2,603,700

within the consolidated entity. Therefore, the gain must be eliminated when we prepare the consolidated income statement.

- *Cost of sales.* Cost of sales must also be reduced by the $80,000 of intercompany sales. Some of the goods sold from one company to the other are still in inventory. Therefore, we must also adjust cost of sales by increasing it for the unrealized profit in the year-end inventory.

  - *Upstream.* Target's gross profit margin for 2003 was 45%. Purchase's inventory contains $10,000 of goods purchased from Target. Therefore, we must increase cost of sales by $10,000 × 45% = $4,500.

  - *Downstream.* Purchase's gross profit margin for 2003 was 30%. Target's inventory contains $6,000 of goods purchased from Target. The unrealized profit is $6,000 × 30% = $1,800. Cost of sales is increased by $1,800.

Unrealized profit in the ending inventory is not the only thing we have to worry about. Remember that there was also $8,000 in unrealized profit in Purchase's ending inventory in 2002. The ending 2002 inventory is also the beginning 2003 inventory. If we include Purchase's beginning inventory in the consolidated cost of sales calculation, we will overstate the opening inventory by $8,000, and thereby *overstate* cost of sales by the same amount. Therefore, we must *reduce* consolidated cost of sales by $8,000.

- *Depreciation expense.* We must continue to amortize the fair value increment on Target's buildings and equipment. As in 2002, the amortization is $200,000 ÷ 10 years, or $20,000. This amount is added to the depreciation expense.

- *Amortization.* Goodwill amortization will be $5,000 again for 2003.

- *Dividends declared.* Target's $20,000 in dividends paid to Purchase must be eliminated.

- *Opening retained earnings.* The opening balances (i.e., the December 31, 2002 balances) must be adjusted for two things: (1) Target's retained earnings balance at the date of acquisition, and (2) adjustments to earnings since the date of acquisition. The 2002 earnings adjustments were for $20,000 amortization of the fair value increment, for $5,000 goodwill amortization, and for $8,000 unrealized profit on upstream inventory sales. All three of these amounts are subtracted from the opening retained earnings to get the correct, adjusted, beginning balance.

Balance sheet

The consolidated balance sheet is shown in Exhibit 4-9. Adjustments are as follows:

- *Accounts receivable.* The intercompany receivable of $500,000 that is included on Target's books must be eliminated.

EXHIBIT 4–9 PURCHASE LTD. CONSOLIDATED BALANCE SHEET (DIRECT METHOD)

Balance Sheet
December 31, 2003

Assets

Current assets:

Cash [490,000 + 70,000]	$ 560,000
Accounts receivable [1,900,000 + 775,000 – **500,000**]	2,175,000
Inventory [300,000 + 60,000 – **4,500 – 1,800**]	353,700
	3,088,700

Property, plant, and equipment:

Land [1,450,000 + 0 **+ 100,000 – 150,000**]	1,400,000
Buildings and equipment [3,800,000 + 500,000 **+ 50,000**]	4,350,000
Accumulated depreciation [1,400,000 + 220,000 – **150,000 + 40,000**]	(1,510,000)
	4,240,000

Other assets:

Investments [1,200,000 + 0 – **1,200,000**]	—
Goodwill [**100,000 × 18/20**]	90,000
Total assets	$7,418,700

Liabilities and shareholders' equity

Liabilities:

Current accounts payable [865,000 + 150,000 – **500,000**]	$ 515,000
Long-term notes payable [500,000 + 0]	500,000
	1,015,000

Shareholders' equity:

Common shares [**Purchase Ltd. shares only**]	3,800,000
Retained earnings [2,575,000 + 835,000 – **600,000**	
– **150,000 – 4,500 – 1,800 – (20,000 × 2) – (5,000 × 2)**]	2,603,700
	6,403,700
Total liabilities and shareholders' equity	$7,418,700

- *Inventory.* The unrealized profits from both the upstream and downstream sales must be eliminated. The upstream amount is $10,000 \times 45\% = \$4,500$; downstream is $6,000 \times 30\% = \$1,800$.

- *Land.* Target's land has been sold to Purchase. Target recorded a gain of $150,000 on the sale. This is an intercompany unrealized profit that must be eliminated. However, there was a fair value increment of $100,000 on the land at the date of purchase. This FVI still must be added on, even though legal title to the land has now been transferred from Target to Purchase.

- *Buildings and equipment.* The date-of-acquisition FVI of $50,000 must be added, just as in 2002.

- *Accumulated depreciation.* Target's date-of-acquisition accumulated depreciation of $150,000 is eliminated; two years' worth of FVI amortization of $20,000 per year is added.

- *Current accounts payable.* Purchase's payables include the $500,000 owed to Target. This intercompany balance must be eliminated.

- *Common shares.* As usual, only the parent's shares are reported on the consolidated balance sheet.

- *Retained earnings.* Consolidated retained earnings is calculated by starting with the book balances of the two companies, and then:

  (1) subtracting Target's date-of-acquisition retained earnings,

  (2) subtracting year-end unrealized profits,

  (3) subtracting the cumulative amount of FVI amortization since the date of acquisition (i.e., $20,000 \times 2$ years), and

  (4) subtracting accumulated goodwill amortization since the date of acquisition ($5,000 \times 2$).

Wholly-Owned
Subsidiaries:
Reporting
Subsequent to
Acquisition

149

Notice that it is not necessary to adjust for the unrealized profit in the beginning inventory when we compute the ending consolidated retained earnings. Target's separate-entity retained earnings already includes the $8,000 previously unrealized profit from 2002, and by *not* making any adjustment, we permit it to flow through to consolidated retained earnings as a now-realized amount. Of course, we are assuming that the beginning inventory has been sold during the period. This is the normal assumption; we only need to be told how much of the intercompany sales is still in ending inventory each year (and the relevant gross profit percentage) in order to make the adjustments for unrealized year-end profit, regardless of which year the intercompany sales occurred.

The calculation for Purchase's consolidated retained earnings for December 31, 2003, is as follows:

Purchase separate-entity retained earnings	$2,575,000
Target's separate-entity retained earnings	+ 835,000
Target's date-of-acquisition retained earnings	−600,000
Unrealized profit on sale of land	−150,000
Unrealized upstream profit in ending inventory	−4,500
Unrealized downstream profit in ending inventory	−1,800
2 years' amortization of FVI in buildings and equipment	−40,000
2 years' amortization of goodwill	−10,000
Purchase's consolidated retained earnings	**$2,603,700**

As we observed earlier in the chapter, we could have obtained the year-end consolidated retained earnings from the bottom of the statement of income and retained earnings, or simply by treating retained earnings as a "plug" once we've calculated all of the other balances. However, it is useful to be able to derive closing retained earnings directly from information given, rather than going through the whole process of constructing a consolidated income statement. And "plugs" are always dangerous—there is no way to tell if the balance sheet really is in balance.

Worksheet approach

The first two numerical columns of Exhibit 4-10 present the trial balances for Purchase and Target at December 31, 2003. We will make the adjustments and eliminations much as we did earlier in the chapter for 2002. Again, for greater clarity, we will use separate columns for the acquisition adjustment and the operations adjustments. As well, we will add yet another column, as we will explain in the following paragraphs. There is no real need to use separate columns—a single adjustment column can be used as long as you allow enough rows under each item to record all of the adjustments.

Acquisition and cumulative adjustments

To consolidate financial statements at the date of acquisition, we make only two adjustments—to eliminate Target's date-of-acquisition shareholders' equity accounts and to allocate the purchase price discrepancy. When we consolidate the statements one year after acquisition, an additional group of adjustments is necessary to adjust the current year's operations for (1) amortization of the fair value increments and goodwill and (2) intercompany transactions and balances.

When we prepare consolidated financial statements more than one year after the acquisition, an additional type of adjustment is necessary. We must adjust the balance sheet accounts for unrealized earnings, fair-value amortization, and goodwill amortization that occurred between the date of acquisition and the *beginning* of the year for which we are preparing consolidated financial statements.

For example, if we prepare consolidated statements for Purchase for 2007, we will provide for $20,000 amortization of the fair-value increment of the buildings and equipment for 2007, just as we did in Exhibit 4-3 for 2002. However, the net amount of the fair-value increment that is included on the *balance sheet* on December 31, 2007, will only be $80,000: $200,000 original increment reduced by six years of amortization at $20,000 per year. Therefore, we first need to make an adjustment for the amortization in the five years *prior* to 2007, and then we can make the adjustment for the 2007 amortization to expense.

In Exhibit 4-10, the three different types of adjustments are shown in three separate columns for clarity. The first adjustment column ("Acquisition") contains exactly the same adjustments as in Exhibit 4-4.

The second adjustment column ("Cumulative") shows the adjustments that are necessary in order to restate the beginning balances (at January 1, 2003) correctly. The adjustments for pre-2003 amortization are as follows:

b1	Retained earnings	20,000	
	Accumulated depreciation		20,000
b2	Retained earnings	5,000	
	Goodwill		5,000

Recall that at the end of 2002, there was unrealized profit of $8,000 in

EXHIBIT 4–10 PURCHASE LTD. CONSOLIDATION WORKSHEET, DECEMBER 31, 2003

December 31, 2003

| | Trial balances | | Adjustments | | | Purchase Ltd. consolidated trial balance |
	Purchase	Target	Acquisition [a]	Cumulative [b]	Current [c]	
Cash	$ 490,000	$ 70,000				$ 560,000
Accounts receivable	1,900,000	775,000			(500,000) **c7**	2,175,000
Inventories	300,000	60,000			(4,500) **c5**	353,700
					(1,800) **c6**	
Land	1,450,000	—	100,000 **a2**		(150,000) **c3**	1,400,000
Buildings and equipment	3,800,000	500,000	50,000 **a2**			4,350,000
Accumulated depreciation	(1,400,000)	(220,000)	150,000 **a2**	(20,000) **b1**	(20,000) **c1**	(1,510,000)
Investments (at cost)	1,200,000	—	(800,000) **a1**			—
			(400,000) **a2**			
Goodwill			100,000 **a2**	(5,000) **b2**	(5,000) **c2**	90,000
Accounts payable	(865,000)	(150,000)			500,000 **c7**	(515,000)
Long-term notes payable	(500,000)					(500,000)
Common shares	(3,800,000)	(200,000)	200,000 **a1**			(3,800,000)
Dividends declared	135,000	20,000			(20,000) **c8**	135,000
Retained earnings,						—
December 31, 2002	(2,330,000)	(635,000)	600,000 **a1**	20,000 **b1**		(2,332,000)
				5,000 **b2**		
				8,000 **b3**		
Sales	(3,000,000)	(400,000)			80,000 **c4**	(3,320,000)
Dividend income	(20,000)	—			20,000 **c8**	—
Gain on sale of land	—	(150,000)			150,000 **c3**	—
Cost of sales	2,100,000	220,000		(8,000) **b3**	(80,000) **c4**	2,238,300
					4,500 **c5**	
					1,800 **c6**	
Depreciation expense	100,000	35,000			20,000 **c1**	155,000
Goodwill amortization expense					5,000 **c2**	5,000
Other operating expenses	440,000	75,000				515,000
	$ —	$ —	$ —	$ —	$ —	$ —

Purchase Ltd.'s inventory. As we explained above, unrealized profit causes the inventory balance to be overstated. When the overstated opening inventory is added to purchases, the goods available for sale are overstated. That, in turn, causes the cost of sales to be overstated. We adjust for this misstatement by decreasing cost of sales and simultaneously decreasing opening retained earnings. We must decrease Target's beginning retained earnings by the amount of unrealized profit that is included therein:

b3 Retained earnings, December 31, 2002   8,000

       Cost of sales   8,000

In effect, what we are doing is transferring the profit on unsold intercompany inventory from the period of Target's book recognition (in 2002) to the year that the inventory was sold externally (in 2003).

Current operations

The third column of adjustments contains all the figures necessary to adjust the balance sheet at the end of the year and the income statement accounts for intercompany transactions during the year.

The first and second adjustments are (1) for the 2003 depreciation on the fair-value increment for buildings and equipment and (2) for the amortization of goodwill for 2003:

c1	Depreciation expense	20,000	
	Accumulated depreciation		20,000
c2	Amortization expense	5,000	
	Goodwill		5,000

The third adjustment is to eliminate the gain that Target recorded when it sold its land to Purchase (i.e., upstream):

c3	Gain on sale of land	150,000	
	Land		150,000

The fourth adjustment is for the intercompany sales during 2003. Total intercompany sales were $60,000 upstream plus $20,000 downstream, a total of $80,000:

c4	Sales	80,000	
	Cost of sales		80,000

Of the upstream sales, $10,000 is still in Purchase's year-end 2003 inventory. Since Target had a gross margin of 45%, unrealized gross profit is $4,500. The fifth adjustment is to increase cost of sales and reduce ending inventory by $4,500:

c5	Cost of sales	4,500	
	Inventory		4,500

Of the $20,000 downstream sales, $6,000 is still in Target's year-end inventory. Purchase's gross margin is 30%, and therefore Target's ending inventory includes $1,800 of unrealized profit:

c6	Cost of sales	1,800	
	Inventory		1,800

At the end of 2003, Purchase borrowed $500,000 from Target. The offsetting receivable and payable must be eliminated before preparing the consolidated financial statements:

c7	Accounts payable	500,000	
	Accounts receivable		500,000

The final adjustment that is made on Exhibit 4-10 is the elimination of the intercompany dividends paid by Target to Purchase:

c8 Dividend income	20,000	
Dividends declared		20,000

After all of the adjustments have been entered on the worksheet, we can cross-add the rows to find the 2003 consolidated trial balance amounts. The amounts in the last column are used to prepare the consolidated statements.

Completed consolidated financial statements

Exhibits 4-11 through 4-13 present the complete consolidated financial statements for Purchase Ltd. as of December 31, 2003. Since financial statements should be comparative statements, the 2003 statements also include the amounts for 2002. A complete set of financial statements must include a cash flow statement. Exhibit 4-13 illustrates a cash flow statement.

The preparation of a consolidated cash flow statement involves no particular challenges. The statement can be prepared by combining the cash flow statements of the separate entities and eliminating intercompany transactions. Alternatively, the statement can be prepared directly from the consolidated income statement, balance sheet, and statement of retained earnings in exactly the same manner as from any other set of financial statements.

Alternative presentation of goodwill amortization

Throughout this book, we will show goodwill amortization on the income statement as a part of operating expenses. However, an alternative presentation is to present goodwill amortization on a separate line, after taxes but just before net operating income (that is, net income before discontinued operations and extraordinary items). Since the amortization is presented after income tax expense has been deducted, the amortization is reported net of tax (if any). Not only can goodwill amortization be presented net-of-tax below other operating income, but also the reporting company can present a supplemental earnings per share (EPS) figure that excludes goodwill amortization.

An example illustrating the separate disclosure of goodwill is shown in Exhibit 4-14 (page 156). NQL reports 1999 "income before goodwill amortiza-

---

EXHIBIT 4–11 PURCHASE LTD. CONSOLIDATED STATEMENT OF INCOME AND RETAINED EARNINGS

Years Ended December 31

	2003	2002
Sales revenue	$3,320,000	$2,645,000
Operating expenses:		
Cost of sales	2,238,300	1,883,000
Depreciation expense	155,000	155,000
Goodwill amortization	5,000	5,000
Other expenses	515,000	270,000
	2,913,300	2,313,000
Net income	$ 406,700	$ 332,000
Retained earnings, January 1	2,332,000	2,000,000
Dividends declared	(135,000)	—
Retained earnings, December 31	$2,603,700	$2,332,000

EXHIBIT 4–12 PURCHASE LTD. CONSOLIDATED BALANCE SHEET

December 31

	2003	2002
Assets		
Current assets:		
Cash	$ 560,000	$ 1,080,000
Accounts receivable	2,175,000	2,450,000
Inventory	353,700	312,000
	3,088,700	3,842,000
Property, plant, and equipment:		
Land	1,400,000	1,400,000
Buildings and equipment	4,350,000	3,550,000
Accumulated depreciation	(1,510,000)	(1,355,000)
	4,240,000	3,595,000
Other assets:		
Goodwill	90,000	95,000
Total assets	$ 7,418,700	$ 7,532,000
Liabilities and shareholders' equity		
Liabilities:		
Current accounts payable	$ 515,000	$ 1,000,000
Long-term notes payable	500,000	400,000
	1,015,000	1,400,000
Shareholders' equity:		
Common shares	3,800,000	3,800,000
Retained earnings	2,603,700	2,332,000
	6,403,700	6,132,000
Total liabilities and shareholders' equity	$ 7,418,700	$ 7,532,000

tion" of $1,647 (thousand). In the notes, the company reports "EPS before good-will amortization" of 10.2¢. After deducting goodwill amortization, net income is $1,185 and EPS becomes 7.4¢.

It is unprecedented to encourage a single item of operating expense to be shown in such a way. Even unusual items are required to be shown pre-tax, and no special EPS presentation is permitted. This alternative treatment was made possible by a December 1999 addendum to Section 1580 of the *CICA Handbook*—the first step in the international harmonization of business combi-nation accounting.

The special treatment of goodwill amortization originated with the FASB in the U.S. The FASB was suffering heavy criticism of their proposal to require the purchase method of accounting for business combinations. Many of the FASB's exposure draft respondents objected vigorously to the requirement to amortize goodwill. Providing the alternative separate presentation of goodwill was a response to that criticism by permitting companies to report pre-amortization operating income and EPS. The AcSB followed suit, in order to maintain con-sistency with the FASB's proposals on business combinations.

This special treatment of goodwill amortization seems to make little sense from an accounting standpoint. It suggests that goodwill amortization is not a

Wholly-Owned
Subsidiaries:
Reporting
Subsequent to
Acquisition

155

EXHIBIT 4–13 CONSOLIDATED CASH FLOW STATEMENT

Years Ended December 31

	2003	2002
Operating activities		
Consolidated net income, as reported	$ 406,700	$ 332,000
Add expenses not requiring cash:		
Depreciation on capital assets	155,000	155,000
Goodwill amortization	5,000	5,000
Changes in working capital items:		
Accounts receivable	275,000	(300,000)
Inventory	(41,700)	(62,000)
Accounts payable	(485,000)	(100,000)
Net cash from operating activities	315,000	30,000
Financing activities		
Increase in long-term notes payable	100,000	—
Dividends declared and paid	(135,000)	—
	(35,000)	—
Investing activities		
Purchase of buildings and equipment	(800,000)	—
Increase (decrease) in cash	$(520,000)	$ 30,000

"real" expense, and that it can be ignored when looking at a company's earnings. But goodwill represents a true cost—the acquiring company gave real consideration for it, just as real as for the acquired company's financial assets and tangible capital assets. If it were not considered to be a true cost it would not be recorded as an asset. In fact, this paid consideration is what distinguishes goodwill in a business combination from internally created goodwill that is not recorded. Recorded goodwill is not an accounting fabrication. It is difficult to rationalize special treatment of goodwill but not of other interperiod allocations, such as other amortization amounts or future income tax allocations.

Note disclosure

While Exhibits 4-11 through 4-13 do present the complete set of statements, they do not present the notes thereto. The notes should contain additional disclosure of Purchase Ltd.'s acquisition of Target, as we discussed at the end of the preceding chapter.

The 1999 edition of *Financial Reporting in Canada* reported on the disclosure of business combinations by 200 surveyed companies from 1996 through 1998. About 43% of the companies reporting business combinations reported by the purchase method. Of the companies reporting purchase-method business combinations, no company provided all the recommended information. Compliance ranged from about 90% for disclosure of the acquiree's name and of the net assets acquired, down to about 70% for description of the acquiree's business. Details of the consideration given were disclosed for about 83% of the acquisitions.[6] The report does not speculate on the reasons for non-compliance with the disclosure

6. *Financial Reporting in Canada 1999*, Twenty-fourth Edition (Toronto: CICA, 1999), p. 125.

EXHIBIT 4–14 NQL DRILLING TOOLS INC. CONSOLIDATED STATEMENT OF OPERATIONS*

(Thousands of Canadian Dollars)	1999	1998	1997
Revenue			
Sales	$51,551	$61,289	$36,390
Direct expenses	22,080	27,611	15,283
Income from operations	29,471	33,678	21,107
Expenses			
General and administrative	16,398	10,946	6,324
Amortization	8,061	4,800	1,932
	24,459	15,746	8,256
Income before interest expense	5,012	17,932	12,851
Interest expense	2,454	825	711
Income before income taxes	2,558	17,107	12,140
Income taxes—current	316	5,874	3,796
—deferred	595	1,401	1,143
	911	7,275	4,939
Income before goodwill amortization	**1,647**	9,832	7,201
Goodwill amortization	**462**	338	790
Income before discontinued operations	**1,185**	9,494	6,411
Discontinued operations	—	313	186
Net income	$ 1,185	$ 9,807	$ 6,597

*For sixteen months ended December 31, 1999 and the years ended August 31, 1998 and 1997.

From Note 16:

	1999	1998	1997
Earnings per share from continuing operations:			
Basic—before goodwill amortization	**10.2¢**	65.9¢	63.2¢
Basic—after goodwill amortization	**7.4¢**	63.6¢	56.2¢

recommendations, but a lack of materiality may have been a factor in at least some instances.

Consolidating parent-founded subsidiaries

The example used throughout this chapter is that of a business combination. Purchase Ltd. acquired control over the net assets of Target at a price that included both fair value increments and goodwill. By using a business combination as the basis for the example, we can fairly comprehensively illustrate the major types of adjustments that may be required when consolidated statements are prepared.

However, we pointed out in Chapter 2 that most subsidiaries are not the result of one corporation's acquiring another in a business combination. Instead, most subsidiaries are formed by their parent to conduct or facilitate some component of the parent's business. The process of consolidation for a subsidiary that was founded and wholly owned by its parent is considerably easier than for a subsidiary that was acquired as a going concern.

Since the investment by the parent was directly in the subsidiary (rather than by buying the subsidiary's shares from another shareholder), the paid-in capital accounts of the subsidiary directly offset the original investment in the investment account of the parent. There are no fair value increments or goodwill to worry about. The lack of fair value increments and goodwill means that there is no periodic amortization of those amounts to adjust for. Consolidating a wholly-owned, parent-founded subsidiary simply requires adjusting for intercompany transactions, eliminating any unrealized profits or losses, and eliminating intercompany receivable and payable balances.

Indirect holdings

In Chapter 2, we pointed out that a parent company might control a subsidiary indirectly through other subsidiaries, rather than by direct ownership. When the parent prepares its consolidated financial statements, not only the direct subsidiaries are consolidated, but also the indirect subsidiaries.

Wholly-Owned
Subsidiaries:
Reporting
Subsequent to
Acquisition

157

Procedurally, indirect subsidiaries can be consolidated in either of two ways. The first is to consolidate by steps, from the bottom up. If P controls A, who controls B and C, then consolidated statements for A can be prepared that include its direct subsidiaries, B and C. A's *consolidated* statements will then include all of the assets and liabilities of B and C just as if A owned them directly, and the investment accounts will have been eliminated. The next step is then to consolidate A's *consolidated* statements with P's statements. If the consolidation is being performed by the direct approach without a worksheet, then the step method is almost certainly the best one to use.

The second procedural approach is to perform the consolidation of all subsidiaries, direct and indirect, on a single worksheet. A single-step worksheet approach may be easiest for those who are performing the consolidation on a computer spreadsheet, since it is relatively easy to include all the subsidiaries on the worksheet with adequate space for explanatory notes. Whichever procedural approach is used, the elimination and adjustment process is no different from that illustrated in this chapter for directly owned subsidiaries.

The process of consolidation is simplified when all subsidiaries use the same accounting policies as the parent. This is fairly easily accomplished with wholly-owned subsidiaries—the parent company's management can specify the subsidiaries' accounting policies. When the same accounting policies are used, there will be no need for the parent to adjust the accounts of the subsidiaries for accounting policy differences.

Summary of Key Points

1. The parent company and each of its subsidiaries will prepare individual, separate-entity, financial statements. These statements are independent of the consolidated statements. Consolidated statements are prepared only for the shareholders of the parent company. The existence of consolidated statements does not eliminate the need for separate-entity statements.

2. Only a balance sheet is necessary when a parent and its purchased subsidiary are consolidated at the date of acquisition. At all subsequent reporting dates, consolidation involves a full set of financial statements.

3. At reporting dates following acquisition, consolidated net income must be adjusted for amortization of fair value increments, amortization of or adjustments to goodwill, and elimination of unrealized profits on intercompany sales. Amortization of fair value increments on tangible and intangible assets

should be based on the estimated remaining useful life of the asset. Amortization of goodwill is not required, but goodwill must be written down if its value for generating future earnings is impaired. If goodwill is amortized, the maximum period is 20 years.

4. Sales of current and non-current assets between a parent and its subsidiaries, or between subsidiaries, should be eliminated. Profits on intercompany sales of assets should be eliminated, unless the asset has been sold to outside third parties.

5. If consolidated statements are not prepared, the parent can report its investment in the subsidiary on either the cost or equity basis. If the equity basis is used for reporting non-consolidated subsidiaries, the parent company's reported net income and retained earnings will be exactly the same as though the statements had been consolidated.

6. Discontinued operations and extraordinary items arising both in consolidated subsidiaries and in equity-reported subsidiaries are reported as such in the parent's income statement. However, a discontinued operation or an extraordinary item may change its status within the broader economic context of the consolidated entity.

7. A complete set of consolidated financial statements should include a cash flow statement. The cash flow statement can be prepared for consolidated statements in exactly the same manner as for separate-entity statements.

8. An alternative presentation of goodwill amortization is to show the amount on a separate line following after-tax operating income but before discontinued operations and extraordinary items. Since this goodwill amortization presentation comes after income tax expense has been deducted, the goodwill amortization is shown net of tax (including future income tax).

Weblinks

International Accounting Standards Committee (IASC)
www.iasc.org.uk/

This site includes a list of current standards, as well as summaries of content and effective dates. Information on the IASC and its work, including standards revision, is also featured.

Financial Accounting Standards Board (FASB)
www.rutgers.edu/Accounting/raw/fasb

The mission of the Financial Accounting Standards Board is to establish and improve standards of financial accounting and reporting for the guidance and education of the public, including issuers, auditors, and users of financial information. Recent exposure drafts are available for download. The publications section includes summaries and status of all FASB statements, a demo of the Financial Accounting Research System, action alerts, and publication lists.

Accounting Standards Board (ASB)
www.cica.ca/cica/cicawebsite.nsf/public/StandardsGuidance

Financial reporting, accounting and auditing provide information essential to economic decision making and accountability. To be useful, this information must be understandable, comparable and reliable. To this end, our objectives are to serve private and public sector communities, and support the capital markets.

Chartered Accountants of Canada (provincial links)
www.cica.ca/

This site provides links to each of the provincial institutes' home pages. Chartered Accountants and CA students organize their responsibilities to protect the public interest through professional self-regulation and to serve clients, employers and their own professional needs through these various sites. How to become a chartered accountant, career connections, and what chartered accountants do are a few of the topics covered.

Self-Study Problem 4-1

Early in 2001, Parco acquired 100% of the shares of Subco by issuing Parco shares worth $10 million. The book value of Subco's net assets at the date of acquisition was $7,000,000. The fair values of Subco's assets were deemed to be equal to their carrying values on Subco's books with one exception: the aggregate fair value of Subco's buildings was $1,400,000 higher than their carrying value.

Parco and Subco enjoyed a trading relationship for many years prior to the combination. In 2000, for example, Subco had sold $1 million of goods to Parco (at a gross margin of 20% on sales), and Parco had billed Subco $300,000 for management services. However, the two companies had no common ownership interest and were not related companies prior to the 2001 business combination.

In 2001, following the business combination, Subco had sales of $1.2 million to Parco. Subco's gross margin remained at 20%. Of the amount sold, $200,000 remained in Parco's inventory at the end of 2001. Parco billed Subco $400,000 for management fees, of which $100,000 remained unpaid at the end of the year. Other information is as follows:

a. Subco reported separate-entity net income of $350,000 for 2001. Subco declared and paid dividends of $150,000 during the year.

b. Parco reported separate-entity net income of $680,000 for 2001, including the dividend income from Subco. Parco declared dividends of $200,000, of which one-quarter were unpaid at year-end.

c. Retained earnings at the date of acquisition were $3,450,000 for Parco and $1,250,000 for Subco.

d. Subco's buildings have an estimated remaining useful life of 14 years. Subco uses straight-line depreciation.

e. Parco's policy is to amortize goodwill over 20 years.

Required:

Determine the following amounts:

a. Parco's consolidated net income for the year ended December 31, 2001.

b. Parco's consolidated retained earnings at December 31, 2001.

c. Parco's equity-basis earnings from Subco for 2001.

Self-Study Problem 4-2

On January 1, 2003, Parent Ltd. (Par) bought 100% of the shares of Subsidiary Inc. (Sub) for $1,084,000 cash. Sub's balance sheet at the date of acquisition is shown in Exhibit 4-15, together with the estimated fair values of Sub's assets and liabilities.

EXHIBIT 4–15 SUBSIDIARY INC. BALANCE SHEET

January 1, 2003

	Book values	Fair values
Cash	$ 80,000	$ 80,000
Accounts receivable	99,000	99,000
Inventory	178,000	195,000
Property, plant, and equipment	800,000	740,000
Accumulated depreciation	(200,000)	
Total assets	$ 957,000	
Accounts payable	$70,000	70,000
Long-term notes payable	200,000	200,000
Common shares	250,000	
Retained earnings	437,000	
Total liabilities and shareholders' equity	$ 957,000	

Additional information is as follows:

a. Sub depreciates its tangible capital assets over 10 years on a straight-line basis, assuming zero residual value.

b. Par amortizes goodwill over 20 years.

c. During 2005, Par sold goods with a cost of $300,000 to Sub for $390,000. At the end of 2005, 20% of those goods remain in Sub's inventory.

d. Sub sold goods costing $100,000 to Par for $150,000 in 2005. At the end of the year, 40% of these goods remain in Par's inventory.

e. Par sold land to Sub on January 1, 2005 for $710,000. The original cost of the land was $500,000 to Par. The gain was netted to "other expenses."

f. On January 1, 2005, Par had inventory on hand that it had bought from Sub for $45,000. Intercompany profit of $12,000 was included in that price.

The separate-entity financial statements for Par and Sub for the year ended December 31, 2005 are shown in Exhibit 4-16.

Required:

Prepare the consolidated financial statements for 2005.

EXHIBIT 4–16 SEPARATE-ENTITY FINANCIAL STATEMENTS FOR 2005

Income Statements
Year Ended December 31, 2005

	Parent Ltd.	Subsidiary Inc.
Sales revenue	$1,200,000	$ 987,000
Cost of goods sold	(800,000)	(650,000)
	400,000	337,000
Other operating expenses	(235,000)	(147,000)
Net income	$ 165,000	$ 190,000
Retained earnings, December 31, 2004	1,153,000	330,000
Retained earnings, December 31, 2005	$1,318,000	$ 520,000

Balance Sheets
December 31, 2005

	Parent Ltd.	Subsidiary Inc.
Assets		
Current assets:		
Cash	$ 120,000	$ 110,000
Accounts receivable	150,000	135,000
Inventory	240,000	195,000
	510,000	440,000
Property, plant, and equipment	1,400,000	910,000
Accumulated depreciation	(510,000)	(320,000)
	890,000	590,000
Other assets:		
Investments (at cost)	1,084,000	
Goodwill	76,000	
	1,160,000	
Total assets	$2,560,000	$1,030,000
Liabilities and shareholders' equity		
Liabilities:		
Accounts payable	$ 142,000	$ 60,000
Long-term notes payable	600,000	200,000
	742,000	260,000
Shareholders' equity:		
Common shares	500,000	250,000
Retained earnings	1,318,000	520,000
	1,818,000	770,000
Total liabilities and shareholders' equity	$2,560,000	$1,030,000

Wholly-Owned
Subsidiaries:
Reporting
Subsequent to
Acquisition

161

Appendix

Income Tax Allocation Subsequent to Acquisition

Introduction and review

The Appendix to Chapter 3 discussed the issue of income allocation as it applies in a business combination, and illustrated the calculation of future income tax (FIT) at acquisition. The essence of income tax allocation for business combinations is that the buyer, *on its consolidated balance sheet,* must calculate future income tax as part of the purchase equation. The future income tax for each asset and liability is based on its temporary difference. The temporary difference is the difference between (1) the tax basis of the asset to the *subsidiary* and (2) the fair value of the asset as it is included on the *parent's* consolidated statement. For the purchase transaction in Chapter 3, which also pertains to this chapter, the amounts are as follows:

	Target's book value (1)	Tax basis for Target (2)	Fair value to Purchase (3)	Temporary difference (3) – (2)
Land	$300,000	$300,000	$400,000	$100,000
Buildings and equipment	350,000	250,000	550,000	300,000
Total	$650,000	$550,000	$950,000	$400,000

Target's book values are included as column (1), but they really are irrelevant for determining the amount of future income tax. They are irrelevant because we need to compare the fair values with the assets' *tax bases,* not with their carrying values on the subsidiary's books. We have put them in the table to emphasize that the tax bases of Target's assets may be different from their carrying values. For income tax allocation, the relevant figures are those in columns (2) and (3).

The temporary differences are shown in the last column. The tax basis for each asset is subtracted from its fair value. If we assume that Purchase's income tax rate is 40%, we must include $400,000 \times 40\% = \$160,000$ as a future income tax liability when we allocate the purchase price. As we explained in the Chapter 3 Appendix, the effect of including the future income tax liability is to increase the amount of the purchase price that is allocated to goodwill.

Post-acquisition tax accounting for fair value increments

The balance in the future income tax account is a function of the temporary differences at each balance sheet date. In a business combination, the temporary difference is the difference between the tax basis of an asset to the tax-paying entity (that is, to the *subsidiary* that legally owns the asset and that deducts the CCA) and its value as reported *on the parent company's consolidated balance sheet* [CICA 3465.17].

In a business combination, we must focus on the fair value increments relating to amortizable capital assets, both tangible and intangible. Residual goodwill in a purchase of shares is not a capital asset, and it is not deductible for tax purposes. There are no tax accounting effects that arise from either recording or amortizing goodwill in a business combination that is accomplished by a share purchase.

For amortizable capital assets, in years subsequent to the acquisition, (1) the fair value increments are amortized and flow into expense, thereby reducing their carrying value, and (2) the assets' tax bases change as the assets are recognized in taxable income (e.g., through CCA). Therefore, the temporary differences change. The change in temporary differences arising from FVI amortization must be recognized on the consolidated balance sheet.

In this chapter, we amortized the fair value increment relating to buildings and equipment. The amortization for each of 2003 and 2004 was $20,000. Therefore, the fair value increment declined from $200,000 at the date of acquisition to $180,000 at the end of 2003 and $160,000 at the end of 2004.

The change in the FVI is only half of the situation. The other half is the tax basis. The tax basis changes because Target continues taking CCA on its buildings and equipment. The overall temporary difference depends on both the FVI amortization and the change in the tax basis. Fortunately, however, we really don't need to know the tax basis of all of the subsidiary's assets in order to adjust for the change in temporary differences during each year.

Remember that the starting point for consolidation is the companies' separate-entity financial statements (or trial balances). The subsidiary will be using tax allocation procedures on its own books. Therefore, the subsidiary will already have recorded the future income tax that relates to temporary differences between its assets' tax bases and their carrying values. All we have to do for consolidation is to supplement that already-reported future income tax amount by recognizing the additional change to the temporary difference that relates to the FVI:

Wholly-Owned
Subsidiaries:
Reporting
Subsequent to
Acquisition

163

Tax basis of Target assets $\left.\right\}$ *Recorded* on Target's books

Carrying value on Target's books

Consolidation value = carrying value + FVI $\left.\right\}$ Added as a consolidation *adjustment*

In essence, therefore, we only have to make an FIT adjustment for the change in the temporary difference that is caused by the FVI amortization. In each of 2003 and 2004, the amortization is $20,000. At an assumed income tax rate of 40%, each year's worksheet adjustment for the additional change in consolidated FIT will be:

Future income tax liability—long term	8,000	
Income tax expense ($20,000 × 40%)		8,000

The adjustment always will be to *reduce* the future income tax liability because FVIs will never increase—they will only decrease. This does not mean that the *overall* temporary difference may not increase. Instead, it means that an increase that might have been recorded on Target's books will be reduced by the additional adjustment in consolidation.

For example, suppose that in 2003, Target recorded depreciation of $35,000 on its buildings and equipment and took CCA of $65,000. The carrying value of buildings and equipment *on Target's books* will be $350,000 − $35,000 = $315,000. The tax basis will be $250,000 − $65,000 = $185,000. The changes can be summarized as follows:

	2002	2003
Tax basis	$250,000	$185,000
Target's carrying value	350,000	315,000
Temporary difference	$100,000	$130,000

From 2002 to 2003, Target's temporary difference for the buildings and equipment increased by $30,000. Target will have *recorded* the appropriate increase in the FIT liability of $12,000 (that is, $30,000 × 40% = $12,000) resulting from the increase in the temporary difference.

Looking now at Purchase's consolidated amounts (i.e., including FVI), the consolidated temporary difference is as follows:

	2002	2003
Tax basis	$250,000	$185,000
Purchase's consolidated value	550,000	495,000
Temporary difference	$300,000	$310,000

The consolidated value of the buildings and equipment acquired in the business combination was initially a Target book value of $350,000 plus FVI of $200,000, for a total fair value of $550,000. One year later, the Target book value has been depreciated to $315,000 and the FVI has been amortized to $180,000—the sum of these two amounts equals the $495,000 shown above.

Overall, the temporary difference relating to the fair values shown on Purchase's consolidated balance sheet is increased by $10,000. The related increase in the consolidated FIT liability is $10,000 × 40% = $4,000. The change in consolidated FIT liability relating to Target's buildings and equipment can be summarized as follows:

	Temporary difference	Future income tax liability
Increase recorded on Target's books	$30,000	$12,000 Cr
Decrease from FVI amortization upon consolidation	20,000	8,000 Dr
Net change in consolidated amounts	$10,000	$ 4,000 Cr

Therefore, when we make the consolidation adjustments relating to future income tax, we need concern ourselves only with the changes in the fair value increments. We can safely assume that the subsidiary has already recorded the FIT arising from the timing differences between the tax basis and the carrying value of its assets and liabilities.

Unrealized profit

The only other income tax aspect that we need to worry about is that relating to unrealized profit. At the end of 2003, there is unrealized upstream profit of $8,000 in inventory. This profit is unrealized only from the viewpoint of the consolidated entity. So far as Canada Customs and Revenue Agency is concerned, Target has earned this profit and will be taxed on it in 2003. The tax, at 40%, will amount to $3,200.

On consolidation, the unrealized profit is eliminated. Since the profit is removed from net income, tax allocation requires that the related taxes also be removed from net income. The adjustment to achieve this is quite straightforward:

Future income tax—current	3,200	
Income tax expense ($8,000 × 40%)		3,200

All unrealized profit eliminations must be accompanied by an adjustment for income tax, deferring recognition of the income taxes paid by the selling company to the period in which the profit is realized.

A reminder: future income tax balances must be segregated between current and long-term. If the unrealized profit relates to a current asset such as inventory (or to a current liability), the *current* FIT balance is affected. If the unrealized profit relates to a non-current asset (such as in an intercompany sale of a capital asset), the *long-term* FIT balance is affected. The classification has nothing to do with the expected timing of the reversal of the temporary difference.

In 2004, the beginning-of-year unrealized profit is recognized in consolidated net income, and therefore the income tax expense also is recognized:

Income tax expense ($8,000 × 40%)	3,200	
Future income tax—current		3,200

Of course, the year-end 2004 unrealized profit must be eliminated, and those eliminations must be accompanied by adjustments to defer recognition of the related income tax expense.

Wholly-Owned
Subsidiaries:
Reporting
Subsequent to
Acquisition

165

Summary

Income tax allocation affects consolidation in two ways:

1. Amortization of the fair value increments changes the consolidated reporting values of tangible and intangible capital assets (except land), and therefore the temporary differences are affected.

2. The tax relating to unrealized profits must be removed from consolidated net income and deferred as part of the future income tax balance(s) on the balance sheet.

Fortunately, we need not worry about making the full adjustment for the changes in consolidated temporary differences for capital assets. The subsidiary company will have recorded the effects of changes in temporary differences between their carrying values and the tax bases. On consolidation, we need only to adjust for the income tax effect of the FVI amortization.

Review Questions

4-1 Define the following terms:
   a. Unrealized profits
   b. Upstream sales
   c. Downstream sales
   d. One-line consolidation
   e. Equity pick-up of earnings

4-2 What is accomplished by the acquisition adjustment when consolidated statements are prepared?

4-3 How would the acquisition adjustment for an acquired subsidiary differ from that for a parent-founded subsidiary?

4-4 What limitations are there on the amortization of goodwill arising from a business combination?

4-5 Why are the fair value increments and decrements on depreciable capital assets amortized? What is the basis for determining the amount of amortization?

4-6 When is it necessary to eliminate the profit on intercompany transactions?

4-7 Explain why the adjustment for unrealized profit in ending inventories appears to *increase* cost of goods sold.

4-8 Explain the difference between the acquisition adjustment and the operations adjustments.

4-9 Why is the equity method of reporting sometimes called the consolidation method of equity reporting?

4-10 How does a parent company's total net assets differ under consolidated reporting as compared to equity reporting for a subsidiary?

4-11 Under equity reporting, how do discontinued operations or an extraordinary item of an investee corporation affect the income statement of the investor corporation?

4-12 How does unrealized profit in the beginning inventories affect the consolidated net income, if the inventories have been sold during the year?

4-13 What disclosure should be made in the financial statements of an acquirer as to the details of a business combination?

4-14 In what general ways will consolidation of a parent-founded subsidiary differ from consolidation of a purchased subsidiary?

4-15 Are consolidated statements required after one corporation directly acquires the net assets of another corporation?

Cases

Case 4-1

McIntosh Investments Ltd.

McIntosh Investments, Ltd. (MIL) is a diversified closed-end investment company that is traded on the Toronto Stock Exchange. Loraine McIntosh, the president, owns 40% of the common shares of MIL. Another 30% are owned jointly by Loraine's brother, Blair, and his long-time companion, Douglas. The 70% ownership by Loraine and her associates gives her control of the company. The remaining 30% of the shares are widely distributed.

On April 1, 2001, the first day of MIL's fiscal year, Loraine succeeded in negotiating the acquisition by MIL of 30% of the outstanding common shares of Efrim Auto Parts, Inc. (EAPI). EAPI was an important supplier of parts to Candide Cars Corporation (CCC), a maker of specialty automobiles ("the best of all possible cars"), which was 40% owned by MIL. Loraine was particularly pleased at being able to arrange the purchase of the shares of EAPI because she was certain that great efficiency could be obtained by having the operations of EAPI and CCC more closely coordinated.

The EAPI shares were purchased from a descendant of the founder of EAPI, Jeffrey Efrim. The shares were purchased for a consideration of $600,000 cash and the issuance of 10,000 shares of MIL common stock. MIL shares were currently being traded on the TSE at $40 per share. In order to help finance the cash part of the deal, Loraine arranged a loan from the Royal Bank of East Coast for $350,000. Appendix 1 presents the balance sheet of EAPI as of March 31, 2001, the end of EAPI's fiscal year.

During the following year, Loraine and her fellow managers took an active interest in the affairs of both CCC and EAPI. CCC became EAPI's major customer, and purchased $2,000,000 of parts from EAPI during fiscal 2002. At the end of fiscal 2002, CCC had parts in inventory that were purchased from EAPI at a cost (to CCC) of $300,000, as compared to only $100,000 of such parts in inventory a year earlier. The attentions of MIL management had increased EAPI's efficiency so that average gross profit on sales rose to 35% in fiscal 2002. EAPI's net income after tax in fiscal 2002 reached a record high of $300,000 after tax, enabling EAPI to declare a dividend of $1.50 per common share on March 31, 2002.

Required:

Determine what impact MIL's investment in EAPI shares and EAPI's fiscal 2002 activities will have on the financial statements of MIL. Where alternatives are possible, state them and briefly explain the alternatives you choose. State any assumptions that you find it necessary to make.

Wholly-Owned
Subsidiaries:
Reporting
Subsequent to
Acquisition

167

APPENDIX 1
EAPI Balance Sheet
March 31, 2001

	Book value	Fair value
Cash	$ 200,000	$ 200,000
Accounts receivable	300,000	300,000
Inventories	400,000	440,000
Equipment (net)	2,100,000	2,400,000
Long-term investment (cost)	300,000	360,000
	$3,300,000	
Accounts payable	200,000	200,000
Debentures outstanding	700,000	600,000
10% preferred shares (4,000 cumulative)	400,000	300,000
Common shares (60,000 shares)	500,000	—
Retained earnings	1,500,000	—
	$3,300,000	

Case 4-2

Fish Crates Limited

You are the CA appointed as the new auditor of Fish Crates Limited (FCL) for the next three years. The requirement for an audit is specified in FCL's debt covenant with the bank.

As part of an on-going expansion program, FCL added two new sizes to its line of fish-crate products. The president of FCL is pleased with the continuing expansion program. Annual sales are $800,000, the highest level in FCL's history and a real achievement for a firm of its size. The president attributes the increase in sales to the exacting standards of quality incorporated in its new products.

"We have never amortized goodwill and don't plan to this year either," the president of FCL stated. "Last year I wrote a note at the bottom of the audit report sent to the bank, stating that amortization of goodwill is unnecessary since goodwill is being built up, not used up. We are building our reputation, which continues to increase our goodwill. I do not agree with the audit report qualification.

"We also wrote off the future income tax balance this year because it doesn't mean anything. In fact, our banker adds the accumulated future income tax balance to retained earnings when he reviews our annual financing proposals. I just couldn't think of any reason why we should pay you to calculate future income taxes when no one uses them."

Required:

Discuss the president's comments.

[CICA, adapted]

Case 4-3

M Aluminum Products

M Aluminum Products (MAP) is a manufacturer of doors, windows, greenhouses, and sunrooms.

In February 2001, MAP's common shareholders arranged for a receiver/manager to take over the management of MAP. The common shares had been owned in equal percentages by Mr. and Mrs. Mansfield since MAP's federal incorporation. In the year ended December 31, 2000, sales of MAP, according to the audited financial statements, had been over $6 million. However, as a result of Mr. Mansfield's illness, and due to uncollected receivables, profits were negligible and the cash and liquid assets position had deteriorated.

In August 2001, the receiver/manager was able to sign an agreement with Eric Cooper, who agreed to buy the common shares of MAP for $90,000 and to have MAP make various other payments to settle with creditors and preferred shareholders, effective September 1, 2001. The agreement was approved by all parties and the court, and Mr. Cooper assumed responsibility for MAP on September 1, 2001. A tax ruling confirmed that for tax purposes, no change in control has occurred, since Mr. Cooper is Mrs. Mansfield's brother.

Mr. Cooper has engaged your firm Hansen & Boyd. You visit MAP's offices and learn that at August 31, 2001, the condensed balance sheet of MAP showed the following (in thousands of dollars):

Assets

Receivables		$1,175
Inventory		530
Land		800
Building, net	(Note 1)	895
Equipment, net	(Note 1)	1,240
Goodwill, net	(Note 2)	610
Franchise	(Note 3)	470
Deficit	(Note 8)	1,120
		$6,840

Liabilities and shareholders' equity

Accounts payable	(Note 4)	$1,060
Notes payable	(Note 4)	800
Mortgage payable	(Note 5)	1,320
Preferred shares	(Note 6)	2,000
Common shares		1,000
Appraisal increase	(Note 7)	660
		$6,840

Additional Information:

1. The building and the equipment are shown at cost to MAP less accumulated depreciation.

2. Goodwill is shown at cost to MAP less accumulated amortization.

3. MAP has local rights to manufacture and distribute some types of aluminum products. The franchise cost of these rights is being amortized over 10 years, which is an estimate of their useful life.

4. The notes payable and accounts payable creditors agreed to accept $0.60 on the dollar, and MAP made payments to them of $1,116,000 on September 1, 2001. Mr. Cooper was owed $100,000 by MAP and therefore received $60,000 on settlement of the debt.

5. The mortgage payable liability was restructured on September 1, 2001, to lower the interest rate to 9% and lengthen the period for repayment of principal from 15 to 20 years. At August 31, 2001, the interest rate of 14% on the mortgage was equal to current market rates. MAP paid $400,000 to the mortgage holders of the restructuring.

6. The preferred shareholders had the option under the agreement to:

   a. have their shares redeemed for $0.30 on the dollar on September 1, 2001; or

   b. have their shares redeemed for $1.00 on the dollar in 10 years, if they waived their 10% dividend.

   All the preferred shareholders are friends of the former owners of MAP. Not surprisingly, therefore, 95% of the preferred shareholders agreed to option a.

7. MAP's land holdings were appraised years ago at $660,000 higher than their cost.

8. The non-capital loss carryforward for income tax purposes is $3,180,000. Before the company got into difficulties, a normal annual taxable income for MAP was $950,000.

In addition to the above-noted items, MAP paid $120,000 in September 2001 to the receiver/manager and the court for their fees.

Mr. Cooper advanced to MAP the monies required to make all payments.

During the negotiations with the receiver/manager of MAP, Mr. Cooper estimated that the assets of the company had the following worth to him as of September 1, 2001:

Receivables	$ 200,000
Inventory	500,000
Land	1,400,000
Building	750,000
Equipment	950,000
	$3,800,000

In order to continue its operations, MAP requires financing. The bank has requested financial statements prepared in accordance with generally accepted accounting principles.

Mr. Cooper is wondering whether he can eliminate the deficit from the balance sheet. He wants you to prepare a balance sheet as at September 2, 2001, so that he can visualize what the assets, liabilities, and shareholders' equity would look like (a) "as is" and (b) after the possible reduction or elimination of the deficit. He wants to know your reasons for whatever you prepare.

Mr. Cooper has to spend most of his time at another business he owns and will therefore have to hire a competent general manager for MAP. The person whom he is considering hiring wants an incentive of either 10% of income after income tax and before bonus, or 5% of income before income tax and bonus.

Mr. Cooper believes that MAP's main assembly line has to be realigned in order to attain better economies of production. The cost of this will be $350,000 and will involve a plant shutdown of three days, plus a weekend or two. The realignment is scheduled for late September 2001.

Most of the employees of MAP will be retained. However, some were dismissed by the receiver/manager before they attained the 10 years of employment necessary for admission to the pension plan. As a result, MAP's actuary believes that a surplus of $390,000 exists in the pension fund.

You have been engaged by Mr. Cooper to assist in all financial accounting, income tax, and related matters that concern his takeover of MAP. Mr. Cooper does not expect to hire a controller for MAP for at least a year. Therefore, he wants a thorough report from you, giving supported recommendations.

Required:

Prepare the report for Eric Cooper.

[CICA]

Problems

P4-1

Officeplus Corporation is a retailer of office supplies and equipment in Vancouver. On March 5, 2001, Officeplus formed a new corporation in Calgary in order to operate the same type of business. Officeplus invested $100,000 cash in exchange for 10,000 common shares in the new subsidiary, to be known as Plus Limited.

During 2001, Plus Limited commenced operations. Most of Plus's initial inventory came from Officeplus. In total, goods that had cost Officeplus $200,000 were sold to Plus at an assigned value of $250,000. These goods were repriced by Plus to sell for $500,000 at retail. At year-end, 30% of the merchandise acquired from Officeplus was still in Plus's inventory.

Officeplus also extended a loan to Plus to finance the start-up costs. A total of $150,000 was lent during the year, of which $80,000 was still owing at year-end. Interest of $10,000 on the loan had been accrued by both companies, of which only $8,000 had actually been paid during 2001.

Condensed balance sheets and income statements of the two companies are presented below, as of December 31, 2001.

Required:

Prepare a consolidated balance sheet and income statement for Officeplus Corporation at December 31, 2001.

Balance Sheets
December 31, 2001

	Officeplus	Plus
Cash	$ 85,000	$ 10,000
Accounts and other receivables	275,000	130,000
Inventories	440,000	60,000
Capital assets	500,000	300,000
Accumulated depreciation	(200,000)	(30,000)
Investment in Plus (at cost)	100,000	—
	$1,200,000	$470,000
Accounts and other payables	$ 300,000	$150,000
Long-term liabilities	270,000	200,000
Common shares	50,000	100,000
Retained earnings	580,000	20,000
	$1,200,000	$470,000

Wholly-Owned
Subsidiaries:
Reporting
Subsequent to
Acquisition

171

Statements of Income and Retained Earnings
Year Ended December 31, 2001

	Officeplus	Plus
Sales	$2,000,000	$600,000
Other income	70,000	—
	2,070,000	600,000
Expenses	1,700,000	540,000
Net income	370,000	60,000
Retained earnings, December 31, 2000	410,000	—
Dividends	(200,000)	(40,000)
Retained earnings, December 31, 2001	$ 580,000	$ 20,000

P4-2

At the end of 2002, the condensed balance sheets and income statements of Officeplus Corporation and Plus Limited were as they appear below. Intercompany activities were as follows:

1. Plus sold all of its opening (i.e., December 31, 2001) inventory including that acquired from Officeplus (see **P4-1**).

2. Plus purchased merchandise from Officeplus for $400,000. This price included a 25% markup over the cost to Officeplus. At year-end, 40% of these goods were still in Plus's inventory.

3. Plus sold to Officeplus some merchandise that Plus had acquired for $120,000. The sale to Officeplus was at a price of $100,000. The merchandise was all in Officeplus's inventory at year-end, but is expected to sell for $150,000 in 2003.

4. Plus fully repaid Officeplus the $80,000 loan that had been outstanding at the beginning of the year, plus $7,000 in interest ($2,000 of the interest pertained to 2001).

5. Officeplus purchased a plot of land in Calgary for $100,000 and resold it to Plus for $140,000.

Required:

Prepare a consolidated statement of income and retained earnings and a consolidated balance sheet for Officeplus Corporation for 2002.

Balance Sheets
December 31, 2002

	Officeplus	Plus
Cash	$ 50,000	$ 10,000
Accounts and other receivables	230,000	60,000
Inventories	470,000	195,000
Capital assets	560,000	420,000
Accumulated depreciation	(230,000)	(60,000)
Investment in Plus	100,000	—
Other investments	140,000	—
	$1,320,000	$625,000
Accounts and other payables	$ 360,000	$250,000
Long-term liabilities	250,000	230,000
Common shares	50,000	100,000
Retained earnings	660,000	45,000
	$1,320,000	$625,000

Statements of Income and Retained Earnings
Year Ended December 31, 2002

Sales	$2,300,000	$720,000
Other income	100,000	—
	2,400,000	720,000
Expenses	2,100,000	650,000
Net income	300,000	70,000
Dividends	(220,000)	(45,000)
Retained earnings, December 31, 2001	580,000	20,000
Retained earnings, December 31, 2002	$ 660,000	$ 45,000

P4-3

On January 1, 2001, Big Inc. acquired 100% of the outstanding shares of Small Corp. for $5,000,000 cash. On this date, Small had shareholders' equity of $4,000,000, including $2,000,000 in retained earnings. Small had buildings and equipment that had a fair value of $600,000 less than book value, inventory that had a fair value of $150,000 greater than book value, and investments that had a fair value of $900,000 greater than book value.

The balance sheets of the two companies on December 31, 2001 are shown below.

Additional Information:

1. The goodwill on Small's books arose from the purchase of another company several years ago, a company that has since been amalgamated into Small. The goodwill is being amortized at the rate of $50,000 per year. It was assumed to have a fair value of zero on January 1, 2001.

2. Small's plant and equipment has an estimated average remaining life of 10 years from January 1, 2001. The net book value of the plant and equipment was $5,000,000 on that date, after deducting $2,000,000 of accumulated depreciation.

3. On January 1, 2001, Big held inventory of $400,000 that had been purchased from Small. Small had sold the merchandise to Big at a 100% markup over cost.

4. On December 31, 2001, Big held inventory of $500,000 that had been purchased from Small during 2001 at 100% above Small's cost.

5. At the end of 2001, Big owed Small $200,000 for merchandise purchased on account.

6. During 2001, Small sold an investment for $400,000. The investment had cost Small $180,000, and had a fair value of $300,000 on January 1, 2001.

7. Big's retained earnings on December 31, 2001 includes dividend income received from Small. Small declared dividends of $200,000 in 2001.

Wholly-Owned
Subsidiaries:
Reporting
Subsequent to
Acquisition

173

Required:

Prepare a consolidated balance sheet for Big Inc. at December 31, 2001.

Balance Sheet
December 31, 2001

	Big	Small
Cash	$ 1,000,000	$ 300,000
Accounts receivable	1,600,000	400,000
Inventories	2,400,000	700,000
Plant and equipment	21,000,000	7,000,000
Accumulated depreciation	(6,000,000)	(2,500,000)
Goodwill	—	400,000
Long-term investments (cost)	5,000,000	1,600,000
Total assets	$25,000,000	$7,900,000
Accounts payable	$ 3,000,000	$ 500,000
Bonds payable	5,000,000	3,000,000
Common shares	7,000,000	2,000,000
Retained earnings	10,000,000	2,400,000
	$25,000,000	$7,900,000

P4-4

On January 1, 2001, Parent Ltd. purchased 100% of the outstanding voting common shares of Sub Ltd. for $2,800,000. Any revaluation arising from the purchase of depreciable assets is to be amortized over 10 years and any goodwill created on consolidation is to be amortized over 20 years, straight-line.

During 2001, the following events occurred:

1. No dividends were paid on the shares by either company.

2. Sub Ltd. sold inventory costing $494,000 to Parent Ltd. for $682,000, 30% of which was not sold at year-end.

3. During 2001, all of the current assets that had a fair market value greater than book value were sold to outside parties or were collected.

4. On July 1, 2001, Parent Ltd. purchased 60% of the outstanding 10% bonds payable of Sub Ltd. for $129,000. These bonds have a 20-year total life with 15 years remaining at January 1, 2001.

5. Parent Ltd. has made no entries in the Investment in Sub Ltd. account following the acquisition.

Condensed trial balance information for Sub Ltd. and Parent Ltd. is shown below.

Required:

Prepare a consolidated statement of income and retained earnings and a consolidated balance sheet for Parent Ltd. for the year ended December 31, 2001.

[CGA–Canada, adapted]

Sub Limited

	Post-closing trial balance January 1, 2001	Fair market value January 1, 2001	Pre-closing trial balance December 21, 2001
Cash	$ 185,000	$185,000	$ 135,000
Accounts receivable, net	432,000	450,000	385,000
Inventory	680,000	730,000	730,000
Land	510,000	570,000	510,000
Buildings & equipment, net	974,000	850,000	963,000
Goodwill	120,000	0	110,000
	$2,901,000		$2,833,000
Current liabilities	$ 320,000	$320,000	$ 310,000
Bonds payable,10%	215,000	215,000	215,000
Common shares	400,000	—	400,000
Retained earnings	1,966,000	—	1,966,000
Sales	—	—	1,430,000
Cost of goods sold	—	—	(867,000)
Depreciation	—	—	(11,000)
Other expenses	—	—	(588,500)
Bond interest expense	—	—	(21,500)
	$2,901,000		$2,833,000

Parent Ltd.
Pre-closing Trial Balance
December 31, 2001

Cash	$ 275,000
Accounts receivable, net	384,000
Marketable securities *	129,000
Inventory	860,000
Land	730,000
Buildings & equipment, net	862,000
Goodwill **	140,000
Investment in Sub Ltd.	2,800,000
	$6,180,000
Current liabilities	$ 395,000
Bonds payable	685,000
Common shares	1,100,000
Retained earnings	3,757,000
Sales	1,930,000
Cost of goods sold	(1,463,000)
Depreciation	(27,000)
Other expenses	(203,450)
Bond interest income	6,450
	$6,180,000

* Bonds of Sub Ltd.
** Not related to Sub Ltd.

Wholly-Owned
Subsidiaries:
Reporting
Subsequent to
Acquisition

175

P4-5

Parent Ltd. acquired 100% of the voting shares of Sub Ltd. on January 1, 2001, for $1,255,000. The financial statement of Sub Ltd. on the date of acquisition was as follows:

Sub Ltd.
Balance Sheet
January 1, 2001

	Book value	Fair Market value
Cash	$ 40,000	$ 40,000
Accounts receivable	110,000	130,000
Inventory	280,000	320,000
Land	310,000	400,000
Depreciable capital assets, net	460,000	495,000
Total	$1,200,000	
Current liabilities	$ 250,000	250,000
Common shares	400,000	—
Retained earnings	550,000	—
Total	$1,200,000	

The inventory will be sold and the accounts receivable collected within seven months, and the depreciable capital assets will be depreciated over 10 years, straight-line, with no salvage value. Any goodwill arising on consolidation will be amortized over 20 years, straight-line.

During 2001, Sub Ltd. sold inventory to Parent Ltd. for $150,000 with a 20% markup on retail. At the end of 2001, $30,000 (at retail) of these goods were still in the inventory. Parent Ltd. sold $200,000 of goods to Sub Ltd. during 2001, with a 25% markup on retail, and $40,000 (at retail) of these were still in inventory at the end of 2001. All of these goods remaining in inventory were sold during 2002.

During 2002, Parent Ltd. sold $180,000 of goods to Sub Ltd. with a 25% markup on retail, and $50,000 (at retail) of these goods were in inventory at the end of 2002. In addition, Sub Ltd. sold goods to Parent Ltd. for $220,000 with a 20% markup on retail, and $60,000 (at retail) of these were still in inventory at the end of 2002. All of these remaining goods were sold during 2003.

The following are the financial statements of the two companies at December 31, 2002:

Balance Sheets
December 31, 2002

	Parent Ltd.	Sub Ltd.
Cash	$ 55,000	$ 40,000
Accounts receivable	140,000	110,000
Inventory	400,000	320,000
Land	670,000	385,000
Depreciable capital assets, net	864,000	520,000
Investment in Sub Ltd.	1,255,000	—
Total	$3,384,000	$1,375,000
Current liabilities	$ 248,000	$ 180,000
Common shares	1,136,000	400,000
Retained earnings	2,000,000	795,000
Total	$3,384,000	$1,375,000

Income Statements
For the Year Ended December 31, 2002

	Parent Ltd.	Sub Ltd.
Sales	$900,000	$845,000
Cost of goods sold	542,000	479,000
Depreciation	120,000	110,000
Other expenses	128,000	126,000
	790,000	715,000
Net income	$110,000	$130,000

Neither company paid any dividends during 2001 or 2002.

Required:

Calculate the following, considering all dates carefully:

1. Consolidated goodwill at December 31, 2002.

2. Investment income, under the equity method, for 2001.

3. Consolidated net income for 2002.

4. Consolidated balance of accounts receivable at December 31, 2002.

5. Consolidated balance of depreciable capital assets at December 31, 2002.

6. Consolidated balance of inventory at December 31, 2002.

[CGA–Canada, adapted]

P4-6

On January 4, 2001, Practical Corp. acquired 100% of the outstanding common shares of Silly Inc. by a share-for-share exchange of its own shares valued at $1,000,000 (**P3-8**). The balance sheets of both companies just prior to the share exchange are shown below. Silly had patents not shown on the balance sheet, but that had an estimated fair value of $200,000 and an estimated remaining productive life of four years. Silly's buildings and equipment had an estimated fair value $300,000 in excess of book value, and the deferred charges were assumed to have a fair value of zero. Silly's building and equipment are being depreciated on the straight-line basis and have a remaining useful life of 10 years. The deferred charges are being amortized over three years. Any goodwill arising from the combination is to be amortized over 20 years.

Wholly-Owned
Subsidiaries:
Reporting
Subsequent to
Acquisition

177

Balance Sheets
December 31, 2000

	Practical	Silly
Cash	$ 110,000	$ 85,000
Accounts and other receivables	140,000	80,000
Inventories	110,000	55,000
Buildings and equipment	1,500,000	800,000
Accumulated depreciation	(700,000)	(400,000)
Deferred charges	—	120,000
	$1,160,000	$740,000
Accounts and other payables	$ 200,000	$100,000
Bonds payable	—	200,000
Future income taxes	60,000	40,000
Common shares*	600,000	150,000
Retained earnings	300,000	250,000
	$1,160,000	$740,000

*Practical = 300,000 shares; Silly = 150,000 shares.

During 2001, the year following the acquisition, Silly borrowed $100,000 from Practical; $40,000 was repaid and $60,000 is still outstanding at year-end. No interest is being charged on the loan. Through the year, Silly sold goods to Practical totalling $400,000. Silly's gross margin is 40% of selling price, and its tax rate is 25%. Three-quarters of these goods were resold by Practical to its customers for $450,000. Dividend declarations amounted to $80,000 by Practical and $50,000 by Silly. There were no other intercompany transactions. The year-end 2001 balance sheets and income statements for Practical and Silly are shown below.

Required:

a. How would the income statement and balance sheet for Practical Corp. differ from those shown below if Practical reported its investment in Silly on the equity basis? Show all calculations.

b. Prepare a complete set of consolidated financial statements for Practical Corp. for 2001.

Balance Sheets
December 31, 2001

	Practical	Silly
Cash	$ 50,000	$ 25,000
Accounts and other receivables	240,000	90,000
Inventories	150,000	80,000
Buildings and equipment	1,300,000	900,000
Accumulated depreciation	(570,000)	(445,000)
Land	—	60,000
Investment in Silly (at cost)	1,000,000	—
Other investments	70,000	30,000
Deferred charges	—	80,000
	$2,240,000	$820,000
Accounts and other payables	$ 150,000	$180,000
Bonds payable	—	170,000
Future income taxes	70,000	45,000
Common shares	1,600,000	150,000
Retained earnings	420,000	275,000
	$2,240,000	$820,000

Statements of Income and Retained Earnings
Years Ended December 31, 2001

	Practical	Silly
Sales	$1,500,000	$900,000
Dividend income	50,000	—
	1,550,000	900,000
Cost of sales	1,000,000	540,000
Depreciation expense	70,000	45,000
Amortization expense	—	40,000
Income tax expense	50,000	25,000
Other expenses	230,000	175,000
	1,350,000	825,000
Net income	200,000	75,000
Retained earnings, December 31, 2000	300,000	250,000
Dividends declared	(80,000)	(50,000)
Retained earnings, December 31, 2001	$ 420,000	$275,000

P4-7

Refer to **P4-6**. During 2002, the following events occurred:

1. Silly Inc. had sales of $800,000 to Practical Corp. Silly's gross margin was still 40% of selling price, and its income tax rate continued to be 25%. At year-end, $120,000 of these goods were still in Practical's inventory.

2. On October 1, 2002, Silly sold its land to Practical for $185,000 (on which income taxes were due for $20,000). Practical paid Silly $85,000 and gave a promissory note for $100,000 that was due in three years at 10% interest per year, simple interest to be paid at maturity.

3. $60,000 that Silly owed to Practical at the beginning of the year was repaid during 2002.

4. Practical paid dividends of $100,000 during the year; Silly paid dividends of $70,000.

The pre-closing trial balances of Practical and Silly at December 31, 2002 are shown below.

Required:

a. Determine Practical Corp.'s equity in the earnings of Silly Inc. for 2002. Determine the balance of the Investment in Silly account on Practical's books at December 31, 2002, assuming that Practical recorded its investment on the equity basis.

b. Prepare a comparative consolidated balance sheet and income statement for Practical Corp. for 2002.

Wholly-Owned
Subsidiaries:
Reporting
Subsequent to
Acquisition

179

Trial Balances
December 31, 2002

	Practical	Silly
Cash	$ 55,500	$ 45,000
Accounts and other receivables	160,000	116,000
Inventories	140,000	75,000
Buildings and equipment	1,700,000	900,000
Accumulated depreciation	(655,000)	(495,000)
Land	185,000	—
Investment in Silly	1,000,000	—
Due from Practical	—	102,500
Other investments	100,000	50,000
Deferred charges	—	40,000
Accounts and other payables	(225,000)	(215,000)
Payable to Silly	(102,500)	—
Future income taxes	(75,000)	(47,500)
Common shares	(1,800,000)	(150,000)
Retained earnings	(420,000)	(275,000)
Dividends paid	100,000	70,000
Sales	(1,680,000)	(1,200,000)
Cost of sales	1,120,000	720,000
Depreciation expense	85,000	50,000
Amortization expense	—	40,000
Income tax expense	31,000	57,000
Other expenses	351,000	244,500
Gain on sale of land	—	(125,000)
Other income	(70,000)	(2,500)
	$ 0	$ 0

P4-8

On July 1, 2001, Parent Ltd. paid $3,620,000 to acquire 100% of the common shares of Sub Ltd., which had a balance sheet at that date as follows:

Sub Ltd.
Balance Sheet
July 1, 2001

	Net book value	Fair market value
Cash	$ 300,000	$ 300,000
Accounts receivable	335,000	350,000
Inventory	575,000	532,000
Capital assets, net	1,765,000	2,090,000
Goodwill	210,000	—
	$3,185,000	
Current liabilities	$ 150,000	$ 170,000
Preferred shares (Note 1)	500,000	—
Contributed surplus preferred share-issue	200,000	—
Common shares (Note 2)	750,000	—
Retained earnings to January 1, 2001	1,450,000	—
Net income, January 1 to July 1	135,000	—
	$3,185,000	

Parent Ltd. and Sub Ltd. have a year-end of December 31.

Notes:

1. Preferred shares: 500,000 authorized, 100,000 issued with $5 stated value, cumulative, redemption price $6 per share, $1 per year dividend paid June 30 and January 1, non-voting. No dividends were paid in 1999, 2000, and 2001 on the preferred shares.

2. Common shares: 2,000,000 authorized, 1,000,000 issued with no par and no stated value. No dividends were paid in 1999, 2000, and 2001 on the common shares.

Required:

Calculate the consolidated goodwill that would be created on the purchase of the common shares of the subsidiary by Parent Ltd.

[CGA–Canada]

P4-9

On January 1, 2000, Parent Ltd. purchased 100% of the shares of Sub Ltd. for $1,085,000. At that time Sub Ltd. had the following balance sheet:

Sub Ltd.
Balance Sheet
January 1, 2000

	Net book value	Fair value
Cash	$ 60,000	$ 60,000
Accounts receivable	120,000	150,000
Inventory—FIFO	180,000	230,000
Capital assets, net	1,500,000	1,350,000
Goodwill	100,000	—
	$1,960,000	
Current liabilities	$ 140,000	140,000
Bonds payable (Note)	800,000	850,000
Common shares	400,000	—
Retained earnings	620,000	—
	$1,960,000	

Wholly-Owned
Subsidiaries:
Reporting
Subsequent to
Acquisition

181

The bonds were issued at par and will mature in 10 years. Sub Ltd. has a receivables and inventory turnover of greater than six times per year. The capital assets have an average of 10 years of remaining life and are being amortized straight-line. The subsidiary's goodwill has 10 years remaining on the amortization period. Any goodwill on consolidation will be amortized on a straight-line basis over 20 years.

In 2000, Sub Ltd. sold inventory to Parent Ltd. for $260,000; the inventory had cost $320,000. At the end of 2000, 25% was still in Parent's inventory but was all sold in 2001.

In 2001, Parent Ltd. sold inventory to Sub Ltd. for $275,000; the inventory had cost $200,000. At the end of 2001, 35% was left in Sub's inventory.

During 2000, the subsidiary earned $875,000 and paid dividends of $50,000. During 2001, the subsidiary incurred a loss of $180,000 and paid dividends of $60,000.

The parent company uses the cost method for the investment in subsidiary and nets almost everything to "Other expenses."

At December 31, 2001, the following financial statements were available:

Balance Sheet
December 31, 2001

	Parent Ltd.	Sub Ltd.
Cash	$ 290,000	$ 75,000
Accounts receivable	850,000	179,000
Inventory	970,000	245,000
Capital assets, net	2,631,000	1,863,000
Goodwill	0	92,000
Investment in Sub Ltd.	1,085,000	0
	$5,826,000	$2,454,000
Current liabilities	$ 450,000	$ 49,000
Bonds payable	0	800,000
Common shares	1,000,000	400,000
Retained earnings	3,026,000	1,385,000
Net income (loss)	1,350,000	(180,000)
	$5,826,000	$2,454,000

Income Statement
Year Ended December 31, 2001

	Parent Ltd.	Sub Ltd.
Sales	$9,865,000	$1,650,000
Cost of sales	8,040,000	1,140,000
Gross profit	1,825,000	510,000
Depreciation	(106,000)	(104,000)
Other expenses	(369,000)	(816,000)
Gain on sale of building	0	230,000
Net income	$1,350,000	$ (180,000)

Required:

a. Prepare a consolidated income statement for 2001.

b. Calculate the amounts that would appear on the consolidated balance sheet at December 31, 2001 for:

(1) Goodwill

(2) Capital assets, net

(3) Bonds payable

[CGA–Canada]

Consolidation of Non-Wholly-Owned Subsidiaries

Introduction

The previous two chapters dealt with the preparation of consolidated statements when the parent company owns 100% of the shares of the subsidiary. Most subsidiaries are wholly owned because they were initially formed by the parent corporation in order to facilitate the conduct of some aspect of the parent's business. As well, acquiring companies usually buy 100% of purchased subsidiaries acquired in a business combination.

Nevertheless, a parent's ownership interest may be less than 100% for either of two reasons:

- in a business combination, the acquiring company (the parent) may buy a majority of the shares, but less than 100%, or

- a parent may form a new subsidiary with the involvement of a non-controlling partner who is providing specialized expertise, management ability, market access, governmental support, etc.

Some parent corporations prefer to purchase significantly less than 100% of the shares in a business combination. The parent then need not invest the full value of the subsidiary's net assets. A less-than-100% investment conserves the parent's liquid resources (if the purchase was for cash) or reduces its share dilution (if the purchase was an exchange of shares). In addition, the maintenance of a significant non-controlling interest in the subsidiary can spread the ownership risk, can provide valuable links with other corporate shareholders, and can maintain a market for the subsidiary's shares.

Non-controlling interests may also exist if the parent initially establishes the subsidiary, but subsequently sells shares in the subsidiary to others. The sale may be of shares originally owned by the parent (i.e., a secondary offering by the parent) or may be of new shares (i.e., a direct or primary offering by the subsidiary). In either case, the parent ends up holding less than 100% of the subsidiary. Subsequent changes in ownership interest will be discussed in Chapter 7.

Conceptual Alternatives

As is the case with most aspects of accounting, there is no single approach to accounting for subsidiaries when a non-controlling interest exists. Conceptually, there is more than one treatment of the non-controlling shareholders' share of the subsidiary's net assets. Two questions arise:

1. Should the non-controlling interest's share of net assets be included in the consolidated balance sheet?

2. If included, should they be shown at their book value on the subsidiary's books or at their fair value as of the date of acquisition?

The answers to these two questions are, to some extent, dependent upon the basic theory of consolidation that is applied to business combinations, as we discussed in Chapter 3. For example, the pooling-of-interests approach assumes that two previously independent businesses combine on equal terms and both carry on jointly and equally. It would be mechanically possible to exclude the non-controlling interest's share of assets from the consolidated balance sheet. But excluding the non-controlling interest's share is inconsistent with the underlying philosophy of the pooling approach, which is that the two companies are combining to jointly and equally carry on the previously separate businesses.

Similarly, the new-entity approach to consolidations would seem to call for inclusion of the non-controlling interest at fair value. To exclude the non-controlling interest or to include it at book value is inconsistent with the underlying conceptual basis of the new-entity method, which is that the newly combined entity is getting a "fresh start" and revaluing all of its assets and liabilities at fair value.

The widest choice of approaches to non-controlling interest exists under the fair-value purchase method. Three alternatives exist:

1. Include only the parent's share of the fair value of the subsidiary's assets and liabilities, and revenues and expenses (excluding the non-controlling interest entirely). This is known as the **proportionate consolidation approach**.

2. Include the parent's share of the fair values of the subsidiary's assets and liabilities, plus the book value of the non-controlling interest's share. This approach is most commonly called the **parent-company approach**. The consolidated income statement would include 100% of the subsidiary's revenues and expenses.

3. Include 100% of the fair value of the subsidiary's assets and liabilities, and 100% of all revenues and expenses. This is usually called the **entity** method, but should not be confused with the new-entity approach to consolidations that was discussed in Chapter 3.

If we include all of the subsidiary's net assets in the parent company's consolidated balance sheet (using either the entity or the parent-company approaches), the combined net assets will exceed the parent's investment in the subsidiary. Therefore, we must balance the *non-controlling interest's* share of assets and liabilities with an amount for non-controlling interest on the liabilities/equity side of the parent company's consolidated balance sheet.

Similarly, if we include 100% of the subsidiary's revenues and expenses in the consolidated income statement, the result will be the combined earnings attributable to *both* the parent's shareholders and the non-controlling interest in the subsidiary. The consolidated statements are reports to the parent's shareholders, not to the outside shareholders in the subsidiary. Therefore, we must subtract the non-controlling interest's share of the earnings of the subsidiary in order to determine the net income attibutable to the parent corporation's shareholders.

Exhibit 5-1 summarizes the alternative approaches to the treatment of the non-controlling interest's share of net assets under each of the three methods of consolidation. As described above, exclusion of the non-controlling interest is

EXHIBIT 5–1 ALTERNATIVE APPROACHES TO REPORTING NON-CONTROLLING INTEREST (NCI)

Consolidation method	Include NCI net assets?	Book value or fair value?	Name of approach
1. Pooling of interest	yes	Book value	Pooling
2. Fair value purchase	**a.** no	—	Proportionate consolidation
	b. yes	Book value	Parent company
	c. yes	Fair value	Entity
3. New entity	yes	Fair value	Entity

known as *proportionate consolidation*, inclusion at book value is known as the *parent-company approach*, and inclusion at fair value is known as the *entity approach*. An exception to this terminology is that under the pooling-of-interests approach, the treatment of non-controlling interest in the subsidiary's net assets is part of the overall concept and approach to pooling, and the "parent company" label is not appropriate under pooling.

As we pointed out in Chapter 2, the general term for shareholdings that do not enable the shareholder to control the enterprise is "non-controlling interests," which is the term used in Section 1590 of the *CICA Handbook*. In the vast majority of cases, the non-controlling interest will in fact be a *minority interest*, i.e., less than 50%. Many corporations continue to use the term "minority interests" in their financial statements rather than the more general term. The reader must be aware that minority interests is a narrower category of non-controlling interests, just as depreciation is a specific form of amortization.

Illustration of the alternative approaches

In order to clarify the conceptual issues underlying the three different approaches to non-controlling interest, we will apply the three alternatives to a simple example. The example uses the same facts as the illustration in Chapter 3, except that less than 100% of the shares are purchased.

Assume that instead of buying 100%, Purchase buys only 70% of the outstanding shares of Target on December 31, 2001, giving 28,000 Purchase shares in exchange. If we assume that the market value of Purchase's shares is $30 per share, then the total cost of the acquisition is $840,000. The post-acquisition balance sheets of Purchase and Target, and the fair values of Target's assets and liabilities, are shown in Exhibit 5-2.

Exhibit 5-3 shows the allocation of the purchase price and derivation of the goodwill. Note that in this case, the goodwill is 70% of the goodwill of $100,000 that resulted from Purchase's 100% purchase of Target in Chapter 3. Note also that the nature of the calculations in Exhibit 5-3 is exactly the same as in Chapters 3 and 4 (Exhibit 4-1), except that only 70% of Target's assets and liabilities are included in the analysis instead of 100%.

Exhibit 5-4 shows the Purchase consolidated balance sheet immediately after the business combination, prepared (by the direct approach) under each of the three alternatives, each of which will be discussed in turn.

Proportionate consolidation

The first column of Exhibit 5-4 shows the Purchase consolidated balance sheet as it would appear using the proportionate consolidation approach. Under this

EXHIBIT 5–2 BUSINESS COMBINATION—PURCHASE OF 70% OF TARGET

Post-acquisition asset positions, December 31, 2001

	Balance sheets		Target
	Purchase Ltd.	Target Ltd.	fair values
Cash	$1,000,000	$ 50,000	$ 50,000
Accounts receivable	2,000,000	150,000	150,000
Inventory	200,000	50,000	50,000
Land	1,000,000	300,000	400,000
Buildings and equipment	3,000,000	500,000	550,000
Accumulated depreciation	(1,200,000)	(150,000)	
Investment in Target Ltd.	840,000		
	$6,840,000	$900,000	
Current accounts payable	$1,000,000	$100,000	(100,000)
Long-term notes payable	400,000	—	
Common shares	3,440,000	200,000	
Retained earnings	2,000,000	600,000	
	$6,840,000	$900,000	1,100,000

EXHIBIT 5–3 ALLOCATION OF PURCHASE PRICE

70% Purchase of Target Ltd., December 31, 2001

Purchase price						$840,000
	Book value	Fair value	Fair value increment	% share	FVI acquired	
Cash	$ 50,000	$ 50,000	—			
Accounts receivable	150,000	150,000	—			
Inventory	50,000	50,000	—			
Land	300,000	400,000	$100,000 × 70% =		$ 70,000	
Buildings and equipment	500,000	550,000	50,000 × 70% =		35,000	
Accumulated depreciation	(150,000)	—	150,000 × 70% =		105,000	
Accounts payable	(100,000)	(100,000)	—			
Total fair value increment					210,000	
Net asset book value	$ 800,000			× 70% =	560,000	
Fair value of assets acquired						770,000
Goodwill						70,000

approach, the Purchase balance sheet includes only Purchase's share of Target's assets and liabilities. Since Purchase does *not* own the remaining 30% of the Target shares, the assets and liabilities that are represented by the *non-owned* shares are *excluded* from Purchase's consolidated statements. The investment account balance of $840,000 is disaggregated and the purchased portion (i.e., 70%) of the fair values is distributed to the appropriate assets and liabilities and to goodwill.

The proportionate consolidation approach takes the view that the only subsidiary assets and liabilities that should be shown on the parent's balance sheet are

EXHIBIT 5–4 ALTERNATIVE ACCOUNTING APPROACHES FOR NON-CONTROLLING INTEREST

Purchase Ltd. Acquires 70% of Target Ltd.
Purchase Ltd. Post-Acquisition Consolidated Balance Sheets
December 31, 2001

	(1) Proportionate consolidation	(2) Parent company	(3) Entity
Assets			
Cash	$1,035,000	$1,050,000	$1,050,000
Accounts receivable	2,105,000	2,150,000	2,150,000
Inventory	235,000	250,000	250,000
Land	1,280,000	1,370,000	1,400,000
Buildings and equipment	3,385,000	3,490,000	3,550,000
Accumulated depreciation	(1,200,000)	(1,200,000)	(1,200,000)
Goodwill	70,000	70,000	100,000
Total assets	$6,910,000	$7,180,000	$7,300,000
Liabilities			
Accounts payable	$1,070,000	$1,100,000	$1,100,000
Long-term notes payable	400,000	400,000	400,000
	1,470,000	1,500,000	1,500,000
Non-controlling interest	—	240,000	360,000
Shareholders' equity			
Common shares	3,440,000	3,440,000	3,440,000
Retained earnings	2,000,000	2,000,000	2,000,000
	5,440,000	5,440,000	5,440,000
Total liabilities and shareholders' equity	$6,910,000	$7,180,000	$7,300,000

those in which the shareholders of the parent have an ownership interest. Because of the strict identification of consolidated assets and liabilities as only those owned by parent shareholders, this approach is also called the **proprietary** method. However, in this text we prefer to avoid using that label because of possible confusion with the proprietary theory of accounting, in which the accounting is performed from the point of view of the residual common shareholders. The proprietary theory of accounting underlies virtually all private enterprise accounting, including the alternative methods of accounting for non-controlling interest, and thus we prefer not to use the term to describe a particular method of consolidation.

The problem with the proportionate consolidation approach for subsidiaries is that it focuses on *ownership* interest rather than on *control*. When a parent controls a subsidiary, the parent controls *all* of the net assets of the subsidiary, not just the proportion represented by the parent's ownership interest. Users of proportionately consolidated statements are not given a complete picture of the resources, obligations, and revenue-generating activities of the combined entity. They have no way of compensating for the deficiency, unless they also are given separate-entity financial statements for the subsidiary, thus enabling them to fill in the missing information. As a result, proportionate consolidation has not been accepted in practice for accounting for controlled subsidiaries.

However, proportionate consolidation presently is the prescribed method in Canada for reporting investments in *joint ventures*. **Joint ventures**, as we noted in Chapter 2, are business ventures entered into by two or more co-venturers to be operating jointly. In a joint venture, no one investor or co-venturer has control over the activities of the venture. Instead, all of the co-venturers must agree on any course of action.

Consolidation normally is based on the concept of *control*; that is, that the reporting entity can control the assets and liabilities of the investee corporation *without the co-operation of others* and can determine the strategic policies of the investee. In contrast, the very nature of a joint venture is that no investor can unilaterally determine the strategic direction or operating policies of a joint venture. Co-operation of the other investors is absolutely essential in a joint venture.

Canada is out of step with the rest of the world. Canada is the *only* country that requires proportionate consolidation for joint ventures. In contrast, international standards call for use of the equity method only. A 1999 international study on joint venture accounting argues that "the conceptual basis for the proportionate consolidation of joint ventures is weak" because the method requires recognition of portions of assets and liabilities that are not under the control of the co-venturer. The study concludes that:

> The equity method of accounting is the most appropriate method for presenting an interest in a joint venture enterprise in the financial statements of the venturer.[1]

There is strong pressure for Canada to harmonize its accounting standards with those of other countries, and therefore it is quite likely that we will see the AcSB propose a change in joint venture accounting in the future.

Parent-company approach

The second column of Exhibit 5-4 shows the Purchase consolidated balance sheet under the parent-company approach. In this approach, *all* of Target's assets and liabilities are reflected in Purchase's consolidated statements in recognition of the fact that Purchase controls all of the Target assets.

The parent-company approach is a strict application of the historical cost basis of accounting. The Parent consolidated assets include:

1. the historical cost of Parent's separate entity assets,

2. the historical cost to Purchase of Purchase's share of Target assets (i.e., the purchase price of Target shares acquired), and

3. the historical cost to *Target* of the 30% portion of the net assets *not* acquired by Purchase.

Since the non-controlling share of net assets has been included, it is necessary to balance these net assets with the amount of Target shareholders' equity that relates to the non-controlling interest (in this example, a minority interest). The consolidated balance sheet includes the 30% of the book value of the Target net assets that relates to minority interest, and therefore the offset is 30% of the Target unconsolidated shareholders' equity (or net assets), which is $240,000.

---

1. J. Alex Milburn and Peter D. Chant, *Reporting Interests in Joint Ventures and Similar Arrangements*, (Financial Accounting Standards Board, 1999), p. 25. This was a G4+1 study for the accounting standards boards of Australia, Canada, New Zealand, the U.K., and the U.S.A., plus the International Accounting Standards Committee.

The parent-company approach can be criticized because it results in the anomaly that the same assets (of Target) are reported on two different bases: fair value for the parent's percentage of each asset, and book value for the percentage of each asset that relates to non-controlling interest. If one of the purposes of consolidated statements is to give the user a view of the total resources controlled by the parent, then it is difficult to rationalize the parent-company approach; Purchase controls the fair value of 100% of Target's assets, not just 70%. Nevertheless, the parent-company approach is the approach recommended in the *CICA Handbook* [CICA 1600.15]. It also is the method in general use around the world.

Entity approach

The third column of Exhibit 5-4 shows the Purchase consolidated balance sheet as it would appear if the entity approach to non-controlling interest were used. The entity approach includes the full fair value of Target's assets and liabilities in the Purchase consolidated balance sheet, rather than just the fair value increments that relate to Purchase's 70% share.

The total fair value of Target's identifiable net assets is $1,100,000, as is shown in Exhibit 5-2. The total amount of Purchase's identifiable net assets is increased by that amount upon consolidation. In addition, Purchase paid $70,000 for goodwill; therefore the total Target goodwill, based on the price that Purchase paid for its 70% interest, could be calculated at $100,000. Since 30% of the goodwill pertains to the Target minority shareholders, minority interest is shown as $360,000, that is: $(30\% \times \$1,100,000) + (30\% \times \$100,000)$.

The assignment of goodwill to the minority shareholders' interest can be defended since if 70% of Target is worth $840,000, then 30% must be worth 3/7 of that amount, or $360,000. Securities laws give some support to this approach because when there has been a block purchase of shares in certain publicly traded companies,[2] an offer to buy non-controlling shareholders' shares must be at least as attractive as the price paid for the majority shares.

However, an acquiring company may be willing to pay a bonus in order to gain control, and it may be *control* of the assets that gives rise to goodwill, not just a non-controlling interest in the assets. That control gives rise to goodwill is evidenced by the fact that many tender offers or takeover bids propose a high price, but offer to buy only enough of the outstanding shares (e.g., 51%) to gain control.

Therefore, a modification of the entity approach provides that only the goodwill actually purchased by the parent is shown on the consolidated balance sheet—no goodwill would be assigned to the non-controlling interest. In that case, the last column of Exhibit 5-4 would differ in two respects: (1) the amount shown for goodwill would be $70,000, and (2) the amount for non-controlling interest would be only $330,000, or 30% of the fair value of Target's identifiable net assets. This approach is called the **parent-company extension approach**.

It should be noted that the *entity* approach to non-controlling interests is consistent with, but not the same as, the *new-entity* approach to consolidated financial statements discussed in Chapter 3. The two should not be mixed up:

- **new entity** is an approach to consolidation that involves the reporting of fair values for the parent's assets and liabilities;

- **entity** is an approach to accounting for the non-controlling interest of non-wholly-owned subsidiaries at fair values.

---

2. For example, those covered by the *Ontario Securities Act* (section 91).

Since the recommended approach for accounting for non-controlling interests around the world is essentially the parent-company approach to the fair-value purchase method, we use that approach in all of the following consolidation illustrations.

Consolidation under the entity approach is very similar; the only difference is that the consolidated assets and liabilities and the non-controlling interest will include the non-controlling interest's share of the subsidiary's fair value increments. Amortization of the non-controlling interest's fair value increments is charged against non-controlling interest on the consolidated balance sheet.

Summary of consolidation approaches

When a business combination occurs, there are two main variables to the consolidation approach: (1) the valuation of the acquired company's net assets, and (2) the valuation of the acquiring company's net assets. The existence of a non-controlling interest introduces a third variable, the valuation of the non-controlling interest's share of the net assets. We can summarize the variables as follows:

1. Valuation of the acquiring company's net assets:
   a. Book value
   b. Fair value

2. Valuation of the parent's acquired (controlling) share in the subsidiary's net assets:
   a. Book value
   b. Fair value

3. Valuation of the non-controlling interest's share of the subsidiary's net assets:
   a. Book value
   b. Fair value
   c. Exclude

Mathematically, there are 12 possible combinations of these alternatives. But as we have already seen, only five are viable, as shown in the last column of Exhibit 5-1.

If 100% of the shares are purchased, the third variable disappears, which leaves four theoretical but three practical alternatives. These are the three alternatives in the first column of Exhibit 5-1.

If a subsidiary was founded by the parent corporation rather than acquired in a business combination, then matters are simplified even further. There is no valuation variable for either the parent or the controlling share of the subsidiary. The only variable is whether to include or exclude the book value of the non-controlling interest's share of net assets.

Consolidation at Date of Acquisition

Direct method

The Purchase consolidated balance sheet at date of acquisition (December 31, 2001—parent company approach) is illustrated in the second column of Exhibit 5-4. In order to clarify the procedure, the process of consolidation is presented in Exhibit 5-5, using two different methods of using the direct approach.

Purchase Ltd. Acquires 70% of Target Ltd.
(Direct Approaches)

Approach A

	Purchase Ltd. unconsolidated net assets	+	Target Ltd. 70% of fair value	+	30% of book value	=	Purchase Ltd. consolidated net assets
Cash	$ 1,000,000		$ 35,000		$ 15,000		$ 1,050,000
Accounts receivable	2,000,000		105,000		45,000		2,150,000
Inventory	200,000		35,000		15,000		250,000
Land	1,000,000		280,000		90,000		1,370,000
Buildings and equipment	3,000,000		385,000		105,000		3,490,000
Accumulated depreciation	(1,200,000)						(1,200,000)
Goodwill			70,000				70,000
Accounts payable	(1,000,000)		(70,000)		(30,000)		(1,100,000)
Long-term notes payable	(400,000)						(400,000)
Non-controlling interest in Target Ltd.					$240,000		(240,000)
Purchase Ltd. net assets	$ 4,600,000		$ 840,000				$ 5,440,000

Approach B

	Purchase Ltd. unconsolidated net assets	+	Target Ltd. net assets 100% of book value	+	70% of FVI	=	Purchase Ltd. consolidated net assets
Cash	$ 1,000,000		$ 50,000				$ 1,050,000
Accounts receivable	2,000,000		150,000				2,150,000
Inventory	200,000		50,000				250,000
Land	1,000,000		300,000		$ 70,000		1,370,000
Buildings and equipment	3,000,000		350,000		140,000		3,490,000
Accumulated depreciation	(1,200,000)						(1,200,000)
Goodwill					70,000		70,000
Accounts payable	(1,000,000)		(100,000)				(1,100,000)
Long-term notes payable	(400,000)						(400,000)
Non-controlling interest in Target Ltd.			(240,000)				(240,000)
Purchase Ltd. net assets	$ 4,600,000		$ 560,000		$280,000		$5,440,000

In Approach A, we can directly obtain the consolidated amount for the assets and liabilities by starting with Purchase's book values and adding 70% of the fair values and 30% of the book values for Target's assets and liabilities. The sum of the amounts in the 30% book value column represents the minority interest, which is extended into the consolidated column. The resultant consolidated net asset balance of $5,440,000 is balanced by Purchase's shareholders' equity: $3,440,000 in common shares and $2,000,000 in retained earnings. Thus the consolidated balance sheet can be prepared from the figures in the last column, plus Purchase's shareholders' equity account balances.

When calculating the consolidated amount of buildings and equipment in Exhibit 5-4, Purchase's accumulated depreciation is carried forward. The accumulated depreciation for Target, however, is netted against the asset account and only the net book value is carried forward. Therefore, the consolidated accumulated depreciation at the date of acquisition is only the amount relating to Purchase's own assets. In future periods, the consolidated accumulated depreciation will include both depreciation on Purchase's own assets plus depreciation on Target's assets *since the date of acquisition* only, including amortization of the fair value increments.

Approach A is a literal representation of the derivation of the consolidated assets and liabilities at the date of acquisition. Target's assets and liabilities are consolidated at 70% of their fair values plus 30% of their book values. A somewhat different approach that yields the same result is presented as Approach B in Exhibit 5-5. In this approach, the Target assets are consolidated at 100% of book value plus the *fair value increment* relating to the 70% of the net assets acquired. Since the net assets' fair value is equivalent to the book value plus the fair value increment, the two approaches are mathematically equivalent. If **BV** denotes book value, and **FV** denotes fair value:

$$70\% \text{ FV} + 30\% \text{ BV} = 70\% \text{ [BV} + (\text{FV} - \text{BV})] + 30\% \text{ BV}$$
$$= (70\% + 30\%) \text{ BV} + 70\% (\text{FV} - \text{BV})$$
$$= 100\% \text{ of book value} + 70\% \text{ of fair value increments}$$

The minority interest, calculated at 30% of Target's net book value, is included in the second column of Approach B as a credit. The sum of the second and third columns is $840,000, which is the purchase price paid by Purchase for 70% of Target's shares. The sums of each of these two columns can be reconciled directly with the analysis of the purchase as was shown in Exhibit 5-3.

Since both approaches give the same result, it makes no difference which one is used. Approach B, however, is a more useful way of looking at consolidation subsequent to the date of acquisition, because we can take the total book value of the assets existing at subsequent balance sheet dates without trying to separate the amounts into those existing at the date of acquisition (for fair values) and those acquired thereafter.

Worksheet approach

Exhibit 5-6 illustrates the worksheet that can be used to prepare the balance sheet at the date of acquisition. The consolidated balance sheet is derived by adding together the separate-entity balances for Purchase and Target in the first and second columns, plus and minus the eliminations and adjustments shown in the third column. The eliminations and adjustments pertain to the original acquisition and consist of two components:

1. elimination of Target's shareholders' equity, and

2. adjustment of Target's net assets by the amount of the fair value increment for which Purchase has paid.

In general journal format, the worksheet adjustments are:

a1	Common shares	200,000	
	Retained earnings	600,000	
	Investment in Target Ltd.		560,000
	Non-controlling interest in Target Ltd.		240,000

EXHIBIT 5–6 CONSOLIDATION WORKSHEET AT DATE OF ACQUISITION,
NON-WHOLLY-OWNED SUBSIDIARY

Purchase Ltd. Acquires 70% of Target Ltd., December 31, 2001

	Trial balances		Adjustments	Purchase Ltd.
	Purchase	Target	& eliminations	Consolidated
Cash	$ 1,000,000	$ 50,000		$ 1,050,000
Accounts receivable	2,000,000	150,000		2,150,000
Inventory	200,000	50,000		250,000
Land	1,000,000	300,000	$ 70,000 **a2**	1,370,000
Buildings and equipment	3,000,000	500,000	(10,000) **a2**	3,490,000
Accumulated depreciation	(1,200,000)	(150,000)	150,000 **a2**	(1,200,000)
Investments (at cost)	840,000	—	{ (560,000) **a1** }	—
			{ (280,000) **a2** }	
Goodwill	—	—	70,000 **a2**	70,000
Accounts payable	(1,000,000)	(100,000)		(1,100,000)
Long-term notes payable	(400,000)	—		(400,000)
Non-controlling interest in Target Ltd.			(240,000) **a1**	(240,000)
Common shares	(3,440,000)	(200,000)	200,000 **a1**	(3,440,000)
Retained earnings	(2,000,000)	(600,000)	600,000 **a1**	(2,000,000)
	$ —	$ —	$ —	$ —

a2 Land	70,000	
Accumulated depreciation	150,000	
Goodwill	70,000	
Buildings and equipment		10,000
Investment in Target Ltd.		280,000

Entry **a1** allocates Target's net asset book value of $800,000 to the non-controlling interest (for 30%) and Purchase's controlling interest (to eliminate the investment account). The recording of non-controlling interest is the only substantive difference between the eliminations for wholly-owned subsidiaries and for non-wholly-owned subsidiaries when we consolidate at the date of acquisition.

The credit to buildings and equipment in **a2** for $10,000 is the net result of eliminating Target's accumulated depreciation of $150,000 at the date of acquisition and recording the fair value increment of $140,000. The total impact of the adjustment on the net of buildings and equipment less accumulated depreciation is to increase net buildings and equipment on the balance sheet by $140,000.

Consolidation One Year After Acquisition

Basic information

For the year ended December 31, 2002 (i.e., one year following the business combination), the following occurred:

1. Target's buildings and equipment will be depreciated over 10 years after the date of acquisition, using straight-line depreciation.

2. Purchase Ltd. will amortize goodwill over 20 years.

3. During 2002, Target sold goods of $55,000 to Purchase. Target's gross margin is 40% of sales.

4. On December 31, 2002, $20,000 of the goods acquired by Purchase Ltd. from Target Ltd. are still in Purchase's inventory. Unrealized profit is $20,000 × 40% = $8,000.

5. During 2002, Target Ltd. paid dividends totalling $30,000. Of this amount, 70% (i.e., $21,000) were received by Purchase Ltd. Since Purchase maintains its investment in Target on the cost basis, the dividends were recorded as dividend income.

Direct method

Exhibit 5-7 shows the separate-entity financial statements for 2002. These statements are very similar to those shown in Exhibit 4-2. The only differences are due to two factors:

1. Purchase acquired 70% instead of 100%, and therefore:
   - investment in Target Ltd. is smaller by $360,000 (i.e., $1,200,000 − $840,000), and
   - Purchase's common share account is less by $360,000 due to the lower value of the shares issued in the acquisition.

2. Although Target declared and paid $30,000 in dividends, just as in 2002 in Chapter 4, Purchase received only 70% of Target's dividends. Therefore, Purchase's dividend income, closing retained earnings, and cash balance are all less by 30% × $30,000 = $9,000.

Purchase's 2002 consolidated statement of income and retained earnings and consolidated balance sheet are shown in Exhibit 5-8 (page 197), as prepared by the direct method. As usual, we assume that Purchase Ltd. is using the cost basis of *recording* its investment in Target Ltd.

Many of the adjustments to the combined Purchase + Target amounts are logical extensions of the adjustments already described in Chapter 4. One important new wrinkle is added, however—the appearance of an amount for *non-controlling interest* in the income statement. We will discuss this adjustment in general terms first, and then we will explain the detailed adjustments.

Non-controlling interest in earnings

In every consolidation of a controlled subsidiary, 100% of the subsidiary's revenues and expenses are added to those of the parent. The income statement shows the total combined revenues and expenses for the entire economic entity.

However, if all of the subsidiary's earnings were distributed to the shareholders as dividends, the parent would receive only the proportion relating to its ownership interest in the subsidiary—the remainder would go to the people or institutions that hold the remaining (or non-controlling) shares. Therefore, we say that the non-controlling proportion of earnings **accrues** to the minority or non-controlling interest.

EXHIBIT 5–7 SEPARATE-ENTITY FINANCIAL STATEMENTS FOR 2002

Income Statements
Year Ended December 31, 2002

	Purchase Ltd.	Target Ltd.
Revenue:		
Sales	$2,400,000	$ 300,000
Dividend income	21,000	—
	2,421,000	300,000
Expenses:		
Cost of sales	1,750,000	180,000
Depreciation expense	100,000	35,000
Other operating expenses	250,000	20,000
	2,100,000	235,000
Net income	$ 321,000	$ 65,000
Retained earnings, December 31, 2001	2,000,000	600,000
Dividends declared	—	(30,000)
Retained earnings, December 31, 2002	$2,321,000	$ 635,000

Balance Sheets
December 31, 2002

	Purchase Ltd.	Target Ltd.
Assets		
Current assets:		
Cash	$ 971,000	$ 100,000
Accounts receivable	2,200,000	250,000
Inventory	250,000	70,000
	3,421,000	420,000
Property, plant, and equipment:		
Land	1,000,000	300,000
Buildings and equipment	3,000,000	500,000
Accumulated depreciation	(1,300,000)	(185,000)
	2,700,000	615,000
Other assets:		
Investments (at cost)	840,000	—
Total assets	$6,961,000	$1,035,000
Liabilities and shareholders' equity		
Liabilities:		
Accounts payable	$ 800,000	$ 200,000
Long-term notes payable	400,000	—
	1,200,000	200,000
Shareholders' equity:		
Common shares	3,440,000	200,000
Retained earnings	2,321,000	635,000
	5,761,000	835,000
Total liabilities and shareholders' equity	$6,961,000	$1,035,000

Consolidation of
Non-Wholly-
Owned
Subsidiaries

195

Be careful here—*accrue* in this sense does not mean that the earnings are recorded on anyone's books the way we usually use the word. The term is used simply to indicate that the parent corporation does not have the right to receive the benefits of shares it does not own.

Because all of the revenues and expenses of the subsidiary are included in the parent's consolidated statements, we must deduct the proportion of the subsidiary's net income that accrues to the benefit of the non-controlling shareholders. This amount is an expense from the viewpoint of the parent company's shareholders. Therefore, an amount for *non-controlling interest in subsidiary's earnings* will appear on the consolidated income statement whenever the parent does not own 100% of the shares.[3]

The amount of the deduction for the non-controlling share of earnings is based on the subsidiary's separate-entity net income, *adjusted for unrealized profits*. We will explain the calculation below.

Statement of income and retained earnings

- *Sales.* The upstream intercompany sales of $55,000 are eliminated.

- *Dividend income.* The dividends paid by Target to Purchase are eliminated: $30,000 × 70% = $21,000.

- *Cost of sales.* Cost of sales is reduced by $55,000 to avoid counting the intercompany sales in cost of goods sold twice. However, this elimination is partially offset by the unrealized profit in Purchase's ending inventory: $20,000 × 40% = $8,000.

- *Depreciation expense.* As usual, the FVI for buildings and equipment must be amortized. But the amortization is based on the ownership proportion, which is now 70% of the full FVI of $200,000. The FVI amortization therefore is $140,000 ÷ 10 = $14,000.

- *Other operating expenses.* Goodwill amortization is added: $70,000 ÷ 20 = $3,500.

- *Non-controlling interest in earnings.* Target Ltd. reported separate-entity earnings of $65,000. However, this amount includes the unrealized profit on the upstream inventory that is in Purchase's ending inventory. The unrealized profit is $20,000 × 40% = $8,000. Before calculating the non-controlling interest in Target's earnings, the unrealized profit must be deducted. The non-controlling interest is:

$$30\% \times (\$65,000 - \$8,000) = 30\% \times \$57,000 = \mathbf{\$17,100}$$

Why do the earnings of the non-controlling interest get reduced just because Purchase Ltd. failed to sell all of its inventory? They don't! The deduction for non-controlling interest has nothing to do with the non-controlling interest's real entitlement to the subsidiary's earnings and dividends. The non-controlling shareholders look at the *subsidiary's* financial statement and receive the *subsidiary's* dividends. The calculation of non-controlling interest is only an adjustment to the *parent's* consolidated statements, not to the subsidiary's separate-entity statements. In effect, the reduction in the non-controlling interest deduction (by 30% of the unrealized upstream profit) is to make up for the fact that consolidated cost of sales was adjusted for 100% of the unrealized profit.

---

3. If the amount is immaterial, it may not be separately disclosed but instead may be included in other expenses. If the amount is material, then it should be shown separately.

EXHIBIT 5–8 PURCHASE LTD. CONSOLIDATED FINANCIAL STATEMENTS

[Purchase owns 70% of Target Ltd.—Direct Method]
Statement of Income and Retained Earnings
Year Ended December 31, 2002

Sales revenue [2,400,000 + 300,000 – **55,000**]	$ 2,645,000
Dividend income [21,000 + 0 – **21,000**]	
Operating expenses:	
Cost of sales [1,750,000 + 180,000 – **55,000** + **8,000**]	1,883,000
Depreciation expense [100,000 + 35,000 + **14,000**]	149,000
Goodwill amortization [+ **3,500**]	3,500
Other expenses [250,000 + 20,000]	270,000
Non-controlling interest in earnings of Target Ltd. [(**65,000 – 8,000**) × **30%**]	17,100
	2,322,600
Net income	$ 322,400
Retained earnings, December 31, 2001 [2,000,000 + 600,000 – **600,000**]	2,000,000
Dividends declared [0 + 30,000 – 30,000]	—
Retained earnings, December 31, 2002	$ 2,322,400

Balance Sheet
December 31, 2002

Assets

Current assets:	
Cash [971,000 + 100,000]	$ 1,071,000
Accounts receivable [2,200,000 + 250,000]	2,450,000
Inventory [250,000 + 70,000 – **8,000**]	312,000
	3,833,000
Property, plant, and equipment:	
Land [1,000,000 + 300,000 + **70,000**]	1,370,000
Buildings and equipment [3,000,000 + 500,000 – **10,000**]	3,490,000
Accumulated depreciation [1,300,000 + 185,000 – **150,000** + **14,000**]	(1,349,000)
	3,511,000
Other assets:	
Investments [840,000 + 0 – **840,000**]	—
Goodwill [**70,000** × **19/20**]	66,500
Total assets	$ 7,410,500

Liabilities and shareholders' equity

Liabilities:	
Current accounts payable [800,000 + 200,000]	$ 1,000,000
Long-term notes payable [400,000 + 0]	400,000
	1,400,000
Non-controlling interest in net assets of Target Ltd. [(**835,000 – 8,000**) × **30%**]	248,100
Shareholders' equity:	
Common shares [**Purchase Ltd. shares only**]	3,440,000
Retained earnings [2,321,000 + 635,000 – **600,000** – **10,500**	
– (**8,000** × **70%**) – **14,000** – **3,500**]	2,322,400
	5,762,400
Total liabilities and shareholders' equity	$ 7,410,500

- *Inventory.* Inventory is adjusted for the $8,000 unrealized profit on upstream sales. Notice that the full amount of unrealized profit is eliminated, not just 70%. This is because Purchase controls Target. If only 70% of the unrealized profit were eliminated, Purchase could inflate its consolidated inventory by buying a lot of merchandise from Target and retaining 30% of the unrealized profit in its reported inventory.

- *Land.* The FVI of $70,000 is added (that is, 70% of the full FVI of $100,000).

- *Buildings and equipment.* Buildings and equipment is *reduced* by $10,000 to reflect the fair value at the date of acquisition, as was the case for consolidation at the date of acquisition.

- *Accumulated depreciation.* Target's date-of-acquisition accumulated depreciation is not carried forward on the consolidated balance sheet. The elimination is for the full amount of the date-of-acquisition accumulated depreciation of $150,000. There are two effects to this adjustment:

  - The net date-of-acquisition value assigned to Target's buildings and equipment is increased by $140,000: (1) the elimination of accumulated depreciation, less (2) the decrease in value assigned to the asset account.

  - The amount remaining in Target's accumulated depreciation is only the depreciation taken *since the date of acquisition.*

  In addition, we must add one year's amortization of the FVI: $140,000 ÷ 10 = $14,000.

- *Investment in Target Ltd.* This account is eliminated completely, of course.

- *Goodwill.* As explained previously, goodwill is $70,000, minus one year's amortization of 1/20th of that amount (i.e., $3,500). The remaining unamortized goodwill is $66,500.

- *Non-controlling interest.* The minority interest in Target's net assets is 30%. Net assets must be adjusted for the unrealized upstream inventory profit of $8,000. Target's adjusted net assets at the end of 2002 is $835,000 − $8,000 = $827,000. Thirty percent of the adjusted net assets is $248,100.

- *Common shares.* Only Purchase Ltd.'s shares are included.

- *Retained earnings.* The starting point is to add the end-of-year balances together. Then several adjustments are necessary:

  - Target's retained earnings balance at the date of acquisition ($600,000) is eliminated.

  - The non-controlling interest's share of the change in Target's retained earnings *since the date of acquisition* is subtracted. Target's retained earnings increased by $35,000, from $600,000 at the date of acquisition to $635,000 at the end of 2002. The adjustment is for $35,000 × 30% = $10,500.

  - Purchase's share of the unrealized inventory profit of $8,000 is deducted: $8,000 × 70% = $5,600.

  - Accumulated amortization of fair value increments is deducted. By the end of 2002, there is only one year's amortization, $14,000.

  - Accumulated amortization of goodwill is deducted, $3,500 for one year.

In summary, the year-end 2002 consolidated retained earnings is:

Purchase separate-entity retained earnings	$2,321,000
Target separate-entity retained earnings	635,000
Target's date-of-acquisition retained earnings	−600,000
Non-controlling interest's portion of Target's share equity	−10,500
Purchase share of unrealized upstream profit	−5,600
2002 amortization of FVI on buildings and equipment	−14,000
2002 amortization of goodwill	−3,500
Consolidated retained earnings, December 31, 2002	$2,322,400

Classification of non-controlling interest on the balance sheet

Throughout this book, non-controlling interest will be shown on the balance sheet as a separate item between liabilities and shareholders' equity. This is the treatment recommended by the *CICA Handbook* [CICA 1600.69] as this book goes to press.

In the accounting profession worldwide, there always has been some unease about the presentation of non-controlling interest on the consolidated balance sheet. Theoretically, items on the equities side of the balance should be a part of either creditors' equity (i.e., liabilities) or shareholders' equity. Having an unidentified floating object between liabilities and shareholders' equity seems contrary to the basic concept of the balance sheet.

IAS 27, which deals with consolidated statements, recommends the separate classification of minority (i.e., non-controlling) interests. But some countries, such as Germany and Australia, require minority interest to be shown in the equity section of the consolidated balance sheet. Japan, on the other hand, requires minority interest to be shown at the end of the liabilities section, because "in Japan minority interest is not thought of as capital, but rather as liability."[4] Yet another alternative comes from the U.K.:

> FRS 4, Capital Instruments (1994), requires minority interest to be analyzed between the aggregate amount attributable to equity interest and the amounts attributable to non-equity interest.[5]

In the U.S., the FASB tentatively decided in early 2000 that non-controlling interest should be shown as a separate component within the shareholders' equity section of the consolidated balance sheet instead of as a separate item between liabilities and shareholders' equity. As this book goes to press, there is no final decision.

The implication of a change in U.S. classification is that the AcSB may consider adopting the U.S. classification approach. It is quite possible that there will be a future change in the recommended balance sheet classification of non-controlling interest.

---

4. *TRANSACC: Transnational Accounting*, (London: KPMG and The Macmillan Press, 1995), edited by Professor D. Ordelheide, University of Frankfurt, page 2007.

5. *Ibid.*, page 2890.

Worksheet approach

Exhibit 5-9 shows the 2002 separate-entity trial balances for Purchase and Target in the first two columns. The trial balances are almost identical to those shown in Exhibit 4-4 for 100% ownership. The differences are:

1. The investment account is for the cost of 70% of the shares, or $840,000, instead of $1,200,000.

2. The Purchase Ltd. common shares are $3,440,000 instead of $3,800,000, reflecting the fact that 28,000 shares were issued to accomplish the business combination instead of 40,000 shares.

3. Purchase's dividend income is only 70% of the $30,000 paid by Target, or $21,000.

EXHIBIT 5–9 PURCHASE LTD. CONSOLIDATION WORKSHEET—PURCHASE LTD. OWNS 70% OF TARGET LTD.

December 31, 2002

| | Trial balances | | Adjustments | | Purchase |
	Purchase Dr/(Cr)	Target Dr/(Cr)	Adjustments Dr/(Cr) [a]	Operations Dr/(Cr) [c]	consolidated trial balance
Cash	$ 971,000	$ 100,000			$1,071,000
Accounts receivable	2,200,000	250,000			2,450,000
Inventories	250,000	70,000		(8,000) **c2**	312,000
Land	1,000,000	300,000	70,000 **a2**		1,370,000
Buildings and equipment	3,000,000	500,000	(10,000) **a2**		3,490,000
Accumulated depreciation	(1,300,000)	(185,000)	150,000 **a2**	(14,000) **c3**	(1,349,000)
Investments (at cost)	840,000	—	{ (560,000) **a1** (280,000) **a2**	}	
Goodwill			70,000 **a2**	(3,500) **c4**	66,500
Accounts payable	(800,000)	(200,000)			(1,000,000)
Long-term notes payable	(400,000)	—			(400,000)
Non-controlling interest in Target Ltd.			{ (240,000) **a1**	(17,100) **c5** 9,000 **c6** }	(248,100)
Common shares	(3,440,000)	(200,000)	200,000 **a1**		(3,440,000)
Dividends declared	—	30,000		(30,000) **c6**	
Retained earnings, December 31, 2002	(2,000,000)	(600,000)	600,000 **a1**		(2,000,000)
					—
Sales	(2,400,000)	(300,000)		55,000 **c1**	(2,645,000)
Dividend income	(21,000)	—		21,000 **c6**	—
Cost of sales	1,750,000	180,000	{	(55,000) **c1** 8,000 **c2** }	1,883,000
Depreciation expense	100,000	35,000		14,000 **c3**	149,000
Goodwill amortization expense				3,500 **c4**	3,500
Non-controlling interest in earnings				17,100 **c5**	17,100
Other expenses	250,000	20,000			270,000
	$ —	$ —	$ —	$ —	$ —

4. The cash is less by $9,000 owing to the smaller amount of dividends received by Purchase from Target: $21,000 instead of $30,000.

Acquisition adjustments

The two adjustments for the acquisition are shown in the third numerical column. Entry **a1** eliminates Target's shareholders' equity accounts and establishes the non-controlling interest's share of Target's net assets at the date-of-acquisition. Entry **a2** adds the fair value increments for Purchase's share of Target's net assets and recognizes the purchased goodwill. Together, these two entries eliminate Purchase's investment account.

Current operations

The fourth numerical column shows the adjustments that are necessary as a result of operations for 2002. These adjustments are similar to those illustrated in Chapter 4 (Exhibit 4-4), except that in this chapter we are assuming 70% ownership rather than 100%. Therefore the non-controlling interest must be accounted for.

The first two adjustments are to eliminate the intercompany sales and to reduce the inventory by the total amount of unrealized intercompany profit:

c1	Sales	55,000	
	Cost of sales		55,000
c2	Cost of sales	8,000	
	Inventory		8,000

Adjustment **c2** is exactly the same adjustment as we made in Chapter 4. The existence of non-controlling interest does not affect this adjustment. The entire inventory will be included in the consolidated balance sheet, and therefore the entire unrealized profit must be eliminated. Similarly, since 100% of Target's revenues and expenses are included in the consolidated income statement, the full amount of the intercompany transactions must be eliminated, not just 70%.

The next two adjustments amortize the fair value increments relating to buildings and equipment and to goodwill:

c3	Depreciation expense	14,000	
	Accumulated depreciation		14,000
c4	Amortization expense	3,500	
	Goodwill		3,500

The amortization is only for the fair value increments relating to the 70% share acquired by Purchase Ltd. Since the minority interest's share of assets and liabilities is being reported at book value, there is no additional amortization relating to the other 30%.

Non-controlling interest in earnings is next. The Purchase Ltd. consolidated income statement will show the total revenues and the total expenses for the two companies. The consolidated income from operations will reflect the entire operations for both companies. However, the shareholders of Purchase will benefit from only 70% of Target's earnings. The 30% share of Target's earnings that increases the equity of Target's non-controlling shareholders must be subtracted to determine consolidated net income from the point of view of Purchase's shareholders.

Target's separate-entity net income must first be adjusted by subtracting any unrealized profits. The $8,000 unrealized inventory profit is subtracted from Target's reported net income of $65,000. Then, we take 30% of the adjusted Target net income of $57,000, which is $17,100. The adjustment is:

c5	Non-controlling interest in earnings of Target (**I/S**)	17,100	
	Non-controlling interest in Target (**B/S**)		17,100

This adjustment may be a bit confusing since the account titles are very similar. The account debited in adjustment **c5** is the *income statement* account. The account credited is the *balance sheet* account.

As for all consolidation adjustments, entry **c5** is a worksheet entry only. *The financial statements of Target as a separate legal entity are in no way affected by the adjustments made in Exhibit 5-9.* Target will still report to its non-controlling shareholders a net income of $65,000 for 2002 and net assets of $850,000 at year-end. Adjustment **c5** is a necessary part of the consolidation process *for Purchase,* but it does not affect the income or financial position of Target itself or the rights of non-controlling shareholders in the earnings of Target.

The final adjustment eliminates the dividends paid by Target. Since 30% of the dividends were paid to Target's minority shareholders, the entry reduces the non-controlling interest to reflect the fact that Target's net assets have been reduced by the payment of dividends:

c6	Dividend income	21,000	
	Non-controlling interest	9,000	
	Dividends declared		30,000

The consolidated statements are for the parent company's shareholders, and therefore 100% of the subsidiary's dividend payments must be eliminated when consolidated statements are being prepared, regardless of the ownership percentage held by the parent company.

After the foregoing adjustments, the balance sheet non-controlling interest is $248,100. This amount is 30% of the book value of the net assets of Target that will be reported in Purchase's consolidated financial statements on December 31, 2002. The amount of non-controlling interest can be verified as follows:

	100%	30%
Target net assets, December 31, 2001	$800,000	$240,000
Target 2002 net income, as reported	65,000	19,500
Target 2002 dividends	−30,000	−9,000
Unrealized profit in inventory	−8,000	−2,400
Target adjusted net assets, December 31, 2002	$827,000	$248,100

All of Target's net assets of $827,000 are included in the consolidated balance sheet, but the non-controlling interest reduces the interest of the Purchase shareholders to their 70% ownership of Target.

Consolidation in Second Subsequent Year

The separate-entity financial statements for the two companies are shown in Exhibit 5-10. Assume that during 2003, the following occurred:

EXHIBIT 5–10 SEPARATE-ENTITY FINANCIAL STATEMENTS FOR 2003

Income Statements
Year Ended December 31, 2003

	Purchase Ltd.	Target Ltd.
Revenue:		
Sales	$3,000,000	$ 400,000
Dividend income	14,000	—
Gain on sale of land	—	150,000
	3,014,000	550,000
Expenses:		
Cost of sales	2,100,000	220,000
Depreciation expense	100,000	35,000
Other operating expenses	440,000	75,000
	2,640,000	330,000
Net income	$374,000	$ 220,000
Retained earnings, December 31, 2002	2,321,000	635,000
Dividends declared	(135,000)	(20,000)
Retained earnings, December 31, 2003	$2,560,000	$ 835,000

Balance Sheets
December 31, 2003

	Purchase Ltd.	Target Ltd.
Assets		
Current assets:		
Cash	$ 475,000	$ 70,000
Accounts receivable	1,900,000	775,000
Inventory	300,000	60,000
	2,675,000	905,000
Property, plant, and equipment:		
Land	1,450,000	—
Buildings and equipment	3,800,000	500,000
Accumulated depreciation	(1,400,000)	(220,000)
	3,850,000	280,000
Other assets:		
Investments (at cost)	840,000	—
Total assets	$7,365,000	$1,185,000
Liabilities and shareholders' equity		
Liabilities:		
Accounts payable	$ 865,000	$ 150,000
Long-term notes payable	500,000	—
	1,365,000	150,000
Shareholders' equity:		
Common shares	3,440,000	200,000
Retained earnings	2,560,000	835,000
	6,000,000	1,035,000
Total liabilities and shareholders' equity	$7,365,000	$1,185,000

1. Target had sales of $60,000 to Purchase; Target's 2003 gross margin was 45%; $10,000 (sales price) of the goods are in Purchase's inventory on December 31, 2003. Unrealized upstream profit therefore is $10,000 × 45% = $4,500.

2. Purchase had sales of $20,000 to Target; Purchase's 2003 gross margin was 30%; $6,000 (sales price) of the goods sold to Target are in Target's 2003 ending inventory. Unrealized downstream profit is $6,000 × 30% = $1,800.

3. Purchase borrowed $500,000 from Target on December 29, 2003. Both companies have reported this as a current item on their separate-entity balance sheets.

4. Target sold its land to Purchase for $450,000. The land originally cost Target $300,000, and its fair value at the date of Purchase's acquisition of Target was $400,000. The gain on the sale ($150,000) is separately disclosed on Target's income statement as an unusual item.

These facts are exactly the same as those used in Chapter 4; they are repeated here for convenience.

Direct method

Statement of income and retained earnings

The consolidated statement of income and retained earnings is shown in Exhibit 5-11. The amounts that require adjustment are as follows:

- *Sales.* The two companies' combined sales of $3,400,000 are adjusted for the $80,000 in intercompany sales.

- *Dividend income.* The intercompany dividends are eliminated.

- *Gain on sale of land.* The $150,000 unrealized gain is eliminated.

- *Cost of sales.* The unrealized profit adjustments to cost of sales are identical to those shown in Chapter 4 for 2003. The non-controlling interest does not affect the adjustments—the entire unrealized profit in opening inventory ($8,000) must be subtracted from cost of sales (thereby increasing net income), and the unrealized profits in the ending inventory ($4,500 and $1,800) must be added.

- *Depreciation expense.* Amortization of the fair value increment on Target's buildings and equipment is added to the book amount of depreciation. As in 2002, the amortization is $140,000 ÷ 10 years, or $14,000.

- *Amortization.* Goodwill amortization will be $3,500 again for 2003.

- *Non-controlling interest in earnings.* Target's book net income of $220,000 is increased by the $8,000 of unrealized profit in the *opening* inventory, and reduced by the unrealized upstream profit in the *closing* inventory ($4,500) and in land ($150,000). Then, we take 30% of that adjusted net income to get the non-controlling interest's share of Target's earnings.

- *Opening retained earnings.* The 2003 opening retained earnings is, obviously, the same as the year-end 2002 retained earnings. The sum of the book balances is reduced by Target's date-of-acquisition retained earnings, by the non-controlling interest's share of earnings since acquisition, by Purchase's share of unrealized upstream profits, and by pre-2003 amortization of FVIs and goodwill.

EXHIBIT 5–11 PURCHASE LTD. CONSOLIDATED INCOME STATEMENT (DIRECT METHOD)

Statement of Income and Retained Earnings
Year Ended December 31, 2003

Revenue:

Sales revenue [3,000,000 + 400,000 – **60,000 – 20,000**]	$3,320,000
Dividend income [14,000 + 0 – **14,000**]	—
Gain on sale of land [0 + 150,000 – **150,000**]	—
	3,320,000

Operating expenses:

Cost of sales [2,100,000 + 220,000 – **60,000 – 20,000 – 8,000** **+ 4,500 + 1,800**]	2,238,300
Depreciation expense [100,000 + 35,000 **+ 14,000**]	149,000
Goodwill amortization [**+ 3,500**]	3,500
Other expenses [440,000 + 75,000]	515,000
Non-controlling interest in earnings [(**220,000 + 8,000 – 4,500 – 150,000**) × 30%]	22,050
	2,927,850
Net income	$ 392,150
Retained earnings, December 31, 2002 [2,321,000 + 635,000 – **600,000** – (35,000 x .30) – (8,000 × .70) **– 14,000 – 3,500**]	2,322,400
Dividends declared [135,000 + 20,000 – **20,000**]	(135,000)
Retained earnings, December 31, 2003	$2,579,550

- *Dividends declared.* Target's $20,000 in dividends are eliminated. Only Purchase's dividends are shown on Purchase's retained earnings statement.

Balance sheet

The consolidated balance sheet is shown in Exhibit 5-12. Adjustments are as follows:

- *Accounts receivable.* The intercompany receivable of $500,000 that is included on Target's books is eliminated.

- *Inventory.* The unrealized profits from both the upstream and downstream sales are eliminated: $4,500 upstream and $1,800 downstream.

- *Land.* We add the FVI for land, and then subtract the $150,000 unrealized gain on the intercompany sale.

- *Buildings and equipment.* The balance is reduced by $10,000, to reflect fair value.

- *Accumulated depreciation.* Target's date-of-acquisition accumulated depreciation of $150,000 is eliminated; two years' worth of FVI amortization of $14,000 per year is added.

- *Investments.* Purchase's $840,000 investment in Target is eliminated.

- *Goodwill.* Goodwill is reduced by two years' amortization of $3,500 × 2 = $7,000. Alternatively, the initial amount of goodwill can be multiplied by the portion of life remaining: $70,000 × 18/20 = $63,000.

EXHIBIT 5–12 PURCHASE LTD. CONSOLIDATED BALANCE SHEET (DIRECT METHOD)

Balance Sheet
December 31, 2003

Assets

Current assets:

Cash [475,000 + 70,000]	$ 545,000
Accounts receivable [1,900,000 + 775,000 – **500,000**]	2,175,000
Inventory [300,000 + 60,000 – **4,500** – **1,800**]	353,700
	3,073,700

Property, plant, and equipment:

Land [1,450,000 + 0 **+ 70,000 – 150,000**]	1,370,000
Buildings and equipment [3,800,000 + 500,000 – **10,000**]	4,290,000
Accumulated depreciation [1,400,000 + 220,000 – **150,000 + 28,000**]	(1,498,000)
	4,162,000

Other assets:

Investments [840,000 + 0 – **840,000**]	—
Goodwill [**70,000** × **18/20**]	63,000
Total assets	$7,298,700

Liabilities and shareholders' equity

Liabilities:

Current accounts payable [865,000 + 150,000 – **500,000**]	$ 515,000
Long-term notes payable [500,000 + 0]	500,000
	1,015,000
Non-controlling interest [(**1,035,000 – 4,500 – 150,000) x 30%**]	264,150

Shareholders' equity:

Common shares [**Purchase Ltd. shares only**]	3,440,000
Retained earnings [2,560,000 + 835,000 – **600,000** – (235,000 × .30) – (**150,000** × **.70**) – (**4,500** × **.70**) – **1,800** – (**14,000** × **2**) – (**3,500** × **2**)]	2,579,550
	6,019,550
Total liabilities and shareholders' equity	$7,298,700

- *Current accounts payable.* The intercompany balance of $500,000 is eliminated.

- *Non-controlling interest.* The non-controlling interest is determined by starting with the total shareholders' equity as reported on Target's separate-entity balance sheet, Exhibit 5-10: $1,035,000. From this amount we must deduct any and all year-end 2003 unrealized upstream profits. There are two unrealized profit amounts, $4,500 in Purchase's inventory and $150,000 from Target's sale of land to Purchase:

Target's shareholders' equity, December 31, 2003	$1,035,000
Unrealized year-end 2003 upstream profits:	
Inventory	–4,500
Land	–150,000
Target's adjusted shareholders' equity	$ 880,500
Non-controlling interest's proportion	× 30%
Non-controlling interest, December 31, 2003	**$ 264,150**

- *Retained earnings.* We start with the book balances of the two companies, and then:

  (1) subtract Target's date-of-acquisition retained earnings,

  (2) subtract the non-controlling interest's share of the change in retained earnings since the date of acquisition: ($835,000 − $600,000) × 30% = $70,500,

  (3) subtract Purchase's 70% share of upstream unrealized profits in land and in ending inventory,

  (4) subtract 100% of unrealized downstream profits,

  (5) subtract the cumulative amount of FVI amortization since the date of acquisition (i.e., $14,000 × 2 years), and

  (6) subtract accumulated goodwill amortization since the date of acquisition ($3,500 × 2).

The calculation for Purchase's consolidated retained earnings for December 31, 2003, is as follows:

Purchase separate-entity retained earnings	$2,560,000
Target separate-entity retained earnings	+ 835,000
Target's date-of-acquisition retained earnings	− 600,000
Non-controlling interest's share of Target's post-acquisition retained earnings	− 70,500
Target's share of unrealized profit on sale of land	− 105,000
Target's share of unrealized upstream profit in ending inventory	− 3,150
Unrealized downstream profit in ending inventory	− 1,800
2 years' amortization of FVI in buildings and equipment	− 28,000
2 years' amortization of goodwill	− 7,000
Purchase's consolidated retained earnings	**$2,579,550**

Worksheet approach

To construct the consolidated financial statements for 2003, we must make the same three types of worksheet adjustments and eliminations as we did for 2003 in Chapter 4:

a Adjust for the acquisition.

b Adjust for the amortization of fair value increments and goodwill and for Target's earnings between the date of acquisition and the *beginning* of 2003.

c Adjust for 2003 unrealized profits and amortization, and eliminate 2003 intercompany transactions and balances.

In addition, we must recognize the non-controlling interest when we make the worksheet adjustments and eliminations for non-wholly-owned subsidiaries. The consolidation worksheet is shown in Exhibit 5-13.

Acquisition and cumulative adjustments

The first adjustment column, **a**, contains the two adjustments for the acquisition. Nothing new there.

The second adjustment column, **b**, contains the balance sheet changes that have occurred since acquisition, but prior to the current year. There are four adjustments in this column, all of which involve a charge against retained earnings:

b1 recognizes the prior years' amortization of the FVI on buildings and equipment. Since only one year has elapsed, this adjustment includes only 2002's amortization. More generally, however, this adjustment will include all FVI amortization from the date of acquisition to the *beginning* of the current year.

b2 provides for the prior years' goodwill amortization.

b3 recognizes the beginning-of-year unrealized upstream profit by reducing cost of sales, thereby increasing consolidated net income.

b4 allocates to non-controlling interests their share of the cumulative change in Target's retained earnings from the date of acquisition to the *beginning* of the current year, adjusted for unrealized upstream profit: ($35,000 − $8,000) × 30% = $8,100.

Current operations

Many of these adjustments are identical to or very similar to those that we have made repeatedly, and we will not repeat all of the adjustments in general journal form. The adjustments can be summarized as follows:

c1 Eliminate the intercompany sales.

c2 Eliminate Target's unrealized profit on upstream sales in Purchase's ending inventory.

c3 Eliminate Target's unrealized profit on upstream sale of land to Purchase.

c4 Eliminate Purchase's unrealized profit on downstream sales in Target's ending inventory.

c5 Adjust for 2003 amortization of FVI on buildings and equipment.

c6 Adjust for 2003 amortization of goodwill.

c7 Eliminate intercompany receivable and payable balances.

c8 Adjust for the non-controlling interest's share of Target's earnings, as adjusted for unrealized profits. The calculation is as follows:

	100%	30%
Target's book net income (Exhibit 5-10)	$ 220,000	$ 66,000
Plus unrealized upstream profit in opening inventory	+ 8,000	+ 2,400
Minus unrealized upstream profit in ending inventory	− 4,500	− 1,350
Minus unrealized profit on upstream sale of land	− 150,000	− 45,000
Target adjusted 2003 net income	$ 73,500	$ 22,050

This calculation shows both a 100% column and a 30% column, but that is not necessary. Any calculation that gets you to the correct answer (and that you feel most comfortable with) is okay.

c9 Eliminate Target's dividends. Of the $20,000, 70% (i.e., $14,000) is eliminated against Purchase's dividend income and 30% ($6,000) is charged to non-controlling interest on the balance sheet.

EXHIBIT 5–13 PURCHASE LTD. CONSOLIDATION WORKSHEET

December 31, 2003

| | Trial balances | | Adjustments | | | Purchase Ltd. consolidated trial balance |
| | | | Acquisition [a] | Operations | | |
	Purchase	Target		Cumulative [b]	Current [c]	
Cash	$ 475,000	$ 70,000				$ 545,000
Accounts receivable	1,900,000	775,000			(500,000) c7	2,175,000
Inventories	300,000	60,000			{ (4,500) c2 (1,800) c4	353,700
Land	1,450,000	—	70,000 a2		(150,000) c3	1,370,000
Buildings and equipment	3,800,000	500,000	(10,000) a2			4,290,000
Accumulated depreciation	(1,400,000)	(220,000)	150,000 a2	(14,000) b1	(14,000) c5	(1,498,000)
Investments (at cost)	840,000	—	{ (560,000) a1 (280,000) a2	—	}	—
Goodwill			70,000 a2	(3,500) b2	(3,500) c6	63,000
Accounts payable	(865,000)	(150,000)			500,000 c7	(515,000)
Long-term notes payable	(500,000)					(500,000)
Non-controlling interest in Target			(240,000) a1	{ (8,100) b4	(22,050) c8 6,000 c9	(264,150)
Common shares	(3,440,000)	(200,000)	200,000 a1			(3,440,000)
Dividends declared	135,000	20,000			(20,000) c9	135,000
Retained earnings, December 31, 2002	(2,321,000)	(635,000)	600,000 a1	{ 14,000 b1 3,500 b2 8,000 b3 8,100 b4		(2,322,400)
Sales	(3,000,000)	(400,000)			80,000 c1	(3,320,000)
Dividend income	(14,000)	—			14,000 c9	—
Gain on sale of land	—	(150,000)			150,000 c3	—
Cost of sales	2,100,000	220,000		{ (8,000) b3	{ (80,000) c1 4,500 c2 1,800 c4	2,238,300
Depreciation expense	100,000	35,000			14,000 c5	149,000
Goodwill amortization expense					3,500 c6	3,500
Non-controlling interest in earnings					22,050 c8	22,050
Other operating expenses	440,000	75,000				515,000
	$ —	$ —	$ —	$ —	$ —	$ —

The Next Steps

Chapters 4 and 5 have worked methodically through the consolidation process at three points in time: the date of acquisition, one year after acquisition, and two years after acquisition. Chapter 4 assumed that the parent owned 100% of the subsidiary shares. Chapter 5 relaxed that assumption and illustrated consolidation when the subsidiary is *not* wholly owned. Through the course of these two chapters, most of the major aspects of consolidation have been illustrated.

The next chapter covers the one remaining major aspect of consolidations—intercompany sale of depreciable or amortizable assets. Then, it presents a general approach to consolidation that can be used at any point in time, freeing us from the methodical process of year-by-year consolidations. We also will take a third and final look at the equity basis of reporting. We'll bet you can hardly wait!

Summary of Key Points

1. When a parent company purchases control of a subsidiary but acquires less than 100% of the subsidiary's shares, the *parent-company* approach to consolidation is used. The subsidiary's assets and liabilities are consolidated with those of the parent (1) at fair value for the parent's share of the subsidiary's net assets and (2) at carrying value for the non-controlling interest's share. The parent-company approach is the widely accepted international practice for controlled subsidiaries.

2. *Proportionate consolidation* is the required consolidation method in Canada for joint ventures, and only for joint ventures. Under proportionate consolidation, only the reporting enterprise's proportionate share of the joint venture's assets and liabilities is included on the investor's consolidated balance sheet. Canada is the only country to require proportionate consolidation for joint ventures. All other countries permit equity-basis reporting only.

3. All of the subsidiary's assets and liabilities are consolidated on the parent's balance sheet, but part of those net assets represents the equity of the non-controlling interests. On the parent's balance sheet, there must be an amount shown for the non-controlling interest's share of the subsidiary's net assets. In Canada, this amount is shown after liabilities but before shareholders' equity.

4. All of the subsidiary's revenues and expenses are included in the parent's income statement, but part of the subsidiary's earnings accrues to the non-controlling interests. Therefore, the parent must deduct an amount for non-controlling interest's share of earnings. The non-controlling interest's share of earnings is reduced by their proportionate share of any upstream unrealized profits.

 Weblinks

Roughneck's Accounting and Financial Glossary
www.dpliv.com/roughnec/Glossary.htm

Accounting terms from A to Z are listed here for quick reference.

Department of Finance and Administration—Australia
www.dofa.gov.au/

Learn about Australia's government operations, parliamentary services, and financial framework, or read one of the many publications, such as the most recent Annual Report, available for downloading.

Canadian Department of Finance
www.fin.gc.ca/fin-eng.html

The Department of Finance Canada is the federal department primarily responsible for providing the Government of Canada with analysis and advice on the broad economic and financial affairs of Canada. Use the Finance Department's bilingual Web site to find news releases and speeches, career information, and budget information.

Self-Study Problem 5-1

On January 10, 2003, Regina Ltd. acquired 60% of the shares of Dakota Ltd. by issuing common shares valued at $150,000. Prior to the acquisition of Dakota, Regina's balance sheet appeared as shown in Exhibit 5-15. The balance sheet of Dakota Ltd. at the date of acquisition is shown in Exhibit 5-14.

EXHIBIT 5–14 DAKOTA LTD.

Balance Sheet
January 10, 2003

	Book value	Fair value
Current assets:		
Cash	$ 10,000	$ 10,000
Accounts and other receivables	20,000	20,000
Inventory	30,000	30,000
	60,000	
Capital assets:		
Land	45,000	80,000
Building	150,000	130,000
Accumulated depreciation	(50,000)	
Equipment	130,000	10,000
Accumulated depreciation	(80,000)	
	195,000	
Total assets	$255,000	
Liabilities:		
Current accounts payable	$ 40,000	40,000
Long-term debenture payable	50,000	50,000
	90,000	
Shareholders' equity:		
Common shares	100,000	
Retained earnings	65,000	
	165,000	
Total liabilities and shareholders' equity	$255,000	

EXHIBIT 5–15 REGINA LTD.

Balance Sheet
December 31, 2002

Current assets:

Cash	$ 50,000
Accounts and other receivables	70,000
Inventory	80,000
	200,000

Capital assets:

Building	260,000
Accumulated depreciation	(40,000)
Equipment	175,000
Accumulated depreciation	(70,000)
	325,000
Total assets	$525,000

Liabilities:

Current accounts payable and accrued liabilities	$ 80,000

Shareholders' equity:

Common shares	220,000
Retained earnings	225,000
	445,000
Total liabilities and shareholders' equity	$525,000

Required:

Prepare a consolidated balance sheet for Regina Ltd., as it would appear immediately following the acquisition of Dakota.

Self-Study Problem 5-2

During 2003, the following transactions occurred between Regina Ltd. and Dakota Ltd. (see SSP5-1):

a. Regina lent $50,000 at 10% interest to Dakota Ltd. on July 1, 2003 for one year. The interest was unpaid at December 31, 2003.

b. During 2003, Regina purchased inventory from Dakota at a cost of $400,000; $100,000 of that amount was still in Regina's inventory at the end of 2003. [Hint: look at Dakota's income statement to compute Dakota's gross profit percentage.]

c. During 2003, Dakota purchased inventory of $200,000 from Regina; $40,000 of that amount was still in Dakota's inventory at the end of 2003.

Other Information:

d. Dakota's building and equipment were estimated to have remaining useful lives from January 10, 2003, of 10 and 5 years, respectively. Straight-line depreciation is being used.

e. Goodwill, if any, is to be amortized over 20 years.

f. No fixed assets were sold or written off during 2003.

The December 31, 2003 separate-entity financial statements for both companies are shown in Exhibit 5-16.

Required:

Prepare the consolidated statement of income and retained earnings and the consolidated balance sheet for Regina Ltd. for the year ended December 31, 2003.

EXHIBIT 5–16 REGINA LTD. AND DAKOTA LTD.

Balance Sheets
December 31, 2003

	Regina Ltd.	Dakota Ltd.
Current assets:		
Cash	$ 28,000	$ 10,000
Accounts and other receivables	110,000	30,000
Inventories	160,000	60,000
	298,000	100,000
Capital assets:		
Land	—	135,000
Buildings	300,000	150,000
Accumulated depreciation	(45,000)	(60,000)
Equipment	200,000	130,000
Accumulated depreciation	(80,000)	(90,000)
	375,000	265,000
Other assets:		
Investment in Dakota Ltd. (at cost)	150,000	—
Total assets	$823,000	$365,000
Liabilities:		
Current accounts payable and accrued liabilities	$ 40,000	$ 80,000
Long-term liabilities	65,000	50,000
	105,000	130,000
Shareholders' equity:		
Common shares	370,000	100,000
Retained earnings	348,000	135,000
	718,000	235,000
	$ 823,000	$ 365,000

EXHIBIT 5–16 REGINA LTD. AND DAKOTA LTD. (cont'd)

Statements of Income and Retained Earnings
Year Ended December 31, 2003

	Regina Ltd.	Dakota Ltd.
Sales	$2,000,000	$1,000,000
Dividend income	24,000	—
Other income	7,000	—
	2,031,000	1,000,000
Cost of sales	1,000,000	600,000
Other operating expenses	886,000	280,000
Interest expense	2,000	10,000
	1,888,000	890,000
Net income	143,000	110,000
Retained earnings, December 31, 2002	225,000	65,000
Dividends declared	(20,000)	(40,000)
Retained earnings, December 31, 2003	$ 348,000	$ 135,000

Self-Study Problem 5-3

Regina Ltd. owns 60% of the common shares of Dakota Ltd., acquired on January 10, 2003. The details of the purchase are given in SSP 5-1, and the trial balances for December 31, 2003, and selected transactions for 2003 are shown in SSP 5-2. The financial statements of both companies (unconsolidated) at December 31, 2004 are shown in Exhibit 5-17.

Additional information:

1. At the beginning of 2004, unrealized upstream profits in inventory amounted to $40,000 held in Regina's inventory (i.e., from upstream sales) and $20,000 in Dakota's inventory (i.e., downstream).

2. During 2004, Dakota sold inventory to Regina for $160,000 at the normal gross margin. One-half of that amount is still in Regina's inventory at year-end.

3. Late in 2004, Regina sold inventory to Dakota at a special price of $40,000. All of these goods are still in Dakota's inventory on December 31, 2004. The cost to Regina of the goods sold to Dakota was $20,000, a 50% gross margin on the selling price.

4. The one-year, $50,000 loan that Regina extended to Dakota on July 1, 2003, was extended for two more years (to July 1, 2006). Simple interest (at 10%) has been accrued by both companies, but no interest will be paid until the principal is repaid.

Required:

Calculate the following amounts for the year ended December 31, 2004:

a. Non-controlling interest in earnings (i.e., on Regina's consolidated income statement).

b. Non-controlling interest (on Regina's consolidated balance sheet), December 31, 2004.

c. Regina's year-end consolidated retained earnings.

EXHIBIT 5–17 REGINA LTD. AND DAKOTA LTD.

Balance Sheets
December 31, 2004

	Regina Ltd.	Dakota Ltd.
Current assets:		
Cash	$ 63,800	$ 2,500
Accounts and other receivables	120,000	27,000
Inventories	130,000	55,000
	313,800	84,500
Capital assets:		
Land	—	135,000
Buildings	380,000	150,000
Accumulated depreciation	(56,200)	(70,000)
Equipment	230,000	170,000
Accumulated depreciation	(68,000)	(47,000)
	485,800	338,000
Other assets:		
Investment in Dakota Ltd. (at cost)	150,000	—
Total assets	$949,600	$422,500
Liabilities:		
Current accounts payable and accrued liabilities	$ 51,600	$ 97,500
Long-term liabilities	180,000	120,000
	231,600	217,500
Shareholders' equity:		
Common shares	370,000	100,000
Retained earnings	348,000	105,000
	718,000	205,000
	$949,600	$422,500

EXHIBIT 5–17 REGINA LTD. AND DAKOTA LTD. (cont'd)

Statements of Income and Retained Earnings
Year Ended December 31, 2004

	Regina Ltd.	Dakota Ltd.
Sales	$2,200,000	$1,100,000
Dividend income	36,000	—
Gain on sale of equipment	10,000	—
Other income	12,000	—
	2,258,000	1,100,000
Cost of sales	1,300,000	660,000
Other operating expenses	864,000	392,000
Interest expense	20,000	18,000
	2,184,000	1,070,000
Net income	74,000	30,000
Retained earnings, December 31, 2003	348,000	135,000
Dividends declared	(74,000)	(60,000)
Retained earnings, December 31, 2004	$ 348,000	$ 105,000

Review Questions

5-1 Define the following terms:
   a. Non-controlling interest
   b. Minority interest
   c. Entity method
   d. Proportionate consolidation
   e. Parent-company approach

5-2 Why do some corporations prefer to control their subsidiaries with less than full ownership?

5-3 How can the inclusion of 100% of a subsidiary's assets on the consolidated balance sheet be justified when the parent owns less than 100% of the subsidiary's shares?

5-4 When all of a non-wholly-owned subsidiary's revenues and expenses are consolidated, what recognition is given to the fact that the parent's share of the subsidiary's earnings is less than 100%?

5-5 Under a pure application of the entity method of reporting minority interest, what value is assigned to goodwill?

5-6 How does the parent-company extension approach modify the entity approach? What is the rationale for this modification?

5-7 Using generally accepted accounting principles, explain why a subsidiary's assets and liabilities are consolidated using two different valuations under the parent-company approach.

5-8 At the date of acquisition, how is the amount of minority interest measured?

5-9 One year after the date of acquisition, how is the amount of minority interest on the balance sheet measured?

5-10 How do unrealized profits on upstream sales affect the minority interest's share of a subsidiary's earnings?

5-11 How do unrealized profits on downstream sales affect the minority interest's share of a subsidiary's earnings?

5-12 How are minority shareholders likely to react to the reduction of their share of the subsidiary's earnings as a result of unrealized profits?

5-13 What is the impact on minority interest of unrealized profits in *beginning* inventories?

5-14 Why are a non-wholly-owned subsidiary's dividend payments completely eliminated even though the parent does not receive all of the dividends?

5-15 What is the effect of the minority interest in earnings on the consolidated cash flow statement?

5-16 In Canada, all of a subsidiary's assets and liabilities are consolidated regardless of the ownership percentage of the parent. Nevertheless, the ownership percentage may affect the amount of the reported (consolidated) assets. Explain.

Cases

Case 5–1

ABC & XYZ

On March 31, 2001, at the end of its fiscal year, ABC Co. acquired 80% of the outstanding shares of XYZ Ltd., at a price in excess of the fair values of XYZ's net assets. At the subsequent annual meeting of XYZ, ABC voted its shares in XYZ in favour of a motion dissolving XYZ and distributing the net assets of the company to the shareholders. An amount equal to 20% of the fair value of the net assets would be distributed in cash to the minority shareholders; all remaining assets and liabilities would be distributed to the majority shareholder (ABC). This plan of dissolution received the required two-thirds majority of the shareholders and was implemented later in 2001.

Required:

Explain how the financial statements of ABC after the dissolution of XYZ would differ from, or be similar to, the consolidated financial statements of ABC had the dissolution not occurred.

Case 5–2

Simpson Ltd.

Simpson Ltd. is a private Ontario corporation controlled by Ted Simpson. The company owns a series of chocolate chip cookie stores throughout Ontario, and also has a wholly-owned Quebec subsidiary that operates stores in Montreal and Quebec City. Because of its lack of stores in Western Canada and its managers' lack of knowledge about that part of the country, Simpson Ltd. has just acquired

70% of the outstanding class A voting shares of Ong Inc. for $6,000,000 cash. Ong Inc. is another cookie store chain that is headquartered in Vancouver and has stores throughout Vancouver and Victoria, as well as in Edmonton, Saskatoon, and Winnipeg.

Ted expects that the acquisition will greatly help the Simpson Ltd. "bottom line," which in turn will help Simpson Ltd. to obtain expanded debt financing because of the greater net income and cash flow. The management of Ong Inc. will not change as a result of the purchase; the former sole owner, John Ong, retains the remaining 30% of the Ong Inc. shares and has agreed to continue as CEO of Ong Inc. for at least five years after the change in control. The president and chief operating officer, Travis Hubner, will also stay on, so there is no reason that the acquired company should not continue to be highly profitable. The condensed balance sheet of Ong Inc. at the date of acquisition is shown in Exhibit 1.

The acquisition was financed mainly by debt; $4,500,000 was borrowed by Simpson Ltd. from the Western Bank of British Columbia, secured by the assets of both Simpson Ltd. and Ong Inc. The bank has requested audited financial statements of both companies on an annual basis, supplemented by unaudited quarterly statements.

Ong Inc. owns the buildings in which some of its stores are located, but most are leased. None of the land is owned. The buildings are being depreciated over 30 years. John has obtained two separate appraisals of the owned buildings; one

EXHIBIT 1

Ong Inc.
Condensed Balance Sheet
May 8, 2001

Assets

Cash		$ 200,000
Accounts receivable		100,000
Inventories—raw materials and supplies		1,200,000
Buildings	$ 7,000,000	
Accumulated depreciation	(1,400,000)	5,600,000
Equipment	$ 3,000,000	
Accumulated depreciation	(1,200,000)	1,800,000
Total assets		$8,900,000

Liabilities and shareholders' equity

Liabilities:		
Accounts payable	$ 350,000	
Accrued expenses	50,000	
Total current liabilities		$ 400,000
Bank loan payable, due May 3, 2001		2,700,000
Future income taxes		1,100,000
Total liabilities		4,200,000
Shareholders' equity:		
Common shares—Class A voting	$ 1,000,000	
Retained earnings	3,700,000	4,700,000
Total liabilities and share equity		$8,900,000

appraisal firm has placed the aggregate current value at $9,500,000, while the second firm arrived at a value of $8,400,000. Ong Inc. owns all of the equipment in its stores; the equipment is being depreciated over 10 years, and is, on average, 40% depreciated. It would cost $3,300,000 to replace the existing equipment with new equipment of similar capacity. Inventories are generally worth their book values, except that the replacement cost of the stock of imported Belgian chocolate in the Vancouver warehouse is $20,000 less than book value because of the strengthening Canadian dollar. On the other hand, the accounts payable shown in Exhibit 1 include an unrealized gain of $10,000 because much of the liability is denominated in Belgian francs.

Required:

Determine, on a line-by-line basis, the impact on Simpson Ltd.'s consolidated assets and liabilities as a result of the acquisition, in accordance with Ted Simpson's objectives in acquiring Ong. Where alternative values could be used, explain the reasons for your selection.

[ICAO]

Case 5–3

Le Gourmand

Le Gourmand is one of Canada's most famous French restaurants. Located 20 kilometres north of Toronto, it draws diners from all over the province to enjoy its fare. One of the attractions at the restaurant is its private label brand of wines; produced, bottled, and aged by Ombre Wines Ltd., located in the Niagara Peninsula.

The owner of Le Gourmand, Francois LeClerc, decided on New Year's Eve to increase the ties between Ombre Wines Ltd. and Le Gourmand Inc.; Le Gourmand is Ombre Wines' largest customer. On January 2, 2001, Le Gourmand Inc. purchased 3,000 common shares of Ombre Wines Ltd. on the open market for $207,000. This left very few common shares still available to the public. The preferred shares were owned by the founders of Ombre Wines, but their children owned many of the common shares and were gradually selling them because none of them wished to take over the business.

Ombre Wines Ltd.'s owners' equity at January 2, 2001 was:

Preferred shares:

Cumulative, 6%, non-voting;

2,000 authorized, 1,000 issued	$ 20,000

Common shares:

7,000 authorized, 6,000 issued	137,000
Retained earnings	170,000
	$327,000

At January 1, 2001, the book values of Ombre Wines Ltd.'s assets approximated fair values except as follows:

	Book value	Fair value
Two identical parcels of land, purchased in January 1989 as an investment; each parcel cost $20,000 and the fair value of each parcel was identical	$40,000	$60,000
The land on which Ombre Wines' factory was located	$70,000	$85,000
Grape press, purchased in January 1996 (useful life when the press was purchased was 10 years, no salvage value)	$20,000	$24,000

In September 2001, Ombre Wines sold one of the parcels of land that it had been holding as an investment (both lots had been put on the market but only one had sold). The proceeds were $18,000. The real estate market had declined badly in 2001. The purchaser, however, had also discovered that Ombre Wines had been using the vacant lots to dump some residue from the wine processing; the land would not be ready to produce crops for at least five years. The purchaser had originally been willing to offer $24,000, but reduced this to $18,000 when the land use was confirmed by his lawyer.

Sales from Ombre Wines to Le Gourmand totalled $100,000 and $120,000 in 2000 and 2001, respectively. At December 31, 2000, Le Gourmand's inventory contained $45,000 of Ombre Wines' wine. A year later, the inventory included $60,000 of Ombre Wines' wine. Of the ending inventory acquired from Ombre Wines, $20,000 had not been paid for as at December 31, 2001. In settlement of part of this payable, Le Gourmand sent some old office equipment to Ombre Wines. The equipment had cost $10,000 and had a net book value at December 31, 2001, of $1,000. Ombre Wines agreed to accept the equipment and to forgive $5,000 of the receivable from Le Gourmand, leaving a balance of $15,000 due from the restaurant. Ombre Wines did not depreciate this office equipment during 2001.

Ombre Wines' most recent dividend declaration was December 31, 1999.

Le Gourmand Inc. writes off goodwill over 20 years. The amortization policy for all capital assets is straight-line.

Francois LeClerc is looking forward to the cash flow from dividends that he hopes his company will receive from Ombre Wines Ltd. each year.

The balance sheets of the two companies at December 31, 2001 and the income statements for the year then ended are presented in Exhibit 1 below.

Required:
Describe the alternative accounting treatments available to Le Gourmand Inc. for its investment in Ombre Wines Ltd. Describe why each alternative is an option and conclude which treatment is appropriate based on your description. Calculate Le Gourmand Inc.'s net income for the year ended December 31, 2001. Show details of all calculations.

[ICAO]

EXHIBIT 1

Balance Sheet
December 31, 2001

	Le Gourmand Inc.	Ombre Wines Ltd.
Assets		
Cash	$ 1,750	$ 16,400
Accounts receivable	—	66,000
Inventory	85,500	134,000
Investment in Ombre Wines	207,000	—
Land	30,000	90,000
Building	40,000	60,000
Equipment	25,000	75,000
	$389,250	$441,400
Liabilities and owners' equity		
Accounts payable	$ 34,000	$ 13,000
Taxes payable	2,150	15,000
Long-term debt	—-	10,000
Future income taxes	1,600	—
Preferred shares	—	20,000
Common shares	155,000	137,000
Retained earnings	196,500	246,400
	$389,250	$441,400

Income Statement
For the Year Ended December 31, 2001

	Le Gourmand Inc.	Ombre Wines Ltd.
Sales	$400,000	$300,000
Gain on transfer office equipment	4,000	—
Loss on sale of land	—	(2,000)
Cost of goods sold	(275,000)	(100,000)
Salaries	(78,000)	(55,000)
General & administration	(4,500)	(3,000)
Depreciation, building	(2,500)	(3,600)
Depreciation, equipment	(3,000)	(8,000)
Interest expense	—	(1,000)
Tax expense (40%)	(16,000)	(51,000)
Net income	$ 25,000	$ 76,400

Case 5–4

Proctor Industries

You, CA, are the senior in charge of an audit of Proctor Industries (PI), a public company in the business of selling plumbing parts wholesale. It is now November 3, 2001—five weeks after PI's year-end of September 30, 2001 and one week before your firm has been asked to discuss the financial statements for PI, including any significant accounting issues, with their audit committee.

PI's unconsolidated annual sales approximate $36 million. It operates through six regional branches with approximately equal sales volumes at each branch.

PI has a 60% interest in Minor Inc., a company located in the United Kingdom. It also has a September 30th year-end and is audited by a firm of chartered accountants in the United Kingdom.

You are at the client's premises reviewing the year-end working papers for Proctor Industries, and you note the following items:

1. PI's unconsolidated net income before income taxes is normally about $2 million.

2. The allowance for doubtful accounts in PI is $200,000. Based on the work performed in this section of the audit, the audit assistant concluded that the allowance should be at least $250,000, and could be as high as $350,000.

3. You have contacted the auditors for Minor Inc.(MI) to obtain their financial statements. However, they are unable to provide you with the audited financial statements since the president of MI refused to sign the management representation letter. He disagrees with the revenue recognition policy insisted on by the auditors of MI and intends to obtain opinions from other audit firms on this issue. The financial statements, under the policy supported by their auditors, show a net loss of $320,000 for the year. MI's current policy for revenue recognition is when items are produced. Their support is that there is a ready market for their supplies that are currently in short supply. PI's revenue recognition policy is when goods are shipped to the customer.

4. There is a new item on PI's balance sheet called "Investments." The working papers indicate that this represents a cash payment in June 2001 for $100,000 for all the common shares of Chemicals Inc. (CI). This company has an August 31 year-end. Although CI has previously never been audited, PI requested, and you have completed, an audit of CI for its August 31, 2001 year-end. The audited financial statements for CI appear in Exhibit 1. CI manufactures household cleaning products. The equipment used in the manufacturing process is not complex and is inexpensive to replace. CI has earned large profits in the past, mainly from government contracts. This year, the financial statements show an after-tax profit of $100,000.

5. An extract of the agreement to purchase CI states that if the company earns more than $1 million per year in any of the next five years, the vendor may buy back the common shares for a price to be determined.

6. One of the legal letters for PI was returned with the following comment:

> Chemicals may be liable for damages arising from the alleged dumping of hazardous chemicals from its Bedford plant into the nearby Black River. As of the current date, a statement of claim has been filed. CI denies these allegations.

The partner has asked you to prepare a memo on the above items for his use in discussions with the audit committee.

Required:

Prepare the memo requested by the partner.

[CICA, adapted]

EXHIBIT 1

Chemicals Inc.
Extracts from Audited Balance Sheet
As at August 31, 2001

Assets

Accounts receivable	$ 900,000
Prepaid expenses	100,000
Inventory	400,000
Capital assets, net	400,000
	$1,800,000

Liabilities and shareholders' equity

Accounts payable	$ 500,000
Common shares (100 issued)	50,000
Retained earnings	1,250,000
	$1,800,000

Problems

P5-1

In January 1999, Paris Ink Company (Paris) purchased 80% of the common shares of Slade Paper Ltd. (Slade) by issuing common shares worth $800,000. At that date, Slade's common shares and retained earnings totalled $250,000 and $340,000 respectively. The net book values and fair values of the net identifiable assets of Slade were the same except for the following:

1. the fair market value (FMV) of inventory was greater than book value by $50,000;

2. the FMV of capital assets had replacement cost that exceeded net book value (NBV) by $120,000, although net realizable value exceeded NBV by only $60,000 (management planned to retain the capital assets throughout their remaining useful life of 12 years); and

3. although the NBV of Slade's bonds payable was $400,000, the FMV was $460,000, due to a decline in the interest rates since the bonds were originally issued. The bonds payable mature on December 31, 2004 and have a nominal rate of interest of 12%. The companies use straight-line amortization for bond premiums and discounts.

The financial statements for Paris and Slade for the year ended December 31, 2001 are presented in Appendix A. Additional information on transactions between Paris and Slade is presented in Appendix B.

Required:

a. Calculate the carrying value of the goodwill on the consolidated financial statements of Paris Ink Company at December 31, 2001. Paris amortizes goodwill on a straight-line basis over 20 years.

b. Prepare a consolidated income statement for Paris Ink Company for the year ended December 31, 2001.

c. Calculate the following balances for Paris Ink Company's consolidated balance sheet as at December 31, 2001:

　　i) inventory

　　ii) minority interest

APPENDIX A

Income Statements
For the Year Ended December 31, 2001

	Paris	Slade
Sales	$3,850,000	$1,650,000
Cost of goods sold	2,550,000	1,120,000
Gross profit	1,300,000	530,000
Expenses		
Administration & selling	550,000	384,000
Amortization	136,000	74,000
Interest	—	56,000
	686,000	514,000
Other income		
Interest & dividends	76,000	4,000
Gain on sale of land	—	100,000
	76,000	104,000
Income before income taxes	690,000	120,000
Income tax expense	260,000	30,000
Net income	$ 430,000	$ 90,000

Balance Sheets
As at December 31, 2001

	Paris	Slade
Assets		
Current assets		
Cash	$ 45,000	$ 80,000
Accounts receivable	655,000	455,000
Inventory	420,000	350,000
Marketable securities	380,000	45,000
Due from Slade	200,000	—
	1,700,000	930,000
Capital assets—net	1,450,000	690,000
Investment in Slade	800,000	—
	$3,950,000	$1,620,000
Liabilities		
Current liabilities		
Accounts payable	$ 665,000	$ 280,000
Note payable to Paris	—	200,000
	665,000	480,000
Bonds payable	—	400,000
Shareholders' Equity		
Common shares	2,500,000	250,000
Retained earnings	785,000	490,000
	$3,950,000	$1,620,000

Appendix B

Additional Information:

1. On July 1, 2001, Paris advanced Slade $200,000, due on July 1, 2002. Interest of 8% is due at maturity.

2. Intercompany sales from Slade to Paris were as follows for 1999–2001:

	1999	2000	2001
Sales	$200,000	$240,000	$250,000
Gross profit margin	32.00%	33.33%	30.00%
Amount remaining in inventory at year-end	$ 60,000	$ 75,000	$100,000

All amounts in closing inventory at the end of each year were sold during the first four months of the following year. Round to the nearest five dollars if necessary.

3. On March 1, 2001, Slade sold land to Paris for $300,000. The original cost of the land was $200,000. Assume this transaction was taxed at the company's normal tax rate.

4. During 2001, Paris sold inventory to Slade for $108,000, which represented a markup of 35% above cost. At December 31, 2001, 20% of these goods remained in inventory.

5. During 2001, Paris paid dividends of $250,000 and Slade paid dividends of $50,000.

6. Paris and Slade pay taxes at 40% and 25% rates, respectively.

[ICAO, adapted]

P5-2

On December 30, 2001, the balance sheets of the Perk Company and the Scent Company are as follows:

	Perk Company	Scent Company
Cash	$ 7,000,000	$ 200,000
Accounts receivable	1,000,000	600,000
Inventory	1,300,000	800,000
Capital assets, net	6,700,000	3,400,000
	$16,000,000	$5,000,000
Current liabilities	$ 3,000,000	$ 200,000
Long-term liabilities	4,000,000	800,000
Common shares	5,000,000	1,000,000
Contributed surplus	—	1,000,000
Retained earnings	4,000,000	2,000,000
	$16,000,000	$5,000,000

For both companies, the fair values of their identifiable assets and liabilities are equal to their carrying values except for the following fair values:

	Perk	Scent
Inventories	$1,000,000	$ 600,000
Capital assets (net)	7,000,000	5,000,000
Long-term liabilities	3,800,000	1,100,000

The following cases are *independent*.

1. On December 31, 2001, the Perk Company purchases the net assets of the Scent Company for $5.5 million in cash. The Scent Company distributes the proceeds to its shareholders in return for their shares, cancels the shares, and ceases to exist as a separate legal entity.

2. On December 31, 2001, the Perk Company purchases 75% of the outstanding voting shares of the Scent Company for $4.5 million in cash. The Scent Company continues to operate as a separate legal entity.

Required:

For each of the two independent cases, prepare a consolidated balance sheet for Perk Company at December 31, 2001, subsequent to the business combination. For the second case, prepare a consolidated balance sheet using *each* of the following four approaches:

a. Fair-value purchase:

    1. Proportionate consolidation

    2. Parent company

    3. Entity

b. New entity

[SMA, adapted]

P5-3

Zoe Ltd. has the following balance sheet at December 31, 2001:

Zoe Ltd.
Balance Sheet
December 31, 2001

Current assets		$ 80,000
Capital assets		
Land	$ 30,000	
Building, net	100,000	
Equipment, net	50,000	180,000
Goodwill, net		20,000
		$280,000
Current liabilities		$ 55,000
Bonds payable		80,000
Common shares		100,000
Retained earnings, Jan. 1, 2001		60,000
Net loss for 2001		(15,000)
		$280,000

On December 31, 2001, Halifax Ltd. bought 70% of the outstanding shares of Zoe Ltd. and paid $190,000. The current fair values of the net assets of Zoe Ltd. on December 31, 2001, are:

Current assets	$ 80,000	Current liabilities	$ 55,000
Land	180,000	Bonds payable	$ 70,000
Building	160,000		
Equipment	20,000		

Halifax Ltd. is an investment company that has assets composed only of cash and short-term marketable investments.

Required:

Calculate the following items, as they would appear on the Halifax Ltd. consolidated balance sheet at December 31, 2001:

a. Land

b. Goodwill

c. Minority interest

[CGA–Canada]

P5-4

Calgary Ltd. acquired a subsidiary, Ottawa Ltd., on July 1, 2001, by paying $200,000 for 70% of the outstanding shares. The fiscal year for both companies is December 31. The balance sheets of Ottawa Ltd. and Calgary Ltd. are shown below.

Required:

Prepare the consolidated balance sheet as at July 1, 2001, for Calgary Ltd., following *CICA Handbook* recommendations.

[CGA–Canada]

Ottawa Ltd.
Balance Sheet
July 1, 2001

	Book values	Fair market values
Current assets	$ 140,000	$140,000
Capital assets		
Land	90,000	150,000
Building, net	215,000	200,000
Equipment, net	60,000	90,000
	$ 505,000	
Current liabilities	$ 70,000	70,000
Bonds payable	210,000	225,000
Common shares	100,000	
Retained earnings, Jan 1, 2000	70,000	
Net income (Jan. 1–July 1)	55,000	
	$ 505,000	

Calgary Ltd.
Balance Sheet
July 1, 2001

	Book values	Fair market values
Current assets	$ 150,000	$100,000
Capital assets		
Land	400,000	700,000
Building, net	550,000	400,000
Equipment, net	360,000	200,000
Investment in Ottawa Ltd.	200,000	
Goodwill	400,000	
	2,060,000	
Current liabilities	$ 60,000	60,000
Bonds payable	200,000	170,000
Common shares	1,000,000	
Retained earnings, July 1, 2001	800,000	
	2,060,000	

P5-5

Qorp Ltd. has the following balance sheet at December 31, 2001.

Qorp Ltd.
Balance Sheet
December 31, 2001

Current assets		$ 85,000
Capital assets		
Land	$ 30,000	
Building, net	120,000	
Equipment, net	50,000	200,000
Goodwill, net		50,000
		$335,000
Current liabilities		$ 65,000
Bonds payable, due 2019		70,000
Common shares		120,000
Retained earnings, Jan. 1, 2001		140,000
Net loss for 2001		(60,000)
		$335,000

On January 1, 2002, Zip Ltd., whose assets are composed entirely of share investments and cash, paid $185,000 for 70% of the outstanding shares of Qorp Ltd. The current fair values of the net assets of Qorp Ltd. on January 1, 2002, were:

Current assets	$ 85,000	Current liabilities	$65,000
Land	75,000	Bonds payable	70,000
Building (net)	180,000		
Equipment (net)	30,000		

Zip Ltd. had the following shareholders' equity on January 1, 2002:

Common shares	$ 480,000
Retained earnings	710,000
	$1,190,000

Required:

a. Assume a consolidated balance sheet is prepared on January 1, 2002. Calculate the dollar amounts for the following items as they would appear on that consolidated balance sheet:

(1) Goodwill

(2) Land

(3) Equipment

(4) Common shares

(5) Retained earnings

(6) Minority interest

b. What does minority interest represent on the consolidated balance sheet?

[CGA–Canada]

P5-6

On January 1, 2001, Big Ltd. purchased 80% of the shares of Small Ltd. for $1,400,000 and, on the same day, Small Ltd. purchased 60% of the shares of Smaller Ltd. for $930,000. Any excess of the purchase price was allocated to goodwill and amortized over 10 years.

At January 1, 2001

	Big Ltd.	Small Ltd.	Smaller Ltd.
Shares	$1,950,000	$1,600,000	$ 500,000
Retained earnings	2,300,000	1,910,000	730,000
	$4,250,000	$3,510,000	$1,230,000

During 2001

Net income (cost basis)	$ 800,000	$ 600,000	$ 300,000
Dividends paid	120,000	100,000	40,000

There were no intercompany transactions.

Required:

Calculate the balance of minority interest as it would be shown on the consolidated balance sheet of Big Ltd., at December 31, 2001.

[CGA–Canada]

P5-7

Parent Ltd. pays $550,000 cash for 70% of the outstanding voting shares of Sub Ltd. on January 1, 2001. The following information was available:

Sub Ltd.
Trial Balance
January 1, 2001

	Book value	Fair value
Cash	$ 40,000	$ 40,000
Inventory	40,000	30,000
Equipment, net	120,000	100,000
Building, net	300,000	360,000
Land	50,000	160,000
	$550,000	
Liabilities	10,000	14,000
Common shares	250,000	—
Retained earnings	290,000	—
	$ 550,000	

During 2001, Sub Ltd. earned $180,000 and paid no dividends. The inventory on hand at January 1, 2001, was sold during 2001. The equipment will be depreciated over 10 years straight-line, the building will be depreciated over 20 years straight-line, and any goodwill will be amortized over 20 years straight-line. The liabilities were paid during 2001. Parent Ltd. uses the cost method of accounting for its investment.

Required:

Prepare the eliminating entries that would appear on the consolidated working papers at December 31, 2001, based on the above information.

[CGA–Canada]

P5-8

On January 1, 2001, Par Ltd. purchased 80% of the voting shares of Sub Ltd. for $906,400. The balance sheet of Sub Ltd. on that date was as follows:

Sub Ltd.
Balance Sheet
January 1, 2001

	Net book value	Fair value
Cash	$ 160,000	$160,000
Accounts receivable	200,000	240,000
Inventory	300,000	380,000
Capital assets, net	900,000	750,000
	$1,560,000	
Current liabilities	$ 150,000	130,000
Bonds payable	400,000	400,000
Discount on bonds payable	(38,000)	(38,000)
Common shares	200,000	—
Retained earnings	848,000	—
	$1,560,000	

The accounts receivable, inventory, and current liabilities have "turned over" by December 31, 2001, and the net capital assets will be amortized over 10 years, on a straight-line basis. Any goodwill created by the purchase will be amortized over 20 years on a straight-line basis.

Additional Information:

1. During 2001, Par Ltd. sold goods costing $100,000 to Sub Ltd. for $140,000. At December 31, 2001, 20% of these goods were still in the inventory of Sub Ltd.

2. In 2001, Sub Ltd. sold goods costing $200,000 to Par Ltd. for $250,000. At December 31, 2001, 30% of these goods were still in the inventory of Par Ltd.

3. In 2001, Sub Ltd. sold land to Par Ltd. for $300,000. The land had cost Sub $240,000.

4. Both companies pay income taxes at the rate of 40%.

The balance sheets and income statements for Par Ltd. and Sub Ltd. at December 31, 2001 are presented below.

Required:

a. Prepare the consolidated income statement for the year ended December 31, 2001.

b. Present the following as they would appear on the consolidated balance sheet at December 31, 2001:
   (1) Net capital assets
   (2) Goodwill
   (3) Retained earnings

[CGA–Canada]

Balance Sheets
December 31, 2001

	Par Ltd.	Sub Ltd.
Cash	$ 200,000	$ 140,000
Accounts receivable	300,000	190,000
Inventories	500,000	460,000
Buildings and equipment (net)	1,200,000	900,000
Investment in Sub Ltd.	906,400	—
Other investments	417,600	—
Total assets	$3,524,000	$1,690,000
Current liabilities	$ 300,000	$ 200,000
Bonds payable	600,000	400,000
Discount on bonds payable	(87,000)	(32,000)
Common shares	500,000	200,000
Retained earnings	2,211,000	922,000
Total liabilities and share equity	$3,524,000	$1,690,000

Income Statements
Year Ended December 31, 2001

	Par Ltd.	Sub Ltd.
Sales	$2,000,000	$2,000,000
Cost of sales	1,400,000	1,700,000
Gross margin	600,000	300,000
Depreciation expense	100,000	90,000
Interest expense	63,000	44,000
Income tax expense	140,000	74,000
Other expenses	124,000	78,000
Investment income	(37,000)	(60,000)
Net income	$ 210,000	$ 74,000

P5-9

On January 1, 2001, the Brown Company acquired 65% of the outstanding shares of the Moran Company in return for cash in the amount of $5,825,000. On this date, the book values and the fair values for the Moran Company's balance sheet accounts were as follows:

	Book values	Fair values
Cash and current receivables	$ 325,000	$ 325,000
Temporary investments	1,560,000	1,000,000
Inventories	3,450,000	1,275,000
Land	2,960,000	3,400,000
Plant and equipment (net)	3,470,000	5,000,000
Total assets	$11,765,000	
Current liabilities	$ 950,000	950,000
Long-term liabilities	2,980,000	2,550,000
Common shares	5,350,000	
Retained earnings	2,485,000	
Total equities	$11,765,000	

On the acquisition date, the remaining useful life of the Moran Company's plant and equipment was 10 years. The long-term liabilities mature on June 30, 2003. The temporary investments were sold during 2001 for $1,200,000, and the inventories were sold during 2001, at normal sales prices. The land is still on the company's books at December 31, 2002. Any goodwill arising from this business combination is to be amortized over 20 years.

The condensed income statements of the Brown Company and its subsidiary, the Moran Company, for the year ending December 31, 2002, are as follows:

	Brown Co.	Moran Co.
Revenues	$12,540,000	$2,535,000
Cost of goods sold	8,970,000	1,460,000
Depreciation expense	2,350,000	375,000
Other expenses	790,000	465,000
Total expenses	12,110,000	2,300,000
Net income	$ 430,000	$ 235,000

Additional Information:

1. The Brown Company carries its investment in the Moran Company using the cost method.

2. Both companies calculate all depreciation and amortization charges using the straight-line method.

3. During 2002, Moran sold merchandise to Brown at sales prices of $500,000. Of this amount, $200,000 is in the December 31, 2002 inventories of the Brown Company. On January 1, 2002, the inventories of Brown contained merchandise purchased from Moran at sales prices of $150,000.

4. During 2002, Brown sold merchandise to Moran for $600,000. One-sixth of this merchandise remains in the December 31, 2002 inventories of Moran. All intercompany merchandise sales are priced to provide the selling company with a gross profit of 25% on sales prices. Both companies use the FIFO cost flow assumption for inventory valuation.

5. During 2002, Moran declared and paid dividends of $125,000, while Brown declared and paid dividends of $210,000.

6. The December 31, 2001 retained earnings balance of Moran was $3,235,000.

7. Both companies pay income taxes at a rate of 40%.

Required:

a. Prepare a consolidated income statement for the Brown Company for the year ending December 31, 2002.

b. Calculate the retained earnings that would be disclosed in the consolidated balance sheet at December 31, 2002.

c. Calculate the minority interest that would be disclosed in the consolidated balance sheet at December 31, 2002.

[SMA]

P5-10

On January 2, 2001, Par Ltd. acquired 80% of the common shares of Eider Ltd. for a cash payment of $1,367,000. The book and fair values of Eider's net assets were as follows on the date of acquisition:

Eider Ltd.
Balance Sheet
January 2, 2001

	Book value	Fair value
Cash	$ 150,000	$ 150,000
Receivables	220,000	270,000
Inventory	330,000	250,000
Capital assets (net)	1,950,000	1,830,000
Total assets	$2,650,000	
Current liabilities	$ 70,000	70,000
Long-term liabilities	680,000	620,000
Preferred shares	250,000	*
Common shares	500,000	
Retained earnings	1,150,000	
Total equities	$2,650,000	

Chapter

Five

234

* Preferred shares have no par value and were issued for $25 per share; 10,000 shares are issued and outstanding. The shares have a $3 per share cumulative dividend that has not been paid for 2000. The shares are callable at their issue price plus a call premium of $2 per share.

Eider Ltd.'s receivables and inventory are expected to turn over within one year. The capital assets have a 10-year remaining life. The long-term liabilities have 15 years to maturity. Any goodwill on consolidation will be amortized over 20 years. Both Par Ltd. and Eider Ltd. have a December 31 fiscal year-end.

Required:

a. Calculate the amount of goodwill arising from Par's acquisition of Eider.

b. Construct a note for Par's consolidated statements for 2001 describing the acquisition of Eider.

[CGA–Canada, adapted]

P5-11

On January 1, 2000, Parent Ltd. purchased 90% of the shares of Sub Ltd. for $975,000. At that time Sub Ltd. had the following balance sheet:

Sub Ltd.
Balance Sheet
January 1, 2000

	Net book value	Fair value
Cash	$ 60,000	$ 60,000
Accounts receivable	120,000	150,000
Inventory—FIFO	180,000	230,000
Capital assets, net	1,500,000	1,350,000
Goodwill	100,000	—
	$1,960,000	
Current liabilities	$ 140,000	140,000
Bonds payable (Note)	800,000	850,000
Common shares	400,000	—
Retained earnings	620,000	—
	$1,960,000	

The bonds were issued at par and will mature in 10 years. Sub Ltd. has a receivables and inventory turnover of greater than six times per year. The capital assets have an average of 10 years of remaining life and are being amortized straight-line. The subsidiary's goodwill has 10 years remaining on the amortization period. Any goodwill on consolidation will be amortized on a straight-line basis over 20 years.

In 2000, Sub Ltd. sold inventory to Parent Ltd. for $260,000; the inventory had cost $320,000. At the end of 2000, 25% was still in Parent's inventory but it was all sold in 2001.

In 2001, Parent Ltd. sold inventory to Sub Ltd. for $275,000; the inventory had cost $200,000. At the end of 2001, 35% was left in Sub's inventory.

During 2000, the subsidiary earned $875,000 and paid dividends of $50,000. During 2001, the subsidiary incurred a loss of $180,000 and paid dividends of $60,000.

The parent company used the cost method for the investment in subsidiary and netted almost everything to "Other expenses."

At December 31, 2001, the following financial statements were available:

Balance Sheet
December 31, 2001

	Parent Ltd.	Sub Ltd.
Cash	$ 400,000	$ 75,000
Accounts receivable	850,000	179,000
Inventory	970,000	245,000
Capital assets, net	2,631,000	1,863,000
Goodwill	0	92,000
Investment in Sub Ltd.	975,000	0
	$5,826,000	$2,454,000
Current liabilities	$ 450,000	$ 49,000
Bonds payable	0	800,000
Common shares	1,000,000	400,000
Retained earnings	3,026,000	1,385,000
Net income (loss)	1,350,000	(180,000)
	$5,826,000	$2,454,000

Income Statement
Year Ended December 31, 2001

	Parent Ltd.	Sub Ltd.
Sales	$9,865,000	$1,650,000
Cost of sales	8,040,000	1,140,000
Gross profit	1,825,000	510,000
Depreciation	(106,000)	(104,000)
Other expenses	(369,000)	(816,000)
Gain on sale of building	0	230,000
Net income	$1,350,000	$ (180,000)

Required:

a. Prepare a consolidated income statement for 2001.

b. Calculate the amounts that would appear on the consolidated balance sheet at December 31, 2001 for:

(1) Goodwill

(2) Capital assets, net

(3) Bonds payable

(4) Minority interest

Ignore the impact of income taxes.

[CGA–Canada]

P5-12

Pop Company acquired 70% of Son Limited on January 1, 2000 for $345,000. On the acquisition date, common shares of Son Limited were $100,000 and $200,000 respectively. The fair market values of Son's identifiable net assets were equivalent to their book value except for capital assets, which were undervalued by $50,000, and long-term debt, which was overvalued by $100,000. The undervalued capital assets have a remaining life of 10 years. The long-term debt matures on December 31, 2004. Any goodwill should be amortized over 10 years. Both companies use the straight-line method of amortization.

Intercompany transactions include the downstream sale of a capital asset in 2000, which included an unrealized profit of $30,000 to be amortized over five years. During 2001, there was an intercompany upstream sale of land for $120,000. The original cost of the land was $95,000. For the year ended December 31, 2001, Pop Company had net income of $244,000 and declared dividends of $10,000. All dividends have been declared and paid on December 31. Pop Company uses the cost method to account for its investment in Son Limited. Shown below are the balance sheets for the parent company and its subsidiary on December 31, 2001.

Balance Sheets
At December 31, 2001

	Pop Company	Son Limited
Current assets	$1,200,000	$250,000
Investment in Son Limited	345,000	—
Capital assets—net	900,000	450,000
Goodwill	—	—
Total assets	$2,445,000	$700,000
Current liabilities	$1,045,000	$ 75,000
Long-term debt	500,000	200,000
Minority interest	—	—
Common shares	500,000	100,000
Retained earnings	400,000	325,000
Total liabilities and equities	$2,445,000	$700,000

Required:

a. Determine consolidated net income for the year ended December 31, 2001. Show all your calculations.

b. Calculate the balances of the following accounts as they would appear in the consolidated balance sheet on December 31, 2001:

   1. Capital assets, net
   2. Minority interest
   3. Goodwill
   4. Retained earnings

c. Prepare the required December 31, 2001 journal entry to eliminate the Investment in Son Limited account.

[CGA–Canada]

Subsequent-Year Consolidations:

General Approach

Introduction

In this chapter, we wrap up the major elements of preparing consolidated financial statements. In the first major section of the chapter, we will discuss one important type of intercompany transaction that we have not examined so far—the intercompany sale of long-term depreciable or amortizable capital assets. There is nothing conceptually new about consolidation eliminations and adjustments for capital assets that are subject to amortization. However, unrealized profit eliminations for intercompany sales of such assets are complicated by the amortization; the amount of unrealized profit declines from year to year.

After we discuss the intercompany sale of capital assets, we will move on to illustrate a general approach to preparing consolidated financial statements. This approach can be used for any consolidation problem, no matter how far in the past the acquisition was. We will free ourselves of the year-by-year illustration that we used in the previous two chapters. The illustration in this section will also demonstrate what happens when an asset that had a fair value increment at the date of the business combination is sold to a third party outside of the consolidated entity.

Finally, we return to the issue of equity-basis reporting. The equity method of reporting was illustrated in Chapter 4, but only for a wholly-owned subsidiary. In this chapter, we will examine equity-basis reporting for non-wholly-owned subsidiaries and significantly influenced affiliates. Then, we will illustrate what happens to the consolidation process when the parent company *records* its investment in a subsidiary on the equity basis.

An Appendix to this chapter presents a discussion and illustration of consolidation adjustments for intercompany purchases of bonds involving premiums and discounts. We have relegated this topic to an Appendix because it is not crucial to understanding the process of consolidation and may seldom be encountered in practice in other than a straightforward manner that is easily handled by a simple elimination. Readers who are not interested in some of the more arcane aspects of consolidation are encouraged to skip over the Appendix and proceed directly to Chapter 7.

Intercompany Sale of Long-Term Assets

General concept

We have repeatedly illustrated that unrealized profits on intercompany sales must be removed from the consolidated net income. The concept of eliminating unrealized intercorporate profits or gains is applicable to *any* sale between members of a group of controlled or significantly influenced companies. The sale need not involve the parent or investor corporation; sales from one subsidiary to another or from one significantly influenced investee corporation to another require elimination of unrealized profit.

The discussion in previous chapters has focused on intercompany sales of inventory and non-depreciable assets (i.e., land). However, any type of asset may be sold, current or long-term, tangible or intangible. Examples of common types of non-inventory sales include:

- sales of customer receivables from an operating to a finance subsidiary,

- sales of investments from one subsidiary to another,

- sales of existing capital assets, and

- construction of new buildings or equipment by one subsidiary for the use of the parent or another subsidiary.

Sales of tangible capital assets may not only be "straight" sales, but may also take the form of capital leases.

Intercompany sales of inventory and other short-term assets result in an unrealized profit in one period that is usually realized in the next period. When the assets sold are long-term, eliminations must continue as long as the asset is in the group of companies. In the case of assets whose carrying value does not change (e.g., land), the same elimination is made year after year.

When the assets have changing carrying values, then the elimination will change each year because the amount of unrealized profit will change each year. Assets with changing carrying values include any depreciable or amortizable capital asset and any instalment-basis financial asset, such as customer notes or capital leases.

Losses on intercompany sales may or may not be eliminated [CICA 1600.27]. The key question is whether or not the loss reflects a real decline in the value of the asset sold. If there is no evidence of impairment of the value of the asset sold, then the intercompany loss on the sale should be eliminated. But if the sale price reflects a new, lower value-in-use for the asset, then the asset should have been written down even without the sale, because the loss on the sale simply reflects a decline in the value of the asset that should have been reflected by a reduction in the carrying value of the asset anyway. Thus, the crucial question in deciding whether or not to eliminate a loss is whether the item that was sold should have been written down had it *not* been sold.

For capital assets, market or resale value may not be relevant for answering this question. An intercompany sale may occur at a fair market price that results in a loss. But a decline in market value (or net realizable value) of productive assets is not normally recognized, as long as the productive usefulness of the asset is not impaired. Book value of a productive capital asset represents its unrecovered cost, not its realizable value. Therefore, a loss on an intercompany sale of a productive asset will normally be eliminated unless the loss reflects a decline in the recoverable cost of the asset.

To illustrate the adjustments for unrealized profits on the intercompany sale of amortizable assets, we will use the example of depreciable capital assets. First we will examine downstream sales (i.e., from the parent to a subsidiary), and then upstream sales (from a subsidiary to the parent).

Downstream sales of amortizable assets

Assume that Company P buys a piece of equipment and sells it to its subsidiary, Company S. The cost to P of the asset is $200,000. P sells it to S for $250,000 at the end of 2002. S will depreciate the asset over 10 years on a straight-line basis, beginning in 2003 (and assuming zero salvage value).

When consolidating the financial statements for 2002, we must reduce the reported value of the equipment from its carrying value on S's books of $250,000 to the actual cost to the consolidated entity (that is, to P) of $200,000. When we prepare the consolidated statements, we must:

- eliminate the $50,000 gain on the intercompany sale from P's revenue, and

- reduce the equipment account by $50,000.

On a consolidation worksheet, the adjustment at the end of 2002 (assuming that amortization will begin in 2003) will appear as follows:

Gain on sale of equipment	50,000	
Equipment		50,000

In 2003, S will begin to depreciate the equipment at the rate of $25,000 per year. Depreciation expense is overstated from the viewpoint of the consolidated entity because the carrying value of the equipment includes unrealized profit. Based on the actual cost of the equipment of $200,000, depreciation expense should only be $20,000 per year. Thus, the year-end 2003 consolidation adjustments must:

1. reduce the cost of the equipment on the balance sheet from $250,000 to $200,000,

2. eliminate the unrealized profit from the opening retained earnings,

3. decrease depreciation expense by $5,000, and

4. reduce accumulated depreciation by $5,000.

In worksheet terms, the adjustments are:

(1)	Retained earnings (opening)	50,000	
	Equipment		50,000
(2)	Accumulated depreciation	5,000	
	Depreciation expense		5,000

On intercompany *inventory* sales, the profit is realized when the inventory is eventually sold to an outside party. On depreciable assets, the profit is realized not by direct sale to outsiders, but rather by using the asset to produce goods or services to be sold to outsiders. The $5,000 depreciation adjustment in 2003 recognizes the realization of one-tenth of the 2002 unrealized profit.

In 2004, the *previously unrealized profit* must be eliminated. So far, there has been only one year's depreciation recognized (i.e., in 2003), which accounts for one-tenth of the unrealized profit. Therefore, the unrealized profit at the *beginning* of 2004 is $50,000 \times 9/10 = $45,000. The $5,000 that has been realized is now in the accumulated depreciation account, which must also be adjusted by:

- reducing retained earnings by $45,000, which is $50,000 \times 9/10,

- reducing accumulated depreciation by the $5,000 depreciation in previous years (one for 2003, so far), and

- reducing the equipment account by the full intercompany profit of $50,000.

As a worksheet adjustment:

(1)	Retained earnings	45,000	
	Accumulated depreciation	5,000	
	Equipment		50,000

In 2004, S will amortize another $5,000 of the intercompany profit in its equipment account. When we prepare the year-end 2004 consolidated statements, we will make exactly the same additional adjustment for 2004 as we made for 2003's depreciation:

- decrease depreciation expense by $5,000, and

- reduce accumulated depreciation by $5,000.

(2)	Accumulated depreciation	5,000	
	Depreciation expense		5,000

In subsequent years, the adjustment for the remaining unrealized gain will reflect the depreciation taken to date. For example, in 2009 we will recognize the fact that the equipment has already been depreciated for six years (2003 through 2008, inclusive). Using the direct approach to consolidation, the line-by-line adjustments will be as follows:

- Equipment—reduce by the full unrealized profit of $50,000.

- Accumulated depreciation—multiply the unrealized profit by the fraction of years elapsed since the intercompany sale (i.e., $50,000 \times 7/10 = $35,000), and subtract that amount from accumulated depreciation balance.

- Depreciation expense—reduce by the current year's depreciation on the unrealized profit ($50,000 \times 1/10).

- *Opening* retained earnings (on the retained earnings statement)—reduce by the four years' unrealized profit on the transaction that remains at the start of the year: $50,000 \times 4/10 = $20,000.

- *Closing* retained earnings—reduce by the remaining three years' unrealized profit on the transaction: $50,000 \times 3/10 = $15,000

The 2009 worksheet adjustments will be as follows:

(1)	Retained earnings ($50,000 \times 4/10)	20,000	
	Accumulated depreciation ($50,000 \times 6/10)	30,000	
	Equipment		50,000

(2) Accumulated depreciation	5,000	
Depreciation expense		5,000

Keeping the two adjustments separate may keep the process clearer and help avoid confusion. However, these can be combined into a single adjusting entry under the worksheet approach:

Retained earnings (opening)	20,000	
Accumulated depreciation ($50,000 × 7/10)	35,000	
Equipment		50,000
Depreciation expense		5,000

By the end of 2012, the asset is fully depreciated and there will be no depreciation expense in subsequent years. The only consolidation adjustment that will be made in 2013 and thereafter (until the asset is retired and written off) will be a cumulative adjustment that has no impact on either consolidated net income or consolidated retained earnings:

Accumulated depreciation	50,000	
Equipment		50,000

Upstream sales of amortizable assets

When the intercompany sale of an amortizable asset is upstream or is horizontal (i.e., between two subsidiaries), the consolidation eliminations are exactly the same as those shown above *if* the selling subsidiary is 100% owned by the parent.

If the selling subsidiary is not wholly owned, then the adjustments are complicated somewhat by the presence of non-controlling interest. For example, assume the same situation as above except that S sells the equipment to P, and P owns 75% of the shares of S. The non-controlling interest will have a 25% interest in the $50,000 gain.

The full $50,000 will be eliminated from consolidated net income in 2002, and the annual amortization of $5,000 also will be eliminated in each of the following 10 years. However, the non-controlling interest will also have to be adjusted for elimination of the unrealized profit. When non-controlling interest is computed for the consolidated balance sheet, the unrealized profit *at the end of the year* must be deducted from the subsidiary's net book value before we multiply by the non-controlling interest's share. The impact on the year-end 2002 balance sheet can be shown as follows:

Non-controlling interest ($50,000 × 25%)	12,500	
Retained earnings ($50,000 × 75%)	37,500	
Equipment		50,000

In 2003, we make the same unrealized profit adjustment again, since none of the unrealized profit had been recognized by the beginning of the year. In addition, we also must make the income statement adjustment, including the portion allocated to non-controlling interest. The two adjustments for 2003 are as follows:

Non-controlling interest ($50,000 × 25%)	12,500	
Retained earnings ($50,000 × 75%)	37,500	
Equipment		50,000

Accumulated depreciation	5,000	
Non-controlling interest in earnings (I/S)	1,250	
Depreciation expense		5,000
Non-controlling interest ($5,000 × 25%)		1,250

At the beginning of 2004, one-tenth of the unrealized profit will have been recognized, and therefore the profit eliminations are for only 9/10ths of the inter-company profit:

(1)	Non-controlling interest ($50,000 × 25% × 9/10)	11,250	
	Retained earnings ($50,000 × 75% × 9/10)	33,750	
	Accumulated depreciation	5,000	
	Equipment		50,000
(2)	Accumulated depreciation	5,000	
	Non-controlling interest in earnings	1,250	
	Depreciation expense		5,000
	Non-controlling interest		1,250

Jumping ahead to 2009, the adjustments will be:

(1)	Non-controlling interest ($50,000 × 25% × 4/10)	5,000	
	Retained earnings ($50,000 × 75% × 4/10)	15,000	
	Accumulated depreciation ($50,000 × 6/10)	30,000	
	Equipment		50,000
(2)	Accumulated depreciation	5,000	
	Non-controlling interest in earnings	1,250	
	Depreciation expense		5,000
	Non-controlling interest		1,250

Each year, the current operations adjustment is the same as long as depreciation is being charged. The cumulative adjustment, however, gradually shifts the total net gain from unrealized (as deductions from retained earnings and non-controlling interest) to realized (as a reduction in accumulated depreciation).

In this discussion, we have assumed that the equipment was a capital asset on the books of the selling company. When a company sells a capital asset, the difference between the book value and the selling price is reported as a gain or loss. However, the selling company may sell long-lived assets that are part of its *inventory*, such as when an equipment manufacturer sells equipment to another company in the consolidated group, either upstream or downstream. In that case, the intercompany sale will be accounted for by the seller as *sales revenue* with offsetting *cost of sales*. This raises no complications in consolidation. The elimination in the year of sale will differ from those shown above only by replacing the debit to *gain on sale of equipment* of $50,000 with a debit to *sales* for $250,000 and a credit to *cost of sales* for $200,000.

Direct amortization

We used a depreciable tangible capital asset in the example above. For such assets, normal practice is to maintain the asset account at the original cost of the asset and to record depreciation in a separate accumulated depreciation account. However, many companies do not maintain a separate accumulation account, especially for intangible capital assets. The annual amortization may be credited directly to the asset account instead.

When the amortization is credited directly to the asset account, the consolidation adjusting entries are a little different. In each entry above, the two amounts for the asset account (equipment) and the accumulated depreciation will be netted together, simplifying the adjustment somewhat. Otherwise, the process is exactly as illustrated above.

For example, suppose that S sells a *patent* to P, instead of equipment. The remaining unamortized cost of the patent on S's books is $200,000, and the selling price to P is $250,000. Assume that S is 75% owned by P. The adjustment for 2002, the year of the sale, will be essentially the same as above:

Non-controlling interest ($50,000 × 25%)	12,500	
Retained earnings	37,500	
Patent		50,000

If the patent will be amortized over 10 remaining years, P will record amortization of $25,000 each year (the $250,000 purchase price for 10 years) by crediting the patent account directly. Remember, however, that the $25,000 annual amortization is overstated by $5,000 due to the $50,000 upstream profit. The 2003 consolidation adjustment to correct for the over-amortization is:

(1) Non-controlling interest ($50,000 × 25%)	12,500	
Retained earnings ($50,000 × 75%)	37,500	
Patent		50,000

(2) Patent	5,000	
Non-controlling interest in earnings	1,250	
Amortization expense		5,000
Non-controlling interest		1,250

This adjustment may appear slightly baffling, because it *increases* the patent account, whereas adjustments for unrealized profit usually *decrease* the asset account. The explanation is that P already credited the patent account for $25,000 in amortization, which includes amortization on the unrealized profit. The first adjustment removed the remaining unrealized profit, and the second adjustment restores the $5,000 over-amortization taken by P.

In 2004, (1) the remaining $45,000 of unrealized profit is removed from the asset account, and (2) the annual amortization is corrected:

(1) Non-controlling interest	11,250	
Retained earnings	33,750	
Patent ($50,000 × 9/10)		45,000

(2) Patent	5,000	
Non-controlling interest in earnings	1,250	
Amortization expense		5,000
Non-controlling interest		1,250

By the *beginning* of 2009, the balance in the patent account will be reduced to $20,000 after six years of amortization. The year-end 2009 adjustments are similar to those above for the cases where there is a separate accumulated depreciation account:

(1) Non-controlling interest ($50,000 × 25% × 4/10) 5,000

  Retained earnings ($50,000 × 75% × 4/10) 15,000

    Patent 20,000

(2) Patent 5,000

  Non-controlling interest in earnings 1,250

    Amortization expense 5,000

    Non-controlling interest 1,250

Subsequent sale of capital assets acquired intercompany

One company may buy a depreciable asset from another in the consolidated group, and then later sell that asset to a third party in an arm's-length transaction. For example, suppose P sells the equipment that it acquired from S for $220,000 at the beginning of 2006. P will recognize a gain of $45,000, the $220,000 proceeds from sale minus the remaining net book value to P of $175,000 (i.e., $250,000 cost to P × 70% remaining useful life).

At the beginning of 2006, there will be 70% of the original gain from the intercompany sale still unrealized. Once the asset has been sold to a third party, the entire remaining unrealized gain must be recognized and added to the gain (or deducted from the loss) on the third-party sale:

Retained earnings 35,000

  Gain on sale of equipment 35,000

Thus the gain on P's sale would be increased by the remaining unrealized profit on S's sale, reflecting the fact that for the consolidated entity as a whole, a profit of $80,000 was realized on the sale of the equipment to an unrelated party:

Sales price		$220,000
Consolidated carrying value:		
Cost to S	$200,000	
Depreciation (3 years @ $20,000)	60,000	140,000
Gain to consolidated entity		$ 80,000

Subsequent-Year Consolidations—General Approach

So far, we have discussed the process of preparing consolidated financial statements (1) at the date of acquisition, (2) one year subsequent to acquisition, and (3) two years subsequent to acquisition. We have explored the basic concepts underlying consolidation and the treatment of non-controlling interest. The major procedural aspects of consolidation have also been presented. In this section, we discuss the general approach to preparing consolidated financial statements at any reporting date subsequent to acquisition, regardless of how long ago the business combination occurred.

Basic conceptual approach

Previous chapters have emphasized that consolidated financial statements must reflect adjustments for three types of events: (1) the acquisition transaction, (2) the cumulative effects of amortization and transactions to the beginning of the current reporting period, and (3) the effects of amortization and transactions in the current period. It doesn't matter whether the three types of adjustments are kept separate or combined.

The general nature of these adjustments is portrayed in Exhibit 6-1 with a time line. The first point of interest on the time line is point **A**, the date of acquisition of the parent's controlling interest in the subsidiary. The consolidation worksheet entry for this event is a constant, and has been thoroughly discussed.

EXHIBIT 6–1 OVERVIEW OF CONSOLIDATION ADJUSTMENTS

1. **Acquisition adjustments**

    a. Eliminate subsidiary's share equity accounts; establish non-controlling interest

    b. Add fair value increments and goodwill

    c. Offset subsidiary's accumulated depreciation against the asset account(s)

2. **Cumulative operations adjustments** to start of the current year (i.e., affecting current year's *beginning*-of-year balance sheet amounts)

    a. Recognize the non-controlling interest's share of subsidiary retained earnings from date of acquisition to *start* of the current year.

    b. Recognize the cumulative amortization of fair value increments (or decrements) and goodwill.

    c. Eliminate the impact of intercompany transactions that affect carrying values:

    i. Gains and losses from intercompany transactions that are still unrealized at the start of the year.

    ii. Flow-through to retained earnings of fair-valued assets and liabilities that have since been sold to third parties.

3. **Current year operations adjustments**

    a. Amortize fair value increments (decrements) and goodwill.

    b. Eliminate the current year's intercompany transactions.

    c. If equity-basis reporting is used, eliminate the subsidiary earnings and dividends that were recorded by the parent.

    d. Realize previously unrealized profits (losses), if they are realized or partially realized in the current year.

    e. Eliminate unrealized profits (losses) arising from intercompany transactions in the current year.

    f. Recognize the non-controlling interest in earnings.

    g. Eliminate year-end intercompany balances.

A Date of acquisition	**B** Start of current year	**C** End of current year

Point **C** on the time line is that most recent point, which is the current balance sheet date. The worksheet adjustments for point **C** and for the year then ended (the time between point **B** and point **C**) have been reviewed several times in the previous chapters and should be reasonably clear by now.

The more problematic adjustment is apt to be that for the time between acquisition (point **A**) and the beginning of the current year (point **B**). We have pointed out that the consolidation adjustments for the intervening period (points **A** to **B**) are essentially *cumulative* adjustments. We can simply accumulate the effects of each year's current operations adjustments, bearing in mind that the net effect of all adjustments to income statement accounts and to previous years' current nonmonetary accounts (e.g., inventories) will usually be reflected in retained earnings. The result will then be the point **A**-to-**B** adjustment when we prepare the consolidated statements for the next accounting period (points **B** to **C**).

If we have the task of preparing only a year-end consolidated balance sheet, then we don't have to worry about point **B** but can adjust the balance sheet amounts directly to year-end balances. For example, there would be no reason to distinguish between fair value amortizations in the current year and those relating to prior years. Although balance-sheet-only consolidations may be encountered in student examination situations, actual accounting practice calls for preparing a full set of financial statements and not just a non-comparative year-end balance sheet. In preparing a full set of financial statements, we need to isolate the adjustments relating to the current period so that we can properly prepare the income statement and the comparative balance sheet.

To illustrate the preparation of consolidated financial statements in any year, we will use a different example than the one used in previous chapters. This example will include an intercompany sale of capital assets to illustrate the adjustments described in the first part of this chapter.

Basic information

On December 31, 2000, Parent Corp. acquired 80% of the outstanding common shares of Sub Ltd. by issuing Parent shares worth $800,000. At the date of acquisition, Sub's shareholders' equity totalled $855,000, consisting of $300,000 in the common share account and $555,000 in retained earnings. Parent acquired 80% of the book value of the net assets, $855,000 × 80% = $684,000.

Some of Sub's assets and liabilities had a fair value that differed from carrying value. Exhibit 6-2 summarizes those assets and liabilities for which there was a fair value increment. The fair value increment for the bonds is a credit, indicating that the fair value of the bonds is higher than the book value. This difference would most likely be caused by a nominal interest rate for the bonds that was higher than the market rate for the appropriate term and risk.

Parent's 80% share of the fair value increments is a total of $76,000. Once the fair value increments have been determined, the purchase transaction can be analyzed. Goodwill is $40,000, as is shown in Exhibit 6-2.

Exhibit 6-3 shows the separate-entity financial statements for Parent and Sub at December 31, 2006, six years after Parent's acquisition of its 80% interest in Sub. Other relevant information is as follows:

1. Sub's machinery had an estimated remaining useful life of 10 years from December 31, 2000. At the date of acquisition, the balance in Sub's accumulated depreciation (on machinery) account was $575,000. Machinery is depreciated on a straight-line basis, assuming no salvage value.

EXHIBIT 6–2 PARENT CORP. BUYS 80% OF SUB LTD.

December 31, 2000

Fair value increments, date of acquisition:

	Excess of fair value over book value [Dr/(Cr)]	
	100%	**80%**
Inventories	$ 10,000	$ 8,000
Machinery	75,000	60,000
Investments	30,000	24,000
Bonds payable	(20,000)	(16,000)
Total	$ 95,000	$ 76,000

Goodwill calculation:

Purchase price		$800,000
Book value of net assets acquired		
($855,000 × 80%)	$684,000	
Fair value increments (above)	76,000	760,000
Goodwill		$ 40,000

2. The bonds had a remaining term of eight years from the date of acquisition. Straight-line amortization is used for bond premiums and discounts.

3. Parent's policy is to amortize goodwill over 20 years.

4. In 2003, Sub sold its investments for a profit of $45,000 over book value.

5. During 2006, intercompany sales were as follows:

   a. Parent had sales totalling $100,000 to Sub at a gross margin of 40% of selling price. On December 31, 2006, $40,000 of the amount sold was still in Sub's inventory.

   b. Sub had sales of $700,000 to Parent at a gross margin of 40% of sales. At year-end, $70,000 was still in Parent's inventory.

   Both companies had a gross margin of 40% of the sales price during 2006.

6. The inventories on January 1, 2006, contained intercompany purchases as follows:

   a. Sub held goods purchased from Parent for $20,000.

   b. Parent held goods purchased from Sub for $100,000.

   The gross margin on intercompany sales held in the beginning inventories was 40% of selling price for both companies. All of the beginning inventories were sold to third parties during 2006.

7. Parent collects royalties from Sub (as well as from other companies). Between January 1, 2001 and December 31, 2005 (that is, prior to the current year), Sub paid a total of $500,000 in royalties to Parent. During 2006, Sub paid $90,000 to Parent for royalties.

8. In 2004, Sub sold machinery to Parent for $91,000. The machinery had originally been acquired by Sub in 2001 for $100,000. Sub had been depreciat-

EXHIBIT 6–3 PARENT CORP. AND SUB LTD. CONDENSED SEPARATE-ENTITY FINANCIAL STATEMENTS

Balance Sheets
December 31, 2006

	Parent	Sub
Assets		
Cash	$ 50,000	$ 20,000
Accounts receivable	150,000	160,000
Inventories	180,000	100,000
Machinery	5,000,000	2,700,000
Accumulated depreciation	(1,770,000)	(1,240,000)
Investment in Sub Ltd. (at cost)	800,000	—
Other investments	100,000	—
Total assets	$ 4,510,000	$ 1,740,000
Liabilities and shareholders' equity		
Accounts payable	$ 450,000	$ 200,000
Bonds payable	300,000	500,000
Total liabilities	750,000	700,000
Common shares	1,200,000	300,000
Retained earnings	2,560,000	740,000
Total shareholders' equity	3,760,000	1,040,000
Total liabilities and shareholders' equity	$ 4,510,000	$ 1,740,000

Income Statements
Year Ended December 31, 2006

	Parent	Sub
Sales revenue	$ 2,000,000	$ 1,500,000
Royalty revenue	150,000	—
Dividend income	75,000	—
Total revenue	2,225,000	1,500,000
Cost of sales	1,200,000	900,000
Other expenses	560,000	411,000
Total expenses	1,760,000	1,311,000
Net income	465,000	189,000
Dividends declared	(300,000)	(90,000)
Retained earnings, beginning of year	2,395,000	641,000
Retained earnings, end of year	$ 2,560,000	$ 740,000

ing the machinery on a straight-line basis over 10 years (i.e., at $10,000 per year), with a full year's depreciation in the year of acquisition and no depreciation in the year of disposal. Thus, the net book value of the machine to Sub was $70,000 at the time of the sale to Parent. After the sale from Sub to Parent, Parent continued to depreciate the machinery over the seven remaining years of its original useful life (i.e., at $13,000 per year beginning in 2004).

A caveat for students

Before we launch into an illustration of consolidation techniques, we would like to caution students about their problem-solving approach to complex consolidation problems.

When we prepare financial statements for a real enterprise, it is rather obvious that balance sheets must balance, and that the full set of four financial statements must **articulate** or tie in to each other. However, when we are attempting consolidations for learning and practice, it may well be beneficial not to worry too much if our balance sheets don't balance! It is possible to spend many hours in an attempt to find the error (or errors) that keep our statements from balancing or from articulating properly. This particularly is a problem when we are using the direct approach, in which the ad hoc nature of the adjustment process denies us the self-balancing feature of the worksheet approach.

Often, the error is very minor—sometimes only a simple arithmetic error. We generally recommend, therefore, that students not get too stressed when their problem solutions don't quite work. This is especially true in examination situations, where time wasted looking for small mistakes will consume valuable time that could be used to answer other questions and problems.

Therefore, we urge all users of this book not to get too upset if your statements don't balance. Even the authors of this book sometimes have trouble getting their solutions to balance!

Direct approach

Statement of income and retained earnings

The consolidated income statement for Parent Corp. is shown in Exhibit 6-4. The calculation of each item of revenue and expense is shown in brackets.

- *Sales revenue.* The consolidated sales are reduced by the intercompany sales during 2006 of $100,000 (downstream) plus $700,000 (upstream).

- *Royalty revenue.* Royalties are reduced by the intercompany royalties of $90,000 paid by Sub to Parent during 2006.

- *Dividend income.* Sub paid dividends of $90,000 during 2006. Of this amount, Parent received $90,000 × 80% = $72,000. The dividend income of Parent is reduced by the amount of the intercompany dividends of $72,000.

- *Cost of sales.* The cost of sales of the two companies is adjusted for (1) the intercompany sales, (2) the unrealized profits in the ending inventories, and (3) the realization of the previously unrealized profits in the beginning inventories:

  - The intercompany sales are $100,000 and $700,000, which are deducted from cost of sales as the offset to the deduction from sales, above.

  - The unrealized profits in the ending inventories are $16,000 for the downstream sales ($40,000 × 40%) and $28,000 for the upstream sales ($70,000 × 40%). These amounts are added to cost of sales.

  - The now-realized profits from the beginning inventory are $20,000 × 40% = $8,000 for downstream sales (in Sub's inventory) and are $100,000 × 40% = $40,000 for upstream sales (in Parent's inventory). These now-realized amounts are subtracted from cost of sales, thereby increasing consolidated net income.

EXHIBIT 6–4 PARENT CORP.

Condensed Consolidated Statement of Income and Retained Earnings
Year Ended December 31, 2006

Revenues

Sales revenue [2,000,000 + 1,500,000 – **100,000** – **700,000**]	$2,700,000
Royalty revenue [150,000 – **90,000**]	60,000
Dividend income [75,000 – **72,000**]	3,000
	2,763,000

Expenses

Cost of sales [1,200,000 + 900,000 – **100,000** – **700,000** + **16,000** + **28,000** – **8,000** – **40,000**]	1,296,000
Other expenses [560,000 + 411,000 – **90,000** + **6,000** + **2,000** – **2,000** – **3,000**]	884,000
Non-controlling interest in earnings of Sub Ltd. [(189,000 + **40,000** – **28,000** + **3,000**) × 20%]	40,800
	2,220,800

Net income	$ 542,200
Retained earnings, December 31, 2005 [2,395,000 + 641,000 – **555,000** – 20% × (641,000 – **555,000**) – **8,000** – **24,000** – (100,000 × 40% × 80%) – (20,000 × 40%) – (6,000 × 5) – (2,000 × 5) + (2,000 × 5) – (21,000 × 5/7 × 80%)]	2,349,800
Dividends declared [300,000 + 90,000 – **90,000**]	(300,000)
Retained earnings, December 31, 2006	$2,592,000

- *Other expenses.* Operating expenses are adjusted for (1) the intercompany royalty expense, (2) the amortization of the fair value increments and goodwill, and (3) for the over-depreciation of the machinery that was sold by Sub to Parent.

(1) Intercompany royalty payments of $90,000 are eliminated.

(2) On a straight-line basis, the $60,000 fair value increment on the machinery is amortized over 10 years at $6,000 per year. The increased value of the bonds of $16,000 is amortized over eight years at $2,000 per year—this amortization is similar to the amortization of any bond premium and is treated as a reduction of interest expense. The goodwill of $40,000 is amortized over 20 years at $2,000 per year.

(3) The depreciation expense relating to the machinery sold intercompany must be adjusted. Parent recorded $13,000 of depreciation on the asset during 2006, but the depreciation based on the cost of the machinery to Sub is only $10,000. Therefore, depreciation expense must be reduced by $3,000.

- *Non-controlling interest in earnings of Sub Ltd.* Exhibit 6-3 shows that Sub's separate-entity net income is $189,000. Parent has equity in only 80% of this amount. The remaining 20% is equity of the non-controlling interest. Before taking the 20%, we must adjust Sub's separate-entity earnings for the realized and unrealized profits from upstream sales. There are three adjustments.

Parent's *opening* inventory contains $100,000 of goods that had been purchased from Sub. The gross profit percentage was 40%, which yields an unrealized gross profit at the beginning of the year of $100,000 \times 40\% = \$40,000$. This amount has been sold to outsiders, and therefore has now been realized. We must add the $40,000 in now-realized profit to Sub's nominal earnings.

Parent's *ending* inventory contains unrealized profit of $70,000 \times 40\% = \$28,000$. We must subtract this amount from Sub's separate-entity net income.

Parent also is depreciating the machinery that had been purchased from Sub in 2004. Parent's depreciation is $91,000 \div 7 = \$13,000$. Depreciation based on the historical cost of the asset to Sub would have been $100,000 \div 10 = \$10,000$. Parent has charged an extra $3,000 in depreciation. Remember that amortization or depreciation constitutes recognition of the benefits of using a capital asset. Therefore, the extra $3,000 represents the realization of part of the previously unrealized intercompany profit. This $3,000 is added to Sub's nominal net income.

After these three adjustments are made, we can simply multiply the result by 20% to find the non-controlling interest's share of the Sub earnings that are included in Parent's consolidated net income.

- *Retained Earnings.* Once the net income for the year has been determined, the ending retained earnings can be calculated. First, however, it is necessary to determine the consolidated retained earnings at the beginning of the current year, January 1, 2006. The opening balance of retained earnings will include Parent's separate-entity retained earnings, plus Parent's share of Sub's retained earnings *since the date of acquisition*, plus and minus adjustments for amortization, unrealized profits, and sale of fair-valued assets. Taking the subtractions and additions to the beginning retained earnings in the order in which they appear in Exhibit 6-4:

  - Sub's retained earnings of $555,000 at the date of acquisition is subtracted.

  - Twenty percent of the increase in Sub's retained earnings since the date of acquisition is subtracted. This is the non-controlling interest's share of the increase in Sub's retained earnings.

  - The $8,000 fair value increment on inventories has flowed through cost of goods sold and into retained earnings. This FVI is subtracted from retained earnings.

  - The $24,000 FVI on investments is subtracted. Item 4 in *basic information* tells us that Sub sold its investments prior to 2006 (in 2003, actually, but the exact date is irrelevant). The profit recognized by Sub on this transaction must be reduced by the amount of the fair value increment *purchased* by Parent. In effect, the gain on the sale *to the consolidated entity* is the difference between the sales proceeds and the cost to the consolidated entity, which is the cost of the investments on Sub's books plus the $24,000 FVI. In general, when fair-valued assets are sold to unrelated purchasers, the fair value increment must be charged against the profit (or added to the loss) on the transaction. Note that the non-controlling interest is unaffected, because the fair value increment related only to the investor's share.

- Unrealized profits at the *beginning* of the year are subtracted:
  - *Upstream*: 80% of the 40% gross margin on $100,000 in Parent's inventory.
  - *Downstream*: 40% gross margin on $20,000 in Sub's inventory.

- We add the accumulated amortization on fair value increments and goodwill to the *beginning* of the year. Five years have elapsed between the acquisition date of December 31, 2000 and the end of the prior year, December 31, 2005.

- *FVI on machinery.* $60,000 FVI at 10% per year for five years equals $60,000 × 5/10 = $30,000 debit to retained earnings.
- *Goodwill.* $40,000 × 5/20 = $10,000 debit.
- *Bonds payable.* $16,000 FVI amortized over eight years on a straight-line basis, $16,000 × 5/8 = $10,000 *credit.*

- Sub sold machinery to Parent in 2004 at a gain over book value of $21,000. The machinery is being amortized over seven years from the date of acquisition. Therefore, Parent is recording depreciation that is $3,000 higher than it should be for the consolidated entity (that is, $21,000 ÷ 7 years = $3,000 per year). Two adjustments are necessary for the beginning retained earnings:
  - Two years' (2004 and 2005) excess depreciation must be added back to retained earnings: $21,000 × 2/7 = $6,000.
  - Parent's share of the remaining unrealized profit must be removed from consolidated retained earnings: $21,000 × 5/7 × 80% = $12,000.

    Notice that the total intercompany profit of $21,000 is divided between the 2/7 that has been realized (through use of the asset) and the 5/7 that remains unrealized at the end of 2005 and the beginning of 2006.

- *Dividends declared.* Parent's consolidated statements show only the dividends paid by Parent Corp.

Note that there is no need to adjust for the royalties paid by Sub to Parent prior to the beginning of 2006. The $500,000 in prior-year royalties has reduced Sub's retained earnings, but has increased Parent's retained earnings by the same amount. On consolidation, the effects are directly offsetting. No adjustment needs to be made for intercompany expenses in prior years, only for unrealized profits.

Balance sheet

Exhibit 6-5 shows the consolidated balance sheet for Parent Corp. at December 31, 2006. Cash, accounts receivable, investments, and accounts payable are simply the sum of the two companies' balances. The common share amount is for Parent only, since this is Parent's balance sheet. The calculations of the other amounts are summarized below:

- *Inventories.* The inventories are reduced by the full amount of the unrealized earnings in the ending inventories, both downstream ($16,000) and upstream ($28,000).

- *Machinery.* First, Sub's accumulated depreciation at the date of acquisition ($575,000) must be offset against the asset account. Then we add the fair value increment of $60,000. This adjustment assumes that all of the machinery to which the fair value increment applies is still held by Sub.

Next, we must adjust for the intercompany sale of machinery. The total upstream unrealized profit of $21,000 is deducted in order to reduce the carrying value of the machinery from the $91,000 reflected on Parent's books to the $70,000 net carrying value that had been on Sub's books. However, the machinery should not be shown in the consolidated machinery account at its net book value to Sub at the time of the intercompany sale, but rather at the full historical cost ($100,000) to Sub. Therefore, the $30,000 accumulated depreciation that existed on Sub's books at the time of the sale must be restored; $30,000 is added

EXHIBIT 6–5 PARENT CORP.

Condensed Consolidated Balance Sheet
December 31, 2006

Assets

Current assets:

Cash [50,000 + 20,000]	$ 70,000
Accounts receivable [150,000 + 160,000]	310,000
Inventories [180,000 + 100,000 **–16,000 – 28,000**]	236,000
	616,000

Capital assets:

Machinery [5,000,000 + 2,700,000 **– 575,000 + 60,000 – 21,000 + 30,000**]	7,194,000
Accumulated depreciation [1,770,000 + 1,240,000 **– 575,000 + (6,000 × 6) + 30,000 – (3,000 × 3)**]	(2,492,000)
	4,702,000

Other assets:

Investments [800,000 + 100,000 + 0 **– 800,000**]	100,000
Goodwill [**40,000 × 14/20**]	28,000
	128,000
Total assets	$ 5,446,000

Liabilities and shareholders' equity

Liabilities:

Current: accounts payable [450,000 + 200,000]	$ 650,000
Long-term: bonds payable [300,000 + 500,000 **+ 16,000 – (2,000 × 6)**]	804,000
Total liabilities	1,454,000
Non-controlling interest in Sub Ltd. [**1,040,000 – (70,000 × 40%) – (21,000 × 4/7)**] × 20%	200,000

Shareholders' equity:

Common shares	1,200,000
Retained earnings [see Exhibit 6-6]	2,592,000
Total shareholders' equity	3,992,000
Total liabilities and shareholders' equity	$ 5,446,000

to the machinery account and is also added to the accumulated depreciation account, below.

- *Accumulated depreciation.* First, Sub's accumulated depreciation at the date of Parent's acquisition ($575,000) is eliminated. Next, the amortization of the fair value increment over the six years between the date of acquisition and the current balance sheet date is added ($6,000 × 6 = $36,000). In addition, the accumulated depreciation of $30,000 that existed on the machinery sold intercompany is restored, as explained in the preceding paragraph. Deducted from accumulated depreciation is three years' annual depreciation adjustment on the intercompany machinery sale (3 years @ $3,000 per year = $9,000).

- *Goodwill.* Goodwill is reduced by six years' amortization at $2,000 per year, or $12,000.

- *Bonds payable.* The fair value increment is added to the book value of the bonds, less the amortization of the increment at $2,000 per year for six years.

An implicit assumption is that all of the bonds outstanding at January 1, 2002, are still outstanding. If any had been retired, then the related amount of fair value increment would have been offset against any gain or loss on retirement, as explained above for the sale of Sub's investments.

- *Non-controlling interest.* The non-controlling interest starts out as 20% of Sub's net assets (i.e., shareholders' equity) at the balance sheet date. On December 31, 2006, Sub's net assets amount to $1,040,000. The non-controlling interest's share of the net asset value is 20%. From that amount must be subtracted the non-controlling interest's share of the unrealized profit from the upstream sales at the end of the year: $70,000 × 40% × 20% = $5,600.

  Also, we must deduct the non-controlling interest's share of the remaining unrealized profit (after tax) from the upstream sale of machinery. Three years have elapsed since the sale, leaving 4/7 of the profit unrealized: $21,000 × 4/7 × 20% = $2,400.

- *Retained earnings.* The year-end retained earnings could be obtained from Exhibit 6-4, but that would take all the fun out of our consolidation. Instead, we should attempt to derive the year-end consolidated retained earnings directly. The year-end consolidated retained earnings consists of:

  1. the parent's year-end separate-entity retained earnings,

  2. plus the subsidiary's year-end separate-entity retained earnings,

  3. minus the subsidiary's date-of-acquisition retained earnings,

  4. minus the non-controlling interests' share of the subsidiary's retained earnings *since the date of acquisition,*

  5. less the cumulative amortization on fair value increments and goodwill from the date of acquisition to the current year-end, and

  6. less unrealized profits (net of non-controlling interest, where appropriate) at the *end* of the year.

The starting point is Parent's separate-entity retained earnings. To that we add 80% of the increase in Sub's retained earnings. Next we deduct the fair value increments relating to inventory at the date of acquisition ($8,000) and investments ($24,000), both of which have been sold prior to this year's balance sheet dates and have flowed through to retained earnings in prior years. Then we deduct the six years' amortization of the fair value increment on machinery, add the six years' amortization of the fair value increment on bonds payable, and deduct six years' amortization of goodwill.

There are three unrealized profit adjustments, two for year-end inventory and one for the machinery. The adjustment for the upstream inventory is $70,000 × 40% × 80% = $22,400. The adjustment for the downstream inventory is $40,000 × 40% = $16,000. The adjustment for Parent's share of the remaining unrealized machinery profit is $21,000 × 80% × 4/7 = $9,600.

The calculation of year-end consolidated retained earnings is summarized in Exhibit 6-6.

EXHIBIT 6–6 CALCULATION OF PARENT CORP. RETAINED EARNINGS

December 31, 2006

1	Parent's separate-entity retained earnings (Exhibit 6-3)	$2,560,000
2	Sub's separate-entity retained earnings (Exhibit 6-3)	740,000
3	Less Sub's retained earnings at the date of acquisition	(555,000)
4	Less non-controlling interests' share of retained earnings since the date of acquisition (740,000 – 555,000) × 20%	(37,000)
5	Less (plus) the cumulative amortization of FVIs and goodwill since the date of acquisition:	
	Less FVI on inventories (sold to third parties)	(8,000)
	Less FVI on investments (sold to third parties)	(24,000)
	Less six years' amortization of FVI on machinery (60,000 × 6/10)	(36,000)
	Less six years' amortization of goodwill (40,000 × 6/20)	(12,000)
	Plus six years' amortization of FVI (premium) on bonds (16,000 × 6/8)	12,000
6	Less year-end unrealized profit on intercompany sales:	
	Less unrealized profit on upstream inventory sales [(70,000 × 40%) × 80%]	(22,400)
	Less unrealized profit on downstream inventory sales (40,000 × 40%)	(16,000)
	Less remaining unrealized profit on machinery sold intercompany [(21,000 × 4/7) × 80%]	(9,600)
		$2,592,000

Worksheet approach

The consolidation worksheet for Parent Corp. at December 31, 2006 is shown in Exhibit 6-7. The first two columns contain the separate-entity financial statements for Parent and Sub. The adjustments are explained below:

Acquisition adjustments

The acquisition adjustments are to

- eliminate Sub's shareholders' equity and establish the date-of-acquisition non-controlling interest,

- recognize the fair value increments (that is, Parent's 80% share thereof) and goodwill, and

- eliminate Sub's accumulated depreciation at the date of acquisition.

Sub's shareholders' equity at the date of acquisition was $855,000, comprised of $300,000 in common shares and $555,000 in retained earnings. The non-controlling interest's share is $855,000 × 20% = $171,000. The adjustment to eliminate Sub's shareholders' equity accounts and to establish the non-controlling interest is as follows:

a1	Common shares	300,000	
	Retained earnings	555,000	
	Investment in Sub Ltd.		684,000
	Non-controlling interest in Sub Ltd.		171,000

EXHIBIT 6–7 PARENT CORP. CONSOLIDATION WORKSHEET

December 31, 2006

	Trial balances		Acquisition [a]	Adjustments Operations Cumulative [b]	Current [c]	Parent Corp. consolidated trial balance
	Parent	Sub				
Cash	$ 50,000	$ 20,000				$ 70,000
Accounts receivable	150,000	160,000				310,000
Inventories	180,000	100,000	8,000 **a2**	(8,000) **b1**	(16,000) **c3** (28,000) **c4**	236,000
Machinery	5,000,000	2,700,000	60,000 **a2** (575,000) **a3**	(21,000) **b5** 30,000 **b6**		7,194,000
Accumulated depreciation	(1,770,000)	(1,240,000)	575,000 **a3**	(30,000) **b6** (30,000) **b1** 6,000 **b5**	(6,000) **c1** 3,000 **c6**	(2,492,000)
Investment in Sub Ltd. (at cost)	800,000		(684,000) **a1** (116,000) **a2**			—
Other investments (at cost)	100,000		24,000 **a2**	(24,000) **b1**		100,000
Goodwill			40,000 **a2**	(10,000) **b1**	(2,000) **c1**	28,000
Accounts payable	(450,000)	(200,000)				(650,000)
Bonds payable	(300,000)	(500,000)	(16,000) **a2**	10,000 **b1**	2,000 **c1**	(804,000)
Non-controlling interest in Sub Ltd.			(171,000) **a1**	(17,200) **b2** 8,000 **b3** 3,000 **b5**	18,000 **c7** (40,800) **c8**	(200,000)
Common shares	(1,200,000)	(300,000)	300,000 **a1**			(1,200,000)
Dividends declared	300,000	90,000			(90,000) **c7**	300,000
Retained earnings, December 31, 2005	(2,395,000)	(641,000)	555,000 **a1**	62,000 **b1** 17,200 **b2** 32,000 **b3** 8,000 **b4** 12,000 **b5**		(2,349,800)
Sales revenue	(2,000,000)	(1,500,000)			800,000 **c2**	(2,700,000)
Royalty revenue	(150,000)				90,000 **c5**	(60,000)
Dividend income	(75,000)				72,000 **c7**	(3,000)
Cost of sales	1,200,000	900,000		(40,000) **b3** (8,000) **b4**	(800,000) **c2** 16,000 **c3** 28,000 **c4**	1,296,000
Other operating expenses	560,000	411,000			6,000 **c1** (90,000) **c5** (3,000) **c6**	884,000
Non-controlling interest in earnings					40,800 **c8**	40,800
	$ —	$ —	$ —	$ —	$ —	$ —

257

Adjustment **a1** eliminates $684,000 of the $800,000 purchase price. The remaining $116,000 purchase price discrepancy pertains to the fair value increments and goodwill. The fair value increments (and Parent's 80% share) and the calculation of goodwill are shown in Exhibit 6-2. The consolidation adjustment to record the FVI and goodwill, and to eliminate the remainder of the purchase price, is as follows:

a2	Inventory	8,000	
	Machinery	60,000	
	Investments	24,000	
	Goodwill	40,000	
	Bonds payable		16,000
	Investment in Sub Ltd.		116,000

The final acquisition adjustment is to offset Sub's accumulated depreciation at the date of acquisition against the machinery account, since the subsidiary's date-of-acquisition accumulated depreciation should not be carried forward in the consolidated balance sheet:

a3	Accumulated depreciation	575,000	
	Machinery		575,000

The acquisition adjustment shown here can be simplified somewhat. The fair value increment relating to inventories has long since flowed through to retained earnings. Similarly, the fair value increment relating to Sub's investments was realized through sale in 2004. Both of these fair value increments can be debited directly to the opening retained earnings. Since we did not take that approach in Exhibit 6-7, it will be necessary to make that transfer to retained earnings as part of the cumulative operations adjustment.

Cumulative operations adjustment

As noted just above, the cumulative operations adjustment will eliminate the fair value increments for inventories and investments by charging them to retained earnings.

Five years have elapsed between the date of acquisition and the *beginning* of the current fiscal year, and therefore five years' amortizations will have occurred. The *annual* amortizations for the FVI (other than inventories and investments) are as follows:

- Machinery: $60,000 FVI ÷ 10-year life = $6,000 depreciation per year.

- Goodwill: $40,000 ÷ 20-year estimated life = $2,000 amortization per year.

- Bonds payable: $16,000 ÷ 8-year remaining life = $2,000 amortization per year.

Cumulatively, the amortizations from the date of acquisition to the *beginning* of the current year amount to:

- Machinery: $6,000 × 5 = $30,000 credited to accumulated depreciation.

- Goodwill: $2,000 × 5 = $10,000 credited to the asset account.

- Bonds payable: $2,000 × 5 = $10,000 *debited* to the liability account.

The cumulative adjustment for the FVIs and goodwill therefore is:

b1 Retained earnings (beginning)   62,000
        Bonds payable   10,000
            Inventories   8,000
            Accumulated depreciation   30,000
            Other investments   24,000
            Goodwill   10,000

The second adjustment is to credit non-controlling interest for their share of the increase in Sub's retained earnings since the date of acquisition. Non-controlling interest is credited for 20% of the increase in Sub's retained earnings between January 1, 2002 and December 31, 2005. Retained earnings increased from $555,000 to $641,000, or $86,000; 20% of that amount is $17,200:

b2 Retained earnings (beginning)   17,200
            Non-controlling interest (B/S)   17,200

The third adjustment is to recognize the unrealized profits in the *beginning* inventories. Parent's opening inventory included $100,000 in goods acquired from Sub. Sub's gross margin was 40%; the unrealized upstream profit was $40,000. Of that amount, 20% pertains to the non-controlling interest:

b3 Retained earnings (beginning)   32,000
        Non-controlling interest (B/S)   8,000
            Cost of sales   40,000

Sub's opening inventories included $20,000 of goods purchased from Parent. At 40% gross margin, the unrealized profit was $8,000:

b4 Retained earnings (beginning)   8,000
            Cost of sales   8,000

The adjustment relating to machinery that was sold intercompany from Sub to Parent is a little more complicated. We will take this item in two steps. First, the *remaining unrealized* intercompany profit must be eliminated. The initial intercompany profit was $21,000. This full amount must be eliminated from the machinery account because Parent's machinery account still contains the full purchase price. However, two-sevenths of that amount has been realized through depreciation at the rate of $21,000 ÷ 7 years = $3,000 per year. Accumulated depreciation must be reduced by the excess depreciation for 2004 and 2005: $3,000 × 2 = $6,000.

The remaining five-sevenths of the original unrealized profit ($21,000 × 5/7 = $15,000) is still unrealized at the *beginning* of 2006. Of that amount, 80% (or $12,000) is in consolidated retained earnings and 20% (i.e., $3,000) pertains to the non-controlling interest. Putting that all together gives us a compound adjustment:

b5 Accumulated depreciation   6,000
        Retained earnings   12,000
        Non-controlling interest (B/S)   3,000
            Machinery   21,000

Adjustment **b5** reduces the machinery from its carrying value on Parent's books ($91,000) to the date-of-sale carrying value on Sub's books ($70,000).

However, on Sub's books, the carrying value was not just in the asset account. Instead, there was $100,000 in the asset account and $30,000 in the accumulated depreciation account. Therefore, the second step is to reinstate the date-of-sale accumulated depreciation:

b6 Machinery	30,000	
Accumulated depreciation		30,000

Current operations adjustments

The first of the current operations adjustments is the 2006 amortization of the fair value increments on machinery and bonds payable and of goodwill. If we combine all three amortization amounts, the net charge to other expenses is $6,000:

c1 Bonds payable	2,000	
Other expenses [net charge]	6,000	
Accumulated depreciation		6,000
Goodwill		2,000

Second is the elimination of intercompany sales. In Exhibit 6-7, we have combined the upstream and downstream intercompany sales transactions into a single amount:

c2 Sales revenue	800,000	
Cost of sales		800,000

Sub's inventory contains goods purchased from Parent (i.e., downstream) amounting to $40,000. The unrealized profit is $40,000 × 40% = $16,000:

c3 Cost of sales	16,000	
Inventories		16,000

Upstream sales of $70,000 are still in Parent's inventory. The unrealized profit is $70,000 × 40% = $28,000:

c4 Cost of sales	28,000	
Inventories		28,000

The royalties that Sub paid to Parent during the year must be eliminated:

c5 Royalty revenue	90,000	
Other expenses		90,000

No adjustment is needed for the $500,000 royalties paid in prior years. That is an extraneous or irrelevant piece of information!

The depreciation that Parent is charging on the machinery purchased from Sub must be reduced to the amount that Sub would have charged had the intercompany sale not taken place. Parent is charging $13,000 per year (i.e., $91,000 ÷ 7), but depreciation on the original cost to Sub would have been $10,000. The "excess" depreciation of $3,000 must be eliminated:

| **c6** | Accumulated depreciation | 3,000 | |
| | Other operating expenses | | 3,000 |

The next step is to eliminate Sub's dividends of $90,000. Eighty percent of the dividends were received by Parent and are offset against Parent's dividend income. The other 20% of the dividends went to the non-controlling interest, and therefore they are offset against the non-controlling interest on the balance sheet:

c7	Dividend income ($90,000 × 80%)	72,000	
	Non-controlling interest (B/S) ($90,000 × 20%)	18,000	
	Dividends paid		90,000

Notice that this adjustment does not completely eliminate the dividend income on Parent's income statement. Parent has other investments as well as its investment in Sub. Parent apparently earned $3,000 in dividends from these other investments.

Finally, we must calculate the non-controlling interest's share of Sub's 2006 net income, *net of unrealized profits*. The starting point is Sub's separate-entity net income of $189,000 (from Exhibit 6-3). To this, we must add the now-realized upstream profit in the opening inventory and deduct the unrealized downstream profit in the ending inventory. In addition, we must add this year's realized profit on the upstream sale of machinery, which is represented by the "excess" depreciation charged by Parent on the machinery:

Sub's separate-entity net income	$189,000
Plus now-realized upstream profit in opening inventory, $100,000 × 40%	+ 40,000
Less unrealized upstream profit in ending inventory, $70,000 × 40%	− 28,000
Plus now-realized profit on upstream sale of machinery, $21,000 × 1/7	+ 3,000
Sub's separate-entity net income adjusted for unrealized profits	$204,000

The non-controlling interest's share of Sub's adjusted earnings, as reported on Parent's consolidated income statement, is $204,000 × 20% = $40,800:

| **c8** | Non-controlling interest in earnings of Sub (I/S) | 40,800 | |
| | Non-controlling interest in Sub (B/S) | | 40,800 |

The result of these adjustments is consolidated net income of $542,200 and consolidated retained earnings of $2,592,000. We can verify these amounts via a separate calculation of Parent's equity in the 2006 earnings of Sub plus a calculation of Parent's year-end 2006 investment based on the equity method. Since equity-basis reporting constitutes one-line consolidation, we should get the same net income and the same retained earnings under the equity method as by consolidation.

Equity-Basis Reporting

To determine Parent's equity in Sub's 2006 earnings, we start with Parent's 80% share of Sub's reported net income of $189,000, or $151,200. This amount must then be adjusted for (1) amortization of fair value increments, (2) previously unrealized profits now realized in 2006, and (3) unrealized profits at the end of 2006. The top section of Exhibit 6-8 illustrates the necessary calculations.

EXHIBIT 6–8 PARENT CORP.'S EQUITY IN SUB LTD.

December 31, 2006

Parent Corp.'s equity in the earnings of Sub Ltd.:

Parent's share of Sub's reported net income: $189,000 × 80%			$151,200
Adjustments:			
Amortization of fair value increments and goodwill:			
Machinery		$ (6,000)	
Bonds payable		(2,000)	
Goodwill		2,000	(6,000)
Unrealized profit in opening inventories:			
Downstream		8,000	
Upstream: $40,000 × 80%		32,000	40,000
Unrealized profit in ending inventories:			
Downstream		(16,000)	
Upstream: $28,000 × 80%		(22,400)	(38,400)
Profit realized through depreciation on machinery sold intercompany: $3,000 × 80%			2,400
Parent's equity in the 2006 earnings of Sub			**$149,200**

Parent Corp.'s investment in Sub Ltd.

Initial investment (cost)			$800,000
Equity in unremitted earnings (net of dividends received from Sub):			
Parent's share of the change in Sub's retained earnings since the date of acquisition: ($740,000 − $555,000) × 80%			148,000
Less amortization of fair value increments and goodwill through 2006:			
Inventories (full amount realized)		$ (8,000)	
Investments (full amount realized)		(24,000)	
Machinery: $60,000 × 6/10		(36,000)	
Bonds payable: ($16,000) × 6/8		12,000	
Goodwill $40,000 × 6/20		(12,000)	(68,000)
Less remaining unrealized profits, December 31, 2006:			
Inventory, downstream		(16,000)	
Inventory, upstream: $28,000 × 80%		(22,400)	
Machinery: $21,000 × 80% × 4/7		(9,600)	(48,000)
Investment in Sub Ltd. (equity basis), December 31, 2006			**$832,000**

After making all the necessary adjustments, including the adjustment relating to the "excess" depreciation taken on the machinery that had been sold intercompany, Parent's equity in Sub's earnings amounts to $149,200. If we take this amount and add it to Parent's net income less the dividends received from Sub, we obtain $542,200, which is exactly the same as the consolidated net income derived on Exhibit 6-4:

Parent separate-entity net income (Exhibit 6-3)	$465,000
Less dividends received from Sub	(72,000)
Plus equity in earnings of Sub (Exhibit 6-8)	149,200
Consolidated net income	$542,200

At the end of 2006, Parent's investment in Sub should amount to (1) the original purchase price to acquire the 80% share, (2) plus 80% of the increase in Sub's retained earnings since the date of acquisition, (3) less amortization and realization of fair value increments and goodwill between the date of acquisition and year-end 2006, and (4) less any unrealized profits at year-end 2006. The lower section of Exhibit 6-8 illustrates this calculation.

The increase in the balance of the investment account since acquisition (that is, $832,000 - $800,000 = $32,000$), plus Parent's separate-entity retained earnings of $2,560,000 at the end of 2006, equals the consolidated retained earnings of $2,592,000. Thus the equity method can be used to double-check the results of the consolidation process.

Consolidation with Equity-Basis Recording

Throughout this book, we have focussed on consolidation when the parent company records its investment in the subsidiary at cost. This is the customary practice, since the cost method simplifies both parent-company bookkeeping and consolidation.

If the parent *records* its investment on the equity basis instead of the cost basis, the consolidation process must be modified accordingly. This is not a big problem. The only differences in the parent's separate-entity accounts between cost-basis and equity-basis reporting are that:

- the investment account includes the parent's share of the subsidiary's unremitted earnings to date (that is, the subsidiary's accumulated net incomes since the date of acquisition minus the dividends paid), in addition to the cost of the acquisition;

- the parent's opening retained earnings includes the cumulative amount of unremitted earnings to the beginning of the year;

- "Equity in earnings of subsidiary" will appear on the parent's separate-entity income statement; and

- the parent will show no dividend income from the subsidiary.

To prepare consolidated statements when the parent uses the equity basis of recording the investment, we must first remove the effects of the equity basis from the parent's accounts or trial balance. Once that is done, we can consolidate the accounts exactly as we have above.

Exhibit 6-9 shows Parent Corp.'s separate entity financial statements for 2006 using both the cost method and the equity method. The accounts that show a difference are highlighted. All other accounts are the same regardless of which recording method is used.

The first step in consolidation when Parent uses the equity basis of recording its investment is simply to reverse the differences between the two bases by undoing the equity recording. Using the amounts in the "difference" column of Exhibit 6-9, we debit for the credit difference (in the equity in earnings account) and credit for the debit differences:

Equity in earnings of Sub Ltd.	149,200	
Investment in Sub Ltd.		32,000
Dividend income		72,000
Retained earnings (opening)		45,200

EXHIBIT 6-9 COMPARISON OF COST-BASIS VS. EQUITY-BASIS RECORDING OF INVESTMENT

Parent Corp.
Balance Sheet
December 31, 2006

	Cost	Equity	Difference Debit/(Credit)
Assets			
Cash	$ 50,000	$ 50,000	
Accounts receivable	150,000	150,000	
Inventories	180,000	180,000	
Machinery	5,000,000	5,000,000	
Accumulated depreciation	(1,770,000)	(1,770,000)	
Investment in Sub Ltd.	**800,000**	**832,000**	**$ 32,000**
Other investments	100,000	100,000	
Total assets	$4,510,000	$4,542,000	
Liabilities and shareholders' equity			
Accounts payable	$ 450,000	$ 450,000	
Bonds payable	300,000	300,000	
Total liabilities	750,000	750,000	
Common shares	1,200,000	1,200,000	
Retained earnings	2,560,000	2,592,000	
Total shareholders' equity	3,760,000	3,792,000	
Total liabilities and shareholders' equity	$4,510,000	$4,542,000	

Income Statement
Year Ended December 31, 2006

	Cost	Equity	
Sales revenue	$2,000,000	$2,000,000	
Royalty revenue	150,000	150,000	
Dividend income	**75,000**	**3,000**	**72,000**
Equity in earnings of Sub Ltd.	**—**	**149,200**	**(149,200)**
Total revenue	2,225,000	2,302,200	
Cost of sales	1,200,000	1,200,000	
Other expenses	560,000	560,000	
Total expenses	1,760,000	1,760,000	
Net income	465,000	542,200	
Dividends declared	(300,000)	(300,000)	
Retained earnings, beginning of year	**2,395,000**	**2,349,800**	**45,200**
Retained earnings, end of year	$2,560,000	$2,592,000	

A slight variation is to leave the subsidiary's dividends received in the equity in earnings account, since they will be eliminated in the consolidation process anyway:

Equity in earnings of Sub Ltd.	77,200	
Investment in Sub Ltd.		32,000
Retained earnings (opening)		45,200

Either adjustment will work equally well. The equity-reversal entry can be made either before starting the consolidation process by adjusting the parent's separate-entity accounts, or by entering the reversing amounts in the consolidation working papers—either direct method or worksheet approach—as the first step after entering the separate entity amounts.

Extraordinary Items and Discontinued Operations

In Chapter 4, we pointed out that subsidiaries' extraordinary items and discontinued operations normally maintain their reporting status in the parent's financial statements, under both equity-basis reporting and consolidated financial statements.

A parent will report a subsidiary's extraordinary item as extraordinary in its own equity-basis or consolidated income statement if the required conditions still are present within the broader economic entity. An extraordinary gain or loss in a subsidiary may become immaterial in the context of the parent's financial reporting, or it may become merely an unusual item that merits separate disclosure but not treatment as an extraordinary item.

Similarly, a subsidiary may decide to discontinue a separable line of business and thus report a discontinued operation. But if that type of discontinued business still remains within the broader economic entity, then it will not qualify for reporting as a discontinued operation in a consolidated (or equity-basis) income statement.

The parent will report only its proportionate share of a subsidiary's extraordinary items and discontinued operations. In consolidation, the non-controlling interest absorbs its share of these gains or losses.

As is always the case with these items, they are reported net of any related income tax. If an item loses its special status and becomes an operating item in the consolidated statements, the tax effect must be added back (to *gross up* the item) and the tax effect is included in operating income tax expense.

Summary of Key Points

1. When amortizable capital assets are sold between related companies, any unrealized profit must be eliminated. Intercompany *losses* on unrealized sales may or may not be eliminated, depending on whether the loss reflects a true decline in the recoverable benefit of the asset. The amount of *unrealized* profit declines as the asset is amortized because amortization reflects the use of the asset and thus the realization of its benefits. For downstream sales, the full amount of unrealized profit is eliminated. For upstream sales (or lateral sales between subsidiaries), the non-controlling interest absorbs its share of unrealized profit.

   An asset that was acquired via an intercompany sale may be sold to outside third parties. When that happens, any remaining unrealized gain must be combined with the recorded gain or loss on the sale.

2. In general, consolidation adjustments fall into three categories: (1) acquisition adjustments, (2) cumulative operations adjustments, and (3) current operations adjustments. For problems that are to be solved by a student, these three may be combined to arrive at a year-end balance sheet or for a single-

year income statement. In practice, however, comparative statements are always required and the distinction between beginning and ending balance sheet amounts must be preserved.

The acquisition adjustments stay the same over time. There is no need to alter them, although they may be modified to reflect changes in asset structure, such as the disposition of fair-valued assets that were acquired but no longer held. In effect, this is a combination of acquisition and cumulative adjustments.

The theory underlying the cumulative operations adjustments is that date-of-acquisition balances must be updated to reflect amortizations and intercompany transactions to the beginning of the reporting year. Amounts such as opening inventories and opening retained earnings must be correctly stated.

Current operations adjustments have two basic functions: (1) to correctly state consolidated end-of-period balances, and (2) to adjust the year's earnings to reflect only transactions with non-related entities.

3. Equity-basis reporting will result in the same parent-company net income and retained earnings as does consolidation. Calculations for equity-basis earnings therefore can provide a useful check on the accuracy of consolidated results.

If the parent company records its investment on the equity basis, the first step in consolidation is to reverse the impact of the entity-basis adjustments. Then, consolidation can proceed as has been described throughout this textbook.

4. A parent company normally will report a subsidiary's extraordinary gains and losses and discontinued operations as such in its consolidated (or equity-basis) income statement. Only the parent's proportionate part of these items is included; the non-controlling interest absorbs its portion of any such items.

Weblinks

FEI (Financial Executives International) Canada
www.feicanada.org/

FEI Canada provides many valuable services to its members including peer networking opportunities; emerging issues alerts; personal and professional development; and advocacy services.

CMA Canada
www.cma-canada.org

CMA Canada represents more than 31,000 Certified Management Accountants (CMAs) and 10,000 CMA candidates and students in Canada. Check out the *Careers* section for a job listing service for employers. *Provinces* links you to information from CMA Canada's provincial and territorial partners; for current CMA information click on *News*. In the *Resources* section you'll find a collection of publications you can purchase on leading-edge management techniques, and articles from CMA Management magazine.

Certified General Accountants Association
www.cga-canada.org

The Certified General Accountants Association of Canada is a national self-regulating association of 60,000 Certified General Accountants and students. CGAs are professional accountants working in industry, commerce, finance, government, and public practice. Find out how to become a CGA, where the jobs are for CGAs, or read past and present articles from *CGA Magazine*.

Self-Study Problem 6-1

Sorrow Limited is an 80%-owned subsidiary of Parks Corporation, a manufacturer of industrial equipment. In 2003, Sorrow purchased a grummling machine from Parks for $100,000. Parks had manufactured the machine at a cost of $60,000. Sorrow uses straight-line depreciation over a 10-year period for its grummling machines, and follows the practice of depreciating its assets by one-half year in both the year of acquisition and the year of disposal. No salvage value is assumed. Single assets accounting (that is, not group depreciation) is used. Sorrow used the machine in its productive operations from 2003 to 2016, in which year it was sold for scrap for $1,000.

Required:

Prepare the adjustments that would be necessary in each of 2003, 2004, 2008, 2015, and 2016 for the grummling machine when preparing Parks Corporation's consolidated financial statements.

Self-Study Problem 6-2

On January 1, 2001, Power Corporation purchased 80% of the outstanding shares of Spencer Corporation for $2,500,000 in cash. On that date, Spencer Corporation's common shares had a carrying value of $2,000,000 and retained earnings of $1,000,000. On January 1, 2001, all of Spencer's identifiable assets and liabilities had fair values that were equal to their carrying values except for:

1. A building that had an estimated fair value of $600,000 less than its carrying value; its remaining useful life was estimated to be 10 years.

2. A long-term liability with a fair value of $500,000 less than its carrying value; the liability matures on December 31, 2008.

Power Corporation's executives estimate that any goodwill that arises from this business combination will have a beneficial life of 20 years.

The income statements of Power Corporation and Spencer Corporation for the year ended December 31, 2005 are shown in Exhibit 6-10. Additional information is as follows:

1. On January 1, 2002, Spencer sold a machine to Power for $210,000. Spencer originally paid $400,000 for the machine on January 2, 1997. At the original date of purchase by Spencer, the machine had an estimated useful life of 20 years with no estimated salvage value. There has been no change in these estimates—the machine still retains its value in use.

2. Both companies use the straight-line method for all depreciation and amortization.

3. During 2004, the following intercompany inventory sales occurred:
   * Power sold $500,000 of merchandise to Spencer, $100,000 of which is in Spencer's inventory at 2004 year-end.
   * Spencer sold $300,000 of merchandise to Power, $70,000 of which is in Power's inventory at the end of 2004.

4. During 2005, the following intercompany inventory sales occurred:
   * Power sold $400,000 of merchandise to Spencer, $90,000 of which is in Spencer's inventory at 2005 year-end.

EXHIBIT 6–10 SEPARATE-ENTITY INCOME STATEMENTS

Year Ended December 31, 2005

	Power	Spencer
Sales	$2,000,000	$ 900,000
Investment income	1,000,000	100,000
Gain on sale of land	—	68,000
Total revenue	3,000,000	1,068,000
Cost of goods sold	1,300,000	500,000
Other operating expenses	960,000	320,000
Total expenses	2,260,000	820,000
Net income	$ 740,000	$ 248,000

- Spencer sold $250,000 of merchandise to Power, $60,000 of which is in Power's inventory at the end of 2005.

5. Intercompany inventory transactions are priced to provide Power with 30% gross margin (on sales price) and Spencer with 40% gross profit (on sales). Both companies use the first-in first-out inventory cost flow assumption.

6. On September 1, 2005, Spencer sold a parcel of land to Power Company for $150,000 that it had originally purchased for $65,000.

7. During 2005, Power declared and paid $250,000 in dividends, while Spencer declared and paid $40,000 in dividends.

8. Power accounts for its investment in Spencer on the cost basis.

Required:

a. Prepare a consolidated income statement for Power Corporation for the year ending December 31, 2005. Show supporting calculations for each amount in the consolidated income statement.

b. Independently, calculate Power Corporation's net income using equity-basis reporting.

[SMA, adapted]

Appendix

Intercompany Bond Holdings

Intercompany bond transactions

On occasion, one company in an affiliated group of companies will buy bonds issued by another company of the group. When the purchase is directly from the issuing company, the transaction is clearly an intercompany transaction. When consolidated financial statements are prepared, the intercompany transaction must be eliminated in order to prevent the intercompany receivable and payable from appearing on the consolidated balance sheet. Only bonds that are held by bondholders who are outside the affiliated group can be shown as a liability of the consolidated entity. As long as the bonds are held within the group, intercompany interest expense (to the issuer) and interest revenue (to the holder) must be eliminated, as well as any amortization of related discount or premium.

When the bonds are retired, the indebtedness and the investment will both be removed from the books. However, if the retirement occurs prior to the maturity date of the bonds, a gain or loss may result on the separate company books. Any such gain or loss must also be eliminated upon consolidation.

In general, intercompany transactions in bonds pose no particular reporting problems for consolidation or for the equity method. Adjustments and eliminations for bond transactions are similar to those that are required for asset transactions. Both offsetting transactions and offsetting balances must be eliminated when consolidated statements are prepared.

Indirect acquisitions of bonds

What if one company within the economic entity buys bonds in an affiliated company not directly from the issuer, but rather from an outside holder of the bonds? In this case, the buying company still ends up holding bonds that are an indebtedness of an affiliated company and that must be eliminated upon consolidation, but the buying price and the issuer's carrying value are likely not to be the same.

While an open-market purchase of an affiliate's bonds is possible, we must point out that it is very rare in Canadian business practice. Its rarity is the reason that we have relegated this discussion to an Appendix instead of including it in the main body of the chapter. For the sake of completeness, however, we will explain the ramifications of such a transaction.

Suppose that SubCorp has a bond issue outstanding that has a face value of $1,000,000, an unamortized premium of $50,000, a nominal interest rate of 12%, and five years remaining to maturity. Non-affiliated investors hold all of the bonds. Market rates of interest have risen above the nominal rate on the bonds, and have caused the market price of SubCorp's bonds to fall. SubCorp's parent, ParCorp, then buys $100,000 face value of the SubCorp bonds on the open market for $90,000.

When consolidated statements are prepared, the intercompany interest must be eliminated, and the amount of the bonds held by ParCorp must be eliminated against the proportionate part of the indebtedness of SubCorp. On ParCorp's books, the bond investment is carried at $90,000; while on SubCorp's books, the bond indebtedness is carried at $105,000 (10% of the $1,000,000 face value and of the $50,000 premium). The problem is how to dispose of the $15,000 difference in carrying values.

To solve this problem, we must look at the substance of the transaction. SubCorp could have used its own cash to purchase the bonds itself. If SubCorp had done so, it would have recognized a gain on the retirement of debt of $15,000. Alternatively, SubCorp could have borrowed $90,000 from ParCorp and used that cash to buy the bonds. SubCorp still would have recognized a gain of $15,000, and an intercompany payable (and receivable) for $90,000 would exist—that payable (and receivable) would be eliminated upon consolidation.

However, instead of lending SubCorp the money, ParCorp simply bought the bonds directly. SubCorp still has a legal liability (to ParCorp) for the bonds, but the substance is that for the consolidated entity, the indebtedness no longer exists. From the viewpoint of the readers of the consolidated statements, the bonds have been retired. Therefore, the $15,000 difference between SubCorp's carrying value and ParCorp's acquisition cost must be treated as a gain when the statements are consolidated and the intercompany bond holdings are eliminated. The Year 1 adjustment will appear as follows, assuming that the bonds were acquired at the end of Year 1 without accrued interest, and that *SubCorp is wholly owned by ParCorp*:

Bonds payable	100,000	
Premium on bonds payable	5,000	
Bond investment		90,000
Gain on retirement of bonds		15,000

In subsequent years, the carrying value of the bonds on SubCorp's books will decrease due to the continuing amortization of the premium. If we assume straight-line amortization, the carrying value to SubCorp will decline by $1,000 per year. This decline is offset by a decrease in SubCorp's interest expense (assuming that the premium amortization is credited directly thereto). Therefore, the Year 2 elimination, including the intercorporate payment of interest, will appear as follows:

Bonds payable	100,000	
Premium on bonds payable	4,000	
Interest income (paid to ParCorp)	12,000	
Bond investment		90,000
Interest expense (for SubCorp)		11,000
Retained earnings		15,000

Each year that ParCorp holds the bonds, the above entry will change only by the decreasing balance of the premium—the decrease in the premium will be offset by a decrease in the credit to retained earnings, reflecting the continuing amortization of the premium. The Year 3 elimination will be:

Bonds payable	100,000	
Premium on bonds payable	3,000	
Interest income (paid to ParCorp)	12,000	
Bond investment		90,000
Interest expense (for SubCorp)		11,000
Retained earnings		14,000

The above example assumes that ParCorp is accounting for its investment in SubCorp's bonds as a portfolio investment and does not amortize the bond purchase discount. If, instead, ParCorp accounts for the bonds as an investment to maturity, then each year ParCorp will amortize one-fifth of its $10,000 purchase discount by charging $2,000 to the bond investment account and crediting it to interest income. In that case, the elimination entry in years subsequent to acquisition will have to reflect the difference in both the investment and the interest income account, as follows:

Year 2

Bonds payable	100,000	
Premium on bonds payable	4,000	
Interest income	14,000	
Bond investment		92,000
Interest expense		11,000
Retained earnings		15,000

Year 3

Bonds payable	100,000	
Premium on bonds payable	3,000	
Interest income (paid to ParCorp)	14,000	
Bond investment		94,000
Interest expense (for SubCorp)		11,000
Retained earnings		12,000

In each of Years 4 and 5, the balance in SubCorp's premium account will decline by $1,000, while the balance of ParCorp's bond investment will rise by $2,000. The combined effect is to reduce the credit to retained earnings in the elimination entry by $3,000 per year, which represents the gradual recognition (through amortization) on both companies' books of the issue premium and purchase discount.

At the end of Year 6, SubCorp will officially retire the bonds, transferring $100,000 to ParCorp for its amount held. The bonds payable and bond investment accounts will disappear from both companies' books, and the only remnant of the bonds that will remain on the pre-consolidation financial statements will be the interest income and expense accounts. These will be eliminated in Year 6 as follows:

Interest income	14,000	
Interest expense		11,000
Retained earnings		3,000

Non-wholly-owned subsidiaries

If SubCorp is not wholly owned by ParCorp, then a question arises as to whether the gain on elimination of the intercompany bond holdings is a gain to SubCorp, to ParCorp, or partially to each. The significance of this question lies in the fact that if all or part of the gain is attributable to SubCorp, then the non-controlling interest will be assigned its proportionate share of the gain.

There are two views of the gain. One is that it is attributable to each corporation based on the difference between the bond's carrying value on the books of the company and the face value of the bonds. This is known as the **par-value approach**. Under this approach, the $15,000 total gain would be attributed as $5,000 to SubCorp and $10,000 to ParCorp. The result is what would have happened if SubCorp had redeemed the bonds at face value. Indeed, if ParCorp holds the bonds until maturity, SubCorp will in fact amortize the $5,000 premium and ParCorp will amortize the purchase discount as a credit to income over the five years. Thus the par-value approach attributes the gain to the two parties in relation to their respective roles as debtor and creditor, as though they were unaffiliated companies.

If SubCorp is 80% owned by ParCorp, then 20% of the $5,000 gain attributed to SubCorp under the par-value approach will be allocated to the non-controlling interest. The Year 1 worksheet elimination entry is:

Bonds payable	100,000	
Premium on bonds payable	5,000	
Non-controlling interest in earnings (I/S)	1,000	
Bond investment		90,000
Gain on retirement of bonds		15,000
Non-controlling interest (B/S)		1,000

However, SubCorp could easily have borrowed $90,000 from ParCorp and retired the bonds itself. In that case, the par-value method would have assigned the entire $15,000 gain to SubCorp. Since there is no difference in substance between ParCorp buying the bonds or lending SubCorp the money to buy the bonds, the second approach to allocating the $15,000 total gain is to attribute it entirely to the issuing corporation—SubCorp in this example. This method is called the **agency approach** because ParCorp is effectively acting as agent for SubCorp when it buys the bonds. The Year 1 elimination entry will appear as follows.

Bonds payable	100,000	
Premium on bonds payable	5,000	
Non-controlling interest in earnings (I/S)	3,000	
Bond investment		90,000
Gain on retirement of bonds		15,000
Non-controlling interest (B/S)		3,000

The non-controlling interest is increased by 20% of the full $15,000 gain.

Unlike the par-value method, the agency method yields the same results regardless of the way in which the bond repurchase transaction was structured. Since the agency method stresses substance over form, many accountants prefer it. Either approach may be encountered in practice, however. The difference between the two is likely to be immaterial, and then the easiest treatment should be used.

In years following ParCorp's purchase of SubCorp's bonds, the eliminating entries will differ from those shown above for Year 1 as a result of the amortization of the issue premium and the purchase discount. Assuming that both are amortized on a straight-line basis over the five years to maturity, SubCorp's premium account will decrease by $1,000 per year and ParCorp's carrying value of the bond investment will increase by $2,000 per year. The resulting combined recognition of $3,000 per year of the spread between the issue and repurchase prices causes the *unrecognized* portion of the spread (i.e., gain) to decline by $3,000 per year, exactly as described in the previous section.

If SubCorp were wholly owned by ParCorp, the $3,000 decline will be reflected in the year-by-year eliminations as a reduction in the amount added (credited) to retained earnings. When SubCorp is not wholly owned, then the change in the unrecognized gain is allocated to retained earnings and non-controlling interest—the relative proportions depend on whether the par-value or the agency approach is being used.

The annual adjustment to eliminate intercompany interest income and expense (assuming that *both* the premium and the discount are being amortized) will be as follows if SubCorp is wholly owned:

Interest income	14,000	
Interest expense		11,000
Retained earnings		3,000

Since the full amount of the gain was recognized on the consolidated statements in Year 1, the separate-entity recognition of the gain through amortization must not be permitted to flow through to the consolidated income statement again. Therefore, the balancing credit is to retained earnings rather than to a gain account.

When SubCorp is only 80% owned, then part of the balancing credit of $3,000 must be allocated to non-controlling interest. The portion allocated depends on the approach used. Under the par-value approach:

Interest income	14,000	
Interest expense		11,000
Non-controlling interest (B/S)		200
Retained earnings		2,800

The $200 represents 20% of the SubCorp $1,000 discount amortization for each year.

Using the agency approach:

Interest income	14,000	
Interest expense		11,000
Non-controlling interest (B/S)		600
Retained earnings		2,400

The $600 represents 20% of the combined amortizations of $3,000 per year.

The eliminating entries for the principal amount (and the related issue premium and purchase discount) are shown in Exhibit 6-11. Under both methods, the combined credits to non-controlling interest and retained earnings are $12,000 at the end of Year 2, down from $15,000 at the bond acquisition in Year 1. The combined credit declines by $3,000 each year as the carrying values of the bonds on both companies' books merge towards the maturity value of $100,000. In Year 6, the bonds mature and are retired; therefore, the only consolidation adjustment relating to the bonds in Year 6 will be for the intercompany interest.

Subsidiary purchase of parent's bonds

The foregoing example dealt solely with the purchase of a subsidiary's bonds by the parent. When the situation is reversed, how do the consolidation adjustments differ?

If the par-value method is used, the non-controlling interest is allocated its share of the difference between the bond's face value and its carrying value on the subsidiary's books. The adjustment is exactly the same as shown above, regardless of whether the subsidiary is the issuer of the bonds or the buyer.

If the agency approach is used, the full gain or loss is attributed to the issuing company. When the issuing company is the parent, there obviously will be no non-controlling interest; the consolidation eliminations will be exactly the same as those illustrated above for wholly-owned subsidiaries.

EXHIBIT 6–11 BOND ELIMINATION ENTRIES, SUBSEQUENT TO ACQUISITION

(amounts in thousands of dollars)

	Year 2	Year 3	Year 4	Year 5
Par-value approach				
Bonds payable	100.0	100.0	100.0	100.0
Premium on bonds	4.0	3.0	2.0	1.0
Bond investment	92.0	94.0	96.0	98.0
Non-controlling interest	0.8	0.6	0.4	0.2
Retained earnings (end)	11.2	8.4	5.6	2.8
Agency approach				
Bonds payable	100.0	100.0	100.0	100.0
Premium on bonds	4.0	3.0	2.0	1.0
Bond investment	92.0	94.0	96.0	98.0
Non-controlling interest	2.4	1.8	1.2	0.6
Retained earnings (end)	9.6	7.2	4.8	2.4

Summary

Direct intercompany bond transactions are treated no differently than other intercompany indebtedness when consolidated statements are prepared. The off-setting liability and investment must be eliminated, as well as all intercompany interest payments and any premium and discount amortizations.

When bonds of an affiliated company are purchased from an unaffiliated holder subsequent to their original issuance, the carrying value of the bonds on the books of the issuer may be different from the cost to the acquirer. The difference in carrying values can be assigned wholly to the issuer of the bonds (the agency approach) or allocated to both the issuer and the buyer on the basis of the face value of the bonds (the par-value approach). The method of allocation will affect the non-controlling interest and the consolidated net income.

The essence of consolidated reporting is to show the assets *and liabilities* that are under the control of the parent company. Since the parent can structure the liability position of the affiliated companies in a number of ways with the same substantive result, the reporting of an in-substance debt retirement should not be affected by the technical manner by which it is accomplished. Only the agency approach achieves substance over form; the par-value approach will yield different consolidated net income depending on the technical structure of the repurchase.

Indeed, the par-value approach can lead to some odd results. For example, if the parent has bonds outstanding that were issued at a premium, then the parent can trigger recognition of a gain in its consolidated income statement by having a non-wholly-owned subsidiary buy the bonds, regardless of the price paid by the subsidiary. The subsidiary could pay a price that is even higher than the carrying value of the bonds on the parent's books, and an overall economic loss to the combined entity would clearly result. But the par-value approach would still attribute a gain to the parent and a loss to the subsidiary, with part of the loss allocated to non-controlling shareholders. Thus the agency approach seems more consistent with the overall objectives of consolidated reporting and with the basic qualitative characteristic of reporting substance over form; as well, it is easier to apply. Nevertheless, both methods can be found in practice.

When part of a bond issue is retired at a gain, GAAP permits the gain to be recognized either in a lump sum or amortized over the remaining life of the bond issue. In this chapter, we have assumed for the sake of simplicity that the gain is recognized in the year of the repurchase.

Self-Study Problem 6-3 (Appendix)

Sweetness Corporation is 70% owned by Passion Limited. At the beginning of 2001, Sweetness issued $1,000,000 in 12%, 10-year bonds for $958,000. On December 31, 2004, Passion purchased 50% of the bonds from their original buyer for $479,000. Passion reports the bond investment as a long-term investment. Both companies calculate amortization on a straight-line basis.

Required:

Construct the eliminating entry for the bonds (including interest) at the following dates, first using the agency approach and then using the par-value method:

a. December 31, 2004

b. December 31, 2006

c. December 31, 2010

Review Questions

6-1 Under what conditions is a profit on an intercompany sale considered to be *unrealized?*

6-2 A capital asset is sold by a subsidiary to its parent company at the asset's fair market value, which is less than the asset's carrying value on the subsidiary's books. Would the unrealized loss on the sale be eliminated upon consolidation? Explain.

6-3 Company P owns 60% of Company S1 and 90% of Company S2. S1 sells inventory to S2 at a profit of $10,000. All the goods are still in S2's inventory at year-end. By what amount should consolidated net income be adjusted to eliminate the unrealized profit?

6-4 Company IR owns 30% of Company IE1 and 40% of Company IE2. IE1 sells inventory to IE2 at a profit of $10,000. All the goods are still in IE2's inventory at year-end. By what amount should IR's equity-basis investment income be adjusted to eliminate the unrealized profit?

6-5 In what way is the profit on intercompany sales of depreciable assets *realized?*

6-6 What is the difference between an *upstream* sale and a *downstream* sale?

6-7 What happens if a company sells a capital asset that is part of its *inventory* to another company in the consolidated group instead of one that is shown as a *capital asset* on the books of the selling company?

6-8 How does the adjustment differ when there is sale of an intangible asset; e.g., patent instead of a capital asset from the subsidiary to the parent?

6-9 Explain the composition of consolidated retained earnings in terms of the parent's and subsidiary's separate-entity retained earnings.

6-10 In what way do consolidation adjustments for the amortization of fair value increments and goodwill for prior years differ from those for the current year?

6-11 When a fair-valued asset is sold by a subsidiary to its parent, how does the amount of the fair value increment affect the unrealized profit elimination?

6-12 When a fair-valued asset is sold to outsiders, what is the disposition of the fair value increment when the statements are consolidated in the year of the sale? What is the disposition of the increment in years following the sale?

6-13 Explain briefly how the process of consolidation differs when the equity method is used by the parent for recording the investment account as compared to the cost method?

6-14 What does the equity-basis balance of the investment account for a subsidiary represent (e.g., cost of the investment, market value of the investment, etc.)?

6-15 Under equity reporting, why are unrealized profits from *downstream* sales deducted from the investor's equity in the earnings of the investee, instead of from the parent's own earnings?

6-16 Parent Company holds debentures of Sub Company that were purchased by Parent as a part of the original issuance by Sub. What eliminations are necessary in preparing Parent's consolidated financial statements?

6-17 Parent Company holds bonds of its subsidiary, Sub Company, that were purchased on the open market at a substantial discount. Upon consolidation of Parent's financial statements, how should the difference in carrying values of the bonds on the two companies' books be reported?

6-18 Explain the difference in concept between the par-value and the agency approaches to eliminating intercorporate bond holdings.

6-19 "Substance over form" is an important qualitative criterion for external financial reporting. Which method of intercompany bond elimination better satisfies this criterion? Explain why.

Cases

Case 6-1

A La Mode Inc.

A La Mode Inc. (ALM) is a retailer of women and children's clothing with stores all across Canada. ALM has been in operation for the last 35 years and is a public company with a year-end of January 31.

Currently, Mr. Jones and Mr. Grenier each own approximately 35% of the voting shares of ALM; the remaining outstanding shares are widely held. They founded ALM in the 1960s, when they were both in their late twenties. Their first store sold clothing for the working woman. It took only a few years until this first store became one of many successful stores. In 1990, they launched a new children's clothing chain.

Mr. Jones is always looking for new challenges. ALM is nearing completion of acquiring an American chain of women's apparel, USA Chic Inc. (CI), to give ALM a gateway to the U.S. market.

ALM has almost completed the acquisition of CI. Mr. Jones and Mr. Grenier already personally own some shares in CI. Mr. Jones estimates if ALM acquires an additional 3,500,000 Class B common shares of CI, ALM could gain control of CI. ALM intends to finance the acquisition of CI shares by issuing convertible debt to a pension fund. The pension fund has agreed to advance $20,055,000 of convertible debt, bearing interest at 8%. The debt will be convertible at the option of the pension fund into multiple-voting shares on May 1, 2000. The exercise price on conversion is to be determined using the average of the 2000 and 2001 consolidated earnings per share (EPS) before discontinued operations and extraordinary items, as reported in ALM's audited financial statements, multiplied by the price-earnings ratio. The average EPS is $0.4228 and the average price-earnings multiplier is 12. Further information on the purchase of CI is included in Exhibit 1.

EXHIBIT 1
NOTES FROM DISCUSSION OF USA CHIC WITH MR. JONES

1. Mr. Grenier and Mr. Jones each own 1,128,600 multiple-voting shares of ALM.

2. ALM proposes to acquire 3,500,000 Class B common shares of CI from the largest shareholder, BCG Inc., an unrelated corporation, for $5.73 per share. BCG Inc. is experiencing serious cash-flow problems and therefore wants to sell its investment in CI. BCG needs to sell at least 3,500,000 shares, which it has agreed to sell to ALM. BCG is also contemplating selling the rest of its investment on the public market. If ALM buys the 3,500,000 shares from BCG Inc., it will be entitled to two seats on the board of directors of CI. The other members of the board include the CEO of CI, a lawyer, and a businesswoman.

3. The shareholdings of CI are as follows:

BCG Inc.	5,998,000	Class B common shares
Mr. Jones and Mr. Grenier	2,869,000	Class B common shares
Public	8,399,000	Class A common shares

4. The CI Class B common shares currently outstanding give the right to two votes per share and are convertible into Class A shares at the holder's option. In all other respects the Class B shares are the same as the Class A shares. A side agreement between ALM and BCG provides that BCG will convert any of its remaining shares in CI to Class A shares before selling to the public.

5. CI is a specialty retailer of moderately priced fashion apparel for women and is well established in the U.S. market. If ALM acquires voting control of this company, ALM will gain a presence in the U.S. market and obtain valuable experience, and will eventually get to open a chain of its clothing stores there. The current CI auditors will remain the auditors for the 2001 year-end.

6. ALM has completed the due diligence process related to the purchase of CI and did not find anything that would alter its decision to go ahead with the acquisition on May 1, 2000. ALM has concluded that the fair value of the assets of CI is approximately the same as their book value.

7. The total shareholders' equity for USA Chic (in Canadian dollars) for January 31, 2000 is $63,046,000. Net income for the first three months of operations (Jan. 31 to May 1, 2000) is anticipated to be $3,076,000.

Mr. Jones and Mr. Grenier would like an analysis of the number of ALM shares that need to be issued to complete the purchase of CI and any implications from the proposed financing arrangement. Mr. Jones is not sure whether ALM can consolidate the results of CI operations in ALM's 2001 financial statements. Mr. Jones was quoted as saying "If possible, ALM would show better EPS, which is of utmost importance to the board."

You work for a CA firm that will be completing the audit of ALM. Your partner has asked you to write a memo addressing the concerns raised by Mr. Jones and Mr. Grenier. In addition, your partner wants you to identify, in a separate memo, audit concerns relating to the purchase of CI.

Required:

Write the report to Mr. Jones and Mr. Grenier and the separate memo requested by the partner.

[CICA, adapted]

Case 6-2

Voice Limited

National Computers (NC) and Hightech Ltd. (HT), two unrelated companies, agreed to share the latest technology in allowing visually impaired individuals to use voice recognition software to complete their banking over the phone (e.g., transferring funds from one account to another, verifying bank balances, paying bills). Eventually they hope to expand the program to allow enquiries about stock market quotes.

On January 1, 2000, NC and HT incorporated a new company, Voice Ltd. (VL). Two classes of VL common shares were issued. Each share in both classes participates equally in the company's earnings. Class A shares are nonvoting, whereas Class B shares are voting. In return for 59 Class A shares and 1 Class B share, NC contributed land with a fair market value of $1,600,000 (NC's book value for the land was $800,000). In return for 39 Class A shares and 1 Class B share, HT contributed cash of $1,000,000.

Of the five-member board of directors of VL, three are nominees of NC and two are nominees of HT. Initially, it was decided that VL would conserve its cash by paying no dividends. Under a written agreement, any change in the dividend policy of VL, and any transactions between VL and either NC or HT, must be approved in advance by both NC and HT. NC has retained the right to select VL's chief executive officer. The primary activity of NC is the manufacturing of personal computers.

Extracts from the income statements and the balance sheets for NC and VL are as follows, ignoring the impact of income taxes:

Income Statements
For the Year Ended Dec 31, 2000

	NC	VL
Sales	$3,300,000	$1,200,000
Cost of goods sold	1,600,000	600,000
	1,700,000	600,000
Depreciation	600,000	200,000
Other operating expenses	700,000	300,000
	1,300,000	500,000
Income before gain	400,000	100,000
Gain on sale of land	800,000	300,000
Net income	$1,200,000	$ 400,000

Balance Sheets
December 31, 2000

	NC	VL
Cash	$1,800,000	$ 500,000
Accounts receivable	400,000	300,000
Inventory	1,500,000	500,000
Investment in VL, at cost	1,600,000	—
Building and equipment, net	1,800,000	600,000
Land	800,000	800,000
	$7,900,000	$2,700,000
Accounts payable	$ 200,000	$ 300,000
Common shares	5,000,000	2,000,000
Retained earnings	2,700,000	400,000
	$7,900,000	$2,700,000

Additional Information:

1. During 2000, VL sold one-half of the land transferred from NC for proceeds of $1,000,000, and recorded a gain of $300,000.

2. A management fee of $150,000, paid to NC by VL during 2000, is included in other operating expenses of VL and sales of NC in the above 2000 income statements.

3. VL's ending inventory includes goods purchased from NC for $400,000. NC's cost for these goods was $275,000. NC's ending inventory includes goods purchased from VL for $250,000. VL's cost for these goods was $150,000.

Required:

The following are four possible alternatives for accounting for NC's investment in VL:

    1. cost

    2. equity

    3. consolidation

a. Discuss the appropriateness of using each of these four alternatives.

b. Calculate NC's net income for 2000 under each alternative (ignore income taxes). Explain any assumptions used.

[SMA, adapted]

Case 6-3

Alright Beverages Ltd.

Alright Beverages Ltd. (AB) was federally incorporated in 1986. In the initial years, the company produced a cranberry drink for sale at sporting and entertainment events in eastern Canada. In 1993, operations were expanded to include sales to bars, restaurants, and fast-food outlets. To penetrate additional markets, AB started manufacturing a wide variety of fruit beverages and acquired the distributorship of another company's fruit concentrate. Sold under the brand name "Fruit Brite," the fruit beverage sales were only moderately successful.

In 1996, a management review indicated that while sales of the new fruit beverage line had increased, AB's cost to manufacture was also greater than that of its competitors. Much of the profit was being made on the distribution of the fruit concentrate.

In an attempt to improve profitability, the company entered the retail market in 1997. To finance the expansion, AB obtained funds from two sources, bank loans and its first public issue of shares. The funds were used to purchase a bottling plant in Toronto and to provide working capital during the first year of operation. The retail operation was administered by a newly incorporated, wholly-owned subsidiary, Fruitbrite Flavours Ltd. (FF). In the first year the company incurred a loss on its retail operations, but subsequent years were profitable.

FF continued to expand until it had a nationwide bottling and distribution network. In major cities, the bottlers were wholly-owned subsidiaries of FF; in smaller cities, the bottlers were independents who bottled other products as well. In all cases, AB sold its fruit concentrate to the bottlers.

In 2000, AB acquired 70% of the shares of Concentrated Vending Ltd. (CV), a manufacturer of fruit beverage vending machines, located in Windsor, Ontario. AB purchased CV at a price well below its proportionate book value, since CV had encountered financial difficulties. AB lent CV funds to finance a plant modernization program. AB contracted with the founders of CV to continue as senior management since AB had no experience in the equipment manufacturing industry. The management contract stipulated that a bonus would be paid, amounting to 20% of CV's income before taxes, in each of the next five consecutive years. Although the plant modernization was successful, CV had difficulty selling enough machines to achieve a break-even point.

Sales of fruit beverages through vending machines were growing rapidly with the increased awareness of the importance of a healthier lifestyle. This was a segment of the market in which the AB group did not participate. Therefore, early in 2002, AB created a wholly-owned subsidiary, VendSell Ltd. (VS). VS buys the machines from CV at regular retail price and then sells them to local operators with the condition that only AB products be sold in the machines. The intent was to place machines in as many locations as possible.

VS sells the majority of machines under conditional sales contracts, in which the buyer agrees to make an initial payment of $500 and payments of $75 per month for the next 48 months, for a total of $4,100. Machine maintenance is the responsibility of the operator. The payment plan was devised with three objectives in mind:

1. To place the maximum number of machines by the use of an easy payment plan.

2. To defer payment of income tax by deducting the full cost of the machines when sold and deferring recognition of the revenue until the cash was collected.

3. To ensure that only AB products were used during the payment period, since title to the machine would not transfer until all payments have been made.

The fruit concentrate for the machines is purchased by the local operators from the bottler in the particular area, who in turn had purchased the fruit concentrate from AB. The operator is charged an amount equal to the cost to the bottler plus 20%.

During 2002, VS expects to buy 8,000 machines from CV at a price of $5,000 each. The machines currently cost CV $3,000 each to manufacture. This cost to CV is significantly lower than in previous years. In order to supply VS, the volume of production in 2003 is expected to be twice that of 2001. As a result, CV expects to show a profit in 2002.

By the end of 2002, VS expects to sell 6,800 machines. The revenue from initial payments will amount to $3,400,000 and VS expects to receive total revenues of $5,100,000 from initial payments and instalments in 2002.

In its annual report for 2001, AB reported after-tax earnings of $4,575,000 on consolidated revenue of $77,970,000. Since CV accounted for less than 10% of AB's consolidated assets, revenues, and income, no segmented information was presented in the 2001 annual report.

Within the management of AB there is disagreement over the proper accounting treatment for the activities of AB, VS, FF, and CV for 2002 and the effect on consolidation and reporting.

Required:

In August 2002, you were engaged as an independent advisor. Prepare a report that:

a. Outlines the major accounting and reporting issues faced by the company and its subsidiaries.

b. Identifies alternative policies to deal with the issues outlined.

c. Provides recommendations on the preferred policies.

[CICA, adapted]

Case 6-4

Computo Ltd.

Every Friday afternoon, the audit staff of the firm of Bowyer & Co. Chartered Accountants meets to discuss various technical and professional client matters. These meetings are used for training, planning audits, or discussing the results of audit work.

Computo Ltd. (CL), a new client, was the subject of discussion at one of these meetings. John Wayne, an audit manager with Bowyer & Co., had made several visits to CL. During these visits, Robert Roy, the president, had explained the operations of his company at some length. He had also described some of CL's accounting practices, including its revenue recognition policies. At this Friday afternoon meeting, Wayne relayed portions of his conversations with Roy and provided background information on the company.

CL, a favourite of the investment community, is a public company with shares listed on Canadian stock exchanges. Its shares, originally issued at $4.50 five years ago, have recently been trading in the $25 to $30 range. Robert Roy owns 65% of the voting shares of CL.

Five months ago, Roy approached the senior partner of Bowyer & Co., stating that he had heard of the firm's excellent reputation and wanted it as his auditor. Roy indicated that CL was growing quickly, and that he wanted Bowyer & Co. to handle all financial affairs for both CL and himself personally.

Roy pointed out that owing to the significance of debt financing, maintaining good relations with CL's various lenders was important. He did not want any difficulties with them resulting from disputes over the financial statements. Also, Roy made it clear that he wanted to maintain the company's rising profit picture. He said it correctly portrayed the growth and innovation of the company and facilitated further expansion.

CL manufactures the hardware and develops the software for Computo, a full line of microcomputers for home and small office applications. Even though CL is faced with strong competition from the well-known products of Dell, Apple, IBM, and others, Roy expects great expansion ahead through franchising and special contracts.

CL operates five company stores in three major cities. In order to expand into more cities and increase its share of the market, CL sells store franchises. The number of franchise stores dealing exclusively in the Computo line is growing quickly. The franchisee is granted the exclusive right to the Computo name and products for a store in a specific area. CL is required to supply advice on store location, and to provide technical training, advertising, and other specified franchise-support activities. Each store handles only the Computo line of microcomputer products, but noncompeting lines of electronic merchandise can also be carried.

New, advanced products with good consumer acceptance are continually emerging as a result of the major expenditures on research and development during the past few years. CL's revenues were growing as the following financial statement excerpts indicate:

	Year Ended December 31, 2001 ($000)	Year Ended December 31, 2000 ($000)
Sales of franchises	$4,520	$2,459
Sales of equipment	2,896	2,270
Continuing fees	898	549
Software and other sales	3,066	1,781

Franchises are sold for a franchise price ranging from $80,000 to $150,000, depending on store location. Terms of payment include a down payment and a series of notes payable to CL with terms ranging from five to ten years. The notes bear interest at rates significantly below the market rate at the time the agreement is signed. The financial arrangements are intended to help the new franchisees become established. CL recognizes the franchise price as revenue when it signs contracts with franchisees. Roy stated that the notes receivable are recorded by CL at face value to conform to generally accepted accounting principles.

Continuing fees are charged as a percentage of each franchisee's monthly sales of the Computo line. These fees are recorded on an accrual basis each month when reports are received from the franchisees. Revenue from both equipment and software sales is recognized when shipments are made from CL's plant.

In common with other growing firms, CL is highly leveraged and owes slightly over $10 million at an average interest rate of nearly 17%. A substantial part of the proceeds from this debt was used to finance research and development. A second major portion was used to finance two special projects. The remainder was used to finance the manufacturing assets for the Computo line.

In 2001, research costs and development costs other than interest were close to $2 million each. CL had capitalized nearly 90% of the total $4 million to match these costs with the applicable future revenues. In addition, CL capitalized the interest on the debt applicable to the research and development expenditures. In Roy's opinion, all these costs would have a highly beneficial effect on CL in the future.

Roy was uncertain about what accounting policy he should use for the interest charges on debt relating to CL's two new special projects. He thought these interest charges should probably be capitalized because the benefits and revenues would flow in a future period.

One project is the design and construction by CL's engineers of a manufacturing facility for a line of virtual certainty games. This project has been under way for nine months and will be completed in the next fiscal year. Production and marketing of the virtual certainty games will commence immediately upon completion of the facility. The other project is the manufacturing of a large number of special-design, computerized components for Canadian Armed Forces equipment. All of the design costs and about 30% of the production costs will be incurred in this fiscal year. Delivery of the components will be made next year.

The interest on the debt related to the manufacturing assets for the Computo line was expensed because Roy said that it would not benefit future periods.

Roy has also discussed CL's subsidiary companies with Wayne. CL has both active and dormant subsidiaries. The eight active subsidiaries consist of the five company stores and three franchise stores. These three franchise stores were acquired when their principals became ill or encountered other problems. CL currently owns all eight stores. The dormant subsidiaries consist of companies that had been acquired by CL from franchisees who wanted out of the business and had closed the stores.

When CL acquired the franchise companies, it bought the shares by issuing notes payable. The interest rate on these notes is at half the market rate at the settlement date. After acquisition, any outstanding notes receivable relating to the original sale of the franchise were treated by CL as increments to the investment in subsidiaries account.

Roy noted with satisfaction that he adhered to a strict policy of amortizing, over 20 years, the excess of the cost of shares of subsidiary companies acquired over their book value at the date of acquisition. Goodwill in the balance sheet was $1,552,000 in 2001 and $1,514,000 in 2000. Roy explained that a large part of these amounts arose on the acquisition of the problem stores.

When CL sells the franchise companies, gains are recorded after contracts are signed, consideration has passed, and initial support conditions have been met. The down payment is received in cash while the remainder of the consideration is recorded as notes receivable. Gains on sales of these companies are included in the income statement under software and other sales.

CL's accounting policy for intercorporate investments is to consolidate all of the companies in which it owns more than a 50% interest. It uses the equity basis for those companies where it holds 50% or less and is able to exercise significant influence.

Considerable discussion of CL's financial and accounting affairs took place during the Friday afternoon meeting. Wayne closed the meeting by summarizing the issues raised and requesting you to prepare a written report on the accounting issues. He asked you to recommend and justify the accounting policies that should be followed.

Required:

Prepare the report for John Wayne.

[CICA, adapted]

Problems

P6-1

Dudes Outfitters, Ltd., is a 70%-owned subsidiary of Trail Ltd. On January 10, 1998, Dudes sold some display cases to Trail Ltd. for $190,000, recognizing a gain of $90,000 before-tax on the transaction. Trail Ltd. depreciated the cases on a straight-line basis over six years, taking a full year's depreciation in 1998.

On February 12, 2001, Trail sold the display cases to an unaffiliated company for $110,000.

Required:

Prepare the appropriate consolidated adjustments relating to the display cases for each year ending December 31, 1998 through 2001, ignoring income tax effects.

P6-2

On January 1, 2000, Sub Ltd., 80% owned by Par Ltd., sold a building to Par Ltd. for $900,000. The building cost Sub $400,000 and was 70% depreciated (at 5% per year). Par will depreciate the building over the six remaining years, straight-line.

Required:

Give the consolidation eliminating entries relating to this transaction for the years ended:

  a. 2000

  b. 2002

[CGA–Canada, adapted]

P6-3

Parent Ltd. owns 70% of the voting shares of Sub Ltd. During 2000, Sub Ltd. sold inventory costing $640,000 to Parent Ltd. for $800,000. At December 31, 2000, Parent Ltd. still had $300,000 of these goods in its inventory, and had not yet paid for $480,000 of the goods. All of the remaining goods were sold in 2001.

Sub Ltd. also sold a piece of land (cost of $188,000) to Parent Ltd. on July 1, 2000, for $260,000, for which Parent Ltd. had issued Sub Ltd. a 5-year, 10% per annum note. The interest will be paid on July 1, 2001.

Required:

a. Prepare the eliminating entries as they would appear on the consolidated worksheet for 2000 and 2001, as related to the foregoing information.

b. Assuming that Sub Ltd. earned $680,000 during 2000 and $880,000 during 2001, calculate the minority interest in the earnings of Sub Ltd.

[CGA–Canada, adapted]

P6-4

Adam Ltd. owns 80% of the outstanding shares of Bob Ltd. Adam Ltd. also owns 70% of the shares of Xena Ltd. During the year 2001, Adam sold $500,000 (cost) of goods (widgets) to Bob at a 30% markup. Xena sold $400,000 (cost) of goods to Adam at a 25% markup.

Adam sold a piece of land (cost $100,000) to Bob for $50,000.

On October 1, 2001, Xena sold land (cost $80,000) and a building (cost $110,000) to Adam for $400,000; 40% of the price was allocated to land and 60% of the price was allocated to building. The building had five years of expected life at October 1, 2001, and was 30% depreciated at that time.

The $400,000 was unpaid at year-end and Adam had agreed to pay $10,000 interest on the unpaid amount.

An inventory count showed that 20% of the widgets that Bob had purchased from Adam were unsold at December 31, 2001. Seventy percent of the gadgets that Adam had purchased from Xena were also unsold.

Required:

Assume that Adam Ltd. uses the cost method of keeping its accounts.

a. Prepare the eliminating entries on the working papers that would be required at December 31, 2001, to prepare the consolidated financial statements.

b. Calculate the effect on the minority interest; by how much would the income to each minority interest be changed? Keep the two subsidiaries separate.

[CGA–Canada, adapted]

P6-5

On June 30, 2001, Pink Ltd. acquired for cash of $20 per share 80% of the outstanding voting common shares of Soft Ltd. Both companies continued to operate as separate entities and both have December 31 calendar year-ends. On June 30, 2001, after closing the nominal accounts, Soft's condensed balance sheet was as follows:

Assets

Cash	$ 700,000
Accounts receivable, net	600,000
Inventories	1,400,000
Capital assets, net	3,300,000
Other assets	500,000
Total assets	$6,500,000

Liabilities and shareholders' equity

Accounts payable	$ 700,000
Long-term debt	2,600,000
Other liabilities	200,000
Common shares	1,400,000
Retained earnings	1,600,000
Total liabilities and shareholders' equity	$6,500,000

On June 30, 2001, Soft's assets and liabilities having fair values different from the book values were as follows:

Fair value

Capital assets, net	$16,400,000
Other assets	200,000
Long-term debt	2,200,000

The difference between the fair values and book values resulted in a gross charge or credit to income for the consolidated statements for the six-month period ending December 31, 2001, as follows:

Capital assets, net	$500,000 charge
Other assets	10,000 credit
Long-term debt	5,000 charge

The amount paid by Pink in excess of the fair value of the net assets of Soft is attributable to expected future earnings of Soft and will be amortized over the maximum period allowable.

On June 30, 2001, there were no intercompany receivables or payables. During the six-month period ending December 31, 2001, Soft acquired merchandise from Pink at an invoice price of $500,000. The cost of the merchandise to Pink was $300,000. At December 31, 2001, one-half of the merchandise was not sold and Soft had not yet paid for any of the merchandise. The 2001 net income (loss) for both companies was as follows:

	Pink	Soft
January 1 to June 30	$350,000	$ (750,000)
July 1 to December 31	600,000	1,250,000

On July 1, 2001, Pink sold Soft a hectare of land (historical cost $200,000) for $80,000 and a building (historical cost $260,000, accumulated depreciation $169,000, i.e., six and a half years of depreciation) for $455,000. Soft will depreciate the asset on the same basis as Pink since the building is expected to be of zero value in three and a half years.

On December 31, 2001, after closing the nominal accounts, the condensed balance sheets for both companies were as follows:

	Pink	Soft
Assets		
Cash	$ 3,500,000	$ 600,000
Accounts receivable, net	1,400,000	1,500,000
Inventories	1,000,000	2,500,000
Capital assets, net	2,000,000	3,800,000
Investment in subsidiary, cost	16,000,000	—
Other assets	100,000	500,000
Total assets	$24,000,000	$8,900,000

Liabilities and shareholders' equity

Accounts payable	$ 1,500,000	$1,800,000
Long-term debt	4,000,000	2,600,000
Other liabilities	500,000	250,000
Common shares	15,000,000	1,400,000
Retained earnings	3,000,000	2,850,000
Total liabilities and shareholders' equity	$24,000,000	$8,900,000

Required:

Prepare a condensed consolidated balance sheet of Pink Ltd. as of December 31, 2001. Show all supporting computations. Ignore the impact of income taxes in your calculations.

[CGA–Canada, adapted]

P6-6

On January 1, 1999, Peter Limited purchased 80% of the outstanding voting common shares of Susan Limited at a cost of $139,200. At acquisition date, the book value of Susan Limited was $161,000, inventory was undervalued by $2,500, and depreciable capital assets were undervalued by $7,500. Relevant information for 2002 is shown below.

Required:

a. Calculate minority interest in net income for 2002 assuming consolidation is appropriate.

b. Calculate minority interest in the consolidated balance sheet as of the end of 2002.

c. Calculate goodwill remaining at the end of 2002, assuming a 20-year amortization period.

d. Calculate consolidated net income for 2002, assuming a 10-year remaining life at acquisition date for capital assets and straight-line depreciation. Note that Peter Limited uses the cost method and that Susan Limited paid dividends during the year.

Reported at End of 2002

	Peter	Susan
Net income	$ 44,000	$ 11,000
Dividends paid	4,000	1,000
Current assets	170,800	40,000
Investment in S (at cost)	139,200	—
Capital assets (net)	330,000	160,000
	$640,000	$200,000
Liabilities	$140,000	$ 30,000
Common shares	400,000	150,000
Retained earnings (end)	100,000	20,000
	$640,000	$200,000

[CGA–Canada, adapted]

P6-7

Anita Company owns a controlling interest in Brian Company and Gabriel Company. Anita purchased an 80% interest in Brian at a time when Brian reported retained earnings of $450,000. Anita purchased a 60% interest in Gabriel at a time when Gabriel reported retained earnings of $100,000. In each acquisition, the purchase price was equal to the proportionate net book value of the acquired company's shares, and the fair values of the assets and liabilities approximated their book values.

An analysis of the changes in retained earnings of the three companies during the year 2001 gives the following results:

	Anita Company	Brian Company	Gabriel Company
Retained earnings, Jan. 1, 2001	$ 742,000	$ 686,000	$ 475,000
Net income for the year	550,000	348,000	310,000
Dividends paid	(250,000)	(200,000)	(150,000)
Retained earnings, Dec. 31, 2001	$1,042,000	$ 834,000	$ 635,000

Gabriel sells some raw materials to Anita. After further processing and assembly, these parts are sold by Anita to Brian where they become a part of the finished products sold by Brian. Intercompany profits included in inventories at the beginning and end of the current year are estimated as follows:

	Jan. 1, 2001 Inventory	Dec. 31, 2001 Inventory
Intercompany profit included on sales from Gabriel to Anita	$70,000	$50,000
On sales from Anita to Brian	60,000	80,000

Brian also rents a building to Gabriel. Gabriel is paying $5,000 per month according to the lease contract. Anita carries its investments on a cost basis. Ignore the impact of income taxes.

Required:

a. Compute the consolidated net income for 2001.

b. Prepare a statement of consolidated retained earnings for 2001.

c. What change would there be in consolidated net income if the three companies had engaged in the same transactions, but all purchases, sales, and lending had been with firms outside the affiliated group? Give the amount of the difference and explain how it is derived.

[SMA, adapted]

P6-8

The following financial statements at December 31, 2001, reflect the ownership by Parco of Subco.

Parco and Subco Ltd.
Individual and Consolidated Balance Sheets
December 31, 2001

	Parco	Subco	Consolidated
Assets			
Current	$ 290,000	$190,000	$ 480,000
Investment in Subco (cost)	310,000	—	—
Capital assets (net)	860,000	200,000	1,060,000
Goodwill	—	—	37,000
	$1,460,000	$390,000	$1,577,000
Liabilities and equities			
Current	$ 90,000	$ 60,000	$ 150,000
Long-term	170,000	—	170,000
Shareholders' equity			
Common shares	800,000	200,000	800,000
Retained earnings	400,000	130,000	424,000
Minority interest	—	—	33,000
	$1,460,000	$390,000	$1,577,000

Additional Information:

1. Parco purchased its interest in Subco on January 1, 1999.

2. There have been no intercompany transactions.

3. Goodwill at acquisition was $20,000. Goodwill is amortized over 20 years.

Required:

Based on the financial statements presented above:

a. What percentage of ownership does Parco have in Subco?

b. What was the balance in Subco's retained earnings account at the date of acquisition?

c. How is the consolidated retained earnings figure of $424,000 calculated?

(Support your answers with calculations.)

[SMA, adapted]

P6-9

On June 30, 1998, Punt Corporation acquired 70% of the outstanding common shares of Slide Ltd. for $3,326,000 in cash plus Punt Corporation common shares estimated to have a fair market value of $1,200,000. On the date of acquisition, the fair market value and book value of each of Slide Ltd.'s assets were generally equal, except for inventory, which was undervalued by $225,000, and capital assets (net), which was overvalued by $1,000,000. The shareholders' equity of Slide at that time was $3,440,000, consisting of:

Common shares	$2,900,000
Retained earnings	540,000
	$3,440,000

Balance sheets at June 30, 2002, are as follows:

	Punt Corp.	Slide Ltd.
Assets		
Cash and marketable securities	$ 4,432,000	$ 321,000
Accounts and other receivables	2,153,000	950,000
Inventory	2,940,000	1,206,000
Capital assets (net)	17,064,000	7,161,000
Other long-term investments	3,038,000	2,240,000
Investment in Slide Ltd.	4,526,000	—
Total assets	$34,153,000	$11,878,000
Liabilities		
Current liabilities	$ 3,025,000	$ 2,090,000
Mortgage note payable	12,135,000	4,000,000
Total liabilities	15,160,000	6,090,000
Shareholders' equity		
Common shares	10,000,000	2,900,000
Retained earnings	8,993,000	2,888,000
Total shareholders' equity	18,993,000	5,788,000
Total liabilities and shareholders' equity	$34,153,000	$11,878,000

Additional Information:

1. Slide Ltd. had income of $1,460,000 for the year ended June 30, 2002. Dividends of $480,000 were declared during the fiscal year but were not paid until August 12, 2002.

2. Slide Ltd. has had an average inventory turnover of four times per year over the last decade.

3. The capital assets that were overvalued on the date of acquisition had a remaining useful life of 20 years.

4. Slide sold goods to Punt during the year ended June 30, 2002, at a gross profit margin of 25%. The opening inventory of Punt at July 1, 2001 included items purchased from Slide in the amount of $160,000. There were no sales from Slide to Punt during the year ended June 30, 2002.

5. Punt sold goods to Slide Ltd. during the current fiscal year at a gross profit margin of 30%. Of the $750,000 of sales, goods worth $200,000 were in Slide's closing inventory at June 30, 2002. None of these intercompany sales still in inventory had been paid for at the fiscal year-end.

6. Both companies follow the straight-line method for depreciating capital assets.

7. The controller of Punt has informed you that the company amortizes goodwill over 20 years.

Required:

Prepare the consolidated balance sheet for Punt Corporation and its subsidiary, Slide Ltd., at June 30, 2002.

[SMA, adapted]

P6-10

Selected items from the adjusted general ledger trial balances at December 31, 2002, of Print Ltd. and its 70% owned subsidiary, Stamp Inc., are given below.

	Print	Stamp
Inventory (FIFO cost) at Dec 31, 2001	$ 60,000	$ 40,000
Other long-term assets—net	200,000	150,000
Common shares	(300,000)	(100,000)
Retained earnings at Dec. 31, 2001	(88,400)	(60,000)
Cash dividends declared in 2002	20,000	15,000
Sales	(210,000)	(200,000)
Purchases	130,000	110,000
Depreciation and amortization expenses	15,000	10,000
Other expenses, including interest	30,000	20,000
Other income, including investment and interest income	(44,800)	—

Additional Information:

1. Print Ltd. acquired a 70% interest in Stamp Inc. on January 1, 1998; on that date, Stamp's shareholders' equity was comprised of common shares, $100,000, and retained earnings, $10,000. On January 1, 1998, the acquisition cost in excess of acquired net assets was assigned:

   • $12,000 to equipment to be amortized over five years on a straight-line basis;

   • $40,000 to goodwill to be amortized over ten years.

2. The inventory (FIFO Cost) balances at December 31, 2002, were $70,000 for Print and $50,000 for Stamp.

3. During 2002, Stamp sold merchandise to Print for $20,000 at a gross profit of $4,000. At December 31, 2002, 50% of this merchandise remained in Print's inventory. Print's December 31, 2001 inventory included unrealized profit of $5,000 on merchandise purchased from Stamp.

4. Stamp did not acquire any merchandise from Print in 2002. However, Stamp's December 31, 2001 inventory included an unrealized profit of $6,000 on goods acquired from Print. Stamp sold all of these goods during 2002.

Required:

a. Calculate the account balance of Print's investment in Stamp at December 31, 2002, by the equity method.

b. Prepare a consolidated income statement for 2002.

c. Prepare a consolidated balance sheet as at December 31, 2002, which is as complete as possible, using the information provided.

[SMA, adapted]

P6-11

On January 1, 1997 ABC Limited purchased 90% of the outstanding common shares of XYZ Limited for $150,000. At that date, XYZ Limited's condensed balance sheet and fair values were as follows:

	Book value	Fair value
Cash	$10,000	$10,000
Land	20,000	30,000
Building (net)	20,000	25,000
	$50,000	
Liabilities	$10,000	10,000
Common shares	10,000	
Retained earnings	30,000	
	$50,000	

Assume a 10-year amortization period for any capital assets and a 20-year amortization period for goodwill.

Required:

a. Assume the following information regarding net income and dividends for XYZ Limited:

Year	Net Income	Dividends
1997	$ 10,000	$ 2,000
1998	12,000	2,000
1999	9,000	2,000
2000	(10,000)	2,000*
2001	10,000	26,000

*The 2000 dividend was a stock dividend.

Calculate the balance in the investment account in ABC's books at the end of 2001 assuming that ABC uses the equity method of accounting in its books.

b. Assume that ABC uses the cost method of accounting for its investment. Prepare a journal entry or entries to reflect the information previously provided for 2000 and 2001.

[CGA–Canada]

P6-12

On April 2, 1999, Curry Ltd. acquired 40% of the outstanding common shares of Jasmine Ltd. by issuing one share of Curry plus $5 cash for each of Jasmine's shares acquired. At the time of purchase, Curry's shares were trading at $25 per share and Jasmine's shares were trading at $28. Jasmine had a total of one million shares outstanding.

At the date of acquistion, the shareholders' equity of Jasmine totalled $18,000,000. The fair values of Jasmine's assets and liabilities were the same as their net book values except for the following capital assets:

	Book value	Fair value
Land	$5,000,000	$8,000,000
Building	6,000,000	5,000,000
Equipment	5,000,000	7,000,000

The building and equipment have estimated remaining useful lives of 10 years and 5 years respectively. Jasmine uses straight-line amortization.

For the year ended March 31, 2000, Jasmine reported net income of $1,500,000. Jasmine's dividend payout was 60% for fiscal 2000.

Required:

For the year ended March 31, 2000, compute: (1) Curry's equity in the earnings of Jasmine and (2) the balance of the investment account at the fiscal year-end, using the equity method. Provide supporting calculations. Assume that Curry uses straight-line amortization for its intangible assets over 20 years.

P6-13

At the 2000 annual meeting for Jasmine's shareholders, Curry nominated seven directors for Jasmine's 12-person board of directors. After some negotiation, five of Curry's nominees were accepted onto the board. During fiscal year 2001 the following occurred:

1. Curry shifted a substantial amount of business to Jasmine. Jasmine became the major supplier of one of Curry's raw materials and had sales totalling $7,000,000 to Curry. Of that total $1,000,000 was in Curry's raw materials inventory at year-end. The other $6,000,000 had been utilized in finished goods, of which one-third was still in inventory on March 31, 2001.

2. Curry began selling some products to Cinnamon Corp. a wholly-owned subsidiary of Jasmine. Fiscal 2001 sales totalled $2,500,000, all within the last two months of the year. At year-end 60% of the sales were still in Cinnamon's inventory.

3. Operating results for fiscal 2001 were reported as follows:

	Curry	Jasmine
Sales	$ 80,000,000	$ 20,000,000
Cost of sales	(56,000,000)	(12,000,000)
	24,000,000	8,000,000
Operating expenses	(6,000,000)	(4,000,000)
Income tax expense	(7,200,000)	(1,600,000)
Net income	$ 10,800,000	$ 2,400,000

Required:

Using the information above and in **P6-12** prepare a schedule(s) in which you:

a. Compute the amount of investment income that Curry should recognize in fiscal 2001 from its investment in Jasmine.

b. Compute the balance of Curry's investment account for its investment in Jasmine at March 31, 2001.

P6-14

On January 1, 1999, Porter Inc. purchased 80% of the outstanding voting shares of Sloan Ltd. for $3,000,000 in cash. On this date, Sloan had common shares outstanding in the amount of $2,200,000 and retained earnings of $1,100,000. The identifiable assets and liabilities of Sloan had fair values that were equal to their carrying values except for the following:

i) Capital assets (net) had a fair value $200,000 greater than its carrying value. The remaining useful life on January 1, 1999, was 20 years with no anticipated salvage value.

ii) Accounts receivable had a fair value $75,000 less than carrying value.

iii) Long-term liabilities had a fair value $62,500 less than carrying value. These liabilities mature on June 30, 2007.

It is the policy of Porter to amortize all goodwill balances over five years. Both Porter and Sloan use the straight-line method for amortization and depreciation. Porter Inc. is a public company and, therefore, is required to follow generally accepted accounting principles.

Additional Information:

1. Between January 1, 1999, and December 31, 2001, Sloan earned $345,000 and paid dividends of $115,000.

2. On January 1, 2000, Sloan sold a patent to Porter for $165,000. On this date, the patent had a carrying value on the books of Sloan of $185,000, and a remaining useful life of five years.

3. On September 1, 2001, Porter sold land to Sloan for $103,000. The land had a carrying value on the books of Porter of $82,000. Sloan still owned this land on December 31, 2002.

4. For the year ending December 31, 2002, the income statements revealed the following:

	Porter	Sloan
Total revenues	$2,576,000	$973,000
Cost of goods sold	1,373,000	467,000
Depreciation expense	483,000	176,000
Other expenses	352,000	153,000
Total expenses	2,208,000	796,000
Net income	$ 368,000	$177,000

Porter records its investment in Sloan using the cost method and includes dividend income from Sloan in its total revenues.

5. Porter and Sloan paid dividends of $125,000 and $98,000 respectively in 2002.

6. Sloan issued no common shares subsequent to January 1, 1999. Selected balance sheet accounts for the two companies at December 31, 2002, were:

	Porter	Sloan
Accounts receivable (net)	$ 987,000	$ 133,000
Inventories	1,436,000	787,000
Capital assets (net)	3,467,000	1,234,000
Patents (net)	263,000	—
Land	872,000	342,000
Long-term liabilities	1,876,000	745,000
Retained earnings	4,833,000	1,409,000

7. During 2002, Porter's merchandise sales to Sloan were $150,000. The unrealized profits in Sloan's inventory on January 1, and December 31, 2002, were $14,000 and $10,000, respectively. At December 31, 2002, Sloan still owed Porter $5,000 for merchandise purchases.

8. During 2002, Sloan's merchandise sales to Porter were $55,000. The unrealized profits in Porter's inventory on January 1, and December 31, 2002, were $1,500 and $2,500 respectively. At December 31, 2002, Porter still owed Sloan $2,000 for merchandise purchases.

Required:

a. Compute the balances that would appear in the consolidated balance sheet of Porter and Sloan as at December 31, 2002, for the following:

(1) Patent (net)

(2) Goodwill

(3) Minority interest

(4) Retained earnings

b. Porter has decided not to prepare consolidated financial statements and will report its investment in Sloan by the equity method. Calculate the investment income that would be disclosed in the income statement of Porter for the year ended December 31, 2002.

[SMA]

P6-15

On January 1, 1995, the Partial Company acquired 80% of the outstanding voting shares of the Sum Company for $3,900,000 in cash. On this date, the Sum Company had $2,000,000 in common shares outstanding and $2,000,000 in retained earnings. Any excess of cost over book value is to be recorded in the consolidated financial statements as goodwill and will be amortized over 14 years. On December 31, 2002, the balance sheets of the two companies are as follows:

Balance Sheets
December 31, 2002

	Partial Company	Sum Company
Cash	$ 3,000,000	$ 1,000,000
Accounts receivable	7,000,000	2,000,000
Inventories	4,100,000	3,000,000
Investment in Sum	3,900,000	—
Capital assets (net)	7,000,000	5,000,000
Total assets	$25,000,000	$11,000,000
Liabilities	$ 5,000,000	$ 3,000,000
Common shares	7,000,000	2,000,000
Retained earnings	13,000,000	6,000,000
Total equities	$25,000,000	$11,000,000

Additional Information:

1. Sum Company sells merchandise to the Partial Company at a price that provides Sum with a gross margin of 50% of the sales price. During 2002, these sales amounted to $1,000,000. The December 31, 2002 inventories of the Partial Company contain $200,000 of these purchases while the December 31, 2001 inventories of Partial contained $100,000 in merchandise purchased from Sum.

2. At the end of 2002, Partial owes Sum $60,000 for merchandise purchased on account. The account is non-interest-bearing.

3. On December 31, 1999, the Partial Company sold equipment to the Sum Company for $550,000. At the time of the sale, the equipment had a net book value in Partial's records of $450,000. The remaining useful life of the asset on this date was 10 years.

Required:

Prepare a consolidated balance sheet for the Partial Company and its subsidiary, Sum Company, at December 31, 2002. Ignore the impact of income taxes.

[SMA, adapted]

P6-16

On December 31, 1998, the Joyce Company purchased 80% of the outstanding voting shares of the Blume Company for $5 million in cash. On that date, the carrying value of the net identifiable assets of the Blume Company totalled $6 million. Both companies use the straight-line method to calculate all depreciation and amortization charges. Goodwill, if any arises as a result of this business combination, is to be amortized over 10 years.

For the year ending December 31, 2002, the income statements for Joyce and Blume are as follows:

	Joyce Company	Blume Company
Sales and other revenue	$12,500,000	$ 5,600,000
Cost of goods sold	8,000,000	4,000,000
Depreciation expense	1,500,000	1,000,000
Other expenses	1,800,000	1,200,000
Total expenses	11,300,000	6,200,000
Income (loss) before extraordinary items	1,200,000	(600,000)
Extraordinary loss	—	(1,400,000)
Net income (loss)	$ 1,200,000	$(2,000,000)

Additional Information:

1. On December 31, 1998, Blume had a building with a fair value that was $220,000 greater than its carrying value. The building had an estimated remaining useful life of 20 years.

2. On December 31, 1998, Blume had inventory with a fair value that was $100,000 less than its carrying value. This inventory was sold during 1999.

3. On January 1, 2000, Blume sold Joyce a machine for $30,000. When Blume had purchased the machine on January 1, 1995, for $80,000, it was estimated that its service life would be 10 years to January 1, 2005. There is no change in this estimate at the time of the intercompany sale.

4. During 2002, Joyce sold merchandise to Blume for $200,000, a price that includes a gross profit of $80,000. During 2002, one-half of this merchandise was resold by Blume and the other half remains in its December 31, 2002 inventories. On December 31, 2001, the inventories of Blume contain merchandise purchased from Joyce on which Joyce had recognized a gross profit in the amount of $25,000.

5. On December 31, 2002, Blume owed Joyce $100,000 on open account.

6. During 2002, Blume sold merchandise to Joyce for $400,000. All of these sales were priced to provide a gross profit to Blume equal to 50% of the sale price. On December 31, 2002, $60,000 of this merchandise remained in the inventories of Joyce. On December 31, 2001, the inventories of Joyce contained merchandise purchased from Blume at a sale price of $150,000. The 2001 gross profit percentage on intercompany sales was the same as for 2002.

7. During 2002, Joyce declared and paid dividends of $300,000, while Blume declared and paid dividends of $100,000.

8. Joyce carries its investment in Blume by the cost method.

9. Between December 31, 1998 and December 31, 2001, Blume earned $4 million and declared dividends of $400,000.

Required:

a. Prepare the consolidated income statement for the Joyce Company and its subsidiary, the Blume Company, for the year ending December 31, 2002. Ignore the impact of income taxes.

b. Calculate the amount of the minority interest that would be shown in the consolidated balance sheet on December 31, 2002.

[SMA]

P6-17

518 850,000

On January 1, 1998, the Perkins Company purchased 70% of the outstanding voting shares of the Staton Company for $860,000 in cash. On that date, the Staton Company had retained earnings of $400,000 and common shares of $500,000. On the acquisition date, the identifiable assets and liabilities of the Staton Company had fair values that were equal to their carrying values except for equipment, which had a fair value $200,000 greater than its carrying value, and long-term liabilities, which had fair values that were $100,000 greater than their carrying values. The equipment had a remaining useful life of 10 years on January 1, 1998, and the long-term liabilities mature on December 31, 2007. Both companies use the straight-line method to calculate all depreciation and amortization.

The trial balance of the Perkins Company and the Staton Company on December 31, 2002, was as follows:

	Perkins	Staton
Cash	$ 50,000	$ 10,000
Accounts receivable	250,000	100,000
Inventories	3,000,000	520,000
Equipment (net)	6,150,000	2,500,000
Buildings (net)	2,600,000	500,000
Investment in Staton (at cost)	850,000	—
Cost of goods sold	2,000,000	400,000
Depreciation expense	300,000	100,000
Other expenses	200,000	150,000
Dividends declared	200,000	20,000
Total debits	$15,600,000	$4,300,000
Current liabilities	$ 300,000	$ 170,000
Long-term liabilities	4,000,000	1,100,000
Common shares	3,000,000	500,000
Retained earnings	4,500,000	1,600,000
Sales revenue	3,500,000	900,000
Other revenues	300,000	30,000
Total credits	$15,600,000	$4,300,000

Additional Information:

1. Perkins carries its investment in Staton on its books by the cost method.

2. During 2001, Perkins sold Staton $100,000 worth of merchandise, of which $60,000 was resold by Staton in the year. During 2002, Perkins had sales of $200,000 to Staton, of which 40% was resold by Staton. Intercompany sales are priced to provide Perkins with a gross margin of 30% of the sales price. Both companies use the first-in, first-out cost-flow assumption.

3. On December 31, 2001, Perkins had in its inventories $150,000 of merchandise purchased from Staton during 2001. On December 31, 2002, Perkins had in its ending inventories $100,000 of merchandise that had resulted from purchases of $250,000 from Staton during 2002. Intercompany sales are priced to provide Staton with a gross margin of 60% of the sale price.

4. Liabilities resulting from intercompany inventory purchases were as follows on December 31, 2002:

Staton owes Perkins	$50,000
Perkins owes Staton	$25,000

5. On January 1, 2001, Staton sold a building to Perkins for $730,000. The — UPSTREAM.
building had the following history on Staton's records:

M.I .

Purchase date:	December 31, 1998
Purchase price:	$490,000 — SIB $480,000
Estimated life at acquisition:	30 years
Estimated salvage at acquisition:	$40,000 — SIB $30,000

The estimates are still applicable on January 1, 2002.

6. Any goodwill arising from the business combination is to be amortized over 20 years.

Required:

Prepare for the Perkins Company and its subsidiary, the Staton Company, the following (ignoring income tax effects for this problem):

a. The consolidated income statement for the year ending December 31, 2002.

b. The consolidated balance sheet at December 31, 2002.

c. A verification or independent calculation of the consolidated retained earnings balance at December 31, 2002.

d. A verification or independent calculation of the minority interest as shown on the consolidated balance sheet at December 31, 2002.

[SMA, adapted]

P6-18

On January 1, 1996, Harriet Company purchased 70,000 of the Smithers Company's outstanding voting shares at a price of $330 per share. This gave them 70% ownership in the company. On that date, Smithers Company had common shares of $16 million and retained earnings of $14 million. At the time of this acquisition, the fair values of Smithers Company's identifiable assets and liabilities were equal to their carrying values; however, Smithers Company had developed a valuable patent that had not been recorded on the company's books. On January 1, 1996, it was estimated that this patent had a fair value of $2.5 million and a remaining useful life of 10 years. If any goodwill arises on this business combination, it is to be amortized over 20 years.

On January 1, 1999, Smithers Company sold a depreciable asset to Harriet Company for $900,000. Smithers Company had purchased the asset on January 1, 1994, at a cost of $920,000, and had subsequently depreciated the asset using the straight-line method over an estimated life of 30 years. There was no change in the estimated life on January 1, 1999.

Between January 1, 1996, and January 1, 2002, Smithers Company had earnings of $6 million and paid dividends of $3 million. Harriet Company uses the cost method to carry its investment in Smithers Company. On January 1, 2002, the retained earnings of Harriet Company amounted to $40 million.

The income statements of the two companies, for the year ended December 31, 2002, are as follows:

	Harriet	Smithers
Revenues	$10,000,000	$2,000,000
Cost of goods sold	6,000,000	1,000,000
Other expenses	2,000,000	600,000
Total expenses	8,000,000	1,600,000
Net income	$ 2,000,000	$ 400,000

During 2002, Harriet Company paid dividends of $1,500,000, while Smithers Company paid dividends of $100,000. The revenues of Harriet Company contain the dividends received from Smithers Company. Also during 2002, 40% of Smithers' revenues resulted from sales to Harriet Company. Half of this merchandise remains in the ending inventories of the Harriet Company. On January 1, 2002, inventories of Harriet contained purchases from Smithers that were sold during 2002 for $150,000. All intercompany sales are priced to provide the selling company with a gross margin of 50% of the sales price.

Required:

a. Compute the following balances for inclusion in the consolidated balance sheet at December 31, 2002:

(1) The net book value of the patent that was owned by Smithers Company when Harriet Company acquired Smithers' shares.

(2) The net book value of the depreciable asset that Smithers sold to Harriet.

(3) Goodwill.

b. Prepare a consolidated income statement for the year ended December 31, 2002, for Harriet Company and its subsidiary, Smithers Company.

c. Prepare a consolidated statement of retained earnings for the year ended December 31, 2002, for Harriet Company and its subsidiary, Smithers Company.

d. Compute the minority interest in the consolidated net assets of Smithers Company at December 31, 2002.

[SMA, adapted]

P6-19

The following are extracts from the consolidated working papers of Pinch Inc. for the year ended December 31, 2002, prior to income tax adjustments.

	Pinch Inc.	Steele Inc.	Consolidated
Cash	$ 10,000	$ 3,225	$ 13,225
Accounts receivable	248,007	169,800	342,807
Inventories (at cost)	109,600	46,900	142,500
Land	18,900	11,500	30,400
Building (net)	46,980	32,000	90,230
Machinery (net)	43,320	12,100	56,935
Investment 12% bonds	100,000	—	100,000
Investment in Steele	118,193	—	—
Goodwill	—	—	3,750
	$695,000	$275,525	$ 779,847
Current liabilities	$219,500	$ 51,700	$ 196,200
Notes payable	50,000	—	50,000
Customer advances	48,000	3,800	51,800
Minority interest	—	—	20,665
Common shares	150,000	100,000	150,000
Retained earnings	227,500	120,650	312,432
	$695,000	$275,525	$ 779,847
Sales	$969,900	$414,300	$1,259,200
Cost of goods sold	824,415	331,440	1,019,855
Gross profit	145,485	82,860	239,345
Operating expenses:			
Selling	67,890	29,400	98,035
General & administrative	39,620	15,500	55,120
Total operating	107,510	44,900	153,155
Operating income	37,975	37,960	86,190
Interest income	12,000	—	12,000
Investment income	37,800	—	—
Income before income taxes	87,775	37,960	98,190
Income taxes	36,860	9,460	46,320
Net income before minority interest	50,915	28,500	51,870
Less minority interest	—	—	3,950
Net income	$ 50,915	$ 28,500	$ 47,920
Opening retained earnings	$221,585	$134,150	$ 309,512
Net income	50,915	28,500	47,920
Dividends	(45,000)	(42,000)	(45,000)
Closing retained earnings	$227,500	$120,650	$ 312,432

Additional Information:

1. Pinch Inc. acquired 90% of the voting shares of Steele Inc. on the open market on January 1, 1998. At that time, all the assets and liabilities of Steele Inc. were recorded at fair market value, except for its building. Both Pinch Inc. and Steele Inc. depreciate their buildings on a straight-line basis over 20 years. The buildings of both Pinch Inc. and Steele Inc. each had an estimated remaining useful life of 15 years on January 1, 1998. Pinch Inc. decided to amortize goodwill over a 20-year period. No acquisitions or disposals of buildings have occurred since 1998 in either company.

2. On December 31, 2001, Pinch Inc. sold a machine to Steele Inc. The machine had a remaining useful life of four years at that date. Both Pinch Inc. and Steele Inc. depreciate machinery on a straight-line basis over five years.

3. In 2002, as in prior years, Steele Inc. sold merchandise to Pinch Inc. Even though Steele Inc. was a subsidiary of Pinch Inc., Steele Inc. still earned its normal gross profit on these sales. On December 31, 2002, Pinch Inc. owed Steele Inc. a balance on these sales.

Required:

a. Is Pinch's investment in Steele Inc. accounted for under the cost or the equity method? Support your answer.

b. Determine the following amounts, showing all calculations:
   (1) The goodwill at the acquisition date
   (2) The fair market value of Steele Inc.'s building at the acquisition date
   (3) Steele Inc.'s retained earnings at the acquisition date
   (4) The intercompany gain or loss on the sale of machinery
   (5) The intercompany sales
   (6) The profit in the ending inventory
   (7) The profit in opening inventory
   (8) The intercompany debt

c. Provide an independent calculation for:
   (1) Consolidated net income of $47,920
   (2) Minority interest of $20,665

[SMA, adapted]

P6-20

On January 2, 1997, Plastic Limited acquired 80% of the outstanding voting shares of Screen Limited for $1,600,000 in cash. The balance sheet of Screen Limited and the fair values of its identifiable assets and liabilities were as follows:

	Book value	Fair value
Assets		
Cash	$ 100,000	$ 100,000
Accounts receivable	300,000	300,000
Inventory	600,000	662,500
Land	800,000	900,000
Building (net)	1,000,000	1,200,000
Patents (net)	200,000	150,000
Total assets	$3,000,000	
Liabilities and shareholders' equity		
Accounts payable	$ 500,000	$ 500,000
14% bonds payable, due December 31, 2006	1,000,000	900,000
Common shares	950,000	
Retained earnings	550,000	
Total liabilities and shareholders' equity	$3,000,000	

At acquisition date, the building had a remaining useful life of ten years with zero net salvage value, while the patent had a remaining economic life of eight years. With respect to any recorded amounts of goodwill, it is corporate policy to amortize such amounts over 20 years.

Both companies use the FIFO method to cost their inventories and the straight-line method to calculate all depreciation and amortization. Plastic Limited uses the cost method to account for its long-term investment in Screen Limited.

The net incomes for the two companies for the year ended December 31, 2002, were determined as follows:

	Plastic	Screen
Sales	$4,000,000	$2,000,000
Gain on sale of land	—	100,000
Dividend revenue	40,000	—
Rental revenue	—	70,000
Total revenue	4,040,000	2,170,000
Cost of goods sold	2,000,000	800,000
Selling and administrative expense	855,000	680,000
Interest expense	250,000	140,000
Depreciation: building	300,000	100,000
Depreciation: equipment	150,000	125,000
Patent amortization	—	25,000
Rental expense	35,000	—
Total expenses	3,590,000	1,870,000
Net income	$ 450,000	$ 300,000

The amount of retained earnings for the two companies for the year ended December 31, 2002, was determined as follows:

	Plastic	Screen
Retained earnings, Jan. 1	$2,000,000	$ 900,000
Add: Net income	450,000	300,000
	2,450,000	1,200,000
Less: Dividends	100,000	50,000
Retained earnings, Dec. 31	$2,350,000	$1,150,000

The balance sheets for the two companies at December 31, 2002, were as follows:

	Plastic	Screen
Assets		
Cash	$ 300,000	$ 150,000
Accounts receivable	800,000	500,000
Inventory	800,000	400,000
Investment in Screen Ltd. (cost)	1,600,000	—
Land	900,000	800,000
Building (net)	1,200,000	400,000
Equipment	3,000,000	1,500,000
Less: accumulated depreciation	1,750,000	300,000
Patents (net)	—	50,000
Total assets	$6,850,000	$3,500,000

Liabilities and shareholders' equity

Accounts payable	$1,000,000	$ 400,000
14% bonds payable, due Dec. 31, 2006	—	1,000,000
Notes payable	2,000,000	—
Common shares	1,500,000	950,000
Retained earnings	2,350,000	1,150,000
Total liabilities and shareholders' equity	$6,850,000	$3,500,000

Additional Information:

1. In 1998, Plastic sold a parcel of land, costing $200,000, to Screen for $300,000. In 2002, Screen sold the land to an unrelated company for $400,000.

2. Screen regularly sells merchandise to Plastic at the same terms it sells to other customers. Intercompany sales totalled $500,000 in 2001 and $600,000 in 2002. At December 31, 2001, Plastic's inventory contained $200,000 of merchandise purchased from Screen. At December 31, 2002, Plastic's inventory contained $150,000 of merchandise purchased from Screen.

3. On January 2, 1999, Screen acquired a piece of equipment for $140,000. The equipment had an estimated useful life of seven years and no salvage value. On January 2, 2001, Screen sold the equipment to Plastic Limited for $80,000. There were no changes in the asset's estimated useful life.

4. Plastic Limited's entire rental expense relates to equipment rented from Screen Limited.

Required:

a. Schedules of calculation and allocation of the purchase price discrepancy.

b. Consolidated income statement (year ended 2002) calculations for:
   (1) Cost of goods sold
   (2) Minority interest
   (3) Interest expense

c. Consolidated balance sheet December 31, 2002, amounts for:
   (1) Net book value of equipment
   (2) Goodwill
   (3) Bonds payable
   (4) Minority interest

Note: Ignore income tax effects for this problem.

[SMA, adapted]

P6-21

On January 1, 1996, Pen Company purchased 80% of the outstanding voting shares of Silk Company for $300,000. Silk's assets and liabilities all had fair values that were equal to their carrying values. The $80,000 excess of purchase price over 80% of the book values of Silk Company's net assets was allocated to goodwill and is being amortized over 20 years. Between January 1, 1996 and January 1, 2002,

Silk Company earned $200,000 and paid dividends of $40,000. Both companies use the straight-line method to calculate depreciation and amortization.

Additional Information:

1. On January 1, 1992, Silk Company purchased a machine for $100,000 that had an estimated useful life of 20 years; on January 1, 1997, Silk Company sold the machine to the Pen Company for $60,000. The estimated useful life of the machine remains unchanged at a total of 20 years (15 years from January 1, 1997).

2. During 2002, Silk Company had sales of merchandise in the amount of $400,000 to Pen Company, of which $60,000 remains in the December 31, 2002 inventories of Pen Company. Pen Company had no sales to Silk Company during 2002, but had sales of $200,000 to Silk Company in 2001. Of these sales, $40,000 remained in the December 31, 2001 inventories of Silk Company. Intercompany sales are priced to provide the selling company with a 40% gross profit on sales prices.

3. On September 1, 2002, Silk Company sold a piece of land to Pen Company for $50,000. The land had been purchased for $35,000. The gain on this land is not considered extraordinary for reporting purposes.

4. During 2002, Silk Company declared dividends of $6,000 and the Pen Company declared dividends of $35,000.

5. During 2002, Silk Company paid Pen Company $10,000 in management fees.

6. On July 1, 2002, Pen Company lent the Silk Company $100,000 for five years at an annual interest rate of 10%. Interest is paid on July 1 of each year for which the loan is outstanding.

Pen Company carries its investment in Silk Company by the cost method. On this date, the income statements of Pen Company and Silk Company for the year ending December 31, 2002, are as follows:

	Pen	Silk
Merchandise sales	$3,000,000	$2,000,000
Investment income	60,000	—
Other revenue	50,000	70,000
Total revenues	3,110,000	2,070,000
Cost of goods sold	1,800,000	1,400,000
Depreciation expense	400,000	400,000
Selling and administrative	500,000	200,000
Total expenses	2,700,000	2,000,000
Income before extraordinary items	410,000	70,000
Loss on sales of investments	—	(26,000)
Net income (loss)	$ 410,000	$ 44,000

Required:

a. Prepare the consolidated income statement for Pen Company and its subsidiary, Silk Company, for the year ending December 31, 2002.

b. Assume that Pen Company does not consolidate its investment in Silk

Company and that the reason for the exclusion from consolidation is such that the equity method of accounting is appropriate. Provide a detailed calculation of Pen Company's ordinary and extraordinary investment income for the year ending December 31, 2002.

[SMA, adapted]

P6-22

On April 1, 2002, Marsh Ltd. purchased 25% of the outstanding common shares of King Corp. for $4,000,000. The book value of King's net assets was $12,000,000, an amount that also approximated their fair value. For the year ended December 31, 2002, King reported net income of $1,600,000 and Marsh reported net income of $10,200,000. King paid dividends of $100,000 in each of the first two quarters of 2002, and $150,000 in each of the last two quarters. There were no intercompany transactions during the year. Both companies generate their incomes fairly evenly throughout the year. Any goodwill is to be amortized over 20 years.

Required:

Compute the amounts that would appear on Marsh's 2002 income statement as income from investment in King, and the balance of the investment account on the December 31, 2002 balance sheet, assuming that Marsh uses:

a. The cost method

b. The equity method

P6-23

North Company has supplied you with information regarding two investments that were made during 2002 as follows:

1. On January 1, 2002, North purchased for cash 40% of the 500,000 shares of voting common shares of Young Company for $2,800,000, representing 40% of the net worth of Young. The book value of Young's net assets was $6,000,000 on January 1, 2002, and this amount approximated the fair value of the net assets. Young's net income for the year ended December 31, 2002 was $900,000. Young paid dividends of $0.80 per share in 2002. The market value of Young's common shares was $15 per share on December 31, 2002. North exercised significant influence over the operating and financial policies of Young.

2. On July 1, 2002, North purchased for cash 20,000 shares representing 5% of the voting common shares of the Mak Company for $500,000. Mak's net income for the six months ended December 31, 2002 was $400,000, and for the year ended December 31, 2002 it was $650,000. Mak paid dividends of $0.40 per share each quarter during 2002 to shareholders of record on the last day of each quarter. The market value of Mak's common shares was $30 per share on January 1, 2002, and $35 per share on December 31, 2002.

Required:

As a result of these two investments, determine the following:

a. What should be the balance in the investment account for North at December 31, 2002?

b. What should be the investment income reported by North for the year ended December 31, 2002?

Show all supporting calculations. Ignore the impact of income taxes. North's management wishes to report the highest net income permissible under GAAP. The equity method of recording investments is used when appropriate for reporting purposes.

[AICPA, adapted]

P6-24

King Oil Company, to maintain closer ties with associated companies in the oil business, decided to purchase holdings of common shares in several companies. The following is a list of activities associated with these acquisitions during 2002.

February 15   Acquired 80,000 shares of Lub Oil Co. at $8 per share representing 70% of the outstanding shares. At date of acquisition, book value of the Lub Oil Co.'s net assets was $800,000. Assets were considered to be valued at market.

April 13   Acquired 140,000 shares of Richman Refineries at $11 per share representing 60% of the outstanding shares. The purchase price corresponds to the underlying book value.

May 17   Acquired 50,000 shares of Discovery Co. Ltd. at $5 per share representing 2% of the outstanding shares.

June 30   Lub Oil Co. announced a loss of $50,000 for the first six months of 2002.

               Richman Refineries announced earnings of $120,000 for the first six months of 2002 and declared a dividend of $0.10 per share.

August 15   Dividend received from Richman Refineries.

October 11   Dividend of $0.05 per share received from Discovery Co. Ltd. with a statement of earnings for the six months ending September 30 indicating net earnings of $60,000.

December 31   Lub Oil Co. announced a loss of $40,000 for the year.

               Richman Refineries announced earnings of $200,000 for the year, including an extraordinary gain of $40,000.

               Discovery Co. Ltd. announced earnings of $90,000 for the nine months ending December 31.

Additional Information:

The King Oil Company's policy is to amortize goodwill over 20 years.

Required:

a. Investments in shares could be recorded and/or reported using either the equity method or cost method. Distinguish between the two methods, indicating under what circumstances each method should be used.

b. Prepare journal entries to record the above transactions in the books of King Oil Company, assuming the use of the equity method of accounting where appropriate for reporting purposes.

[SMA, adapted]

P6-25

Slater Company purchased 30% of the outstanding voting shares of Rogan Company for $1,500,000 in cash on January 1, 2000. On that date, Rogan Company's shareholders' equity was made up of common shares of $3 million and retained earnings of $1 million. There were no differences between the carrying values and the fair values of any of its net identifiable assets or liabilities. The net income and dividends declared and paid by Rogan Company for the two years subsequent to its acquisition were as follows:

	2000	2001
Net income (loss)	$(200,000)	$180,000
Dividends	50,000	60,000

The income statements for the year ending December 31, 2002, prior to the recognition of any investment income, for Slater and Rogan Companies are as follows:

	Slater	Rogan
Sales	$3,000,000	$550,000
Other revenues	200,000	—
Total revenues	3,200,000	550,000
Cost of goods sold	1,500,000	300,000
Other expenses	300,000	50,000
Total expenses	1,800,000	350,000
Income before extraordinary items	1,400,000	200,000
Extraordinary loss	—	30,000
Net income	$1,400,000	$170,000

During 2002, Slater Company declared and paid dividends of $120,000, while Rogan Company declared and paid dividends of $80,000. Rogan Company declares and pays its dividends on December 31 of each year.

Required:

a. Assume that Slater can exercise significant influence over the affairs of Rogan. Provide the following:

(1) The income statement of Slater Company, including recognition of any investment income or loss, for the year ending December 31, 2002.

(2) The balance in the investment in Rogan Company account as it would appear on the December 31, 2002, balance sheet of Slater Company.

Goodwill, if any, is to be amortized over 20 years.

b. Assume that Slater cannot exercise significant influence over the affairs of Rogan. Provide the journal entry of Slater Company related to its investment in Rogan Company for 2002.

[SMA, adapted]

P6-26

Beluga Ltd. is a wholly-owned subsidiary of Orcas Ltd. On January 1, 1995, Beluga issued $200,000 of 5%, 10-year bonds payable for $240,000. The interest is paid annually, on December 31. On January 1, 2002, Orcas Ltd. purchased $50,000 face value of the Beluga bonds for $41,000.

Required:

a. Give the eliminating entries relating to the bonds as they would appear on the consolidated worksheet at December 31, 2002.

b. Assume instead that Beluga is 75% owned by Orcas. Give the eliminating entries for the bonds at December 31, 2002, using:

(1) Agency method

(2) Par-value method

[CGA–Canada, adapted]

P6-27

Poseidon Ltd. (P Ltd.) bought 80% of the voting shares of Submarine Ltd. (S Ltd.) for $470,000 at January 1, 2002. S Ltd. had the following balance sheet at that date:

Submarine Ltd.
Balance Sheet
January 1, 2002

Cash	$ 10,000
Accounts receivable	30,000
Inventory	50,000
Land	150,000
Capital assets, net	200,000
	$440,000
Current liabilities	$ 20,000
Bonds—20-year, 15% interest	100,000
Common shares	100,000
Retained earnings	220,000
	$440,000

The fair values, on January 1, 2002, of S Ltd.'s assets were:

Inventory	$ 90,000
Land	$220,000
Capital assets, net	$170,000

The bonds on S Ltd.'s balance sheet were issued on January 1, 2002, at face value; interest is paid July 1 and December 31.

All inventory on the books of S at January 1, 2002, was sold during the year. P sold $400,000 (cost of goods) to S for $500,000 during 2002, and 20% of the inventory was on hand at the end of the year. P sold land to S (cost $30,000) for $90,000. P purchased $60,000 face value of S's bonds on July 2, 2002, for $64,000. The premium will be amortized straight-line over the remaining life of the bonds. Any goodwill will be amortized over 20 years. S's plant and equipment have 10 years (straight-line amortization) remaining.

S had a net income of $100,000 for 2002 and paid no dividends.

The balance sheets for the two companies at December 31, 2002 are:

	P Ltd.	S Ltd.
Cash	$ 70,000	$ 15,000
Accounts receivable	100,000	45,000
Inventory	240,000	80,000
Land	600,000	240,000
Capital assets, net	800,000	250,000
Investment in subsidiary equity*	550,000	—
Investment in bonds of subsidiary	63,898	—
	$2,423,898	$630,000
Current liabilities	$ 80,000	$110,000
Bonds	—	100,000
Common shares	1,000,000	100,000
Retained earnings	1,343,898	320,000
	$2,423,898	$630,000

*Includes only the parent's share of subsidiary net income.

Required:

Calculate the balances of the following selected accounts, at December 31, 2002, that would appear on the consolidated balance sheet. Ignore income taxes for this problem.

a. Inventory

b. Land

c. Capital assets

d. Bonds payable

e. Retained earnings

[CGA–Canada]

P6-28

Colin Ltd. has a 70%-owned subsidiary, Alice Ltd., with whom it conducted the following transactions during 2002:

1. Purchased $80,000 of merchandise from Alice Ltd. (cost Alice Ltd. $60,000).

2. Sold merchandise to Alice Ltd. for $160,000 at 20% markup on cost.

3. Sold land to Alice Ltd. (cost $70,000) for $1.

4. Purchased equipment on July 1, 2002, from Alice Ltd. for $150,000 (cost $150,000, 30% depreciated to date of sale, 10% per year straight-line). Colin Ltd. recorded no depreciation.

5. Colin Ltd. purchased $100,000 face value of 10-year bonds (four years left to redemption) for $96,000. The bonds were on the books of Alice Ltd. at par. The interest rate is 10% but was not paid during the year. (Assume the bonds were held by Colin Ltd. for the entire fiscal period.)

6. At the end of the year, Colin Ltd. had 30% of the intercompany merchandise on hand and Alice Ltd. had 10% of the intercompany merchandise on hand.

7. Alice Ltd. earned $360,000 during the year and paid $60,000 in dividends.

Required:

Prepare the eliminating entries that would be required on the working papers leading to consolidated financial statements at the fiscal year-end, December 31, 2002.

[CGA–Canada, adapted]

P6-29

Your assistant is preparing consolidated financial statements at December 31, 2002, for your company and has come to you with the following problems:

1. Subone Ltd., a 70%-owned subsidiary, sold land and buildings to Parent Ltd. for $1,180,000 ($300,000 was allocated to the land). The land cost Subone Ltd. $200,000; the building cost $1,400,000 and was 45% (i.e., nine years) depreciated at the date of sale. Parent Ltd. took a full year's depreciation on the building and will depreciate it over the original remaining life. Subone Ltd. took no depreciation on the building in 2002.

2. Subtwo Ltd., a 90%-owned subsidiary, purchased $600,000 of Parent Ltd.'s bonds on July 1, 2002, in the open market for $680,000. The bonds have a 12% interest rate, which will be paid on January 5, 2003, and will be due on January 1, 2006. All consolidated income statement adjustments arising from inter-company bond transactions are to be allocated between the two parties.

3. On December 1, 2002, Subthree Ltd. split their shares four to one. Prior to the split, Parent Ltd. owned 90% of the shares (90,000 shares) of Subthree Ltd. and had the account "Investment in Subthree Ltd." on the books at $2,400,000 cost basis.

Additional Information:

	At December 31, 2001		At December 31, 2002	
	Subone Ltd.	Parent Ltd.	Subone Ltd.	Parent Ltd.
Land	$4,000,000	$8,100,000	$4,200,000	$8,400,000
Buildings, net	5,200,000	9,320,000	4,982,000	9,178,000
Depreciation expense	460,000	530,000	420,000	570,000
Investment in bonds	—	—	668,571	—
Interest income (total from all sources)	—	—	111,000	—
Bonds payable	—	$2,000,000	—	$2,000,000
Discount on bonds	—	(130,000)	—	(97,500)
Interest expense (total on all debt)	—	368,070	—	392,462

	During 2002	
	Subone Ltd.	Subtwo Ltd.
Net income	($421,000)	$400,000
Dividends	—	20,000

Ignore the impact of income taxes.

Required:

a. For each item in problems 1 and 2 above, calculate the amounts that would appear on the consolidated financial statements for 2002.

b. For problem 3, calculate the amounts that would be in the investment in subsidiary account and the journal entries that would appear on the books of Parent Ltd. If no journal entries are needed, explain why.

c. Calculate for Subone Ltd. and Subtwo Ltd. the amount for minority interest that would appear on the consolidated income statement for 2002.

[CGA–Canada]

P6-30

On January 1, 1998, Portly Company purchased 75% of Slim Company at a cost of $4,500,000. On that date, the net identifiable assets of Slim Company had carrying values of $5,500,000. All the assets and liabilities of Slim Company had carrying values that were equal to their fair values, except from capital assets that had a fair value $200,000 greater than their carrying value, and long-term liabilities that had a fair value $100,000 less than their carrying value. The capital assets had a remaining useful life of 15 years and are being depreciated by the straight-line method. The long-term liabilities mature on January 1, 2004. Goodwill, if any, is to be amortized over a period of 20 years.

On December 31, 1999, Slim Company issued 8% coupon bonds payable with a par value of $500,000. The bonds are sold at 105% and mature on December 31, 2009. On January 1, 2002, Portly Company purchased one-half of these bonds in the open market for $230,000 in cash.

On January 1, 2000, Slim Company sold a patent to Portly Company for $400,000. The carrying value of this patent on the books of Slim Company on this date is $500,000 and its remaining useful life is five years.

The income statements of the two companies for the year ending December 31, 2002, are as follows:

	Portly	Slim
Total revenues	$3,200,000	$1,400,000
Cost of goods sold	2,000,000	700,000
Other expenses	500,000	300,000
Total expenses	2,500,000	1,000,000
Net income	$ 700,000	$ 400,000

Additional Information:

1. During 2002, Slim Company sold merchandise to Portly Company for $200,000. Of this merchandise, $100,000 was still in the inventories of Portly Company on December 31, 2002. On December 31, 2001, the inventories of Portly Company contained merchandise purchased from Slim Company for $75,000. All of Slim Company's sales to Portly Company were priced to provide a gross margin on sales prices of 20%.

2. During 2002, Portly Company sold merchandise to Slim Company for $500,000. All of this merchandise has been resold by Slim Company to individuals outside the consolidated entity. This merchandise was priced to provide Portly Company with a gross margin on sales prices of 25%.

3. Portly Company carries its investment in Slim Company at cost.

4. During 2002, Slim Company declared and paid dividends of $120,000, while Portly Company declared and paid dividends of $200,000.

5. Both Portly and Slim are merchandising companies. As a result, cost of goods sold consists entirely of merchandise that has been purchased and resold.

   All of their other types of expenses have been aggregated under the heading of "Other expenses."

Required:

The consolidated income statement for the year ending December 31, 2002, for Portly Company and its subsidiary, Slim Company, is being prepared to facilitate this process. You are to provide detailed calculations for each of the following:

a. Consolidated total revenue. (Any gain on the intercompany bond purchase would be included here.)

b. Consolidated cost of goods sold.

c. Consolidated other expenses. (Any loss on the intercompany bond purchase would be included here.)

d. The minority interest to be disclosed in the consolidated income statement for the year ending December 31, 2002.

e. Consolidated net income for the year ending December 31, 2002. This calculation should be independent of the expenses and revenues calculated in the preceding parts of this question.

[SMA, adapted]

P6-31

On January 1, 2002, Paco Ltd. purchased 70% of the common shares of Scot Ltd. for $506,100.

Financial data for Scot Ltd. are as follows:

Scot Ltd.
Balance Sheet
January 1, 2002

	Book value	Fair market value
Cash	$ 56,000	$ 56,000
Accounts receivable	102,000	108,000
Inventory	197,000	180,000
Capital assets, net	750,000	700,000
	$1,105,000	
Current liabilities	$ 140,000	140,000
Long-term liabilities		
Bonds payable at 12% interest	300,000	300,000
Bond discount	(60,000)	(60,000)
Preferred shares	175,000	—
Common shares	200,000	—
Retained earnings	350,000	—
	$1,105,000	

Additional Information:

1. Accounts receivable will be collected within the year.

2. Inventory is on the FIFO method and has a turnover of two times per year.

3. The capital assets are being written off over 10 years on a straight-line basis.

4. Any goodwill on the purchase will be amortized over 20 years on a straight-line basis.

5. The bond discount is being amortized over the remaining 10 years on a straight-line basis. Interest is payable semi-annually.

6. The preferred shares are noncumulative, nonparticipating, and redeemable at par ($100) plus a $2 premium.

During the year the consolidated entity had the following intercompany transactions:

1. Scot Ltd. sold a building that had a cost of $300,000, and had accumulated depreciation of $180,000 at the date of sale, to Paco Ltd. for $195,000 cash. (This building was being depreciated over 10 years straight-line with no residual value, but no depreciation had been recorded for the year 2002 to the date of sale.) It is company policy that assets receive a full year's depreciation in the year of acquisition and none in the year of disposal. It is also company policy that the acquiring company amortize the asset over the remaining life of the asset.

2. On July 1, 2002, Paco Ltd. purchased one-half of the bonds payable of Scot Ltd. for $107,250. It is company policy that the purchaser be allocated any gain or loss on an intercompany transaction of this nature.

3. On September 1, 2002, Paco Ltd. sold land costing $135,000 to Scot Ltd. for $175,000.

Financial statements of Paco Ltd. and Scot Ltd. as at December 31, 2002 are:

Balance Sheets
December 31, 2002

	Paco Ltd.	Scot Ltd.
Cash	$ 145,500	$ 85,000
Accounts receivable	300,000	200,000
Inventory	500,000	400,000
Bond investment	109,500	—
Capital assets, net	1,000,000	800,000
Investment in subsidiary (cost)	506,100	—
	$2,561,100	$1,485,000
Current liabilities	$ 100,000	$ 331,000
Long-term liabilities		
Bonds payable at 12% interest	—	300,000
Bond discount	—	(54,000)
Preferred shares	—	175,000
Common shares	400,000	200,000
Retained earnings	2,061,100	533,000
	$2,561,100	$1,485,000

Income Statements
Year Ended December 31, 2002

	Paco Ltd.	Scot Ltd.
Sales	$ 900,000	$ 800,000
Cost of goods sold	500,000	500,000
	400,000	300,000
Less:		
Depreciation	(80,000)	(70,000)
Interest expense	—	(42,000)
Other expenses	(100,000)	(80,000)
Plus:		
Interest income on bonds	11,250	—
Gain on sale of land	40,000	—
Gain on sale of building	—	75,000
Net income	$ 271,250	$ 183,000

Required:

a. Calculate the consolidated goodwill that would appear on the consolidated balance sheet at December 31, 2002.

b. Prepare the consolidated income statement for the year 2002.

c. Calculate the following, as they would appear on the consolidated balance sheet at December 31, 2002:

(1) Inventory

(2) Fixed assets, net

(3) Bond discount

(4) Minority interest (Be precise.)

[CGA–Canada]

P6-32

On January 1, 2002, AN Holdings Ltd. (AN) purchased 20% of the outstanding common shares of DUN Development Inc. (DUN) for $400,000, of which $100,000 was paid in cash and $300,000 is payable without interest on December 31, 2004. AN's incremental borrowing rate at the time of purchase was 8%. AN also paid $20,000 to a business broker who helped find a suitable business and negotiated the purchase.

At the time of the acquisition, the fair values of DUN's identifiable assets and liabilities were equal to their carrying values, except for an office building that had a fair value in excess of book value of $200,000 and an estimated remaining useful life of 20 years. DUN's shareholders' equity on January 1, 2002 was $1,300,000.

During 2002, DUN reported a net income of $250,000 and paid dividends of $100,000.

Required:

a. Determine the amount of goodwill amortization for 2002 relating to AN's investment in DUN. Assume a 10-year amortization period for goodwill.

b. Prepare the journal entry to record AN's investment in DUN on January 1, 2002 and any journal entries relating to the loan payable.

c. Prepare all other journal entries relating to the investment in DUN for 2002 under the:

i) cost method

ii) equity method

[CGA–Canada]

Strategic Investments: Additional Aspects of Share Capital

Introduction

The preceding chapters have provided a thorough overview of accounting for intercorporate investments, especially for preparing consolidated financial statements. This chapter will round out the discussion by examining two additional facets of intercorporate investments that frequently arise.

The first facet concerns different classes of shares. Throughout the preceding chapters, we have implicitly assumed that there is only one class of outstanding share—voting common. Very often, however, there are two or more classes of shares outstanding. What happens then? What ownership percentage does a parent possess if the parent owns differing amounts of the different classes of share, or none at all of certain classes? The first section of this chapter will discuss this issue. Actually, the problem is not a complicated one, so the first section of the chapter should be easy sailing.

The second facet, one that will consume most of this short chapter, is that an investor corporation may change the level of ownership in an investee. Often an investor will *increase* its ownership. Investments that are achieved through a series of purchases rather than just one are called **step purchases**. At first, the accumulation may simply be a portfolio investment. But as more shares are acquired, the investor may achieve *significant influence* or even *control*. Since the financial reporting varies for these different stages of investment, how do we move from one to the other?

An investor corporation may also *decrease* its level of ownership, usually (but not only) by selling a portion of its share holdings. What are the ramifications of a reduction in ownership percentage?

It is possible to spend a great deal of time examining the issue of changes in ownership interest. However, we will take only a general look at accounting for ownership changes. We will leave complex transactions in the real world to the expertise of specialists.

Preferred and Restricted Shares of Investee Corporations

Introduction

Throughout our discussion of intercorporate investments, we have dealt entirely with voting common shares. In all of the examples in the previous chapters, none of the investments was in senior or preferred shares, and none of the investee corporations (either subsidiaries or significantly influenced companies) had preferred shares in their capital structure.

The percentage of ownership interest affects the consolidation process in several ways, including:

- the proportion of the fair value increments of Sub's assets that is included on Parent's balance sheet,

- the amount assigned to non-controlling interest,

- the amount of the purchase price assigned to goodwill, and

- the amount of consolidated net income.

Consolidated net income (and equity-basis net income) is affected because the allocation of the purchase price to fair value increments and goodwill affects annual amortization expense.

This section discusses the effect of preferred and restricted shares on the investor's reporting of intercorporate investments. First, we will examine the effect that investee preferred shares have on the investor's ownership interest. Then we will briefly look at the accounting for an investment in preferred shares. After discussing preferred shares, we will look at *restricted common shares*—those that have reduced (or non-existent) voting rights.

Effect of preferred shares on investor's ownership interest

It is not unusual for a subsidiary or a significantly influenced investee corporation to have preferred shares outstanding. The parent or investor corporation may not own all or any of the preferred shares. For example, one company may acquire 100% of the common shares of another, while third parties continue to own the subsidiary's preferred shares. How does the existence of the subsidiary's preferred shares affect the parent company's ownership interest? Can the parent be said to own 100% of the subsidiary even though the parent does not own the preferred shares?

A simple example will help to demonstrate the issue. Suppose that Sub has total shareholders' equity of $1,000,000, consisting of $400,000 in preferred shares (redemption value) and $600,000 in common shares and retained earnings. Assume further that Parent buys all of Sub's common shares for $1,200,000. What is Parent's ownership interest in Sub?

Two alternatives seem to exist. First, Parent can be said to own 100% of Sub because Parent owns 100% of the voting shares and can elect 100% of the board of directors. Alternatively, it can be argued that Parent owns less than 100% because there is an outstanding ownership interest of $400,000 in Sub. Parent's ownership interest may be viewed as being either 60% or 75%:

- at book value, Parent owns shares representing $600,000 of the $1,000,000 total shareholders' equity, which is 60%; or

- based on market values, the parent owns shares worth $1,200,000 of the total value of the outstanding shares—common shares valued at $1,200,000 plus $400,000 redemption value of the preferred shares—which is 75%.

To resolve the issue, we can first approach the problem from the standpoint of measuring earnings. If Parent owns 100% of the common shares of Sub, then Parent has an interest in all of the residual earnings of Sub. Sub must pay (or provide for) the preferred dividends out of net income; all of the remaining earnings accrue to the benefit of the common shareholders. Parent must report 100% of Sub's residual earnings.

When consolidated statements are prepared, then all of Sub's revenues and expenses are included, and the deduction for non-controlling interest in earnings of Sub will consist solely of the dividend entitlement of Sub's preferred shareholders.

On the equity basis, Parent will pick up 100% of Sub's earnings after provision for the preferred dividends. Therefore, when reporting its share of Sub's earnings either by consolidation or on the equity basis, Parent will report 100% of Sub's earnings less the prior dividend claim of the preferred shareholders.

A similar conclusion may be reached by looking at the issue from the viewpoint of the balance sheet. If Parent is viewed as owning only 60% (or 75%) of Sub, then only 60% (or 75%) of the fair value increments for Sub's net assets will be included on Parent's consolidated balance sheet. By implication, the remainder of the fair value increments would benefit the non-controlling shareholders.

However, the non-controlling interest in preferred shares is not a residual interest. Instead, it is a fixed amount determined by call or redemption value of the preferred shares, plus any dividends in arrears. Increases in the value of Sub's assets increase only the common share equity—preferred shareholders do not benefit, except perhaps by the reduced risk of dividend non-payment. Therefore, Parent's purchase of 100% of the Sub common shares should be viewed as an acquisition of 100% of the Sub net assets, less the claim on those assets represented by the preferred shares.

Exhibit 7-1 shows the assignment of the purchase price, assuming that the fair value of Sub's net assets is $1,350,000. The preferred share equity is subtracted in order to find the net asset value for common equity. The fair value of the preferred equity is determined by the preferred shareholders' claim on assets. This claim is measured by the shares' call price or redemption value plus dividends in arrears, if any. Call prices are usually higher than par values or issue prices, and thus fair value is likely to be higher than book value.

Strategic
Investments:
Additional
Aspects of
Share Capital

319

EXHIBIT 7–1 ALLOCATION OF PURCHASE PRICE—PARENT BUYS 100% OF SUB COMMON SHARES BUT NO PREFERRED

	Sub		Fair value increment
	Book value	**Fair value**	
Purchase price	$1,200,000	$1,200,000	
Net assets	$1,000,000	1,350,000	$ 350,000
Less preferred share equity	400,000	440,000	40,000
Common share equity acquired	600,000	910,000	310,000
Goodwill		$ 290,000	290,000
Purchase price discrepancy	$ 600,000		$ 600,000

In Exhibit 7-1, the preferred equity fair value of $440,000 is subtracted from the net asset fair value of $1,350,000. The result, $910,000, is the fair value of the net assets *acquired through purchase of the common shares*. The residual purchase price is allocated to goodwill: $1,200,000 − $910,000 = $290,000.

Investment in preferred shares

In the preceding section, we assumed that outsiders owned all the preferred shares. However, the parent may own some of the subsidiary's preferred shares as well as its common shares.

On the books of the parent, the cost of the shares will be debited to an investment account. When consolidated statements are prepared, the parent's investment account for the preferred shares must be eliminated, as must the portion of the subsidiary preferred share equity that is owned by the parent.

Similarly, preferred dividends paid by a subsidiary to its parent are intercompany transfers and will be eliminated on consolidation. Consolidated earnings (or the equity-basis earnings) must include the parent's share of the subsidiary's net income after provision only for the portion of preferred dividends paid or payable to outside shareholders.

The cost of the preferred shares to the parent will most likely be different from the carrying value of the preferred shares on the subsidiary's balance sheet. If the parent purchased the preferred shares on the open market, it is obvious that the cost of the shares will be different from the par or other carrying value. It is less obvious that a difference may exist even when the preferred shares were purchased directly from the subsidiary.

Any premium on the shares that was paid by the parent will be included in the investment account. However, that premium will not be a part of preferred shareholders' equity in the subsidiary's accounts because the preferred shareholders have an equity in the subsidiary only to the extent of their redemption value.

From the viewpoint of the consolidated entity, subsidiary preferred shares owned by the parent do not exist—they have the same general status as do intercompany receivables and payables, and must be eliminated. When there is a difference in the preferred share carrying value, the worksheet elimination entry must be balanced by a debit or credit for the difference. This difference is charged or credited to the shareholders' equity on the consolidated balance sheet, generally to a contributed surplus account for that class of shares, if one exists. Otherwise, the charge or credit is to retained earnings. In effect, the shares are treated as having been retired.

Restricted shares

Much of Canadian enterprise is conducted by family-controlled corporations. As these corporations grow, it frequently becomes impossible to finance them adequately without going to the public equity markets. If shares are sold to the public, however, the controlling shareholders risk losing control of "their" companies, which the shareholders are loath to do.

To raise equity capital without losing control, family corporations issue **restricted shares** to the public. A restricted share is just like a regular common share, except that it either has no voting rights or has sharply reduced voting rights. Restricted shares usually share equally with regular shares in dividends and in assets upon dissolution, although they can be subordinated in those regards as well.

There are well over 200 listings of restricted shares on the Toronto Stock Exchange. A prime example is Canadian Tire, whose 78 million Class A non-voting shares comprise about 96% of the outstanding shares but are permitted to elect only 20% of the Canadian Tire directors.

As we described above, a prime motivation for issuing restricted shares is to raise equity capital while maintaining control in the hands of the original group of shareholders. Earnings usually accrue to all shareholders equally, but the voting power resides wholly or mainly in the hands of a few. This situation raises the question as to how to treat restricted shares in consolidated financial statements when a parent controls the voting shares but does not own the restricted shares. There are two separate issues: (1) control and (2) percentage of ownership.

Strategic

Investments:

Additional

Aspects of

Share Capital

321

Control

Control exists when the investor has sufficient votes (or a combination of votes and convertible securities that can be converted into voting shares) to elect a majority of the board of directors and thereby determine the strategic policies of the corporation. If an investee has restricted shares, control exists when the investor has more than half the votes, regardless of the proportion of shares owned.

For example, suppose that The Odyssey Inc. has 1,000 shares of regular common shares outstanding and 10,000 restricted shares. The regular shares have ten votes each, while the restricted shares have one vote each. The total number of votes available is 20,000: 10,000 for the regular shares plus 10,000 for the restricted shares. A takeover could occur when a buyer acquires 10,001 of the available 20,000 votes. It doesn't matter whether the buyer acquires all of the regular shares plus one restricted share, or 10,000 restricted shares plus one regular share, or any linear combination thereof.

Restricted shares sometimes have a **coattail provision**, which is a provision that comes into effect when a buyer attempts to buy control of a company. If a control block is about to change hands, then the restricted shares may become fully voting shares for limited purposes. For example, Bombardier Inc. has Class A shares that have ten votes per share and Class B shares that have one vote per share. Class B shares are convertible to Class A on a one-for-one basis at the option of the holder in the event that the controlling shareholders (the Bombardier family) accept an offer to acquire substantially all of the Class A shares. In such an event, therefore, the Class B shareholders can participate equally with the Class A shareholders if control of the company changes.

The nature of coattail provisions differs significantly between companies, and they do not exist at all for many (if not most) companies. But when coattail provisions exist, the number of shares that must be *held* in order to maintain control is quite different from the number of shares that must be *purchased* in order to acquire control.

Percentage of ownership

The second issue that relates to restricted shares in an investee corporation's equity structure is how to treat the percentage of ownership for consolidation or equity reporting purposes. It is important not to confuse the proportion of votes with the proportion of common equity investment. The crucial question is how much of the investee's earnings are available to the investor. If the restricted shares participate equally with the regular shares in dividends, then the investor's ownership percentage is simply the proportion of shares owned relative to the total number of shares outstanding, regular and restricted.

For example, The Odyssey Inc. has a total of 11,000 shares outstanding in the two classes. If the common shares are equal in dividend participation and an acquirer obtains 1,000 regular shares plus one restricted share, then the owner-ship percentage for consolidation purposes is 1,001/11,000 or about 9%. If, on the other hand, control was obtained by buying all 10,000 restricted shares plus one regular share, then the ownership percentage is 10,001/11,000, or about 91%. It is obvious, therefore, that it is quite possible to have control of a sub-sidiary while still having a non-controlling interest of over 90%!

In summary, the key points to remember are that (1) when determining con-trol, count *votes*, but (2) when determining non-controlling interest, look at *par-ticipation in earnings and dividends*. The two measures are not the same when restricted shares exist in an investee corporation.

Changes in Ownership Interest

Step purchases

Throughout the preceding chapters, we have implicitly assumed that an investor corporation acquires its ownership interest in another company at a single point in time. However, an investor corporation may acquire its shares in an investee corporation in several steps or by gradual accumulation over a period of time, sometimes over several years. Sequential purchases are known as **step purchases** or **step acquisitions**.

We have seen that when an investor corporation acquires a significant portion of the shares of an investee corporation, fair values and goodwill must be meas-ured and amortized in future years, when appropriate. When a subsidiary is con-solidated, consolidated assets include the subsidiary's assets at book values plus the fair value increments and goodwill for the controlling interest's share only. The valuation of assets and the measurement of income are affected when the investor or parent increases its proportion of ownership. There are three situa-tions involving increases in ownership interest:

- An investor holds shares in another corporation as a portfolio investment, and then acquires sufficient additional shares to give the investor significant influ-ence over the investee. The investor's reporting will shift from the cost basis to the equity basis when significant influence is achieved.

- An investor has significant influence in the investee and then acquires enough additional shares to give the investor control over the investee. The investor's reporting then changes from equity-basis reporting to consolidation.

- An investor buys additional shares without affecting the nature of the report-ing for the investment. The investor may have significant influence and may increase the size of its non-controlling position. Similarly, the investor may control the investee and prepare consolidated statements, and additional share purchases simply increase the parent's controlling interest. In these cases, the method of reporting does not change, but the increase in ownership interest nevertheless does have an impact on the financial reporting of the investor corporation.

In the next section, we will focus on increases in the ownership percentage of controlled investees, i.e., subsidiaries. In the later sections, increases in non-controlling interests will be discussed, including those situations that call for a change in reporting practice.

Example: Increase in controlling interest

Assume that on December 31, 2002, Parent Corporation (PC) acquires 60% of the shares of Subsidiary Corporation (SC) for $600,000. The condensed balance sheets for PC and SC are shown in Part 1 of Exhibit 7-2, together with the fair values for SC.

Part 2 of Exhibit 7-2 shows the allocation of the purchase price. PC paid a price that was $270,000 above the book value of the 60% share of net assets acquired; of this amount, $180,000 is estimated to be the FVI on capital assets and the remainder ($90,000) is goodwill.

The consolidated balance sheet for PC on the date of the acquisition is shown in Exhibit 7-3. PC's consolidated assets include 100% of the book values plus 60% of the FVIs of SC's assets. Non-controlling interest is 40% of the net book value of SC's net assets.

For the next step, assume the following additional information:

- In 2003, SC reported net income of $70,000 and paid $20,000 in dividends.

- The remaining useful life of SC's capital assets is 10 years from December 31, 2002.

Strategic
Investments:
Additional
Aspects of
Share Capital

323

EXHIBIT 7–2 PARENT CORPORATION ACQUISITION OF SUBSIDIARY CORPORATION

December 31, 2002

1. Net asset positions subsequent to acquisition

	Parent book values	Subsidiary Book values	Subsidiary Fair values
Current assets	$1,000,000	$ 400,000	$ 400,000
Capital assets (net)	1,900,000	1,100,000	1,400,000
Investment in Subsidiary Corporation	600,000	0	
Total assets	$3,500,000	$1,500,000	
Liabilities	$1,500,000	$ 950,000	– 950,000
Common shares	400,000	100,000	
Retained earnings	1,600,000	450,000	
Total liabilities and shareholders' equity	$3,500,000	$1,500,000	
Net asset fair value for Subsidiary Corporation			$ 850,000

2. Allocation of purchase price

	Subsidiary Corporation		
	Book values	Fair values	Fair value increments
Current assets	$ 400,000	$ 400,000	0
Capital assets (net)	1,100,000	1,400,000	$ 300,000
Liabilities	(950,000)	(950,000)	0
	$ 550,000	850,000	$ 300,000
Parent's ownership share		× 60%	× 60%
FV of net assets acquired		510,000	**180,000**
Purchase price		600,000	
Goodwill		$ 90,000	90,000
Total purchase price discrepancy			$ 270,000

EXHIBIT 7–3 PARENT CORPORATION CONSOLIDATED BALANCE SHEET

December 31, 2002

Current assets (1,000,000 + 400,000)	$1,400,000
Capital assets (1,900,000 + 1,100,000 + **180,000**)	3,180,000
Goodwill	90,000
Total assets	$4,670,000
Liabilities (1,500,000 + 950,000)	$2,450,000
Non-controlling interest (**550,000 × 40%**)	220,000
Common shares, Parent Corporation	400,000
Retained earnings	1,600,000
Total liabilities and shareholders' equity	$4,670,000

- Goodwill will be amortized over 15 years.

- There were no intercompany transactions during 2003.

The separate-entity balance sheets for PC and SC at December 31, 2003, are shown in Part 1 of Exhibit 7-4.

So far, there has been nothing new in this analysis. But now, assume that PC buys an additional 10% of the shares of SC for $140,000 cash on January 2, 2004. The additional 10% increases PC's ownership interest in SC to 70%. When we prepare a consolidated balance sheet using the new percentage of ownership, we seem to have two choices for consolidating SC's net assets:

1. Include 100% of book value on January 2, 2004, plus 70% of the fair value increments at January 2, 2004; or

2. Include 100% of book value on January 2, 2004, plus 60% of the fair value increments at December 31, 2002, plus 10% of the fair value increments at January 2, 2004.

Under the first alternative, the second purchase (of 10%) will trigger a general revaluation of the assigned costs from the first purchase. The purchase price is viewed as a total cost of $740,000 (i.e., $600,000 for 60% plus $140,000 for 10%) for a 70% share interest. Fair value increments and goodwill will be recalculated based on the difference between 70% of the net asset fair values *on January 2, 2004* and the total purchase price.

Proponents of this first alternative argue that a general reallocation based on fair values at the date of the latest purchase is desirable because it recognizes the fair value of the subsidiary's assets at a single point in time. The second alternative, on the other hand, includes pieces of fair values of the same assets at different points in time, resulting in a hodgepodge of valuations that are meaningless when added together.

The problem with the first approach is that it results in reallocating costs based on values that were not in effect at the time of purchase. When Parent Corporation bought its initial 60% interest in Subsidiary Corporation, the fair value of the capital assets was $1,400,000. The purchase price of $600,000 implicitly recognizes that fair value, not the fair value of $1,500,000 that existed one year later. If the fair value of $1,500,000 had existed at the time of the initial purchase, then the cost of the 60% share interest may well have been higher

Strategic
Investments:
Additional
Aspects of
Share Capital

325

EXHIBIT 7–4 PARENT AND SUBSIDIARY

1. Condensed separate-entity balance sheets, December 31, 2003

	Parent	Subsidiary
Current assets	$1,000,000	$ 500,000
Capital assets (net)	1,900,000	1,000,000
Investment in Subsidiary (at cost)	600,000	0
Total assets	$3,500,000	$1,500,000
Liabilities	$1,300,000	$ 900,000
Common shares	400,000	100,000
Retained earnings	1,800,000	500,000
Total liabilities and shareholders' equity	$3,500,000	$1,500,000

2. Parent Corporation consolidated balance sheet, December 31, 2003

Current assets (1,000,000 + 500,000)	$1,500,000
Capital assets [1,900,000 + 1,000,000 + (**180,000 × 9/10**)]	3,062,000
Investment in Subsidiary (600,000 – **600,000**)	0
Goodwill (**90,000 × 14/15**)	84,000
Total assets	$4,646,000
Liabilities (1,300,000 + 900,000)	$2,200,000
Non-controlling interest (**600,000 × 40%**)	240,000
Common shares	400,000
Retained earnings (see below)	1,806,000
Total liabilities and shareholders' equity	$4,646,000

Consolidated shareholder's equity, December 31, 2003

Separate entity retained earnings, December 31, 2003:	
Parent	$1,800,000
Subsidiary	500,000
Less Subsidiary's share equity at date of acquisition	– 450,000
Less non-controlling interest's share of S's earnings since date of acquisition [(**600,000 – 550,000**) × **40%**]	– 20,000
Less amortization:	
FVI on capital assets (**180,000 × 1/10**)	– 18,000
Goodwill (**90,000 × 1/15**)	– 6,000
Consolidated shareholders' equity, Parent Corporation	$1,806,000

than the $600,000 paid. The first method is seriously flawed, therefore, because it reallocates the cost on the basis of values that did not underlie the initial purchase price.

As well, the second approach is more in accordance with the historical cost concept. The historical cost of each purchase is represented by the fair values of the net assets acquired at each acquisition date. Fair values at an earlier date are irrelevant for measuring the value (and thus the cost) of assets acquired at a later date.

Canadian accounting practice calls for the second alternative for reporting the effect of step purchases in consolidated financial statements [CICA 1600.13]. Using this alternative, the assigned valuations for the first purchase are left untouched by the second purchase. The cost of the second purchase ($140,000 for 10%) is allocated to fair value increments and goodwill at the date of the purchase as a separate investment. This allocation is shown in Exhibit 7-5. FVI of $50,000 is allocated to capital assets on the 10% share acquired. The remaining $30,000 purchase price discrepancy is goodwill.

EXHIBIT 7–5 PARENT ACQUIRES AN ADDITIONAL 10% OF SUBSIDIARY

January 2, 2004

Allocation of purchase price

	Subsidiary Corporation		
	Book values	Fair values	Fair value increments
Current assets	$ 500,000	$ 500,000	0
Capital assets (net)	1,000,000	1,500,000	$500,000
Liabilities	(900,000)	(900,000)	0
	$ 600,000	1,100,000	$500,000
Parent's new ownership share acquired		× 10%	× 10%
FV of net assets acquired		110,000	**50,000**
Purchase price		140,000	
Goodwill		**$ 30,000**	30,000
Total purchase price discrepancy			$ 80,000

The pro-forma consolidated balance sheet is shown in Exhibit 7-6. Current assets are reduced (compared to Exhibit 7-4) by $140,000, the amount expended to buy the additional 10%. The total amount of goodwill on the pro-forma consolidated balance sheet is $114,000 at January 2, 2004, as follows:

Goodwill from 60% purchase on December 31, 2002	$ 90,000
Less amortization for 2003	− 6,000
Plus goodwill from 10% purchase on January 4, 2003	+ 30,000
Goodwill after second purchase	$114,000

EXHIBIT 7–6 PARENT CORPORATION PRO-FORMA CONSOLIDATED BALANCE SHEET

January 2, 2004

Current assets (1,000,000 + 500,000 − **140,000 purchase price**)	$1,360,000
Capital assets [1,900,000 + 1,000,000 + **(180,000 × 9/10)** + 50,000]	3,112,000
Goodwill [**(90,000 × 14/15) + 30,000**]	114,000
Total assets	$4,586,000
Liabilities (1,300,000 + 900,000)	$2,200,000
Non-controlling interest **(600,000 × 30%)**	180,000
Common shares	400,000
Retained earnings	1,806,000
Total liabilities and shareholders' equity	$4,586,000

In 2004 and following years, the two goodwill amounts will be amortized separately, as will the two fair value increments assigned to the capital assets.

Increases in equity-basis investments

Equity-method accounting is intended to yield the same net income and investor-corporation retained earnings as would consolidation. Therefore, it will come as little surprise that when an investment is being reported on the equity basis, the same principles apply for step acquisitions as were discussed above in accounting for consolidated subsidiaries. In general, each significant purchase of shares is accounted for separately, with separate estimates of fair values and goodwill at each date of purchase. For practical purposes, numerous small purchases can be grouped together and treated as a single purchase [CICA 1600.11].

An investor corporation may increase its ownership in a significantly influenced company to the point where the investor becomes the majority shareholder and consequently controls the investee. Once control is achieved, consolidation becomes appropriate, rather than equity-basis reporting. Since the equity method is completely consistent with the parent-company approach to consolidation, shifting from equity reporting to consolidation poses no additional problems.

Strategic
Investments:
Additional
Aspects of
Share Capital

327

Acquisition of significant influence

One further situation that should briefly be considered is where the initial purchase (or purchases) is reported on the cost basis because significant influence does not exist, but an additional purchase does give significant influence to the investor corporation.

For example, suppose that an investor buys an initial stake of 18% in an investee corporation. The initial purchase of 18% does not give significant influence to the investor, and the investment is reported on the cost basis.

Subsequently, the investor buys an additional 12%, resulting in a 30% ownership interest. The additional acquisition gives the investor significant influence. A change in the reporting basis from the cost basis to the equity basis therefore is required. Any purchase price discrepancy must be allocated to fair value increments and goodwill.

When the purchase of the additional 12% is made and equity-basis reporting becomes appropriate, three alternative approaches to accounting for the acquisition are possible:

1. Treat the total cost of both the 18% and the 12% acquisition as an acquisition of 30% of the fair value of the investee's net assets at the date of the second acquisition.

2. Treat the two purchases independently by (a) allocating the cost of the 12% purchase to 12% of the investee's fair values on the date of purchase, and (b) retroactively allocating the cost of the earlier 18% purchase on the basis of the fair values of the investee's net assets at the date of the first purchase.

3. Continue to report the first purchase on the cost basis, but account for the second purchase on the equity basis.

The first two of these three alternatives are the same as the two alternative reporting practices discussed earlier in the section on accounting for step purchases of consolidated subsidiaries. In that section, we saw that the second alternative is recommended because it treats each purchase as a separate transaction and yields results that are most similar to direct purchase of assets.

The discussion in the previous sections was based on the premise that all of the purchases of shares had been reported on the equity basis. Subsequent purchases would not affect the accounting for previous purchases. However, a different situation exists when the earlier purchases were reported on the cost basis, as we are assuming in this section. The subsequent acquisition of significant influence calls for a change in accounting policy for the investment, and thus we must re-examine the alternatives.

The third alternative, that of leaving the first purchase on the cost basis, clearly is unsound. This alternative results in different reporting practices for two transactions that meld together in substance. The 18% interest and the 12% interest are not wielded individually by the investor; it is the total of 30% that is exercised and that gives rise to significant influence.

The second alternative is consistent with the approach described in the previous sections, when there is an increase in the percentage ownership of a controlled subsidiary or an already significantly influenced investee.

A practical problem arises, however. It is likely to be difficult, if not impossible, to obtain fair-value estimates retroactively to the time of the first purchase. In addition, since the first purchase is likely to have been relatively small, the refinement obtained by retroactive restatement may be immaterial to the investor corporation's financial reporting and thus not worth the effort. As a result, the first alternative is usually applied in practice. The *CICA Handbook* states that the total cost of all purchases is allocated to net assets and goodwill on the basis of fair values at the date on which the equity method is first deemed appropriate [CICA 1600.11].

Decreases in Ownership Interest

On occasion, an investor corporation may reduce its share of ownership of a subsidiary or of a significantly influenced affiliate. A reduction may be the result of either of two occurrences:

- The investor may sell part of its holdings, thereby directly reducing its ownership percentage.

- The investee may issue new shares, thereby indirectly reducing the investor's ownership interest, assuming that the investor does not buy a proportionate part of the new offering.

The financial reporting impact is similar whether applied to parent-subsidiary relationships or to equity-basis investments. Therefore, we will explicitly discuss only reductions in interest experienced by a parent corporation. The same principles apply to significantly influenced investees.

Sale of part of an investment

When a parent corporation sells part of its investment in a subsidiary, the accounting *on the parent's books* is quite straightforward. The investment account must be reduced by the proportionate part of the carrying value of the investment, and the difference between the carrying value of the investment and the proceeds from the sale is a gain or loss on the sale. The difficulty is in measuring the carrying value of the investment.

Since investments normally are recorded on the cost basis, it is tempting to view the carrying value as being simply the proportionate part of the cost of the investment. However, the *recorded* carrying value is not the same as the *reported* carrying value. The reported carrying value is the net asset value of the subsidiary as reported in the parent's consolidated balance sheet.

For example, assume that on December 31, 2002, Parent Corporation acquired 30,000 of the 50,000 outstanding shares (i.e., 60%) of Subsidiary Corporation for $20 per share, or $600,000 total. The net book value of the shares on the date of acquisition is $11 per share, or a total of $330,000 for the acquired shares. The purchase price discrepancy of $270,000 is allocated $180,000 to FVI on capital assets and $90,000 to goodwill. (Note that these are the same amounts that we used in the previous section, Exhibit 7-2.)

On January 1, 2004, Parent's management decides to reduce Parent's share of Sub to the minimum of 51% needed to retain control. Therefore, Parent sells 4,500 of its Sub shares (15% of its 60% ownership interest) for $30 per share: 4,500 shares × $30 = $135,000. The effect on PC's consolidated balances is to reduce Parent's equity in Sub's net assets by 15%. Note that the key word is *equity*. The assets and liabilities for Sub that are included in Parent's 2003 consolidated balance sheet (Exhibit 7-4) are as follows:

Strategic
Investments:
Additional
Aspects of
Share Capital

329

Current assets	$ 500,000
Capital assets [1,000,000 + (**180,000** × **9/10**)]	1,162,000
Goodwill (**90,000** × **14/15**)	84,000
Liabilities	−900,000
Non-controlling interest (**600,000** × **40%**)	−240,000
Parent's consolidated equity in Subsidiary's net assets	$ 606,000

Fifteen percent of Parent's consolidation equity in Sub's net assets is $606,000 × 15% = $90,900. The gain on the sale is the difference between the sale proceeds and the surrendered 15% equity in Sub's net assets: $135,000 − $90,900 = $44,100. The difference between the surrendered equity and the recorded cost of the 15% interest represents Parent's equity in Sub's increase in net asset value since acquisition, which must be credited to Parent's retained earnings.

The entry to record the sale *on Parent's books* is as follows (assuming that Parent carries its investment in Sub at cost on its books):

Cash	135,000	
Investment in SC (cost basis: 600,000 × 15%)		90,000
Retained earnings (90,900 − 90,000)		900
Gain on sale of investment (135,000 − 90,900)		44,100

The credit to retained earnings simply records 15% of the unremitted adjusted earnings of Sub that Parent has already recognized in its consolidated financial statements for 2003 but that has not been recorded on Parent's books. The unremitted earnings can be verified as follows:

Increase in Sub's shareholders' equity since acquisition (600,000 − 550,000)	$ 50,000
Less non-controlling interest's share (50,000 × 40%)	− 20,000
Less amortization of FVI on capital assets (180,000 × 1/10)	− 18,000
Less amortization of goodwill (90,000 × 1/15)	− 6,000
Parent's equity in unremitted earnings of Sub	$ 6,000
Proportion of Parent's ownership interest being sold	× 15%
Unremitted earnings related to sold portion of investment	$ 900

These entries are no different in substance from any entry to record the sale of part of an investment. However, the sale of part of Parent's interest in Sub has implications that a sale of a portfolio investment does not have. The sale will affect consolidated net assets, non-controlling interest (which has now risen to 49%), and Parent's equity in the earnings of Sub. In order to evaluate the impact of the sale, we must disaggregate the equity-basis carrying value of $606,000.

Issuance of shares by subsidiary

At first glance, it may appear that issuance of new shares by the subsidiary to outside parties should not affect the parent. The parent corporation still holds the same number of shares, and the cost of acquiring those shares is not directly affected by the new issue of the subsidiary.

However, it is not quite so simple. While it is true that the number of shares held by the parent is not changed, the percentage of ownership *is* changed. After the issuance, the parent owns a smaller percentage of the subsidiary and the non-controlling interest is larger.

Under the purchase method of accounting for business combinations, the parent is considered to have purchased a proportionate share of the fair value of the subsidiary's net assets. If a subsidiary issues additional shares to outsiders, then new capital is brought into the subsidiary, thereby increasing its net asset value. But the parent's *proportionate* interest in the increased net asset value is *decreased*. The parent's equity in the subsidiary is affected by both factors, the increase in the subsidiary's net assets and the decrease in the parent's proportionate interest.

To illustrate the impact of a new issue, assume that on January 1, 2004, Subsidiary Corporation issues 8,824 new shares to outside interests for net proceeds of $264,706 (about $30 per share). The new issue will increase Sub's total outstanding shares to 58,824, and will thereby reduce Parent's holdings of 30,000 shares to 51% of the total, the same level of ownership that we used in the example in the previous section. Before the new issue, Sub had total shareholders' equity of $600,000 (including common shares of $100,000). The new issue increases the total to $864,706 by raising the amount in the common share equity account to $364,706. Parent formerly owned 60% of $600,000 book value; now Parent owns 51% of the $864,706 book value.

The change in the net assets of Sub and Parent's share thereof is illustrated in Exhibit 7-7. As a result of Sub's new issue of shares, Parent's equity in the book value of Sub's net assets has increased from $360,000 to $441,000 (that is, $864,706 × 51% = $441,000). But the change in book value is not the only impact that Sub's new issue has on Parent's equity in Sub. Parent now has an interest in only 51% of the date-of-acquisition fair value increment on Sub's net assets and only 51% of the goodwill. Parent will include in consolidated net income only 51% of Sub's future net income. If Parent continues to amortize 60% of the fair value increment and goodwill, Parent will be understating its share of Sub's earnings.

Therefore, the fair value increment and the goodwill must be adjusted to reflect Parent's lessened interest. Parent's ownership interest has declined from 60% to 51%, a decline of nine percentage points, or 15% of the original 60% interest. The unamortized fair value increment attributable to Parent's equity declines by 15%, from $162,000 (i.e., $180,000 × 9/10) to $137,700 (that is, $180,000 × 9/10 × 85%), and goodwill declines to $84,000 × 85% = $71,400. These decreases in Parent's equity partially offset the increase in Parent's share of the net book value, with the result that the equity underlying Parent's investment in Sub increases from $606,000 to $650,100 as shown at the bottom of Exhibit 7-7.

Strategic
Investments:
Additional
Aspects of
Share Capital

331

EXHIBIT 7–7 CHANGE IN PARENT'S SHARE OF SUBIDIARY'S NET ASSETS AFTER NEW SHARE ISSUE

	Before new share issue		After new share issue	
	100%	**60%**	**100%**	**51%**
Current assets	$ 500,000	$300,000	$ 764,706	$390,000
Capital assets (net)	1,000,000	600,000	1,000,000	510,000
Total assets	$1,500,000		$1,764,706	
Liabilities	$ 900,000	(540,000)	$ 900,000	(459,000)
Common shares	100,000		364,706	
Retained earnings	500,000		500,000	
Total liabilities and share equity	$1,500,000		$1,764,706	
Parent's equity in NBV of Sub		$360,000		$441,000
Parent's share of FVI:				
$180,000 x 9/10		162,000		
$180,000 x 9/10 x 85%				137,700
Goodwill:				
$90,000 x 14/15		84,000		
$90,000 x 14/15 x 85%				71,400
Parent's equity in FV of Sub's net assets		**$606,000**		**$650,100**

The net change in Parent's equity in Sub amounts to $44,100. This amount is exactly the same as the profit that was recognized in the previous section when Parent sold part of its holdings. Thus the general impact of a reduction in the parent's proportionate interest in the subsidiary is the same regardless of whether the reduction is the result of a sale by the parent or a new issue by the subsidiary.

The $44,100 gain can be viewed in one of two ways: (1) as a gain, to be reflected in consolidated income, or (2) as a capital transaction, to be credited directly to contributed capital.

Under the parent-company approach to consolidations, the consolidated financial statements are prepared from the viewpoint of the shareholders of the parent corporation. A reduction in ownership interest in a subsidiary is deemed to be a voluntary disposal of part of an investment. When a subsidiary issues new shares, the parent's decision not to purchase all or part of the new issue is voluntary, and thus the reduction in interest is voluntary. Also, since the parent controls the subsidiary, the parent must have agreed to the new issue in the first place. Gains on the voluntary disposal of investments are normally treated as income.

Furthermore, it would be inconsistent to treat gains on sales of the parent's shareholdings as income while treating gains from new issues as a capital transaction. Thus the recommended Canadian practice is to treat the credit as a gain to be reported in consolidated net income [CICA 1600.45].

Nevertheless, there is some unease in the professional accounting community about taking the gain into the income statement. It can be argued that capital for a parent and its subsidiary can be raised by issuing shares in either corporation, and that the accounting results for the consolidated entity should be the same regardless of whether the parent or the subsidiary issued the shares. When the parent issues shares, there is no gain or loss recognized on the capital transaction. But when the subsidiary issues shares, a gain may be recognized. Therefore, a parent corporation may raise capital for a consolidated group *and* recognize a gain in the process by having a subsidiary issue new shares instead of the parent.[1]

In the example used above, the new share issue resulted in a gain to Parent and an equivalent increase in Parent's equity in Sub. However, it also is possible for a loss to occur. The break-even point between a gain and a loss will be the price that is equal to the average consolidation carrying value of Sub's net assets per share.

Before the change in ownership interest, the consolidation carrying value of Parent's ownership interest was $606,000 (see Exhibit 7-7). Dividing this amount by the number of shares held by Parent yields $606,000 ÷ 30,000 = $20.20 per share. Any sale of shares by Parent *or* an issuance of new shares by Sub at a price higher than $20.20 will result in Parent's reporting a gain. Any price lower than $20.20 will result in a loss.

Summary of Key Points

1. Corporations often have more than one class of shares outstanding. Control is defined by the ability of the investor to elect a majority of the directors of an investee company. Therefore, the crucial issue for determining *control* is not the number of shares of different classes that are held, but the number of votes controlled, directly or indirectly.

   The level (or percentage) of ownership for consolidation calculations, however, depends on the investor's interest in the investee's residual earnings. Preferred shares normally are entitled only to a stated dividend, and therefore do not enter into the percentage of ownership calculation. Restricted (or non-voting) common shares, on the other hand, do usually participate in earnings pro rata with fully voting common shares. The ownership percentage for consolidation is based on the investor's proportionate share in residual earnings (that is, after preferred share dividend entitlements), which will often be different from the percentage of voting power held by the investor.

2. If a parent owns preferred shares in a subsidiary, the parent's investment and the subsidiary's preferred shares are offset and eliminated upon consolidation. Any difference between the purchase price to the parent and the carrying value on the subsidiary's books must be offset against consolidated share equity, either to a contributed surplus account or to retained earnings.

3. Strategic investments often are made not all at once, but through a series of transactions that accumulates to a significant influence level or that achieves control. This is known as a *step acquisition.* In step acquisitions, each step is treated as a separate purchase transaction, with fair value increments and goodwill calculated at that point in time.

   An exception to this general principle is made when the initial purchases are reported on the cost basis, and significant influence or control is obtained later. It is not feasible to retroactively calculate fair value increments and goodwill for the earlier purchases. Therefore a single cumulative purchase transaction analysis is made when significant influence is first obtained.

4. An investor that controls or has significant influence in an investee corporation may decrease its ownership percentage. The decrease can be either direct, by selling part of its share holdings, or indirect, when the investee issues addi-

1. See Lynne Clark, "Demystifying Dilution," *CA Magazine,* (May 1993), pp. 62–64, for a discussion of this and related issues.

tional shares to the public or to other shareholders. In either case, a gain or loss must be determined and reported as part of the investor's net income. Calculation of the gain or loss is based on the change in the investor's consolidation carrying value (or equity-basis carrying value), even though the investor is likely to be carrying the investment on its books at cost.

The break-even point between a gain and a loss on any such decrease is the amount of the investor's pre-reduction consolidation interest in the investee's net assets, divided by the number of shares held by the investor.

Weblinks

Strategic
Investments:
Additional
Aspects of
Share Capital

333

Bombardier Inc.
www.bombardier.com

Beginning in 1942 as a snowmobile manufacturing company, Bombardier Inc. is now a multinational company that assembles transit vehicles, aircraft, and many recreational vehicles. Read more about Bombardier's products, financial information, and history at their Web site.

Canadian Tire Corporation
www.canadiantire.ca

Canadian Tire Retail and its Associate Dealers offer consumers approximately 85,000 stock-keeping units of Automotive parts and accessories, Sports and Leisure, and Home products. Visit this site to shop online at Canada's popular hardware store, or use the store locator to find the Canadian Tire store location nearest you.

Toronto Stock Exchange
www.tse.com

The main page shows the TSE index and links to news items, investor centre, listed companies, TSE regulation services, participating organizations, conference centre, market data services, career centre, investor information, corporate news, and SEDAR filings (public company filings).

Self-Study Problem 7-1

The capital structure of 212°F Corporation contains the following amounts of share capital:

Preferred shares—1,000,000 issued and outstanding,	
$8 dividend per year, cumulative, non-participating, non-voting	$ 10,000,000
Class A common shares—600,000 issued and outstanding	30,000,000
Class B common shares—50,000 issued and outstanding	50,000
Retained earnings	84,950,000
Total shareholders' equity	$125,000,000

The preferred shares do not participate in dividends beyond their designated $8 per share. The call price for the preferred is $12 per share. The Class A common shares have one vote per share. The Class B common shares carry 15 votes per share. The two classes of common shares participate equally in dividends on a share-per-share basis.

Numbers Incorporated holds the following quantities of 212°F shares:

- 40,000 Class A common shares, purchased at $75 per share, and

- 44,000 Class B common shares, purchased at $85 per share.

Required:

  a. What proportion of votes is held by Numbers? Does Numbers control 212°F?

  b. When Numbers reports its investment in 212°F by consolidation or on the equity basis, as appropriate, what is 212°F's total ownership share?

  c. What is the amount of the non-controlling interest in 212°F?

Self-Study Problem 7-2

The balance sheet for Subco Ltd. at July 1, 2003 is shown in Exhibit 7-8. On that date, Parco Ltd. purchased 6,000 common shares of Subco for $312,500 and thereby attained significant influence over the affairs of Subco.

EXHIBIT 7–8 SUBCO LTD.

Balance Sheet
July 1, 2003

	Book value	Fair value
Cash	$ 75,000	$ 75,000
Inventory	200,000	250,000
Tangible capital assets, net	800,000	750,000
	$1,075,000	
Current liabilities	$ 50,000	50,000
Long-term liabilities	150,000	150,000
Common shares, 20,000 issued and outstanding	200,000	
Retained earnings at January 1, 2003	575,000	
Net income, 2003 to date	100,000	
	$1,075,000	

    Subco amortizes its tangible capital assets over 10 years straight-line and its intangible capital assets over 20 years. The inventory is expected to turn over six times per year and is on a FIFO cost allocation system.

    Consolidation goodwill is to be amortized over a period of 20 years. On September 1, 2004, Parco purchased 3,000 more shares of Subco for $183,500. The balance sheet of Subco and the related fair values are shown in Exhibit 7-9.

    Between September 1 and December 31, 2004, Subco had net income of $30,000 and paid no dividends.

    On January 1, 2005, Parco sold 4,000 of its shares in Subco for $300,000.

Required:

Calculate Parco's gain or loss on disposal of the Subco shares on January 1, 2005.

[CGA–Canada, adapted]

Strategic
Investments:
Additional
Aspects of
Share Capital

335

EXHIBIT 7–9 SUBCO LTD.

Balance Sheet
September 1, 2004

	Book value	Fair value
Cash	$ 80,000	$ 80,000
Inventory	190,000	200,000
Tangible capital assets, net	1,020,000	1,200,000
	$1,290,000	
Current liabilities	$ 40,000	40,000
Long-term liabilities	150,000	150,000
Common shares, 20,000 issued and outstanding	200,000	
Retained earnings at January 1, 2004	775,000	
Net income, 2004 to date	125,000	
	$1,290,000	

Review Questions

7-1 Corporation S has 100,000 shares of common stock and 100,000 shares of non-voting preferred stock outstanding. Corporation P owns 60,000 of S's common shares and 45,000 of S's preferred shares. When P prepares its financial statements, what proportion of S's earnings will be reflected in P's net income?

7-2 S Corporation has 10,000 shares of common stock and 10,000 shares of non-voting preferred stock outstanding. The preferred stock carries a cumulative dividend of $10 per share per year. S reported net income of $600,000 for the year just ended. If P Corporation owns 7,000 of S's common shares and 2,000 of S's preferred shares, how much of S's net income will be included in P's net income for the year just ended?

7-3 When a subsidiary has both common and preferred shares outstanding, how is the parent's proportionate ownership interest determined?

7-4 If a parent company has purchased some of its subsidiary's preferred shares at a price higher than the carrying value of the shares on the subsidiary's books, how is the difference treated when the parent prepares consolidated financial statements?

7-5 What is a *restricted share*?

7-6 Irene Ltd. has 500,000 common shares outstanding, consisting of 100,000 regular shares with ten votes each and 400,000 restricted shares with one vote each. The shares participate equally in dividends on a share-for-share basis. Gordon Inc. owns 165,000 of the 500,000 shares, 65,000 regular plus 100,000 restricted.

a. Does Gordon control Irene?

b. What proportion of Irene's earnings would be included in Gordon's equity-basis earnings?

7-7 What is a *coattail provision*?

7-8 What is meant by a *step purchase*?

7-9 P Ltd. acquired 51% of S Inc. by means of a tender offer on April 1, 2000. On February 14, 2002, P increased its ownership of S by an additional 19% through additional purchases. How would P determine the total goodwill pertaining to its 70% interest in S?

7-10 When a step acquisition has occurred, why are the fair value increments of the subsidiary's net assets not measured entirely at the date of the last purchase?

7-11 P Corp. owned 40% of the voting shares of S Ltd. and exercised significant influence over the affairs of S. Subsequently, P acquired an additional 20% of S's shares. How would the additional acquisition affect the nature of P's reporting of its investment in S?

7-12 P Inc. owned 22% of S Corp. and reported the investment on the cost basis. Subsequently, P acquired an additional 20% interest; the additional shares gave P the ability to significantly influence the affairs of S. How would the fair value increments and goodwill be determined for the 42% total interest?

7-13 When an investor corporation holds a cost-basis investment in an investee corporation, and then acquires sufficient shares to have significant influence, why is the equity method *not* applied retroactively to the date of the first purchase?

7-14 What are two basic ways in which a parent company can decrease its ownership interest in a subsidiary?

7-15 Why would a parent company want to decrease its share of a subsidiary?

7-16 When a parent company sells part of its investment in a subsidiary, how is the gain or loss on the sale determined?

7-17 When a parent sells part of its investment in a subsidiary, how is the consolidated balance sheet affected?

7-18 When a parent's ownership interest in a subsidiary declines, why would consolidated assets change even though the parent still has control over the same assets?

7-19 Why does the issuance by the subsidiary of new shares to outsiders affect the parent's consolidated assets?

7-20 Why does the parent corporation recognize a gain or loss when the subsidiary issues new shares to third parties?

7-21 How can one determine whether the issuance by a subsidiary of new shares to outsiders will result in a gain or a loss to the parent company?

Cases

Case 7-1

Major Developments Corporation

John "Calc" Gossling is one of Canada's foremost real estate investment analysts. He works for the firm of Bouchard Wiener Securities Inc. (BWS). His job is to do research and make recommendations on the stock of publicly traded companies, independent of any interest his employer may have in the companies. The research gets published and is used by investors in making their investment decisions. He is noted for his superb number-crunching ability, scathing comments, and accurate analysis. In late 1989, he correctly predicted the end of the real estate bubble, which occurred about two years later. His writing style is in marked contrast to the traditional dry prose of most investment analysts.

Major Developments Corporation (Major) is a publicly traded company operating primarily in the real estate sector. Major has a March 31 year-end and in 2000 reported revenues of $704 million and after-tax income of $118 million. The company buys and sells commercial real estate properties and manufactures commercial elevator components (its original business before it got into real estate). Major survived the recession of the 1990s, and during that time purchased a number of commercial "jewels" at bargain prices. In 1999, Major ventured overseas, acquiring properties in three Asian countries.

Major's share price climbed steadily from 1995 until July 11, 2000. On that date BWS released a stunning research report by Gossling on Major (see extracts in Exhibit 1). The report caused an uproar, as it claimed that many of Major's accounting policies in 2000 were misleading and therefore not in accordance with Canadian generally accepted accounting principles. It further claimed that the company was overvalued and had poor prospects because of its real estate portfolio mix.

The stock had been trading in the $15–16 range but immediately dropped to around $9. BWS profited from the decline in the stock price because it held a significant short position in Major's stock. Within four days, lawyers working for Major launched a legal suit against BWS, claiming damages plus a full retraction of all statements made and published in a national newspaper.

BWS's legal counsel is now examining various courses of action. To help prepare for the case, counsel has hired Brick & Mortar, Chartered Accountants, to provide a report on the validity of the positions of each of the parties on the disagreements over accounting policies as well as any other relevant advice. You, CA, work for Brick & Mortar. You have obtained a copy of Major's 2000 annual report (see extracts in Exhibit 2). Major's lawyers have provided the information in Exhibit 3.

Required:

Prepare a draft report to legal counsel for the partner to review.

EXHIBIT 1

EXTRACTS FROM JOHN GOSSLING'S RESEARCH REPORT

—I have done a detailed review of Major's 2000 annual report. I approached management of the company with a detailed list of further questions, but management did not respond in the four days that I gave them.

—It is my contention that in 2000, Major clearly violated Canadian generally accepted accounting principles (GAAP), as set out in the *Handbook of the Canadian Institute of Chartered Accountants*, on a number of issues. I am saying that the accounting is wrong, not just aggressive.

—Major's accounting for its real estate loans really takes the cake for non-compliance. The company consolidates the assets and results of two corporations to whom it has granted loans when it does not own any shares in either of the two companies.

—I don't like the accounting in Major's non-real estate business. There is no question it is misleading. Starting in 2000, the company specifically states in the financial statement notes that revenue (and profit I might add) is recognized on product that is still sitting in the company's warehouse.

—How can Rely Holdings, a company that lost $750,000, in which Major had acquired an additional 25% interest for $5 million, be valued at over $29 million? The valuation of Rely Holdings makes no sense.

—How can a company capitalize costs incurred for properties that were never acquired? Clearly these costs cannot be considered assets, and it is misleading to do so.

—It is absurd that Major continues to recognize the revenue from properties in certain economically unstable Asian countries. It is unlikely that the money will be collected. Major should write off these buildings immediately instead of recognizing revenue from them.

—Major has not followed GAAP in its accounting for the dividend in kind declared during the year. Thirteen days after the dividend was declared, the only tenant in the only property owned by NC Tower Inc. went bankrupt (reference: *The Financial Journal*, dated February 26, 2000, p. 13) so the value attributed cannot be accepted. Furthermore, the dividend has still not been paid, as the regulators are still looking into it.

Recommendation on Major Developments Corp.

Price earnings multiplier based last fiscal year	12.7
Overall rating on their stock	underperform
Recommendation	sell

EXHIBIT 2

EXTRACTS FROM MAJOR DEVELOPMENTS CORPORATION'S 2000 ANNUAL REPORT

Note 1: Accounting Policies

The company incurs significant costs in investigating new properties for purchase. Costs incurred in investigating any and all properties, whether or not these properties are ultimately purchased by the company, are capitalized as part of the cost of properties actually acquired. These costs are amortized over the useful lives of the properties acquired.

Economic problems in certain Asian countries where the company owns properties have made collection of rental revenues from these properties difficult at this time. The company expects that, once the difficulties in these countries have been resolved, amounts owed will be collected in full. It is the company's policy to accrue the revenue from these properties.

Revenue on product sales is recognized when the goods are shipped to the customer. In the case of "bill and hold" sales, revenue is recognized when the goods are placed in the company's designated storage area.

The consolidated financial statements include the accounts of Major and its majority-owned subsidiaries and, commencing prospectively in fiscal 2000, the accounts of companies in which Major has no common share ownership but to which it has advanced loans that are currently in default. The equity method is used for investments in which there is significant influence, considered to be voting ownership of 20% to 50%.

Note 14: Investments

	2000	1999
Rely Holdings	$29,640,000	$25,000,000

In 2000, Major purchased an additional 25% interest in Rely Holdings Inc. for $5 million. Major now owns 48% of Rely Holdings Inc. Major accounts for its investment on an equity basis. In 2000, Major recorded a loss of $750,000 from Rely Holdings Inc.

Note 24: Dividend in Kind

On February 10, 2000, the Board of Directors of Major declared a $0.20 dividend in kind on each common share, consisting of five common shares of NC Tower Inc. The NC Tower Inc. shares had an appraised value of $0.04 each and a carrying value of $0.018 per share. The stock exchange on which Major is listed has raised certain objections to the transaction, and the matter is currently being investigated. Management expects approval for the transaction to be granted in the near future. During the year, Major reported a gain on disposal of $11 million and a charge to retained earnings of $20 million to account for the declaration of the dividend.

Strategic
Investments:
Additional
Aspects of
Share Capital

339

EXHIBIT 3

EXTRACTS FROM INFORMATION PROVIDED BY MAJOR'S LAWYERS

1. Major's auditor has always provided an unqualified report on the audited financial statements of Major, including the 2000 financial statements.

2. Major has a legal opinion that the two loans are in default (Item A), and a third party opinion (Item B) that the default permits consolidation of these companies.

   Item A

   "…In my opinion, loan 323 to Skyscraper Inc. and loan 324 to Wenon Corporation are in default as of February 1, 1999, under the aforesaid terms of default of the respective loan agreements, dated the 12th day of August, 1997. The lender has the right under law and contract to repossess said aforementioned properties, for the purposes of realization on the loans, subject to restrictions of right under clause 43.(b)…"

   [Matthew Krebs, Q.C.]

   Item B

   "Based on facts set out in the attached document, we concur that it is acceptable, under Canadian generally accepted accounting principles, for Major to consolidate Skyscraper Inc. and Wenon Corporation."

   [Jesse & Mitchell, Chartered Accountants]

3. "Bill and hold" refers to a practice whereby a customer purchases goods but the seller retains physical possession until the customer requests shipment. Delivery is delayed at the purchaser's request, but the purchaser accepts both the title to the goods and the related billing.

[CICA]

Case 7-2

Brand Drug Limited

In the course of the audit of Brand Drug Limited (BDL), CA, while reviewing the draft financial statements for the year ended August 31, 2001, noticed that BDL's investment in National Pharmaceuticals Limited (NPL) was valued on the cost basis. In 2000, it had been valued on the equity basis. Representing a 22% interest in NPL, this investment had been made 10 years ago to infuse fresh equity, with a view to protecting BDL's source of supply for drugs.

BDL's controller informed CA that NPL had suffered a large loss in 2001, as shown by the May interim financial statements. BDL's representative on NPL's board of directors had resigned because BDL's purchases from NPL now constituted less than 5% of its total purchases. In addition, NPL had been uncooperative in providing profit data in time to make the year-end equity adjustment. Consequently, BDL's controller had revised the method of accounting for the investment in NPL.

CA then found out that BDL's managers are planning a share issue in 2002 and do not want their earnings impaired by NPL's poor performance. However, they are reluctant to divest themselves of NPL in case the rumoured development by NPL of a new drug to reduce the impact of colitis materializes.

When CA approached NPL's managers, they refused to disclose any information on NPL's operations. CA then learned from a stockbroker friend that NPL's poor results were due to its market being undercut by generic drug manufacturers. The loss had been increased when NPL's management wrote off most of NPL's intangible assets. CA summarized the relevant information on the treatment of the investment for his audit file (Exhibit 1).

Required:

Discuss the matters raised above.

[CICA, adapted]

EXHIBIT 1

CA'S NOTES ON INVESTMENT IN NPL'S SHARES

Extracts from BDL's draft financial statements for the year ended August 31, 2001, in thousands of dollars:

	2001 (Draft)		2000 (Actual)	
Investment in NPL (Note 3)	$25,000	(1)	$27,400	(2)
Retained earnings:				
Opening balance	$ 6,500		$ 2,350	
plus: net earnings	4,500		7,300	
	11,000		9,650	
less: prior period				
adjustment (Note 1)	(2,400)		—	
dividends	(2,250)		(3,150)	
Closing balance	$ 6,350		$ 6,500	

Note 1: Represents original cost. The 2000 balance has been reduced by the amount of previously recorded equity interest of $2.4 million. In the nine months ended May 31, 2001, NPL reported a net loss of $140 million after writing off development and patent costs as extraordinary items.

Note 2: Valued on equity basis. Equity adjustment for 2000 involved the elimination of $5.5 million unrealized profit included in ending inventory, on sales from NPL to BDL. The unrealized profit in BDL's ending inventory for 2001 amounts to $1.5 million.

Note 3: Stock market trading in NPL's common shares has been heavy in 2001. Prices for the year are as follows:

August 31, 2000:	$22.00
February 28, 2001:	$ 4.00
August 31, 2001:	$12.00

BDL owns 2,000,000 common shares of NPL; in neither 2000 nor 2001 did NPL declare or pay any dividends.

Strategic

Investments:

Additional

Aspects of

Share Capital

341

Case 7-3

Grand Investments Limited

Grand Investments Limited is a large Canadian public company that holds investments in four subsidiaries. The company and its subsidiaries all pay combined federal and provincial income taxes at the rate of 50%.

Three subsidiaries, A Sub Limited, B Sub Limited, and C Sub Limited, are all 100% owned; D Sub Limited is 60% owned.

A Sub Limited is in the publishing business. It publishes several trade magazines, a monthly family magazine, and some books, usually of a technical nature.

B Sub Limited prints and sells greeting cards. It also prints calendars, business cards, etc., on a contract basis. In addition, it prints the books published by A Sub Limited.

C Sub Limited has large forestry holdings in Canada. Most of the forests are used for pulp and paper production. The company manufactures many grades of paper and virtually all of the production is sold to A Sub Limited and B Sub Limited. C Sub Limited also produces lumber, much of which is sold to builders near its manufacturing plants, but about 20% of which is sold to D Sub Limited.

D Sub Limited is a real estate development company. It operates around two large cities and owns substantial tracts of land near those cities. Zoning by-laws require that the land be fully serviced before buildings are put up. Several years ago, the company started building houses, but because the zoning restrictions had led to a shortage of serviced land, it expanded its operations into the servicing of land. It then began servicing industrial lots and building industrial plants and buildings.

For the year ended June 30, 2002, consolidated financial statements had been presented to the shareholders accompanied by an audit report, which was unqualified. Reported consolidated net income was $800,000. Shortly after that year-end, CA was appointed auditor of Grand Investments Limited.

During the course of the audit of D Sub Limited for the year ended June 30, 2003, CA found that one of the company's major building contracts was construction of an office building for A Sub Limited. By June 30, 2003, $10,000,000 had been incurred by D Sub Limited in construction of the building, estimated to cost $12,000,000 on completion.

CA had known that A Sub Limited was planning a major expansion. Largely, the expansion consisted of converting A Sub Limited's monthly family magazine into a weekly news magazine, to make A Sub Limited more able to compete with certain large periodicals. It meant, however, that the company had to expand its facilities considerably. CA had been under the impression that no progress billings had yet been received with respect to the new building.

On checking into the matter further, CA found that part of the reason for this was that the building qualified for a government grant and that grants of the type involved are paid by the government on behalf of the owner of the building to the builder. On the strength of certain commitments made by A Sub Limited as to the ultimate cost of the building and the number of jobs that would be created, D Sub Limited had, in May, 2002, received $4,000,000 towards the grant, which was equal to 50% of the $8,000,000 cost incurred on the building to that date and 25% of the total contract price of $16,000,000. The building was 60% complete at that date.

Also, prior to June 2002, D Sub Limited required more money to finance the construction. Instead of sending a progress billing to A Sub Limited, however, it was decided to obtain lumber from C Sub Limited for the houses under construction, but not to pay for it. The price charged to D Sub Limited was $5,500,000. The cost of the lumber to C Sub Limited was $5,000,000. The lumber shipments were received in the accounts of D Sub Limited by a charge to inventory and the credit was treated as a revenue item.

C Sub Limited then obtained an advance payment of $5,500,000 from A Sub Limited for the large quantities of paper that would be required when the news magazine went into production. This payment was recorded by A Sub Limited as prepaid expense.

D Sub Limited's accounting practice, unlike many development companies, was to present a balance sheet that segregated working capital items from non-working capital items. D Sub Limited used the percentage-of-completion basis of accounting.

No consolidation adjustments had been made in respect to the building for the year ended June 30, 2002, or the $5,500,000 shipment of lumber.

Required:

Outline the financial accounting and reporting issues that must be resolved in presenting consolidated financial statements for the year ended June 30, 2003, with comparative figures. State how these issues should be resolved and give the additional consolidating journal entries that should have been made at June 30, 2002. Ignore the impact of income taxes in your calculations.

[CICA, adapted]

Problems

P7-1

On July 1, 2001, Super Corp. purchased 80% of the common shares and 40% of the preferred shares of Paltry Corp. by issuing Super Corp. shares that had a total market value of $4,900,000. On that date, Paltry's shareholders' equity accounts appear as follows:

Common shares, no par (300,000 shares)	$3,000,000
Preferred shares, no par (10,000 shares)	1,100,000
Other contributed capital	400,000
Retained earnings	1,500,000
	$6,000,000

Paltry's preferred shares are cumulative and nonparticipating and carry a dividend rate of $15 per year per share. The dividends are paid at the end of each calendar quarter. The redemption price of the preferred shares is $100 per share. At the time of Super's purchase, the Paltry preferred shares were selling on the market at $95.

The fair values of Paltry's net assets were identical to their book values on July 1, 2001. Super Corp.'s policy is to amortize goodwill (if any) over 20 years.

During 2001 and 2002, Paltry's net income and dividends declared (common and preferred) were as follows:

Strategic

Investments:

Additional

Aspects of

Share Capital

343

Years Ended December 31

	Net income	Dividends
2001	$600,000	$400,000
2002	$800,000	$450,000

All preferred dividends were declared and paid quarterly, as due. Paltry earns its income evenly throughout the year.

Required:

a. Determine the amounts at which each of Super's investments in the common and preferred shares of Paltry should appear in Super's balance sheet on December 31, 2001, and on December 31, 2002, assuming that Super does not consolidate Paltry. Show all calculations clearly.

b. Assume that on January 2, 2003, Super Corp sells 1,000 of its Paltry preferred shares. Determine the balance remaining in the investment account for the preferred shares after the sale.

P7-2

Consult **P7-1**. Assume that on January 2, 2003, Super sells 1,000 of its preferred shares and 50,000 of its common shares in Paltry. The sale nets $106 per preferred share and $20 per common share.

During 2003, Paltry earns net income of $200,000, pays the preferred dividends for only the first three quarters, and pays no common dividends.

Required:

a. Determine the gain or loss to be reported by Super that arose from the sale of the preferred and common shares of Paltry.

b. Determine the balances of the investment accounts to be reported by Super on December 31, 2003, assuming that Super does not consolidate Paltry.

P7-3

On January 2, 2002, Playful Inc. purchased 60% of the outstanding common shares of Serious Ltd. for $7,000,000.

Serious's condensed balance sheet at that time was as follows:

Current assets	$ 8,000,000
Capital assets	19,000,000
	$27,000,000
Current liabilities	$ 5,000,000
Long-term liabilities	10,000,000
Shareholders' equity:	

Common shares (100,000, no par)	$2,500,000	
Preferred shares (100,000, no par, $4 dividend, callable at $45; cumulative and non-voting)	4,200,000	
Retained earnings	5,300,000	
		12,000,000
		$27,000,000

The fair value of Serious's assets was the same as their book value except for capital assets, which had a fair value of $22,000,000. The capital assets have a remaining useful life of 15 years. Goodwill on the purchase, if any, will be amortized over 20 years.

On October 1, 2002, Playful purchased 20,000 of Serious's preferred shares at $35 per share. There were no dividend arrearages. Serious declared the fourth-quarter preferred dividend on December 15, 2002, payable on January 15, 2003, to holders of record on December 30, 2002.

The condensed balance sheets for both Playful and Serious were as follows on December 31, 2002:

	Playful Inc.	Serious Ltd.
Current assets	$12,000,000	$ 7,000,000
Capital assets	20,000,000	22,000,000
Investments (at cost)	7,700,000	—
	$39,700,000	$29,000,000
Current liabilities	$10,000,000	$ 6,000,000
Long-term liabilities	5,000,000	10,000,000
Shareholders' equity:		
Common shares	8,000,000	2,500,000
Preferred shares	—	4,200,000
Retained earnings	16,700,000	6,300,000
	$39,700,000	$29,000,000

Required:

Prepare a consolidated balance sheet for Playful Inc. at December 31, 2002.

P7-4

Pike Ltd. is a producer of plastics that uses oil in the manufacturing process. To ensure a reliable supply of oil at current prices, on January 1, 1998, the company purchased 80% of the common shares and 25% of the preferred shares of Spike Ltd. for $205,000. The preferred shares were purchased at their stated value of $5 each. On the date of acquisition, Spike Ltd.'s shareholders' equity was as follows:

Preferred 6% cumulative, 20,000 shares outstanding	$100,000
Common, no par value, 200,000 shares outstanding	200,000
Retained earnings	100,000
	$400,000

On January 1, 1998, the fair values of net identifiable assets of Spike Ltd. were equal to their book values except for oil-related capital assets, which were worth $200,000 less than their recorded values. All allocations of the excess of purchase price over book value are to be amortized over 10 years.

Additional Information:

1. Spike Ltd. had incurred minor losses in the two years prior to acquisition, and was expected to operate at a break-even level after acquisition. On January 1, 1998, $5,000 of accumulated potential tax benefits in respect to noncapital losses were unrecorded by Spike Ltd.

2. During 2002, Spike sold oil to Pike at a price of $500,000, which included a markup of 5% on cost. The price at which Spike was selling to Pike was well below fair market value for oil, and the policy of 5% markup on cost had been followed since acquisition. On December 31, 2002, Pike's ending inventories included $42,000 in oil (some of which was in manufactured products and work-in-progress) purchased from Spike. This closing inventory represented a 20% reduction of 2001's closing inventory of oil purchased from Spike. Pike's oil inventory turns over twice per year.

3. On January 1, 2002, Spike sold capital assets to Pike for proceeds of $20,000. These assets had a net book value of $40,000 and a remaining useful life of four years.

4. During 2002, as a result of a "Save the Environment" movement, Pike's uninsured warehouse, which had a net book value of $100,000, was blown up and destroyed. The land on which the warehouse was situated was then sold to Spike at a gain of $2,000.

5. On January 1, 2002, Spike's preferred dividends were one year in arrears. During 2002, Spike paid $20,000 in dividends to common shareholders.

6. During 2002, Pike's share capital consisted of 100,000 common shares. Pike's long-term debt consisted of 10% debentures that are convertible into 100,000 common shares.

7. Summarized adjusted trial balances as at December 31, 2002, are as follows:

Strategic

Investments:

Additional

Aspects of

Share Capital

345

	Pike	Spike
Cash	$ 35,000	$ 34,000
Accounts receivable	112,000	53,000
Inventories	210,000	40,000
Land	27,000	35,000
Capital assets (net)	905,000	429,000
Investment in Spike	205,000	—
Accounts payable	(281,000)	(74,000)
Long-term debt	(500,000)	(190,000)
Preferred shares	—	(100,000)
Common shares	(250,000)	(200,000)
Retained earnings	(388,000)	(62,000)
Dividends paid	—	32,000
Revenues	(1,794,000)	(1,190,000)
Dividend income	(19,000)	—
Cost of sales	1,148,000	840,000
Other expenses	492,000	333,000
Loss on disposal of capital assets	98,000	20,000
	$ 0	$ 0

Required:

In accordance with generally accepted accounting principles, calculate the following. (Show all calculations and supporting analysis. Ignore the impact of income taxes.)

a. Consolidated earnings per share, basic and fully diluted, for 2002.

b. The following consolidated balance sheet accounts at December 31, 2002:
  (1) Inventory
  (2) Land
  (3) Capital assets
  (4) Goodwill
  (5) Minority interest
  (6) Retained earnings

[SMA]

P7-5

On January 1, 2001, McCleod, Inc. paid $700,000 for 10,000 shares of Daga Company's voting common shares, which was a 10% interest in Daga. At that date, the net assets of Daga totalled $6,000,000. The fair values of all of Daga's identifiable assets and liabilities were equal to their book values. McCleod does not have the ability to exercise significant influence over the operating and financial policies of Daga. McCleod received dividends of $0.80 per share from Daga on October 1, 2001. Daga reported net income of $500,000 for the year ended December 31, 2001.

On July 1, 2002, McCleod paid $2,300,000 for 30,000 additional shares of Daga Company's voting common shares, which represents a 30% investment in Daga. The fair values of all of Daga's identifiable assets net of liabilities are equal to their book values of $6,500,000. As a result of this transaction, McCleod has the ability to exercise significant influence over the operating and financial policies of Daga. McCleod received dividends of $1.05 per share from Daga on April 1, 2002, and $1.40 per share on October 1, 2002. Daga reported net income before taxes of $600,000 for the year ended December 31, 2002, and $300,000 for the six months ended December 31, 2002. McCleod amortizes goodwill over a 20-year period.

Required:

a. Prepare a schedule showing the income or loss before income taxes for the year ended December 31, 2001, which McCleod should report from its investment in Daga in its income statement issued in March 2002.

b. During March 2003, McCleod issues comparative financial statements for 2001 and 2002. Prepare schedules showing the income or loss before income taxes for the years ended December 31, 2001 and 2002 that McCleod should report from its investment in Daga. Show supporting computations in proper format.

[AICPA, adapted]

Strategic
Investments:
Additional
Aspects of
Share Capital

347

P7-6

The December 31, 2001, balance sheets of Enrico Corporation and its subsidiary, North Corporation, are presented below:

	Enrico Corporation	North Corporation
Assets		
Cash	$ 167,250	$101,000
Accounts receivable	178,450	72,000
Notes receivable	87,500	28,000
Dividends receivable	36,000	
Inventories	122,000	68,000
Capital assets	487,000	252,000
Accumulated depreciation	(117,000)	(64,000)
Investment in North Corporation	240,800	
	$1,202,000	$457,000
Liabilities and shareholders' equity		
Accounts payable	$ 222,000	$ 76,000
Notes payable	79,000	89,000
Dividend payable		40,000
Common shares	400,000	100,000
Retained earnings	501,000	152,000
	$1,202,000	$457,000

Additional Information:

1. Enrico initially acquired 60% of the outstanding common shares of North in 1999. This purchase resulted in no difference between cost and net assets acquired. As of December 31, 2001, the percentage owned is 90%. An analysis of the investment in North account is as follows:

Date	Description	Amount
Dec. 31, 1999	Acquired 6,000 shares	$ 70,800
Dec. 31, 2000	60% of 2000 net income of $78,000	46,800
Sept. 1, 2001	Acquired 3,000 shares	92,000
Dec. 31, 2001	Subsidiary income for 2001	67,200*
Dec. 31, 2001	90% of dividends declared	(36,000)
		$240,800

*Subsidiary income for 2001:	
60% of $96,000	$57,600
30% of $96,000 × 33 1/3%	9,600
	$67,200

North's net income is earned evenly over the year. The excess of cost over the net assets acquired is to be amortized over 60 months.

2. On December 13, 2001, North declared a cash dividend of $5 per share of common stock, payable to shareholders on January 7, 2002.

3. During 2001, Enrico sold merchandise to North. Enrico's cost for this merchandise was $68,000, and the sale was made at 125% of cost. North's inventory at December 31, 2001 included merchandise purchased from Enrico at a cost to North of $35,000.

4. In December 2000, North sold merchandise to Enrico for $67,000, which was at a markup of 35% over North's cost. On January 1, 2001, $54,000 of this merchandise remained in Enrico's inventory. This merchandise was subsequently sold by Enrico at a profit of $11,000 during 2001.

5. On October 1, 2001, Enrico sold excess equipment to North for $55,000. Data related to this equipment is as follows:

Book value on Enrico's records	$45,000
Method of depreciation	Straight-line
Estimated remaining life on October 1, 2001	10 years

6. Near the end of 2001, North reduced the balance of its intercompany account payable to Enrico to zero by transferring $10,000 to Enrico. This payment was still in transit on December 31, 2001.

Required:

Prepare the consolidated balance sheet for Enrico Corporation as of December 31, 2001. Supporting computations should be in proper format.

[AICPA, adapted]

P7-7

On December 31, 2000, Black Company acquired 20% of the outstanding voting shares of Harvest Company for $2.5 million in cash. On that date, the shareholders' equity of Black Company was as follows:

Common shares	$6,000,000
Retained earnings	3,000,000
Total	$9,000,000

Also on this date, all of the identifiable assets and liabilities of Black Company had fair values equal to their carrying values except for capital assets, which had a fair value that was $200,000 greater than its carrying value. The capital assets had a remaining useful life of 10 years and were being depreciated by the straight-line method.

On December 31, 2002, Black Company acquired an additional 40% of Harvest Company's outstanding voting shares in return for cash in the amount of $6.5 million. At this date, the shareholders' equity of Black Company was as follows:

Common shares	$ 6,000,000
Retained earnings	9,000,000
Total	$15,000,000

Strategic
Investments:
Additional
Aspects of
Share Capital

349

At the time of this second purchase, all of the identifiable assets and liabilities of Black Company had fair values equal to their carrying values except for capital assets, which had a fair value that was $800,000 greater than its carrying value. The remaining useful life of the capital assets is 10 years and it is being depreciated by the straight-line method.

Any goodwill arising on either of the preceding purchases should be amortized over a period of 20 years from the date of the purchase.

There were no intercompany transactions in any of the years 2000 through 2004.

On December 31, 2004, the balance sheets of the two companies were as follows:

	Black	Harvest
Net monetary assets	$ 8,000,000	$ 4,000,000
Investment in Harvest (cost)	9,000,000	—
Capital assets (net)	14,000,000	12,000,000
Total	$31,000,000	$16,000,000
Common shares	$10,000,000	$ 6,000,000
Retained earnings	21,000,000	10,000,000
Total	$31,000,000	$16,000,000

Required:

Prepare for Black Company and its subsidiary, Harvest Company, a consolidated balance sheet at December 31, 2004. All calculations should be shown. Assume that the initial purchase had given Black Company significant influence in Harvest Company.

[SMA]

P7-8

Pine Ltd. had the following transactions in the shares of Sap Ltd.:

Year	Date	%*	Cost	Equity Jan. 1	Equity Dec. 31	Goodwill
2001	January 1	30%	$ 70,000	$150,000	$220,000	$25,000
2002	January 1	35%	110,000	220,000	300,000	33,000
2003	July 1	6.5%	—	300,000	410,000	—

*Of Sap Ltd.'s shares.

The income of Sap Ltd. is earned evenly over the year.

Any excess of purchase price over book value is attributable solely to goodwill, which will be amortized over 20 years.

Sap Ltd. has 100,000 shares outstanding.

The July 1 transaction is a sale of shares by Pine Ltd. The proceeds were $50,000. Pine uses the equity method of recording investments where appropriate.

Required:

Prepare the journal entries for Pine Ltd. for 2001, 2002, and 2003, up to July 2, 2003, assuming no dividends.

[CGA–Canada, adapted]

P7-9

On October 1, 2002, XYZ Ltd. sold its 80% interest in the subsidiary, Sub Ltd., for $2,430,000. Prior to the date of sale, XYZ Ltd. had recorded the investment in a subsidiary account on the *cost* basis, which showed $1,100,000. At the date of sale, the consolidated entity had a residual unamortized revaluation of the capital assets (from the original purchase price discrepancy) of $260,000 and unamortized goodwill arising from the acquisition of the subsidiary of $148,500. The goodwill was being amortized at the rate of $12,000 per year. There were no intercompany transactions between the parent and the subsidiary.

At the date of the sale, October 1, 2002, the balance sheet of Sub Ltd. was:

Sub Ltd.
October 1, 2002

	Net Book Value	Fair Market Value
Cash	$ 110,000	$ 110,000
Receivables	180,000	180,000
Inventory	510,000	570,000
Capital assets, net	950,000	880,000
	$1,750,000	
Current liabilities	$ 124,000	124,000
Common shares	300,000	
Retained earnings	1,006,000	
Income—Jan.1-Oct. 31, 2002	320,000	
	$1,750,000	

XYZ Ltd.'s 2001 and 2002 consolidated balance sheets were as follows:

XYZ Ltd.
Consolidated Balance Sheet
December 31

	2001	2002
Cash	$ 256,000	$1,420,000
Receivables	368,000	246,000
Inventory	742,000	538,000
Capital assets, net	1,720,000	845,000
Goodwill	160,000	—
	$3,246,000	$3,049,000
Current liabilities	$ 422,000	$ 115,000
Minority interest	261,200	—
Common shares	500,000	500,000
Retained earnings	2,062,800	2,434,000
	$3,246,000	$3,049,000

Strategic
Investments:
Additional
Aspects of
Share Capital

351

The net income for the year for the consolidated entity was $371,200, but this was after the extraordinary item for the gain on the sale of the subsidiary. No dividends were paid. The consolidated depreciation expense was $104,000, which included the depreciation of the capital asset revaluation. Ignore the impact of income taxes on the sale.

Required:
Calculate the gain on the sale of the subsidiary.
[CGA–Canada, adapted]

P7-10

Big Limited has three subsidiaries, all 80% owned, and, at December 31, 2002, they have the following balance sheets:

	Sub 1 Limited	Sub 2 Limited	Sub 3 Limited
Cash	$ 200,000	$ 120,000	$ 140,000
Receivables	400,000	230,000	250,000
Inventory	1,040,000	590,000	610,000
Capital assets, net	1,320,000	890,000	920,000
	$2,960,000	$1,830,000	$1,920,000
Current liabilities	$ 260,000	$ 140,000	$ 150,000
Common shares	600,000	400,000	500,000
Retained earnings	2,100,000	1,290,000	1,270,000
	$2,960,000	$1,830,000	$1,920,000

Selected balance sheet information of Big Limited as at December 31, 2002, with respect to each subsidiary is as follows:

	Sub 1 Limited	Sub 2 Limited	Sub 3 Limited
Investment in Sub	$2,470,000	$1,252,000	$1,536,000
Capital asset, unamortized revaluation	300,000	(200,000)	—
Goodwill	280,000	—	120,000
Number of shares outstanding	100,000	100,000	10,000

The "Investment in Sub" account for each subsidiary is kept on the equity basis and includes all entries for 2002, with the exception of the following:

On the last day of the year, after all the accounts had been brought up to date but before the closing entries had been made, the subsidiaries had the following transactions:

1. Sub 1 Limited issues a 100% stock dividend to all common shareholders.

2. Sub 2 Limited issues shares equal to 10%, or 10,000 shares of the present outstanding amount, to the minority interest shareholders for $38 per share.

3. Sub 3 Limited purchases and retires 10% or 1,000 shares of the outstanding shares from the minority interest for a price of $150 per share.

Big Limited will consolidate the subsidiaries but has kept the investment in subsidiary accounts on the equity basis.

Required:

Considering that the parent company is using the equity method for its investment in subsidiary accounts, prepare a separate journal entry(ies) to record the above events for each subsidiary on the parent company's books. If no journal entry on the parent's books is needed, then explain why. Indicate any gain or loss that would appear on the consolidated financial statements. If no gain or loss is present, explain why. Support your answer fully.

[CGA–Canada, adapted]

P7-11

Presented in Exhibit 1 are the trial balances (unconsolidated) for the year ended December 31, 2002, of Graham Company and its subsidiary, Kraker Company.

Additional Information:

1. On January 3, 2000, Graham acquired from Wendy Kraker, the sole shareholder of Kraker Company, for $440,000 cash, both a patent valued at $40,000 and 80% of the outstanding shares of Kraker. The net book value of Kraker's shares on the date of acquisition was $500,000, and the book values of the individual assets and liabilities were equal to their fair market values. Graham charged the entire $440,000 to the account designated "Investment in stock of Kraker Company." The patent, for which no amortization had been charged, had a remaining legal life of four years as of January 3, 2000.

2. On July 1, 2002, Graham reduced its investment in Kraker to 75% of Kraker's outstanding common shares, by selling shares for $70,000 to an unaffiliated company at a profit of $16,000. Graham recorded the proceeds as a credit to its investment account.

3. For the six months ended June 30, 2002, Kraker had net income of $140,000. Graham recorded 80% of this amount on its books of account prior to the time of sale.

4. During 2001, Kraker sold merchandise to Graham for $130,000, which was at a markup of 30% over Kraker's cost. On January 1, 2002, $52,000 of this merchandise remained in Graham's inventory. This merchandise was subsequently sold by Graham in February 2002, at a profit of $8,000.

5. In November 2002, Graham sold merchandise to Kraker for the first time. Graham's cost of this merchandise was $80,000, and the sale was made at 120% of cost. Kraker's inventory at December 31, 2002, contained merchandise that was purchased from Graham at a cost to Kraker of $24,000.

6. On December 31, 2002, there was a $45,000 payment-in-transit from Kraker Company to Graham Company. Accounts receivable and accounts payable include intercompany receivables and payables.

7. In December 2002, Kraker declared and paid cash dividends of $100,000 to its shareholders.

8. On December 31, 2002, Graham purchased 50% of the outstanding bonds issued by Kraker for $58,000. The bonds mature on December 31, 2006, and were originally issued at a discount. On December 31, 2002, the balance in Kraker's account for unamortized discount on bonds payable was $2,400. It is the intention of the management of Graham to hold these bonds until their maturity.

Strategic
Investments:
Additional
Aspects of
Share Capital

353

Required:

Prepare a consolidated balance sheet and statement of income and retained earnings for Graham Company as of December 31, 2002.

[AICPA, adapted]

EXHIBIT 1

Graham Company and Subsidiary Trial Balances
December 31, 2002

	Graham Company	Kraker Company
Assets		
Cash	$ 486,000	$ 249,600
Accounts receivable	235,000	185,000
Inventories	475,000	355,000
Capital assets	2,231,000	530,000
Investment in Kraker Co.	954,000	—
Investment in bonds of Kraker Co.	58,000	—
	$ 4,439,000	$ 1,319,600
Liabilities and owners' equity		
Accounts payable	$ (384,000)	$ (112,000)
Bonds payable	—	(120,000)
Unamortized discount on bonds payable	—	2,400
Common shares		
Graham Company	(1,200,000)	—
Kraker Company	—	(250,000)
Retained earnings Jan.1, 2002	(2,100,000)	(640,000)
Dividends paid	170,000	100,000
Sales	(4,000,000)	(1,700,000)
Cost of sales	2,982,000	1,015,000
Operating expenses	400,000	377,200
Dividend income	(75,000)	—
Subsidiary income	(232,000)	—
Interest expense	—	7,800
	$(4,439,000)	$(1,319,600)

P7-12

On January 1, 1998, Proctor Ltd. became the largest shareholder of Sandy Ltd. by acquiring 30% of the outstanding voting shares of Sandy Ltd. for $250,000. On January 1, 2000, Proctor Ltd. purchased an additional 50% of Sandy Ltd.'s shares for $570,000. Sandy Ltd.'s shareholders' equity section at each date of acquisition was as follows:

	January 1, 1998	January 1, 2001
Common shares	$700,000	$700,000
Retained earnings	30,000	116,000
	$730,000	$816,000

On January 1, 1998, the fair value of Sandy Ltd.'s inventory was $30,000 greater than its carrying value. On January 1, 2001, the fair value of Sandy Ltd.'s inventory was $20,000 greater than its carrying value. Also on January 1, 2001, Sandy Ltd. had a favourable operating lease contract on one of its buildings, with rental payments well below market rent. The fair value of the difference between the remaining contractual payments and market rent of an equivalent property was estimated to be $160,000. As of January 1, 2001, there were three years remaining in the lease contract. Proctor Ltd. amortizes any recorded amount of goodwill over 20 years.

The net incomes for the two companies for the year ended December 31, 2002, were determined as follows:

	Proctor Ltd.	Sandy Ltd.
Sales	$2,100,000	$735,000
Dividend revenue	50,400	—
	2,150,400	735,000
Cost of goods sold	1,058,050	469,000
Selling & administrative	910,350	175,000
	1,968,400	644,000
Net income	$ 182,000	$ 91,000

The amount of retained earnings for the two companies at December 31, 2002, was determined as follows:

	Proctor Ltd.	Sandy Ltd.
Retained earnings, Jan. 1	$787,500	$130,000
Add: Net income	182,000	91,000
	969,500	221,000
Less: Dividends	87,500	63,000
Retained earnings, Dec. 31	$882,000	$158,000

The condensed balance sheets for the two companies at December 31, 2002, were as follows:

	Proctor Ltd.	Sandy Ltd.
Assets		
Current assets	$ 510,000	$388,000
Investment in Sandy Ltd. (at cost)	820,000	
Other assets	1,570,000	536,000
Total assets	$2,900,000	$924,000
Liabilities and shareholders' equity		
Current liabilities	$ 200,000	$ 66,000
Bonds payable	300,000	—
Common shares	1,518,000	700,000
Retained earnings	882,000	158,000
Total liabilities and shareholders' equity	$2,900,000	$924,000

Strategic

Investments:

Additional

Aspects of

Share Capital

355

Additional Information:

1. On average, the inventory of Sandy Ltd. turns over four times a year.

2. During 2001, Sandy Ltd. sold inventory costing $140,000 to Proctor Ltd. for $175,000. One-quarter of these goods was in Proctor Ltd.'s inventory on December 31, 2001. During 2002, Sandy Ltd. sold inventory costing $168,000 to Proctor Ltd. for $210,000. One-third of these goods was in Proctor Ltd.'s inventory on December 31, 2002.

3. Equipment with a remaining useful life of three years was sold to Sandy Ltd. from Proctor Ltd. on January 2, 2001, for $270,000. The equipment, which originally cost $400,000 and had accumulated depreciation of $100,000 at the date of transfer, was being depreciated on a straight-line basis over four years by Proctor Ltd. Annual depreciation of $90,000 was recorded by Sandy Ltd. for the equipment during 2001 and 2002.

Required:

Prepare the following in accordance with generally accepted accounting principles:

a. Fully labelled schedules of calculation and allocation of the excess of the purchase price over book value at each date of acquisition.

b. A consolidated statement of income for 2002.

c. A consolidated statement of retained earnings for 2002.

Show all supporting calculations.

[SMA, adapted]

P7-13

On December 31, 1999, Plummer Company acquired 70% (7,000 common shares) of Summer Company for $950,000. On the acquisition date, all of the identifiable assets and liabilities of Summer had fair values that were equal to their carrying values except for the equipment, which had a fair value of $200,000 more than its carrying value and a remaining useful life of 10 years. The only other purchase price discrepancy adjustment relates to consolidated goodwill of $40,000, which is to be amortized over 20 years. Plummer uses the cost method to record its investment in Summer. The following financial information is available about the two companies.

	Plummer	Summer
Retained earnings, Dec. 31, 1999	$333,000	$ 72,000
Net income, 2000	137,000	26,000
Dividends declared, 2000	(60,000)	(10,000)
Retained earnings, Dec. 31, 2000	410,000	88,000
Net income, 2001	110,000	30,000
Dividends declared, 2001	(50,000)	(15,000)
Retained earnings	$470,000	$103,000

During 2000, Plummer sold merchandise inventory to Summer for $72,000. On December 31, 2000, a portion of inventory remained unsold. An unrealized profit of $15,000 remained in this ending inventory.

On January 1, 2001, Plummer sold 1,000 of its shares to Summer for $150,000.

Required:

a. Determine consolidated net income for the year ended December 31, 2000.

b. Determine the gain or loss on the sale of the 1,000 shares of Summer sold by Plummer in 2001.

c. Determine consolidated retained earnings at December 31, 2001.

[CGA]

P7-14

On December 31, 1999, PC Company acquired 60% of the 10,000 outstanding voting shares of SL Limited for $295,000. The balance sheet and fair market values for SL Limited were:

SL Limited
Balance Sheet
At December 31, 1999

	Book value	Fair market value
Cash	$ 100,000	$100,000
Accounts receivable	250,000	250,000
Inventory	300,000	250,000
Capital assets (net)	800,000	900,000
	$1,450,000	
Accounts payable	$ 300,000	325,000
Bonds payable	800,000	800,000
Common shares	100,000	
Retained earnings	250,000	
	$1,450,000	

The capital assets have a remaining useful life of 10 years. The bonds mature on December 31, 2003.

On December 31, 2000, SL issued an additional 6,000 shares to PC for $130,000. The variance between the purchase price and the fair market values of $400,000 is to be allocated to goodwill. This goodwill will be amortized over four years.

SL had a net income of $60,000 for the year ended December 31, 2000 and $70,000 for the year ended December 31, 2001. SL declared and paid $5,000 in dividends in 2000, and $10,000 in 2001.

Required:

Calculate the balance in the investment in SL Limited account on December 31, 2001 assuming PC uses the equity method.

[CGA]

Strategic
Investments:
Additional
Aspects of
Share Capital

357

P7-15

On January 1, 1999 Pumpkin Company acquired 70% of the 10,000 outstanding voting shares of Squash Limited for $769,000. The balance sheet and fair values for Squash Limited were:

Squash Limited
Balance Sheet
At December 31, 1999

	Book value	Fair market value
Cash	$ 120,000	$120,000
Accounts receivable	190,000	180,000
Inventory	240,000	270,000
Capital assets (net)	700,000	820,000
	$1,250,000	
Accounts payable	$ 330,000	330,000
Common shares	500,000	
Retained earnings	420,000	
	$1,250,000	

The capital assets had a remaining useful life of 20 years. Any goodwill should be amortized over 10 years. Squash had a net income of $50,000 for the year ended December 31, 1999 and $80,000 for the year ended December 31, 2000. Squash paid dividends of $5,000 in 1999 and paid dividends of $10,000 in 2000.

On January 1, 2001 Pumpkin sold 1,000 of the Squash shares for $130,000.

Required:

a. Calculate the balance in the investment in the Squash account before and after the sale of the 1,000 shares, assuming Pumpkin uses the equity method.

b. Calculate the gain/loss on the sale of the 1,000 shares.

[CGA]

Segmented and

Interim Reporting

Introduction

The previous six chapters developed the concepts and procedures underlying consolidated financial statements. In our discussion, we pointed out that consolidated statements give the reader a broad view of the complete economic entity and of the aggregate resources under the control of the parent corporation. The focus of consolidated statements is *aggregation*—combining business activities across all lines of business and all separate legal entities within the consolidated group and reporting on an annual basis.

In contrast, this chapter deals with *disaggregation*—reporting for smaller parts of the enterprise and for shorter periods of time.

Consolidated statements conceal the financial position and results of operations for the separate entities and business lines comprising the consolidated whole. All of the business activities are combined and condensed in the consolidated statements. A financial statement user cannot discern the relative importance and profitability of the different lines of business that the consolidated entity may be engaged in. Nor can a user ascertain the company's risk exposure in its various types of activities. To help the financial statement reader, accounting standards call for supplemental disclosure on business segments. Segment disclosure is intended to overcome some of the limitations of consolidated statements. Reporting on segments will be the first major topic in this chapter.

The second major topic deals with reporting on the results of operations for a period of time that is shorter than a year. Public companies in Canada and the United States are required to issue *interim reports* to their shareholders on a quarterly basis. In other countries, interim reporting for public companies is usually semi-annual. Since many estimates, allocations, and business practices are based on a yearly cycle of activity, reporting for short periods of time raises more difficulties than we might at first suspect.

Segmented Reporting

Introduction

When a company is engaged in several lines of business, it is difficult for an investor or creditor to appraise the future earnings and cash flow prospects for the firm and to evaluate the riskiness of the company's business. Each type of business will be affected by different factors relating to markets, supply, competition, etc. An analyst can make reasonable predictions of cash flow and earnings only on the basis of information *not* included in the consolidated financial statements.

Another problem with consolidated financial statements is that they can mask poor investments in lines of business that are unrelated to the main business of the corporation. Managers sometimes go into ventures that turn out not to perform as anticipated. The poor performance may be the result of management's misjudging the risks involved in a new venture, may be due to a lack of management experience in the new line of business, or may be caused by any number of other reasons. While bad investments and unwise ventures will adversely affect the parent's operating performance, the true dimensions of a fiasco may be hidden when unsuccessful ventures are consolidated with the successful parts of the business. Performance evaluation by external users therefore can be made more difficult by consolidated statements.

The response of accounting standard setters to the problems posed by consolidated reporting has been to require **segmented reporting**, which is the disaggregation of consolidated results into the major different types of businesses in which a consolidated entity engages. Also known as "line of business" reporting, segmented reporting helps analysts to understand how the risks and rewards inherent in different lines of business are affecting and will affect the corporation. Segmented reporting also reduces the likelihood of poorly performing lines of business being concealed by the consolidated results.

Line of business reporting is intended to enable financial-statement readers to evaluate the risk that a company is exposed to in its various types of activities. As well, however, there is risk inherent in operating in different parts of the world. Therefore, segment reporting also extends to reporting on operations by geographic area.

Segmented reporting addresses the problems cited above for consolidated statements, but it does not directly address the need of some users for reporting by a separate legal entity. Only if there is a correspondence between segments and corporate entities is the shareholder or creditor able to gain some insight into the viability of the individual corporation in which she or he has a stake. A remedy is available to those who need legal-entity reporting, however—simply request separate-entity financial statements. Such statements are always prepared because they are necessary for income tax purposes.

Over 30 countries have some form of segmented reporting requirements. Some requirements provide minimal guidance. Others require disaggregated disclosures through adoption of IAS 14, "Reporting Financial Information by Segment" (revised 1997). While segmented reporting is widespread, Canada and the U.S. generally provide the most guidance in defining segments and designating the reporting requirements.

In Canada, the recommendations on segmented reporting are contained in Section 1701 of the *CICA Handbook*. The recommendations are quite broad, and permit substantial flexibility in reporting. The AcSB worked in conjunction with the FASB in the U.S. in developing a single standard for the two countries. The current segment reporting recommendations became effective in 1998.

Applicability

Unlike almost all other sections of the *CICA Handbook*, Section 1701 applies only to *public* companies—those that have either shares or bonds traded in the public capital markets, either on an exchange or over the counter.[1] This section of the *CICA Handbook* therefore does not apply to most companies in Canada, although the recommendations can be used as a guideline for private companies. Banks or other holders of privately placed debt can also require the borrower to

---

1. The requirements also apply to co-operative business enterprises (such as United Grain Growers), deposit-taking institutions (e.g., banks and credit unions), and life insurance companies.

provide segmented results. More commonly, however, banks require borrowers to supply separate-entity statements rather than segmented breakdowns of consolidated results.

In formulating the recommendations in Section 1701, the AcSB was cognizant of the benefit-cost relationship in presenting segmented information. In general, the AcSB preferred to recommend disclosure only of information that was already readily available within the reporting enterprise, mainly from the management accounting system. Thus, some of the variability that exists in practice is the result of differing management accounting systems.

The focus of the segment disclosure recommendations is on reportable operating segments. There are two key words here—*operating* and *reportable*. Not all operating segments are reportable. We will clarify the distinction in the following discussion.

In addition to reporting on their definable operating segments, companies should report additional enterprise-wide information about:

- products and services,

- geographic areas, and

- major customers.

Operating segments

Identifying operating segments

The first step is to identify the segments to be reported. In some instances, identifying operating segments is no problem. If a telephone company buys a gas pipeline company, it is clear that those are two distinct segments; they share no resources, market, management expertise, or common costs, except at the top corporate level. Operationally, there is no similarity.

In other instances, however, it is more difficult to identify operating segments than one perhaps might expect. The *CICA Handbook* cites three aspects to defining an operating segment [CICA 1701.10-1701.12]:

1. It is a component of the enterprise that is expected to generate revenues and incur expenses. A segment need not be generating revenues currently, but should be expected to do so in the normal future course of its activity.

2. Discrete financial information on the business component is regularly available through the company's internal financial reporting system.

3. The business component's operating results are reviewed regularly by the enterprise's "chief operating decision maker," which normally will be the COO (chief operating officer), the CEO (chief executive officer), or the president. This officer will use the various business components' financial information to make resource allocation decisions within the enterprise.

Clearly, the guidelines focus on the decision-making process within the enterprise. The accounting system must provide the information as a matter of routine, and that information must be used by senior management for allocating resources within the company.

Normally there will be a manager in charge of the business component, and that manager will interact and negotiate directly with the chief operating decision maker about the segment's plans, results, and resources. In a matrix organization, where one manager is responsible for geographic areas and another is responsible for products or services across the entire enterprise, the *CICA Handbook* recommends that the operating segments be defined on the basis of products and services [CICA 1701.15].

Some operating segments may be quite separate when defined by the criteria described above, and yet can be combined for segment reporting. For example, the business components may serve the same general market, although not necessarily the same customers. If the products are complementary, or are substitutes for each other, then the enterprise may simply be horizontally integrated in the same market rather than being in two different segments. Some of Canada's major wineries are owned by beer companies. Beer and wine are likely to have different segment managers and distinct financial reporting, and may be viewed by senior management as two different segments. But since both beer and wine serve the same general market, it may make sense to report only one alcoholic beverages segment rather than two segments.

The degree of vertical integration can also be used as a criterion for segmentation. A company may produce a raw material, refine it, convert it into manufactured products, and sell the products through its own chain of stores. Is the company in three segments (resources, manufacturing, and retailing) or in one vertically integrated segment? The answer depends on the relative independence of the various levels of the business and the degree of reliance by each on the others. If substantially all of the raw material goes into the enterprise's own manufacturing plants, and the output of the plants is sold mainly through the company's stores, then the high level of interdivisional product flows suggests that there is only one integrated segment.

On the other hand, if the three levels of business operate fairly autonomously, buying materials from external suppliers and selling intermediate outputs on the open market, then the enterprise would seem to be in separate segments rather than in just one.

Different companies with seemingly comparable operations could quite legitimately segment their results differently. One company may report several related operating segments, while another company with seemingly similar segments may choose to report the segments together as a single, dominant, integrated segment. The second company's lack of segmented reporting may suggest that the sales between divisions account for the bulk of each division's revenues, and that sales to third parties may not be sufficiently important to justify segmentation.

Reportable segments

There is a difference between an *identifiable* segment and a *reportable* segment. To be reportable, a segment must be separately identifiable, but in addition must satisfy at least one of the criteria or guidelines set out in Section 1701. The general guidelines for reporting an operating segment are that a segment is considered reportable if it comprises 10% or more of the enterprise's:

- total revenues, including sales between segments,

- operating profits, *or*

- combined assets of all operating segments.

Only one of the 10% tests needs to be met. If an operating segment does not meet any of these criteria, it can be combined with another related segment or lumped into an "other" category. In general, at least 75% of the enterprise's consolidated revenues should be disclosed by operating segment.

Management can choose to report segments that do not meet any of the 10%

criteria. However, the *CICA Handbook* suggests that 10 segments may be a reasonable upper limit for disclosure [CICA 1701.27].

In applying the 10% guideline for profits, a problem arises when some of the operating segments operate at a loss while others are profitable. The offsetting effect of profits and losses reduces the size of the company's total profit (or loss), and thereby would reduce the level of segment profit or loss that would satisfy the 10% criterion. The approach taken by the AcSB to dealing with the offsetting effect is that the 10% profit guideline should be applied to the *larger* of:

1. 10% of the combined profits of all of the segments that reported profits, *or*

2. 10% of the combined losses of all of the segments that operated at a loss for the period.

For example, suppose that a company has six operating segments:

Segment	Operating profit (loss)
A	$ 25,000
B	(10,000)
C	15,000
D	30,000
E	(35,000)
F	40,000
Total	$ 65,000

The total profit is $65,000, and all of the segments have profits or losses that are higher than 10% of that amount. However, the sum of the profitable segments is $110,000 while the sum of the losses is $45,000. The basis for applying the 10% guideline is the larger of those two amounts, or $110,000. Any segment that has a profit or a loss larger than $11,000 is reportable. Under that criterion, segment B ceases to be a reportable segment (although it still may meet one of the other criteria).

The definition of "profit" is intentionally ambiguous. The recommendations make no reference as to how the profit is measured. It may be pre-tax or after-tax, and it may or may not include costs such as interest expense, allocated head office expenses, etc. The profit measure is defined simply as "the measure reported to the chief operating decision maker for purposes of making decisions about allocating resources to the segment and assessing its performance" [CICA 1701.32]. In other words, segment profit is measured on the same basis the company measures it in its internal reporting system. Therefore, a financial statement reader must be extremely cautious in trying to compare segment profits between different enterprises.

It is quite possible for an identifiable segment to satisfy one of the 10% criteria in one year and not the next, or vice versa. Therefore, the determination of reportable segments must be based on more than a one-year view. If a segment is likely to exceed a 10% guideline more often than not, then it probably should be reported *each* year even if it may not meet the guideline every year.

The qualitative criterion of *consistency* suggests that the same segment breakdown should be reported each year until a significant shift in relative importance of lines of business causes a segment to drop below the 10% guidelines more or less permanently. The guidelines should also be used to identify emerging segments, those that are increasing in importance in the consolidated enterprise.

Information to be reported

The two basic pieces of information that should be reported for each segment are:

- total assets, and
- a measure of profit or loss.

Notice that the requirement is specifically for "a" measure of profit—there is no suggestion as to how profit should be measured. The profit measure is whatever the company's senior management uses to evaluate the segment.

The *CICA Handbook* gives a list of items to be disclosed for each reportable segment. However, these items are reported only *if* they are reviewed regularly by the chief operating decision maker. Regular review can be either (1) by their inclusion in the measure of segment profit that is used by senior management or (2) by being separately reported and reviewed. The information to be disclosed is as follows [CICA 1701.30–31]:

- Revenues, separately disclosed by:
  - sales to external customers
  - inter-segment sales
- Interest revenue and interest expense, normally disclosed separately
- Revenues, expenses, gains, or losses arising from unusual non-recurring transactions
- Income tax expense or benefit
- Extraordinary items
- Amortization of capital assets and goodwill
- Total expenditures for additions to capital assets and goodwill
- Significant non-cash items other than amortization
- Information about investees that are subject to significant influence:
  - equity in earnings
  - amount of investment

The *CICA Handbook* recommends that the reporting enterprise explain the basis for determining reportable segments. Also, the company should present a general description of the products and services from which each segment derives its revenues [CICA 1701.29].

The basis for reporting segment information to the chief operating decision maker will often be based on non-consolidated data. Therefore, a reconciliation of the segmented sales, profits, and assets to the amounts in the consolidated financial statements is recommended [CICA 1701.35].

Enterprise-wide disclosures

Products and services

We stated above that the company should disclose the nature of each segment's products and services. However, a company may not have separate reportable segments but still may have a series of different product types or services. In that case, the company should disclose the revenues from each group of similar products and services.

Geographic areas

One of the primary tasks of a financial statement reader is to assess the potential business risks that are facing an enterprise. Several aspects of business risk are related to the countries or geographic areas in which the company does business. Risks relate to both revenue potential and asset exposure. If a Canadian company generates significant amounts of revenue in Europe, for example, European revenues (and profits) will be threatened if the Euro weakens in relation to the Canadian dollar. As the Euro declines, Canadian services and products become more expensive in terms of Euros. Or, if the company maintains its prices in Euros, the Canadian-dollar profit margin will decline as the Euro declines. Similarly, assets located in certain geographic areas may be a source of risk. The risk can arise either politically (e.g., political instability) or economically (e.g., high inflation).

To help investors assess risk, the *CICA Handbook* recommends that companies disclose the extent to which their sales are to foreign vs. domestic customers, and also the breakdown between domestic and foreign assets. The specific recommended disclosures are as follows [CICA 1701.40]:

- total revenues from external customers in foreign countries

- total revenue from sales to external customers in the company's home country

- total assets and goodwill that are located in foreign countries

- total amount of capital assets and goodwill that are located in the company's home country

In many cases, the domestic-foreign breakdown is provided as part of the segment disclosure. If the segment disclosures contain all of the appropriate information, then no additional reporting is necessary. Otherwise, the company should disclose these four pieces of information for the consolidated enterprise as a whole.

Major customers

Another major risk factor is the extent to which a corporation is dependent upon one or a few major customers. What will happen to the company if 45% of its services are provided to a customer that goes bankrupt?

Because of the risk inherent in relying on major customers, a reporting enterprise should disclose "information about the extent of its reliance on its major customers." Not too surprisingly, the guideline is 10%. If the company relies on a single customer for 10% or more of its revenue, the company should disclose the total amount of revenues from each such customer and the segment or segments that generate those total revenues. Customers under common control are considered to be a single customer.

Note that there is no requirement to disclose the *name* of the important customer or customers. This may be viewed as a shortcoming. If one or more companies in the retail clothing business is in financial jeopardy, it may not be terribly helpful to a financial-statement reader to know that a significant part of a clothing manufacturer's revenue comes from a retail clothing chain without knowing the name of the chain.

Examples of segmented reporting

There is no prescribed format for the reporting of information by segments; the method of presentation is left entirely up to the preparers. In the following paragraphs, we will discuss three quite different examples of segment disclosure.

The first example, Exhibit 8-1, is Petro-Canada.[2] Petro-Canada reports two business segments, plus a general corporate column that the company calls

---

EXHIBIT 8–1 PETRO-CANADA SEGMENT DISCLOSURE

December 31, 1999
(millions of Canadian dollars)

Note 2—SEGMENTED INFORMATION

The Company operates in two business segments:

Upstream, comprising: exploration, development, production, transportation and marketing activities for crude oil, natural gas, propane, field liquids, sulphur and oil sands; and extraction of liquids from natural gas.

Downstream, comprising: purchase and sale of crude oil; refining crude oil into oil products; and distribution and marketing of these and other purchased products.

Financial information by business segment is presented in the following table as though each segment were a separate business entity. Inter-segment transfers of products, which are accounted for at market value, are eliminated on consolidation. Shared Services includes investment income, interest expense and general corporate revenue and expense. Shared Services assets are principally cash and short-term investments and other general corporate assets.

	Upstream	Downstream	Shared Services	Consolidated
Revenue				
Sales to customers and other revenues	$1,174	$4,975	$ (2)	$6,147
Inter-segment sales	516	14	—	
Segment Revenue	$1,690	$4,989	$ (2)	
Earnings				
Earnings (loss) before the following:	$ 930	$ 335	$ (66)	$1,199
Depreciation, depletion, and amortization	399	158	1	558
Exploration expense	78	—	—	78
Interest	—	—	141	141
Provision for (recovery of) income taxes				
—current	52	192	(97)	147
—deferred	152	(121)	11	42
Reorganization costs	—	—	—	—
Net Earnings (Loss)	$ 249	$ 106	$(122)	$ 233
Capital and Exploration Expenditures				
Property, plant and equipment and exploration expenditures	$ 793	$ 220	$ 8	$1,021
Deferred charges and other assets	(3)	(5)	13	5
	$ 790	$ 215	$ 21	$1,026
Total Assets	$5,052	$3,301	$ 308	$8,661
Capital Employed	$3,525	$2,084	$ 98	$5,707

---

2. In its annual report, Petro-Canada presents this information in a three-year comparative format. To simplify and clarify the example, we have included only the 1999 columns.

"shared services." The presentation of a "corporate" or "shared services" column is not unusual; many companies use this approach in order to facilitate the reconciliation process. But this is not actually a business segment because it is not generating revenues by offering products or services to customers. Remember that one of the components for defining an operating segment is that it is *expected* to generate revenue. The table ends with a "consolidated" column; therefore, the segment table also serves as the reconciliation table for each of the revenue and expense items that Petro-Canada reports.

Petro-Canada shows segment revenues segregated between revenues from outside customers and revenues from inter-segment sales. For the upstream division, about 30% of the sales are to the downstream segment. When a substantial proportion of a company's sales are between segments, the reported amount of the revenue will depend on the transfer pricing policy that the company uses. A relatively small change in the transfer price can cause a substantial change in segment profit not only for the selling segment, but also for the buying segment. In Exhibit 8-1, Petro-Canada states that "inter-segment transfers of products... are accounted for at market value... ," and therefore the segment results may be quite appropriately stated. Nevertheless, it is best to be quite cautious about interpreting the segment earnings figures whenever substantial inter-segment sales occur.

The company reports that, in the upstream division, it earned $249 million on capital employed of $3,525 million, a return of 7%. As well, we can see that the company reported these earnings on gross revenue of $1,690 million. But it is difficult to interpret this earnings level, because we do not know how much profit (if any) the company is including in its inter-segment sales price.

The second example (Exhibit 8-2) is from the annual report of Cadillac Fairview Corporation. This company defines its three segments largely in geographic terms—two segments in Canada and one in the United States. The company could be viewed as being in a single business segment—commercial property development and operation—but apparently the company assesses its operations along the three lines described and thus reports three segments. As well, this presentation satisfies the requirement for geographic information.

Cadillac Fairview uses a basic measure of "net operating income" for its segment evaluation. Most of the individual items that are in the *CICA Handbook*'s list of recommended disclosures are not included in the company's segment earnings measure. These items are disclosed on an overall corporate basis in the reconciliation that follows the segment information.

Exhibit 8-3 shows the segmented information for a company that has only one reportable operating segment, Creo Products Inc. Creo has significant sales outside of Canada and therefore the company reports its geographic revenue sources. Of its total revenue, only a little over 2% is from Canadian customers. The company also reports that it had one major customer in 1997, but none at or above the 10% disclosure requirement in 1998 or 1999.

Finally, Exhibit 8-4 (at the end of this chapter) illustrates segmented disclosure within the context of interim reporting.

Interim Reporting

Introduction

All enterprises issue financial reports at least once a year. One of the basic postulates of accounting is *periodicity*—it is feasible to break the life of an organization

EXHIBIT 8–2 CADILLAC FAIRVIEW CORPORATION SEGMENT DISCLOSURE

October 31, 1999
(thousands of Canadian dollars)

10. Segmented Information

The Corporation has three reportable segments: retail and office properties in Canada and retail properties in the United States. Evaluation of segment operating performance is based on net operating income, defined for this purpose as rental revenue less property operating expenses. Decisions relating to investment and financing activities are made on a corporate basis. The accounting policies of the segments are the same as those described for the Corporation in Note 2—Accounting Policies.

Information by reportable segment as at and for the year ended October 31, 1999:*

	Canada		United States	
	Retail	**Office**	**Retail**	**Total**
Rental revenue	$ 502,932	$ 270,223	$145,365	$ 918,520
Property operating expenses	(195,707)	(146,943)	(54,268)	(396,918)
Net operating income	$ 307,225	$ 123,280	$ 91,097	$ 521,602
Real estate assets	$2,565,791	$1,197,500	$833,373	$4,664,664
Real estate investing activities	$ 216	$ 71,983	$168,494	$ 240,693

Reconciliations of net operating income and real estate assets from reportable segments are as follows:

	1999	1998
Net operating income from reportable segments	$ 521,602	$ 445,226
Revenue (expense) not allocable to reporting segments:		
Management and development fees	16,384	17,065
Interest	7,902	8,607
Interest expense	(214,701)	(202,128)
General and administrative expense	(36,723)	(32,977)
Capital taxes expense	(10,200)	(9,800)
Depreciation and amortization expense	(118,255)	(92,368)
Operating income	$ 166,009	$ 133,625
Real estate assets from reportable segments	$4,646,664	$4,486,312
Amounts receivable	58,341	56,259
Other assets	245,620	120,641
Total assets	$4,950,625	$4,663,212

* Cadillac Fairview also presents a similar table for the prior year. We have omitted that table in this exhibit.

into discrete time periods and to report meaningfully on financial performance during that period. However, periodicity is usually applied within the context of an annual reporting cycle.

Interim reporting is the issuance of general purpose financial statements for any period of time of *less* than one year. Interim statements may be prepared for external use or for management's internal use only. Public companies are required to submit quarterly reports to their shareholders. For example, the *Ontario Securities Act* (Section 76) requires comparative quarterly statements consisting of an income statement and a cash flow statement (Regulations, Section 7). The

EXHIBIT 8–3 CREO PRODUCTS INC. SEGMENT DISCLOSURE

September 30, 1999
(thousands of Canadian dollars)

14. SEGMENTED FINANCIAL INFORMATION

The Company operates in a single reportable operating segment relating to digital prepress equipment. The Company generated revenue from the development and sale of digital prepress equipment to customers in the following geographic segments:

Revenue Generated by Geographic Region	Years Ended September 30		
	1999	1998	1997
Canada	$ 4,059	$ 3,193	$ 3,134
U.S.	105,953	71,927	62,441
Europe	56,252	41,655	15,718
Japan	2,647	5,316	9,936
Other	9,412	6,757	4,354
	$178,323	$128,848	$95,583

There were no customers representing 10% or more of the total revenue in the year ended September 31, 1999, or the 1998 fiscal year. There was one customer in 1997 representing approximately 10% of total revenue.

The Company has capital assets located in:

Location of capital assets	September 30	
	1999	1998
Canada	$37,678	$31,914
Other	3,040	2,232
	$40,718	$34,146

securities acts of six other provinces also require interim statements.[3] Interim reports need not be audited.

Another common use of interim statements is for internal management use. Internal interim reports may be monthly rather than quarterly, and may be more detailed than those prepared for external release. Although interim reports may be prepared in less detail than the annual statements and will include more estimates, it would be a rude shock to managers and shareholders alike if the annual statements were not consonant with the operations as described by the interim statements. Thus interim statements should be prepared in a manner that is consistent with the annual statements.

General principles of application

Section 1751 of the *CICA Handbook* contains explicit recommendations for the preparation of interim statements. This section was revised in 2000 (effective for 2001) to conform more closely with International Accounting Standard (IAS) 34 and to harmonize the Canadian standard with interim reporting standards in the United States. To a large extent, the revision merely caught up with existing practice. For example, the prior Canadian standard did not require an interim balance

---

3. Those not mentioning interim statements in their securities acts are New Brunswick, Newfoundland, and Prince Edward Island.

sheet, but the vast majority of companies already provided one in their interim reports.

Section 1751 applies to companies that are required by law or regulation to prepare interim reports [CICA 1751.02]. In effect, however, the section applies almost exclusively to *public* companies, as private companies are not required to issue interim statements unless required to do so by regulation. But regulators (e.g., for financial institutions) usually have their own specific requirements about the information to be reported. Of course, companies that voluntarily prepare consolidated statements are encouraged to follow the recommendations also.

Public companies do not issue a full set of financial statements and notes as their interim results. Interim financial statements are briefer than annual financial statements and more of an *exception reporting* principle is used for note disclosure—only new or changed accounting policies are disclosed.

The period covered by the interim statements varies somewhat depending on the type of statement. Interim income statements should report on both the individual interim period and on the year to date [CICA 1751.16(b)]. For example, the third-quarter income statement will show operating results both for the third quarter and for the year-to-date cumulative amounts for the first three quarters.

The retained earnings statement and the cash flow statements, in contrast, report only on a year-to-date basis [CICA 1751.16(c) and (d)]. The balance sheet will be as of the reporting date, of course; there is no such thing as a year-to-date balance sheet, since that statement reports on financial condition at a point in time.

All financial statements need to have a basis for comparison. Interim statements produced for external users are normally prepared on a comparative basis. In most statements, the comparison is with the same period of the preceding year. For the balance sheet, however, the comparison is with the previous year-end balance sheet [CICA 1751.16(a)]. For internal reports, budgeted figures for the period may provide a more relevant basis for comparison.

A company normally will use the same accounting policies for interim statements as it uses for the annual financial statements. If there are exceptions, those are to be disclosed [CICA 1751.14(a)]. The interim statements should indicate that they should be read in conjunction with the company's previous annual financial statements, since fuller information is available in the annual statements than in the interim statement.

Segment information should also be presented in the interim statements [CICA 1751.14(e)]. Segment information should include at least the following:

- segment revenues, segregated between inter-segment revenues and those to external customers

- segment profit (loss)

- segment assets if there has been a significant change from the amounts reported in the previous annual statements

- any changes in the basis of segmentation or the method of reporting segment profit

- reconciliation of segment earnings to consolidated earnings for the interim period

The interim segment information is essentially the same as that required in the annual financial statements.

The periodicity problem

At first glance, it may appear that the preparation of interim statements poses no special problems. Since the same accounting principles are used as for the annual reports, the interim period would seem to require only the same application of accounting, but for a shorter period.

Unfortunately, the situation is not quite so simple. Accounting for an annual period poses major problems of allocation and estimation. Revenue recognition can present significant difficulties, the costs of tangible and intangible capital assets must be allocated, and future costs must be estimated in order to achieve matching. When these accounting problems are confronted for a period shorter than a year, their significance increases proportionately.

Estimation errors will have a much larger impact on the operating income for a month or a quarter than they will on the operating income for a year. Cut-off procedures are not likely to be as stringent for the unaudited interim statements, and interim inventories are most likely to be estimated or to be taken from perpetual inventory records whose accuracy has not been verified by a physical count.

Not only will estimation errors have a greater impact, but also the materiality threshold will be lower because the amounts on the income statement and cash flow statement will be only about one-fourth of the annual amounts. Estimation variances that might be ignored in the annual statements (with the higher materiality threshold) become significant in the quarterly statements. The result may be that the reliability of interim statements will intrinsically be less than for annual statements.

Additional estimation and allocation problems arise as the result of the shorter accounting period. Some costs and revenues are seasonal or annual in nature, and interim statements require allocations where none would be required for annual statements.

For example, annual insurance costs pose no problems if the accounting period is a year, but how should the cost be allocated if the period is a month? An easy answer would be to allocate one-twelfth of the cost to each month. However, suppose that the insurance is an expensive public liability policy for an amusement park that is open all year, but that does the bulk of its business in the summer months. Should the cost be allocated by time or by volume of activity in order to match the cost with the revenue?

Another example is a factory that shuts down in the month of August for a vacation for all production employees. The fixed costs of the factory during August could be viewed as a cost to be allocated to all of the interim periods, or as a cost of the individual period in which August falls. Similarly, annual costs such as retooling costs or once-a-year major maintenance costs could either be allocated, or could be allowed to fall into the interim period in which they occur.

Some costs are determined not only on an annual basis, but also *after* the end of the year. Customer rebates, sales bonuses, and income taxes are examples of these costs. Should an attempt be made to estimate and allocate these costs, or should they be allowed to fall into the last interim period?

As the preceding examples suggest, there are two basic approaches to the preparation of interim statements. The interim period can be viewed either as a distinct and separate accounting period of its own (the **discrete approach**), or as a part of a year (the **integral approach**).

Discrete approach

Under the discrete or *separate-period* approach, each interim period is accounted for by using the company's normal accounting policies applied to the interim period as though it were a year. A company's policy may be to expense immediately all costs that may have future benefits that are difficult to measure, such as development costs or factory retooling costs. Under this accounting policy, deferred charges and credits are normally not carried on the balance sheet. A company that follows such a policy will also apply it to the interim periods under the discrete approach. Costs will be permitted to fall into the period in which they are incurred, even though they may be annual costs that benefit other interim periods.

This approach implicitly recognizes that since revenues and expenses are likely to be "lumpy," the interim earnings are also going to be lumpy, and are not just a proportionate part of the annual earnings. This approach treats the insurance costs, vacation costs, or retooling and maintenance costs as period costs for the quarter rather than allocating them to the other periods.

On the other hand, a company could follow a general accounting policy of capitalization and amortization of costs that benefit future periods. If this policy is followed, then there could be an attempt to allocate costs that are incurred in early periods to later periods, and to accrue costs in early periods that will not be incurred until later periods. There still would be no attempt to normalize costs and revenues, however, by spreading out seasonal costs such as heating, seasonal maintenance, annual bonuses, etc., or by spreading out seasonal revenues.

Under the discrete approach, income taxes are viewed as cumulative. Income taxes are accrued for the first period based on the net operating income for the period. Income taxes for the second period will be based on the *additional* taxes payable as a result of the operations for the second period, and so forth. If a loss occurred in the first period, no benefit will be recognized. Future income taxes would be provided for all temporary differences arising during the interim period, even if the temporary difference is expected to reverse within the taxation year.

Integral approach

Under this approach, the interim period is viewed simply as a part of the longer period of a year. Expenses are allocated across the interim periods in such a way as to portray the company's likely annualized operating results. Theoretically, if a company is heading for a year in which the operating margin (net income divided by sales) is 10%, then the interim statements should reflect that fact. Under this view, the interim statements should be the best predictor available of the company's operating results for the year.

For the examples cited above, the integral approach will allocate the insurance costs proportionately to the volume of business, and will allocate the costs of the plant closing, the annual retooling and maintenance costs, and the estimated bonuses and rebates to all of the interim periods. In an extreme application of the approach, revenues could be annualized using statistical techniques similar to those used for macroeconomic, seasonally adjusted statistics; however, it is doubtful that revenue would ever be statistically smoothed in practice.

Income taxes are viewed as an annual expense to be allocated to interim periods in proportion to the pre-tax interim net income. There will be no separate computation of income taxes for the interim period as though it were a separate taxation period, and timing differences will be determined on an annual basis and allocated to the interim periods. An income tax benefit will be recognized for a first-quarter loss if the company expects to earn a profit for the tax year as a whole.

Application in practice

For internal interim reports, the discrete approach will almost always be used. The comparative amounts for internal users are likely to be budgeted figures for the period (perhaps supplemented by the previous year's figures), and budgets generally include major costs as expenses of the period in which they occur. Controllability is a concern in budgeting, and costs allocated from previous periods are not controllable in the later periods to which they are allocated. Also, internal reports frequently do not include any estimates of income tax, thereby removing one major estimation problem.

For public interim statements, reporting is guided by Section 1751 of the *CICA Handbook*. Interim statements should include the same headings and subtotals that appear in annual financial statements. All of the line-item disclosures that are required by the *CICA Handbook* for annual statements should also be disclosed (e.g., interest expense, income tax expense, and amortization) [CICA 1751.11]. As well, basic and fully diluted earnings per share should be presented on the face of the interim income statement.

Note disclosure in interim statements is much abbreviated from annual disclosure. A statement reader is presumed to have access to the previous year-end financial statements, and much of the information in the notes thereto will not be significantly different for the interim periods. As mentioned previously, the exception principle comes into play here—to the extent that there are significant changes, the company should provide note disclosure. Such changes include changes in accounting policy, changes in strategic investments, restructurings, extraordinary items, and discontinued operations. Subsequent event disclosure is also required.

For measuring interim period operating results, Section 1751 generally favours the discrete approach, "each interim period standing alone as an independent reporting period" [CICA 1751.19]. Generally, costs and revenues should be accrued or deferred at the end of interim periods only if those same costs or revenues would normally be accrued or deferred at the end of the fiscal year.

However, the recommendations also contain some aspects of the part-of-year approach, as described in the following paragraphs. Therefore, the *CICA Handbook* approach might better be characterized as a "modified discrete" approach.

Two specific exceptions pertain to inventories [CICA 1751.26]. Certain types of standard cost variances may be deferred if those variances are expected to be offset by the end of the year. Also, under LIFO inventory procedures, a dip into the base stock (i.e., "old" prices) should not be recognized if the inventory is expected to be replaced by the end of the year.

Another general exception arises for costs that are determined only on an annual basis. The section specifically discusses year-end bonuses, contingent lease payments, and income taxes. The section uses the terminology of "constructive obligation" to rationalize these exceptions, but the basic point is simply that companies can estimate or project the determining factors for the entire year and accrue the costs in the interim statements. For example, contingent rents may be based on annual sales in excess of a contractual minimum. In a strict application of the discrete approach, no accrual for contingent rent is made until the threshold level of sales is achieved. Section 1751, however, permits this type of cost to be spread out over the several interim periods—an application of the integral approach.

When purchases are made under an annual volume rebate or discount scheme, the section suggests different approaches for the buyer and seller [CICA 1751.B26]. If attainment of the required level of sales to qualify for the rebate is likely, the seller should recognize the contingent liability. The buyer, on the other hand, recognizes the contingent benefit only when the required level of sales has been achieved—the integral approach is used for the seller and the discrete approach for the buyer. Although these are conflicting treatments from the viewpoint of interim reporting, these treatments are consistent with the recommendations for contingencies, in which contingent liabilities are recognized when they are likely and measurable [CICA 3290.12], but contingent gains are recognized only when they are realized [CICA 3290.20].

Income tax expense presents a special problem. Under the discrete approach, income tax for each quarter would be calculated on the year-to-date taxable income. The increase (or decrease) in income tax from the previous quarter would be that quarter's tax expense. This is consistent with the general approach espoused in Section 1751:

> Amounts of income and expenses reported in the current interim period will reflect any changes in estimates of amounts reported in prior interim periods of the fiscal year. The amounts reported in prior interim periods are not retroactively adjusted. [CICA 1751.25]

However, the AcSB recommends that interim income tax expense be estimated by using the estimated average annual effective income tax rate [CICA 3471.B13]. The average rate will differ from the marginal rate only under a two-rate tax system or a progressive tax system, in which higher levels of income are taxed at a different rate than lower levels. Instead of accruing income tax at the lower rate in the early quarters, the average rate applicable to the management's estimate of the full year's earnings year should be used. The average rate should be used even if the early quarters show a loss and even if the overall earnings for the year are expected to be zero.

The benefits of an income tax loss in an interim period are recognized in that period if:

- the loss will be offset by taxable income in the other interim periods of that year,

- the loss can be used as a tax loss carryback to a prior year, or

- it is more likely than not that the benefit of the loss will be realized as a tax loss carryforward.

For example, suppose that a company has a loss of $50,000 in the first quarter but expects to earn $120,000 over the following three quarters. If the expected average tax rate is 30%, the first quarter interim income statement will show an income tax *benefit* or recovery (i.e., a negative tax expense, or a credit) of $50,000 × 30% = $15,000. The following quarters will show a positive income tax expense totalling $120,000 × 30% = $36,000. The total income tax expense for the year will be $36,000 − $15,000 = $21,000, based on cumulative net income of $70,000 for the year (i.e., $120,000 − $50,000).

If an income tax loss is not expected to be offset by taxable profits in the other interim periods of the current year, the benefit is recognized only if it is more likely than not that the benefit will be realized in future years.

Illustrative interim statement

Exhibit 8-4 shows NRG's second-quarter 2000 interim statements. Although the new requirements of Section 1751 were not in effect in 2000, NRG's interim report seems to comply with the AcSB's revised recommendations in every material respect except possibly for the lack of segment asset disclosure in Note 5.

The NRG Group Inc. is described as follows in the introductory comments to its second quarter 2000 interim report:

> The NRG Group Inc. is an operating Internet incubator, venture capital and advisory company. NRG is a resource for youth-oriented companies, brands, products and institutions and invests financial and human resource capital in start-up and early stage technology, Internet and e-commerce companies.[4]

The company has three operating units:

- NRG Factory, an operating Internet incubator

- NRG Ventures, a venture capital and investment arm

- NGR Solutions, a consulting service

The full interim statements are reproduced in Exhibit 8-4, except for four pages of introductory comments about the company's performance, including a segment-by-segment description of activities. We can make a few observations about this interim report.

As explained briefly in Note 1, NRG does not present comparative information on its interim income statement or cash flow statement. The reason is that the corporation was founded on November 16, 1999, and therefore there is no comparable earlier period.

NRG's accounting policy for investments is to carry investments at market value. This is a general accounting policy, not one that relates exclusively to the interim statements. As a result, the income statement and the segment information (Note 5) report both realized and unrealized gains and losses on investments.

Note 3 reports on the acquisition of The NRG Group Inc. by 2FundEcom on March 10, 2000. Although 2FundEcom was the acquirer, the companies amalgamated immediately after the acquisition and assumed the NRG name. Note 4 discloses that approximately 9.3 million shares were issued to acquire NRG. Since there were about 11.6 million shares outstanding prior to the acquisition, this does not appear to have been a reverse takeover.

The purchase price allocation is disclosed in Note 3, in accordance with the recommendations of both Section 1571 and Section 1580. Most of the purchase price was allocated to goodwill: $15,131 \times $27,350 = 55\%$. Goodwill is being amortized over five years.

Although NRG is a new company and therefore lacks comparative information, it is a good example of an interim report.

---

4. The company's Web site is www.thenrggroup.com, in case you'd like more information!

EXHIBIT 8–4 INTERIM FINANCIAL STATEMENTS

THE NRG GROUP INC.
Interim Balance Sheets
As at June 30, 2000 and December 31, 1999
(In thousands of dollars)

	(Unaudited) June 30, 2000	(Audited) December 31,1999
ASSETS		
Cash and cash equivalents	$12,889	$2,023
Accounts receivable and other assets	573	40
Investments (note 2)	32,266	5,082
Capital assets, net	607	—
Goodwill, net (note 3)	14,249	—
Future tax assets	979	8
	$61,563	$7,153
LIABILITIES AND SHAREHOLDERS' EQUITY		
Liabilities		
Accounts payable and accrued liabilities	$ 772	$ 103
Future tax liabilities	6,447	366
	7,219	469
Shareholders' equity		
Share capital (note 4)	53,269	5,945
Retained earnings	1,075	739
	54,344	6,684
	$61,563	$7,153

See accompanying notes to the financial statements.

EXHIBIT 8–4 INTERIM FINANCIAL STATEMENTS (continued)

THE NRG GROUP INC.
Interim Statements of Income (Loss)—Unaudited
Three and six months ended June 30, 2000
(In thousands of dollars, except share and per share amounts)

	Three months ended June 30, 2000	Six months ended June 30, 2000
Revenue and income		
Consulting revenues	$ 413	$ 455
Interest income	144	150
	557	605
Expenses		
General and administrative	2,200	2,531
Sales and marketing	184	233
Amortization	33	36
	2,417	2,800
Gain (loss) before income taxes, goodwill charges, realized and unrealized gain (loss) on investments	(1,860)	(2,195)
Realized gain (loss) on investments	(4,308)	(4,308)
Unrealized gain (loss) on investments	(22,812)	7,781
Income (loss) before income taxes and goodwill charges	(28,980)	1,278
Provision for (recovery of) income taxes	(8,963)	59
Income (loss) before goodwill charges	$(20,017)	$ 1,219
Goodwill charges	(757)	(883)
Net income (loss) for the period	(20,774)	336
Retained earnings—beginning of period	21,849	739
Retained earnings—end of period	$1,075	$ 1,075
Earnings (loss) per common share before goodwill charges:		
Basic	$(0.74)	$0.06
Fully diluted	$(0.74)	$0.06
Earnings (loss) per common share:		
Basic	$(0.76)	$0.02
Fully diluted	$(0.76)	$0.02
Weighted average number of common shares outstanding:		
Basic	27,227,177	20,991,293
Fully diluted	27,227,177	20,642,263

See accompanying notes to the financial statements

EXHIBIT 8–4 INTERIM FINANCIAL STATEMENTS (continued)

THE NRG GROUP INC.
Interim Statements of Cash Flows—Unaudited
Three and six months ended June 30, 2000
(In thousands of dollars)

	Three months ended June 30, 2000	Six months ended June 30, 2000
Cash provided by (used in):		
Operations:		
Net income (loss) for the period	$(20,774)	$ 336
Items not involving cash:		
Amortization of capital assets	33	36
Realized (gain) loss on investments	4,308	4,308
Unrealized (gain) loss on investments	22,812	(7,781)
Goodwill charges	757	883
Foreign exchange loss	27	27
Net change in non-cash working capital balances	(8,619)	(1)
	(1,456)	(2,192)
Investing:		
Purchase of capital assets	(391)	(489)
Purchase of investments	(1,411)	(2,273)
	(1,802)	(2,762)
Financing:		
Issuance of common shares	13,411	16,885
Repayment of bank indebtedness	—	(765)
Repayment of short-term loans	—	(300)
	13,411	15,820
Increase in cash	10,153	10,866
Cash—beginning of period	2,736	2,023
Cash—end of period	$ 12,889	$12,889

See accompanying notes to the financial statements.

EXHIBIT 8–4 INTERIM FINANCIAL STATEMENTS (continued)

THE NRG GROUP INC.
Notes to Unaudited Interim Financial Statements
Three and six months ended June 30, 2000

1. Comparative Figures

The prior year figures on the Statements of Income (Loss) and Cash Flows for the three and six months ended June 30, 2000 are not shown as 2FundEcom Inc., the originating corporation, was incorporated on November 16, 1999.

2. Investments

Investments consist of the following:

Venture investments:

	June 30, 2000 (000s)	December 31,1999 (000s)
Investments in publicly-traded companies		
MedcomSoft Inc.	$10,170	$1,631
Starfire Technologies International Inc.	698	678
Chinadotcom Corporation	2,160	—
	13,028	2,309
Investment in privately-held company		
StreetViews Inc.	3,990	2,773
Total Venture investments	17,018	5,082
Factory investments		
Charity.ca	6,897	—
Sportslink	5,158	—
EyeReturn	3,193	—
Total Factory investments	15,248	—
Total Investments	$32,266	$5,082

3. Acquisition

On March 10, 2000, 2FundEcom ("the Company") acquired all of the issued and outstanding shares of The NRG Group Inc. ("Old NRG") by issuing 9,280,970 shares of the Company and 349,030 options to acquire common shares of the Company to the shareholders of Old NRG. Immediately following the acquisition, the Company and Old NRG amalgamated. The amalgamated entity carried on business as The NRG Group, Inc. ("NRG").

EXHIBIT 8–4 INTERIM FINANCIAL STATEMENTS (continued)

Total purchase price consists of the following:

	(000s)
Value of common shares and options assumed	$27,150
Acquisition cost	200
Total purchase price	$27,350

The purchase price allocation is as follows:

	(000s)
Accounts payable	$ 243
Prepaid expenses	2
Income taxes recoverable	21
Investments	18,500
Capital assets, net	155
Goodwill	15,131
	34,052
Bank indebtedness	(765)
Accounts payable and accrued liabilities	(287)
Due to related party	(600)
Future tax liabilities	(5,050)
Net assets acquired	$27,350

Goodwill will be amortized on a straight-line basis over five years.

4. Share Capital

Share capital consists of the following:

	Number of common shares	Stated amount (000s)
Authorized		
Unlimited common shares		
Issued		
Outstanding, December 31, 1999	11,570,000	$ 5,945
Shares issued for cash	200,000	100
Shares issued to acquire Old NRG	9,280,970	27,350
Shares issued to Chinadotcom	4,146,625	6,463
Shares issued on the initial public offering	6,000,000	13,411
Balance at June 30, 2000	31,197,595	$53,269

Details of outstanding stock options at June 30, 2000 are as follows:

Number of stock options granted and outstanding	Exercise price	Expiry date
349,030	$0.104 - $0.208	December 16, 2004
1,906,500	$2.50	March 13, 2005–May 18, 2005

EXHIBIT 8–4 INTERIM FINANCIAL STATEMENTS (continued)

5. Segment Information

	Three months ended June 30, 2000 (000s)		
	Solutions	**Investing**	**Total**
Revenues	$ 413	$ —	$ 413
Unrealized gain (loss) on investments	—	(22,812)	(22,812)
Realized gain (loss) on investments	—	(4,308)	(4,308)
Interest			144
	413	(27,120)	(26,563)
Segment operating gain (loss)	(601)	(28,490)	(28,947)
Amortization			(790)
Income (loss) before income taxes			$(29,737)

	Six months ended June 30, 2000 (000s)		
	Solutions	**Investing**	**Total**
Revenues	$ 455	$ —	$ 455
Unrealized gain (loss) on investments	—	7,781	7,781
Realized gain (loss) on investments	—	(4,308)	(4,308)
Interest			150
	455	3,473	4,078
Segment operating gain (loss)	(701)	1,865	1,314
Amortization			(919)
Income (loss) before income taxes			$ 395

Investing includes the operations of NRG Ventures and NRG Factory.

Approximately 87% of the Company's consulting revenues during the six months ended June 30, 2000 were earned from four customers.

Summary of Key Points

1. Segmented reporting is intended to provide information to enable financial statement readers to assess the risk and return that a company generates in its different lines of business. Segment information reveals performance aspects that are concealed by the aggregated nature of consolidated statements.

2. The recommendations for segment reporting apply only to public companies, with a few exceptions. Basically, segment information is provided for reportable operating segments. An *operating* segment is one that has a separate responsibility reporting line directly to the company's chief operating officer for evaluation and resource allocation. A *reportable* segment is an operating segment that accounts for at least 10% of the consolidated company's revenues, profits, or assets.

3. The corporation should report the total assets and a measure of profit or loss for each reportable segment. Detail, as prescribed by the *CICA Handbook*, should be provided for specific income statement line items *if* those items are

reviewed regularly by the chief operating decision maker. As well, the corporation should report certain enterprise-wide information on products and services, on the geographic distribution of revenues and assets, and on customers that account for 10% or more of the company's revenues.

4. Interim financial statements are those that are issued for any period less than a year. Public companies are required to issue interim statements—quarterly in the United States and Canada, semi-annually in most other countries. The *CICA Handbook* recommendations on interim reporting apply only to companies that are required to prepare interim statements by law or regulation.

5. Interim statements should consist of a balance sheet, income statement, cash flow statement, retained earnings statement, and notes that explain deviations from or exceptions to the accounting policies and major estimates that are used for the annual statements. The statements can be condensed, but should include all of the subtotals and totals that the company uses in its annual statements, and should include those line items specifically required by the *CICA Handbook*. The company should disclose extraordinary items, discontinued operations, restructurings, and acquisitions and other changes in strategic investments.

6. The *CICA Handbook* approach to interim statements is very similar to that taken in the U.S. and by international accounting standards. The underlying philosophy is the *discrete* approach, in which each interim period is treated as a distinct time period. Exceptions exist, however, for certain types of expense that are calculated only on an annual basis, such as bonuses, contingent rent, income tax, and quantity discounts (for the seller). For these items, the *integral* or *part-of-year* approach is used. The annual amount is estimated and apportioned to the interim periods.

Weblinks

Petro-Canada
www.petro-canada.ca/

Aimed at corporate and individual customers, this Web site outlines Petro-Canada's position on clean fuels, retailer opportunities, media releases, and investor information.

Cadillac Fairview
www.cadillacfairview.com

With a 9.3 billion dollar portfolio, Cadillac Fairview is one of North America's largest investors, owners, and managers of commercial real estate. The company focuses on high quality retail centres and office properties in Canada and the United States. Their Web site includes the portfolio highlights, annual reports, media information, and leasing opportunities.

Inniskillin Wines Inc.
www.inniskillin.com/

One of Canada's largest wineries, Inniskillin is situated in the Niagara Peninsula and was the first winery granted an estate licence in Canada. Advice on how to pair wine with food, online ordering forms, and descriptions of current wines are available here.

8-1 In a diversified corporation, why is prediction of future earnings and cash flow difficult when only consolidated statements are presented?

8-2 How can segmented reporting mask poor investments?

8-3 What are the objectives of segmented reporting?

8-4 When a corporation reports financial information by segments, do the segments correspond to specific subsidiaries?

8-5 What type of company is required to provide segmented reporting?

8-6 How does the AcSB consider benefit-cost relationships for segmented reporting?

8-7 How can an operating segment be identified?

8-8 What are the guidelines for determining whether an operating segment is *reportable*?

8-9 Companies L and D both operate food processing plants, and both operate a chain of retail food stores. Company L transfers all of the output from its processing plants to its stores, while Company D's processing plants produce private-label products for other retailers. How might the segment reporting of the two companies differ?

8-10 What does the *CICA Handbook* consider a reasonable upper limit for the number of segments to disclose?

8-11 How is profit defined for determining operating segments?

8-12 How much of the consolidated enterprise's business activity must be reported in operating segments in order to satisfy the requirements of the *CICA Handbook*?

8-13 Where some operating segments operate at a loss and others are profitable, how is the problem of offsetting considered in applying the 10% guidelines for reporting?

8-14 What is the reason for requiring companies to report geographic segments?

8-15 What data must be reported for each geographic segment? How do these data differ from the data reported for industry segments?

8-16 How is the risk of relying on major customers considered in segmented reporting?

8-17 Explain briefly why interim reporting poses problems different from those of annual reporting.

8-18 What type of companies does Section 1751 of the *CICA Handbook* apply to for interim reporting?

8-19 What does the *exception reporting* principle mean for note disclosure in interim reporting?

8-20 What basis of comparison is used for interim financial statements?

8-21 What are the two basic approaches to the preparation of interim statements?

8-22 Which approach to interim statements is recommended by the *CICA Handbook*?

8-23 Under the discrete or separate-period approach to interim statements, how would an annual, one-time expenditure such as retooling cost be reported? How would the reporting differ under the integral or part-of-a-year approach?

8-24 How does the measurement of income tax expense differ between the two approaches to interim reporting?

8-25 When the quarterly statements of a public Canadian company are reported, are the same financial statements prepared as for annual reporting?

Cases

Case 8-1

Ermine Oil Limited

Ermine Oil Limited (Ermine) is a fully integrated Canadian oil company. Ermine commenced as a petroleum exploration company and was very successful in its oil field discoveries. In order to attain market security and improve profits, Ermine was forced to embark on a program of vertical integration. It first acquired a refining division and then marketing and transportation divisions. From the beginning, management appreciated the integrated nature of the business, and production was transferred between divisions at standard cost. The management control system recognized the exploration, refining, and transportation divisions as cost centres and the marketing division as a revenue centre. While the exploration, refining, and transportation divisions did make external sales, historically, none of these divisions' external sales accounted for 10% of Ermine's total sales. However, in the last fiscal year, due to unusual world market conditions, the transportation division's sales accounted for 11% of Ermine's total sales. Over 90% of Ermine's sales were within Canada, with the balance spread over many countries worldwide. Ermine did not feel it was necessary to disclose segmented information in its annual financial statements.

Beluga Petroleum Limited (Beluga) was similar to Ermine in size and also in scope of operations except that, in addition, it had a chemical division. However, Beluga was a subsidiary of a foreign oil company and its divisions were each organized as profit centres with products transferred between divisions at world market prices. Each division purchased and sold products extensively to outside companies. In addition, about 15% of Beluga's sales were export, almost exclusively to the U.S. In its annual financial statements, Beluga showed segmented information by the five divisions (exploration, refining, transportation, chemical, and marketing) and sales were divided between domestic and export operations.

Required:

Discuss how both Ermine and Beluga could report differently with respect to disclosure of segmented information, and yet be in accordance with generally accepted accounting principles.

[SMA]

Case 8-2

Interim Reporting

In today's rapidly changing financial markets, financial-statement users are demanding more information, released more promptly than in the past. To respond to these needs the *CICA Handbook* has recently issued a revised Section 1751 for Interim Reporting.

At a professional update session to outline the accounting changes to the *CICA Handbook* two members engaged in a lively discussion. One member is a controller of an international public company, while the other member is a senior financial analyst in a securities firm.

Financial Analyst: My review of the *CICA Handbook* leads me to conclude that the objectives of interim reporting should be the same as those of annual reporting.

Controller: I disagree. Interim reports are aimed at different users, serve different purposes, and must be published more quickly than annual reports. It follows that the underlying objectives should also differ.

Financial Analyst: Regardless of the content of interim reports, the interim operating results should be measured on the same basis as the annual results because the interim period is an integral part of the annual period.

Controller: I agree that there is a measurement problem for interim reporting, but I don't see that there is a simple solution. For example, I find it difficult to make interim estimates for various expenses given the cyclical nature of our business. After all, the interim period is only a portion of the annual period.

Required:

Prepare a memo discussing the main issues raised in the preceding conversation. [CICA, adapted]

Problems

P8-1

Tech Company sells personal computers, mainframes, and software in more than seven countries. The company is required to file financial statements annually with a securities commission. The controller has just compiled the following information on last year's revenues:

Revenues (in millions)

Personal computers	$47
Mainframes	26
Software	3
	$76
United States	$18
Canada	22
Europe	15
Asia	9
Africa	6
South America	6
	$76

Required:

Which of the above should be reported as an operating segment and a geographical segment in a note to the financial statements?

[CICA, adapted]

P8-2

The Fellows Corporation has internal reporting for four divisions. The following data have been gathered for the year just ended.

	Div. A	Div. B	Div. C	Div. D
Interdivisional sales	$100,000	$ 20,000	—	—
External sales	10,000	200,000	$150,000	$400,000
Direct divisional expenses	50,000	120,000	30,000	100,000
Allocated joint costs	—	—	70,000	110,000
Depreciation	35,000	40,000	25,000	45,000
Capital expenditures	20,000	60,000	80,000	160,000
Identifiable assets	185,000	215,000	125,000	245,000

1. Division A sells over 90% of its output to Division B on a cost-plus basis.

2. Divisions C and D share production facilities. Joint product costs, depreciation, capital expenditures, and much of the identifiable assets are allocated one-third to Division C and the remainder to Division D.

3. Unallocated corporate expenses not included above amount to $115,000.

Required:

a. From the preceding information, what are the operating segments that should be reported by the Fellows Corporation? Explain your recommendation fully.

b. Prepare a schedule of supplementary financial information by segments, in accordance with the *CICA Handbook* recommendations based on the information provided above, together with a condensed consolidated income statement.

P8-3

The following information is available for World Wide Corporation's operating subsidiaries throughout the world, in thousands of Canadian dollars:

	External Sales	Sales to Operating Regions	Identifiable Assets	After-tax Profit
Canada	$ 40,000	$200,000	$ 20,000	$ 5,000
United States	190,000	40,000	80,000	4,500
Europe	150,000	20,000	70,000	9,000
Asia	30,000	—	15,000	3,500
South America	40,000	—	20,000	5,000
General Corporate	—	—	30,000	3,000*
Consolidated	$450,000		$235,000	$30,000

*Investment income, less general corporate expenses.

Required:

Determine which regions you would suggest reporting as geographic segments, as defined by the *CICA Handbook*. Identify the characteristics that led to your choices.

P8-4

This year, for the first time, Samson Corporation must report supplementary information by operating segment. The controller has prepared the following note for inclusion in the annual report.

Segmented Data

Your company operates in several different operating segments. Selected financial data by division are provided below, in thousands of Canadian dollars.

	Men's Wear	Tires	Other	Consolidated
Sales to outsiders	$400	$200	$300	$ 900
Sales between divisions	50	10	60	120
Total sales	$450	$210	$360	$1,020
Operating profit	$ 15	$ 40	$ 20	$ 62
Capital expenditures	$ 5	$ 25	$ 30	$ 70
Assets	$ 65	$240	$ 90	$ 455

During the year, your company had exported sales that resulted in gross profit of $50,000.

Required:

Criticize the note as prepared by the controller. Identify any missing information, either numerical or verbal, and indicate errors in presentation.

P8-5

The Shaw Navigational Company is a public Canadian corporation that operates a fleet of ships on the Great Lakes. In common with other Great Lakes shipping companies, rates are quoted and revenues are collected in U.S. dollars, regardless of the location or nationality of the shipper. Over 90% of Shaw's consolidated gross revenues, operating profits, and identifiable capital assets relate to the shipping business, and thus Shaw's management claims exemption from segmented reporting requirements on the grounds that shipping represents their only operating segment. In 2002, Shaw's consolidated net income was $1,200,000.

Shaw does have two subsidiaries that are not in the shipping business. One is a bus company that operates on intercity routes in Manitoba, and that is consolidated with the shipping operation. The bus fleet has recently been modernized, and the new buses have been acquired by means of leases rather than by an outright purchase.

The other subsidiary, which is reported on the equity basis, is a casualty insurance company located in Michigan. About 20% of the insurance company's business involves Great Lakes shipping, although mainly for shipping companies other than Shaw. Shaw's equity in the earning of the insurance company amounted to $180,000 in 2002.

Required:

Comment on management's assertion that Shaw is exempt from segment reporting because they operate in one line of business.

P8-6

The High End Company is a retail department store chain. The company's fiscal year ends on the Saturday closest to January 31 of each year. The company is publicly held and submits quarterly financial statements to the shareholders.

Like most retail establishments, High End operates at a loss for most of the year, but generally recovers the losses in the fourth quarter to finish the year with a profit. In fiscal year 2001, the company reported pre-tax net income of $2,000,000, and paid taxes at a rate of 45%.

In the first quarter of 2002, the company suffered a loss of $1,500,000 before taxes. In the second quarter, economic conditions improved slightly, but the cumulative 6-month loss was $2,600,000, the worst in the company's history. Nevertheless, management predicted that the losses would be recovered as the economy improved, and forecast a break-even performance for the year as a whole.

The loss did decline in the third quarter, to a cumulative loss of $1,300,000; the fourth quarter almost completely wiped out the loss, ending the year with a fiscal pre-tax loss of only $100,000.

Required:

Assume that tax losses can be carried back for only one year. Determine the provision for income taxes that should be reported on High End's interim income statements for fiscal year 2002, assuming:

a. That each quarter is reported separately, not cumulatively.

b. That each quarter is reported cumulatively.

P8-7

Smith and Quarter Ltd. experienced the following events during the first quarter of 2002:

1. The annual sales catalogue was developed and provided on-line, at a cost of $1,000,000.

2. Programming and consulting fees were incurred for annual updates of the Internet site, at a cost of $500,000.

3. Owing to a strike at the principal supplier's factory, Smith and Quarter's inventory fell to the lowest level in 14 years. Smith and Quarter uses the LIFO method for financial reporting.

4. A notice of assessed value for property taxes was received. The tax assessment will be received and be due in the second quarter. Taxes for 2002 are estimated at $400,000.

5. Smith and Quarter uses the declining-balance method for depreciation. The total depreciation for 2002 on assets held at the start of the year will be $1,600,000.

6. The company's top management receives annual bonuses based on 10% of annual net income after taxes.

Required:

For each event reported above, indicate what impact it would have on the first-quarter interim report under each approach to interim statements:

a. The integral or part-of-year approach.

b. The discrete or separate-period approach.

Foreign Currency
Transactions

Introduction

Many corporations engage in some form of international activity. The range of possible activities is vast. At one extreme is the company that has only an occasional transaction in a foreign currency. At the opposite extreme is the corporation with a network of foreign subsidiaries that operates on a global basis.

We find most Canadian companies between these two extremes. Transborder transactions are very common, accounting for about 40% of Canada's GDP. About 80% of those transactions are with the United States. Canadian companies that have a large volume of transactions in a foreign country may establish a subsidiary in that country. A smaller number of companies establish (or buy) manufacturing or direct service subsidiaries outside Canada. The Canadian population base and GDP are small, in world terms. Therefore, a Canadian company cannot become a significant international player until most of its activity is outside of Canada.

Canadian companies that have international operations may be Canadian home-grown companies, such as Bombardier Inc., Nortel Networks Corp., McCain Foods Ltd., or Magna International Inc. Other Canadian companies with extensive cross-border or international business may be Canadian subsidiaries of foreign parents. For example, three of the five largest corporations in Canada are the subsidiaries of U.S. automobile corporations.

Regardless of the home country of a Canadian corporation, the accounting issues are the same. Essentially, there are two major issues:

* Accounting for transactions (and balances) in foreign currencies

* Translating and consolidating foreign operations

This chapter will deal with the first of these problems, including the issue of exchange rate risk exposure and hedging. The following chapter, Chapter 10, will discuss the consolidation problems that arise when a domestic company has subsidiaries outside Canada.

Foreign Currency Transactions

Many companies conduct at least some of their business activities in countries other than that in which they are based. Whenever a Canadian corporation has transactions with principals in foreign countries, the corporation is engaged in **foreign transactions**. The transactions may be conducted in Canadian dollars. For example, Bombardier Inc. could sell subway cars to Mexico City at a price stated in Canadian dollars. If the price of a foreign transaction is stated or *denominated* in Canadian dollars, then no unusual accounting problems arise from the fact that the customer (or supplier) is in a foreign country.

However, it is quite common for a Canadian company to engage in foreign transactions that are denominated in a foreign currency. For example, a Canadian electronics manufacturer may buy all of its semiconductor chips from the United States at prices quoted in U.S. dollars. Or a carpet manufacturer who regularly sells its carpets in the United Kingdom may quote prices in pounds sterling.

A transaction is **denominated** in a foreign currency whenever the monetary value of an explicit or implicit contract between the two parties to the transaction is defined in terms of a currency other than the company's reporting currency. Transactions that are denominated in a foreign currency are called **foreign currency transactions**. Such transactions include borrowing and lending money, selling products at a price stated in a foreign currency, or purchasing goods from a supplier in another country.

It is not the national location of the other party to the transaction that makes it a foreign currency transaction—it is the type of currency in which the transaction takes place. Even a transaction between two Canadian corporations can be a foreign currency transaction. Some products are sold world-wide in U.S. dollars, especially commodities such as oil and gold and wheat. On the other hand, if a foreign supplier offers a product to a Canadian company and quotes the price in Canadian dollars, then the transaction is *not* a foreign currency transaction from the viewpoint of the buying company.

For example, suppose that CanCorp, a Canadian corporation, borrows one million dollars from a New York bank. CanCorp receives the loan in U.S. dollars and promises to repay the loan in U.S. dollars. CanCorp will have a liability of US$1,000,000. However, assuming that CanCorp prepares its financial statements in Canadian dollars, the balance sheet cannot show the one million dollars. The value of the loan must be converted into Canadian dollars before it can be reported on the company's balance sheet.

Another key factor is that the currency for the transaction is not the enterprise's *reporting currency*. Most Canadian corporations report in Canadian dollars, but some report in U.S. dollars because the bulk of their transactions are in that currency. In such cases, the Canadian dollar becomes the foreign currency for reporting purposes, because the Canadian dollar must be converted to U.S. dollars for financial reporting.

Whenever a Canadian company carries on business in a foreign currency, a problem arises from the fact that the company's accounting records and financial statements are in Canadian dollars (normally), while some of the transactions are in a foreign currency. To report the results of the transactions that were denominated in foreign currencies, we must translate these transactions or the results thereof into Canadian dollars.

Causes of exchange rate changes

Before launching into a discussion of accounting for foreign currencies, we will pause and consider briefly the reasons that exchange rates change. Near the end of World War II (i.e., in 1944), the world's major trading countries established fixed exchange rates among the major currencies. This was known as the Bretton Woods Agreement, named after the place where the international agreement was negotiated and signed. These fixed exchange rates were intended to facilitate international commerce by eliminating the exchange rate fluctuations that made international financial transactions so risky.

Fixed exchange rates remained in effect for over 25 years, but there was increasing strain on the system as national economies developed at different rates and in different ways. The fixed rate system did not permit natural economic adjustments in response to the flow of funds and balance of payments. Finally, in 1971, the Bretton Woods Agreement was abandoned and exchange rates were permitted to fluctuate freely in the economic marketplace.

Why do exchange rates fluctuate? Some short-run changes in exchange rates are the result of speculation in the money markets. Over the longer run, however, exchange rates are related to two economic phenomena: (1) differential inflation rates and (2) relative interest rates.

If Country A experiences inflation that is in excess of inflation in Country B, then the currency in Country A will decline in value relative to Country B's currency. The relative change in exchange rates will be approximately equal to the relative change in purchasing power of the currency; a fixed nominal amount of Country A's currency will buy less after a period of inflation than the equivalent nominal amount of Country B's currency, and therefore the relative values of the two currencies will be adjusted through the money markets to recognize the fact that Country A's currency will not buy as much any more. This is known as the **purchasing power parity (PPP)** concept.

An alternative concept for explaining changes in exchange rates is that changes in rates are a reflection of a difference in interest rates between countries; this is known as the **Fisher Effect**, after the eminent economist who developed the theory.

Inflation rates and interest rates are related. A country that has a higher inflation rate will have higher interest rates. Both differentials will have an impact on the exchange rate, and the net result will be a currency that declines in value relative to the currency of countries with lower inflation (and lower interest rates). It is difficult (and perhaps pointless, for accounting purposes) to unravel the impact of PPP and the Fisher Effect empirically.[1]

The consequence of the interaction of inflation, interest rates, and exchange rates has particular consequence for the translation of foreign operations, a topic that we will discuss extensively in the next chapter. The translation of foreign operations must be undertaken only in full recognition of the economic significance of the resultant translated amounts. Certain translation methods have the implicit effect of adjusting for relative inflation between the host country and the home country, while other methods disconnect the financing of foreign assets from the investment in the assets themselves. Either approach may be appropriate in particular circumstances, but the choice of translation method should be made with full awareness of the economic significance of the reported amounts and not be approached as a purely mechanical exercise.

Transactions and current balances

Transactions

Suppose that on December 5, 2001, Domestic Corporation sells 100 units of its product in Germany for one hundred thousand Euros, or €100,000. To record this sale on its books, Domestic Corporation must translate the sale into the equivalent amount in Canadian dollars. If we assume that the exchange rate on the date of sale was €1 = Cdn$1.25 (that is, that each Euro is worth $1.25, or

---

1. One empirical test, for example, found that purchasing power parity is the central tendency for exchange rate movements, although "there are significant deviations from PPP theory for some years. The theory's validity increases as the length of the period is increased." Robert Z. Aliber and Clyde P. Stickney, "Accounting Measures of Foreign Exchange Exposure: The Long and Short of It," *The Accounting Review* (January 1975), pp. 44–57.

that one dollar is worth €0.80), then the Canadian equivalent is $125,000. The sale can be recorded as follows, assuming that it was a sale on account:

Accounts receivable	125,000	
Sales		125,000

The amount of the sale in its Canadian equivalent will then be added to the other domestic and foreign sales without further difficulties.

If the German customer pays the amount owing on December 21, Domestic Corporation will receive €100,000. If the exchange rate is €1 = $1.27 on the payment date, Domestic will receive $127,000 when the Euros are converted to Canadian dollars. Domestic will debit cash for $127,000 and credit accounts receivable for $125,000. The $2,000 difference represents a gain that has been realized by Domestic because the value of the Euro went up while Domestic was holding a receivable that was denominated in Euros. If the exchange rate had gone down instead of up, Domestic would have realized a loss instead of a gain.

The gain on the exchange rate change could be treated in either of two ways: (1) by increasing the amount of revenue recognized by $2,000, or (2) by crediting a separate gain account. The difference may seem minor, since both treatments will result in an increase in net income in the same period. The alternative treatments can have a substantive impact, however, when a company buys inventory or capital assets in a foreign currency and the exchange rate changes between the date of purchase and the date of payment. Any exchange gain or loss realized by holding the liability could either be added to the cost of the assets acquired or be treated as a gain or loss of the period.

The first approach, to attach exchange gains and losses to the asset or the revenue that results from the initial transaction, is known as the **one-transaction theory** because the accrual and the cash settlement are viewed as a single economic event. The second approach is called the **two-transaction theory**; the accrual (i.e., the sale or purchase) is viewed as one economic event while the eventual cash settlement (collection of the receivable or payment of the liability) is treated as a separate financing activity. Under the two-transaction theory, exchange gains and losses normally flow through directly to the income statement in the period that they occur.

The two-transaction theory has been more widely adopted and is the one reflected in the recommendations in Section 1650 of the *CICA Handbook*. The financing component of a foreign currency transaction is separated from the purchase or sale itself because the cash flow is controlled by the domestic company, and the results of such essentially speculative activity should not be hidden in gross revenue or in the cost of assets. The financing component can be controlled because the company has options—purchases can be paid for by bank drafts at the time of the transaction; receivables can be sold to banks or finance companies, or can be financed by the sale of credit "paper" denominated in the same currency; the foreign currency denominated payable or receivable can be hedged (which is the subject of the second part of this chapter); and so forth.

Under the two-transaction approach, the collection by Domestic of the €100,000 receivable will be recorded as follows:

Cash (€100,000)	127,000	
Accounts receivable		125,000
Foreign currency exchange gain		2,000

Current monetary balances

Now assume instead that the receivable is not collected until January 25, 2002, and that the fiscal year of Domestic Corporation ends on December 31. The receivable was initially recorded on Domestic's books at $125,000, but actually the receivable is for €100,000. If the Euro is worth $1.28 on December 31, then the value of the €100,000 receivable is $128,000, a $3,000 gain over the original recorded amount of the transaction. The accounting problem then becomes whether or not to recognize the change in value of the foreign-currency-denominated monetary balance on the balance sheet and, if it is recognized on the balance sheet, then whether or not the gain should be taken into income.

The recognition issue arises whenever foreign transactions result in current *monetary* balances at the balance sheet date. **Monetary balances** are those that are fixed in a given amount of currency, such as receivables and payables. The alternatives are as follows:

1. Report the current monetary balance at the historical rate, with note disclosure of the effect of the changed exchange rate.

2. Report the current monetary balance at the current rate; treat the gain/loss as a deferred credit/debit on the balance sheet and defer recognition on the income statement until the amount is **settled** (that is, until the receivable or payable is paid).

3. Report the current monetary balance at the current rate, and include the gain or loss in income for the period.

In our example, the €100,000 sale resulted in an account receivable at the balance sheet date of $128,000 when translated at the current rate (that is, at the rate in effect at the balance sheet date). The impacts of applying each of the three alternatives listed above are illustrated in Exhibit 9-1, assuming that the receivable is settled on January 25, 2002, when the Euro is worth $1.275.

The first approach, that of simply leaving the receivable balance at the historical amount of $125,000, is certainly the easiest of the three alternatives.

EXHIBIT 9–1 ALTERNATIVE APPROACHES TO REPORTING EXCHANGE GAINS AND LOSSES

Years Ended December 31

	2001		2002
	Balance sheet	Income statement	Income statement
1. *Historical rate:*			
Receivable balance	$125,000 Dr		
Foreign currency gain			$2,500 Cr
2. *Current rate—deferred gain:*			
Receivable balance	$128,000 Dr		
Deferred foreign currency gain	$ 3,000 Cr		
Foreign currency gain			$2,500 Cr
3. *Current rate—current recognition:*			
Receivable balance	$128,000 Dr		
Foreign currency gain/loss		$3,000 Cr	$ 500 Dr

Proponents of this approach argue that since the amount has not yet been settled, it is premature to recognize any gain or loss. A gain recognized in the current year may well be offset in the following year if the exchange rate declines before the balance is paid. Since any gains or losses on current balances can be viewed as temporary, the balance should best be left at the exchange rate that was in effect at the date of the transaction, consistent with the historical cost concept. Of course, parenthetical or note disclosure can be made of the current rate equivalent at the balance sheet date.

Under the historical rate approach, the gain or loss will be recognized only when the transaction is settled and the gain or loss is realized:

December 5, 2001:

| **1a** Accounts receivable | 125,000 | |
| Sales | | 125,000 |

January 25, 2002:

1b Cash (€100,000 × $1.275)	127,500	
Accounts receivable		125,000
Exchange gains and losses		2,500

A lower-of-cost-or-market (LCM) approach can also be taken—recognize losses but defer gains.

Under the second alternative, the change in the Canadian dollar equivalent of the €100,000 balance is recognized by reporting the balance on the balance sheet as $128,000 rather than as $125,000. The $3,000 gain, however, is not recognized as a component of income in fiscal 2001, but is carried on the balance sheet as a *deferred credit* until the account is settled. The initial sale and the adjustment of the account at year-end would be:

December 5, 2001:

| **2a** Accounts receivable | 125,000 | |
| Sales | | 125,000 |

December 31, 2001:

| **2b** Accounts receivable | 3,000 | |
| Deferred foreign currency gain | | 3,000 |

If the balance is subsequently paid in January when the exchange rate is €1 = $1.275, the entry to record the receipt of the €100,000 will be as follows, assuming that the preceding entry has been recorded on Domestic's books and not just on the financial statement working papers:

2c Cash	127,500	
Deferred foreign currency gain	3,000	
Accounts receivable		128,000
Foreign currency gain		2,500

Under this approach, the net gain on the transaction is reflected in net income in the period in which the account is paid. Here too, a lower-of-cost-or-market rule could be applied, with gains deferred but losses recognized when they occur.

The third approach recognizes the change in the balance owing, but also recognizes the gain in the income statement. The adjusting entry will be:

December 5, 2001:

3a Accounts receivable   125,000

            Sales   125,000

3b Accounts receivable   3,000

            Foreign currency gain   3,000

If the account is subsequently settled when the Euro is worth $1.275, the entry to record the payment will be:

3c Cash   127,500

            Foreign currency loss   500

            Accounts receivable   128,000

Under this approach, the change in the current equivalent of the foreign currency balance is recognized in income in the period in which it occurs. Since $3,000 of the gain occurred in December, that gain is recognized in income in the income statement for the year ended December 31, 2001. After the fiscal year-end, the exchange rate declined slightly, and the resultant loss that occurred in January will be included in income for that period.

The proponents of the third alternative argue that it has two advantages over the other approaches:

1. It shows the account balances at the current Canadian-dollar equivalent of amounts legally owing (e.g., €100,000) at the balance sheet date.

2. It reflects in net income the impact of the economic events of the period—specifically, the impact on the reporting enterprise of changes in the exchange rates.

The third alternative is the one recommended in Section 1650 of the *CICA Handbook* [CICA 1650.18 and 1650.20], and therefore is widely used in practice.

Practical expedients

As a practical matter, companies that engage in a large volume of foreign currency transactions may not actually use the current rate for translating each transaction. If, for example, a company has thousands of sales transactions in U.S. dollars during a year, it is impractical to check on the current exchange rate (the *spot rate*) every time a sale occurs. Instead, the sales may be accumulated for a period of time and a single rate applied to the aggregate.

Alternatively, a company might use the rate at the beginning of each month for that month's transactions. Each of these approaches is an expedient for accounting for a large volume of transactions. Minor differences between the actual spot rate and the rate used for translation of the transactions will be adjusted for when the accounts are settled, or when the monetary account balances are adjusted to the current rate on the balance sheet date.

Some companies use a *pre-determined standard rate* for translating foreign currency transactions. If a company uses a profit-centre approach for evaluating its managers, it may be desirable to remove the effects of uncontrollable currency fluctuations from the profit centre's operating results so that the managers are not held accountable for factors beyond their control. The total amount of current monetary balances will then be adjusted to the current rate for external reporting.

Nonmonetary balances

The foregoing discussion has focused on the translation of current *monetary* balances. If the foreign currency transaction was not a sale but was, for example, a purchase of inventory, then the transaction will result in *two* balance sheet amounts—(1) an account payable and (2) inventory. The account payable is a monetary balance and will be treated exactly as the account receivable discussed above, assuming that the two-transaction approach is used.

The inventory, however, is a *nonmonetary balance*. A **nonmonetary balance** is, by definition, *not* an amount that is fixed in terms of a currency and does not represent a claim against monetary resources. Therefore, nonmonetary balances are not affected by changes in the exchange rate. If inventory is carried at historical cost, then the historical cost of inventory that was purchased with a foreign currency is simply the domestic currency equivalent of the foreign currency *at the date of the purchase*. Nonmonetary balances are carried at historical exchange rates because that is the historical cost.

An exception arises when a nonmonetary asset is reported on the balance sheet at current value rather than at historical cost. For example, suppose that Domestic Corporation purchased gold in U.S. dollars and that Domestic reports its gold inventory at current market value. If the current market value is quoted in U.S. dollars, it makes no sense to take a current value and translate it at a historical rate. In order to report the current value of the investment in Canadian dollars, the current value in U.S. dollars must be converted into Canadian dollars at the current exchange rate.

Long-term balances

The foregoing discussion dealt exclusively with current transactions and with current asset and current liability balances that arise from foreign currency transactions. Similar problems and alternatives also arise for long-term balances. If the long-term balances are *nonmonetary* assets carried at historical cost, then the carrying value is not adjusted for changes in the exchange rate. This treatment is exactly the same as that discussed above for historical-cost inventories. But if the balances are long-term monetary balances, then the accounting treatment might be different than that for short-term monetary balances.

The most common type of long-term foreign currency balance in Canada is undoubtedly long-term debt that has been raised outside of Canada, most commonly in the United States. Long-term monetary balances may also arise from activities such as long-term leasing, mortgage financing, or other long-term financing provided to a customer, client, or affiliate.

When long-term monetary balances are denominated in a foreign currency, the question again arises as to whether or not the balances should be shown on the balance sheet at the current exchange rate. And if the current rate is used, then what should be done with the gains or losses due to changes in the exchange rate?

The basic range of alternative treatments includes all of those cited above for short-term monetary balances, plus one additional possible treatment for the gain or loss. The added alternative is to record the translation gain (or loss) as a deferred credit (or deferred charge) and amortize it over the remaining life of the balance.

For example, assume that Domestic Corporation issues bonds in England on January 1, 2002, for one million pounds sterling (£1,000,000). On that date, the exchange rate was £1 = Cdn$1.80. Domestic Corporation therefore received $1,800,000 from the bond issue. The bonds will mature in five years, on January 1, 2007. At the fiscal year-end of December 31, 2002, the value of the

British pound has fallen to $1.75. The alternative valuations of the bonds payable are (1) at the historical rate of $1.80, or $1,800,000, or (2) at the current rate of $1.75, or $1,750,000 total. If the current rate is used, then there are three alternative treatments of the $50,000 gain:

1. Defer the gain until the bonds are retired and the gain is realized.

2. Recognize the gain immediately in income.

3. Defer the gain and amortize it over the five years until maturity (at $10,000 per year, if straight-line amortization is used), including the current year, 2002.

Defer until realized

Prior to the effective date of the current version of Section 1650 of the *CICA Handbook* (July 1983), the most common method of valuing long-term bonds in Canada was to leave the bonds at the historical rate, with note disclosure of either the amount at the current rate or the currency in which the debt must be paid, or both. Such disclosure then enabled users to make their own adjustments if they wished to do so.

The then-common treatment for bonds seems on the surface to be in conflict with the common treatment for short-term balances, which was to report them at current rates. The conflict is not so illogical as it may at first appear, however. Short-term monetary balances represent assets that will be realized or liabilities that will require payment in liquid assets within the next year. There is little doubt that settlement of the balances will directly affect the reporting company's financial position in the near future, and that exchange rate fluctuations are the real economic events that trigger the realization of gains and losses on short-term balances.

Exchange rate fluctuations that affect long-term balances, however, have a much more tenuous impact on the financial position of the company. Exchange gains or losses on long-term debt will not be realized for many years in the future, if at all. Since the amount of debt that is denominated in foreign currencies may be quite large, gains or losses arising from this debt can have a substantial impact on reported earnings. Domestic Corporation may recognize the $50,000 gain on its income statement in 2002, but if the pound strengthens in 2003, Domestic will then recognize a loss in 2003. Neither the gain in 2002 nor the loss in 2003 is realized, and neither may suggest what the value of the pound will be in 2007 when the bond issue matures.

Another reason for the popularity of the historical rate for long-term debt was that the debt might effectively never be repaid. If the corporate policy is to refinance the debt when it comes due, then it can be argued that no gain or loss is realized even at maturity because it is refinanced in replacement debt in the same foreign currency.

Finally, a third justification offered for the use of the historical rate was that, in some instances, the debt is used to finance nonmonetary assets in the foreign country in which the debt is issued. The assets will generate foreign currency revenue (through either use or sale) that will be available to service the debt.

For example, a Canadian company could buy a building in Chicago to use as a U.S. sales headquarters and finance the building by a mortgage from a Chicago bank. The mortgage will be denominated in U.S. dollars. When the company prepares its financial statements (in Canadian dollars), it will include the Chicago building at its historical cost, computed at the historical exchange rate.

If the mortgage on that building is translated at the current exchange rate, then the company will be recognizing a gain or loss on the debt without recognizing any change in the value of the building and without recognizing that the U.S.-dollar revenue that is being generated by the sales office will be used to pay the mortgage payments. Since a revenue stream in U.S. currency will be available through the use of the building to pay the U.S. debt, the company has no real exposure to exchange rate changes.[2] Thus it is argued that the related asset and liability should be reported in a similar manner—at the historical exchange rate.

Immediate recognition

The second alternative is to restate the long-term balances at the current exchange rate at the balance sheet date, and to report the change in the dollar-equivalent as a gain or loss for the period. This approach will result in a balance sheet that fully reflects the current value of long-term monetary balances in terms of the Canadian dollar.

Any gains or losses arising from translating the balances at the current rate are reported in the income statement because the change in the exchange rate is an economic event of the period. This year's change in rates is not related to future periods; the movement of the exchange rates in the future is dependent upon economic conditions in future periods. Therefore, deferral of all or part of the gains or losses to future periods can be viewed as inappropriate for both income measurement and balance sheet valuation.

A counter-argument is that gains or losses on the market value of long-term monetary balances are not ordinarily reported, even for domestic balances. If a company's bonds decline in price on the bond market, no gain is reported on the income statement unless the company actually buys back the bonds at a discount. If a change in exchange rates is viewed simply as an added component of market value, then consistency of treatment with domestic bonds would suggest that no gain or loss should be reported on foreign-currency-denominated bonds unless the company actually extinguishes or refinances the debt.

Defer and amortize

Canadian corporations incur an appreciable amount of their long-term debt in foreign currencies. Because of the size of the currency gains and losses that can arise from short-term changes in exchange rates, there was considerable resistance to the original intent of the AcSB to require current recognition of exchange gains and losses. As a result, the AcSB's recommendation in Section 1650 is that exchange gains and losses on long-term monetary items should be deferred and amortized over the remaining term to maturity (if any) of the receivable or obligation [CICA 1650.23].

Those public Canadian corporations that had substantial amounts of foreign-currency-denominated long-term debt outstanding welcomed this recommendation. Management believed that, over the life of the debt, losses in some years would offset gains in other years. As a result, the impact of exchange gains and losses on the income statement would be minimal.

Unfortunately, it isn't quite as simple as that. There are two factors that undermine the expectation that "it will all even out." One is that, on a year-by-year basis, exchange rates do not rise and fall so much as they tend to exhibit intermediate and long-term trends. The U.S. dollar has changed direction a couple of times, but it enjoyed a virtually continuous increase in value (relative to the

---

2. This is known as an *implicit hedge,* and will be discussed more fully later in this chapter.

Canadian dollar) from 1976 to 2000. As well, the Swiss franc and Japanese yen have shown almost continuous increases in value relative to the Canadian dollar over 40 years. When the exchange rate for a particular country's currency tends to go in one direction for several years rather than fluctuate, gains and losses do not cancel out over the long term.

The second factor that works against the expected smoothing effect of the defer-and-amortize approach is that each year's exchange gain or loss is amortized over a shorter period than that of the preceding year. In the last year that the debt is outstanding, the entire exchange gain or loss for that period must be recognized, *plus* proportionate amortization of all the preceding years' gains and losses. When the exchange rate has moved more or less continuously in the same direction, the effect of defer-and-amortize is to accentuate the income statement effect of the changes, rather than to ameliorate or smooth them.

The *CICA Handbook* recommends that the net unamortized balance of deferred exchange gains and losses "should be recorded as a deferred charge or as a deferred credit" [CICA 1650.25]. The reason for showing the deferred amounts apart from the liability balances to which they relate is that if the deferred amounts are added to or subtracted from the liability balance, the effect would be to restate the balance back to historical cost. Despite the *CICA Handbook* recommendation, some companies nevertheless do include the deferred gains and losses with long-term debt.

Impending changes

International accounting standards do not recognize the defer-and-amortize approach. IAS 21 says simply that "exchange differences ... should be recognized as income or as expenses in the period in which they arise" [IAS 21, ¶15].

Although the defer-and-amortize approach is the recommended Canadian approach at the time of writing this edition, the recommendation may be changed before long. In December 2000 the AcSB announced (on the CICA Web site) the issuance of an exposure draft in January 2001 to eliminate the defer-and-amortize method for unrealized translation gains and losses on noncurrent monetary assets and liabilities. The AcSB proposes that the new rules will take effect in 2002. This is the third attempt in ten years by the AcSB to eliminate defer-and-amortize. This attempt is likely to be successful!

The world is moving toward *mark-to-market* for reporting financial instruments. **Mark-to-market** means that financial instruments are reported on the balance sheet at their fair value at the balance sheet date. Foreign currency balances (and hedges of those balances, as we shall discuss later) will be reported at current exchange rates, and all gains and losses will flow through to net income.

While the AcSB had issued no proposals in this regard by the end of 2000, both the FASB and the IAS are already moving in that direction. The international accounting standard (IAS 39) requires fair value reporting for financial *assets*, but "fair valuation of liabilities is the subject of several studies currently being undertaken by the Joint Working Group," which includes Canada.[3]

---

3. IAS 39 (1998), paragraph 15.

Debt without fixed maturity

In order to defer and amortize exchange gains and losses over the remaining life of the long-term debt, the debt must have a specified (or ascertainable) maturity date. Sometimes, long-term debt has no such maturity date. The debt may be repayable at the option of the debtor or the creditor (with notice), or may be contingent upon some event or events that are written into the debt contract and that trigger a repayment clause.

Note that we are referring here to debt that is classifiable as *long-term*; a long-outstanding loan that is callable by the lender on short notice (e.g., operating loans extended by a bank that depend on the borrower's adherence to covenants) would be classified as a current liability and therefore is not included in our current discussion.

When debt that is properly classifiable as long-term debt has no fixed maturity, then there is no definite period over which to amortize the annual exchange gains and losses. These gains and losses therefore are recognized in income, just as are gains and losses on short-term monetary balances [CICA 1650.22], assuming that eventual repayment will be required.

Some corporations issue debt that never needs to be repaid. Such debt is referred to as **perpetual debt**; the option to call or retire lies exclusively with the borrower. An example of perpetual debt is the Air Canada $882 million in subordinated perpetual debt outstanding at the end of fiscal 1999. Air Canada has outstanding perpetual debt of 54 billion Japanese yen, 500 million Swiss francs, and 200 million deutsche marks. By issuing the bonds in foreign countries that have low levels of inflation, a favourable interest rate is obtained. Air Canada pays only 2.6% on its yen debt (which comprises about half of the total perpetual debt) and is paying an average of 5.7% on its Swiss franc and deutsche mark debt.

In substance, perpetual debt is the equivalent of preferred shares; it carries a fixed rate of return but is not redeemable by the holder. Perpetual debt is useful to corporations with limited access to new share equity financing. In addition, the interest is tax deductible, whereas preferred share dividends must be paid out of after-tax earnings.

Since perpetual debt has no maturity date, the effects of exchange rate changes will never be realized. Therefore, perpetual debt is reported on the balance sheet at its historical exchange rate. The Air Canada perpetual debt is carried at its historical book value of $882 million, even though the value in Canadian currency was $1,365 million at the year-end 1999 exchange rates.

Accounting for Hedges

Nature of hedging

When a company holds a receivable denominated in a foreign currency, there will be a loss if the foreign currency falls in value relative to the Canadian dollar. Conversely, a loss on a foreign-currency-denominated liability will occur if the foreign currency strengthens or increases in value relative to the Canadian dollar. To protect against foreign currency losses, companies frequently *hedge* their monetary foreign currency balances.

Hedging is the creation of an offsetting balance in the same foreign currency. If a company is holding a receivable of one million Japanese yen, the risk of gain or loss can be neutralized by incurring a liability of ¥1,000,000 for an equal term.

There are several ways of hedging. The most common is to enter into a *forward contract* with a bank or currency dealer. If a receivable is being hedged, then the company will contract to pay a bank an equivalent amount of foreign currency in exchange for Canadian dollars at a specified rate at a specified time in the future.

Some major currencies are also traded in a *futures* market. Futures markets for agricultural products are well known. Wheat, oats, and corn are traded on the commodities exchanges, as well as cattle, cotton, copper, coffee, orange juice, plywood, and heating oil. The commodity that is of immediate concern here is money. On the Chicago Mercantile Exchange, for example, one can buy a futures contract for Canadian dollars, U.S. dollars, Euros, British pounds, or Japanese yen, among others. Futures contracts are for standard terms (e.g., 30, 60, 90, and 180 days) and for limited denominations and currencies.

In this chapter, we focus on forward contracts rather than on futures contracts, since forward contracts are the most common form of hedge in Canada. Forward contracts are individually negotiated and thus can be tailored to suit the needs of the hedger in terms of currency type and contract duration.

Forward contracts and futures contracts are examples of *secondary* or *derivative instruments*. **Derivative instruments** are those that do not themselves represent financial contracts but that derive their value from transferring one or more of the financial risks inherent in an underlying primary financial instrument.

Another example of a derivative instrument is a **currency swap**, wherein corporations in two different countries agree to guarantee the payment of each other's interest and principal on foreign-currency-denominated long-term debt. A Canadian company with outstanding U.K. sterling debt may enter into a currency swap agreement with a U.K. company that has outstanding Canadian-dollar debt.[4] Each party to the agreement thereby converts its foreign currency exposure to a fixed domestic equivalent, effectively eliminating exchange rate risk.

For example, the 1999 Air Canada annual report discloses that only about 23% of the company's $3,296,000,000 total long-term debt is in Canadian dollars. The other 78% is in foreign currencies, including U.S. dollars, Swiss francs, deutsche marks, Japanese yen, U.K. sterling, and French francs. The company uses currency swaps as one of several types of hedges. The MD&A states that "longer term swap arrangements were in place effectively converting 250 million deutsche mark debt into Canadian dollar debt and 239 million Canadian dollar debt into Japanese yen debt." Why would a Canadian company convert Canadian-dollar debt into yen debt? Because "annual Japanese yen cash flow surpluses provide a natural hedge to fully cover yen interest and principal payments," according to the MD&A.

Other derivative instruments include *interest rate swaps* and *foreign currency options*. Air Canada uses all of these options for managing the risk on its long-term debt. A detailed examination of derivative instruments is beyond the scope of this book.[5] Our concern in this chapter is with forward contracts rather than with swaps and options.

---

4. In practice, swaps are usually more complicated than this example and may involve more than two companies. Swaps normally are arranged through financial intermediaries, usually banks.

5. For a good discussion of hedging through options, see "When Risk's Not an Option" by Paul Farrelly, *CA Magazine* (January 1990), pp. 30–37.

Hedge accounting recommendations—old versus proposed

The accounting for hedges is prescribed, in general terms, by Section 1650 of the *CICA Handbook*. The discussion below describes the AcSB's recommended policies as they exist at the time of writing this book. However, major changes are in the works.

We pointed out earlier that both the IAS and the FASB are moving towards fair valuation of long-term debt. Already, IAS 39 requires that financial assets be reported at fair values. **Financial assets** includes not only primary instruments such as accounts or notes receivable, but also secondary instruments such as the foreign currency receivables that are created as hedges of foreign currency liabilities. If the derivative instrument (i.e., a forward contract) is reported at market value while the offsetting primary instrument (i.e., the liability that has been hedged) is reported at historical book values, the gain or loss on the hedge will be recognized (even if it is deferred) while the offset loss or gain will not be recognized. Obviously, the reporting for financial assets and financial liabilities would be inherently inconsistent.

In December 2000, the Joint Working Group issued a draft standard on accounting for financial instruments. The draft standard proposed that the working group member countries adopt new reporting principles for financial instruments. The key proposals are:

- measurement of virtually all financial instruments at fair value (i.e., mark-to-market),

- recognition of all exchange gains and losses in the income statement in the period in which the changes in value occurred, and

- elimination of special accounting for hedges.

If and when the AcSB adapts Canadian standards to comply with these new recommendations, much of the following discussion on hedge accounting will become irrelevant. However, the timing of any change is uncertain. There will be great resistance to mark-to-market, except for those few Canadian companies that are listed in the U.S. or abroad and must follow either FASB standards or international standards. Switching from book values to market values for both primary financial instruments and their derivatives (e.g., forward contracts) will be a controversial step.

The move to fair valuation also is being strongly resisted by private companies because they do not have public investors who need information on risk exposure. Nevertheless, the AcSB is dedicated to the concept of international harmonization, which seems to be an irresistible force in Canadian accounting.

In the remainder of this chapter, we will base our discussion on the recommendations of Section 1650 of the *CICA Handbook*.

Hedging a monetary position

To illustrate the use of hedging, suppose that on October 20, 2000, Domestic Corporation sells some of its product in Germany for €100,000. At the date of the sale, the Euro is selling at a current or **spot rate** of $1.2717 in Canadian funds. As a result of the sale, Domestic has acquired a foreign currency monetary balance (account receivable) of $127,170. If Domestic wishes to protect itself against a possible exchange loss caused by a fall in the value of the Euro, Domestic can buy a forward contract for an equivalent amount of Euros. Assuming that the receivable will be collected in 90 days (on January 18, 2001), Domestic can buy a contract for the *payment* of €100,000 90 days hence. The commitment to pay €100,000 will offset the commitment to receive €100,000 from the German customer.

In October 2000, a 90-day forward contract for Euros is available for $1.2740. Domestic contracts to deliver or pay €100,000 in 90 days, and the contract will be for $127,400. The $230 difference between the current value of €100,000 ($127,170) and the price of the forward contract ($127,400) reflects the anticipated change in the exchange rate over the next month. In effect, Domestic is selling the Euros that it will receive from the German customer. But since Domestic will not receive the Euros for 90 days, the contract to deliver the Euros will not be executed until then.

As a result, Domestic will have a *receivable* (from the customer) that is denominated in Euros, but will also have a *payable* that is denominated in Euros. The Euro receivable and the Euro payable are due at the same time. The two financial instruments will fluctuate in tandem as the Euro exchange rate changes—a gain on one instrument will be exactly offset by a loss on the other.

The entries to record **(a)** the sale of the merchandise and **(b)** the sale of the Euros for delivery in the future will be as follows:

October 20, 2000:

1(a) Accounts receivable (€100,000)   127,170

   Sales   127,170

   [sale of merchandise for €100,000 on account]

1(b) Forward contract receivable (in Cdn $)   127,400

   Forward contract payable (€100,000)   127,400

   [purchase of a forward contract to deliver €100,000]

In the second entry, it appears that the receivable and the payable for the forward contract are offsetting. However, this is not really the case. The receivable is fixed in terms of Canadian dollars and represents the amount to be received by Domestic when Domestic delivers the Euros. The payable, on the other hand, is denominated in Euros; the actual dollar equivalent will change as the price of the Euro changes. Thus the receivable from the customer and the payable to the purchaser of the forward contract are both denominated in a foreign currency—Euros.

Assume that Domestic's fiscal year ends on January 31. On January 18, 2001, the customer pays €100,000 to Domestic, and Domestic delivers the Euros in execution of the forward contract. Also assume that the spot rate for the Euro is $1.2500 on the settlement date. The receipt of the €100,000 from the customer will be recorded as follows:

January 18, 2001:

1(c) Cash (€100,000 @ 1.2500)   125,000

   Exchange gains and losses   2,170

      Accounts receivable (€100,000 @ 1.2717)   127,170

   [receipt of €100,000 from customer, on account]

There is a loss of $2,170 due to the fact that the exchange rate fell during the 90-day period.

To execute the forward contract that is now due, Domestic will **(d)** deliver €100,000 and **(e)** receive the contracted amount of $127,400 in return. The entries to record this transaction will appear as follows:

January 18, 2001:

1(d) Cash	127,400	
Forward contract receivable (in Cdn$)		127,400
[receipt of cash from the buyer of the forward contract]		

1(e) Forward contract payable	127,400	
Exchange gains and losses		2,400
Cash (€100,000 @ 1.2500)		125,000
[payment of €100,000 to fulfil the forward contract obligation]		

Domestic recognizes a *loss* of $2,170 on the receivable and *gain* of $2,400 on the forward contract. The net amount is a gain of $230. The existence of this net gain may suggest that the forward contract was not completely successful at eliminating risk, but that is not the case. The $230 gain is the difference between the spot rate on the date of the original sale and the forward rate, multiplied by the amount of the foreign currency balance being hedged: €100,000 × ($1.2717 − $1.2740).

What the hedge really does is limit any possible gain or loss to a known amount, the spread between the spot rate and the forward rate. The same net gain will exist in our example regardless of the actual exchange rate at the settlement date.

For example, suppose that instead of a rate of $1.2500, the actual spot rate on the settlement date was $1.2850. The three entries to record the receipt from the customer and the settlement of the forward contract will then be as follows:

1(c2) Cash (€100,000 @ 1.2850)	128,500	
Accounts receivable		127,170
Exchange gains and losses		1,330
[receipt of €100,000 from customer, on account]		

1(d2) Cash	127,400	
Forward contract receivable (in Cdn$)		127,400
[receipt of cash from the buyer of the forward contract]		

1(e2) Forward contract payable	127,400	
Exchange gains and losses	1,100	
Cash (€100,000 @ 1.2850)		128,500
[payment of €100,000 to fulfil the forward contract obligation]		

Settlement of **1(c2)** the customer receivable and **1(e2)** the forward contract results in a gain of $1,330 and a loss of $1,100 respectively, for a net gain of $230, exactly as when the spot rate was $1.2500.

In the example that we have used above, the forward rate happened to be higher than the spot rate, resulting in a net gain. Forward rates may be either higher or lower than the spot rate. The spread between the spot rates depends on

(1) the interest rate differential between the two countries and (2) how the market predicts the rate will move.

The spot and forward rates for four major currencies on October 20, 2000 are shown in Exhibit 9-2. The forward rates for the Euro and the Japanese yen were both higher than the spot rates and rose as the term rose. The forward rates for the U.S. dollar and the British pound sterling, in contrast, were lower than the spot rate and declined throughout the 12 months.

A three-month hedge of a receivable denominated in pounds at the above rates will lock the hedger into a *loss*, since the forward rate for the pound is less than the spot rate. But the loss would be quite minor in comparison to the potential loss from an unprotected position. The day-to-day change in the spot rate can easily be larger than the spread between the spot and forward rates quoted above. Thus the small certain loss can be viewed as the cost of insurance against a possibly substantial speculative loss. Of course, hedging also eliminates the possibility of realizing a gain as well.

When the forward rate is higher than the spot rate, the contract has a **premium**. When the forward rate is less, then a **discount** exists. If the hedge is of a foreign currency *receivable*, as above, a premium results in a gain while a discount results in a loss.

Conversely, if the hedge is of a foreign currency *liability*, a premium results in a loss while a discount causes a gain. The following table summarizes this relationship:

	Net result if a forward contract is priced at a:	
Item being hedged	**Premium**	**Discount**
Monetary assets	gain	loss
Monetary liability	loss	gain

Alternative recording methods

In the example above, the forward contract was recorded by means of a journal entry that assigned equal values to the receivable and the payable. In addition to this first method of recording, there are two other methods of recording the hedge that yield the same result and that may be more appropriate if the transaction spans a year-end.

EXHIBIT 9–2 FOREIGN CURRENCY RATES

October 20, 2000
(in Canadian-dollar equivalents)

	U.S. dollar	British pound	Euro	Japanese yen
Spot rate	1.5129	2.1866	1.2717	0.013870
1 month forward	1.5118	2.1862	1.2726	0.013935
3 months forward	1.5108	2.1860	1.2740	0.014058
6 months forward	1.5095	2.1855	1.2758	0.014242
12 months forward	1.5065	2.1834	1.2790	0.014616

Source: The Globe and Mail, October 21, 2000. The reported data were prepared by BMO Nesbitt Burns, Capital Markets.

The first alternative (which we will refer to as the *second method*) is to record the receivable at the Canadian dollar value that is established by the forward contract at $1.2740. The liability is recorded at the Euro spot rate of $1.2717, which is the amount of the hedge—that is, the amount of the receivable as recorded at the date-of-sale spot rate. The difference between the receivable of $127,400 and the payable of $127,170 is the premium on the forward contract. Since the premium will not be realized until the settlement date, it should be treated as a deferred gain. Under this approach, the initial entry to record the purchase of the forward contract will be as follows:

October 20, 2000:

2(b)	Forward contract receivable (€100,000 × 1.2740)	127,400	
	Forward contract payable		127,170
	Deferred exchange gains/losses		230
	[purchase of forward contract]		

When the account receivable is collected and the forward contract is settled, the entries will appear as follows (assuming a spot rate at settlement date of $1.25):

January 18, 2001:

2(c)	Cash (€100,000 × $1.25)	125,000	
	Exchange gains and losses	2,170	
	Accounts receivable		127,170
	[receipt of €100,000 cash from the customer @ $1.25]		
2(d)	Cash	127,400	
	Forward contract receivable		127,400
	[receipt of payment on forward contract, as established in Cdn $]		
2(e)	Forward contract payable	127,170	
	Deferred exchange gain	230	
	Exchange gains and losses		2,400
	Cash (€100,000 @ $1.25)		125,000
	[payment of obligation of €100,000 on forward contract]		

The net result will be the same as in the earlier example, a net exchange gain of $230.

Recording the premium or discount on the forward contract at the date of entering into it may seem to complicate the recording of the transaction. However, the purpose is to identify the gain or loss in order to facilitate its appropriate treatment between the contract date and the settlement date. As is discussed in the next two sections, the premium or discount is not always recognized solely at the settlement date. When the contract spans two fiscal periods, part of the premium or discount is recognized in the income statement or as part of the cost of an asset at the end of the reporting period.

The second alternative (i.e., the *third method*) of handling the forward contract on the books is to not record it formally at all until the settlement date. A forward contract is, by its very nature, an *executory contract*. An **executory contract** is a contract that represents an agreement by two parties to perform in the future. For accounting purposes, no liability or receivable is normally deemed to exist for an executory contract until one of the parties has actually performed, or *executed* the contract. Under a forward contract, neither party will perform until the settlement date, and thus no accounting recognition is necessary for the contract. The liability and the receivable relating to the contract will not be recorded, and on the settlement date, the net gain or loss will flow out of the cash transactions:

January 18, 2001:

3(c)	Cash (€100,000 @ $1.25)	125,000	
	Exchange gains and losses	2,170	
	Accounts receivable (book balance)		127,170
	[receipt of €100,000 from customer, on account]		
3(d)	Cash (Cdn. dollar forward contract receivable)	127,400	
	Exchange gains and losses		2,400
	Cash (€100,000 forward contract payable)		125,000
	[settlement of forward contract @ $1.25 spot rate]		

The disadvantage of this approach is that since the premium or discount has not been explicitly recognized on the books (as it is under the second method), it is easy to overlook when adjustments are made at year-end.

The three approaches to recording the forward contract are shown in a comparative format in Exhibit 9-3. Note that the two entries for the sale and the collection of the receivable from the customer are identical under all three methods. The accounting for the hedge does not affect the accounting for the primary transactions.

Since a forward contract is an executory contract, the forward contract receivable and payable will not be shown on the balance sheet under the recommendations of Section 1650. This is true even if the forward contract has been recognized in the accounts by the second recording method. If the end of an accounting period occurs between the time that the contract is entered into and the settlement date, the receivable and the payable (and the related premium or discount) will be offset against each other, and any remaining balance is treated as a deferred debit or deferred credit on the balance sheet.

Of course, if and when Section 1650 is changed or is overridden by new mark-to-market requirements for all financial instruments, the value of both sides of a foreign contract *will* be reported on the balance sheet, regardless of the recording method used. At the time of writing, however, the value of derivative instruments must only be *disclosed*, but not included on the face of the balance sheet.

The third method, of treating the forward contract as an executory contract and thus not formally recording it, is the most common in practice. Therefore, we will restrict our subsequent discussion to this method alone.

The previous paragraphs described the accounting for an *asset* exposure. In that case, a monetary asset that already exists is being hedged. Similar treatment is given to a monetary *liability*, such as an account payable that is denominated in a foreign currency. However, the corporation will then be buying a contract to *receive* a foreign currency instead of to deliver a foreign currency. A forward contract to receive creates a foreign-currency-denominated receivable that offsets the risk inherent in the foreign-currency-denominated liability.

EXHIBIT 9–3 ALTERNATIVE RECORDING METHODS FOR HEDGING CONTRACTS

(Assuming January 31 fiscal year-end)

	Method 1*		Method 2*		Method 3*	
October 20, 2000:						
a Accounts receivable	127,170		127,170		127,170	
Sales		127,170		127,170		127,170
b Forward contract receivable	127,400		127,400			
Forward contract payable		127,400		127,170		
Deferred exchange gains/losses				230		
January 18, 2001						
c Cash	125,000		125,000		125,000	
Exchange gains and losses	2,170		2,170		2,170	
Accounts receivable		127,170		127,170		127,170
d Cash (Canadian dollar contract)	127,400		127,400		127,400	
Exchange gains and losses						2,400
Forward contract receivable		127,400		127,400		
Cash (€100,000)						125,000
e Forward contract payable (as recorded)	127,400		127,170			
Deferred exchange gains/losses			230			
Exchange gains and losses		2,400		2,400		
Cash (€100,000)		125,000		125,000		

* Methods:

1. Recording forward contracts at contract and spot rates, with no deferral of premium or discount.

2. Recording forward contracts at contract rates, with recognition of future (deferred) premium or discount.

3. No recording of forward contract until settlement.

Intervening year-end

The foregoing illustration dealt with the simplest situation, in which all of the related events occurred within the same accounting period. A slight complication arises when financial statements must be prepared after the forward contract is entered into but before the settlement date. The complication involves the disposition of the premium or discount.

The premium or discount represents the only gain or loss that arises on a hedged monetary position. In the previous example, the gain of $230 was recognized only on the settlement date. However, if the contract is outstanding for more than one accounting period, in which period should the gain or loss be recognized?

Since the premium or discount is the benefit or cost of limiting the risk exposure of the company over the period of time in which the monetary asset or liability being hedged is outstanding, the premium or discount is allocated over all the periods affected. In addition, we must report the account receivable in Canadian dollars at the spot rate equivalent as of the balance sheet date.

To illustrate, we can slightly modify the previous example by assuming that Domestic's fiscal year ends on December 31 instead of January 31. There will be a financial statement reporting date between the October 20 sale and the

January 18 settlement date. Assume also that the spot rate for the Euro on December 31 is $1.2600.

If the receivable were *not* hedged, the entries relating to **(a)** the sale at a rate of $127,170, **(b)** the year-end adjustment of the account receivable balance to $126,000 at the December 31 spot rate of $1.2600, and **(c)** the settlement at $1.2500 would be as follows:

October 20, 2000:

(a) Account receivable (€100,000 @ 1.2717)   127,170

      Sales   127,170

    [sale for €100,000 when the spot rate = $1.2717]

December 31, 2000:

(b) Exchange gains and losses   1,170

      Account receivable   1,170

    [reduce receivable to year-end spot rate: €100,000 × ($1.2600 − $1.2717)]

January 18, 2001:

(c) Cash (€100,000 @ 1.2500)   125,000

    Exchange gains and losses   1,000

      Account receivable   126,000

    [receipt of cash to settle the €100,000 receivable at the January 18 spot rate of $1.25]

In the absence of a hedge, the exchange gain/loss is recognized in the period in which it occurred. Of the total $2,170 exchange loss, $1,170 occurred in 2000 and $1,000 occurred in 2001.

If the receivable is hedged, however, no gain/loss is recognized because it will be offset by a loss/gain on the forward contract liability on the settlement date. Since the receivable balance must be adjusted to the current rate on the balance sheet date (December 31), any gain or loss on exchange rate changes is deferred.

When the receivable is hedged, the year-end adjustment to the customer receivable is as follows:

December 31, 2000:

    Deferred exchange gains and losses   1,170

      Account receivable   1,170

    [reduce receivable to year-end spot rate: €100,000 × ($1.2600 − $1.2717)]

In addition, a proportionate part of the premium will be recognized as a benefit for the year ended December 31, 2000. The elapsed time between the sale (and hedge) and the end of the fiscal year is 72 days. Therefore, 72/90ths of the premium is allocated to 2000:

December 31, 2000:

    Unrealized forward premium   184

      Exchange gains and losses   184

    [premium recognized = $230 × 72/90 days = $184]

When the customer's account is settled, the entry to record the receipt of €100,000 (at the January spot rate of $1.2500) will be:

January 18, 2001:

Cash (€100,000 × $1.25)	125,000	
Exchange gains or losses	2,170	
Account receivable		126,000
Deferred exchange gain		1,170

The settlement of the forward contract will be recorded as follows:

January 18, 2001:

Cash	127,400	
Exchange gains and losses		2,216
Unrealized forward premium		184
Cash (€100,000 × $1.25)		125,000

The exchange loss of $2,170 recognized from settlement of the customer's account is offset against the $2,216 exchange gain from settlement of the forward contract. The net result is a gain of $46, the remaining 18/90ths of the discount that is allocable to 2001. Instead of using an unrealized forward discount account, the premium amortization could simply be charged or credited to the deferred exchange loss account.

The premium or discount on a forward contract is allocated to the periods during which the contract is outstanding because the cost of the contract is thereby assigned to the periods that receive the benefit of the protection.

Hedging a commitment

So far, we have discussed the accounting and reporting only for hedges of monetary assets and liabilities. These are receivables or payables that appear on the books of the company as the result of transactions that have already occurred. However, companies frequently have *commitments* to buy or to sell goods or services.

Commitments do not immediately result in any receivables or liabilities being recorded on the company's books because the commitments are executory contracts that have not yet been performed by either party. Nevertheless, the risk exposure to foreign currency exchange rate fluctuations begins with the commitment and not with the formal recording of a transaction in the accounts. To offset the risk that is inherent in a contract commitment, companies often hedge the commitment. The terms of the hedge establish the cost of the goods or services. The *CICA Handbook* recommends that "when a purchase or sale of goods or services in a foreign currency is hedged before the transaction, the Canadian dollar price of such goods or services is *established by the terms of the hedge*" [CICA 1650.52, emphasis added].

For example, assume that Domestic Corporation issues a purchase order to Français Ltée. on October 31, 2001, to purchase a machine for 200,000 Euros. The machine is delivered on November 30, and payment is made on January 31, 2002. Domestic has a December 31 fiscal year-end.

Domestic Corp. finalized the decision to purchase the machine on October 31, based on the Canadian-dollar equivalent cost of the machine at that time. If the Euro appreciates significantly in value between October 31 and the payment date, Domestic will incur substantial additional cost for the machine. Therefore, it is common for a purchaser to hedge a commitment as soon as the purchase contract is signed and the foreign-currency cost of the asset or service is established. Of course, Domestic will not recognize a liability on the balance sheet until the machine has been delivered.

Suppose that on October 31, 2001, the spot rate for the Euro is €1 = Cdn$1.25. The €200,000 initial commitment is equivalent to Cdn$250,000. Domestic Corp. hedges its Euro commitment by entering into a forward contract to *receive* €200,000 on January 31, 2002. Assume that the three-month forward rate for the Euro is $1.22 on October 31. The cost of the machine is established at the forward rate: €200,000 × $1.22 = $244,000.

By November 30, 2001, the spot rate declines to $1.24 per Euro. On that date, the machine is delivered and the monetary liability is recorded at $248,000 (€200,000 × $1.24). The cost of the machine is recorded at the forward rate of $1.22. The difference between the liability and the asset cost is the discount on the forward contract. At the settlement date, whatever gain or loss arises *since the date of the commitment* on the liability to Français Ltée. will be offset by an equal loss or gain on the forward contract. Therefore, *the value of the forward contract establishes the cost of the machine.*

Using the more common *executory contract method* of accounting for the hedge (i.e., the third method presented in Exhibit 9-3), the hedge itself is not explicitly recognized in the accounts. The entry to record the liability is:

November 30, 2001:

Machinery (€200,000 × $1.22)	244,000	
Deferred foreign exchange gains and		
losses [€200,000 × ($1.24 – $1.22)]	**4,000**	
Accounts payable (€200,000 × $1.24)		248,000

The discount reduces the cost of the machine. However, in order to balance the entry, we must temporarily charge the discount to a deferral account (which we have highlighted in colour in this series of entries). This deferral will be eliminated at settlement date, as we shall illustrate shortly.

On December 31, 2001, the liability must be adjusted to the year-end spot rate for balance sheet purposes. If we assume that the year-end spot rate is $1.20, the adjustment is as follows:

December 31, 2001:

Accounts payable [€200,000 × ($1.24 – $1.20)]	8,000	
Deferred foreign exchange gains and losses		**8,000**

The gain arising from the decrease in the exchange rate from $1.24 to $1.20 will be offset against a corresponding loss on the forward contract. Therefore, the loss is deferred until the settlement date by crediting the amount of the adjustment to a deferred exchange gains and losses account.

On January 31, 2002, Domestic pays €200,000 to Franççais Ltée. when the spot rate is $1.26. Simultaneously, the forward contract is settled. The two entries to record these events are as follows:

January 31, 2002:

Accounts payable (€200,000 × $1.20)	240,000	
Deferred foreign exchange gains and losses	**12,000**	
Cash (€200,000 × $1.26)		252,000
[payment of €200,000 to the supplier]		

Cash (€200,000 × $1.26)	252,000	
Cash (Cdn. dollar forward contract liability)		244,000
Deferred foreign exchange gains and losses		**8,000**

[settlement of forward contract]

The debit to accounts payable is for the balance in that account as adjusted to the spot rate on the last balance sheet date, December 31, 2001. In both entries, the foreign currency amount of €200,000 is translated at the January 31 spot rate of $1.26. The credit to cash in the second entry is for the Canadian dollar liability that was established by the forward contract, at the forward rate of $1.22.

After the transaction is complete, the foreign currency gains and losses all cancel out:

- A deferred *debit* of $4,000 (relating to the discount on the forward contract) is recorded when the machine is received and the initial supplier liability is recognized.

- A deferred *credit* of $8,000 is recorded when the account payable is adjusted to the year-end spot rate on December 31, 2001.

- Payment of the Euro-denominated account payable results in an additional *debit* of $12,000.

- Settlement of the forward contract establishes a *credit* of $8,000.

In total, the deferred exchange gains and losses account has $16,000 in debits and $16,000 in credits—the foreign exchange gains and losses successfully balance out, and the discount is reflected in the capitalized cost of the asset.

This example illustrated the purchase of an asset. The same principles apply if the purchase is of services rather than of an asset.

If the company were *selling* assets or services priced in a foreign currency, the same procedures also would apply, except that the recognized monetary item would be a receivable instead of a payable; any discount or premium on the forward contract would be reflected in sales revenue.

Implicit hedges

Explicit hedges, as discussed above, occur when a monetary balance is deliberately created in order to offset a contrary monetary balance arising from real business transactions. Implicit hedges, however, may arise when foreign currency monetary balances (usually liabilities) are incurred to finance assets or revenue-generating activities in a foreign country.

Earlier in this chapter, we cited an example of a company that borrowed in U.S. dollars to finance acquisition of a building in Chicago to serve as a U.S. sales office. Similarly, a company might borrow U.S. dollars as secondary financing for receivables that are denominated in U.S. dollars. In both cases, an *implicit* hedge arises because an offsetting asset/liability position is created as the result of business transactions rather than for the sole (or *explicit*) purpose of creating a hedge.

In the first example, the implicit hedge is a nonmonetary asset that may effectively hedge a monetary liability exposure. In the second example, a monetary liability arises that effectively hedges a monetary asset position. The exposure is always a monetary balance, but the implicit hedge could be either monetary or nonmonetary.

When the implicit hedge is by a monetary balance, each year's foreign exchange gains and losses for both the asset and liability balances are offset against each other and are deferred until settlement, regardless of whether the balances are short term or long term [CICA 1650.54(a)].

When a liability balance is implicitly hedged by a nonmonetary asset, it probably is not the asset itself that provides the hedge; the real hedge usually is the *net revenue stream* generated by the asset. Under such circumstances, exchange gains/losses on the liability are deferred until maturity of the debt (which may be in instalments, as with a term loan or mortgage). Any exchange losses or gains arising from the foreign currency revenue stream will also be deferred and offset against the deferred gains/losses on the liability balance [CICA 1650.53].

While the concept of designating a nonmonetary asset (or the revenue stream therefrom) as an implicit hedge is intuitively appealing, it gives rise to unresolved difficulties in execution. It is unlikely that a nonmonetary asset would be sold at the same time that a long-term liability balance is paid, and therefore there would be no gain/loss on the nonmonetary asset to offset the deferred exchange rate loss/gain on the liability. The accumulated deferral will therefore have to be written off somehow when the debt is settled, either to income or to the carrying value of the asset. The *CICA Handbook* provides no guidance. Two eminent Canadian professional accountants summarize the use of nonmonetary assets as hedges as follows:

> The logic of all this is not supportable. The CICA recommendation overlooks the essential nature of a hedging instrument, namely that its value can be *relied upon* to fluctuate proportionate to changes in the foreign exchange rate. That simply cannot be said about a piece of real estate, or any other nonmonetary assets.[6]

When the designated hedge is a revenue stream, the *CICA Handbook* recommends that each year's revenue be "translated at the exchange rate in effect when the revenue stream is identified as a hedge" [CICA 1650.53]. The difference between the historical rate at which revenues are translated and the current rate at which the concomitant cash and receivables are translated would be offset against the exchange gains/losses on the balance being hedged.

The side effect of such a procedure is to distort current revenues; the effect is at least as great and certainly more obscure than simply crediting or charging the annual gain or loss on the foreign currency balance directly to income each year. In addition, the *CICA Handbook* recommendation implies that long-term debt is serviced by a revenue stream, rather than by *net* revenue or by net cash flow from operations.

These difficulties in actually accounting for implicit hedges in a logical manner have led to the conclusion that:

> All in all..., it is strongly arguable that leaving the accounting alone would provide a more faithful representation of what is actually occurring. The fact of the matter is that revenue in any year ought to be translated at the exchange rate in effect in that year, not a rate in effect some time earlier. The gain or loss on exchange rate movements occurs when the rate changes, not some years later when cash is collected to pay off the changed liability.[7]

These difficulties have not prevented Canadian companies from designating either nonmonetary assets or revenue streams as implicit hedges. What compa-

6. Ross M. Skinner and J. Alex Milburn, *Accounting Standards in Evolution, Second Edition* (Toronto: Pearson Education Canada, Inc., 2001), p. 457. Chapter 21 of this book contains an excellent discussion of the alternatives in accounting for foreign currencies and hedges.

7. *Ibid.*, p. 459.

nies appear to be doing is simply deferring exchange gains and losses on implicitly hedged liabilities until settlement and then rolling the accumulated deferral into a gain or loss on retirement.

The whole problem of accounting for designated hedges arose because Section 1650 recommends that long-term monetary balances be reported at current exchange rates. The problem did not arise when companies were permitted to report long-term liabilities at historical exchange rates. The irony in the present situation is that many companies, by (1) designating a hedge, (2) deferring the exchange gains/losses on the liability, (3) adding/subtracting the deferred amounts to/from the liability balance, and (4) recognizing the deferred amounts at settlement, are accomplishing a reporting result that is exactly the same as if the liability were reported at the historical exchange rate in the first place!

The IASC limits the use of nonmonetary assets as implicit hedges and does not recognize foreign currency revenue streams as hedges. The IASC Board has indicated that:

> A foreign currency liability should be accounted for as a hedge of a non-monetary asset [or vice-versa] in only very limited circumstances. The Board agreed that this objective can be achieved only if it is probable that the asset will be converted into the necessary foreign currency funds at the date of settlement of the liability. The Board rejected an approach based on the asset generating sufficient cash flows to service and settle the liability.[8]

Generally, the IASC permits designation of a hedge only if "the hedge is expected to be highly effective" [IAS 39, ¶142(b)]. The IASC views a hedge as being *highly effective* only if:

> ... at inception and throughout the life of the hedge, the enterprise can expect changes in the fair value or cash flows of the hedged item to be almost fully offset by the changes in the fair value or cash flows of the hedged instruction. [IAS 39, ¶146]

IAS 39 sets the range of "almost fully offset" to be satisfied if the change in the value of the hedge is not less than 80% nor more than 125% of the change in the value of the hedged item.

Imperfect hedges

In the preceding discussions, we have made some implicit simplifying assumptions. In all examples, we have assumed that a *perfect hedge* is possible. A **perfect hedge** is a hedge that is:

- of the exact amount of exposure,

- for the exact period of exposure,

- in the currency of exposure.

In practice, hedges do not always work out so neatly.

A practical problem for companies that engage in a large volume of foreign transactions (usually sales or purchases of inventory) is that hedging each individual transaction is too cumbersome. Instead, a company may attempt to hedge the net *balance* of its exposure by hedging the balance monthly.

---

8. *IASC Update*, December 1992, p. 2.

Since the hedges are not related to specific transactions, the gains and losses arising from the forward contracts cannot be directly matched to, and offset against, gains and losses arising from the settlement of foreign currency receivables and payables. Instead, all gains and losses tend to be recognized in income when they occur, with only approximate matching.

Hedging may also be sub-optimal for a corporation as a whole, but optimality may not be achievable. Companies with many operating divisions or subsidiaries—either in one country or in many countries—may not be able to assess their exposure to exchange rate fluctuations for the enterprise as a whole. As a result, foreign currency risk management is left to the discretion of the managers of the individual operating companies or divisions.

For example, an asset exposure in one operating division may be offset by a liability exposure in another division. Each division may hedge, which will be effective but will increase transactions costs unnecessarily. On the other hand, one division may hedge while the other does not, thereby effectively *increasing* the currency risk exposure for the corporation as a whole.

When locally effective hedges become ineffective or dysfunctional for the company as a whole, one can argue that they should not be accounted for as hedges but instead all exchange gains and losses should be taken into income in the period they occur. However, a company's reporting should reflect the management style of the enterprise, and local hedges should be reported as such even if they are ultimately ineffective.

Summary of Key Points

1. Exchange rates change for several reasons. Some changes, especially short-term fluctuations, are the result of the speculative activities of money market traders. The more fundamental causes for changes in exchange rates are (1) differential inflation rates between countries and (2) differences in interest rates. Differential inflation rates cause exchange rates to change to compensate for the changing purchasing power between currencies. Exchange rates also change in response to investment opportunities that are caused by international interest rate differentials.

2. Many, if not most, Canadian corporations engage in international activities to some extent. Foreign currency transactions are very common; the value of the transaction is fixed in a currency other than the enterprise's reporting currency. Foreign currency transactions must be recorded on the corporation's books at their equivalent in Canadian dollars at the time of the transaction. For revenues, expenses, and nonmonetary balances, the amounts that are established by the initial transaction are not changed at subsequent reporting dates.

3. Monetary balances arising from foreign currency transactions must be translated at the spot rate at the balance sheet date. Current monetary balances are reported at their Canadian dollar equivalent at the balance sheet date. If there has been a change in the exchange rate during the period of time between the creation of the balance (by a transaction) and the balance sheet date, the exchange gain or loss is recognized in income in the period in which it arose.

   For exchange gains and losses on long-term debt of fixed maturity, Canadian GAAP uses a unique approach: each year's gain or loss is deferred and amortized over the years until maturity, including the current year. In contrast, international standards (and U.S. standards) require that each year's exchange gain or loss be recognized immediately in income.

4. Monetary balances may be hedged. Hedging protects the enterprise from unexpected changes in exchange rates. If a current monetary balance is hedged, any exchange gain or loss is deferred until settlement of the hedge; any gain/loss from the outstanding balance will be offset by a corresponding loss/gain from the hedge. The premium or discount on the hedge is allocated to the periods during which the hedge is in effect.

Long-term monetary balances can be hedged by means of a series of successive shorter-term forward contracts or by derivative instruments such as currency swaps. The gains and losses on these contracts and swaps, along with the gains and losses on the monetary balances, should be deferred until either termination of the hedge or payment of the balance. Any premium or discount on forward contracts is allocated to the accounting periods during which the hedge is outstanding.

5. When a commitment is made to acquire nonmonetary assets and the commitment is hedged, the historical cost of the asset is determined by the terms of the hedge. The premium or discount on the hedge is included in the asset cost.

6. Long-term monetary liabilities may be hedged by nonmonetary foreign assets or by net revenue flows. Such hedges are called implicit hedges because there is no explicit contract providing for a hedge. When there is an implicit hedge, the reporting enterprise defers recognition of any exchange gains and losses on the monetary balance until realization because the nonmonetary asset is assumed to generate the foreign currency cash flows that will be used to retire the debt. Gains and losses on the cash flows are presumed to offset losses and gains on the debt.

7. Companies with a large volume of foreign currency transactions may not attempt to achieve perfect hedges. A perfect hedge is one in which the hedging currency, the term of the contract, and the amount of the exposure are all exactly the same as for the primary financial instrument. Instead, companies may manage their foreign currency exposure on a broader scale, either within operating divisions or for the company as a whole. Month-end balances may be hedged instead of individual receivables and payables, and individual operating units may conduct their own hedging operations that may not be optimal for the enterprise as a whole.

Weblinks

McCain Foods Ltd.
www.mccain.com

Did you know that nearly one-third of all the world's French fries are produced by McCain Foods? Learn more about this multinational company by downloading one of many PDF files that outline executive profiles, current technologies, and company history.

Magna International
www.magnaint.com

Magna International Inc. is a leading global supplier of technologically advanced automotive systems. This company employs more than 59,000 people at 166 manufacturing divisions and 32 product development and engineering centres throughout North and South America, Europe and Asia. Visit Magna's comprehensive Web site to discover more information.

Bretton Woods Agreement
www.haigh999.freeserve.co.uk/bretton.htm

Read about the origins of the Bretton Woods Agreement and its lasting achievements at this Web site.

Bank of Canada Exchange Rates
www.bankofcanada.ca/en/exchange.htm

Use this site to research exchange rates, currency converter, and monthly averages from 1990 to the present. It also contains an article explaining the important role of exchange rates in Canada's economy.

Self-Study Problem 9-1

On December 31, 2000, Debtor Limited issued €5,000,000 in debentures to a private investment company located in Frankfurt, Germany. The debentures are due on December 31, 2003. Debtor Limited is a privately held Alberta company that reports to its shareholders and creditors in Canadian dollars using Canadian GAAP. Debtor did not hedge its Euro-denominated debt, and has not identified an implicit hedge. Over the life of the bonds, the exchange rates for the Euro were as follows:

Date	Canadian dollar equivalent
December 31, 2000	$1.27
December 31, 2001	$1.30
December 31, 2002	$1.34
December 31, 2003	$1.35

Required:

Calculate the amount of gain or loss that will appear on Debtor Limited's income statement for each of 2001, 2002, and 2003, following the recommendations of Section 1650 of the *CICA Handbook*.

Self-Study Problem 9-2

On December 2, 2002, Domestic Corporation sold merchandise to a Taiwanese customer for one million New Taiwan Dollars (NTD). The NTD was worth $0.0500 on the date of the sale. On December 3, 2002, Domestic entered into a forward contract with its bank to deliver NTD1,000,000 in 60 days at a rate of $0.0520.

Domestic's fiscal year ended on December 31, 2002. The NTD was worth $0.0510 at year-end. On February 1, 2003, the customer paid the balance owing, and Domestic also settled the forward contract. The exchange rate on the settlement date was $0.0525.

Required:

a. In general journal form, record the entries in 2002 and 2003 relating to the account receivable and to the forward contract, assuming the hedge is recorded as an executory contract.

b. How would the entries relating to the account receivable differ if Domestic had not hedged the receivable?

Self-Study Problem 9-3

On October 14, 2003, Buycorp signed a contract with Sellco, a U.S. company, to purchase a piece of equipment for US$200,000. The equipment was to be delivered on December 1, 2003, with payment to be made (in U.S. dollars) no later than January 30, 2004.

Having signed the contract, Buycorp immediately arranged a forward contract through the company's bank for US$200,000 as a hedge against the commitment. The spot rate for the U.S. dollar was $1.20 on October 14; the forward rate was $1.22.

Sellco delivered the equipment to Buycorp on December 7, 2003, slightly late owing to customs delays at the border. The spot rate on that date was $1.18, as compared to $1.19 on December 1. On December 31, 2003, the spot rate was $1.19. Despite the late delivery, Buycorp paid the amount due on January 30, 2004, per the contract. The spot rate was $1.24 on January 30.

Required:

Prepare journal entries to record the acquisition of the equipment and the related hedge on Buycorp's books through January 30, 2004. Buycorp's fiscal year ends on December 31.

Review Questions

9-1 Distinguish between foreign currency *transactions* and foreign *operations*.

9-2 What country is the most common site for international transactions by Canadian corporations?

9-3 Distinguish between *fixed* rates of exchange and *floating* rates of exchange.

9-4 Explain why floating exchange rates are risky for a company that conducts part of its business in a foreign currency.

9-5 What are the primary causes of changes in exchange rates over the long run?

9-6 Distinguish between *foreign transactions* and *foreign currency transactions*.

9-7 A Canadian corporation has a subsidiary in the United States. The subsidiary has numerous transactions denominated in U.S. dollars. Is the Canadian corporation thereby engaged in foreign currency transactions? Explain.

9-8 CarpCorp, a Canadian company, bought a machine from the United States for US$100,000 when the exchange rate was Cdn$1.20. The liability for the machine was paid when the exchange rate was Cdn$1.25. At what cost should the machine be recorded in the accounts, assuming (1) the one-transaction theory and (2) the two-transaction theory?

9-9 CarpCorp bought inventory from the United Kingdom when the pound was worth Cdn$1.80. When the year-end balance sheet was prepared, the pound was worth Cdn$1.70. If the account payable for the inventory was unpaid at year-end, and the amount of the purchase was 5,000, how should the liability be reported on the balance sheet? How should the change in the value of the pound be reported (if at all)?

9-10 What is the argument for recognizing exchange gains or losses on current monetary balances in income in the year of the gain or loss rather than in the year of settlement?

9-11 A mutual fund has investments in shares in U.S. companies that are traded on the American Stock Exchange. The mutual fund reports its investments at current value. What exchange rate should the fund use in translating the investments when the balance sheet is prepared?

9-12 Why would some companies decide to use a *pre-determined standard rate* for translating foreign currency transactions?

9-13 Explain the difference between a *monetary balance* and a *nonmonetary balance.*

9-14 Why had many companies followed a practice of reporting their foreign-currency-denominated debt at the historical exchange rate on the balance sheet?

9-15 Why is the issue of accounting for long-term foreign-currency-denominated balances more important in Canada than in the United States?

9-16 If the foreign currency in which a bond is denominated fluctuates in value relative to the Canadian dollar, what will be the effect of the defer-and-amortize procedure that is recommended in the *CICA Handbook*?

9-17 What method is the world moving toward for reporting financial instruments?

9-18 What method does IAS 39 require for reporting *financial assets*?

9-19 Explain what perpetual debt is and the appropriate accounting for any exchange gains and losses.

9-20 What is the purpose of *hedging*?

9-21 CarpCorp has a liability of FF400,000. If CarpCorp wants to hedge the liability, should the company enter into a forward contract to *buy* francs or to *sell* francs?

9-22 Does hedging eliminate all gains and losses arising from a foreign currency exposure? Explain.

9-23 Why is a forward contract viewed as an executory contract?

9-24 Why is the discount or premium on a forward contract allocated to the periods during which the monetary balance and the hedge are outstanding, rather than being recognized in the period of settlement?

9-25 What is the proposed new accounting for hedges?

9-26 How does hedging a *commitment* differ from hedging a liability?

9-27 CharCo signs a contract to buy a special-order machine from a Swiss manufacturer. CharCo then hedges the commitment. How will the Canadian-dollar cost of the machine be determined?

9-28 When might a nonmonetary asset be considered a hedge of a long-term monetary balance?

9-29 What practical difficulties arise in financial reporting when a foreign currency revenue stream is designated as an implicit hedge of a long-term monetary liability?

Cases

Case 9-1

Canada Cola

Canada Cola Inc. (CCI) is a public company engaged in the manufacture and distribution of soft drinks across Canada. Its primary product is Canada Cola ("Fresh as a Canadian stream"), which is a top seller in Canada and generates large export sales.

You, CA, met with Jim MacNamara, the partner in charge of the CCI engagement, to commence planning for the upcoming audit of CCI.

During this meeting the partner informed you that early this year CCI entered into an agreement with the government of Russia and has commenced the manufacture and sale of Canada Cola in Russia. A short summary of the agreement is contained in Exhibit 1. The partner would like you to prepare a detailed report that discusses the accounting and auditing implications of this new division of CCI for this engagement.

EXHIBIT 1

SUMMARY OF AGREEMENT

1. The Russian government will provide the land and the building for the plant. It will make no further investment.

2. CCI will install bottling machinery costing $5 million in the Russian plant. Once installed, the machinery may not be removed from Russia.

3. CCI will be required to provide the funds for the initial working capital. CCI will sell U.S. dollars to the Russian government in exchange for local currency (rubles).

4. CCI will be wholly responsible for the management and daily operations of the plant. Canadian managers will be transferred to Russia.

5. CCI will be permitted to export its cola syrup to Russia at CCI's Canadian cost.

6. CCI and the Russian government will share equally in the profits from the sale of Canada Cola in Russia.

7. Although foreign currency can be converted into rubles, rubles cannot be converted back into any foreign currency. Therefore, the Russian government will sell vodka to CCI (at the prevailing export price in Russia) in exchange for the rubles CCI earns in profits. CCI will be permitted to export this vodka to Canada, where it may be sold in the Canadian domestic market only.

Required:

a. Prepare the report for the partner.

b. Explain how your recommendations would differ for accounting if CCI formed a separate subsidiary, compared to a division, to run the operations in Russia.

[CICA]

Case 9-2

Video Displays, Inc. (Part A)

Video Displays, Inc. (VDI) is a privately held corporation chartered under the *Canada Business Corporations Act*. The corporation was formed in 1998 by four engineers who found themselves jobless after their previous employer (Argo Corporation) discontinued the production of television sets in Canada.

One of the sidelines of Argo had been the assembly of video display units (VDUs). A VDU is the basic chassis containing the cathode ray tube and related components that are used in video-display computer terminals, in computer game sets, and in word processors. When Argo discontinued production, the four engineers purchased some of Argo's assembly and testing equipment and formed VDI.

VDI has been fairly successful because it is the only Canadian producer of VDUs. Some computer terminal manufacturers have a policy of obtaining their components in the country in which they manufacture the terminals, and thus VDI has enjoyed the benefits of local-sourcing policies since it is the only Canadian producer.

In 2000, VDI needed additional debt financing. After being refused by several Canadian banks, the executives of VDI went to New York, where on March 1, they quickly obtained a five-year, 12% term loan of $3,000,000 (U.S.) from Citibank, interest payable annually on the anniversary date of the loan. The U.S. dollar was worth Cdn$1.20 on March 1, 2000. By the end of 2000, the exchange rate had slipped to $1.18.

In 2001, VDI extended its operations into the United States by contracting with an electronics component distributor in Cambridge, Massachusetts. The U.S. distributor supplies component assemblies to small manufacturers, and saw an opportunity to sell VDI's VDUs to independent manufacturers of computer terminals and word processors. The December 31, 2001, VDI unadjusted trial balance showed a balance due from the U.S. distributor of $500,000. The 2001 shipments to and payments from the distributor are shown in Exhibit 1. VDI gave the distributor US$60,000 on April 4 as an accountable advance for financing promotional expenses. By December 31, 2001, the distributor had spent and accounted for $40,000 of this advance. At the end of 2001, the exchange rate was Cdn$1.25 to US$1.00.

Required:

Explain the impact of the transaction described above on VDI's financial statements on December 31, 2001. Where alternatives are possible, state them and explain your choice of approach. Be as specific as possible. Assume that all amounts are material.

EXHIBIT 1

CURRENT ACCOUNT WITH U.S. DISTRIBUTOR 2001*

	Dr	Cr	Balance
Feb. 1: Shipment (US$100,000)	$115,000		$115,000
April 1: Shipment (US$180,000)	207,000		322,000
May 1: Payment (US$100,000)		$118,000	204,000
July 1: Shipment (US$200,000)	240,000		444,000
Aug. 30: Payment (US$150,000)		186,000	258,000
Nov. 15: Shipment (US$200,000)	242,000		500,000

* In Canadian dollars.

Case 9-3

Graham Enterprises Limited

Graham Enterprises Limited (Graham) has just negotiated the purchase of an office building for £20 million in London, England, which is to be used as the head office of its newly incorporated wholly-owned European operating subsidiary, Graham Overseas Limited (GOL). Transfer of ownership to GOL is to be made on January 1, 2002. Graham has arranged a loan for £20 million to finance the purchase through its bankers. The loan, to be dated January 1, 2002, is at 12% and is repayable in 20 equal annual instalments commencing January 1, 2003. The loan would be made to GOL, which would make all interest and principal payments in pounds sterling.

The building will be depreciated on a straight-line basis over 20 years. Assume the following exchange rates: January 1, 2002, £1 = $2.50; December 31, 2002, £1 = $2.00.

Required:

Discuss fully the options available to Graham in structuring its relationship to GOL, and evaluate the impact of each alternative on the consolidated financial statements. Show all supporting calculations.

[SMA]

Problems

P9-1

On January 1, 2000, a Canadian company, Canuck Enterprises Ltd., borrowed 200,000 U.S. dollars from a bank in Seattle, Washington. Interest of 7% per annum is to be paid on December 31 of each year during the four-year term of the loan. Principal is to be repaid on the maturity date of December 31, 2003. The foreign exchange rates for the first two years were as follows:

January 1, 2000	Cdn$1.38 = US$1.00
December 31, 2000	Cdn$1.41 = US$1.00
December 31, 2001	Cdn$1.35 = US$1.00

Required:

Determine the exchange gain/loss on the loan to be disclosed in the financial statements of Canuck Enterprises Ltd. for the years ended December 31, 2000 and 2001.

[CGA]

P9-2

PT Limited began purchasing parts from China. The Chinese currency is renminbi (R$). PT entered into the following transactions in 2000 and 2001:

November 1, 2000	Ordered machine parts from the Chinese supplier for R$2,000,000. The supplier promised to deliver the machine parts at the beginning of December, and payment is expected on January 15, 2001.
December 1, 2000	Received shipment of the machine parts.
December 31, 2000	Acquired a forward contract to receive R$2,000,000 on January 15, 2001 as a hedge of the accounts payable to the Chinese supplier. The forward contract rate was R$1 = Cdn$0.16. PT treats all forward contracts as executory contracts.
January 15, 2001	Received R$2,000,000 on the forward contract; paid R$2,000,000 to the Chinese supplier in settlement of the payable.

Spot rates were as follows:

November 1, 2000	R$1 = Cdn$0.15
December 1, 2000	R$1 = Cdn$0.18
December 31, 2000	R$1 = Cdn$0.17
January 15, 2001	R$1 = Cdn$0.19

Required:

Prepare the journal entries for these transactions, including any adjusting entries needed at the December 31, 2000 fiscal year-end. Specify if no entry is required on any specific date(s).

[CGA]

P9-3

Domestic Corp., a Canadian company, sells its products to customers in the United Kingdom at prices quoted in pounds sterling. On November 14, 2001, Domestic sold and shipped goods that had cost $160,000 to produce to an English company for £200,000. On December 20, Domestic received an international draft for part of the amount due, £80,000. At year-end (December 31), the remaining £120,000 were unpaid.

On February 12, 2002, Domestic received payment of the remaining £120,000.

Required:

In general journal form, prepare journal entries to record the above events, and any adjustments necessary at year-end. Exchange rates (Canadian dollar equivalent to £1) are as follows:

November 14	1.80
December 20	1.85
December 31	1.87
February 12	1.84

P9-4

At the end of the fiscal year, December 31, 2001, Export Ltd. finds itself with two accounts receivable in pesos:

1. From a sale on July 1, 2001, and due to be collected on December 1, 2002, for 3,000,000 pesos.

2. From a sale on September 1, 2001, and due to be collected on December 1, 2004, for 6,000,000 pesos.

   Exchange rates (spot):

$1 = 160 pesos	July 1, 2001
$1 = 174 pesos	September 1, 2001
$1 = 180 pesos	December 31, 2001
$1 = 110 pesos	December 1, 2002
$1 = 90 pesos	December 31, 2002

Chapter
Nine

424

Required:

Prepare the journal entries for December 31, 2001, and December 1 and December 31, 2002, assuming that the foreign exchange risk is *not* hedged.

[CGA–Canada]

P9-5

At the beginning of 2001, Domo Industries Ltd. obtained a four-year loan of US$200,000 from a bank in New York City. At the time of the loan, the U.S. dollar was worth Cdn$1.20. At the end of 2001, the exchange rate had changed to US$1.00 = Cdn$1.24. By the end of 2002, the U.S. dollar was worth Cdn$1.30.

During 2002, Domo Industries Ltd. sold goods to a German customer for 400,000 deutsche marks. At the time of the sale, the mark was worth $0.50. The customer paid one-fourth of the amount due later in the year, when the mark was worth $0.47. By the end of 2002, the mark had declined in value to $0.45.

Required:

Determine the impact of the transactions described above on Domo Industries' financial statements for the year ended December 31, 2002, assuming that the current recommendations of Section 1650 of the *CICA Handbook* are followed.

P9-6

Drory, Ltd. is a private corporation. On March 30, 2002, the company negotiated a five-year loan from Chase Manhattan bank for $2,000,000 in U.S. funds. At the inception of the loan, the U.S. dollar was worth $1.50 in Canadian funds.

Drory's fiscal year ends on September 30. At fiscal year-end, 2002, the exchange rate was US$1.00 = Cdn$1.56. Drory prepares its financial statements in Canadian dollars.

Required:

List the alternative reporting treatments for the loan and any related gain or loss in Drory's 2002 financial statements. For each alternative:

a. Determine the amounts and the financial statement presentation.

b. Briefly state the arguments in *favour* of each alternative.

c. State whether the alternative is acceptable within the recommendations of the *CICA Handbook*.

P9-7

Wayne Ltd. purchased a capital asset from France, which arrived on November 1, 2002, priced at 1,500,000 French francs. The company hedged the debt with a forward contract at the time the machine arrived in Vancouver, since the final price was not known prior to that time. The debt is due February 1, 2003. Relevant exchange rates are:

Spot rate
November 1, 2002	$1 = 6 French francs
December 31, 2002	$1 = 5 French francs

Hedge rate at November 1, 2002
$1 = 5.4 French francs

Required:

a. Prepare the journal entries for 2002 to record the above information.

b. Assuming instead that the debt was due February 1, 2004, and there was no hedge, prepare for 2002 the journal entries to record the above information.

[CGA–Canada]

P9-8

On May 5, 2002, Roy Corp. purchased inventory from a Japanese supplier, and gave the supplier a 90-day note for ¥20,000,000. On the same date, Roy entered a forward contract with its bank to receive ¥20,000,000 in 90 days. The spot rate for the yen was $0.0095. The forward rate was $0.0100.

Required:

Prepare general journal entries to record the purchase, the hedge, and final settlement of both the note and the hedge, assuming each of the following spot rates at the settlement date:

a. $0.0095

b. $0.0100

c. $0.0093

d. $0.0102

P9-9

On October 15, 2001, Zap Limited sold merchandise to two companies in Portugal. In the first transaction, the price was 3,000,000 escudos and was to be paid in 90 days. Worried about the exposure to the exchange risk, the company hedged the receivable for a 90-day period with a forward contract.

In the second transaction, the price was 3,600,000 escudos and the date of payment was November 15, 2004. Due to the difficulty of getting a forward contract to match the date payment is due, the company decided to remain in an "unhedged" position on this receivable.

Exchange rates (for purposes of this question, all months have 30 days):

October 15, 2001, spot rate	$1 = 800 escudos
December 31, 2001, spot rate	$1 = 910 escudos
January 13, 2002, spot rate	$1 = 945 escudos
October 15, 2001, forward 90-day rate	$1 = 926 escudos
December 31, 2002, spot rate	$1 = 775 escudos

Required:

Ignoring closing entries:

a. Prepare all the related journal entries required for the first sale for 2001 *and* 2002.

b. Assuming instead that the company had not hedged the receivable from the first sale in any way, prepare the appropriate journal entries for 2001 *and* 2002 to record this situation.

c. Prepare all the related journal entries for the *second* sale for 2001 *and* 2002.

[CGA–Canada, adapted]

P9-10

Following are transactions of Import Ltd., a company engaged in importing products into Canada.

September 1, 2002: Incurred a liability for 1,000,000 pesos, due February 1, 2003, for purchasing inventory.

October 1, 2002: Incurred a liability for 6,000,000 yen, due November 1, 2003, for purchasing inventory.

November 1, 2002: Incurred a liability for 22,000 Russian rubles, due March 1, 2004, for purchasing inventory.

Exchange Rates:
September 1, 2002

$1 = 150 pesos	Spot rate
$1 = 120 pesos	Forward contract rate

October 1, 2002

$1 = 800 yen	Spot rate
$1 = 950 yen	Forward contract rate

November 1, 2002

$1 = 1.80 rubles	Spot rate
$1 = 1.60 rubles	Forward contract rate

December 31, 2002
$1 = 100$ pesos
$1 = 1,000$ yen
$1 = 1.50$ rubles

Required:

Parts a and b, below, are based on different policies regarding hedging. Answer each part as an independent problem.

a. Import Ltd. did not hedge or cover its exchange risk position. Prepare the journal entries for 2002. The company has a December 31 year-end.

b. At the time of each transaction, Import Ltd. paid $100 for a forward contract, which was a perfect and complete hedge against the foreign exchange risk. Prepare the journal entries for 2002. The company has a December 31 year-end.

[CGA–Canada, adapted]

P9-11

Harley Ltd., a manufacturer of motorcycles located in Burnaby, B.C., successfully negotiated a contract to sell 100 small motorcycles to the police department of Fairbanks, Alaska. The contract price for the cycles was US$10,000 each. The contract was signed on May 12, 2002, with payment to be made by October 1. Harley then entered into a forward contract to hedge against changes in the U.S. dollar exchange rate.

Delivery of the motorcycles began on June 11 and continued in 20-cycle lots at two-week intervals until the last delivery on August 30, 2002. The buyer then paid the US$1,000,000 contract price when due, and Harley settled with the bank.

The exchange rates were as follows:

	Canadian equivalent of US$1.00	
	Spot rate	Forward rate
May 12, 2002	$1.15	$1.18
June 11–August 30, 2002	1.10	1.08
October 1, 2002	1.12	1.14

Required:

a. What amounts relating to the sale and the hedge would appear on Harley's income statement and balance sheet for the year ended December 31, 2002?

b. Assume instead that Harley's year-end was August 30. What amounts would appear on Harley's financial statements at August 30, 2002?

P9-12

Chan Can Corporation (CCC), a Canadian corporation, engaged in the following transactions in late 2001 and early 2002:

December 2   Purchased sheet aluminum from a U.S. subsidiary of a Canadian aluminum company for US$160,000, payable in 60 days.

December 2   Acquired a forward contract to receive US$160,000 in 60 days, as a hedge of the account payable. The forward contract rate was Cdn$1.10.

December 20   Sold large cans to a Buffalo canner for US$200,000, due in 60 days.

January 31   Received US$160,000 on the forward contract; paid US$160,000 to the aluminum company.

February 18   Received US$200,000 from the Buffalo canner.

Spot rates for the U.S. dollar were as follows:

December 2	$1.37
December 20	1.42
December 31	1.44
January 31	1.50
February 18	1.47

Required:

Prepare journal entries for these transactions, including any adjusting entries needed at the December 31, 2001, year-end.

Reporting Foreign
Operations

Introduction

The previous chapter explored the problems and alternatives that arise from foreign currency transactions. When a company carries out a substantial volume of business in a foreign country, it is common for the company to establish a separate operation in the host country. Usually the foreign operation is incorporated, although incorporation is not essential—the foreign operation could be a branch, an unincorporated joint venture, or a partnership.

Ordinarily, the foreign operation maintains its own bank accounts in the currency of the host country and conducts its business in that currency. The prices in which it sells its product or service, pays its employees, and buys its supplies and assets is the host country's currency. Periodically, the foreign operation will summarize its activities in some form of financial statement and will send this statement of activities to the parent company. The statement or statements of the foreign operation will be presented in the host country currency. When the parent company incorporates the results of the foreign operation into its own financial statements, the statements of the foreign operation must be translated into the reporting currency of the parent company. Thus, the problems of *translating foreign operations* arise.

Translation Methods

To illustrate the nature of the problem, assume that Domestic Corporation decides to establish a sales subsidiary in the country of Pantania. Domestic's legal representatives in Pantania draw up the papers for a corporation in that country, to be named Forsub Ltd. The founding board of directors of Forsub is nominated (by Domestic) and Forsub begins operating. One hundred common shares of Forsub are issued to Domestic Corporation for 500 pants per share, the pant being the local currency of Pantania. Forsub will record the investment *in Pantanian pants* (P) as follows:

Cash	P50,000	
Common shares		P50,000

If the pant is worth two dollars Canadian at the time of the transaction, then P50,000 will be worth $100,000 and Domestic will record the investment on its books at cost as it would any initial investment:

Investment in Forsub Ltd.	$100,000	
Cash		$100,000

Now, suppose that after receiving the cash, Forsub begins organizing itself for operations by acquiring some inventory for P20,000 (partially on account) and land for P40,000. To finance this purchase, Forsub issues five-year bonds amounting to P25,000. The transactions would be recorded as follows on Forsub's books:

Cash	P25,000	
Bonds payable		P25,000
Inventory	P20,000	
Cash		P15,000
Accounts payable		5,000
Land	P40,000	
Cash		P40,000

At the time of these transactions, the exchange rate is still P1 = $2. Forsub's balance sheet will then appear as follows:

Cash	P20,000	Accounts payable	P 5,000
Inventory	20,000	Bonds payable	25,000
Land	40,000	Common shares	50,000
		Total liabilities and share-	
Total assets	P80,000	holders' equity	P80,000

A short while later, Domestic Corporation's fiscal year-end occurs. Since Forsub is a subsidiary of Domestic, Domestic will be expected to consolidate Forsub. As with any subsidiary that is consolidated, the investment account is eliminated and Forsub's assets and liabilities are added to those of the parent company in Domestic's balance sheet.

However, Forsub's assets and liabilities are expressed in pants, not dollars. It is necessary to convert Forsub's assets and liabilities to Canadian dollars before consolidation is possible; we must translate the *results* of Forsub's transactions for the period, as reflected in the Forsub balance sheet, rather than the individual *transactions* as we discussed in the preceding chapter. As might be expected, there are several ways in which the results of foreign operations can be translated.

Temporal method

One approach to translating Forsub's balance sheet is to begin by translating all of the accounts that represent cash or claims payable in cash at the exchange rate that exists at the balance sheet date. Forsub has P20,000 in cash, and Domestic could instruct Forsub to remit the cash to the parent company, such as by declaring a dividend.

If Forsub's cash balance were remitted to Domestic on the balance sheet date, it would be convertible directly into Canadian dollars at the spot rate. The rate at the balance sheet date is known as the **current rate**. If the current rate was P1 = $2.30, then P20,000 would be equivalent to $46,000. Other assets that represent cash claims, such as notes receivable and accounts receivable, would also be translated at the exchange rate in effect at the balance sheet date.

Claims against cash are also translated at the current rate. All accounts payable, notes payable, bonds payable, and similar liabilities would be translated at the current rate because they are all payable in cash. In addition, nonmonetary assets that are reported in the financial statements at their *current value* (such as certain types of inventory or investments) are translated at the current rate because their carrying value represents an amount that can be converted to cash.

Nonmonetary items that are reported at historical cost are translated at the exchange rate in effect at the date of the transaction that created the nonmonetary items. The rate on the date of the transaction is known as the **historical rate**. In essence, the temporal approach uses the same translation rules as we described in the previous chapter for monetary and nonmonetary balances arising from foreign currency transactions.

For Forsub Ltd., the nonmonetary items are inventory and land, both purchased when the rate was P1 = $2.00. Thus, these two assets would be translated at the $2.00 historical rate, while the cash and bonds would be translated at the $2.30 current rate.

Note that the historical rate is $2.00 because that was the rate existing at the time that the inventory and land were purchased. The fact that the rate was also $2.00 when the original investment in Forsub was made by Domestic is coincidental. If the land had been purchased when the rate was $2.10 and the inventory was bought when the rate was $2.15, then those would be the historical rates used for translating each account balance.

The only account on the Forsub balance sheet that we have not yet discussed is the common shares. Since this is a nonmonetary item, it is logical that it should be translated at the historical rate of $2.00. This account will be eliminated when Forsub is consolidated. Since the offsetting account in Domestic's balance sheet is the investment in Forsub account, the subsidiary's common share account should be translated at the historical rate in order to facilitate the elimination on consolidation.

In summary, the accounts on Forsub's balance sheet would be translated as follows under the temporal method:

Item	Rate
Cash	Current
Inventory	Historical
Land	Historical
Bonds payable	Current
Common shares	Historical

Since the accounts are being translated at two different rates, the translated balance sheet will not balance until we allow for a *translation gain or loss*. The total gain or loss will be the amount needed to balance the translated balance sheet, and it is a loss of $3,000 in this example. With this addition to the balance sheet, the translated balance sheet of Forsub Ltd. will appear as shown in the last column of Exhibit 10-1.

The $3,000 loss can be derived directly from the information given about Forsub's transactions. There are three components to the loss. The first is a gain of $6,000 on the balance of cash. Forsub originally received P50,000 in cash when the exchange rate was $2.00, and obtained another P25,000 from the issuance of bonds.

While the rate was still $2.00, the company purchased land and inventory, thereby reducing the cash balance to P20,000. The company then held this balance of cash while the exchange rate rose to $2.30. The increase in the exchange rate meant that the P20,000 balance was worth $46,000 at the end of the fiscal year (P20,000 × $2.30) as compared to only $40,000 (P20,000 × $2.00) when

EXHIBIT 10–1 TRANSLATION OF BALANCE SHEET, TEMPORAL METHOD*

Forsub Ltd.
December 31, 2001

Exchange rate, December 31, 2001: P1.00 = Cdn$2.30

	Balance on Forsub's books	Exchange rate	Translated amount
Cash	P20,000	$2.30	$ 46,000
Inventory	20,000	2.00	40,000
Land	40,000	2.00	80,000
Total assets	P80,000		$166,000
Accounts payable, current	P 5,000	$2.30	$ 11,500
Bonds payable, long term	25,000	2.30	57,500
Common shares	50,000	2.00	100,000
Translation gain (loss)	—		(3,000)
	P80,000		$166,000

Calculation of net translation loss:

Cash	P 20,000	asset × ($2.30 – $2.00) =	$ 6,000	gain
Accounts payable	(5,000)	liability × ($2.30 – $2.00) =	(1,500)	loss
Bonds payable	(25,000)	liability × ($2.30 – $2.00) =	(7,500)	loss
Net	P(10,000)	liability × ($2.30 – $2.00) =	$(3,000)	loss

* The monetary/nonmonetary method yields the same result in this example.

the cash was received. Thus, holding a cash balance when the exchange rate rose resulted in an increase in the equivalent amount in Canadian dollars, a gain of $46,000 – $40,000 = $6,000.

The second component of the $3,000 translation loss is a loss of $1,500 on the accounts payable. Forsub still owes P5,000 to its trade creditors, but the dollar equivalent of this amount has changed from $10,000 (P5,000 × $2.00) to $11,500 (P5,000 × $2.30). In Canadian dollar terms, the value of the debt has risen, thereby resulting in a loss.

The final component of the overall translation loss arises from the bonds payable. The P25,000 in bonds were issued when the exchange rate was $2.00, or a Canadian equivalent of $50,000. At year-end, the Canadian equivalent of the bond indebtedness is $57,500, at the year-end exchange rate of $2.30. Therefore, a loss of $7,500 ($50,000 – $57,500) has arisen as a result of holding a liability that is denominated in pants as the Canadian equivalent increased because of changes in the exchange rate.

By breaking the translation loss down into its component amounts, we can see that the loss of $3,000 is really a net amount arising from a loss of $9,000 ($1,500 + $7,500) on monetary liabilities less a gain of $6,000 on holding cash. This information is summarized at the bottom of Exhibit 10-1. We will examine the nature of this loss and its accounting implications more extensively later in the chapter.

For the moment, however, note that the only items that give rise to translation gains or losses are those account balances that are translated at the *current* rate. The net amount of balances that are translated at the current rate is the measure of the foreign operation's **accounting exposure** to currency rate fluctuations. In Exhibit 10-1, the accounting exposure is a net monetary liability balance of P10,000: (P20,000 – P5,000 – P25,000). The translation loss is P10,000 × ($2.30 – $2.00) = $3,000.

Balances that are translated at historical rates do not give rise to translation gains or losses because the rate at which they are translated does not change. The net amount of the exchange gain or loss can be calculated by looking only at the net changes in those balances that are translated at the current rate.

Different methods of translation will yield different accounting exposures and different amounts of gain or loss. Indeed, as we will demonstrate shortly, a translation loss that arises under one method often becomes a gain under a different method. These accounting gains and losses usually do not adequately reflect the economic impacts on the company of exchange rate fluctuations. This issue will be addressed after our discussion of the alternative methods, in the subsection entitled "Accounting Exposure vs. Economic Exposure."

Monetary/Nonmonetary method

A second method of translating the results of foreign operations is known as the **monetary/nonmonetary method**. Monetary items are translated at the current rate, while *all* nonmonetary items are translated at historical rates. The only difference in theory between this approach and the temporal method is in the treatment of nonmonetary amounts that are reported at current value; the temporal method translates these items at the current rate while the monetary/nonmonetary method translates them at historical rates.

The difference between these two methods is more apparent than real. Most companies carry all of their nonmonetary balances at historical cost. For these companies, there will be no difference in results, whether the monetary/nonmonetary method or the temporal method is used. Both methods will result in the translation of monetary assets and liabilities at the current rate, and translation gains and losses will arise to the extent that the exchange rate has changed during the period. Nonmonetary items, all of which are carried at historical cost, will be translated at their individual historical rates, and no translation gains or losses will arise from this. A difference in translation results between the two methods will arise only for those few companies carrying one or more of their nonmonetary items at market value, current value, or current replacement cost.

Because of the consistency in treatment of current value balances (whether monetary or nonmonetary) in the temporal method, the temporal method really is just a refinement of the monetary/nonmonetary method rather than being a distinct method. In the remainder of this chapter, we will drop any explicit reference to the monetary/nonmonetary method and will refer to this related pair of methods simply as the temporal method.

Relationship of temporal method to transaction accounting

In Exhibit 10-1, we translated Forsub's year-end balances by using the temporal method, and we calculated a gain on the balance of cash and a loss on the balance of bonds and accounts payable. An important characteristic to note about the temporal method is that *it yields exactly the same results in terms of the translated amounts as would have resulted from translating each transaction separately*. In substance, the temporal method views the operations of the foreign company as though the transactions had been carried out directly by Domestic Corporation operating from its home base in Canada.

Exhibit 10-2 illustrates the individual transactions as they would have been recorded by Domestic if they had been direct transactions. The first transaction shows the depositing of $100,000 in the Bank of Pantania—this amount is translated to P50,000 by the bank. The remaining transactions record the issuance of the bonds and the purchase of the inventory and land, recorded in the equivalent amount of Canadian dollars.

At year-end, it is necessary to record the monetary foreign-currency-denominated balances at their current equivalents. These adjustments (for cash, accounts payable, and bonds payable) result in a net foreign currency loss of $3,000. The impact of these individual transactions on Domestic Corporation's balance sheet would be exactly the same as translating Forsub's balance sheet by the temporal method and consolidating.

EXHIBIT 10–2 DIRECT TRANSACTIONS EQUIVALENT TO FORSUB'S TRANSACTIONS

If the parent company had engaged in the transactions directly instead of through Forsub, the transactions would have been recorded on Domestic's books as follows:

a	Cash (in Bank of Pantania)	100,000	
	Cash (in Canadian bank)		100,000
	[to record transfer of cash for Pantanian bank account]		
b	Cash (in Pantania)	50,000	
	Bonds payable		50,000
	[to record issuance of bonds in Pantania]		
c	Inventory (cost = P20,000)	40,000	
	Cash (in Pantania)		30,000
	Accounts payable (P5,000)		10,000
	[to record purchase of inventory in Pantania, paid in pants]		
d	Land (cost = P40,000)	80,000	
	Cash (in Pantania: P40,000)		80,000
	[to record purchase of land in Pantania, paid in pants]		

Year-end adjusting entries, December 31, 2001:

e	Cash [P20,000 × (2.30 − 2.00)]	6,000	
	Foreign currency gains/losses		6,000
	[to adjust the cash balance to the year-end current rate]		
f	Foreign currency gains/losses	1,500	
	Accounts payable [P5,000 × (2.30 − 2.00)]		1,500
	[to adjust the accounts payable balance to the year-end current rate]		
g	Foreign currency gains/losses	7,500	
	Bonds payable [P25,000 × (2.30 − 2.00)]		7,500
	[to adjust the bonds payable balance to the year-end current rate]		

Current-rate method

An alternative approach to the translation of the results of foreign operations is to translate *all* of the asset and liability balances at the current rate. Only the shareholders' equity accounts are translated at the historical rate, as shown in Exhibit 10-3.

Under the current-rate method, the total assets of Forsub translate to $184,000 as compared to $166,000 under the temporal method. The much larger amount is due to the fact that under the temporal method, the large non-monetary assets were translated at the lower historical rate. Conversely, if the exchange rate had declined during the period, the total assets would be less under the current-rate method than under the temporal method.

When the current-rate method is used, the net balance of those balance sheet accounts that are translated at the current rate will always be a net *asset* balance. Since all of the assets and all of the liabilities are translated at the current rate, the total assets will exceed the total liabilities, and the balance that is exposed to gains and losses from fluctuations in the exchange rate will be the excess of the assets over the liabilities. This net balance is obviously equal to the shareholders' equity in the foreign operation, or its net asset value.

Thus, under the current-rate method, the *accounting exposure* to currency fluctuations is always measurable as the net assets of the foreign subsidiary. Under the temporal method, in contrast, the exposure could be either a net asset or net liability balance, depending on whether monetary assets exceed monetary liabilities, or vice versa.

A distinct characteristic of the current-rate method is that the proportionate amounts of the various asset and liability accounts do not change when the balance sheet is translated. For example, bonds are 31% of Forsub's total assets in pants (P25,000 ÷ P80,000), and they continue to be 31% of total assets in dollars ($57,500 ÷ $184,000). Under the temporal method, however, the proportion changes from 31% to 35% ($57,500 ÷ $166,000).

EXHIBIT 10–3 TRANSLATION OF BALANCE SHEET, CURRENT-RATE METHOD

Forsub Ltd.
December 31, 2001

Exchange rate, December 31, 2001: P1.00 = Cdn$2.30

	Balance on Forsub's books	Exchange rate	Translated amount
Cash	P20,000	$2.30	$ 46,000
Inventory	20,000	2.30	46,000
Land	40,000	2.30	92,000
Total assets	P80,000		$184,000
Accounts payable, current	P 5,000	$2.30	$ 11,500
Bonds payable, long term	25,000	2.30	57,500
Shareholders' equity	50,000	2.00	100,000
Translation gain (loss)*	—		15,000
	P80,000		$184,000

* *Calculation of net translation gain:*

   Translation gain = net asset position × change in exchange rate
      = P50,000 × ($2.30 – $2.00)
      = $15,000 gain

Many people feel that this characteristic is an advantage of the current-rate method—the "true" financial position of Forsub is that shown by the balance sheet in pants, and the process of currency translation should not change this picture of the foreign operation. As one eminent author puts it, "It is analogous to painting a stone wall; the colour may change, but the bumps remain; the wall is the same as before, just a different colour."[1]

Current/Noncurrent method

As its name implies, the current/noncurrent method distinguishes between assets and liabilities on the basis of whether they are current or noncurrent assets or liabilities. Current items are translated at the current exchange rate and noncurrent items are translated at their historical rate.

The results of translating Forsub's balance sheet by this method are shown in Exhibit 10-4. The net balance of items that are translated at the current rate is equal to the net working capital, or current assets minus the current liabilities. For Forsub, the net working capital is P35,000, and thus the accounting exposure is also P35,000. Since the exposure is a net *asset* position and the exchange rate rose by $0.30 during the period, there is a translation gain of $10,500 (P35,000 × $0.30).

Some accountants view this method as nonsense and claim that it has no underlying theoretical basis. But before the temporal method was imposed by the AcSB, the current/noncurrent method was used by the vast majority of companies in Canada.[2] Was this accounting nonsense?

EXHIBIT 10–4 TRANSLATION OF BALANCE SHEET, CURRENT/NONCURRENT METHOD

Forsub Ltd.
December 31, 2001

Exchange rate, December 31, 2001: P1.00 = Cdn$2.30

	Balance on Forsub's books	Exchange rate	Translated amount
Cash	P20,000	$2.30	$ 46,000
Inventory	20,000	2.30	46,000
Land	40,000	2.00	80,000
Total assets	P80,000		$172,000
Accounts payable, current	P 5,000	$2.30	$ 11,500
Bonds payable, long term	25,000	2.00	50,000
Common shares	50,000	2.00	100,000
Translation gain (loss)*	—		10,500
	P80,000		$172,000

* *Calculation of net translation gain:*

Translation gain = net working capital × change in exchange rate
= (P40,000 current assets − P5,000 current liabilities) × ($2.30 − $2.00)
= P35,000 × $0.30 = $10,500 gain

---

1. Dr. Pierre Vezina, *Foreign Currency Translation: An Analysis of Section 1650 of the CICA Handbook* (Toronto: CICA, 1985), p. 6.

2. *Financial Reporting in Canada*, various biennial editions (Toronto: CICA).

Under the current/noncurrent method, management has some control over the accounting exposure to exchange rate fluctuations. If the net working capital is maintained at zero (i.e., current assets = current liabilities), then there will be no net balance translated at the current rate, and thus no translation gain or loss. If the size of the foreign operation or operations is significant in comparison to the domestic operation, then management may well consider the avoidance of recognizing an unrealized translation gain or loss as a significant benefit. However, management convenience is not normally considered to be an adequate justification for using an accounting method.

The real reason for using the current/noncurrent method involves the concept of an *implicit hedge*. The current assets may have a large component of nonmonetary assets such as inventory. Inventory is translated at historical cost. But inventory will be converted to cash, and therefore constitutes a hedge against the current monetary liabilities. Both the current assets and the current liabilities will be realized within the next year, and the gains from one will tend to offset the losses from the other. Thus, it is logical to translate both the current assets and current liabilities at the current exchange rate.

Similarly, the long-term assets (most likely capital assets) often are financed by the long-term monetary liabilities, and constitute an implicit hedge against them. Since the gains or losses from the long-term items will be realized only over the long run, the noncurrent items are translated at the historical rate, and any foreign currency gains or losses *will be recognized only when they are realized.*

Neither of the alternate methods of translation can achieve a similar result. The temporal method translates the monetary liabilities at the current exchange rate but leaves the related capital assets at the historical rate, thereby forcing recognition of a possibly substantial unrealized gain or loss. The current-rate method translates both the noncurrent assets and the noncurrent liabilities at the current exchange rate, thereby permitting the long-term assets and liabilities to offset each other and reducing the potential gain or loss, but then the balance of the capital assets goes up and down in response to unrealized currency rate changes.

Empirical research has suggested that the validity of Purchasing Power Parity and the Fisher Effect indicates that most assets and liabilities are not really exposed to exchange gains and losses over longer periods of time but that for shorter periods they are. "Over relatively short horizons (two or three years), all assets and liabilities tend to be exposed."[3] These findings suggest that while the current/noncurrent method is not ideal, it may come closer to reflecting the realities of exchange rate risk than the other methods presently available.

Whatever its merits, the current/noncurrent method has no place in the authoritative pronouncements of Canada, the United States, or the International Accounting Standards Committee. It is a shunned alternative.

Summary of translation methods

The three translation methods can be summarized as follows:

1. Temporal method
   a. Translates all monetary and current value items at the current exchange rate; translates all nonmonetary historical cost items at their individual historical rate.

3. Robert Z. Aliber and Clyde P. Stickney, "Accounting Measures of Foreign Exchange Exposure: The Long and Short of It," *The Accounting Review* (January, 1975), p. 52. Another useful reference is Thomas J. O'Brien, "Accounting versus economic exposure to currency risk," *Journal of Financial Statement Analysis* (Summer 1997), pp. 21–29.

b. Yields an accounting exposure to exchange rate fluctuations of the net balance of monetary and current value assets and liabilities, depending on the financial structure of the company.

c. Does not give effect to implicit hedges of monetary items by offsetting nonmonetary items.

2. Current-rate method

a. Translates all assets and liabilities at the current rate, whether current or noncurrent and whether monetary or nonmonetary.

b. Yields an exposure to exchange rate changes that is always a net asset position, equivalent to the owners' equity in the foreign operation.[4]

c. Preserves the proportionate relationships between the various balance sheet items; does not "distort" the statement compared to the way it would appear in local currency.

3. Current/Noncurrent method

a. Translates current assets and current liabilities at the current exchange rate; translates long-term assets and liabilities at their individual historical rates.

b. Yields an exposure to exchange rate changes that is equal to the net working capital position of the foreign operation.

c. Permits "managing" of the current rate exposure through working capital management.

d. Implicitly treats nonmonetary items as hedges against offsetting monetary balances within each of the current and noncurrent groups of accounts.

While the temporal method does not in itself treat nonmonetary assets (or the revenue stream therefrom) as hedges of monetary liabilities, such hedges may be identified and recognized under the temporal method, as we discussed in the "implicit hedges" section of the previous chapter on foreign currency transactions.

So far, we have been treating the net translation gain or loss under each of the methods as a balance sheet item. However, there actually are various treatments possible *under each method* of translation. Before we consider these alternative treatments of the translation gain or loss, however, we should further address the issue of *exposure*.

Accounting Exposure vs. Economic Exposure

Throughout the foregoing discussion, we have pointed out that under each translation method, we can anticipate the nature of the translation gain or loss. We know which items will be translated at the current exchange rate, and only those amounts will give rise to a translation gain or loss. If we know which way the exchange rate is moving, then we can predict whether the translation will result in a gain or a loss for the current period.

We have also observed that since the different methods translate different accounts at the current exchange rate, a given movement in the exchange rate may cause a gain under one method but may cause a loss under another method. In the case of Forsub, above, we calculated a loss of $3,000 under the temporal

---

4. This is true unless the foreign operation has more liabilities than assets, in which case the owner's equity will be a deficit and there will be a net liability position rather than a net asset position.

method, a gain of $15,000 under the current-rate method, and a gain of $10,500 under the current/noncurrent method.

The net balance of those balance sheet amounts that we translated at the current exchange rate is the *accounting exposure* to fluctuations in the foreign exchange rate. This exposure arises as the result of the accounting method of translation that we are using at the time. If a translation gain or loss is to be reported on the financial statements of the parent corporation, then the qualitative characteristic of "representational faithfulness" (in the FASB and *CICA Handbook* sets of criteria) or "isomorphism" (in the CICA Study Group set) should be present. In other words, is there really an *economic* gain to the parent when an accounting gain is reported?

It can be argued that when a Canadian company holds an asset that is denominated in a foreign currency and that currency rises in value against the Canadian dollar, the company experiences an economic gain because the asset increases in value as measured in dollars. Since a Canadian company's equity in a foreign operation is necessarily a net asset position, then one could argue that an increase in the exchange rate will result in a gain to the parent because that net investment will be worth more as a result of the change in the rate.

Such an argument, however, does not take into consideration the impact of changes in the relative values of the currencies on the earnings ability of the foreign subsidiary. In most instances, the foreign operation exists as a going concern that is expected to contribute favourably to the profits of the parent. Therefore, it makes sense to evaluate the impact of currency realignments on the earnings ability of the foreign operation. This impact is known as the **economic exposure** of the foreign operation. The economic exposure is much more complicated than the accounting exposure because many more factors are involved than simply the mechanical aspects of the translation method and the direction of change in the exchange rates.

Suppose, for example, that the business of Forsub Ltd. is to import a product from Canada and to sell it in Pantania. The cost to produce the product is $10.00, and it is sold in Pantania at P6. When the exchange rate is P1 = $2.00, the value of the sale is $12.00 (P6 × $2), resulting in a gross profit of $2.00 ($12 − $10) to Domestic Corporation. But if the exchange rate goes up to P1 = $2.30, the value of each sale will then be $13.80, for an increased gross profit of $3.80. In such a situation, the increase in the value of the pant is a real gain in economic terms. Forsub will either have a larger profit on its sales (if it maintains the same selling price in pants), or it may decrease its price and increase its volume of sales in Pantania (owing to the price elasticity of demand). Either way, Domestic may be better off as a result of the increase in the value of the pant.

Now, suppose instead that the business of Forsub is to produce a product from materials in Pantania and then to transfer the product to Domestic Corporation for sale in Canada. The product costs P10 to produce in Pantania, and sells for $25 in Canada. When the exchange rate is P1 = $2.00, the cost of production is the equivalent of $20, yielding a gross margin of $5. An increase in the value of the pant to $2.30 will cause the production cost to rise to $23 in Canadian dollars, thereby lowering the gross margin to $2.00. In this situation, an increase in the value of the pant can be disadvantageous to Forsub and Domestic Corporation. Instead of being a gain, a rise in the value of the pant is actually a loss in earnings ability.

Of course, things are not really all that simple. Exchange rates do not change autonomously, but are the result of other economic factors, such as relative rates of inflation and interest rate differentials in the various countries. If the value of the pant increased because of high inflation in Canada, then Domestic may be able to charge a higher price for the product and maintain or possibly even increase the relative gross margin on it.

The point is that the economic impact of changes in exchange rates is quite complex and will vary from company to company and situation to situation. The economic exposure is a result of the economic characteristics of the foreign operation, such as the sources of its raw materials, the sources of its debt financing, the market in which its products are sold, the price elasticity of demand for its products, and much more. Economic exposure is forward-looking. *Economic exposure is the impact of an exchange rate change on the present value of future cash flows.*

Accounting exposure, like many other accounting measurements, is historically oriented. It measures the mechanical impact of translating the results of past transactions. The economic exposure is not determinable from the accounting exposure, since the accounting exposure is mechanical in origin and is not necessarily indicative of the earnings impact of a change in exchange rates.

However, application of the concept of representational faithfulness leads to the conclusion that, in any situation, the preferred accounting translation method is the one that yields an accounting exposure that best reflects the economic exposure. If an increase in the exchange rate is likely to have a beneficial economic impact on the foreign operation and the consolidated subsidiary, then the accounting translation method should yield a translation gain when the exchange rate goes up, rather than a loss.

Alternatives for Reporting Translation Gains and Losses

So far in this chapter, we have treated the gain or loss arising from the translation of the balance sheet of a foreign operation simply as a balancing figure on the balance sheet. However, several alternatives are available for the disposition of these gains or losses. All but one of the alternatives have already been discussed in Chapter 9. The broad alternatives are:

1. Recognize the net gain or loss immediately in the consolidated income statement.

2. Disaggregate the net gain or loss and recognize each component in accordance with the treatment of similar types of *transaction* gains or losses.

3. Defer until realized, as a balancing amount in the consolidated balance sheet (e.g., as a separate component of shareholders' equity).

Each of these alternatives can be applied under any one of the three methods of translation described in the earlier sections of this chapter. However, some of the alternatives are more logical under certain of the methods, as we shall see later.

Immediate recognition

Immediate recognition of all exchange gains and losses was the alternative adopted by the FASB in 1975, *SFAS No. 8*, which caused a considerable furor. The FASB considered the various alternatives and found them all lacking. The Board concluded, however, that current recognition was the least misleading or artificial treatment: "...Rate changes are historical facts, and the Board believes that users of financial statements are best served by accounting for the changes as they occur. It is the deferring or spreading of those effects, not their recognition and disclosure, that is the artificial process" [SFAS 8, ¶198].

Since the Board works on the premise that the users of financial statements are sophisticated, it felt that users would understand that the translation gains and losses were unrealized and would not be misled by recognizing the net gains or losses in income.

While the Board was probably correct in assessing the reaction of an efficient market, they failed to anticipate the reactions of managers to the prospect of showing possibly substantial unrealized gains or losses on their companies' income statements. The market as a whole could no doubt properly evaluate the translation gains and losses, but managers were concerned about individuals' reactions to reported amounts, especially losses. The losses would affect net income from operations and therefore would affect earnings per share, dividend payout ratios, and profit-sharing and bonus calculations, as well as certain debt-covenant calculations such as times-interest-earned.

Furthermore, the translation gains and losses were a product of the accounting exposure and were not necessarily an indication of the economic exposure of the company. Empirical research following the implementation of *SFAS No. 8* indicated that many managers with no economic exposure were taking actions to minimize the accounting exposure of their companies, even though those actions might be dysfunctional or represent a misallocation of resources. Some managers were engaging in massive hedging operations in order to offset possible losses from an accounting exposure in a foreign operation. The point of hedging, however, is to offset one economic exposure with another economic exposure in the opposite direction. If hedging is used to offset an artificial accounting exposure, then a real economic exposure is created by the hedge in order to offset a mechanical translation-method "paper" loss.

Other managers were reorganizing the financial affairs of their foreign subsidiaries in order to reduce the accounting exposure. If we assume that the managers made the best decisions in the financial structure of the subsidiaries in the first place, then changes in those decisions as the result of an accounting exposure must be changes that are less than optimal in economic terms.

An additional problem that was perceived by researchers was that the actions of managers to cover their accounting exposures were placing considerable pressure on the U.S. dollar. Ironically, the foreign currency fluctuations that were causing managers to take possibly dysfunctional actions were themselves causing greater fluctuations in the value of the U.S. dollar.

In response to the objections of many people and to the research findings, the FASB reconsidered its position on the disposition of translation gains and losses and issued *SFAS No. 52* in 1981, only six years after *SFAS No. 8* had been issued. The FASB concluded that, in certain circumstances, the translation gains and losses should not be recognized in income, but should instead be reported on a cumulative basis as a separate component of shareholders' equity.

The experience in the United States with *SFAS No. 8* clearly indicated the practical inadvisability of mandating the current recognition of translation gains and losses in all cases. Those instances in which current recognition seems particularly inappropriate are when the foreign operation is substantially autonomous in its activities.

If a foreign operation functions as a separate business unit, then recognition of a translation gain or loss is apt to be misleading because the accounting exposure is not indicative of the economic exposure. The FASB concluded that current recognition "produces results that are not compatible with the expected economic effects of changes in exchange rates" [SFAS No. 52, ¶88].

Disaggregation

The second of the broad approaches to the disposition of translation gains and losses is that of disaggregating the net gain or loss and treating each component individually. Under this alternative, gains and losses arising from monetary items would be treated in the same manner as foreign currency *transactions*, as described in the preceding chapter.

Some foreign operations are extensions of the parent's domestic business. Examples include foreign sales offices and foreign production centres that have no real economic autonomy. Since the parent is directly involved in the foreign operation, the parent is, in effect, using the subsidiary as a facilitating mechanism for a series of foreign currency transactions. Therefore, it is logical to apply the same recognition principles to foreign operations that are interdependent with the parent as would be applied to foreign currency transactions.

The disaggregation alternative is inappropriate for relatively autonomous operations. Disaggregation implies that the parent has direct involvement with the subsidiary, and that the assets and liabilities of the subsidiary should be viewed as directly controlled assets and obligations of the parent. But if the foreign operation is engaged in its own day-to-day activities with little direct interaction from the parent, perhaps arranging its own financing and using the foreign profits to retire the debt, then the parent does not have direct control of the subsidiary's assets and liabilities.

Deferral

The third alternative is to indefinitely defer income statement recognition of the translation gain or loss. The cumulative translation gain or loss will be reported as a balance sheet item. A gain or loss is recognized in income only when the foreign operation is liquidated or significantly wound down. Therefore, the gain or loss would be recognized only when realized by liquidating the investment or a significant portion thereof.

This alternative seems to be appropriate for autonomous operations. There are two possible arguments for deferral of cumulative translation gains and losses:

1. the gain or loss is the result of a mechanical process of translating from a foreign currency into the reporting currency, and thus has no real economic impact on the reporting entity, or

2. the gain or loss is real, but that it has not been realized and is not likely to be realized by the parent corporation.

When translation gains and losses are accumulated directly on the balance sheet, they could be treated as deferred credit or debit, or they could be placed directly in shareholders' equity. Treatment of the cumulative gain or loss as a deferred credit or charge would imply that the translation gain or loss is a liability or an asset. Since there is no logic to support this view, the cumulative foreign currency adjustment is treated as a separate component of consolidated shareholders' equity.

The Two Solitudes: Integrated vs. Self-Sustaining Operations

We discussed above the three general alternatives for reporting translation gains and losses for foreign operations. In practice, not only in Canada but also in international accounting standards and in the U.S., two of the three alternatives are applied. The one alternative that is *not* used is the first one, recognizing all gains and losses immediately in the income statement. As we saw above, that alternative has been tried and found inadequate.

The other two approaches are used in practice, not only in Canada, but around the world. Practice is quite consistent, world-wide. To apply two different approaches, we must define the circumstances under which each can be used. The distinction essentially is on the basis of whether the foreign operation operates as an extension of the parent's operation (i.e., as a branch) or is quite autonomous in its operations. In Canada, the distinction is between (1) integrated and (2) self-sustaining foreign operations. Essentially, integrated operations are those that are interdependent with the parent, while self-sustaining operations are those that are relatively autonomous.

The *CICA Handbook* definition of an **integrated operation** is that it is:

> ...a foreign operation which is financially or operationally interdependent with the reporting enterprise such that the exposure to exchange rate changes is similar to the exposure which would exist had the transactions and activities of the foreign operation been undertaken by the reporting enterprise [CICA 1650.03].

Such operations usually are treated as revenue centres or cost centres from a management accounting standpoint. Integrated operations are largely or entirely dependent on the parent, either for a source of product or for disposition of production. Interdependent foreign operations are a direct arm of the parent and the parent controls the assets and liabilities of the subsidiary. The IASC calls such operations "foreign operations that are integral to the operations of the reporting enterprise."

The *CICA Handbook* calls independent or autonomous foreign operations *self-sustaining*. The definition of a **self-sustaining foreign operation** is:

> ...a foreign operation which is financially and operationally independent of the reporting enterprise such that the exposure to exchange rate changes is limited to the reporting enterprise's net investment in the foreign operation. [CICA 1650.03]

Unfortunately, this definition combines elements of independence with aspects of assumed economic exposure. As the previous section pointed out, economic circumstances seldom are so simple as to permit a company to declare that its economic exposure is limited to its net investment in the foreign operation.

Section 1650 provides a set of six criteria to aid preparers in deciding whether a foreign operation is self-sustaining. In essence, they are as follows:

a. Are the cash flows of the operation independent of the parent?

b. Are prices responsive to local market conditions?

c. Are the sales made primarily in foreign markets?

d. Are operating costs, products, and services obtained primarily in the foreign country?

e. Are the day-to-day operations financed from its own operations?

f. Does the foreign operation function without day-to-day transactions with the parent?

The U.S. FASB and the international accounting standards have similar guidelines.

It must be emphasized that these are only *guidelines*, not *rules*. Applying the guidelines is not a matter of score-keeping (e.g., four "yes" versus two "no") but is an exercise of professional judgement in determining the substance of the relationship between the domestic parent and its foreign operation(s).

An implicit assumption is that foreign operations can be categorized as *integrated* or *self-sustaining* with little ambiguity. Integrated and self-sustaining are really the two ends of a continuum, and many foreign operations fall in between the two extremes, with some aspects of each type of operation. In particular, the operations of world-wide corporations tend to be neither integrated nor self-sustaining, but to display aspects of both. The selection of translation method from among the limited alternatives currently offered in the *CICA Handbook* therefore becomes a matter of professional judgement.

In the U.S., the FASB defines the accounting treatment on the basis of the foreign operation's *functional currency*. The **functional currency** is the currency in which the bulk of the foreign operation's transactions are carried out. For example, if the foreign operation is financed by its parent, acquires its product from the parent, and remits payment for the product (and perhaps also for licence fees and management fees) in U.S. dollars, then the functional currency is the U.S. dollar rather than the local currency. The means of defining the basis for translation is different in the U.S. than in Canada, but the net result is essentially the same.

Integrated foreign operations

By definition, integrated operations operate as extensions of the parent company in a foreign country. Therefore, their operations are viewed simply as a series of foreign currency *transactions*. The results obtained by translating the financial statements of the foreign operation should appear as though the parent had engaged in the foreign currency transactions directly, rather than through a foreign subsidiary.

The method used for translating integrated operations should be compatible with that used for reporting the results of foreign currency transactions. The method that accomplishes this objective is the *temporal method*. Therefore, the *CICA Handbook* recommends the temporal method for translating integrated foreign operations [CICA 1650.29].

Since the objective of translating integrated operations is to achieve the same results as for foreign currency transactions, the disposition of the translation gains and losses that arise from translating integrated foreign operations is treated in the same manner as for transactions [CICA 1650.31]. That is, under the recommendations of Section 1650, the cumulative gain or loss is disaggregated and reported as follows:

1. In the current year's net income, to the extent that the gain or loss relates to:

   a. current monetary transactions and balances, and

   b. current year's amortization of deferred gains and losses on long-term monetary balances.

2. As a deferred charge or deferred credit, to the extent that the gain or loss relates to monetary balances of fixed maturity and represents the portion being deferred to future years under a defer-and-amortize policy.

3. As a part of retained earnings, to the extent that the gain or loss has been recognized in previous years' income.

We will demonstrate the application of this disaggregation in the following sections. When the defer-and-amortize recommendation for gains and losses on long-term monetary items is removed from Section 1650, the disaggregation will be much simpler:

1. As a part of retained earnings, to the extent that the cumulative gain or loss has been recognized in previous years' income.

2. In the current year's net income, to the extent that the cumulative gain or loss arises from changes in exchange rates during the current period.

Specific assets or liabilities in an integrated foreign operation could be hedged by the parent. In that case, any gain or loss arising from the hedge would be offset against the exchange loss or gain on the hedged balance [CICA 1650.54]. The *CICA Handbook*'s provisions for designating a monetary or nonmonetary balance (or the revenue stream therefrom) as an implicit hedge, as was discussed in Chapter 9, also are applicable to integrated foreign operations.

Self-sustaining foreign operations

A self-sustaining foreign operation is viewed as being an individual, autonomous foreign business entity. The parent company's accounting exposure to exchange rate changes is limited to the net investment of the parent in the foreign subsidiary. Therefore, the AcSB recommends the use of the *current-rate method* for translating the financial statements of self-sustaining operations [CICA 1650.33]. The net gain or loss that arises from translating self-sustaining operations is not recognized on the income statement, but is reported as a separate component of shareholders' equity [CICA 1650.34]. As we explained above, this treatment is recommended because:

1. the accounting exposure may not be indicative of the economic exposure, and

2. this exchange gain or loss has no direct effect on the activities of the reporting enterprise.

The translation gains or losses from self-sustaining foreign operations will continue to accumulate in the shareholders' equity account. Section 1650 recommends that companies disclose "the significant elements which give rise to changes" in the accumulated amount in the shareholders' equity account [CICA 1650.39], but many companies simply summarize the changes in the balance without any attempt to disclose "significant elements," presumably because it is difficult (if not irrational) to try to segregate the components of a net investment.

If the parent's net investment in the subsidiary is decreased, a proportionate part of the accumulated amount will be transferred from shareholders' equity to net income [CICA 1650.38]. Thus, as long as dividends declared by a self-sustaining subsidiary do not exceed current earnings, and as long as the parent does not sell part of its investment in the subsidiary, none of the translation gain will be recognized in income.

The parent may choose to hedge its net investment in a self-sustaining subsidiary. Any gains or losses from the hedge will be offset against the cumulative translation loss or gain in the separate component of shareholders' equity [CICA 1650.55].

Operations in hyper-inflationary economies

An exception to the general recommendation to use the current-rate method for self-sustaining operations arises when the self-sustaining operation is in a country that has a high inflation rate. Some countries historically have had very high rates of inflation, sometimes well over 100% per year. Historical-cost financial statements will show long-term nonmonetary assets at a cost that is expressed in currency of a far different purchasing power than the current exchange rate suggests. One solution is to adjust the foreign operation's financial statements for changes in the price level in the foreign country, and then to translate the adjusted statements. But since price level adjustments are not normally included in primary financial statements in Canada, the AcSB has rejected this approach.

Instead, the recommendation is to use the *temporal method* for translating the statements of operations in highly inflationary economies [CICA 1650.33]. In substance, the effects of inflation are removed from the foreign accounts by restating the accounts using the historical exchange rates for nonmonetary items. Of course, the effects of Canadian inflation are still present in the accounts, but the relative difference in inflation rates between Canada and the foreign country is adjusted for by using the temporal method. The AcSB does not provide guidelines as to what constitutes a "highly inflationary" economy, but the similar recommendations in the FASB's *SFAS No. 52* suggest that an inflation rate of 100% over a three-year period (that is, averaging 26% per year, compounded) would be highly inflationary. However, the FASB guideline is absolute, whereas the *CICA Handbook* criterion is relative to the Canadian inflation rate.

Application of Section 1650 Recommendations

Integrated operations

Let us return to the introductory example of Domestic Corporation and its Pantanian subsidiary, Forsub Ltd. We determined earlier in the chapter that under the temporal method of translation, there was a net translation loss of $3,000 in the first year. If Forsub is an integrated subsidiary, the temporal method is used, and the net translation loss of $3,000 will be disaggregated *on Domestic Corporation's statements.*

Exhibit 10-1 shows that the $3,000 loss is composed of three components:

- a $6,000 gain from holding cash,

- a $1,500 loss from the accounts payable, and

- a $7,500 loss from the bonds payable.

The current items account for a net gain of $4,500 ($6,000 gain less $1,500 loss). This entire gain is recognized currently in net income. The loss arising from the bonds, however, will be amortized over the life of the bonds. Since the bonds have a five-year life, one-fifth of the $7,500 loss, or $1,500, is recognized in income in the current year. The remaining $6,000 will be capitalized and reported on the balance sheet as a deferred debit, to be charged to expense at the rate of $1,500 per year over the remaining four years.

In summary, then, application of the *CICA Handbook* recommendations to Forsub Ltd. as an integrated foreign operation will result in a net translation gain of $3,000 being reported on Domestic's 2001 income statement: the $4,500 net gain from the current accounts (cash and accounts payable), less the $1,500 current year amortization of the loss from the bonds. Domestic's December 31, 2001, balance sheet will show a deferred debit of $6,000 for the unamortized portion of the loss on the bonds payable.

Self-sustaining operations

Instead, suppose that Forsub Ltd. is treated as a *self-sustaining* foreign operation. Then the current-rate method is appropriate—the entire translation gain or loss will be reported as a separate component of Domestic Corporation's shareholders' equity. Exhibit 10-3 shows that the current-rate method yields a net translation gain of $15,000, none of which is included in net income.

Obviously, a key facet of applying the AcSB recommendations is the determination of whether a foreign operation is integrated or is self-sufficient. Bear in mind, however, that if the foreign operations are relatively minor or if the parent is not otherwise constrained to follow the *CICA Handbook* recommendations, it may be simpler and no less informative to apply the current-rate method across the board to all foreign subsidiaries and to report the translation gains or losses either in the parent's consolidated shareholders' equity or in income.

Extending the example

Earlier in this chapter, we described the initial transactions for the establishment of Forsub Ltd. by Domestic Corporation. After Forsub was established, the subsidiary purchased land and inventory and issued bonds. Exhibits 10-1, 10-3, and 10-4 illustrate translation of Forsub's balance sheet accounts under three different translation methods. For simplicity, we assumed that Forsub had no operating revenues or expenses for the first year, 2001 (even though, strictly speaking, there should have been some bond interest accrued). While we did point out that some of the translation gain or loss may be taken into income in 2001, it is taken into income by the *parent* company and reported on the consolidated income statement.

Now let us make the example more realistic by looking at Forsub's financial statements for the next year, 2002. Forsub Ltd.'s separate-entity balance sheet and income statement are shown in Exhibit 10-5. Additional information is as follows:

1. At the beginning of 2002, Forsub purchased some equipment for P30,000; the equipment has an expected useful life of six years.

2. Total sales for 2002 were P60,000, and purchases of inventory amounted to P30,000.

3. The ending inventory was purchased in the last quarter of the year, when the exchange rate was $2.45.

4. The exchange rate at December 31, 2002, was $2.50; the average rate during the year was $2.40.

EXHIBIT 10–5 FORSUB LTD. FINANCIAL STATEMENTS, 2002

Balance Sheet
December 31, 2002

Assets		Liabilities and shareholders' equity	
Cash	P 15,000	Accounts payable, current	P 22,000
Accounts receivable	15,000	Bonds payable, long term	25,000
Inventory	10,000		47,000
Land	40,000	Common shares	50,000
Equipment	30,000	Retained earnings*	8,000
Accumulated depreciation	(5,000)		58,000
Total assets	P105,000		P105,000

* No revenues or expenses were recognized in 2001, the only previous year.

Income Statement
Year Ended December 31, 2002

Sales revenue		P 60,000
Cost of sales:		
Beginning inventory	P20,000	
Purchases	30,000	
Ending inventory	(10,000)	40,000
Gross margin		20,000
Operating expenses:		
Depreciation	5,000	
Interest expense	3,000	
Other expenses	4,000	12,000
Net income		P 8,000

Current-rate method

The translation of Forsub's account balances by using the current-rate method is shown in Exhibit 10-6. All of the assets and liabilities are translated at the year-end exchange rate of $2.50. The shareholders' equity accounts are translated at the historical rates:

- common shares at the rate that existed at the time of the initial investment, and

- retained earnings at the rate that existed at the time the earnings were recognized.

In this example, the only amount in retained earnings is the current earnings for 2002, and thus the translated amount is the same as that shown on the translated income statement. The balancing figure for the balance sheet is the cumulative translation gain of $25,800.

Under a pure application of the current-rate method, the income statement would also be translated at the year-end rate. However, Exhibit 10-6 shows the income statement being translated at the average rate for the year rather than at the year-end rate. This is known as the **average-rate approach** to the current-rate method, and is used primarily in order to ensure additivity of the interim

EXHIBIT 10–6 TRANSLATION BY CURRENT-RATE METHOD, 2002

Exchange rate, December 31, 2002: P1.00 = Cdn$2.50
Average exchange rate for 2002: P1.00 = Cdn$2.40

Balance Sheet
December 31, 2002

	Local currency (pants)	Exchange rate	Translated amounts (C$)
Assets			
Cash	P 15,000	$2.50	$ 37,500
Accounts receivable	15,000	2.50	37,500
Inventory	10,000	2.50	25,000
Land	40,000	2.50	100,000
Equipment	30,000	2.50	75,000
Accumulated depreciation	(5,000)	2.50	(12,500)
Total assets	P105,000		$262,500
Liabilities and shareholders' equity			
Accounts payable, current	P 22,000	2.50	$ 55,000
Bonds payable, long term	25,000	2.50	62,500
	47,000		117,500
Common shares	50,000	2.00	100,000
Retained earnings	8,000	(below)	19,200
Cumulative translation gain (loss)*	—		**25,800**
	58,000		145,000
Total liabilities and shareholders' equity	P105,000		$262,500

Income Statement
Year Ended December 31, 2002

	Local currency (pants)	Exchange rate	Translated amounts (C$)
Sales	P 60,000	$ 2.40	$144,000
Cost of sales:			
Beginning inventory	20,000		
Purchases	30,000		
Ending inventory	(10,000)		
	40,000	2.40	96,000
Gross margin	20,000		48,000
Operating expenses:			
Depreciation	5,000	2.40	12,000
Interest expense	3,000	2.40	7,200
Other expenses	4,000	2.40	9,600
	12,000		28,800
Net income	P 8,000		$ 19,200

* *Cumulative exchange gain:*

2001 gain on P50,000 net investment: P50,000 × ($2.30 − $2.00) = $15,000

2002 gain on P50,000 net investment: P50,000 × ($2.50 − $2.30) = 10,000

2002 gain on retained earnings: P8,000 × ($2.50 − $2.40) = 800

Cumulative translation gain $25,800

earnings figures of the parent company. Both Section 1650 and *SFAS No. 52* recommend the use of the average rate rather than the year-end rate for income statement amounts.

On the income statement, all items are translated at the current (average) rate, regardless of the type of revenue or expense, assuming that the revenue and expense accrued evenly through the year. Allocations of past costs, such as depreciation, are translated the same as are current costs, such as interest expense. As a result, the translated amount of net income is also equal to the current (average) rate times the net income as expressed in pants.

The cumulative translation gain of $25,800 that arises under the current-rate method can be broken down into three components:

1. the $15,000 gain arising from the first year's change in the exchange rate from $2.00 to $2.30 (Exhibit 10-3),

2. an additional $10,000 gain in the current year, 2002, caused by a further increase in the exchange rate from $2.30 to $2.50, and

3. an $800 gain on the retained earnings from the period of their generation (mid-2002) to the end of 2002, during which period the exchange rate changed from $2.40 to $2.50.

These components of the cumulative gain are summarized at the bottom of Exhibit 10-6.

Temporal method

If, instead, the accounts of Forsub Ltd. are translated by using the temporal method, then the procedure is somewhat more complicated. Exhibit 10-7 illustrates the application of the temporal method for 2002.

The monetary assets and liabilities are translated by using the current rate. The nonmonetary assets are translated at their historical rates. It is assumed that the ending inventory was purchased when the exchange rate was $2.45, and thus that is the historical rate for inventory. The specific historical rate for land is $2.00 and for the equipment is $2.30. The accumulated depreciation must be translated at the same rate as was used for the gross asset cost.

On the income statement, the revenues and expenses are translated at the rates that were in effect at the time that the revenues were realized or the costs incurred. For many revenue and expense items, realization coincides with recognition, so that the historical rate is essentially the same as the average rate for the period as was used in the current-rate method. Although the result is the same for some income statement items, the concept is quite different.

Under the current-rate method, cost of sales could be translated simply by taking the cost of sales in pants and multiplying it by the average exchange rate for the period. Under the temporal method, however, the cost of sales amount must be derived by multiplying the beginning inventory by its historical rate of $2.00, adding the purchases at the historical/average rate of $2.40, and subtracting the ending inventory at its historical rate of $2.45. The resulting figure for cost of sales, $87,500, *cannot be derived directly by multiplying any exchange rate by the cost of sales in pants, P40,000.*

Similarly, any depreciation or amortization expense must be translated at the exchange rates that existed at the time the original costs were incurred. In this example, the only such expense is the depreciation of the equipment. Since the equipment was purchased when the rate was $2.30, the depreciation expense must be translated at $2.30. Other expenses are translated at the rate that existed

EXHIBIT 10–7 TRANSLATION BY TEMPORAL METHOD, 2002

Exchange rate, December 31, 2002: P1.00 = Cdn$2.50
Average exchange rate for 2002: P1.00 = Cdn$2.40

Balance Sheet
December 31, 2002

	Local currency (pants)	Exchange rate Type	Exchange rate Amount	Translated amounts (Cdn$)
Assets				
Cash	P 15,000	C	$ 2.50	$ 37,500
Accounts receivable	15,000	C	2.50	37,500
Inventory	10,000	H	2.45	24,500
Land	40,000	H	2.00	80,000
Equipment	30,000	H	2.30	69,000
Accumulated depreciation	(5,000)	H	2.30	(11,500)
Total assets	P105,000			$237,000
Liabilities and shareholders' equity				
Accounts payable, current	P 22,000	C	2.50	$ 55,000
Bonds payable, long term	25,000	C	2.50	62,500
	47,000			117,500
Common shares	50,000	H	2.00	100,000
Retained earnings	8,000			28,200
	58,000			128,200
Total liabilities and shareholders' equity	P105,000			$245,700
Cumulative translation gain (loss)[Exhibit 10-8]				$ (8,700)

Income Statement
Year Ended December 31, 2002

	Local currency (pants)	Exchange rate Type	Exchange rate Amount	Translated amounts (Cdn$)
Sales	P 60,000	H/A	$2.40	$144,000
Cost of sales:				
Beginning inventory	20,000	H	2.00	40,000
Purchases	30,000	H/A	2.40	72,000
Ending inventory	(10,000)	H	2.45	(24,500)
	40,000			87,500
Gross margin	20,000			56,500
Operating expenses:				
Depreciation	5,000	H	2.30	11,500
Interest expense	3,000	A	2.40	7,200
Other expenses	4,000	H/A	2.40	9,600
	12,000			28,300
Net income	P 8,000			$ 28,200

Exchange rate types:

C = current, year-end rate

A = average rate for the year

H = historical rate for the individual item

H/A = historical rate, assumed to be the average for the year when they were *accrued.* It does not matter whether they have been paid in cash or not. Thus interest expense and other expenses have been translated at the average rate for the year.

The net income that results from using the temporal method amounts to $28,200 before considering any components of the translation loss. This amount cannot be derived directly from the original net income of P8,000—it must be obtained by working through the income statement and translating all of its individual components by the appropriate historical rates. Note that the temporal method net income of $28,200 is quite different from the current-rate method net income of $19,200. This difference is due to the lags in expense recognition of two types of costs: inventory and depreciable capital assets.

Translation of Forsub Ltd.'s accounts to dollars results in total assets of $237,000, as compared to total equities of $245,700. The cumulative translation loss therefore is $8,700. In Exhibit 10-7, the cumulative translation loss is shown as a single amount pending disposition, rather than being distributed to the income statement, the balance sheet, or both. The reason is that when the foreign operation's statements are translated, the translation gain or loss is not part of the statements of the subsidiary, but is an amount that must be allocated or assigned *on the parent's consolidated statements.*

Allocating the translation loss—temporal method

We know from Exhibit 10-1 that $3,000 of the $8,700 cumulative translation loss arose in 2001, and therefore that the loss arising in 2002 must be the remainder, or $5,700. The $5,700 loss for 2002 has two components:

1. a loss arising from the long-term liability of the bonds payable, and

2. a loss from the net current items.

The loss on the bonds payable is the P25,000 balance times the exchange rate *change* during the period, $2.30 to $2.50: P25,000 × ($2.50 − $2.30) = $5,000 for 2002. The remainder of $700 is attributable to the current items.

The gain or loss from holding current monetary assets and liabilities can be computed by analyzing the flow of these items. Unlike the bonds payable in this example, the current assets and liabilities are not constant throughout the year. The impact of the exchange gains and losses must be measured only for the period of time that the current monetary items are in the enterprise. For example, sales revenue increased current monetary assets, either as cash or as accounts receivable, by P60,000. Assuming that the sales were even throughout the year, we can measure the gain from holding monetary assets resulting from the sales by multiplying the P60,000 by the change in the exchange rate from the average for the year ($2.40) to the end of the year ($2.50). Similarly, the current expenses (or expenditures) that caused either a decline in monetary assets or an increase in monetary liabilities must be taken into account.

The easiest way to measure the net gain or loss from the current monetary assets and liabilities is to construct a funds-flow statement, with funds defined as net current monetary assets. Starting with the beginning-of-year balance of these net assets, we can add the inflows and subtract the outflows, to arrive at the year-end balance of net current monetary assets expressed in pants. We then need only to convert each balance or flow at the exchange rate in effect at the time of the balance or flow, and find the difference at year-end between the balance in foreign currency and the derived amount in domestic currency.

Such a funds-flow statement is shown at the top of Exhibit 10-8. The ending balance in pants is P8,000, as can be verified by referring to Exhibit 10-5. The

EXHIBIT 10–8 TEMPORAL METHOD—ANALYSIS OF CUMULATIVE TRANSLATION LOSS, 2002

	Local currency (pants)	Exchange rate	Translated amounts (Cdn$)
Amounts arising in 2002:			
Current monetary items:			
Balance, January 1, 2002	P15,000	$2.30	$ 34,500
Changes during 2002:			
Sales revenue	60,000	2.40	144,000
Inventory purchases	(30,000)	2.40	(72,000)
Interest expense	(3,000)	2.40	(7,200)
Other expenses	(4,000)	2.40	(9,600)
Purchase of equipment	(30,000)	2.30	(69,000)
Derived balance, December 31, 2002			20,700
Actual balance, December 31, 2002	P 8,000	2.50	20,000
Net exchange loss from current monetary items, 2002			700
Long-term debt:			
2002 loss due to change in exchange rate:			
P25,000 × ($2.50 − $2.30)			5,000
Total exchange loss for 2002			5,700
Amounts relating to previous periods (Exhibit 10-1):			
Current monetary items (gain)	$ (4,500)		
Long-term debt	7,500		
Loss from previous years			3,000
Cumulative translation loss, December 31, 2002			**$ 8,700**

year-end balance is equivalent to $20,000 at the balance sheet date. The sum of the inflows and outflows, however, when translated at the rates in effect during the year, amounts to $20,700. In effect, the $20,700 shows what the ending balance of the net current monetary assets would have been if Domestic Corporation had maintained all of its Pantanian balances in dollars rather than in pants, and had converted to and from dollars only on the transaction dates. Since the actual dollar-equivalent balance of the accounts in pants is only $20,000, Domestic Corporation has suffered a loss of $700 by having Forsub Ltd. hold balances in pants.

The remainder of Exhibit 10-8 summarizes the remaining amounts included in the $8,700 cumulative translation loss at December 31, 2002. As we stated above, a total of $3,000 of the loss pertains to 2001, while the remaining loss of $5,700 pertains to 2002.

When Domestic Corporation consolidates Forsub Ltd., the total cumulative translation loss of $8,700 must be included somewhere in Domestic's consolidated financial statements. The temporal method is intended to yield the same result as if Domestic had carried out the foreign transactions directly. Therefore, the *translation* loss must be reported in Domestic's consolidated statements in a way that duplicates the treatment of gains and losses from foreign currency *transactions*.

In Chapter 9, we saw that the unique Canadian approach to gains and losses on long-term monetary items has been to defer and amortize those gains and losses over their remaining term (including the current year). The defer-and-amortize approach significantly complicates the disposition of the translation loss. However, since that unique Canadian approach is about to be eliminated, we will not illustrate its application, but will instead look only at the soon-to-be-adopted approach that is used everywhere else in the world.

When the defer-and-amortize approach is *not* used, the consolidation process is quite straightforward:

- The portion of the cumulative translation gain or loss that relates to *prior years* is included in opening consolidated retained earnings.

- The portion of the gain or loss that relates to the *current year* is reported in the consolidated income statement, along with any foreign currency gains and losses of the parent.

For Domestic, the $8,700 year-end 2002 cumulative translation loss will be reported as follows:

- The $3,000 loss that arose in 2001 will be included in consolidated retained earnings for January 1, 2002.

- The $5,700 loss pertaining to 2002 will be reported as an expense (i.e., foreign exchange loss) in Domestic's consolidated income statement for the year ending December 31, 2002.

Comparison of accounting implications

Exhibit 10-9 compares the reporting implications of judging a foreign operation to be either *self-sustaining* or *integrated*. The decision to report a foreign subsidiary as one type or the other will determine the translation method to be used, which in turn will decide (1) whether the translation effect will be a gain or a loss and (2) how that gain or loss will be reported in the parent's consolidated financial statements.

EXHIBIT 10–9 COMPARISON OF ACCOUNTING FOR FOREIGN OPERATIONS		
Accounting issue	**Self-sustaining**	**Integrated**
Translation method	Current-rate method	Temporal method
Basis of accounting exposure	Net investment in subsidiary (usually a net asset position)	Net monetary items (most often a net liability position)
Most likely translation gain/loss:		
If foreign currency is strengthening	Exchange gain	Exchange loss
If foreign currency is weakening	Exchange loss	Exchange gain
Accounting treatment of gain/loss:		
Arising from previous years	Report as separate component of shareholders' equity	Include in opening consolidated retained earnings
Arising in the current year	Report as separate component of shareholders' equity	Report in consolidated income statement
Indication of true economic exchange risk exposure?	No relationship	No relationship

In Exhibit 10-9, we have assumed that the defer-and-amortize approach to accounting for translation gains and losses on long-term monetary items is eliminated. We have also assumed that, in most cases, the amount of foreign-currency-denominated liabilities exceeds the foreign-currency-denominated assets. This is the most common scenario, because a foreign subsidiary usually obtains debt financing locally.

Remember, however, that the accounting exposure does not reflect the economic exposure. There is no necessary relationship between the direction of change in a foreign currency and its impact on the economic contribution of the foreign operation to its parent's welfare.

Summary of Key Points

1. A domestic Canadian corporation may establish a subsidiary in another country. When that happens, the parent has a foreign operation. The separate-entity financial statements of the foreign operation will be stated in terms of the host country's local currency. In order to prepare consolidated financial statements, the parent must translate the foreign currency statements of the subsidiary into the parent's reporting currency (normally Canadian dollars, but sometimes U.S. dollars).

2. There are four methods for translating foreign operations: the temporal method, the monetary/nonmonetary method, the current/noncurrent method, and the current-rate method.

3. The temporal method translates all monetary assets and liabilities at the exchange rate at the balance sheet date, known as the *current rate*. Nonmonetary assets and liabilities are translated at historical rates, except for those that are carried at current value. For current-valued nonmonetary assets, the current rate is used. The monetary/nonmonetary method is similar to the temporal method, except that current-valued nonmonetary assets are translated at historical exchange rates.

   The temporal method achieves the same translated amounts as would have arisen if the parent corporation had carried out all of the foreign operations directly, as a series of foreign currency transactions, instead of through a foreign subsidiary.

4. The current-rate method translates all balance sheet amounts at the current rate as of the balance sheet date. Income statement amounts usually are translated at the average rate for the year.

5. The current/noncurrent method is based on an underlying assumption of an implicit hedge. Monetary long-term liabilities are assumed to be implicitly hedged by the long-term nonmonetary assets, primarily capital assets.

6. In a world of fluctuating exchange rates, all translation methods will yield a translation gain or loss. The apparent foreign currency gain or loss is not a real economic gain or loss, however. Accounting gains and losses are the result of the *accounting exposure* to foreign currency fluctuations, and are a mechanical result of the translation method used. Economic exposure to foreign currency fluctuations is the result of real economic impacts on the foreign subsidiary's operations, and cannot be measured by accounting methodologies. Any correspondence between accounting exposure and economic exposure is purely coincidental.

7. Translation gains and losses can be (1) recognized in income immediately, (2) disaggregated in accordance with the treatment given to *transaction* gains and losses, or (3) deferred. Immediate recognition has been tried (in the U.S.) and subsequently rejected. The two remaining methods are both in use, even though they give diametrically opposed results. Disaggregation is the approach applied to foreign operations that are integral to the parent's operations. These are called *integrated foreign operations*. Deferral, as a separate component of the parent's shareholders' equity, is the approach used for foreign operations that operate autonomously, known as *self-sustaining foreign operations*.

8. The translation gain or loss that arises from translating the statements of an integrated foreign operation must be disaggregated and reported in a manner that is consistent with reporting foreign currency transactions. Under Section 1650, this requires allocation of the total translation gain or loss to (1) retained earnings, to the extent that gains and losses relate to previous periods, (2) current earnings, for the current year's gain or loss relating to current monetary or current-valued assets and liabilities, plus the current year's share of amortization of gains and losses relating to long-term monetary items, and (3) deferral to future periods of the unamortized portion of gains and losses relating to long-term monetary items. When the Canadian practice of defer-and-amortize for long-term items is eliminated, the gains and losses relating to all monetary (and current-valued) assets and liabilities will flow directly into income.

Weblinks

The Canadian Academic Accounting Association
www.stmarys.ca/partners/caaa/caaa2.htm

The Canadian Academic Accounting Association (CAAA) is an organization comprised of accounting educators, professional accountants, and others who are involved in, and concerned about, research and education in accounting and related areas.

The Electronic Accountant
www.electronicaccountant.com

Visit this site to access news and critical accounting industry information. Topics include newswire, weblinks, commentary, discussion groups, feature articles, and accounting/tax software exhibit halls.

Bank of Canada Inflation Calculator
www.bankofcanada.ca/en/inflation_calc.htm

The Inflation Calculator uses monthly consumer price index (CPI) data from 1914 to the present to show changes in the cost of a fixed "basket" of consumer purchases, including food, shelter, transportation, clothing, and recreation.

Strategis
strategis.ic.gc.ca

Industry Canada's home page provides business information and statistics on markets, industries, company sourcing, business partners and alliances, products, international trade, business management, microeconomies, regulations, and research laboratories.

Self-Study Problem 10-1

Early in 2001, Irene Corporation established a subsidiary in Simonia. The subsidiary was named Gordon Limited, and Irene's investment was $1,250,000.

When this investment was translated into Simonian Frasers (the currency of Simonia), the initial capitalization amounted to SF500,000.

Gordon Limited negotiated a 3-year bank loan of SF200,000 from a Simonian bank when the exchange rate was $2.40. The company purchased depreciable capital assets for SF600,000 (exchange rate = $2.30).

The company then began operations. Due to an accumulation of cash through operations, Gordon invested SF200,000 in *nonmonetary* temporary investments during 2002. The exchange rate at the time of the investments was $1.90. At the end of 2002, Gordon's comparative balance sheet and income statement are as shown in Exhibit 10-10.

Other exchange rate information for the Simonian Fraser is as follows:

2001 average	$2.20
2001 year-end	$2.00
2002 average	$1.70
2002 year-end	$1.50

Required:

Assume that Gordon Limited is a self-sustaining subsidiary. Determine how the financial statement amounts shown in Gordon's balance sheet and income state-

EXHIBIT 10–10 GORDON LIMITED

Income Statement
Years Ending December 31

	2002	2001
Revenue	SF300,000	SF220,000
Depreciation expense	60,000	60,000
Interest expense	40,000	40,000
Other expenses	120,000	80,000
	220,000	180,000
Net income	SF 80,000	SF 40,000

Balance Sheet
December 31

	2002	2001
Assets		
Cash	SF 30,000	SF160,000
Accounts receivable	40,000	30,000
Temporary investments (at cost)	200,000	—
Tangible capital assets	600,000	600,000
Accumulated depreciation	(120,000)	(60,000)
Total assets	SF750,000	SF730,000
Liabilities and shareholders' equity		
Accounts payable, current	SF 10,000	SF 20,000
Notes payable, due January 1, 2004	200,000	200,000
	210,000	220,000
Common shares	500,000	500,000
Retained earnings	40,000	10,000
	540,000	510,000
Total liabilities and shareholders' equity	SF750,000	SF730,000

ment will affect Irene Corporation's consolidated statements for *each* of 2001 and 2002, including disposition of the cumulative translation gain or loss.

Self-Study Problem 10-2

Refer to the information in **SSP10-1** and Exhibit 10-10. Assume instead that Gordon Limited is an integrated foreign operation, as defined by Section 1650 of the *CICA Handbook*.

Required:

a. Translate Gordon's 2001 financial statements.

b. Disaggregate the 2001 translation gain or loss. Prove the amount of gain or loss relating to current monetary items. Indicate how the translation gains or losses would appear on Irene Corporation's consolidated statements.

c. Translate Gordon's 2002 financial statements.

d. Determine the amount of translation gain or loss on the current monetary items for 2002.

Review Questions

10-1 Distinguish between foreign currency *transactions* and foreign currency *operations.*

10-2 Explain the difference between the current rate and historical rate used for translation.

10-3 Explain what a *translation gain or loss* is and how it arises.

10-4 Explain the differences between these four translation methods:
   a. Monetary/nonmonetary
   b. Temporal
   c. Current rate
   d. Current/noncurrent

10-5 Which assets and liabilities of a foreign operation are translated at the same rate under all of the translation methods?

10-6 Why is the common share account of a foreign subsidiary translated at the historical rate under all translation methods?

10-7 Under what circumstances will the monetary/nonmonetary method yield the same results as the temporal method?

10-8 Which translation method views the foreign subsidiary's operations as though they were foreign currency transactions of the parent?

10-9 Why do balances that are translated at historical rates not give rise to translation gains or losses?

10-10 What is meant by the *accounting exposure* of a foreign operation? How is the accounting exposure measured?

10-11 How does the accounting exposure under the temporal method differ from the accounting exposure under the current-rate method?

10-12 For a given foreign operation for a given accounting period, is it possible for the accounting exposure under the temporal method to result in a translation loss, while the accounting exposure under the current-rate method results in a translation gain? Explain.

10-13 Some people consider a translation method to be desirable when it results in the same *relative* values for the translated assets and liabilities as for the untranslated amounts. Which method or methods achieve this result?

10-14 Prior to 1983, when the temporal method was imposed by the AcSB, what was the most common translation method used by Canadian companies for their foreign operations?

10-15 Explain how the current/noncurrent method assumes the existence of an *implicit hedge*.

10-16 Define *economic exposure*. Distinguish between economic exposure and accounting exposure.

10-17 What is the basic criterion by which the appropriateness of a translation method should be judged in a specific situation?

10-18 In the case of many foreign operations, gains and losses arising from translation will not be realized by the parent corporation. What then is the argument in favour of immediate recognition of translation gains and losses in the parent's consolidated income statement?

10-19 Forop Ltd. is a foreign subsidiary of Domop Inc. Domop's accounting exposure to exchange rate changes when translating the accounts of Forop is a substantial net liability exposure. Domop's management expects the foreign currency in which Forop operates to increase in value relative to the Canadian dollar; such an increase will result in a large translation loss. The management of Domop proposes to enter into a forward contract to receive an equivalent amount of foreign currency in order to hedge against the potential translation loss. Would you recommend that Domop's management follow their proposed course of action? Explain.

10-20 Distinguish between *self-sustaining* foreign operations and *integrated* foreign operations.

10-21 What translation method is recommended by the *CICA Handbook* for *integrated* foreign operations? Why is this method recommended?

10-22 What recommendation does the *CICA Handbook* make regarding the financial statement disposition of translation gains or losses for integrated foreign operations? Why?

10-23 How can management decide whether a foreign operation is integrated or self-sustaining?

10-24 Mammoth Corporation has subsidiaries in thirteen different countries, operating in ten different currencies. Do all thirteen have to be viewed the same way, or can some be considered integrated operations while others are considered self-sustaining?

10-25 What translation method is recommended in the *CICA Handbook* for *self-sustaining* foreign operations?

10-26 Why does the *CICA Handbook* recommend that the cumulative translation gain or loss from self-sustaining foreign operations be shown as a separate component of consolidated shareholders' equity?

10-27 Under the current-rate method, why are the revenue and expense accounts translated at exchange rates that existed during the year, rather than at the current rate at the balance sheet date?

10-28 How does the translation of cost of goods sold differ between the current-rate method and the temporal method?

10-29 How does the translation of depreciation and amortization differ under the current-rate method as opposed to the temporal method?

10-30 Explain how the translation gain or loss on current monetary items can be computed. Is the amount of gain or loss affected by the translation method used?

10-31 What is the impact of hyper-inflation on the translation method for a self-sustaining operation?

Cases

Case 10-1

Elite Distributors Limited

Elite Distributors Limited is a Canadian public company that has been undergoing rapid expansion. The company is based in a major Canadian seaport, and several years ago found it necessary to open a sales office in the United States, in order to transact business directly in that country.

Elite also has a wholly-owned subsidiary, located in Singapore, that manufactures one of the main products that Elite sells in Canada. Substantially all of the Singapore subsidiary's sales are to Elite. There is a second (80% owned) subsidiary, located in the Republic of Ireland, that was acquired in an attempt to diversify. This company sells exclusively through its own sales offices throughout Northern Europe, and has very few transactions with Elite, except for the regular payment of dividends.

Required:

Recommend the appropriate accounting policies for Elite to follow with respect to each of these foreign operations. Support your recommendations.

[SMA]

Case 10-2

Care Inc.

Care Inc. (CI), a national manufacturer and retailer of women's shoes, purchased 100% of the common shares of ShoeCo, a footwear manufacturing company located in a foreign country. CI financed the purchase of ShoeCo's shares through a loan from a Canadian bank. To obtain this financing, CI had to offer one of its Canadian manufacturing plants as security. ShoeCo will continue to be managed and operated by locals and be responsible for obtaining operational loans.

ShoeCo sells most of its production to its domestic market. Previously a supplier of CI's, ShoeCo will continue to supply about 10% of its production to CI. CI has established a contract with ShoeCo fixing the quantity and the price in Canadian dollars.

Required:

a. State whether ShoeCo is an integrated or a self-sustaining operation of CI, and explain how you reached your conclusion.

b. Describe both the temporal and current-rate translation methods. Which method would CI use?

[CICA]

Case 10-3

Multi-Communications Ltd.

Multi-Communications Ltd. (MCL) is a Canadian-owned public company operating throughout North America. Its core business is communications media, including newspapers, radio, television, and cable. The company's year-end is December 31.

You, CA, have recently joined MCL's reporting office as a finance director, reporting to the chief financial officer, Robert Allen. It is October 2002. Mr. Allen has asked you to prepare a report discussing the accounting and auditing issues that may arise with the auditors during their visit in November.

MCL's growth in 2002 was achieved through expansion into the United States by acquiring a number of newspapers, television, and cable operations. Since the U.S. side of MCL's operations is now significant, management will be reporting its financial statements in U.S. dollars. Shareholders' equity at the beginning of the period was $220 million, including a separately disclosed cumulative foreign exchange gain of $45 million. Management merged this balance with retained earnings because "the operations it relates to are no longer considered foreign for accounting purposes, and as a result no foreign currency exposure will arise."

With recent trends to international free trade, MCL decided to position itself for future expansion into the South American market. Therefore, in 2002 MCL bought a company that owns a radio network in a country in South America that has high inflation. MCL was willing to incur losses in the start-up since it was confident that in the long run it would be profitable. The South American country has had a democratic government for the last two years. Its government's objectives are to open the country's borders to trade and lower its inflation rate. The government was rather reluctant to let a foreign country purchase such a powerful communication tool. In exchange for the right to buy the network MCL agreed, among other conditions, not to promote any political party, to broadcast only pre-approved public messages, and to let the government examine its books at the government's convenience. Management has recorded its investment in the books using the cost method.

In 2002, MCL acquired a conglomerate, Peter Holdings (PH), which held substantial assets in the communications business. Over the past three months, MCL has sold off 80% of PH's non-communication-related businesses. In the current month, MCL sold PH's hotel and recreational property business for $175 million, realizing a gain of $22 million ($14.5 million after tax). The assets related to the non-communications businesses were scattered throughout the U.S. and MCL lacked the industry expertise to value them accurately. Management therefore found it difficult to determine the net realizable value of each of these assets at the time PH was acquired.

Newspaper readership has peaked leaving no room for expansion. In 2001, to increase its share of the market, MCL bought all the assets of a competing newspaper for $10 million. In 2002, MCL ceased publication of the competing newspaper and liquidated the assets for $4.5 million.

In 2002, MCL decided to rationalize its television operations. Many of PH's acquisitions in the television business included stations in areas already being served by other stations operated by MCL. MCL systematically identified stations that were duplicating services and did not fit with MCL's long-range objectives. These assets have been segregated on the balance sheet and classified as current. The company anticipates generating a gain on the disposal of the entire pool of assets, although losses are anticipated on some of the individual stations. Operating results are capitalized in the pool. Once a particular station is sold, the resulting gain or loss is reflected in income.

Nine stations are in the pool at the present time. In 2002, three were sold, resulting in gains of $65,000 after tax. Losses are expected to occur on several of the remaining stations. Although serious negotiations with prospective buyers are not underway at present, the company hopes to have disposed of them in early 2003. In order to facilitate the sale of these assets, MCL is considering taking back mortgages.

In 2002, MCL estimated the fair market value of its intangible assets at $250 million. Included as intangibles are newspaper and magazine circulation lists, cable subscriber lists, and broadcast licences. Some of these assets have been acquired through the purchase of existing businesses; others have been generated internally by operations that have been part of MCL for decades.

Amounts paid for intangibles are not difficult to determine; however, it has taken MCL staff some time to determine the costs of internally generated intangibles. In order to increase subscriptions for print and electronic media, MCL spends heavily on subscription drives by way of advertisements, cold calls, and free products. For the non-acquired intangibles, MCL staff have examined the accounting records for the past 10 years and have identified expenditures totalling $35 million that were expensed in prior years. These costs relate to efforts to expand customer bases. In addition, independent appraisers have determined the fair market value of these internally generated intangibles to be in the range of $60 to $80 million. In order to be conservative, management has decided to reflect these intangibles on the December 31, 2002 balance sheet at $60 million.

The market values of companies in the communications industry have been escalating in the past few years, indicating that the value of the underlying assets (largely intangibles) is increasing over time. MCL management would prefer not to amortize broadcasting licences, arguing that these licences do not lose any value, and in this industry, actually increase in value over time.

One of the items included in the intangible category is MCL's patented converter, which was an unplanned by-product of work being done on satellite communications devices a few years ago.

MCL has sold $25 million of its account receivables to a medium-sized financial intermediary, PayLater Corp. The receivables are being re-sold to a numbered company whose common shares are owned by PayLater Corp. MCL receives one-half of the consideration in cash and one-half in subordinated non-voting redeemable shares of the numbered company, bearing a dividend rate of 9%. The dividend payments and share redemption are based on the collectibility of receivables. The purchase price is net of a 4% provision for doubtful accounts. MCL has recorded a loss of $1 million on this transaction. PayLater has an option to return the receivables to MCL at any time for 94% of their face value.

To combat the arrival of a direct broadcast satellite that transmits multiple TV signals to antennas, the communication industry has been developing its own interactive communication services at a cost of over $6 billion. This service will allow viewers to interact with banks, shops, and other viewers through the television. MCL hopes this will maintain its market share of viewers.

MCL has invested in the installation of fibre optic cable, which can transmit far more, far faster than conventional cable. The cost of the cable itself is negligible. MCL will be using it for transmission between its stations in two major Canadian cities. MCL needed only six cables to link all its television and radio stations between the two cities, but it decided to put in 36 cables since it was doing the digging anyway. To date, MCL has sold 6 cables and charges a monthly fee to new owners to cover their share of maintenance expenses. MCL is leasing 10 other cables for 15-year periods.

Required:

Prepare the report.

[CICA]

Case 10-4

Johnston Co. Ltd.

Johnston Co. Ltd. is a medium-sized Canadian company, incorporated in 1974, whose shares are traded on the Toronto Stock Exchange. It began its operations as a processor and distributor of frozen Portobello mushrooms, but quickly branched out until it provided a full line of Canadian specialty foods. Some of these products were processed by Johnston itself, while others were processed by Johnston under contract with other Canadian companies.

The company's strategic plan calls for steady growth in sales and earnings. Accordingly, expansion into the lucrative United States market in 2004 is under serious consideration. A major concern is changes in the exchange rate of the Canadian and American dollar because the company has received very different predictions from various analysts with respect to this.

Johnston is considering the following proposals. The first proposal involves setting up sales offices in the United States with orders filled from Johnston's Canadian warehouses. The sales offices would be responsible for sales, billing, and collections. All transactions would be in U.S. dollars.

Alternatively, Johnston is considering establishing a wholly-owned subsidiary in the United States to process and distribute a full line of specialty foods. It has not yet decided how to finance the purchase of the plant and equipment for this subsidiary.

The president has asked you, the controller, to prepare a report for possible use at a meeting of the board of directors. Specifically, he wants you to recommend which of the above proposals is preferable with respect to the impact of each on current and future income. He wants you to fully support your recommendation and to limit your discussion to foreign currency translation issues, ignoring hedging and income tax considerations.

Required:

Prepare the report to the president.

[SMA, adapted]

Case 10-5

Video Displays, Inc. (Part B)

In early 2002, Video Displays, Inc. (VDI) became dissatisfied with the perform-ance of the U.S. distributor of its video display units (see **Case 9-2**) and decided to establish its own sales subsidiary in the United States. Consequently, in February 2002, VDI formed Vidisplay Corp. (VC) under the laws of California. Vidisplay Corp. would sell the VDI video display units (made in Canada) directly to the U.S. computer terminal and word processing manufacturers. The units would be imported into the United States from Canada, and the price to VC would be the manufacturing cost to VDI plus 10%. Since VC is a subsidiary of VDI, VC would be far better suited to deal with manufacturers than was the independent U.S. distributor. VC would be able to speak directly to VDI and would be able to negotiate design changes in order to make VDI's units meet the manufacturer's needs and specifications.

VDI had a reputation for high quality and excellent quality control, which are vital factors from the viewpoint of the computer terminal manufacturers. Therefore, VC was able to generate significant sales rather quickly. In the first four months of operation, VC obtained orders for over 6,000 units at an average price of about $250.

VDI's primary competition was from the Far East, particularly from Taiwan. Most of the cost of a video display unit can be attributed to the cost of parts, which makes up about 70%–80% of the total cost. Since the labour component of cost is small, there is little direct labour cost advantage in Taiwanese produc-tion. However, most of the cathode ray tubes (the single most costly component) are produced in Taiwan, and the CRT producers had simply integrated forward into the production of video display units.

In mid-2002, the U.S. dollar strengthened considerably against all major for-eign currencies. However, owing to the strong dependence of the Canadian dol-lar on the U.S. economy, and high interest rates in Canada (which were competitive with U.S. interest rates), the Canadian dollar fell less against the U.S. dollar than did most other currencies. Thus, while the prices of Canadian goods fell in terms of the U.S. dollar, the fall was less than that of goods from other countries.

By the end of 2002, VC had delivered 4,800 units to its U.S. customers and had on hand 1,400 additional units, which were acquired from VDI in December, and were being held by VC pending final acceptance by the cus-tomers. VC's furniture and equipment were acquired in February and March, and were financed by VDI's capital investment and a $1 million four-year loan from the Bank of America.

Required:

a. Translate the income statement and balance sheet for Vidisplay Corp., the U.S. subsidiary, into Canadian dollars under each of the following translation methods:

1. Current/noncurrent

2. Temporal

3. Current rate

Assume that the average exchange rate for VC's 2002 operating period was US$1 = Cdn$1.30, and that the amount payable by VC to VDI is a liability of Cdn$260,000.

b. Evaluate the results of the three alternative translation methods in light of the economic risk exposure of Vidisplay Corp. Which method is most likely to reflect in VDI's statements the impact of foreign currency fluctuations on Vidisplay's operations? Which method seems most appropriate for VDI to use, given the nature of Vidisplay's operations and its relationship with the parent, VDI?

Vidisplay Corp.
Trial Balance
December 31, 2002
(in U.S. dollars)

	Dr	Cr
Cash	$ 50,000	
Accounts receivable	800,000	
Inventory	300,000	
Furniture and equipment	350,000	
Accumulated depreciation		$ 50,000
Accounts payable		75,000
Due to Canadian parent company		200,000
Note payable (due March 1, 2006)		1,000,000
Common shares		100,000
Sales		1,200,000
Cost of sales	1,000,000	
Operating expenses	100,000	
Income tax expense	25,000	
	$2,625,000	$2,625,000

Assumed exchange rate for US$1.00:

December 31, 2001			Cdn$1.15
2002: January	1.16	July	1.30
February	1.20	August	1.25
March	1.20	September	1.30
April	1.24	October	1.28
May	1.25	November	1.32
June	1.30	December	1.36
December 31, 2002			1.40

Case 10-6

Hi-Tech Industries Ltd.

Hi-Tech Industries Ltd. is a corporation formed under the provisions of the *Canada Business Corporations Act*. Its shares are held by a small group of private investors. Hi-Tech is a company that is engaged primarily in various facets of computer applications and computer software development. It carries out its business mainly through a series of wholly-owned subsidiaries.

In 1999, Hi-Tech acquired 100% of the shares of Geo Dataserve, Inc., a computer service bureau located in Houston, Texas. The purchase was for cash, and was financed by borrowing 80% of the necessary funds from a Houston bank on a five-year renewable term loan. The remaining 20% was financed by liquidating some of Hi-Tech's temporary investments.

Geo Dataserve (GDI) had developed a large database of information on geographic mapping. They sold computing time (access to their database) to business clients in the Houston area. The company specialized in providing geographic data, using special programs that had been developed by GDI. However, the company would rent computer time, either in-house or time-sharing, for any purpose. The range of services went from straight time rental, with no provisions of programs or processing expertise, to full-service computer applications, operating essentially as though GDI were the data-processing department of the client company.

By 1999, the computer service bureau industry was in a depression, owing to a sharp decline in processing costs that enabled clients to acquire their own in-house micro- and minicomputers. In addition, GDI had been unable to develop any new geographic mapping applications. GDI had fallen into a state of profit decline in the early 1990s; the profits turned to losses in 1998 and 1999. The declining fortunes of GDI made it possible for Hi-Tech to acquire the company at a price significantly below the fair market value of GDI's facilities and the estimated value of its customer base.

In order to turn GDI back into a profitable business, Hi-Tech undertook a series of moves. The first was to lend GDI the money to reorganize its operations and to update much of the peripheral equipment, especially the terminals and printers located in clients' premises.

The second was to supply GDI with a new geographical mapping application involving the establishments of property tax reassessments that had been developed by Hi-Tech's other subsidiaries. GDI paid a royalty for the use of the software. But the software gave GDI an important technological edge in its market through providing clients with a capability that could not be matched by direct competitors or duplicated on the small computers that had seriously eroded the computer-service-bureau market.

Third, Hi-Tech organized a software development division in GDI to extend many of Hi-Tech's other products and services into the lucrative corporate market in the southwest United States. Most, but not all, of this new division's activities were directed from the Canadian operations; it was expected that the division would become more self-sufficient sometime in the future, and would perhaps then be spun off from GDI as a separate company.

The most recent move was the acquisition in 2002 of GDI's major service bureau competitor in Houston, McClean Service Corp. Hi-Tech purchased all of the outstanding shares of McClean by using funds obtained primarily by having GDI declare a substantial dividend. Hi-Tech then had McClean sell all of its assets to GDI for $1 and liquidated McClean. GDI sold most of the McClean assets and transferred the McClean customers and applications to the GDI equipment. This last move was expected to complete the earnings turnaround for GDI; GDI was expected to make a positive contribution to Hi-Tech's consolidated earnings for the first time in 2002.

In 1999, 2000, and 2001, Hi-Tech had used the current-rate method of translation for GDI because it seemed the easiest method to use. However, the company was considering broadening its equity base through the sale of additional shares to new investors, and the management of Hi-Tech was considering engaging an auditor and striving for a "clean" audit opinion.

Management therefore retained an accounting advisor to inform Hi-Tech on the reporting implications for 2002 of the investments in GDI and McClean, as well as on any other matters relating to their U.S. activities.

Required:

Assume the role of the accounting advisor. Write the requested report to the managers of Hi-Tech.

Case 10-7

Verena Manufacturing Limited

Verena Manufacturing Limited (Verena) is a Canadian manufacturer of breast cancer screening equipment. United Kingdom Imports Limited (Imports) was one of Verena's foreign customers. In December of 2001, the owner of Imports advised Joan Bowyer, the president of Verena, that, as a consequence of a heart attack he had suffered earlier in the year, he wished to sell Imports. Bowyer and other managers at Verena judged that the purchase of Imports would be desirable. The negotiations that ensued were amicable and brief, and Verena purchased Imports for 1.2 million U.K. pounds in cash on January 1, 2002. Verena paid the full price on that date.

Verena's comptroller, Peter Thomas, knew that Bowyer wished to be able to show a high return on equity from Imports—a point she could use as part of the justification of the purchase of Imports to Verena's shareholders. He also knew that Bowyer initially planned to operate Imports as a sales branch for Verena's products. However, the choice of an advantageous method of currency translation might call for another way of organizing Imports. If this turned out to be the case, Thomas wished to present this alternative to Bowyer. Finally, he wanted to minimize any exchange losses, as Verena was planning a public offering of its own shares in 2002. He had reasons to believe that the Canadian dollar would likely strengthen against the United Kingdom pound during 2002.

Thomas began his analysis by preparing, according to Canadian generally accepted accounting principles, the balance sheet of Imports for the date of acquisition, January 1, 2002, with his best estimates of the forecast balance sheet as at December 31, 2002 (see Exhibit 1), and the forecast statement of earnings and retained earnings for 2002 (see Exhibit 2). He then obtained the relevant historical Canadian dollar equivalents of one United Kingdom pound, and the relevant estimates of forecast exchange rates (see Exhibit 3).

Required:

a. Which generally accepted method of foreign currency translation would show the higher earnings for Verena? Why?

b. Which method should Thomas recommend and how should Imports be organized in order to use this method?

[SMA, adapted]

EXHIBIT 1

United Kingdom Imports Limited
Balance Sheet
(in Thousands)

	Actual 1/1/02 U.K. Pound	Forecast 31/12/02 U.K. Pound
Net monetary assets	£ 200	£ 360
Inventory	500	650
Capital assets:		
Buildings and equipment	2,500	2,800
Less accumulated depreciation	(1,000)	(1,560)
	£2,200	£2,250
Long-term debt (Note 1)	£1,000	£1,000
Shareholders' equity:		
Common shares	1,100	1,100
Retained earnings	100	150
	£2,200	£2,250

Note 1: The 10%, £1 million long-term debt was issued at face value on January 1, 1999, and is due on December 31, 2005.

EXHIBIT 2

United Kingdom Imports Limited
Forecast Statement of Earnings and Retained Earnings
For the Year Ending December 31, 2002
(in Thousands)

	U.K. Pound
Sales	£10,000
Cost of sales: Opening inventory	500
Purchases	8,000
	8,500
Closing inventory	650
	7,850
Gross profit	2,150
Selling and administration	1,140
Depreciation (Note 1)	560
Interest	100
	1,800
Income before income taxes	350
Income taxes	140
Net income	210
Retained earnings (1/1/02)	100
	310
Dividends (Note 2)	160
Retained earnings (31/12/02)	£ 150

Notes:

1. Depreciation is calculated straight-line over five years. A full year's depreciation is taken in the year of acquisition. No disposals are anticipated for 2002.

2. To be declared and paid December 31, 2002.

EXHIBIT 3

Canadian Dollar Equivalents of One United Kingdom Pound

Historical Rates

January 1, 2000, date of purchase of buildings and equipment by Imports	$5.00
November 15, 2001, date of purchase of 1/1/02 inventory balance by Imports	$2.10
January 1, 2002	$2.00

Forecast Rates

2002 average rate	$1.80
July 1, 2002, scheduled date of purchase of additional capital assets	$1.75
December 31, 2002	$1.50
Average rate for December 31, 2002, closing inventory assuming FIFO accounting flow of goods	$1.70

Case 10-8

Vulcan Manufacturing Limited

Vulcan Manufacturing Limited (VML) is a Canadian-based multinational plastics firm, with subsidiaries in several foreign countries and worldwide consolidated total assets of $500 million. VML's shares are listed on a Canadian stock exchange. Since 2000, the company has included supplementary current cost information in its annual report.

VML is attracted by the growing demand for its products in developing countries. In recognition of trade barriers designed to encourage domestic production in those countries and in order to service local demand, VML incorporated a foreign subsidiary in a South American country on September 1, 2001. The subsidiary, South American Plastics Inc. (SAPI), manufactures patented sheet-plastic and sells virtually all of its output locally. Also, almost all labour and raw materials are provided locally. SAPI finances its day-to-day activities from its own operations and local borrowing.

During 2001 and 2002, the South American country suffered an inflation rate of more than 100%, accompanied by substantial devaluation of the local currency and a drastic increase in interest rates. The government is expected to impose wage and price controls in 2003. The inflation rate is expected to stabilize at more moderate levels sometime in 2003 or 2004.

The chief financial officer (CFO) of VML has recently received SAPI's draft financial statements for the year ended August 31, 2002, together with some comments prepared by SAPI's controller. (Extracts from the draft financial statements and controller's comments are provided in Exhibits 1 and 2.) He is somewhat surprised by the return on investment of nearly 12%. This figure is well above the target rate agreed upon for bonus purposes, which was set at 3% in recognition of start-up costs associated with the first year of operations. The apparently favourable performance will result in large bonuses having to be paid to SAPI's management.

Increases in SAPI's domestic selling price have kept pace with the general rate of inflation and with increases in input prices and borrowing costs in the South American country. The CFO is satisfied that the inflation and devaluation the country has experienced has not seriously affected SAPI's cash flows from operations.

VML assesses its exposure to exchange rate changes on a worldwide basis. Each subsidiary is required to submit to head office a report on its projected foreign currencies position for the upcoming quarter. The report lists receivables and payables and other committed cash flows to be settled in various currencies during the upcoming quarter. The CFO makes decisions on appropriate hedging strategies once such reports are received. SAPI's report for the first quarter of the 2002–03 fiscal year has just been received (Exhibit 3).

In the annual report to Canadian shareholders for the year ended August 31, 2002, the CFO wants to communicate to shareholders the economic impact that inflation and devaluation in the South American country have had on VML's investment in SAPI. He is concerned that gains or losses arising from translation of the statements in accordance with Section 1650 of the *CICA Handbook* will mislead shareholders. The CFO believes that the exchange gains and losses will obscure the true impact of foreign inflation and devaluation on SAPI's economic value in Canadian dollar terms. He has called the audit partner and you, the CA in charge of the audit, into his office. The following conversation ensues:

CFO: We have to issue our financial statements soon, and we have to apply Section 1650 to our South American subsidiary. I must confess that I don't know Section 1650 as well as you two do. My staff tells me that we must use the temporal method this year, due to the local hyperinflation, although I confess that I don't see why. Apparently we will have a choice between the temporal method and the current-rate method once the inflation rate stabilizes, which I expect to happen in 2003 or 2004. I am very reluctant to use the temporal method on this year's statements. It forces me to include fictitious gains and losses in our consolidated income statement.

Partner: Your staff is correct in stating that the *CICA Handbook* requires the use of the temporal method for the year just ended. However, shareholders should not be misled by exchange gains or losses in consolidated income provided that they are fully disclosed as such.

CFO: I guess I just do not understand Section 1650. For example, how might the adoption of the current-rate method in 2003 or 2004 improve matters? It seems to me that an overall exchange loss will arise, if the rate keeps on going down. What does the loss mean? As long as our subsidiary's cash flows keep pace with local inflation, it will be able to maintain its expected rate of profitability and therefore its ability to pay dividends to us. Yet shareholders will see an exchange loss!

Partner: I will have CA prepare a report that explains to you how the exchange gains or losses under either translation method tie in with the notion of risk underlying Section 1650. We will also explain how this notion alleviates your concern about communicating the true economic risk to shareholders. CA will recommend ways to tell the whole story to shareholders.

CFO: Sounds great. I would also like CA to provide advice on any other important issues related to SAPI. For starters, I have some concerns about the way our bonus plan for SAPI's management is working. One possibility I am considering is to evaluate SAPI's performance in Canadian dollar terms.

That afternoon, you and the partner meet in his office to discuss the report requested by the CFO. SAPI has just appointed its auditors for the year ended August 31, 2002. In addition to the report for the CFO, the partner asks you to prepare a draft letter to SAPI's auditors specifying areas of suspected audit risk as well as other pertinent guidelines.

Required:

Prepare the report to the CFO and the draft letter to SAPI's auditors.
[CICA]

EXHIBIT 1

South American Plastics Inc.
Extracts from Draft Financial Statements Balance Sheet
August 31, 2002
Foreign Currency Units* (in Thousands)

	2002
Assets	
Current	
Cash	FCU 10,020
Marketable securities, at cost	3,120
Accounts receivable	93,000
Inventory, at cost	67,200
Prepaid expenses	8,040
	181,380
Capital assets	143,111
Less accumulated depreciation	14,311
	128,800
	FCU310,180
Liabilities and shareholders' equity	
Current	
Revenue received in advance from customer	FCU 10,000
Accounts payable	38,400
Taxes payable	4,920
Other payables	11,820
	65,140
Noncurrent	
Long-term debt	157,200
Shareholders' equity	
Common shares	51,000
Retained earnings	36,840
	87,840
	FCU310,180

*A Foreign Currency Unit (FCU) is a unit of the currency used in the South American country in which SAPI is located.

EXHIBIT 2

South American Plastics Inc.
Controller's Comments on Financial Statements

1. Opening Balances

   SAPI's balance sheet on September 1, 2001, consisted of cash of FCU 208,200,000, long-term debt of FCU 157,200,000, and common stock of FCU 51,000,000.

2. Marketable Securities

   The marketable securities, portfolio equity investments in a number of local companies, were purchased when one FCU = $0.30. The investments are considered temporary and can be sold easily on short notice. The aggregate market value for the securities at August 31, 2002, is FCU 3,000,000.

3. Inventories

   Inventories were purchased when one FCU = $0.30. The Canadian parent company, Vulcan Manufacturing Limited, values inventory at the lower of cost and replacement cost. The aggregate replacement cost of the inventory is FCU 100,000,000.

4. Prepaid Expenses

   The amounts, representing prepaid rent and property taxes, were paid when one FCU = $0.25.

5. Capital Assets

   Capital assets were purchased shortly after the date of SAPI's formation, at a time when one FCU = $0.40. The current replacement cost of the capital assets (in their current condition) is FCU 200,000,000.

6. Current Liabilities

   All current liabilities were incurred at a time when one FCU = $0.25.

7. Long-Term Debt

   The debt represents a floating interest rate loan that will be repaid in foreign currency units on August 31, 2005.

8. Retained Earnings

   No dividends were paid during the 2001–02 fiscal year.

9. Exchange Rates

September 1, 2001	1 FCU = $0.40
August 31, 2002	1 FCU = $0.20
Average rate for the period:	
September 2001 to August 2002	1 FCU = $0.30

EXHIBIT 3

South American Plastics Inc.
Projected Foreign Currencies Position Report
Prepared by the Controller
First Quarter of the Fiscal Year
Beginning September 1, 2002
(in Thousands)

	Foreign Currency Units (FCU)	Deutsche Marks
Amounts to be received during first quarter of the fiscal year beginning September 1, 2002:		
Accounts receivable at August 31, 2002	FCU 20,000	
Foreign currency purchase contract at August 31, 2002 (Note 1)	—	DM 5,000
Signed sales commitments from customers at August 31, 2002 (Note 2)	7,500	7,000
	27,500	12,000
Amounts to be paid during first quarter of the fiscal year beginning September 1, 2002:		
Accounts, taxes, other payables at August 31, 2002	50,000	—
Signed purchase commitments to suppliers at August 31, 2002 (Note 3)	8,500	5,000
	58,500	5,000
Net exposed position in various currencies for first quarter of the fiscal year beginning September 1, 2002	FCU(31,000)	DM 7,000

Note 1:

Represents a deutsche mark forward contract to receive 5,000 deutsche marks, maturing on November 1, 2002.

Note 2:

Represents a one-time sales order from a customer in Germany, to be delivered and settled during October 2002.

Note 3:

Represents an amount owing to a German supplier to be paid on November 15, 2002, for equipment to be delivered in October 2002.

Problems

P10-1

On December 31, 2000 CL Limited, a Canadian company, acquired 100% ownership of British Company, a company based in London, England. Information for the translation of the foreign subsidiary is presented in Exhibit 1. Sales, purchases, operating expenses, and interest expense all occurred evenly throughout the year. The 2002 beginning inventory was acquired when the exchange rate was £1.00 = $2.15. The 2002 ending inventory was acquired on October 1, 2002 when the exchange rate was £1.00 = $2.25. The land was acquired on December 31, 2002. Dividends are declared and paid on December 31. The bonds mature on December 31, 2005.

Required:

Using the information provided in Exhibit 1 calculate the following amounts:

a. Using the current-rate method, determine British Company's:

   (1) Cost of goods sold

   (2) Amortization expense

   (3) Equipment (net)—December 31, 2001

   (4) Equipment (net)—December 31, 2002

   (5) Common shares

   (6) Dividends—2002

b. Using the temporal method, determine British Company's:

   (1) Cost of goods sold

   (2) Amortization expense

   (3) Equipment (net)—December 31, 2002

   (4) Bonds payable—December 31, 2002

   (5) Gain on current monetary items

   (6) Deferred loss on long-term bonds—December 31, 2002.

[CGA]

EXHIBIT 1

Data Table

Dates	Exchange Rate: No. of Cdn$ = 1£
December 31, 2000	2.00
October 1, 2001	2.10
December 31, 2001	2.20
October 1, 2002	2.25
Average rate 2002	2.30
December 31, 2002	2.40
Other Relevant Information:	
Issue of common shares	2.00
Acquisition of capital assets	2.25
2001 retained earnings rate	2.10

British Company
Income Statement
Year Ended December 31, 2002

(Dr) Cr	£
Sales	4,500,000
Cost of goods sold	
Beginning inventory	(400,000)
Purchases	(1,500,000)
Ending inventory	600,000
	(1,300,000)
Amortization expense	(300,000)
Other operating expenses	(1,000,000)
Interest expense	(300,000)
Total expenses	(2,900,000)
Net income	1,600,000

British Company
Balance Sheet
Year Ended December 31, 2001

	£
Cash	200,000
Accounts receivable	700,000
Inventory	400,000
Equipment (net)	3,200,000
Total assets	4,500,000
Accounts payable	600,000
Bonds payable	2,000,000
Common shares	1,500,000
Retained earnings	400,000
Total liabilities & equities	4,500,000

British Company
Balance Sheet
Year Ended December 31, 2002

	£
Cash	100,000
Accounts receivable	100,000
Inventory	600,000
Land	1,300,000
Equipment (net)	2,900,000
Total assets	5,000,000
Accounts payable	100,000
Bonds payable	2,000,000
Common shares	1,500,000
Retained earnings, 2001	400,000
Income, 2002	1,600,000
Dividends	(600,000)
Total liabilities & equities	5,000,000

P10-2

On January 2, 2002, EL Limited established a subsidiary in Mexico City, Mexico. The subsidiary was named GC Company and the cost of EL's investment was Cdn$1,000,000. When this investment was translated into Mexican pesos, the cost of the investment was p5,000,000. On January 2, 2002, GC obtained long-term debt of p1,000,000 from a bank in Mexico City when the exchange rate was p1.00 = Cdn$0.20. The long-term debt must be repaid at the end of 4 years. The opening balance sheet for GC on January 2, 2002, is shown below:

GC Company
Balance Sheet
January 2, 2002

Current monetary assets	p6,000,000
Long-term debt	p1,000,000
Common shares	p5,000,000
	p6,000,000

The December 31, 2002 balance sheet and income statement for GC are shown below:

GC Company
Income Statement
December 31, 2002

Revenues	p3,200,000
Amortization expense	300,000
Operating expenses	2,200,000
Total expenses	2,500,000
Net income	p 700,000

GC Company
Balance Sheet
December 31, 2002

Current monetary assets	p2,800,000
Capital assets	4,900,000
Accumulated amortization	(300,000)
	p7,400,000
Current monetary liabilities	p 900,000
Long-term debt	1,000,000
Common shares	5,000,000
Retained earnings	500,000
	p7,400,000

The relevant exchange rates for the Mexican peso were as follows:

January 2, 2002	p1.00 = Cdn$0.20
Average for 2002	p1.00 = Cdn$0.22
December 31, 2002	p1.00 = Cdn$0.24

During 2002, GC purchased capital assets when the exchange rate was p1.00 = Cdn$0.21. Dividends were declared and paid when the exchange rate was p1.00 = Cdn$0.23. Revenues and other expenses were incurred evenly throughout the year.

Required:

a. Calculate the exchange gains/losses for the temporal and current methods to be disclosed on the December 31, 2002, balance sheet and income statement.

b. Translate the 2002 balance sheet and income statement for GC assuming:

(i) GC is a self-sustaining foreign operation

(ii) GC is an integrated foreign operation

[CGA]

P10-3

On January 1, 2001, Woods Ltd. formed a foreign subsidiary that issued all of its currently outstanding common shares on that date. Selected captions from the balance sheets, all of which are shown in local currency units (LCU), are as follows:

	2002	2001
Accounts receivable, net of allowance for uncollectable accounts of 2,200 LCU at December 31, 2002 and 2,000 LCU at December 31, 2001	40,000	35,000
Inventories, at cost	80,000	75,000
Capital assets, net of accumulated depreciation of 31,000 LCU at December 31, 2002 and 14,000 LCU at December 31, 2001	163,000	150,000
Long-term debt	100,000	120,000
Common stock, authorized shares par value 10 LCU per share, issued and outstanding 5,000 shares at December 31, 2002 and December 31, 2001	50,000	50,000

Additional Information:

Exchange Rates

January 1, 2001 to July 31, 2001	2.1 LCU to $1
August 1, 2001 to October 31, 2001	1.9 LCU to $1
November 1, 2001 to June 30, 2002	1.8 LCU to $1
July 1, 2002 to December 31, 2002	1.6 LCU to $1
Average rate for 2001	2.0 LCU to $1
Average rate for 2002	1.7 LCU to $1

Accounts Receivable—Analysis

	2002	2001
	(in LCUs)	
Balance beginning of year	37,000	—
Sales (36,000 LCU per month in 2002 and 31,000 per month in 2001)	432,000	372,000
Collections	423,600	334,000
Write-offs (May 2002 and December 2001)	3,200	1,000
	42,200	37,000

Allowance for Uncollectable Accounts

	2002	2001
	(in LCUs)	
Balance beginning of year	2,000	—
Provision for uncollectables	3,400	3,000
Write-offs	3,200	1,000
	2,200	2,000

Inventory, FIFO Basis

	2002	2001
	(in LCUs)	
Balance beginning of year	75,000	—
Purchases (June 2002 and June 2001)	335,000	375,000
Less: Inventory at year-end	80,000	75,000
Cost of goods sold	330,000	300,000

On January 1, 2001, Woods' foreign subsidiary purchases land for 24,000 LCU and capital assets for 140,000 LCU. On July 1, 2002, additional equipment was purchased for 30,000 LCU. Capital assets are being depreciated on a straight-line basis over a 10-year period with no salvage value. A full year's depreciation is taken in the year of purchase.

On January 15, 2001, 7% bonds with a face value of 120,000 LCU were sold. These bonds mature on July 15 and January 15. The first payment was made on July 15, 2001.

Required:

Prepare a schedule translating the selected captions above into Canadian dollars at December 31, 2001, and December 31, 2002, using the temporal method. Show supporting computations in good form.

[CGA–Canada, adapted]

P10-4

Efren Ltd. is a foreign subsidiary of a Canadian parent located in the country of Matos. The balance sheet accounts of Efren are as follows, stated in mats (M):

Cash	M 20,000
Accounts receivable	10,000
Inventory (at market)	60,000
Capital assets	200,000
Accumulated depreciation	(80,000)
Long-term note receivable	50,000
Total assets	M260,000
Accounts and notes payable	M 40,000
Bonds payable	150,000
Common shares	70,000
Total equities	M260,000

Additional Information:

1. Efren Ltd. is wholly owned by Hialea Corp. Hialea established Efren when the mat was worth $2.00.

2. The capital assets were purchased when the mat was worth $2.40.

3. The bonds payable were issued when the exchange rate for the mat was $2.30.

4. The long-term note receivable arose when the mat was worth $2.60.

5. The inventory was purchased when the mat was worth $2.80.

6. The current exchange rate for the mat is $3.00.

Required:

a. Translate the balance sheet accounts of Efren Ltd. into Canadian dollars, using each of the following methods:

(1) Current rate

(2) Current/noncurrent

(3) Monetary/nonmonetary

(4) Temporal

In each case, treat the translation gain or loss as a single, balancing figure.

b. For each method, calculate:

(1) The accounting exposure

(2) The additional gain or loss that would result if the exchange rate one year hence was $3.50, assuming no change in the balance sheet accounts in mats.

P10-5

Kantor Corp. is a wholly-owned subsidiary of Windsor Inc., and is located in the country of Zinnia. The currency of Zinnia is the zin (Z). At December 31, 2002, the balance sheet accounts of Kantor Corp. appeared as follows:

Cash	Z 10,000
Accounts receivable (net)	20,000
Inventory	30,000
Temporary investments	40,000
Capital assets	100,000
Accumulated depreciation	(30,000)
Long-term investments	40,000
Total assets	Z210,000
Accounts payable	Z 20,000
Long-term note payable	60,000
Future income taxes	10,000
Common shares	100,000
Retained earnings	20,000
Total equities	Z210,000

Additional Information:

1. The inventory is valued at current market value. It was purchased when the zin was worth $0.53.

2. The cash is all held in Zinnian banks, and the accounts receivable and payable are all denominated in zins.

3. The long-term note was signed on December 31, 2000, and is due on December 31, 2005. It is denominated in zins.

4. The initial investment (in the common shares) by Windsor Inc. was made on December 31, 1999.

5. The capital assets were purchased on March 31, 2000, and are being depreciated over 10 years on a straight-line basis.

6. The temporary investments are carried at lower-of-cost-and-market. They were purchased for Z50,000 when the zin was worth $0.65. At the end of 2002, their net realizable value was less than cost.

7. The long-term investments are also carried at lower-of-cost-and-market. They were purchased when the zin was worth $0.72. Their net realizable value on December 31, 2002 was Z52,000.

8. The future income taxes arose as the result of temporary differences between CCA for tax purposes and depreciation for accounting.

9. The Canadian dollar equivalent of the zin has been as follows:

December 31, 1999	$0.80
March 31, 2000	0.75
December 31, 2000	0.70
December 31, 2001	0.60
December 31, 2002	0.50

The average rate for each year has been midway between the rates at the beginning and end of the year.

Required:

In columnar format, translate the balance sheet accounts of Kantor Corp., using each of the following methods. Treat the translation gain or loss as a single amount to balance the statement.

a. Current rate

b. Current/noncurrent

c. Monetary/nonmonetary

d. Temporal

P10-6

Refer to **P10-5**. Kantor Corp. had net working capital at January 1, 2002 of Z60,000. Net income retained by Kantor Corp. for 2002 was Z10,000.

Required:

To the extent possible from the information given, determine how the translation gain or loss should be incorporated into Windsor Inc.'s (the parent's) financial statements for 2002, in accordance with the current recommendations of the *CICA Handbook*, assuming that Kantor Corp. is:

a. a self-sustaining foreign operation.

b. an integrated foreign subsidiary.

P10-7

The income statement for 2002 for Hilary Co., expressed in Coker francs (CF), is as follows:

Sales revenue	CF3,000,000
Cost of goods sold:	
Beginning inventory	CF 200,000
Purchases	1,000,000
	CF1,200,000
Ending inventory	400,000
	CF 800,000
Depreciation	300,000
Other operating expenses	900,000
Interest expense	200,000
Total expenses	CF2,200,000
Net income	CF 800,000

Hilary Co. is 100% owned by Bryan Inc., a Canadian corporation.

Sales revenue, purchases of inventory, and operating expenses (except depreciation) all occurred evenly through the year. Interest expense accrued throughout the year, but was all paid at the end of the year. The beginning inventory was purchased on October 1, 2001, when the exchange rate was $0.82; the ending inventory was purchased on November 1, 2002, when the exchange rate was $0.93. The capital assets were acquired when the exchange rate was $0.70. Other exchange rate information is as follows:

December 31, 2001	$0.85
Average for 2002	$0.90
December 31, 2002	$0.95

Required:

Translate the income statement into Canadian dollars, using:

a. The current-rate method

b. The temporal method

P10-8

Refer to **P10-7**. The comparative year-end balance sheets for Hilary Co. were as follows:

	2001	2002
Cash	CF 500,000	CF 200,000
Accounts receivable	300,000	400,000
Inventory	200,000	400,000
Land	—	500,000
Equipment (net)	2,000,000	1,700,000
Total assets	CF3,000,000	CF3,200,000
Accounts payable	CF 400,000	CF 500,000
Bonds payable	1,800,000	1,800,000
Common shares	500,000	500,000
Retained earnings	300,000	400,000
Total equities	CF3,000,000	CF3,200,000

The common shares were issued when the exchange rate was $0.60.

The land was purchased at the end of 2002. The bonds were issued at the end of 2000, and mature at the end of 2006. The exchange rate at the end of 2000 was $0.70. Dividends are declared and paid at the end of each year. The retained earnings at the end of 2001 were earned at an average rate of $0.75.

Required:

a. Translate the 2001 and 2002 balance sheets, using the current-rate method. (Note that each year's balance sheet is translated at the current rate *at that year's balance sheet date.*)

b. Translate the 2001 and 2002 balance sheets, using the temporal method.

c. Calculate the net change in the cumulative translation gain or loss for 2002, under each translation method.

d. Determine how the translation gain or loss would be shown on the parent company's 2002 consolidated financial statements, assuming:

   (1) That Hilary Co. is self-sustaining

   (2) That Hilary Co. is an integrated foreign operation

Follow the *CICA Handbook* recommendations.

P10-9

Parent Ltd. has a 100% owned subsidiary in a foreign country, Ruritania, and the subsidiary, Turic Inc., has submitted to you its financial statements in the foreign currency (SNATS). In your professional judgement, this is a "self-sustaining" subsidiary.

Turic Inc.
Balance Sheet (in SNATS)
December 31, 2002

	SNATS
Cash	340,000
Accounts receivable	410,000
Inventory	750,000
Capital assets	1,200,000
Accumulated depreciation	(380,000)
	2,320,000
Current liabilities	210,000
Long-term liabilities	400,000
Common shares	200,000
Retained earnings, at January 1, 2002	1,310,000
Net income for 2002	200,000
	2,320,000

Turic Inc.
Income Statement (in SNATS)
Year Ended December 31, 2002

	SNATS
Sales	980,000
Cost of goods sold	660,000
	320,000
Depreciation	30,000
Other expenses	90,000
Net income	200,000

Exchange Rates

December 31, 2002	$1 = 92 SNATS
December 31, 2001	$1 = 80 SNATS
2002 average	$1 = 86 SNATS

The following information relates to the financial statements and provides additional data:

1. The inventory is kept on a FIFO cost system. The opening inventory was composed of 246,000 SNATS at an applicable exchange rate of $1 = 75 SNATS and 304,000 SNATS at an applicable exchange rate of $1 = 78 SNATS. The purchases during the period were 360,000 SNATS at an exchange rate of $1 = 83 SNATS and 500,000 SNATS at an exchange rate of $1 = 86 SNATS. (The exchange rates listed are the exchange rates in effect at the date of the transaction. The subsidiary acquired all of its assets and incurred all of its debts within Ruritania.)

2. The capital asset account is composed of land, 390,000 SNATS, purchased when the exchange rate was $1 = 65 SNATS and buildings, 810,000 SNATS, purchased when the exchange rate was $1 = 68 SNATS.

3. The long-term liabilities were issued at January 1, 2002, and are due at January 1, 2007.

4. The retained earnings of 1,310,000 SNATS at January 1, 2002, would translate, using the *temporal method*, to $46,778.

5. The retained earnings accumulated at an average rate of $1 = 70 SNATS.

6. Parent Ltd. purchased the common shares of the subsidiary when the exchange rate was $1 = 62 SNATS.

Required:

Using Section 1650 of the *CICA Handbook*, prepare the Canadian dollar financial statements using the *current-rate* method for Turic Inc. for the year 2002.

[CGA–Canada, adapted]

P10-10

Dom Ltd. has a subsidiary, Tarzan Inc., in the country of Tarzania, which uses the Tar as its currency. Preparatory to consolidating this 100% owned subsidiary, the financial statements must be translated from Tars to Canadian dollars, but the person responsible for the translation has quit suddenly and left you with a half-finished job. Certain information is available but the rest you must determine.

Tarzan Inc.
(in Tars)
Financial Statements
For the Year Ended December 31, 2002

Cash	T 100,000
Accounts receivable	200,000
Inventory (1)	400,000
Land	500,000
Buildings (2)	800,000
Accumulated depreciation	(300,000)
Total assets	T1,700,000
Accounts payable	T 250,000
Note payable (3)	400,000
Common shares	300,000
Retained earnings at January 1, 2002	600,000
Net income—2002	150,000
Total liabilities and equity	T1,700,000

Notes:

1. The opening inventory was 500,000 Tars and the purchases during the period were 500,000 Tars. Tarzan Inc. uses a periodic LIFO inventory system. The opening inventory had an exchange rate of Cdn$1 = 3.1 Tars, and the purchases were made 30% from the parent and 70% from the local area. The local area purchases were made evenly throughout the year, and the purchases from the parent were recorded by the parent at $35,714.

2. There were two buildings and one piece of land. The land and building number 1 (300,000 Tars) were acquired when Tarzan Inc. *was formed by Dom Ltd.* The exchange rate at that time was Cdn$1 = 2 Tars. Building number 2 was acquired when the exchange rate was Cdn$1 = 3.2 Tars. The depreciation expense is proportional to the purchase prices. The accumulated depreciation relating to building number 2 is 200,000 Tars.

3. The note payable is due on January 1, 2006, and was created on July 1, 2002.

4. The other expenses were incurred evenly throughout the year.

The opening retained earnings translated into Cdn$181,818.

Exchange Rates:

January 1, 2002	Cdn$1 = 3.7 Tars
2002 average, July 1, 2002	Cdn$1 = 3.9 Tars
December 31, 2002	Cdn$1 = 4.1 Tars

Required:

Assume that Tarzan Inc. is "integrated." Prepare the financial statements of Tarzan Inc. in Canadian dollars. Show your calculations in good form.

[CGA–Canada]

P10-11

Investco Ltd. is a Canadian real estate and property developer that decided to hold a parcel of land in downtown Munich, Germany for speculative purposes. The land, costing DM12,000,000 (deutsche marks) was financed by a five-year bond (DM9,000,000), which is repayable in deutsche marks, and an initial equity injection by Investco of DM3,000,000. These transactions took place on January 1, 2002, at which time a German subsidiary company was created to hold the investment. Investco plans to sell the land at the end of five years and use the deutsche mark proceeds to pay off the bond. In the interim, rent is being collected from another company, which is using the land as a parking lot.

The 2002 year-end draft financial statements of the German subsidiary company are shown below (assume that rental revenue is collected and interest and other expenses are paid at the end of each month).

Required:

a. Prepare the translated 2002 income statements and balance sheets at December 31, 2002, following Canadian generally accepted accounting principles and assuming

   (1) the German subsidiary is an integrated foreign operation as defined in Section 1650 of the *CICA Handbook*; and

   (2) the German subsidiary is a self-sustaining foreign operation as defined in Section 1650.

b. Which translation method better reflects Investco's *economic exposure* to exchange rate movements? Explain.

c. Which translation method would Investco be required to use? Explain.

d. Assume that, instead of incorporating a German subsidiary, Investco carries the investment (land, debt, etc.) directly on its own books. Some accountants would argue that it is inappropriate to reflect any portion of an unrealized exchange gain or loss on the bond in the 2002 income statement because the land serves as an effective hedge. Explain the reasoning behind this position. Would this approach be acceptable? Explain.

[SMA, adapted]

German Subsidiary
Income Statement
For the Year Ended December 31, 2002

		DM
Rental revenue		1,000,000
Interest expense	990,000	
Other expenses	10,000	1,000,000
Net income		0

Balance Sheet
December 31, 2002

Cash	—
Land	12,000,000
	12,000,000
Bond (due December 31, 2006)	9,000,000
Common shares	3,000,000
	12,000,000

Assume the following exchange rates:

January 1, 2002	1 DM = $.35
December 31, 2002	1 DM = $.50
Average, 2002	1 DM = $.43

P10-12

Sentex Limited of Montreal, Quebec, has an 80%-owned subsidiary, Cellular Company Inc., which operates in Erewhon, a small country located in Central America. Cellular was formed by Sentex and Erewhon Development Inc. (located in Erewhon) on January 1, 2002. Advantages to Sentex of locating in Erewhon are easy access to raw material, low operating costs, government incentives, and the fact that the plastics market of Erewhon is not well developed. All management, including the Chief Operating Officer, Mr. V. Globe, has been appointed by Sentex. Top management of Cellular is paid directly by Sentex.

Cellular makes plastic coatings from petrochemical feedstock purchased from Mexico. The process is automated but still uses significant amounts of native Erewhonese labour. The government of Erewhon has determined that this type of development is good for the country, and has underwritten 22,000 cuzos (local currency of Erewhon) of staff training expenses in 2002 by reducing the taxes payable by Cellular. This employment assistance is not expected to continue in the future.

Approximately 75% of total sales by Cellular is made to Sentex, which uses the plastic coatings in its Montreal operations. These coatings are generally of a heavy grade and require special set-up by Cellular. The Sentex orders are handled directly by Mr. Globe and his assistant, Mr. A. Oppong, and the price is set on the basis of variable costs of manufacture, plus freight, and a 30% markup, less applicable export tax incentives. The export tax incentive received by Cellular has been about 1,000 cuzos per order. Plastic coatings are also sold to both commercial and wholesale outlets in Erewhon, with commercial users constituting 20% of the total sales revenue of Cellular.

Cellular has agreed with the Erewhon government not to pay any dividends out of profits for two years. After that, it is anticipated that the majority of profits will be remitted by Cellular to Sentex and its other major shareholder, Erewhon Development Inc.

The opening balance sheet of Cellular Company Inc. at January 1, 2002, was as follows:

(in cuzos)

Cash	30,000	Long-term debt	180,000
Capital assets	350,000	Common shares	200,000
	380,000		380,000

All debt financing was provided by Sentex. The debt was incurred on January 1, 2002, in cuzos, and is secured by the assets of Cellular.

Cellular Company Inc.
Income Statement
For the Year Ended December 31, 2002
(in cuzos)

Sales			600,000
Cost of goods sold*			400,000
Gross margin			200,000
Selling and administrative expenses		70,000	
Interest		20,000	90,000
Net income before taxes			110,000
Local taxes		33,000	
Less allowance for:			
Export incentive	6,500		
Training costs	22,000	28,500	4,500
Net income after taxes			105,500

*Cost of Goods Sold Schedule (in cuzos)

Material purchases	300,000
Labour	70,000
Depreciation	120,000
Total	490,000
Less Inventory at Dec. 31, 2002	(90,000)
Cost of goods sold	400,000

Cellular Company Inc.
Balance Sheet
December 31, 2002 (in cuzos)

Assets

Current assets

Cash	25,000
Notes receivable	100,000
Accounts receivable	65,000
Inventories (at cost)	90,000
	280,000

Capital assets (at cost less accumulated depreciation of 120,000)	230,000
Land (for future development)	10,000
	520,000

Liabilities

Current liabilities

Accounts payable	30,000
Taxes payable	4,500
	34,500

Long-term liabilities	
10% bonds payable, due January 1, 2009	180,000
	214,500

Share equity

Common shares	200,000
Retained earnings	105,500
	305,500
	520,000

Additional Information:

1. Raw material and labour costs were incurred uniformly throughout the year.

2. Sales were made uniformly throughout the year.

3. The capital assets were acquired on January 1, 2002, and are depreciated using the sum-of-the-years'-digits method over four years.

4. The note receivable is a 90-day non-interest-bearing note received from a customer in exchange for merchandise sold in October.

5. Land was purchased on December 31, 2002, for 10,000 cuzos.

6. Cost of sales and inventory include depreciation of 98,000 cuzos and 22,000 cuzos respectively.

7. The exchange rates for 2002 were as follows:

January 1, 2002	1 cuzo = Cdn$2.00
Average for 2002	1 cuzo = Cdn$1.82
December 31, 2002	1 cuzo = Cdn$1.65

Required:

Sentex is in the process of preparing consolidated financial statements for the year ended December 31, 2002.

a. Which method of translation should Sentex use, according to Canadian generally accepted accounting principles? Justify your selection, using the information from the question.

b. Translate into Canadian dollars at December 31, 2002, according to Canadian generally accepted accounting principles, the following balance sheet accounts of Cellular Company Inc.

(1) 10% bonds payable

(2) Capital assets (net)

c. Calculate the translation gain/loss on the accounts of Cellular Company Inc. and show its disposition, according to Canadian generally accepted accounting principles.

[SMA]

P10-13

Garnet Enterprises Limited, a Canadian company, formed a 100%-owned foreign subsidiary on January 1, 2000. Shown below is the balance sheet at December 31, 2000, for Howell Company, the foreign subsidiary. The balance sheets translated into Canadian dollars using the temporal and current-rate methods are shown below:

		Temporal	Current Rate
Current assets	h1,050,000	$420,000	$420,000
Capital assets—net	450,000	225,000	180,000
Total assets	h1,500,000	$645,000	$600,000
Current liabilities	h 650,000	$260,000	$260,000
Long-term liabilities	600,000	240,000	240,000
Deferred exchange gain	—	50,000	—
Common shares	100,000	50,000	50,000
Net income—2000	150,000	45,000	67,500
Cumulative exchange loss	—	—	(17,500)
Total liabilities and equity	h1,500,000	$645,000	$600,000

Exchange rates:

January 1, 2000	1.00 hopi = Cdn$0.50
Average 2000	1.00 hopi = Cdn$0.45
December 31, 2000	1.00 hopi = Cdn$0.40

Additional Information:

1. Capital assets were acquired January 1, 2000, for h500,000. There have been no other capital asset acquisitions or disposals during the year. Amortization expense for 2000 was h50,000.

2. Revenues and operating expenses were incurred uniformly throughout the year.

3. The h600,000 long-term liabilities were issued on January 1, 2000, and mature on January 1, 2006.

4. Net assets on January 1, 2000, were h100,000 in current monetary assets from the issuance of common shares.

Required:

a. Using the temporal method:
   (1) Prepare a reconciliation of the exchange gain/loss.
   (2) Prepare a schedule showing how the net income of $45,000 was derived.

b. Using the current-rate method:
   (1) Prepare a reconciliation of the cumulative exchange loss.
   (2) Show how the net book value of the capital assets on the December 31 balance sheet was derived.
   (3) Show how the net income of $67,500 was derived.

[CGA]

Financial Reporting for Non-Profit Organizations

Introduction

Most study of accounting focuses on business enterprises. However, there are many organizations in Canada that are not businesses. Schools, universities, hospitals, social service agencies, performing arts organizations, museums, trade associations, unions, political parties, and philanthropic foundations are a few examples of the *non-profit organizations* that have an important place in our society. In addition, governments themselves, the entire public sector of the economy, are organizations that are not businesses.

Overall, close to 20% of all Canadian employment is in non-profit organizations or governments. The larger segments are health care, education, and the various levels of government and government services. Indeed, *non-business organizations* comprise a larger component of the economy than manufacturing.

Given the importance of non-business organizations, not only in Canada but world-wide, it is somewhat surprising that so little attention is given to this important segment of the economy in accounting courses. Generally, it is only when students reach the advanced level that they are introduced to the particular problems faced by non-profit organizations and by governments. Well, better late than never! This chapter provides an overview of accounting for non-profit organizations. Chapter 12, Public Sector Financial Reporting, discusses accounting for governments and government services.

Overview of Non-Business Organizations

As a first step, we must make a distinction between *non-business* and *non-profit* organizations. A **non-business organization** is any organization except a private enterprise operating for profit. The general category of non-business organizations can be roughly divided into three groups: (1) governments, (2) governmental units, and (3) non-profit organizations.

Governmental accounting is the body of principles and practices that has been developed for record keeping and reporting by the various levels of government: municipal, regional, provincial, territorial, and federal. Governmental accounting is usually regulated by law, although the accounting and reporting principles on which the law is based were developed by governments and by professional organizations. In Canada, the pronouncements of the CICA's Public Sector Accounting Board influence financial reporting by governments.

Governmental units are organizations that are set up by governments in order to carry out some aspect of their policy. Governmental units include organizations such as school boards, public housing authorities, parking authorities, public cemeteries, water systems, and electric utilities. Such units may be incorporated, but they are **corporations without share capital** and must be distinguished from **Crown corporations**, such as the Canadian National Railway Company, which are business corporations having the government as the only shareholder. Some governmental units do carry on some type of business (e.g., local transportation systems), but they are public sector organizations rather than private enterprises. Therefore, they fall within the general classification of non-business organizations.

Non-profit organizations are non-business and non-governmental organizations that function as educational, scientific, charitable, artistic, or social agencies. The term "social agency" covers a lot of ground, since a social agency can range anywhere from an amateur baseball club to a hospital, with the Salvation Army, the Liberal Party of Canada, and the Kiwanis in between.

Terms other than "non-profit organization" (or "not-for-profit organization") are often used to describe the widely diverse types of organizations that are in this sector of the economy. One alternative is "third sector" (as distinguished from the other two sectors, public and private). Another alternative is "volunteer organizations," because they frequently use the services of volunteers for delivering the organization's services. Also the directors of non-profit organizations are generally prohibited from being paid, and thus are volunteer directors. "Public service sector" is also used, although this phrase can be too easily confused with the "public sector." In this book we will use the term *non-profit organization* (*NPO*).[1]

It is neither possible nor necessary to draw a clear line between governmental units and non-profit organizations. Canadian universities, for example, usually are established as independent corporate entities. But they are dependent on governments for most of their funding and they carry out part of government's educational policy. Similarly, hospitals and public utilities are semi-independent corporations that have some characteristics of governmental units. For accounting purposes, the distinction between non-profit organizations and governmental units is not crucial. The objectives of both are similar, and there is more variation within the broad group of non-profit organizations than there is between non-profit and governmental units.

Governments, on the other hand, have quite different financial statement objectives because of the sources of their funds, their ability to tax, and their legal reporting obligations. In this chapter, we focus on non-profit organizations, including governmental units. Our discussion of governmental financial reporting is in Chapter 12, Public Sector Financial Reporting.

Characteristics of Non-Profit Organizations

There are four very fundamental ways in which non-profit organizations (NPOs) differ from business enterprises:

1. NPOs have *members* instead of owners; there are no residual economic interests.

---

1. Robert Anthony, somewhat annoyed by the use of "not-for-profit," analyzed the relative use of non-profit and not-for-profit in the NPO literature. He found that *non-profit organization* was used in 90% of article abstracts and book titles, 81% of U.S. federal court documents, and 77% of U.S. state laws [Anthony, *Should Business and Nonbusiness Accounting Be Different?*, p. 102]. The term "not-for-profit" seems to have evolved from a concern that people will be overly literal in taking "non-profit" to mean business corporations that are operating at a loss, which is rather like fearing that naive users will think an asset is a small donkey.

2. The organization has a different "bottom line." The organization's objectives may be to serve the common good rather than to maximize net income or generate a return on investment.

3. The nature of revenues and their relationship to costs differs significantly from those of businesses. As well, the sources of revenue often sharply restrict the flexibility of the organization to use that revenue.

4. The suppliers of funds (who are the primary users of the financial statements) are not providing capital in order to earn a return on their investment. Therefore, financial reporting objectives often differ significantly from the profit sector.

These four characteristics profoundly affect the nature of NPO financial reporting. We will expand upon each of these characteristics in the following sections.

No owners

Non-profit organizations have no owners. Regardless of whether an NPO is incorporated or unincorporated, no one has a right to the residual earnings of the organization. Legally, incorporated NPOs are *corporations without share capital*. Since NPOs have no owners, they have no transferable ownership interest.

Although NPOs have no shareholders, they do have *members* who elect the board of directors.[2] The constitution of the organization specifies the conditions for membership. Membership may either be *open* or *closed*.

In an **open membership**, the conditions for membership are clearly specified in the constitution or bylaws of the organization, and membership is available to anyone who is able to fulfil the membership requirements. A **closed membership** exists when the members are designated by the board of directors. Membership is *closed* because it is not automatically open to all qualified individuals who apply, and because the board has the power to change the requirements for membership at any board meeting. In some non-profit organizations, the directors are the *only* members of the organization—in effect, the board elects itself.

A different "bottom line"

NPOs exist in order to perform a service. Since there are no residual economic interests, financial performance on its own is not a primary objective. Obviously, an NPO must remain financially viable in order to continue to operate and to fulfil its service objectives, but financial viability is a *means to an end* rather than being the end itself as is the case with business enterprises.

Businesses provide goods and services to individuals (or to organized groups such as other businesses) at a price. Price is the rationing mechanism, but it also provides the revenue that finances the cost of providing the goods and services. Goods and services that are consumed by individuals and that are rationed are referred to as **private goods and services**.

Non-profit organizations may also provide private goods and services. This is particularly true in NPOs such as sports or social clubs, wherein the primary objective of the organization is to provide services to its members. Private goods are also provided by organizations such as trade unions and professional organizations.

---

2. In some NPOs, the members elect only some of the directors, while other directors are appointed by stakeholder groups, such as government or constituency groups.

However, an NPO may provide goods and services that are not intended to benefit specific individuals but rather to benefit groups within society at large, or the common welfare. Greenpeace, for example, is engaged in environmental awareness activities that benefit society as a whole. The Canadian Cancer Society is engaged not in helping individuals, but rather in supporting cancer research and in increasing public awareness of cancer (and understanding for those who are afflicted with it). The benefits of the activities of organizations such as Greenpeace and the Canadian Cancer Society are available to all individuals within the "target" group either free or at a nominal charge—these benefits are known as **collective goods and services**. Other examples of collective goods include accounting standard-setting, AIDS awareness programs, anti-racism campaigns, and art and museum exhibitions.

Collective goods are not provided by business enterprises; collective goods are provided only by governments and by non-profit organizations. Because there is no parallel in the private sector, proprietary accounting is of little help in designing financial reports for providers of collective goods. Accounting standard setters have implicitly acknowledged this fact in providing for different accounting principles for governments (as we will discuss in Chapter 12).

The accounting policies of an NPO are not driven foremost by a need to determine residual interest, as is the case with shareholders in a business corporation. NPOs do, of course, have a residual both of net assets and of revenues less recognized costs, but measurement of the residual through the use of proprietary accounting does not usually drive the measurement system or the financial reporting. The residual is less of a "net income" construct and more of a true residual: *what is left over.*

Relationship between revenue and costs

In business enterprises, the providers of revenue are the beneficiaries of the business's goods and services. There is a direct link between the service performed, the beneficiary of the service, and the generation of revenue. Therefore, much of proprietary accounting focuses on *matching* of revenue with the costs incurred to generate that revenue.

In some NPOs, there is a similar link. Clubs, private societies, and religious organizations generate revenue primarily from their members and spend that revenue primarily on activities and services that benefit their members. For convenience, we can refer to those organizations wherein the members are the primary (or only) beneficiary of the organization's goods and services as being **self-beneficial organizations**. The members provide the primary revenues, and they receive the benefits of the goods and services.

However, many other types of NPOs do not derive their primary revenues from the beneficiaries of their services. Instead, most social service agencies and arts organizations obtain the bulk of the revenue from governments or private donors, or both. When the beneficiaries of the goods and services are different from the providers of the resources, the NPO is a **public-beneficial organization**.[3]

A key aspect of public-beneficial NPOs is that their revenue is largely independent of the costs. The revenue comes from one group, but the money is spent on serving a different group. This is very different from businesses, where the costs are incurred to earn the revenue. Therefore, non-profit organizations (and governments) need expenditure controls that are markedly different from those normally encountered in private enterprise.

---

3. Charitable organizations are sometimes called "beneficial organizations," which is the same idea.

Businesses measure their expenses in relation to revenue, thereby using the cost/revenue relationship as a control device. When revenues are received by an NPO as a block grant, the relationship between costs and revenues is broken and costs must be controlled directly. The budgetary and management reporting system is designed to prevent managers from exceeding their *spending* authority; *expenditures* become more a focus than *expenses.*

Some or all of the donations or grants received by a non-profit organization may be restricted for particular uses or programs. The donor wants assurance that the funds were used for the intended purpose. The accounting and reporting system must be able to match expenditures to specific programs or purposes. Funds are not transferable from one program to another; therefore, it may not be meaningful to combine revenues and expenditures relating to different programs into a single operating statement for the NPO as a whole.

For example, a school or university will have a large amount of operating funds (grants from government and fees received from students) that are specifically designated for operating the educational programs. The operating funds cannot be used for buildings or for ancillary activities such as providing free parking for faculty or low-cost meals for students. The school will receive separate capital grants that can be used only for capital projects such as new buildings or substantial renovations, and they will also have scholarship funds that must be used only for student aid. Therefore, the accounting and financial reporting system of many NPOs must be able to distinguish between the various funds and be able to show that the various restrictions have been observed.

Objectives of Financial Reporting

The primary users of the financial statements of a non-profit organization are the suppliers of its funds. Funds are derived from (1) members, (2) granting agencies, (3) the general public, and (4) creditors. The objective of financial statements for non-profit organizations "focuses primarily on information needs of members, contributors and creditors" [CICA 1000.11]. In general, the financial reporting objectives for non-profit organizations are:

- Stewardship

- Measuring the cost of services rendered

- Cash flow prediction

- Management evaluation

The first two objectives are the primary objectives; cash flow prediction and management evaluation tend to flow from satisfying the first two objectives. The relevance and priority of the primary objectives depends on the characteristics of the non-profit organization.

If a public-beneficial organization provides collective goods and services using funds donated by the public, *stewardship reporting* of the resources provided by the contributors is most likely to be the primary objective. Greenpeace is a good example. Measurement of the cost of Greenpeace's environmental protection activities is of limited usefulness; there is no meaningful measure of output and thus no useful cost of providing services can be determined. The emphasis in NPO reporting often is on disposition of the resources provided for specific purposes or programs rather than on the costs of services provided. This is an *input* base of reporting rather than the *output* basis that we are accustomed to in business reporting.

On the other hand, a public-beneficial organization may provide private goods and services on a *cost recovery basis*. An overnight hostel for homeless people may be supported by reimbursement on a fee-for-service basis from the city government. The city is the source of funds, and the city will want to know the cost per bed per night; the city may support several such programs and will want to compare the efficiency of the services provided. In such a case, measuring the cost of service becomes the primary reporting objective, and an output base of reporting similar to that used by business enterprises is appropriate.

A distinctive feature of NPO financial reporting is a strong commonality of interest amongst the various users of the statements. Members, managers, directors, and creditors need to see the organization and its programs in the same light as do the major providers of the resources. Managers and directors are accountable to the resource providers for the disposition of resources entrusted to their care. Creditors are also aware that future cash flows may be coming from the suppliers of resources (e.g., government ministries) rather than from the sale of goods and services. Therefore, there often is a strong dominant influence by the providers of the resources in shaping financial reporting objectives and thereby determining accounting policies. This is particularly true of public-beneficial organizations that are providing goods and services (either private or collective) with a fixed revenue base.

Primary Reporting Issues

There are several important reporting issues that shape the financial reporting of non-profit organizations. The primary reporting issues for an NPO are:

1. Expense versus expenditure reporting

2. Capital assets

3. Segregation of resources

4. Donated goods and services

5. Accounting for pledges

6. Accounting for a collection (e.g., museums)

7. Defining the reporting entity

8. Consolidated reporting

We will discuss these issues first, and then we will examine the basic reporting options that are available to NPOs. An NPO should choose the option that better meets their users' needs, as illuminated by the reporting issues.

Expense versus expenditure reporting

There are three different bases on which the resource outflows of any organization can be recognized in the statement of operations:

- *Disbursement* basis: outflows are recognized only when the cash is paid out or disbursed (i.e., a strict cash basis of reporting).

- *Expenditure* basis: outflows are recognized when liabilities are incurred or cash is paid out (i.e., accrual accounting applied to liabilities).

- *Expense* basis: outflows are recognized when goods and services are used in the operations (i.e., a "full accrual" basis of reporting).

Non-profit organizations must decide whether they are going to recognize their costs on the basis of disbursements, expenditures, or expenses. *If* they have a GAAP constraint, the *CICA Handbook* requires the expense basis.

A disbursement basis may be suitable for small organizations with minimal accrued expenses or payables. The use of a strict cash basis, however, may result in reported expenditures that do not properly reflect the commitments made by the organization during the reporting period. Strict cash basis reporting can cause an organization to lose control of its resource management and to lose track of what it owes.

The real choice therefore is between recognizing costs in the statement of operations on the basis of *expenditures* or *expenses*. The expenditure basis has little equivalency in the private sector, where we normally think in terms of expenses. But the notion of expenses is related to the concept of profit, which generally does not exist in the non-profit sector.

The CICA's *Terminology for Accountants* defines **expenditure** as "a disbursement, a liability incurred, or the transfer of property for the purpose of obtaining goods or services . . . ."[4] Note that the emphasis is on *obtaining* goods and services instead of on *using* goods and services, which is the focus of expense.

The expenditure basis means that costs are recorded in operations when incurred, either by disbursing cash or by incurring a liability. Supplies, for example, would be recognized in the statement of operations when acquired rather than when used—no supplies inventory would appear on the balance sheet. In contrast, the expense basis means that goods and services are recognized in the statement of operations when they are used in performing the organization's service.

An expenditure basis is most appropriate when service and program outputs are difficult to measure and therefore there is no clear basis for allocating expenses or measuring efficiency. A clear example would be any form of public or collective good wherein there is no specific beneficiary and no revenue derived from the costs incurred. Specific activities may be clearly defined but the general operations of the organization cannot be specifically related to programmatic goals with measurable outputs. An expenditure basis is also appropriate for programs wherein fixed-grant revenues are intended to finance variable-cost services, as in public-beneficial organizations that derive their primary revenues from block grants by government ministries or foundations.

In contrast, the expense basis is likely to be most appropriate when the NPO is delivering goods or services to individuals and needs to measure the cost of providing those goods or services. For example, hospitals may use an expense basis so that they know the cost of specific services. Revenue providers, such as the provincial governments, often use comparative cost information (that is, from many different hospitals) to evaluate the efficiency of individual hospitals.

On the other hand, it may be useful to exclude certain costs from the cost-of-services calculation when those costs fall outside of the funding guidelines that have been established by the funding agency (i.e., the provincial Ministry of Health). The most notable such cost is the cost of capital assets, which leads us directly to our next major reporting issue—capital assets.

4. *Terminology for Accountants*, Fourth Edition (Toronto: CICA, 1992), p. 88.

Capital assets

Capital asset accounting is controversial largely because of the various methods that NPOs use to finance asset acquisitions. Some NPOs must fund their asset acquisitions through operating revenue (including non-restricted donations), while others may acquire major long-term assets only by special grants or donations. As a result, three different approaches used for accounting for capital assets have developed:

1. Charge to operations immediately (an expenditure basis).

2. Capitalize and depreciate (an expense basis).

3. Capitalize but *not* depreciate.

Charging to operations immediately is the expenditure basis as applied to capital assets. It is possible to use an expenditure basis for capital assets while using an expense basis for other costs. The main reason for the popularity of this approach in the past relates to the nature of the revenue used to acquire the assets.

Many funding organizations (especially government granting agencies and ministries) restrict NPOs' use of operating revenues to operating expenditures, *excluding* capital asset acquisition. Separate grants are given as capital grants for the acquisition of capital assets, and the funding organizations usually prohibit the inclusion of depreciation in the operating accounts. When a capital grant is given, the revenue from the grant is matched to the cost of acquiring the asset in the period of acquisition, and no capitalization or depreciation occurs.

Sometimes capital grants are given only for major assets such as for buildings, while smaller acquisitions (such as furniture or computers) must be financed through the operating grants. In that case, different accounting policies sometimes have been used for the two types of assets due to the differing relationship to revenues.

It has been argued that depreciation is a cost of providing services and that depreciation should therefore be recorded regardless of the way in which the assets were financed. For example, the FASB has argued that "using up assets in providing services . . . has a cost whether those assets have been acquired in prior periods or in the current period and whether acquired by paying cash, incurring liabilities, or by contribution."[5] Similarly, the *CICA Handbook* recommends that capital assets of limited life should be amortized, and that amortization should be included in the NPO's operating statement as an expense [CICA 4430.13].

Even in organizations where revenue comes from general donations rather than from government grants, expenditures for major depreciating capital assets may be financed by means of special capital fund-raising campaigns. There is no intent on the part of either the organization or the donors that part of the cost of assets be charged against operations. If depreciation is taken in periods following the acquisition, then the organization will show a deficit in those periods even if fund-raising activities are sufficient to cover the expenditures for the period (or, conversely, if expenditures are held to the level of the revenue raised).

Depreciation accounting makes sense under two circumstances:

1. the cost of replacing capital assets must be recovered from general revenues, or

2. evaluation of efficiency requires that the cost of *all* inputs, including capital assets, be included in the measurement of outputs.

---

5. Statement of Financial Accounting Standard No. 93, *Recognition of Depreciation by Not-for-Profit Organizations* (FASB, 1987), ¶20.

An expense basis that includes depreciation seems appropriate for self-beneficial organizations and for private goods that are paid for on a fee-for-service basis, regardless of whether the payer is the direct beneficiary or is an outside funder (e.g., a hostel that receives reimbursement from a city for overnight accommodation of homeless people).

The third approach to reporting capital assets is to capitalize the assets and never charge the cost to operations. This approach makes sense when (1) asset replacement or renewal is separately funded or (2) the assets do not decline in value or in usefulness.

When an organization receives separate funding for its capital acquisitions and replacements, it is a form of double-counting to deduct depreciation from operating funds. The usual approach in such circumstances is to charge the full cost of the acquisition against the capital grant when it is received; this approach achieves matching of the revenues and related expenditures. However, the disadvantage of immediate write-off is that the assets do not appear on the balance sheet.

The *CICA Handbook* recommends that NPOs capitalize and amortize all capital assets (except that land is not amortized, of course). Smaller NPOs need not comply with this recommendation. The exemption applies to any organization with gross annual consolidated revenues of less than $500,000.

Segregation of resources

NPOs often receive revenue grants that are earmarked for specific purposes. When the use of the revenue is specified by the donor, the revenue is called a **restricted fund**. If the resources are earmarked by the NPO's board, they are called a **board-designated fund**. The distinction is important because a board can change its mind and remove its own designation. A restriction imposed by an external donor cannot be reversed or changed by the board.

When restricted funds exist, they generally are reported separately for two reasons:

- the donor and other external users need to see that the funds are being used for the proper purposes, and

- the NPO needs to show that restricted funds are not available for general purposes and cannot be transferred to general operations.

One way of accomplishing segregated reporting of restricted funds is through the use of *fund accounting*. **Fund accounting** has been defined as follows:

> Accounting procedures in which a self-balancing group of accounts is provided for each accounting unit established by legal, contractual or voluntary action, especially in governmental units and non-profit organizations.[6]

The focus of fund accounting is on keeping track of resources that are designated for specific purposes, in order to avoid mixing up resources that are intended for diverse purposes and to ensure that management fulfils its stewardship responsibility for proper disposition of the resources. A single non-business organization can have several (or many) such accounting entities. The extent to which funds need to be segregated in an organization is largely a matter of common sense due to the type of contributions they receive and the users' needs.

6. *Terminology for Accountants*, Fourth Edition (Toronto: CICA, 1992), p. 99.

The basic principles of fund accounting are described in the Appendix to this chapter.

Donated goods and services

It is not unusual for people and businesses to donate goods and services instead of (or in addition to) money. Indeed, the very nature of most NPOs and volunteer organizations means that much of the work is being carried out by volunteers through contributed services. As well, companies often choose to donate goods or services, such as an airline that provides free transportation to a sports organization to fly athletes to major competitions. An accounting issue arises from nonmonetary donations—should the donated goods and services be assigned a value and reported in the statements?

In some cases, goods or services are donated as a way of helping the organization to raise money. The goods or services are sold or auctioned off, and the organization ultimately receives cash in exchange for the donated goods or services. In such instances, the inflow of cash determines the value of the donation, and the amount of cash received must be recorded as a donation by the nonprofit organization.

More commonly, however, the goods and services are donated in order to assist the organization to achieve its objectives. The United Way, for example, receives substantial donations of executive time from businesses to help manage its campaigns. Should the United Way assign a value to the donated time?

When donated goods or services are assigned a value and recorded by the organization, the credit to revenues offsets the debit to expenditures and there is no impact on the net operating results. However, the absolute values of the revenues and expenses are affected, and it is possible that management's performance could be evaluated differently.

For example, one measure of the efficacy of a fund-raising organization is the proportion of funds raised that are consumed as fund-raising expenses. An organization that spends only 10% of the donations to obtain those donations is perceived as doing a better job than one that spends 40% of the funds it raises. But if the 40% organization is paying for all of the services it receives, while the 10% organization is using enormous amounts of volunteer effort, are the financial results of the two organizations really comparable? If the 10% organization were to record the value of its donated effort, its cost ratio may rise to 60%. Thus the recording of donated goods and services can have an impact on the perceptions of the readers of the statements, at least in terms of performance evaluation.

For stewardship reporting, the advantages of reporting the value of donated goods and services are not so clear. If the primary objective of the statements is to report on how management used the funds at their disposal, then reporting donated services on the statements may only impair the reporting objective, because it will appear that management had more funds at its disposal than was actually the case.

Practice has varied considerably. Recording and reporting the value of donated goods and services seems to have been the exception rather than the rule in the past. The *CICA Handbook* states that:

> An organization may choose to recognize contributions of materials and services, but should do so only when a fair value can be reasonably estimated and when the materials and services are used in the normal course of the organization's operations and would otherwise have been purchased. [CICA 4410.16]

While the general recommendation for donated goods and services is permissive (i.e., "may"), the suggested recommendation for donated capital assets is stronger. The *CICA Handbook* recommends that donated capital assets "should" be recorded at fair value. When the fair value cannot be reasonably determined, the capital asset should be recorded at nominal value [CICA 4430.06].

Some capital assets may be partially contributed or donated. For example, a builder may construct a new addition to a building at cost rather than fair market value. In this situation, the capital asset would still be recorded at fair value with the donated portion being recognized as a contribution.

Other *CICA Handbook* recommendations call for disclosure of the accounting policies used and the nature and amount of any donated goods or services recorded.

Accounting for pledges

A **pledge** is "a promise to contribute cash or other assets" [CICA 4420.05]. Pledges are therefore a form of contribution receivable. However, a recognition problem arises because pledges are not legally binding. A donor may give a pledge, but may subsequently decide not to actually give the money. In business, accounts receivable are routinely recognized because there has been an *exchange*— the customer or client has received goods or services and therefore has an obligation to pay. For an NPO donor, there is no exchange, but only a one-way promise that can be rescinded, retracted, or ignored by the donor.

An NPO can recognize a pledge as a receivable on its balance sheet if both of two criteria are met: (1) the amount can be reasonably estimated, and (2) ultimate collection is reasonably assured.

The amount is not usually in doubt. Most pledges are for cash, and are payable within a fairly short period of time. Even cash pledges may be uncertain in amount, however, if they depend on future events. For example, a business may promise to contribute 1% of its revenue from sales of a certain product. Even though the contribution will be in cash, the amount will not be known until the sales results are known.

The estimation criterion may also not be met when the pledge is not in cash but is in the form of a non-cash asset. It may be impossible to get a reasonable estimate of the value of the asset until it is in the NPO's hands and can be reliably assessed. As well, the donation may be contingent on some future event, such as the donor's death, which makes both the timing *and* value of the donation uncertain.

The dual criteria of measurability and collectibility often are difficult to achieve for many non-profit organizations. Most NPOs prefer not to count their cash before it has been received. Therefore, revenue is usually recognized only when the amount is collected. For example, the accounting policies note of the Canadian Cancer Society states:

> Revenues from campaign and in-memoriam donations are recognized on a cash basis, with no accrual being made for amounts pledged but not received.

Accounting for a collection

Some non-profit organizations (e.g., museums and art galleries) are dedicated to building and maintaining a *collection*. A **collection** is defined as "works of art, historical treasures or similar assets" [CICA 4400.03] that meet *all* three criteria:

1. The asset(s) must be available to be seen or used (e.g., for education or research) by the public.

2. The collection needs to be maintained and protected.

3. If an asset from the collection is sold, the proceeds from its sale cannot be used for the operations of the NPO. The funds must be used to acquire new pieces for the collection or to help in meeting the second criteria—to care for the collection.

Classification as a *collection* is important because the *CICA Handbook* recommendation to capitalize capital assets does not apply to collections. Instead, the NPO has three options:

- capitalize with no depreciation,

- capitalize and depreciate, or

- disclose only.

The most common alternative is simply to disclose the *existence* of a collection. Although reporting or disclosing the *value* of a collection may be desirable, the practice is not generally followed. Estimates of the value of assets inevitably are unreliable, difficult to verify, and may not be free from bias. In addition, there is a cost associated with having independent appraisals made, and most institutions would prefer not to incur that cost.

Defining the reporting entity

There are many types of relationships that may exist between legally distinct but operationally similar NPOs that are under common control. As a result, the definition of the reporting entity is not as simple as it is for business enterprises.

For example, some arts organizations and social service organizations have a *foundation* that serves primarily to raise money for the main organization. The foundation usually has a board of trustees that is drawn directly from the board of directors of the principal operating arts or social service organization that it controls. Therefore, both the foundation and the operating agency are under common control.

Since the foundation is a legally separate organization, it could report separately from the operating agency. If reporting were done on this basis it would be difficult to evaluate the operations of the operating agency because a large part of the revenues (or the expenses) would be "hidden" in the foundation's statements. Unless the reader of the operating agency knows that the foundation exists, he or she will have difficulty evaluating the agency's financial position or the results of its operations.

To reduce this problem, the *CICA Handbook* recommends that an organization report each controlled organization either by consolidating that entity or by providing specific disclosure [CICA 4450.14]. The obvious issue is what constitutes "*control.*"

The most common indicator that control exists is when one organization has the right to appoint the majority of another NPO's board of directors. However, there may be other factors that indicate control for an NPO. Other possible indicators include (1) significant economic interest, (2) provisions in the organization's charter or bylaws, (3) or common or complementary objectives [CICA 4450.06]. Clearly, professional judgement is required for determining whether control exists.

Consolidated or combined statements

The previous section discussed the issue of consolidation of related entities, which is the usual connotation of consolidation, as we have seen in Chapters 2 through 8 of this book. However, there is another aspect of consolidation that is unique to non-business organizations: to what extent should separate funds and restricted resources be *consolidated* or *combined* on the organization's financial statements?

If there are a large number of separate funds under control of management, separate reporting of the operations and balance sheet of each fund would result in quite a voluminous report, even though columnar formats could be used for conciseness. Separate reporting by funds may clarify the status of each individual fund for stewardship reporting purposes, but may obscure the overall financial position of the organization and the results of its operations.

On the other hand, consolidation of the various funds may hide important characteristics of individual funds, and may impede stewardship reporting. In a research report for the FASB, Professor Robert Anthony observed that:

> Although reports on a funds basis are more difficult to understand than reports on an aggregated basis, especially by users who are accustomed to reading financial statements of business organizations, the complexity is necessary in order to report the realities of a complex situation.[7]

The AcSB supports consolidated reporting. The *CICA Handbook* recommends that the *balance sheet* show "totals for the organization as a whole, to gain complete understanding of the total resources presented" [CICA 4400.09]. The recommendation for a consolidated total does not rule out separate reporting of funds (or of programs), but simply states that everything should be added together at the end.

Note that the requirement is only for a total for the balance sheet. The operating statement need not have a total column under one of the two methods permitted by the *CICA Handbook*, the restricted fund approach, because to provide a total for the operating statement would suggest that the funds are interchangeable between funds, which clearly is not the case for restricted funds.

While this recommendation for aggregating all of the resources on the balance sheet may seem relatively innocuous, reporting of organization-wide totals implicitly suggests that resources can be moved from fund to fund or program to program. Many NPOs oppose the recommendation for consolidated reporting for that reason.

There is a middle ground between fully detailed fund reporting and full consolidation. Similar types of funds or funds with similar objectives can be combined for reporting purposes. All of the ancillary, self-supporting activities of a university, such as the bookstore, food services, parking, and residences can be grouped together because they are similar types of funds. Also, all the student aid funds can be combined for reporting purposes since they serve a similar objective.

The funds do not need to have the same treatment for reporting on all the financial statements. Funds (or groups of funds) can be reported separately on the statement of operations, but combined on the balance sheet. Conversely, the funds may be combined on the statement of operations, but reported separately on the balance sheet and the cash flow statement. As we will discuss below, an

---

7. Robert Anthony, *Financial Reporting in Nonbusiness Organizations: An Exploratory Study of Conceptual Issues* (Stamford, Connecticut: Financial Accounting Standards Board, 1978), p. 111.

NPO may account in different ways for different funds or programs. When such is the case, it is impossible to meaningfully consolidate the various funds or programs.

GAAP for Non-Profit Organizations

In the sections above, we have briefly described the substantial differences between NPOs and businesses. These differences include the nature of the organizations, the financial reporting objectives, and the specific reporting issues. Due to these differences, it is not surprising that GAAP for NPOs developed quite differently from that for business enterprises. In recognition of these differences, NPOs had for many years been exempted from the reporting recommendations of the *CICA Handbook*.

However, the AcSB began taking an interest in NPO financial reporting in the late 1980s, and in 1996 issued a substantial set of recommendations that were aimed at making NPO financial statements look a lot like business enterprises. Not only did NPOs get their own set of sections in the *CICA Handbook*, but also most of the other sections (e.g., pensions and leases) of the *CICA Handbook* were applied to NPOs for the first time. Generally speaking, the AcSB declined to acknowledge the differences between NPOs and business organizations, implying that whatever is good for business reporting must be good for NPO reporting too.

Initially, the AcSB proposed that NPO financial statements should look virtually identical to business statements, with no provision for segregation of funds. However, opposition to that proposal was sufficiently strong to prompt the AcSB to propose two different approaches that NPOs can use:

- the restricted fund method, in which funds can be segregated for financial reporting, and

- the deferral method, in which all funds are combined in the financial statements without distinction between restricted and unrestricted funds.

If an NPO has at least one restricted fund (that is, restricted by the *donor*), management can choose either of the two methods. If there are no restricted funds, then the deferral method must be used.

Many NPOs are not constrained by GAAP and do not need to comply with the *CICA Handbook* recommendations. These organizations may use a reporting method that is mandated by their primary funding agency, such as the Ministry of Health or the Ministry of Social Services. Alternatively, they may follow a more traditional expenditure-based reporting system.

In the following sections we will explain the various methods of reporting. The first is the expenditure-based approach, which we are calling the "traditional" method. Then we will look at the two methods recommended by the *CICA Handbook*. It is important to understand that this is not a theoretical discussion—*all of these methods are used in practice*.

Many organizations use a dual reporting approach. They may use one of the AcSB's recommended methods in order to obtain an audit opinion, and then use an expenditure-based set of statements to satisfy their primary user's needs. Such an approach is somewhat costly, since it involves extensive year-end adjustments to get from an expenditure approach to one of the *CICA Handbook* expense approaches.

Types of Financial Statements

The *CICA Handbook* recommends that NPOs prepare the following four financial statements [CICA 4400.05]:

1. Balance sheet

2. Statement of operations

3. Statement of changes in net assets

4. Cash flow statement

The second and third statements will often be combined into a single statement of operations and fund balances. A separate cash flow statement need not be prepared if the statement would contain no new information that is not apparent from the statement of operations [CICA 4400.52]. As a result, many NPOs report only two statements: (1) a balance sheet and (2) a statement of operations and changes in net assets.

The statements should be in a comparative format, with comparisons to the previous year. There may also be comparisons to budgeted amounts. In addition to the statements themselves, there should be notes to the financial statements.

This list of statements looks deceptively simple. The statements do not look much different from those that we are accustomed to seeing for businesses. The differences can be great, however. As we will discuss shortly, the presentation will depend on whether the NPO has selected the *deferral method* or *restricted fund method* for recognizing contributions.

Reporting Options

Traditional method

In the sections above on reporting issues, we outlined the basic nature of NPO financial reporting as it developed throughout the 20th century. Generally speaking, most NPOs used the following reporting practices:

- Revenues were recognized when received; accruals were rare.

- Resource *outflows* were recognized when the cost was incurred or when the liability was incurred. Accruals were almost never made for items such as pensions, leases, or vacation pay. The general tendency was to report on a flow-of-funds accrual basis, without interperiod allocations.

- Capital assets may or may not have been recorded on the balance sheet, but depreciation was used only for funds that conducted activities that were expected to be self-supporting on a cost-recovery or profit-making basis.

- Funds were segregated on the balance sheet, and separate statements of operations were used for different funds (or for different groups of funds of similar nature).

- Funds rarely were totalled on the statement of operations; the balance sheet more often showed a total for all funds.

- Related organizations were not consolidated.

Many NPOs still follow these practices, usually because that is what their donors or funding agencies want in order to see what the organization's managers have done with the resources placed at their disposal during the year. When audit requirements force an NPO to use an expense basis of reporting, there sometimes are interesting note disclosures that alert users to the difference between expenditure and expenses. An example is the following note from a social services agency's annual report:

Accounting for vacation pay

In accordance with generally accepted accounting principles, the Centre uses the accrual basis of accounting for vacation pay. As a result, the deficit in the Operating Fund amounts to $209,297 at fiscal year-end, of which $199,568 relates to the accrual for vacation pay. In accordance with the Ministry's funding policy, vacation pay is funded on a cash basis and therefore the funding related to this liability has not been reflected in these financial statements.

In other words, the deficit (and a related liability) appears in the financial statements almost entirely because the Centre is required by the *CICA Handbook* to accrue vacation pay. However, the funding agency will support those costs only on a pay-as-you-go basis. There is no doubt that the Ministry will cover those costs, but no revenue can be accrued because the Ministry doesn't owe the money yet!

The accounting policies that are used under the traditional expenditure-based method are shown in Exhibit 11-1, along with those recommended by the methods proposed in the *CICA Handbook*.

CICA Handbook methods

The *CICA Handbook* recommends two alternative methods of accounting, the *deferral method* or the *restricted fund method*. Before we discuss and demonstrate these two methods, we must first explain the three different types of contributions—restricted contributions, endowment contributions, and unrestricted contributions.

Restricted contributions are contributions that are *restricted by the donor* for specific purposes or uses. They may not be used for other purposes, and the system of accounts must maintain the integrity of the donation and its purpose. Restricted contributions must be distinguished from **board-designated funds**, which are funds that the board of directors has earmarked for a specific purpose. The board can decide to reverse its *internal restriction*, and therefore internal restrictions do not have the same importance for financial reporting as do true restricted funds.

An **endowment contribution** is a special type of restricted contribution. Not only is the contribution restricted in purpose, but also the principal amount of the contribution cannot be spent. The contribution must be invested in an endowment fund and only the earnings on the investment can be spent for the intended purposes. An example is a scholarship fund within a university. The principal amount to establish the scholarship is maintained and interest earned on that principal is used to provide scholarships.

An **unrestricted contribution** is provided without any restrictions on its use by the organization. Basically, it is any contribution that does not meet the definition of either a restricted contribution or an endowment contribution.

The differences between these types of contributions are critical to remember as we discuss the NPO reporting options. The recognition and presentation of different types of contributions on the financial statement differs among these methods. Fund accounting will be discussed briefly in an Appendix to this chapter.

The two methods can be briefly described as follows:

- The **deferral method** can be used by any NPO. Under this method, no distinction is made between different funds or groups of resources in the balance sheet or the statement of operations. A full accrual basis is used, including the accrual of pledges and full interperiod allocation of revenues and expenses in accordance with the recommendations of the *CICA Handbook* for business enterprises. Capital assets must be capitalized and amortized. Restricted revenues must be deferred and matched to the expenses that they were intended to fund.

- The **restricted fund method** may be used by any NPO that has at least one fund or resource group that is restricted by an outside donor. Under this method, the NPO presents a separate operating statement for each fund (or group of similar funds)—no totals for the organization need appear on the statement of operations because the funds are not interchangeable. The balance sheet should present totals for the organization as a whole, however. Accrual accounting is applied and capital assets are capitalized, but amortization does not have to be charged to general operations; amortization can be charged to a separate capital fund instead. In contrast to the deferral method, however, revenue usually is recognized in the appropriate fund when it is received (or accrued) rather than when the expenses are incurred.

The choice of method depends primarily on the users and their needs. If the organization wants the simplest financial statements they may select the first alternative. If the primary purpose is to show information on specific activities or programs, or if there is a large number of external users who have imposed restrictions, the second alternative may be more appropriate.

Exhibit 11-1 compares some of the fundamental characteristics of these two methods, as well as comparing them to the traditional method.

Deferral method: business-type accounting

This method is conceptually similar to that used by business enterprises, at least on the surface. The concept behind this method is to match the revenues with the associated expenses. The revenue is recognized as the related expenses are incurred.

Unrestricted contributions are recognized as revenues in the current period. They are available for any use by the organization.

The treatment of *restricted contributions* depends on the purpose for which they have been restricted by the donor. If the contribution is for expenses of the current period, the contribution should be recognized as revenue in the current period. If the contribution is for expenses of a future period, it is recorded as *deferred revenue* until the related expense is recognized.

Note that this matching process is reversed from our normal expectation in business enterprise accounting. For businesses, the usual focus is on recognizing revenue first, and then matching expenses to that revenue. If there are related costs that will be incurred in the future (e.g., warranty expense), those future costs are estimated and recognized in the period in which the revenue has been recognized to achieve matching.

Under the deferral method of NPO accounting, the matching process is reversed. First, the expenses are recognized, and then the revenue is matched. If revenue is received prior to the expense, the revenue must be deferred until the expense is recognized. Note that the deferral is until the *expense* is recognized, not

EXHIBIT 11–1 ALTERNATIVE APPROACHES TO NPO FINANCIAL REPORTING

		CICA Handbook recommendations*	
Accounting practice	Traditional approach	Restricted fund method	Deferral method
Accrual of pledges	Not done	Required if recognition criteria are met	Required if recognition criteria are met
Revenue recognition	Recognize when realized	Recognize when realized	Match to expense recognition
Expense or Expenditure basis	Expenditure	Expense	Expense
Capital assets:			
Capitalize	Sometimes	Required*	Required*
Charge to operations	Seldom	Not required (may use separate fund)	Required*
Combine funds in "Total" column:			
Statement of operations	Seldom	Not required	Required
Balance sheet	Seldom	Required	Required
Consolidation of related organizations	Not done	Required	Required
General application of *CICA Handbook* (e.g., pensions, leases, expense accruals)	Not done	Required	Required

* Not required for NPOs with consolidated gross revenue of less than $500,000 [CICA 4430.03].

the *expenditure*. If a restricted contribution is for a capital asset, the treatment depends on whether or not that asset will be depreciated. If the asset is depreciated, the revenue will be deferred and recognized on the same basis as the amortization of the specific asset that has been purchased.

For example, suppose that a donor contributes $30,000 to a social agency on December 13, 2002. The donation is restricted for the purchase of a new van. The van will be purchased in 2003. The van will be depreciated over three years, straight-line. When the contribution is received, the credit will be to deferred revenue:

December 13, 2002:

Cash	30,000	
Deferred revenue (restricted—van)		30,000

If the van is purchased on January 27, 2003, the transaction will have no immediate impact on the statement of operations:

January 27, 2003:

Capital asset—van	30,000	
Cash		30,000

At the end of 2003, the agency will record $10,000 in depreciation. Simultaneously, the same amount of revenue will be recognized:

December 31, 2003:

Depreciation expense	10,000	
Accumulated depreciation—van		10,000
Deferred revenue (restricted—van)	10,000	
Revenue		10,000

Under the deferral method, all revenues from all funds are added together in the statement of operations. If the restricted revenue were recognized when it is received or when the van is purchased, the agency would show restricted revenue that is not matched by an expense; and any unmatched revenue will lead financial statement readers to believe that the NPO has more revenue available for unrestricted purposes than it really does.

To avoid showing revenue without any related expenses, *endowment contributions* are recognized as direct increases in net assets in the current period because they will never be available to meet expenses of the organization. Remember we said that net assets *may* be shown in a separate statement or combined with the statement of operations.

Restricted fund method

The second method is based on the concepts of fund accounting that have been used in non-profit organizations for many years. A number of separate funds (i.e., self-balancing sets of accounts) are used in order to segregate the three basic different types of contributions: (1) restricted funds, (2) endowment funds, and (3) the general fund (or operating fund) for unrestricted contributions.

Under the restricted fund method, the *CICA Handbook* does recommend that the resources and liabilities of the various funds be added together for a "total" column on the balance sheet. However, there is no requirement that the various funds be added together on the statement of operations. The whole point of this method of accounting is to recognize that restricted and endowed funds are not interchangeable with unrestricted funds, and that a deficit in the operating fund cannot be remedied by transferring money from the restricted funds to the operating fund.

As a result, an NPO might show a surplus under the one-column operating statement of the deferral method, when all of the funds are added together. But under the restricted fund method of reporting, the funds are segregated and it will be apparent to the financial statement user that the restricted and endowment funds cannot be used for general operating purposes.

Another important distinction between the deferral method and the restricted fund method is that depreciation and amortization on capital assets does not need to be charged to the operating fund under the restricted fund method. Depreciation and amortization can be segregated in the capital asset fund instead. This eliminates one of the major objections that many NPOs have to the idea of business-style accounting—that depreciation is charged against operations that are not intended to recover the costs of capital assets, if the assets have been acquired through special grants or fund-raising drives.

It is the organization's option as to how many restricted funds they wish to have on their statements. An NPO may decide not to have a separate fund for smaller restricted contributions. Instead, smaller funds can be combined into a single larger restricted fund. For example, the many different scholarship and bursary endowments in a college or university are combined into a single "financial aid endowment fund."

EXHIBIT 11–2 SAMPLE NPO FINANCIAL STATEMENTS—DEFERRAL METHOD

Statement of Financial Position
December 31, 2001
(in thousands)

	2001	2000
Assets		
Current assets		
Cash and term deposits	$ 520	$ 280
Accounts receivable	150	160
Supplies	160	60
	830	500
Investments	570	200
Capital assets, net	1,000	1,100
Total assets	$2,400	$1,800
Liabilities, deferred contributions, and net assets		
Current liabilities		
Accounts payable & accrued liabilities	$ 70	$ 10
Current portion mortgage payable	10	10
	80	20
Mortgage payable	120	130
	200	150
Deferred contributions:		
Capital	600	720
Other deferred contributions	110	—
	710	720
Net assets:		
Externally restricted	150	100
Invested in capital assets	280	250
Internally restricted	100	200
Endowments	570	200
Unrestricted	390	180
	1,490	930
Total liabilities, deferred contributions, and net assets	$2,400	$1,800

EXHIBIT 11–2 SAMPLE NPO FINANCIAL STATEMENTS—DEFERRAL METHOD (continued)

Statement of Operations
Year Ended December 31, 2001
(in thousands)

	2001	2000
Revenues		
Grants and contributions	$2,140	$2,400
Amortization of capital contributions	120	100
Other revenue	1,400	1,200
	3,660	3,700
Expenses		
Salaries	2,790	2,800
Amortization of capital assets	200	260
Other expenses	480	460
	3,470	3,520
Excess of revenues over expenses	$ 190	$ 180

Statement of Changes in Net Assets
Year Ended December 31, 2001
(in thousands)

Net assets	Externally restricted	Invested in capital assets	Internally restricted	Endow- ments	Unrestricted	Total
Balance, January 1	$100	$250	$ 200	$200	$ 180	$ 930
Excess (deficiency) of revenues over expenses	50	(80)			220	190
Investment in capital assets		110			(110)	—
Endowment contribution				370		370
Internally imposed restrictions			(100)		100	—
Balance, December 31	$150	$280	$ 100	$570	$ 390	$1,490

Even though funds may be combined, their distinct nature should be preserved. Restricted donations and endowment donations are not combined with unrestricted donations. Unrestricted contributions are recognized as revenue in the *general fund* in the current period. This is similar in treatment to the deferral method.

The accounting for restricted contributions depends on whether or not there is a separate restricted fund for that contribution. If there is a separate restricted fund, it is recognized as revenue in the current period in that fund. If there is no separate fund, it is *recognized in the general fund using the deferral method* of accounting for contributions. Therefore, restricted contributions are treated differently depending on whether or not they are shown in a separate fund.

Endowment contributions are recognized as revenues in the *endowment fund* in the current period. Note the difference here between the two reporting methods. The restricted fund method shows the contributions as *revenue* in a separate fund. In contrast, the deferral method shows endowment contributions as a direct increase in net assets—there is no revenue recognition on the statement of operations.

Notice also that under the restricted fund method, contributions in separate restricted and endowment funds are recognized currently rather than being deferred. When restricted funds are shown separately, there will be no confusion about whether excess revenue is available for general use. The use of a restricted fund makes it clear to users that those resources are not available for general operations. Matching of revenues to expenses is not of concern in this reporting framework, and therefore there is no need to defer recognition of the revenue.

The restricted fund method of accounting tends to result in a higher level of revenue than does the deferral method. The reasons are that (1) restricted revenues often are recognized earlier because there is no need to defer recognition of the revenue until the expense has been recognized, and (2) contributions to endowment funds are recognized as revenue under the restricted fund method but not under the deferral method. Therefore, the selection of accounting method may place an organization over the size test for capitalizing capital assets (i.e., average revenues of less than $500,000) if the restricted fund method is used, but not if the deferral method is used.

Illustration of Reporting Methods

Deferral method

Exhibit 11-2 (pages 510 and 511) gives an illustration of a simple set of NPO financial statements prepared by using the deferral method. This organization has all three types of funds—endowment, restricted, and unrestricted—but the statements do not have to be prepared on the restricted fund method. Any NPO can use the deferral method.

There are three statements: a balance sheet (statement of financial position), a statement of operations, and a statement of changes in net assets. In the first two statements, there is no distinction made between the resources in the various funds.

However, notice that on the balance sheet, there is not just one amount for capital, shown here as "net assets" (other often-used headings are *fund balances, net resources available,* or *accumulated excess of revenues over expenditures*). Instead, there are five different fund balances shown. This is an important option in NPO accounting. Even when the deferral method is used, the net resources that relate to each fund may be shown separately on the balance sheet. By using this approach, users can see that, although the total fund balances amount to $1,490, only $390 of that amount is unrestricted and is available for future operations.

The third statement reconciles the beginning and ending balances of each of the fund balances shown on the balance sheet. If the balance sheet shows more than one fund balance, then the beginning balance must be reconciled to the ending balance for each fund.

On the statement of changes in net assets, observe that the total column shows a surplus of $190 (i.e., excess of revenues over expenses). This statement reveals that:

- the surplus in the unrestricted fund actually was $220;

- the contributions to the endowment fund of $370 were not included in revenues on the statement of operations;

- capital assets of $110 were purchased from unrestricted funds during the year; and

- the board reversed an internal restriction by $100, releasing those funds for general unrestricted use.

Restricted fund method

Exhibit 11-3 shows the same organization, but this time using the restricted fund method of reporting. Only two statements are presented, a balance sheet and a combined statement of operations and changes in net assets. A cash flow statement is considered to be unnecessary because the cash flows are apparent from the other statements.

In this approach, detailed balance sheets are presented for the operating fund, for each restricted fund (research and capital assets), and for the endowment fund. We can see, for example, that of the total current assets of $830, only $680 are for unrestricted use.

Revenue recognition also is quite different between the two methods. Notice that in the balance sheet in Exhibit 11-3, there is no liability for deferred revenue. That is because revenue is recognized when realized in the restricted fund method. The endowment is in a separate fund, and therefore the contributions to the endowment fund are recognized as revenue *for that fund* in the restricted

EXHIBIT 11–3 SAMPLE NPO FINANCIAL STATEMENTS—RESTRICTED FUND METHOD

Statement of Financial Position
December 31, 2001
(in thousands)

	Operating fund	Research fund	Capital asset fund	Endowment fund	2001 Total	2000 Total
Current assets						
Cash and term deposits	$370	$150			$ 520	$ 280
Accounts receivable	150				150	160
Supplies	160				160	60
	680	150			830	500
Investments				$570	570	200
Capital assets, net	200		$800		1,000	1,100
Total assets	$880	$150	$800	$570	$2,400	$1,800
Current liabilities						
Accounts payable & accrued liabilities	$ 70				$ 70	$ 10
Current portion, mortgage payable	10				10	10
	80				80	20
Mortgage payable			$120		120	130
Total liabilities	80		120		200	150
Fund balances						
Externally restricted	110	$150			260	100
Invested in capital assets	200		680		880	970
Internally restricted	100				100	200
Endowments				570	570	200
Unrestricted	390				390	180
Total fund balances	800	150	680	570	2,200	1,650
Total liabilities and fund balances	$880	$150	$800	$570	$2,400	$1,800

EXHIBIT 11–3 SAMPLE NPO FINANCIAL STATEMENTS—RESTRICTED FUND METHOD (continued)

Statement of Operations and Changes in Net Assets
Year Ended December 31, 2001
(in thousands)

	Operating fund	Research fund	Capital asset fund	Endowment fund
Revenues				
Grants and contributions	$1,650	$640		$370
Other revenue	1,400			
	3,050	640		370
Expenses				
Salaries	2,300	490		
Amortization of capital assets	200			
Other	480			
	2,980	490		
Excess (deficiency) of revenues over expenses	70	150		370
Fund balance, January 1	640	—	$770	200
Interfund transfers	90		(90)	
Fund balance, December 31	$ 800	$150	$680	$570

fund method. In the deferral method, the endowment contributions are not recognized as revenue.

Since revenue recognition is different, the total fund balances are different between the two methods. Notice that the total fund balances (or "net assets") shown in Exhibit 11-2 is $1,490, while in Exhibit 11-3 the total fund balances amount to $2,200.

In order to avoid complicating the presentation, we have omitted the 2000 comparative data for the statement of operations in Exhibit 11-3. In practice, comparative information would be presented either by putting more columns in the statement or by providing another statement in identical format for the prior year. The restricted fund approach tends to present a lot of numbers. But the numbers are necessary in order to try to grasp the real operating situation of the organization.

The Chore of Users: Unravelling GAAP

We pointed out earlier in the chapter that the users of NPO financial statements often are interested in the organization's use of the resources given to help the organization accomplish its mandate. There are two aspects to this interest—(1) stewardship over the resources themselves, and (2) effectiveness in accomplishing the organization's objectives. Unfortunately, the annual financial statements of an NPO usually do not satisfy either goal very well.

Stewardship is difficult to assess because the expense basis of reporting that is recommended by the AcSB often is in conflict with users' interest in how the organization *spent* the money given to it—expenditures rather than expenses.

Sometimes the organization tries to help users by pointing out the impact of major unfunded accruals, such as the vacation pay example cited earlier in the chapter.

The deferral method makes it especially difficult to unravel the financial performance of any NPO that has restricted funds. Some universities, for example, have chosen to use the deferral method, adding together unrestricted funds, restricted funds, endowment funds, and enterprise accounts into a single set of numbers. The "bottom line" in such a situation is meaningless. If there is a surplus, is it a surplus that can be used for future operations (i.e., unrestricted), or is the surplus due to restricted funds that hide a deficit in the general fund? If the university shows a deficit, is it a deficit in the operating funds or is it because the university is losing piles of money on its enterprises, such as the bookstore or food operations? It is impossible to unravel the reasons for either a surplus or a deficit when the deferral method is used in an NPO that has restricted donations.

The difficulty of evaluating *efficiency* in an NPO has led to a demand for a greater volume of non-financial data as supplementary information in non-business financial statements. Data on the level of services performed or activities accomplished, membership levels, contributors, etc., can be provided. For example, a CICA Research Study on NPOs recommends that non-profit organizations provide the following information along with their annual financial statements:[8]

- The nature and objectives of the organization

- Plans for the future

- Significant events during the year and their relationship to or impact on the financial results

- Any unusual or important items or trends in the financial statements

- Important non-financial information

It would be most useful if quantitative supplementary information were audited. Sometimes the audit opinion does cover at least some such information, but normally the supplementary information is outside the scope of the audit opinion. Auditors find it difficult to verify independently most non-financial data unless it is directly tied into the accounting and reporting system. Therefore, financial statement readers have to accept supplementary information largely on trust.

Unfortunately, there have been instances of over-enthusiastic managers issuing inflated performance data in order to enhance the apparent efficiency or effectiveness of the organization. For example, one Canadian film festival was alleged to have announced attendance figures that were in excess of the combined maximum seating capacities of their theatres! But this type of behaviour is undoubtedly the exception rather than the rule.

Budgetary Control and Encumbrance Accounting

By now, you will have seen that accounting for non-profit organizations is quite different from accounting for business enterprises. But we are not done yet. There are two other special aspects of NPO accounting. We will conclude this chapter

8. Canadian Institute of Chartered Accountants, *Financial Reporting for Non-Profit Organizations* (Toronto: CICA, 1980), pp. 41–42.

with an overview of these two special accounting techniques—*budgetary control accounts* and *encumbrance accounting*.

Budgetary control accounts

A unique characteristic that is often used in fund accounting is the practice of formally incorporating budgetary accounts into the accounting system. **Budgetary accounts** enable a running comparison of budgeted with actual amounts (of revenue and expenditure) and a monitor of the level of expenditure.

It is quite possible to accomplish the same result without formally including the budget in the accounting system; many businesses routinely have budget vs. actual comparisons on their internal statements. The difference in non-business organizations, and especially in governments, is that when strict expenditure limits are in effect, a formalized system acts as an internal control, so that managers are not permitted to issue purchase orders that will push the expenditure total above the budgeted limit. The comparison between the budget and the combined total of expenditures is constant and routine, rather than being occasional and special.

We will not go into the technical aspects of budgetary control accounts here. There are many books that explain the mechanics of fund accounting and budgetary accounts in exquisite detail. It will be sufficient to say simply that the nature of the budgetary accounts is to create a self-balancing set of accounts *within* the regular accounting system, normally within the general or operating fund. In general, the bookkeeping approach that is used for budgetary accounts is as follows:

- Budgeted revenues are *debited* to an account that serves as an offset to actual revenues (which are credits). The difference between the budgeted and actual revenues is automatically shown within the system by netting the actual against the budgeted amounts. A net debit balance indicates that actual revenues are falling short of the budget, while a net credit balance shows that revenues are exceeding budget.

- Budgeted *expenditures* (not *expenses*) are shown as credits. The level of detail matches the level of expenditure control that has been mandated by the board of directors (or, for governments, by the legislature). The budget balance is the upper limit of permitted expenditures. Managers and employees will not be permitted to make additional commitments once the budget limit has been met.

The budget limits on expenditure are enforced by means of an encumbrance system.

The encumbrance system

The **encumbrance system** records the estimated cost of commitments in the formal accounting system when the commitments are made rather than when a legal liability has arisen. For example, purchase orders for supplies are recorded as an *encumbrance* at the estimated cost of the supplies when the purchase order is issued, even though no liability (in both a legal and an accounting sense) exists until the supplier delivers the supplies. In theory, an encumbrance system could be used in private enterprise accounting—encumbrances are not necessarily limited to fund accounting. In practice, encumbrance accounting is unique to governments and NPOs.

The objective of using an encumbrance system is to keep track of the commitments that an organization's managers have made for the acquisition of goods and services. If there is a budgetary or legislative limit on the total amount of expenditure that a manager can make during the year, then use of the encumbrance system keeps the manager from overcommitting the organization and running up a large deficit.

Even in the absence of fixed budgetary limits, encumbrances can be used simply as an aid to planning and control. This is particularly true when commitments on the same budget amount can be made by several people within the organization. When control is decentralized, an encumbrance system improves regulation and communicates to managers and to the people making the expenditures just what the actual level of commitment is.

The encumbrance system is widely used in governmental accounting; budget amounts are legislated maxima that must not be exceeded. In NPOs, however, whether or not an encumbrance system is used depends on the nature of the organization and its operations. In fact, encumbrance accounting can be used in some parts of an organization and not in others, and for some types of expenditure (such as for supplies) and not others (such as salaries). The system is most appropriate when the following conditions are present:

1. The organization, fund, or activity is a cost centre with a maximum expenditure limit *or* has no relationship between costs and revenues.

2. Goods and services acquired discretionally are a significant part of the total budget.

3. There is a significant lag between the commitment (e.g., purchase order) and the receipt of the purchased items.

4. Levels of activity (and expenditure) within the organizational unit are not affected in the short run by an autonomous demand, either external to the organization or from other parts of the organization.

5. Reporting is on an expenditure basis rather than an expense basis.

6. Responsibility for making commitments and expenditures is decentralized throughout a large organization.

If, in contrast, a small organizational unit must vary its level of activity in response to market demand for its services, if it is able to generate revenues to cover expenses, and if externally acquired goods and services are either of little consequence or are received very shortly after ordering, then there is little reason to use an encumbrance system.

Encumbrance systems are used to control costs when expenditure limits are basically fixed and are not tied to revenue or activity levels. If these conditions do not exist, then encumbrances are of limited usefulness. Also, if only a very small part of expenditures is discretionary rather than being tied to longer-term employment or supply contracts, then there is little point to using encumbrances.

A Final Example

We will end this chapter with an example of NPO financial statements. Exhibit 11-4 shows the basic 1999 statements for the Canadian Cancer Society. As is common in NPO reporting, the Canadian Cancer Society (CCS) takes a slightly eclectic approach. The balance sheet has only one column (for each year), which

EXHIBIT 11–4 SAMPLE NPO FINANCIAL STATEMENTS

Canadian Cancer Society
Consolidated Statement of Resources
(In thousands of dollars)

Year ended September 30, 1999, with comparative figures for 1998

	1999	1998
Assets		
Current assets:		
Cash, including interest bearing accounts	$ 9,696	$ 9,905
Accounts receivable	2,122	2,343
Prepaid expenses	1,724	2,004
Investments	26,478	24,812
	40,020	39,064
Deferred pension costs	2,456	2,382
Capital assets (note 2)	11,335	11,402
	$53,811	$52,848
Liabilities and Resources		
Current liabilities:		
Accounts payable	$ 3,085	$ 3,196
Research contribution payable to National Cancer Institute of Canada	1,723	4,143
Deferred revenue	2,968	2,171
	7,776	9,510
Obligation for post-retirement benefits other than pensions	4,356	3,997
Resources:		
Externally restricted	3,160	3,308
Invested in capital assets	11,335	11,402
Internally restricted	14,297	15,388
Unrestricted	12,887	9,243
	41,679	39,341
Commitments (note 7)		
	$53,811	$52,848

See accompanying notes to consolidated financial statements

EXHIBIT 11–4 SAMPLE NPO FINANCIAL STATEMENTS (continued)

**Consolidated Statement of Financial Activities —
Operations and Externally Restricted Resources
(In thousands of dollars)**

Year ended September 30, 1999, with comparative figures for 1998

	Operations		Externally restricted	
	1999	1998	1999	1998
Revenues				
Campaign	$ 36,942	$36,784	$ 782	$ 941
Special events	20,736	20,027	—	2
In Memoriam	12,751	12,132	—	—
Bequests	24,832	25,005	124	—
Other income	4,849	3,822	680	527
Investment income	2,351	2,088	138	127
Expenditures	102,461	99,858	1,724	1,597
Grants and fellowships:				
Research grants — NCIC (note 4)	41,376	42,551	—	—
Research grants to other organizations	282	65	870	946
Fellowships and professional education	342	428	13	15
Grants to lodges and health centres	598	518	—	15
General purpose grants	—	143	—	—
	42,598	43,705	883	976
Functional disbursements:				
Public education	14,283	14,049	618	295
Patient services	18,765	18,171	239	407
Fundraising — general	14,346	13,141	55	23
Fundraising — special events	4,848	3,968	—	—
Administration	5,267	5,290	19	66
	57,509	54,619	931	791
	100,107	98,324	1,814	1,767
Excess of revenues over expenditures before the undernoted	2,354	1,534	(90)	(170)
Pension plan credit	74	989	—	—
Increase (decrease) in resources	$ 2,428	$ 2,523	$ (90)	$ (170)

See accompanying notes to consolidated financial statements

EXHIBIT 11–4 SAMPLE NPO FINANCIAL STATEMENTS (continued)

Consolidated Statement of Changes in Resources
(In thousands of dollars)

Year ended September 30, 1999, with comparative figures for 1998

	Externally restricted	Invested in capital assets	Internally restricted	Unrestricted	1999 Total	1998 Total
Resource balances, beginning of year	$3,308	$11,402	$15,388	$ 9,243	$39,341	$40,762
Adjustment for change in accounting policy (note 3)	—	—	—	—	—	(3,774)
	3,308	11,402	15,388	9,243	39,341	36,988
Increase (decrease) in resources	(90)	—	—	2,428	2,338	2,353
Additions to capital assets	(62)	926	(316)	(548)	—	—
Amortization of capital assets	—	(993)	—	993	—	—
Appropriations (note 5)	4	—	(775)	771	—	—
Resource balances, end of year	$3,160	$11,335	$14,297	$12,887	$41,679	$39,341

See accompanying notes to consolidated financial statements

Consolidated Statement of Cash Flows
(In thousands of dollars)

Year ended September 30, 1999, with comparative figures for 1998

	1999	1998
Cash provided by (used in):		
Operating activities:		
Increase in resources	$2,338	$2,353
Items not involving cash:		
Amortization of capital assets	993	1,388
Gain on disposal of capital assets	—	(18)
Increase in deferred pension costs	(74)	(989)
Increase in deferred revenue	797	449
Increase in obligation for post-retirement benefits other than pensions	359	371
Change in non-cash operating working capital	(2,030)	(4,846)
	2,383	(1,292)
Investing activities:		
Capital asset additions	(926)	(3,945)
Proceeds on disposal of capital assets	—	18
Decrease (increase) in investments	1,666	6,672
	(2,592)	2,745
Increase (decrease) in cash	(209)	1,453
Cash, beginning of year	9,905	8,452
Cash, end of year	$9,696	$9,905

See accompanying notes to consolidated financial statements

might lead one to believe that the statements are prepared on the deferral method.

However, the statement of operations has two columns for each year—operations and externally restricted. There is no total column. Therefore, the CCS must be using the restricted fund method. This is confirmed in the accounting policy note (not reproduced in Exhibit 11-4), which states that "the Society follows the restricted fund method of accounting for contributions."

The statements are headed as "consolidated" statements. The notes explain that "these financial statements include the financial activities and financial position of the ten provincial Divisions and the National Operations of the Canadian Cancer Society."

The consolidated statement of changes in resources contains the reconciliation of beginning fund balances (called "resource balances" in the CCS statements) with the ending balances. In this statement, there are four columns for the current year as contrasted with two columns in the operating statement. The four-column reconciliation in the statement of changes corresponds with the four balances shown under "resources" on the balance sheet.

Finally, the CCS does present a cash flow statement. In 1999, the adjustments to operating activities almost balance out, resulting in little change in the starting point of the surplus as shown in the operating statement (i.e., $2,338). In 1998, however, the adjustments did not net to a minor amount. Instead, the accrual-basis *surplus* of $2,353 is converted into a cash flow *deficit* of $1,292.

As supplementary disclosure, the CCS financial statements include a schedule of *disbursements* by functional classification, as shown in Exhibit 11-5. The rows are disbursements by type of expenditure (in alphabetical order), while the columns are the primary activities of the CCS. Of the total disbursements of $58,440 in 1999, about 25% were spent on public education and 33% were spent on patient services. Administration consumed about 9%, while fundraising and special events used 33%.

Summary of Key Points

1. Non-profit organizations are significantly different from business enterprises. The primary differences are that (1) they have members, but no owners; (2) they do not exist to generate a return on investment; (3) expenses are not usually incurred in order to generate revenue; and (4) the suppliers of funds usually do not receive the benefits of an NPO's activities.

2. The objectives of financial reporting tend to emphasize (1) stewardship and (2) measuring the cost of services. Most NPOs obtain their funding from members, external donors, and public or government granting agencies. These donors need to see how the organization used the resources that were given to it during the year. Therefore, there often is a heightened interest in stewardship reporting—what did the managers do with the funds entrusted to their care? Accounting for expenditures becomes an important reporting objective.

   Some NPOs provide goods and services to individuals on a cost recovery basis. In such cases, a primary reporting objective is to measure the cost of providing those services. The emphasis then falls on expense accounting rather than expenditure accounting.

EXHIBIT 11–5 CANADIAN CANCER SOCIETY

Consolidated Schedule —
Operations and Restricted Functional Disbursements
(In thousands of dollars)

Year ended September 30, 1999, with comparative figures for 1998

	Public education	Patient services	Administration	Fundraising and special events	1999 Total	1998 Total
Aid and service to hospitals and clinics	$ —	$ 29	$ —	$ —	$ 29	$ 59
Amortization of capital assets	364	304	186	139	993	1,231
Boarding, home care, and housekeeping	—	3,194	—	—	3,194	2,567
Camps	—	587	—	—	587	385
Campaign organization and office expenses	—	—	—	1,774	1,774	1,625
Cancer Education in the Workplace	91	1	—	—	92	101
Cancer Information Service	1,100	784	10	5	1,899	1,987
Computers and services	333	264	189	150	936	558
Councils on Smoking and Health	154	—	—	—	154	116
Dressings	—	67	—	—	67	48
Drugs	—	344	—	—	344	566
Education, evaluation, and research studies	306	252	—	62	620	501
Emotional support	—	87	—	—	87	222
Equipment, furniture, and fixtures	184	140	89	46	459	487
Exhibits, fairs, displays, and posters	212	5	1	6	224	206
Films and videos	13	4	—	6	23	16
Insurance	31	25	17	11	84	137
Meetings and conferences	411	286	228	315	1,240	1,115
Membership and grant — U.I.C.C.	80	—	—	—	80	19
Miscellaneous	249	233	138	188	808	687
Occupancy	1,261	1,021	593	415	3,290	3,162
Ostomy supplies	—	67	—	—	67	56
Other medical supplies	—	118	—	—	118	111
Pamphlets, materials, bulletins, and reports	592	389	22	293	1,298	1,582
Planned Giving	—	—	—	101	101	31
Postage and courier	255	198	119	857	1,429	1,630
Professional fees	326	264	160	200	950	1,095
Publicity — newspaper, radio, and T.V.	53	27	3	361	444	486
Repairs and maintenance	116	105	87	84	392	280

EXHIBIT 11–5 CANADIAN CANCER SOCIETY (continued)

	Public education	Patient services	Administration	Fundraising and special events	1999 Total	1998 Total
Salaries and benefits	7,820	5,780	3,052	6,965	23,617	22,210
Special events, gross expenses	—	—	—	4,848	4,848	3,968
School Education Programme	31	—	—	—	31	33
Stationary and supplies	236	181	120	1,973	2,510	2,298
Telephone and fax	332	246	151	120	849	873
Transportation of patients	—	3,706	—	7	3,713	3,797
Travel	310	224	106	234	874	990
Volunteer development and recognition	41	72	15	89	217	175
	$14,901	$19,004	$5,286	$19,249	$58,440	$55,410

3. There are many reporting issues that are unique to NPOs and governments. Unlike business enterprises, NPOs often have resources that are restricted for specific uses. They also receive donated goods and services. Accounting for pledges and for capital asset acquisitions also becomes problematic. Finally, there often is a problem in simply identifying the reporting entity and implementing consolidated reporting.

4. There are three basic approaches to accounting for NPOs. One is the traditional, expenditure-based approach, using fund accounting. Restricted funds are reported separately from unrestricted funds. Capital assets seldom are capitalized and amortization is rarely charged to operations. Capital assets often are funded by special grants or by special fund-raising drives, and operating funds are not expected to bear the costs of the capital assets.

   This method is most commonly used by smaller NPOs—those with gross revenues of less than $500,000—who are not required to follow the AcSB's recommendation for capitalizing capital assets.

5. The *CICA Handbook* recommends two other methods of reporting: the deferral method, or the restricted fund method. The deferral method can be used by any NPO. The restricted fund method can be used only by an NPO that has at least one restricted fund.

   The deferral method adds all of the various funds together into a single total column. No segregation is reported, except that separate fund balances may be reported in the balance sheet. The individual reported fund balances then are reconciled in a statement of changes in fund balances.

   The restricted fund method permits segregated reporting for restricted and endowment funds. The funds do not need to be added together on the statement of operations, although a total column should be provided on the balance sheet.

6. An accounting procedure that is unique to NPOs and governments is the use of budgetary accounts within the formal set of accounts. The purpose of budgetary accounts is to control the level of expenditure, and also to permit an automatic comparison of budget versus actual amounts at every reporting date. Expenditure limits are enforced by means of encumbrance accounting.

Encumbrance accounting records an obligation as soon as a purchase order is issued, thereby reducing the amount of available funds that can be committed to other purchases.

Appendix

Fund Accounting

Introduction

In non-profit organizations and in governments, the maintenance of financial capital is not of high concern; indeed, it may not be a concern at all. Because costs are not incurred in order to generate revenue (except in certain self-sustaining or cost-recovery activities), there is not the same need to measure consumption of goods and services. Instead, the emphasis is on controlling expenditures and keeping within budget. The change in emphasis has resulted in the development of *fund accounting*, one of the three fundamentally different accounting systems that are in general use.[1]

Fund accounting has three attributes, any or all of which may be useful in accounting for specific non-business organizations. The three attributes are (1) the segregation of funds by purpose or restriction, (2) the ability to account for commitments, and (3) the capacity to incorporate budgetary controls directly into the accounts. As we discussed in the main body of Chapter 11, the restricted method of accounting for contributions has specifically designated funds. In this Appendix we will discuss fund accounting as an option, even when the deferral method is used.

In fund accounting, there is a set of self-balancing accounts for each separately-identified fund. Therefore, each fund will also have its own financial statements. The statements for some funds will be very simple, while those for other funds can be very complex. A plethora of interfund transfers complicates matters further, particularly if the transfers are not clearly identified in the financial statements. To avoid a fragmented approach to financial reporting, many NPOs combine similar funds for external reporting. For example, a university will not report each scholarship fund separately, but will combine them all into a single set of accounts for financial statement purposes.

This brief Appendix will outline the major characteristics of fund accounting and will describe the basic different types of funds. The bookkeeping aspects will not be presented herein, however. The technical aspects of fund accounting are dealt with in many other books, large and small, that are readily available.

1. The first system is *proprietary accounting*—the basis for all business enterprise accounting. The second is *fund accounting*. The third system is *entity accounting*, wherein economic institutions are viewed as entities generating value added. The value added is distributed to the factors of production without adopting the point of view of any particular factor (such as the suppliers of capital, as in proprietary accounting). Entity accounting is the basis for all macro-economic accounting, such as the national income accounts. It also is useful in developing countries for enterprise accounting (instead of proprietary accounting) because the enterprise accounts then fit into the framework of the macro-economic systems, which aids in guiding development.

Purpose of fund accounting

Fund accounting has been defined as: "Accounting procedures in which a self-balancing group of accounts is provided for each accounting unit established by legal, contractual or voluntary action, especially in governmental units and non-profit organizations."[2]

The focus of fund accounting is on keeping track of resources that are designated for specific purposes, in order to avoid mixing up resources that are intended for diverse purposes and to ensure that management fulfils its stewardship responsibility for proper disposition of the resources. A single non-business organization can have several (or many) such accounting entities.

As the definition of fund accounting suggests, funds can be created as the result of legal or regulatory requirements, by contract with donors or grantors, or voluntarily by the directorate of the organization. As discussed in the chapter, the different types of fund restrictions fall into three categories: endowed funds, and externally and internally restricted funds.

Fund balances may also be *appropriated.* Appropriations in fund accounting are no different from appropriations of retained earnings in businesses; there is no segregation of funds, but simply an indication that the board or legislature intends to devote some of the resources of a particular fund to an indicated purpose.

The extent to which funds need to be segregated in an organization is largely a matter of common sense. When a donor gives a contribution that is earmarked for a specific purpose, there must be some way of ensuring that the contribution is used only as intended. If an organization operates an ancillary enterprise in order to perform a service or to raise money, it makes sense to segregate all the revenues and costs of that enterprise in order to measure the net cost of providing the service or the net revenue raised. Thus there are no hard and fast rules as to the types of funds that an organization may have.

Fund-basis *recording* does not necessarily imply fund-basis *reporting.* It is common to consolidate several or all funds when preparing the financial statements, especially the statement of operations. The balance sheets can also be consolidated.

Types of funds

There are several different types of funds. Distinctions between types of funds generally relate to either the nature of the activity being carried out by the fund or to restrictions on the uses of monies, or both. Terminology varies somewhat, thereby adding to the confusion. We will distinguish among six basic types of funds. In addition, there are two types of *account groups.* The nature of the different types of funds and account groups is discussed below.

Operating or general funds

Non-profit organizations tend to use the term *operating fund* or *general fund* for the central fund of the organization that bears the costs of conducting the organization's primary functions, and into which unrestricted funds flow. An organization can have more than one operating fund if it conducts more than one primary function, and if it were desirable for managerial purposes to keep the assets, liabilities, and the revenues and expenses of the primary functions separate. But if the revenues, expenses, assets, and liabilities are not directly assignable to

2. *Terminology for Accountants,* 4th Edition (Toronto: CICA, 1992), p. 99.

the various functions, then segregation is not really feasible and only a single operating fund will be maintained.

Maintaining separate *funds* should not be confused with maintaining separate *accounts* within the operating fund for different activities. In modern computerized accounting systems, it is easy to have a triple classification of each account:

- by type or object of revenue or expenditure
- by fund
- by program or activity

Special or reserve funds

A special fund is a fund created to record the resource flows associated with a special project or event. Special funds could be created by an NPO, for example, to carry out a specific research project, to conduct a special event such as a benefit concert, or to institute a new program using a special grant from a donor or a government grantor. Special funds may generate their own revenue (as for a fund-raising event), may be carried out with funds voluntarily segregated by the directorate of the organization and transferred from the operating fund, or may be financed by restricted grants from outside the organization.

Separate reserve funds often are not necessary; the same result (in an operating sense, not an obfuscation sense) often can be obtained by appropriating or designating part of the fund balance in the general fund.

Self-sustaining or enterprise funds

This type of fund accounts for those activities that generate their own revenues to recover their costs, and thus are segregated from the other funds both for control purposes and for performance appraisal. Self-sustaining funds are also known as *enterprise* funds or *revolving* funds. Self-sustaining funds may be created by money advanced from the general fund. In such instances, the amount advanced is a receivable in the general fund accounts and a liability in the self-sustaining fund accounts; the interfund obligation is eliminated if consolidated statements are prepared.

Capital funds

A capital fund (or *plant* fund) is one in which the resources are intended for use for capital improvements or new capital assets. The fund may be a restricted fund if it contains monies given specifically for capital purposes only, as with a capital grant by a province to a hospital. Capital funds may also be board-designated funds, if the capital was appropriated by the board of directors for capital improvements rather than being externally restricted by the donor. If a capital fund contains both restricted amounts and designated amounts, then the fund balance should segregate the net resources within each category.

Capital funds may be used to account for both assets acquired and liabilities incurred, such as mortgages and bonds. The term "capital" can thereby apply to both sides of the balance sheet: to long-term assets (capital used) and to long-term liabilities (capital provided).

If capital funds are not used to keep track of assets and/or liabilities, then one of the *account groups* discussed below may be used.

Fiduciary funds

A fiduciary fund is any fund that is held in trust for outside parties. An organization may hold funds in trust for other organizations or groups, and not be entitled to any of the benefits of the funds. For example, a church or university may hold cash and provide accounting services for clubs or subgroups within the organization but the funds are those of the clubs and not those of the church or university that is functioning as trustee. Similarly, employee pension funds are sometimes administered by a non-profit organization for the benefit of its employees. *Fiduciary funds* can also be called *trust, agency,* or *custodial* funds.

The distinction between trust funds and reserve funds is that trust funds are legally restricted for specified uses, while reserve or special funds are board-designated funds.

Endowment funds

The capital in an *endowed fund* cannot be disbursed at all. The purpose of the endowed fund may also be restricted. Endowment funds, scholarship funds, and loan funds are examples. The income arising from the investment of the fund capital may or may not be disbursed. If the income can be disbursed, it may be restricted (i.e., as to purpose), depending on the conditions of the donor. Sometimes, a fund is endowed only for a designated period of time, after which the capital becomes available for use as directed by the donor.

Endowed funds are sometimes expended on a constant rate of return basis. Under this approach, a given percentage of a fund's net asset *value* may be expended each year, regardless of the actual earnings of the fund. The percentage generally reflects long-term expectations for inflation-free investment earnings, such as from 3% to 5%. The intent is to permit the organization to use a predictable amount of income each year for the fund's operating purpose, without worrying about the vagaries of the investment market in any particular year. In addition, establishing the permissible expenditure at a "real" rate of return permits the endowment to accumulate enough additional principal to offset the erosive effects of inflation on the real value of the return.

The distinction must be clear between a fund that is legally restricted by the donor and one that is voluntarily restricted by the organization's directors. Voluntary restrictions can be reversed at a later date by the directors. Only funds in which the capital is non-expendable by order of the donor should be called endowed funds.

Account groups

In addition to the types of funds explained above, non-business organizations can also have one or two *groups* of accounts. Groups differ from funds in that there are no liquid assets within the group; the group is simply a self-balancing set of accounts that is intended to keep track of assets and liabilities that may otherwise not be included within the control systems of the organization.

One type of group is the *capital asset group.* Acquisitions of new capital assets are generally treated as current expenditures of the fund making the acquisition, such as the operating fund.[3] In order to include the cost of the capital assets on the organization's balance sheet, the assets may be recorded as a debit to an asset

---

3. The principal exceptions would be in self-sustaining or enterprise funds in which capital assets are capitalized and depreciated.

account within a group of capital asset accounts, with an offsetting credit to a fund balance or group balance account. The offsetting credit is often to an account that identifies the source of financing for the asset. In this manner, the organization's long-term sources of financing for its capital assets can be identified. The group really represents a collection of memorandum entries; there are no resources or transactions relating to the group itself.

Capital asset groups are used largely for control purposes and to permit consolidated reporting that shows all of the organization's assets and liabilities. When a non-business organization chooses to capitalize its capital assets (if a GAAP constraint exists), an alternative practice is to capitalize the asset within the capital fund, the operating fund, or whichever other fund has expended the resources to acquire the capital assets.

The second type of account group is the *long-term liability group*. In government accounting, this group has traditionally been called the bonded debt group. The purpose of this group is to keep track of outstanding long-term obligations. This group is used almost exclusively by senior governments—most local governments in Canada are not permitted to issue long-term debt, and NPOs seldom have long-term debt except for property mortgages and occasional bank term loans.

The liability group is used by governments to keep track of the overall debt obligations and repayment schedules. The group also can be used to keep track of loan guarantees that the government has handed out, but few governments do bother to track their guarantees—a control weakness that various auditors general have pointed out from time to time!

Fund accounting and the segregation of funds

In theory, each fund is a separate group of accounts. In practice, however, it is not always necessary to be so formal about the individual funds. For example, suppose that an organization receives a special grant to produce its literature in French translation. Technically, this is a donation that is restricted to a specific use and would call for the establishment of a special fund. More likely, however, the organization will create a single control account in its operating fund and credit the grant to that account. All expenditures relating to the translation and production of the French materials will be charged to that account, so that the account balance corresponds to what would be the fund balance if a separate set of accounts had been established. A subsidiary set of accounts can be maintained in support of the control account, if desired.

Interfund transfers

Transfers between funds create a potential problem area for financial reporting. The problem arises from the difficulty of making the distinction between three types of transfers: (1) interfund loans, (2) redesignations of fund balances by the board of directors, and (3) expenditures by one fund that are revenues to the other. The first type of transfer results in a receivable in the lending fund and a payable in the borrowing fund; the expectation is that the loan will be repaid sometime in the foreseeable future. Interfund loans will show on the balance sheets of the individual funds and on their statements of changes in financial position, but will not affect the statement of operations or the fund balances. Interfund loans would be eliminated in consolidated statements.

Redesignation of fund balances by the board represents a permanent shift of resources from one fund to another. These transfers should be reflected in the statement of changes in fund balance for both the paying and the receiving funds, but should not result in an offsetting receivable and payable or have any impact on the statement of operations. If, on the other hand, the transfer is recognition that one fund is using the services of another fund and is paying for the services rendered, then the transaction should flow through the statement of operations of *both* funds.

A problem that exists in practice in NPOs is that the accounting treatment of the transaction may be determined more by management's desire to influence the reported operating results rather than by the real nature of the transaction. If the operating fund has a substantial surplus, for example, management may redesignate part of the fund balance and transfer the surplus to another fund (e.g., the capital fund). Rather than report the transfer simply as a fund balance transfer, management may list it as an expenditure in the operating fund in order to bring down the apparent surplus so that potential donors won't think that the organization doesn't really need more money.

A similar ploy is not to transfer the surplus to another fund but simply to make an appropriation within the operating fund, separating the fund balance into appropriated and unappropriated amounts, and to charge the appropriation against operations as though it were an expenditure instead of simply debiting the fund balance. Unfortunately, both ploys are common in practice, making the "bottom line" of the statement of operations even less meaningful than it already is (due to the multiplicity of alternative accounting policy choices, almost all of which affect the bottom line).

Any reader of the financial statements of a government or NPO must watch for interfund transfers, not because there is anything wrong with them per se, but because they can be used to hide a variety of sins!

Summary of Key Points

1. Fund accounting is a system of accounting that segregates an organization's resources into a series of separate, self-balancing account sets. Each fund will have its own financial statements, at least in theory. In practice, separate funds of a similar nature usually are combined for external financial reporting. Fund basis *recording* does not necessarily lead to fund basis *reporting*.

2. A desirable attribute of fund accounting is that it encompasses techniques for maintaining budgetary control over the actions of managers. Fund accounting also enables senior management to ensure that restricted funds are used only for the proper purposes.

3. There are several different types of funds. Every organization has an operating or general fund, through which the principal operating activities of the organization are conducted. In addition, an organization may have a variety of special funds, enterprise funds, capital funds, fiduciary funds, and endowment funds.

4. In addition to funds, NPOs and governments often have account groups. The two types of account groups are the capital asset group and the long-term liability group. Each of these groups is a control mechanism for assets or liabilities that are not otherwise recorded on the balance sheet. There are no liquid resources in either capital asset or liability groups.

5. Interfund transfers present a special opportunity for management to affect the "bottom line" of segregated funds. Surpluses and deficits can be "managed" by the adroit use of interfund transfers. Caveat emptor!

Weblinks

Salvation Army
www.salvationarmy.org

The Salvation Army works in over 100 countries using more than 140 languages. Their worldwide program includes accommodation for the homeless, a network of drug addiction centres, anti-suicide counselling, and help for the blind and other physically challenged people.

Kiwanis Club
www.kiwanis.org

Founded in 1915 and headquartered in Indianapolis, Indiana, Kiwanis International is a thriving organization of service- and community-minded individuals who support children and young adults around the world. Service projects include working to stop substance abuse, helping the elderly, promoting literacy, supporting youth sports and recreation, responding to disasters, and aiding specific persons in need.

Greenpeace
www.greenpeace.org

Saving ancient forests, condemning the use of nuclear power, and outlawing genetic engineering are just a few of the mandates of Greenpeace. Learn how you can help from their informative Web site.

Canadian Cancer Society
www.cancer.ca

This site provides a wealth of information about cancer: research and statistics, listings of Canadian Cancer Society events, and volunteer opportunities are some of the topics covered.

Review Questions

11-1 What proportion of Canadian employment is in non-profit organizations?

11-2 Who owns non-profit organizations?

11-3 Why are non-profit organizations sometimes called "voluntary organizations"?

11-4 What distinguishes non-business organizations from business organizations?

11-5 What is the difference between *non-business* organizations and *non-profit* organizations?

11-6 What distinguishes non-profit organizations from governmental units?

11-7 Who elects the directors of a non-profit organization?

11-8 Distinguish between an *open membership* non-profit organization and a *closed membership* organization.

11-9 Explain what is meant by a "self-perpetuating board."

11-10 What are *collective goods and services*? What types of organizations offer collective goods and services?

11-11 What types of organizations offer *private goods and services*?

11-12 Describe the ways in which the nature of revenue in non-profit organizations can differ from business enterprises.

11-13 What is a *public-beneficial organization*? Explain how a public-beneficial organization differs from a *self-beneficial organization*.

11-14 Why might the revenues of an NPO not be derived from the recipients or beneficiaries of its goods and services?

11-15 Who are the primary users of the financial statements of non-profit organizations?

11-16 What are most likely to be the two primary objectives of financial reporting for NPOs?

11-17 What objectives of financial reporting for businesses do not exist for non-business organizations?

11-18 If the emphasis in accounting for many non-profit organizations is on the control of cash flows, why is the accrual basis recommended?

11-19 Explain the difference between the *expense basis*, the *expenditure basis*, and the *disbursements basis* of reporting.

11-20 Why in the past did many non-profit organizations not capitalize their capital assets?

11-21 What alternative approaches are there to accounting for capital assets in non-profit organizations?

11-22 What is the size test for capital assets?

11-23 What is the distinction between a *restricted fund* and a *board-designated fund*?

11-24 Why would an organization want to report the value of donated services in its statement of operations?

11-25 What is a *pledge* and what are the criteria for recognizing pledges?

11-26 What is a *collection* and what criteria are required for something to be defined as a collection?

11-27 How could consolidation hide important characteristics of individual funds?

11-28 Why might it be possible for a non-profit organization to combine the statement of operations with the statement of changes in net assets?

11-29 Explain the distinction between the *restricted fund method* and the *deferral method*.

11-30 What types of financial statements will a non-profit organization normally issue?

11-31 How standardized are the statements of non-profit organizations, as compared to business organizations?

11-32 Explain the differences between a *restricted contribution, board-designated fund, endowment contribution,* and an *unrestricted contribution.*

11-33 How are *restricted contributions* recognized in the deferral method compared to the restricted fund method? What is the difference if there is no separate fund in the *restricted fund method* for that contribution?

11-34 Does the restricted fund method or the deferral method of accounting tend to result in a higher level of revenues?

11-35 Why is non-financial supplementary information often needed for performance evaluation?

11-36 Explain the purpose of recording budgetary amounts in the accounts.

11-37 When budgetary accounts are used, why is the amount for estimated revenues a debit instead of a credit?

11-38 What is an *encumbrance*?

11-39 What is the purpose of an *encumbrance system*?

Cases

Case 11-1

Gold Development

Gold Development (GD), a newly incorporated non-profit organization with a December 31 year-end, will offer low-rent housing services for people with low income.

GD reports to Logimex, a government agency that requires audited annual financial statements to be filed. Mr. Bilodeau, the project originator and administrator of GD, is not familiar with the preparation of financial statements.

GD received a non-repayable grant from Logimex in February 2001 for the construction of an eight-storey apartment building. Construction began in April 2001.

Residents will start to move into the apartment building between October and December 2001, although it will not be entirely completed until the end of December 2001. By December 2001 all the apartments should be rented.

GD receives donations from companies and individuals in the region. It has received pledges from large, well-known companies for the next five years, and pledges from individuals for the current and next year. Pledge amounts have been set out in writing on forms signed by the donors.

For a nominal salary, Mr. Bilodeau manages the organization with the help of his wife and the local priest, both of whom are volunteers.

Required:

a. Explain to Mr. Bilodeau what is meant by "reporting on a restricted fund accounting basis" according to the *CICA Handbook.*

b. Advise Mr. Bilodeau on the appropriate accounting for the above issues assuming that GD decides to report on a restricted fund accounting basis.

Case 11-2

Youth Singers

Youth Singers (YS) is a non-profit organization that was formed in 1992 by Nancy, a retired professional singer. Members of the choir range in age from 8 to 20. The choir has won a number of major singing competitions across North America and is producing its first CD next month. The choir plans to record an annual CD of its Christmas concert.

Nancy is in charge of YS's daily operations. All major decisions need to be approved by the board of directors. Initial financing for YS came solely from private donations. A fund-raising committee was recently formed to raise funds for special projects. Last year, YS qualified for two government grants. These grants require audited financial statements to be submitted on an annual basis. YS has attached a set of financial statements to government grant applications in the past. Canada Customs and Revenue Agency also requires financial statements in order to provide tax receipts for donors.

Your CA firm has a policy of supporting its staff to volunteer their time to NPO activities. You have recently joined YS as a member of their board of directors and have volunteered to assist with all accounting issues. Details on past accounting policies are provided in Exhibit 1.

You have been asked to prepare a report identifying any changes you would make to the current accounting policies for the next board of directors' meeting.

Required:

Prepare the draft report to the board of directors.

EXHIBIT 1

ACCOUNTING POLICIES AND OTHER INFORMATION

1. Donation—Original Historic Sheet Music

   A donor recently died, leaving in her will a large selection of sheet music to YS. It is impossible to verify the value of this donation due to its historical value. The music will be performed by the choir during concerts. The original sheet music will be displayed in a glassed-in case.

2. Annual Pledges

   Every Christmas, YS holds an annual benefit concert. At this time, YS holds a major fund-raising drive and asks all concert guests to provide a donation or pledge an amount. All pledges are recognized when the pledge is made by the donor.

3. Capital Assets

   All capital assets are recorded at their market value as determined by the finance director. During 2001, a local music store provided sheet music stands at manufacturer's direct costs of $20,000. Purchasing these stands at retail prices would have cost $40,000.

4. Revenues

   Individual choir members started providing singing lessons during 2001 as a source of fund-raising. The revenue during 2001 from lessons was $50,000. Annual revenue from all sources was $200,000 in 2000 and $280,000 during 2001.

5. Amortization

Capital assets are not amortized.

Case 11-3

Finest Art Gallery

Finest Art Gallery (Finest) is a major art gallery in Toronto. Finest has the largest collection of art in Canada and has five major exhibits a year. Finest is a non-profit organization with funding received primarily from private contributors and government grants.

The board of directors turns over its members every three years. A new board was just announced for 2000 to 2003. The new board has a number of younger members who have rejuvenated a previous idea to expand a new section of the gallery for the work of children. This would require major fund-raising over the next few years. It is anticipated that this addition would attract a wider audience to the gallery and encourage young children to become interested in art at an early age.

The new board, although energetic and ambitious, lacks knowledge of accounting. Board members were recruited for their marketing skills and love of art. They have asked you, CA, to assist them over the next few months to select accounting policies and provide recommendations for changes to their existing policies. They want to comply with any *CICA Handbook* recommendations for non-profit organizations, but are not familiar with the *Handbook's* content. You have committed to preparing a report for the next board meeting outlining specific accounting policies. If you recommend any changes, they must be fully supported. The board is concerned with the costs involved with preparing financial statements and wants to minimize these costs.

After the meeting with the board of directors you sat down and reviewed their financial statements for 2000. Notes from your review are included in Exhibit 1.

A set of financial statements has been provided to any donors who requested them in the past. In addition, government agencies require a set of audited financial statements as a requirement for government grants.

Required:

Prepare the report for the board of directors.

EXHIBIT 1

NOTES TAKEN FROM A REVIEW OF THE 2000 FINANCIAL STATEMENTS

1. The financial statements include a Statement of Income and Expenditures and a Statement of Financial Position. A Cash Flow Statement was not prepared since it was felt that it does not provide meaningful information.

2. Revenues for 2000 included the following:

Memberships	$ 600,000
Admission fees	800,000
Government grants	2,000,000
Contributions	450,000
Endowment fund revenue	950,000

3. Admission fees are recognized as money is collected. Contributions are recognized when a pledge is made by the donor. Notes to the financial statements segregate the number of restricted and unrestricted contributions. Restricted funds include any amounts donated for a specific purpose and amounts segregated by the board for future expansion or special projects.

4. All capital assets are recorded at a dollar to have a nominal amount provided on the financial statements. No amortization is taken on these assets. A recent review of the capital assets indicated the following items. The amounts were estimated by one of the board of directors:

Office equipment	$ 500,000
Automobiles	70,000
Facilities	10,000,000
Artwork	unable to estimate

5. During 2000 the roof was replaced on the art gallery. The cost of this work was $260,000. This amount was expensed. In addition, a new air-conditioning unit was installed to protect the artwork from damages due to temperature changes. The cost was $300,000. To finance the purchase of the new air-conditioning system a piece of artwork was sold.

6. Volunteer services are not recorded.

Case 11-4

CKER-FM Ethnic Radio

In the fall of 2000, eight wealthy businesspeople from the same ethnic background formed a committee (CKER committee) to obtain a radio licence from the Canadian Radio-Television and Telecommunications Commission (CRTC). Their goal is to start a non-profit, ethnic community radio station for their area. They plan to call the station CKER-FM Ethnic Radio (CKER). It will broadcast ethnic music, news and sports from their country of origin, cultural information, ethnic cooking, and other such programs, seven days a week.

The station's capital requirements are to be financed by memberships, donations, and various types of loans. It is expected that the on-going operations will be supported by advertising paid for by businesspeople from that ethnic community and by the larger business community targeting that ethnic audience, as well as by donations and memberships.

It is now March 2001, and the CRTC has announced that hearings will start in one month on a number of broadcasting licence applications, including the CKER committee's application. The CKER committee members are fairly confident about the viability of their proposal; however, they have decided to seek the advice of a professional accounting firm to assist with the endeavour. The CKER committee has engaged Maria & Casano, Chartered Accountants, for the assignment, as three of the five partners of the firm are from the same ethnic community. The partner in charge of the assignment has stated that the firm will donate half its fee for the work.

You, CA, work for Maria & Casano and have been put in charge of the assignment. You have met with the CKER committee and various volunteers associated with the project. Information gathered on station start-up is contained in Exhibit 1. Exhibit 2 provides other information on the CKER committee's proposal. The partner has asked you to prepare a draft report to the committee members discussing the viability of the proposed radio station over the initial three-year period. Since the committee members are fairly confident that they will receive the licence, the partner has asked you to recommend accounting policies for the transactions that CKER is contemplating. Your report must also cover other significant issues that the station will face after it commences operations.

Required:

Prepare the draft report.

EXHIBIT 1

INFORMATION ON STATION START-UP

1. Costs to date have totalled $50,000 and are mostly transportation and meeting costs, as well as postage. These costs have been paid for personally by the CKER committee members.

2. To approve the licence application, the CRTC must see written commitments to finance the station's start-up costs and operating losses in the first two years. Remaining costs to obtain the licence, excluding donated legal work, are expected to be about $8,000, and will be paid by CKER committee members.

3. If the CRTC approves the licence application, the CKER committee will immediately set up a non-profit organization and apply to Canada Customs and Revenue Agency (CCRA) for charitable status, which it will likely receive.

4. Fairly exhaustive efforts to obtain commercial financing have failed. As a result, four wealthy individuals have volunteered to provide CKER with the financing for the start-up. They will each personally borrow $25,000 from financial institutions and give the funds to the station. These individuals expect the loan to be cost-free to them, as the station will make the interest and principal payments.

5. A "Reverse Lifetime Contribution" program will be instituted. Under this program a donor will pay the station a capital sum of at least $50,000. The station can do whatever it wants with the funds, but it will repay the donor an equal annual amount calculated as the capital sum divided by 90 years less the individual's age at the time of contribution. Upon the death of the donor, the station will retain the balance of the funds. Currently, a 64-year-old station supporter has committed $78,000, and seven other individuals are considering this method of assisting the station.

6. Initially, the station is to broadcast with a 2,500-watt signal. Within three to four years it hopes to obtain commercial financing for a second transmitter that will boost the power of the signal and the broadcast range.

EXHIBIT 2

OTHER INFORMATION ABOUT PLANS FOR THE STATION

1. The CKER committee has analyzed census and other data to determine the potential market for the station. Engineering studies have mapped out the area that will be covered by the broadcast signal. There are about 1.1 million people in the target listening area. The latest Canadian census shows that 14% of the population comes from the target ethnic group. By applying a conservative factor of 50% to these findings, the CKER committee has

arrived at a listenership figure of about 5.6% or about 62,000 people. The CKER committee has found that about one in five of the businesses in the area are run by members of the ethnic community, many of whom would like a medium for reaching their own people through direct advertising.

2. The amount of time expected to be devoted to commercials per hour is four minutes in year one, five minutes in year two, and six minutes in year three. Advertising cost per minute, discounted to 25% below the current market rate, will be:

Prime time (6 hours a day)	$40
Regular time (10 hours a day)	$30
Off-peak (8 hours a day)	$25

Advertising time will be sold by salespeople whose remuneration will be a 15% commission.

3. Miscellaneous revenue from renting out the recording studio when not in use by CKER could approach $3,000 per month in year three, but will start out at about $2,200 per month.

4. At least 120 people have committed to pay a $125 annual membership fee. Membership carries no special privileges other than to be identified as a supporter of the station. Membership is expected to grow by 20% per year.

5. Start-up capital expenditures are as follows: transmission equipment $61,000; broadcast studio equipment $62,000; and production studio equipment $40,000. Administration and other costs, including rent, are expected to total about $1,237,000 per year and will not increase when advertising sales increase.

6. The committee believes that there are no GST implications related to running the station, since it is a non-profit venture.

7. About one-third of the person-hours needed to run the station are expected to come from volunteers.

[CICA]

Case 11-5

European Exchange Club

On August 15, 1998, the European Exchange Club (EEC) was formed in an effort to create a united social group out of several separate regional clubs in the vicinity of the city of Decker, located in central Canada. The purpose of the group is to combine resources to meet the recreational, cultural, and social needs of their collective members. EEC was formed through the collaboration of the following clubs and their memberships:

	Members
The Canadian Russian Society	12,300
The Italian Club of Canada	10,800
Portuguese Cultural Foundation	4,100
Association of Greeks of the World	2,700
The German Groups	1,100
Other	1,700
	32,700

It is now December 2002, and EEC's executives have spent the past few years planning and preparing for the club's operation. The club's community centre is expected to be fully completed next year. Its facilities will include the following:

- a multi-purpose building to house banquets, meetings, and arts activities

- hiking trails

- indoor/outdoor tennis facilities

- bicycle trails

- baseball diamonds

- an indoor/outdoor pool

- a soccer field

The multi-purpose building is 75% complete, and EEC's executives have stated that it is "approximately within budget." Estimated building costs were outlined in a 1998 feasibility study as follows:

Construction cost	$2,300,000
Site preparation costs	400,000
Furniture and fixtures	550,000
Consulting fees	120,000
Miscellaneous	80,000
	$3,450,000

The four hectares of land on which the facility is built were provided by the provincial government by way of a five-year lease at $1 a year. The Italian Club of Canada contributed the adjacent land of 60 hectares. Previously, this land had been leased to a farmer for $54,000 a year. The 64 hectares will be used for the following projects, which will incur the additional costs listed below:

Hiking trails	$ 595,000
Baseball diamonds	30,000
Soccer field	22,000
Bicycle trails	95,000
Indoor/outdoor pool	700,000
Indoor/outdoor tennis facilities	300,000
	$1,742,000

In addition to these development costs, the club faces annual operating costs of approximately $740,000, outlined in Exhibit 1. John Mendez-Smith, the newly elected president of the club, has approached your firm, Young and Kerr, Chartered Accountants, to prepare a report that provides recommendations on accounting, finance, and internal control issues. You took the notes appearing in Exhibit 2 at a meeting with the club's president and executive committee.

Required:

Prepare the requested report for the president.

EXHIBIT 1

EUROPEAN EXCHANGE CLUB YEARLY BUDGET

Operating revenues	
Membership fees	$ 91,000
Social rentals	185,000
Meeting rentals	50,000
Sports rentals	23,000
Concessions	61,000
Fund-raising events	225,000
Total operating revenues	$635,000
Operating costs	
Salaries	$363,000
Administrative costs	39,000
Maintenance	126,000
Utilities	112,000
Educational scholarships	100,000
Total operating costs	$740,000

EXHIBIT 2

NOTES FROM MEETING

1. Under the lease agreement with the province, EEC is responsible for maintenance and all costs of improvements. The lease agreement provides for 20 renewal terms of five years' duration each. Renewal is based on the condition that EEC makes the club's services available to all present and future EEC member clubs and their membership.

2. EEC has requested an operating grant from the provincial government. Its proposal requests the province to provide EEC with annual funds to cover 50% of "approved" operating costs incurred to provide services to all club members.

   The city of Decker wishes to construct an arena and a swimming pool and has opposed the provincial operating grant. The city has asked to be the first in line for available provincial funds. The province has informed EEC that if funds are granted, EEC will have to supply audited financial statements of the organization for all future fiscal year-ends.

   The committee members suspect that they will have to compromise on their proposal and are having problems determining the minimum annual funds required by the club from the province.

3. The Russian and Italian clubs have been arguing with other clubs over the equalization payments required from each club. Currently, each club makes payments to EEC based upon their proportionate membership. Payments for each calendar year are made on February 1 of the following year.

4. The accounting function is a major concern of the member club representatives. In particular, they have raised the following issues:

   a) Several fund-raising events are organized by individual member clubs.

   b) Any donations to EEC are received through the member clubs.

   c) No accounting has been made of services donated to EEC by the members of the individual clubs.

d) EEC has approached a bank to assist in future phases of the club's development. The bank has informed EEC that it is interested in asset values and EEC's ability to repay the loans.

[CICA]

Case 11-6

Art Gallery

You have been hired to prepare a report for the board of directors of a large art gallery. The board of directors has just reviewed the annual financial statements of the art gallery. The board members are dissatisfied with the financial information provided in the financial statements. You have been provided with the following information.

The principal activity of the art gallery is the acquisition and exhibition of modern and contemporary pieces of art. The gallery is open to the general public on a daily basis, and has special exhibits for specific interest groups. Each year the gallery has a number of fund-raising activities to help support operating costs and the acquisition of art. These activities are organized by the support staff, but rely on volunteers to staff the various functions. The major fund-raising activity is an Annual Rennaise Telethon (ART), which solicits pledges from corporations and individuals and has been very successful.

Capital assets, in addition to the pieces of artwork, include a building, maintenance equipment, office furniture, and fixtures. The building that houses the art gallery is a large Victorian mansion that was donated by a local prominent family several years ago. Because the building has been designated a heritage property, utilities are provided by the local utility companies for a nominal fee of one dollar a year. As well, the municipal government has exempted the gallery from paying property taxes. Funding for capital asset acquisitions comes from various granting agencies and from fund-raising activities of the gallery.

The gallery also operates a gift shop on a break-even basis, with the objective of attracting visitors to the gallery. The gift shop has a small staff of salaried employees, but also operates with the assistance of a number of volunteers. The gift shop has an annual inventory of $175,000, on annual sales of approximately $1 million.

The gallery has a support staff of 17 employees, a curator, and a director who is responsible for the overall operation of the gallery. The total operating budget for the gallery is $4.2 million.

Required:

Prepare a report addressing the concerns of the board of directors of the art gallery. Your report should include a brief description of the purpose and objective of a fund accounting system. As well, you have been asked to recommend the different types of funds that would be most appropriate for the gallery. A discussion of relevant accounting policies is also required.

[CGA]

Case 11-7

Reporting Objectives

You have recently been appointed auditor of three different organizations. The first organization is a mining company that was formed a year ago to develop a gold mining site in northern Ontario. The largest single part of the initial investment was provided by a major, publicly held mining company in exchange for 36% of the common shares. The remaining shares were issued publicly in the over-the-counter market, where they are very thinly traded. The company is still in the development stage and does not expect to commence production for at least another year.

The second organization is a non-profit secondary school that provides courses for students who intend to pursue a career in one of the performing arts. The school is fully recognized by the provincial Ministry of Education, which provides about 50% of the school's operating budget. Another 20% of the operating funds are provided by the Ministry of Culture and Recreation, while the remainder is derived from student fees and by fund-raising in the private sector. The school occupies an old public high school building that was no longer being used by the city; the school acquired the building on a 20-year lease from the city's board of education.

The third organization is a labour union for the graduate students at a major university. The union receives its funding from dues that are mandatorily deducted by the university from the earnings of all members of the bargaining unit, whether they are members of the union or not. A portion of the funds is sent to the union's parent national organization, and another part is set aside for the strike fund, which is held and invested by a trustee until such time as it is needed to pay striking union members.

Required:

Explain how the objectives of financial reporting would likely differ for these three organizations.

Case 11-8

Rosen Hall (Part A)

Rosen Hall is a 2,700-seat concert hall located in the centre of a large Canadian city. The hall was completed three years ago as a replacement for an aging and deteriorating concert hall. The older hall remains in use at a sharply reduced activity level, pending accumulation of sufficient funds to renovate it extensively.

The new hall cost approximately $30 million to build. Of that amount, two-thirds were provided by the various levels of government. The remaining one-third was paid for privately, although fund-raising is still going on in order to retire the $8 million loan that is still outstanding. The largest single private contribution was provided by the Rosen family, in memory of S. L. Rosen, a famous publisher of accounting textbooks; the hall was named after Rosen in appreciation of the donation.

Both the new and old halls are governed by an independent board of governors. A sizeable full-time professional staff operates both halls, although the old hall requires very little of their time. The professional staff is augmented by a substantial operating crew of ushers, bartenders, and cleaning and maintenance personnel. Both halls are expected to be self-supporting, although "manageable" deficits on the new hall were anticipated by the board in the first couple of years. Any profits derived from the operation of the new hall will be put towards renovations of the old hall, which Rosen Hall replaced.

The primary tenant of the new hall is the City Symphony Orchestra, which gives about 120 concerts per year in the hall. The hall is also rented to other performing groups for both afternoon and evening performances. The board of governors of the hall has established its own series of concerts, bringing in performing artists and orchestras from around the world. The board's own concert series is an important part of the hall's total activities, and helps to ensure that it is in use most of the time, a necessary condition to enable the hall to meet its costs.

Required:

What are the issues that arise for reporting the financial results of the activities under control of the hall's board of governors? Outline the objectives of reporting in this situation, and how the issues and characteristics of reporting for non-profit organizations apply.

Case 11-9

Rosen Hall (Part B)

The primary purpose and activity of Rosen Hall (see **Case 11-8**) is the rental of the hall for concerts (and occasional large meetings). The hall is rented for approximately 400 events during the year, at rates that vary depending on the day of the week, the time of day, the support staff (ushers, etc.) needed, and whether the bars are in operation. The rental is less if the bars are operational because the profits from the bars go to the hall and not to the renting organization.

In addition to renting the main hall, however, Rosen Hall also rents several other spaces in the building. The lobby area is available for rental, either when the main hall is not in use or in conjunction with rental of the main hall, such as for a reception preceding or following a concert. A rehearsal hall also exists underneath the main stage, which is available for rental. Banquet rooms are also below the auditorium and are rented out.

The hall administration also engages in certain ancillary services (in addition to operation of the bars). There is an outside dining area around a reflecting pool that is operated in the summer months. The food is catered by a nearby restaurant, as the hall has no kitchen facilities. A shop in the main lobby is open during the daytime and during concerts, and offers a wide variety of CDs, books, posters, and other items relating to music or to the hall. The CD business has, in fact, been very successful and has expanded rapidly. A 500-car underground garage is situated beneath the hall. The garage's operation, including routine cleaning and maintenance, is contracted to City Park Inc., a city-wide operator of parking facilities.

General maintenance of the hall is programmed and budgeted in advance, but unexpected maintenance requirements arise from time to time, especially as the hall is relatively new and some aspects of its mechanical and architectural systems are innovative. Because of the nature of the materials used in the hall (i.e., the light-coloured carpets, the wall coverings, and the glass and mirrors), regular cleaning is essential. Cleaning expenditures are closely controlled, but the extent of cleaning is somewhat dependent on the frequency of use of the hall's spaces and on the weather (especially for the carpets).

The staff for the box office is separate from the staff for the operation of the hall itself. The box office has its own computerized ticketing operation and sells the tickets for virtually all of the attractions that appear in the hall, except for those of its major user, the City Symphony Orchestra, which sells its tickets through Ticketron. Events that are not sponsored by the hall's board of governors are assessed a flat fee for box office service plus 50 cents per ticket sold.

Overall, the hall is expected at least to break even on its operations. The board of governors for the hall has no other sources of revenue, although deficits can be financed temporarily through borrowings. Ideally, the board would like to see the hall become a net generator of funds, so that the funds can be used to renovate the older concert hall, which the board also operates.

Required:

Discuss the form that the accounting and reporting system for Rosen Hall should take. Be as specific as possible.

Case 11-10

The New Canadian Counselling Centre

The New Canadian Counselling Centre (NCCC) is a non-profit organization dedicated to professional counselling of individuals who have recently moved into the urban Canadian environment and who are having difficulty in adjusting to their new lifestyle and surroundings. NCCC also offers peer counselling for people who do not need the services of a professional psychologist, psychiatrist, or social worker.

The professional counsellors who work for NCCC do not rely on NCCC for their primary income. Almost without exception, the counsellors have primary employment with a hospital or other social agency, or have private practices. The reason is that since NCCC is not government supported, the counsellors provide their services at substantially below their market rates.

Originally, NCCC operated out of rented offices. Two years ago, however, the organization was able to buy a downtown town house, with the aid of a substantial bequest that was restricted to providing funds for permanent quarters. The bequest not only permitted NCCC to purchase the house, but also to establish an endowment fund to help maintain the premises. The earnings of the fund are not sufficient to provide for all of the maintenance costs, but do contribute significantly to the cost.

NCCC does not qualify for participation in the province's health care program because it does not limit its patients to those referred by other health practitioners. About half of its operating funds are obtained from fees charged to patients on a scale that is tied to each individual's ability to pay. Another 25% of the budget is provided by social fund-raising organizations, and the remainder is raised through private donations.

The organization does not have any accumulated surplus, and thus has no way to support a deficit except by further financial sacrifices by its counsellors. The peer counsellors are not paid, and there is no charge for their services. There is a two-person, full-time administrative staff.

Required:

Outline the objectives of financial reporting as they pertain specifically to NCCC. What accounting policies seem appropriate for this organization?

Public Sector

Financial Reporting

Introduction

This chapter continues on with an overview of the accounting for *non-business organizations*. The focus of this chapter is on public sector reporting or accounting for governments and government services. Formal accounting policies for this sector have been slow in developing. Little interest was shown until the 1980s. Since the establishment by the CICA in 1981 of the Public Sector Accounting and Auditing Board (PSAAB*)*, now the Public Sector Accounting Board (PSAcB*)*, interest has grown and continues to develop with new accounting policies. The most recent of these developments, a draft strategic plan issued by the PSAcB in 2000, proposes changes to the current senior government reporting model.

This chapter continues our discussions of the non-business sector of the economy, focusing on the accounting for governments and government services.

Contrast Between NPOs and Governments

At the beginning of Chapter 11, we drew a distinction between governments, governmental units, and non-profit organizations. All three are *non-business organizations*, and they have several distinguishing characteristics in common. All three types of non-business organization:

- have no investors,

- may provide both private and collective goods and services,

- may derive the bulk of their revenues from sources other than the sale of goods and services,

- have funds that are restricted for specific purposes, and

- have revenues that are not responsive to the demand for services.[1]

All of these characteristics were discussed in Chapter 11. These characteristics have led to financial reporting for governments that is very similar to that for NPOs. Governments (1) use fund accounting, (2) may use different accounting policies for different funds, (3) may report their activities on an expenditure basis,[2] (4) may not report on a fully consolidated basis, and (5) cannot clearly define the reporting entity.

---

1. Indeed, governments have revenues that are inversely related to the demand for services in recessions; e.g., the demand for services goes up while the tax revenues fall.

2. A preliminary views document, *General Standards of Financial Statement Presentation*, issued in July 2000, will eliminate the use of the expenditure basis. Instead, the focus will be on a "net debt model" and expenses rather than expenditures.

Despite the many similarities between non-profit organizations and governments, there are some differences between the two types of organizations. One of the most basic differences is the nature of the financial statement user group. Each non-profit organization has clearly identifiable primary stakeholders who have specific information needs. The financial reporting objectives of NPOs must be directed towards the needs of their primary funders. In contrast, governments have a legal reporting requirement to their legislatures or city councils, and they also have a far larger potential user group.

Consequently it is quite difficult to be very specific about who the users of government financial statements really are. One can say that all Canadian citizens are interested in the financial results of the federal government, for example, but such a statement is difficult to translate to meaningful reporting objectives that will help us make a choice from amongst alternative accounting policies or families of policies.

We must make one more distinction to fully understand public sector accounting. This is the difference between a *government business organization* compared to the non-business government organizations discussed in the above section. The *CICA Handbook* suggests that a **government business organization** [CICA 1300.21]:

- is a separate legal entity with the power to contract in its own name and that can sue and be sued;

- has been delegated the financial and operational authority to carry on a business;

- sells goods and services to individuals and organizations outside of the government reporting entity as its principal activity; and

- can, in the normal course of its operations, maintain its operations and meet its liabilities from revenues received from sources outside of the government reporting entity.

It is important to remember these distinctions between business and non-business organizations during the following discussion.

Public Sector Reporting Standards

Until the decade of the 1980s, there was not much interest demonstrated by professional accountants in governmental reporting. Since 1980, however, there has been quite a bit of interest in developing governmental reporting, and both the CICA and the Canadian Certified General Accountants' Research Foundation have been quite active.

We pointed out in Chapter 11 that the domain of accounting standard setting for non-profit organizations in Canada is in the hands of the CICA's Accounting Standards Board. The efforts of the AcSB to date have largely been attempts to apply business enterprise GAAP to NPOs.

In contrast, the CICA has explicitly removed standard setting for governments from the AcSB. In 1981, the CICA established the Public Sector Accounting and Auditing Board (PSAAB). Effective October 1, 1998, the CICA created the Public Sector Accounting Board (PSAcB) and transferred responsibility for assurance and related services to the Assurance Standards Board. Effective in March 1999, the *CICA Handbook* was split into two sections, the *Public Sector Accounting Recommendations* and the *Public Sector Assurance Recommendations.*

In this chapter we will focus on the work of the Public Sector Accounting Board (PSAcB). The PSAcB's mandate is to:

- serve the public interest by issuing recommendations and guidance with respect to matters of accounting in the public sector, and

- strengthen accountability in the public sector through developing, recommending and gaining acceptance of accounting and financial reporting standards of good practice.[3]

In 2000, the PSAcB approved a draft strategic plan that set out five overriding objectives for the next five years. The proposed objectives are to:

- issue recommendations and guidance that enhance the usefulness of public sector financial statement information;

- issue pronouncements that enhance the usefulness of public sector financial and non-financial performance information;

- engage interest and debate by improving stakeholders' understanding of public finances;

- efficiently coordinate activities with other accounting standard-setters and other public sector related organizations; and

- provide the PSAcB's program of standard-setting and communications effectively, efficiently and economically.[4]

By early 2000, the PSAcB had issued twenty-two public sector accounting recommendations, nine auditing recommendations, and one auditing guideline. The Board's accounting recommendations are "intended to apply to all governments unless specifically limited in individual statements."[5]

This is where the distinction between business and non-business government organizations becomes important. Government business organizations, government business-type organizations, and government non-profit organizations are provided guidance in the *CICA Handbook*—instead of the *Public Sector Accounting Handbook.*[6]

In addition, not all of the recommendations apply to all levels of government. The first accounting recommendation applies to all governments; two apply specifically to senior governments (i.e., the 13 federal, provincial, and territorial governments); two apply specifically to local governments; and the remaining 18 apply to specific items. There is a very strong similarity between the recommendations for senior and local governments.

---

3. PSAB "Introduction to Public Sector Accounting Recommendations," revised March 1999, ¶01.

4. PSAB "Draft Strategic Plan," issued 2000.

5. PSAB "Introduction to Public Sector Accounting Recommendations," revised March 1999, ¶04.

6. *Ibid.*, Appendix 1.

The compliance issue

PSAcB recommendations are just that: *recommendations*, not *requirements* for most levels of government. Other types of organizations may have compelling reasons to comply with recommendations of the *CICA Handbook*, but such is not the case with governments and the recommendations of the PSAcB.

As we discussed in Chapter 1, many corporations acts and securities acts require corporations to adhere to the recommendations of the *CICA Handbook*, thereby giving the *CICA Handbook*'s recommendations considerable clout. For publicly traded corporations especially, the recommendations of the *CICA Handbook* essentially become *requirements* through the power of the securities acts. In contrast, non-profit organizations are not compelled to comply with the *CICA Handbook* unless their principal funders insist; as we have seen in the previous chapter, funders often have their own reporting requirements that take precedence in shaping an NPO's financial reporting, regardless of whether a qualified audit opinion is the result.

For most levels of government, there is no mechanism to compel compliance with the PSAcB recommendations. Governmental financial reporting is governed by legislation, which may be either extensive or virtually non-existent at different levels and in different provinces and territories. Senior governments are not audited by external auditors, but by the governments' auditors general. Auditors general are not required to report in accordance with the recommendations of the PSAcB. Local governments usually are audited by external auditors, although some major cities have their own city auditor. Local government auditors are required to report in accordance with provincial legislation governing municipal reporting. Some local governments are now required to report in compliance with the PSAcB based on provincial legislation.[7]

A letter dated April 12, 2000 from the Ontario Ministry of Municipal Affairs and Housing announced the requirement for municipalities in Ontario to comply with the PSAcB:

> Adopting PSAcB means that there will be a national standard setting authority that is committed to addressing accounting and financial issues of local governments. A nationally focused body such as PSAcB ensures completeness and consistency in financial reporting. PSAcB will ensure that both in the short and long term, municipalities are provided an ongoing, open, consultative forum for developing municipal accounting and financial reporting standards.

While there is no compliance mechanism for the PSAcB accounting recommendations, the recommendations can serve as a useful guide to auditors general and city auditors. The recommendations give the auditors an authoritative lever for persuading government authorities to improve their financial reporting. Ultimately, the PSAcB recommendations can guide provincial legislatures in stipulating requirements for local and provincial governmental reporting as illustrated in the above quote.

A new standard-setting body such as the PSAcB can make progress only if the initial recommendations are largely a codification of existing practices. Changes or improvements in existing practice can then be "eased" into practice with greater likelihood of acceptance, even when there is no legal requirement that forces compliance.

---

7. The British Columbia and Ontario governments, effective January 1, 2000, require municipalities in their jurisdictions to follow the recommendations for local governments in the *Public Sector Accounting Recommendations*.

An example of non-compliance because it did not codify existing practice is the reporting recommendation issued in 1997 to incorporate capital assets into government financial statements. As we will discuss later, changes are being proposed to revise the general standards of financial presentation to adopt existing practice and reduce non-compliance.[8]

Objectives of Governmental Reporting

The issue of government reporting objectives has not suffered from a lack of attention. Several research studies have examined the users and uses of financial statements and, not surprisingly, have come up with a wide variety of both.

In 1980, the CICA issued a research study entitled *Financial Reporting by Governments* (*FRG*) that focused on financial reporting by senior governments. This research study formed the basis of PS 1400, "Objectives of Financial Statements." The study classified the users of the financial reports of governments as fitting into five categories: (1) policy makers, (2) legislators, (3) program administrators, (4) investors, and (5) the general public.[9] Each of these five groups will have advisors. The advisors or analysts for each group can be viewed as being a part of that group rather than a separate user group.

The *FRG* study states the financial reporting objectives for senior governments as follows:[10]

1. To facilitate evaluation of economic impact

2. To facilitate evaluation of program delivery choices and their management

3. To demonstrate stewardship and compliance with legislative authority

4. To display the state of the government's finances

The PSAcB incorporated the information from this study in issuing PS1400, "Objectives of Financial Statements," applicable to federal, provincial, and territorial governments. PS1400 suggests the following five objectives for financial statements:

1. To communicate reliable information relevant to the users' needs which is clearly presented, understandable and timely

2. To provide accounting of financial affairs and resources

3. To demonstrate accountability for financial affairs and resources

4. To account for sources, allocation and use of government resources and show how activities financed and cash requirements met

5. To display the state of government's finances.[11]

An extensive CGA Research Foundation study of the actual reporting practices of local governments found a lack of focus in local government reporting.

---

8. A Preliminary Views Document issued July 2000 based on recommendations from the supporting paper "Senior Government Reporting Model," issued July 2000, proposes to eliminate the Statement of Tangible Net Assets.

9. CICA, *Financial Reporting by Governments* (CICA, 1980), pp. 24–27.

10. *Ibid.*, pp. 27–29.

11. PSAB 1400 "Objectives of Financial Statements of Federal, Provincial and Territorial Governments," issued Sept 1997.

Professor Beedle, the study's author, credited the lack of focus to the absence of guidance or authoritative pronouncements and to the government's attempt to use the general purpose financial statements to be all things to all people:

> Faced with this paucity of guidance and authoritative pronouncements, present Canadian practice in accounting reports of local governments seems to stab at satisfying an undefined range of users and their needs without (with exceptions) specifically defining those users, their needs, or the objectives of the reports. . . . The result in many cases is a complex, scarcely comprehensible set of reports requiring specialized expert accounting knowledge in the government field. There is a failure to realize that "general purpose statements are not all purpose statements, and never can be."[12]

In 1985 the CICA also published a research study, *Local Government Financial Reporting* (*LGFR*). The *LGFR* study group and PS1700, "Objectives of Financial Statements for Local Governments," consider Beedle's findings and the diverse set of potential users of government financial statements in establishing the specific objectives for local government reporting.

The study group recognized that it is necessary to make a distinction between *general purpose* and *special purpose* financial reporting. While such a distinction is hardly new, it is important in governmental reporting because it makes it clear that the general purpose reports that go to the citizenry at large may be quite different from special purpose reports that are prepared for making specific operational decisions such as resource allocation or performance evaluation of major programs and activities. PS 1700.27 states that:

> Financial statements cannot be expected to fulfil all of the needs served by a local government's financial reporting system. Local governments produce various financial reports in addition to financial statements. For example, there are reports prepared by individual entities, reports to measure and report on the performance of individual programs and activities, and special purpose reports designed to meet particular needs of specific users. In addition, local governments set out their financial plan in the Budget. Thus, certain information is better provided, or can only be provided, by financial reports other than financial statements.[13]

Qualitative Characteristics

The *FRG* study group conducted interviews with a sample of representatives from various categories of users of governmental financial reports. Not surprisingly, the users expressed a wide diversity of needs. However, the users tended to stress similar qualitative characteristics of good financial reports. The report cites four qualities that were stressed by the interviewees. These four qualities are (1) comparability among governments, (2) consistency between years, (3) completeness, and (4) timeliness. The users were particularly emphatic about comparability:

> Almost above everything else, users wanted to compare the reports of various governments. This meant they wanted consistency among governments in the basis for:

12. A. Beedle, *Accounting for Local Government in Canada: The State of the Art* (Vancouver: The Canadian Certified General Accountants' Research Foundation, 1981) p. 73.

13. PSAB 1700 "Objectives of Financial Statements for Local Governments," issued March 1995, ¶27.

- defining the reporting entity to make clear what kinds of Crown corporations were included and excluded;
- classifying and reporting revenues, expenditures, assets and liabilities; and
- reporting government debt including contingent debt.

They also wanted consistency, to the extent possible, between the Public Accounts and various statistical compilations of government figures (e.g., the National Accounts) and the ability to reconcile two sets of figures where differences in basis are justified by the different purposes served by the two sets of figures.[14]

The PSAcB incorporated qualitative criteria into its Objective 1:

> Financial statements should communicate reliable information, relevant to the needs of those for whom the statements are prepared, in a manner that maximizes its usefulness. As a minimum, this requires information that is clearly presented, understandable, timely and consistent. [PS 1400.23]

Types of Financial Statements

The financial statements for governments are very similar to those for non-profit organizations. The PSAcB recommends that federal and provincial governments present four financial statements [PS 1500.31]:

- statement of financial position
- statement that reports the surplus or deficit in the accounting period
- statement of changes in financial position
- statement of tangible capital assets

A CICA Supporting Paper, "Senior Government Reporting Model" (issued in July 2000) recommends focusing on economic rather than financial resources. It proposes the following four statements:

- statement of financial position
- statement of operations
- statement of changes in net debt
- statement of cash flow

This paper supports the current focus on the importance of net debt as an indicator of the government's finances but also recognizes the importance of providing information about the costs of providing government services. The paper recommends that the financial statements have four features.

First, the paper recommends that governments issue a statement of operations that shows the excess (or deficiency) of revenues over *expenses*.[15] This recommendation attempts to move away from the expenditure basis of reporting and towards full accrual accounting. In addition, this proposed statement is easier to understand because it has a separate statement to show changes in net debt.

14. *Financial Reporting by Governments* (CICA, 1980), p. 31.

15. CICA, "Senior Government Reporting Model," July 2000, p. 25.

Second, the statement of financial position would report net debt, and then would deduct non-financial assets from net debt to measure the government's accumulated surplus or deficit.[16] The current recommendation is for reporting the assets and liabilities to measure financial condition. The difference between the liabilities and financial assets are measured at the end of the year.

Third, the new statement of changes in net debt would reconcile a government's total expenses for the period to its spending on operations (i.e., expenditures) for the period. The statement would also report (1) the capital spending in the period, (2) the extent to which total government spending was financed by revenues earned in the period (i.e., the change in net debt in the period), and (3) the opening and closing net debt balances.[17]

This new statement shows the importance of net debt as an indicator of the government's finances. It also focuses attention on the operating cost of government services compared to capital. Full disclosure is provided in this statement of the amount of capital spending. For that reason, the paper recommended that the statement of tangible capital assets be eliminated. Additional note disclosure on tangible capital assets is now recommended.

Fourth, there would be a statement of cash flow. This statement calculates the cash flow from operating activities using the indirect method that adjusts the surplus or deficit for the accounting period to the amount of cash used or available from operations. Capital acquisitions are included as an operating activity for the government.[18]

This cash flow statement replaces the current statement of changes in financial position. This is consistent with the changes to the rest of the *CICA Handbook*. The inclusion of capital acquisitions as an operating activity illustrates that capital assets embody future service potential not future cash flows.

This preliminary views document applies to federal, provincial, and territorial governments only. Changes have not been recommended yet for local governments. Currently, the PSAcB recommends that local government financial statements "should include, as a minimum, a statement of financial position, a statement of financial activities, and a statement of changes in financial position" [PS 1800.07].[19]

Note the subtle difference between the "statement that reports the surplus or deficit in the accounting period" and a "statement of financial activities." The latter expression is much less specific.

Also, with local governments there is no requirement to include a statement of tangible capital assets. This is further explained by the statement, "Many local governments do not have adequate physical information to report fully on their acquired physical assets. Therefore, they are encouraged to collect information about their physical assets"[PS 1800.30].[20]

16. *Ibid.*, p. 25.

17. *Ibid.*, p. 25.

18. *Ibid.*, p. 25.

19. PSAB 1800 "General Standards of Financial Statement Presentation for Local Governments," issued March 1995, ¶07.

20. *Ibid.*, ¶30.

Major Reporting Issues

The primary reporting issues for governments are quite similar to those of NPOs:

- Cash versus accrual

- Expenditure versus expense

- Capital assets

- Consolidation and the reporting entity

- Restricted assets and revenues

In addition, governments have major reporting issues concerning liabilities. Liability issues do not arise for NPOs, because NPOs don't issue long-term debt.

Cash vs. accrual

The cash versus accrual debate in government accounting is similar to that for NPOs. The choices are between cash, modified cash or modified accrual, and full accrual. As was discussed in Chapter 11, full accrual is sometimes used to include the full range of interperiod allocations, and therefore this book uses the term *modified accrual* to mean accrual of assets and liabilities without necessarily allocating the costs on an expense basis. Similarly, *LGFR* discussed accrual and observed that:

> Some accountants feel that the accrual basis embraces:
>
> - Recognition of a materials and supplies inventory.
>
> - Recognition of long-lived assets and depreciation thereon.

Without arguing the merits of such interpretations, this study prefers to regard these as matters distinct from the accrual basis.[21]

Up until the preliminary views document, the PSAcB supported a modified accrual accounting (i.e., without necessarily including expense-basis allocations). There are two main advantages to reporting on a modified accrual basis:

1. Operations can be reported on an expenditure or expense basis rather than simply on a disbursements basis; this makes it less likely that government managers will be tempted to manipulate cash payments to suppliers and others in order to "manage" the reported surplus or deficit.

2. Accrual is essential in order to measure and report the government's liabilities. Liability reporting is a major issue in governmental accounting, and will be discussed briefly later in this chapter.

The vast majority of governments use a modified accrual basis. Now that governments have had time to adapt to the modified cash basis of accounting from the cash basis, the proposed model as mentioned earlier supports a move towards full accrual accounting by eliminating the option of reporting expenditures.

---

21. *Local Government Financial Reporting* (Toronto: CICA, 1985), p. 43.

Expense vs. expenditure basis

Initially PSAcB recommendations supported the use of an expenditure basis of reporting rather than an expense basis. The *LGFR* study group provided the following support for the expenditure basis:

> While the cost of operating may have some place in enterprises (which can be accommodated in *separate* financial reports to their constituents), the "significant" users of local government financial reports contemplated by this study have little interest in costs. They are much more interested in whether inflows of resources are adequate to meet outflows. They are not interested in when resources are used up and which periods benefited from them.[22]

An expenditure basis has been the normal reporting practice for both senior and local governments. This reality is reflected in PS 1700.102, for example, which recommends that financial statements for local governments should report *expenditures* of the accounting period by function.

The expenditure basis is consistent with the budgetary control that governmental managers must exercise. If governments were to report on an expense basis, then they would be "required" by the accounting system to raise sufficient revenues to offset the expenses, even if the expenses gave rise to no obligation for cash outflows in the current period. Alternatively, expenses could be significantly lower than expenditures; the government could break even on an expense basis while running a substantial deficit on an expenditure basis.

Gradually, there has been a shift from the expenditure basis to a modified accrual basis. Particularly notable is PS 3250, in which the Board recommends pension accounting that is consistent with the recommendations of Section 3461 of the *CICA Handbook*, an expense-basis recommendation. PS 3250 recommends that, when a defined benefit pension plan is in effect, pension costs should be determined in accordance with the accrued benefit method, and that actuarial gains and losses (i.e., from changes in assumptions or from experience) should be amortized over the expected average remaining service life of the related employee group.[23] The PSAcB supports its recommendations by pointing to the importance of measuring liabilities, and an expenditure is defined as the incurrence of a liability. However, the pension recommendations seem to be substituting one actuarial measure of expense for whatever actuarial expenditure is called for by the pension agreement.

With the proposed recommendations of the "Senior Government Reporting Model" there is a further shift from a modified accrual to a full accrual basis. Their model analyzes the characteristics of governments and reporting implications, and stresses the importance of identifying the net cost of services, net debt, and capital spending. The following comment from the study illustrates the rationale for accrual accounting.

> A move towards full accrual accounting and reporting of the consumption of tangible assets supports the new thinking and reorganization of governments in Canada. The current model is a stepping-stone towards the target destination of a reporting model that sees the deferral of expenditures and measurement of the net cost of services as the ultimate goal.[24]

22. *Ibid.*, p. 32.

23. PSAB 3250 "Employee Pension Obligations," issued March 1995.

24. CICA's "Senior Government Reporting Model," July 2000, p. 19.

Capital assets

Historically, Canadian governments almost universally reported capital assets on an expenditure basis. There are exceptions for certain types of activities, such as for publicly-owned utilities and other enterprise activities that operate on a cost-recovery basis. There also are differences in the fund bases used, largely reflecting differences in the ways that capital assets are financed. But in general, capital assets were seldom capitalized and are almost never depreciated except in utility or other self-sustaining funds.

One of the reasons for this method is that governments did not have or maintain systems that enabled them to report fully on acquired physical assets. The "Senior Government Reporting Model" states "many jurisdictions initially expressed reluctance to adopt the capital asset recommendations. However, these jurisdictions that have updated their computer systems have generally acquired fixed asset modules as part of their upgrade systems."[25] PS 1800 recognizes this problem at the local government level: "many local governments do not have adequate financial information to report fully on their acquired physical assets."[26]

LGFR recommended that all capital assets be shown on the balance sheet, regardless of whether or not the initial charge for the asset was to expenditure, and that the source of financing of those assets be shown. However, the *LGFR* study group concluded that depreciation accounting is not appropriate in the general purpose statements. Instead of reporting depreciated amounts, governments should carry their capital assets "at their initially recorded value until they reach the end of their useful economic lives, when they should be written off."[27]

PS 1500 also favours the recording and reporting of capital assets and requires as one of the statements a statement of tangible capital assets. However, as discussed previously, the "Senior Government Reporting Model" recommends replacing this statement with disclosure. PS 3150, "Tangible Capital Assets," recommends that capital assets be recorded at cost and amortized. If the government uses an expense basis of accounting, amortization would be charged as an expense in the statement of operations.[28]

The "Senior Government Reporting Model" identifies the following problem when governments use the expenditure basis of accounting:

> A principal reason for modification of the existing model is that it discourages reinvestment in long-lived assets because of short-term difficulties. Often, true deficits in infrastructure and investments in needed new technology are postponed indefinitely making eventual replacement increasingly more difficult. Governments that have adopted balanced budget legislation have an additional constraint on capital spending because the current model requires the cost of capital acquisitions be charged as expenditures at the time of acquisition when calculating the annual results of the government.[29]

The study also supports moving towards full accrual accounting and the reporting of the consumption of tangible capital assets as a reflection of the ultimate goal of reporting the net cost of services.[30]

---

25. *Ibid.*, p. 18.
26. PSAB 1800, ¶30.
27. *Local Government Financial Reporting* (Toronto: CICA, 1985), p. 24.
28. PSAB 3150 "Tangible Capital Assets," ¶11, ¶21, and ¶23.
29. CICA's "Senior Government Reporting Model," July 2000, p. 18.
30. *Ibid.*, p. 19.

One of the reasons the report cites in support of full accrual accounting is that the presentation of government financial reports on an expense basis would make the information in such reports more understandable to many potential users who are familiar with expense-based accounting as commonly applied in profit-oriented enterprises and non-profit organizations.[31] However, as discussed in Chapter 11, this is an area of disagreement for governments as well as for NPOs.

PS 1500 and 3150 include infrastructure assets (e.g., roads and water mains), heritage assets (e.g., monuments, historic buildings, and works of art), donated assets, and defence assets.

Consolidation and the reporting entity

All governments use fund accounting, wherein a separate self-balancing group of accounts is provided for each program or major operating activity. Resources are allocated by the legislature for specified purposes, and some revenues are specifically designated for special purposes. Governments sometimes issue bonds in order to finance specific capital projects; special tax assessments are levied in order to cover the costs of specified local improvements. Fund accounting therefore is ubiquitous.

Fund *accounting* need not lead to fund-basis *reporting*. Detailed reporting on individual funds causes a multiplicity of statements and an inability to get an overview of the financial condition and operations of the government. While fund-basis accounting is appropriate, financial statements can and should group together the various activities of the government into those activities and programs of similar nature, so that statement users can get some idea about the resource flows associated with the major activities of the government. This is similar to fund accounting using the deferral method of reporting in NPOs, except that the activity groupings may be larger.

In Chapter 11, we discussed the problem of defining the reporting entity for non-profit organizations. This problem not only exists for governments as well, but is actually much more severe. PS 1300 addresses the issue in "Financial Reporting Entity" for all levels of government and further guidance is provided in PS 2500—"Basic Principles of Consolidation." In June 2000, the PSAcB approved a project "Defining the Reporting Entity" to provide further guidance since new activities and organizational types have arisen since PS 1300 was released. The final report was to be released in February 2001 to provide guidance on applying the criteria of accountability, ownership, and control.

Government activities are carried out through a very complex set of ministries, agencies, Crown corporations, quasi-business enterprises, and non-profit organizations formed by government for the purpose of carrying out parts of government's policies. When financial statements are prepared for a government, which of the many bodies that are directly or indirectly related to the government are to be included in the statements? PS 1300 recommends that the government reporting entity include all agencies and organizations that are owned or controlled by government and that are directly accountable for their financial affairs (either through a minister or directly to the legislature or local government council).[32] The definition of the reporting entity excludes those organizations that are instruments of government or that are dependent on government but that are not directly accountable to government. As a result, hospitals and universities would be excluded from the reporting entity.

31. *Ibid.*, p. 18.

32. PSAB 1300 "Financial Reporting Entity," issued May 1999, ¶07.

Ownership exists when the government "has created or acquired the organization with public resources" and holds title to the organization's assets or owns sufficient voting shares to appoint a majority of the organization's directors.[33] The PSAcB views control as existing through legislation or through appointment of an organization's senior management or a majority of its directors.[34] While the inclusion of controlled organizations may seem intuitively appealing, there are real practical problems involved in such a recommendation.

For example, school boards are a part of local government, but they are usually administered by a separately elected board of trustees that has its own financial responsibility. Consolidation of the school board's financial results with those of the municipality would only decrease the usefulness of the financial statements, because it would be impossible to tell whether excessive expenditure, for example, was the responsibility of the school board or of the city council. Another example is an art gallery that has 11 of its 18 board members appointed by the provincial government. Although the gallery was created by a special Act, and although a majority of the board members are appointed by government, the gallery functions completely independently of government. The directors are *appointed* by the province, but they do not *represent* the province.

PS 1300 also addresses the question of how organizations that constitute parts of the reporting entity should be reported in the financial statements. In general, the conclusions of the statement are that (1) investments in entities that are not controlled by the government (portfolio investments) should be reported on the cost basis,[35] (2) investments in business or quasi-business enterprises, such as public utilities or transportation companies, should be reported on a modified equity basis,[36] and (3) the financial statements of all other organizations or agencies that are part of the reporting entity should be consolidated with the government's own financial statements.[37]

Restricted assets and revenues

An issue similar to NPOs that we discussed in Chapter 11 is the reporting of restricted assets and revenues. Governments may also have restrictions by external parties or other governments that limit the use of assets or revenues. PS 3100 makes similar distinctions to NPOs between external restrictions that are imposed by an external party and internal restrictions or internally restricted entities. The recommended method for external restrictions is similar to the deferral method of recognizing contributions. PS 3100.11 states "External restrictions should be recognized as revenue in the period in which the resources are used."[38] Internal restrictions or designated assets are treated differently since the government can change its mind through changing legislation. To provide information to the users, disclosure is required of all internal restrictions and designated assets.

33. *Ibid.*, ¶11.

34. *Ibid.*, ¶14.

35. *Ibid.*, ¶33.

36. *Ibid.*, ¶28. Under the modified equity method, the net profit or loss of the business enterprise is included in the government's statement of operations (net of dividends or distributions) and is added to the investment account related to that enterprise.

37 *Ibid.*, ¶20.

38. PSAB 3100 "Restricted Assets and Revenues," issued June 1997, ¶11.

Liability measurement

Reporting the liabilities of government is a bigger deal than may be apparent on the surface. The problem starts with those governments that are still reporting on a cash basis; there is not even any measurement of current liabilities. Therefore, the first step is to get cash-basis governments to move to accruing their liabilities.

The second step is the recording of long-term debt. Unlike NPOs, senior governments issue debt instruments, often in very large quantities, which frequently are denominated in foreign currencies. When debt instruments are issued, the proceeds are credited to revenue. PS 1500 and 1800 both recommend that governments should report their "liabilities at the end of the accounting period, segregated by main classification."[39] The debt should be shown as a liability even when the proceeds have been reported as revenue. This is accomplished by means of a debt "group" of accounts that can be consolidated into the balance sheet when the general purpose financial statements are prepared. Further guidance on long-term debt specifying disclosure requirements is provided in PS 3230, "Long-term Debt."

A third type of liabilities is that of *commitments*. PS 1500 and PS 1700 require that material financial commitments should be disclosed.[40] Specific guidance on pensions is provided in PS 3250.

A fourth type of liability is that of *contingencies*. In particular, senior governments have a habit of guaranteeing others' debts, sometimes as a part of a legislated program such as small business loans or student loans. Contingencies should not be reported as liabilities on the balance sheet, but they should be disclosed.[41] Unfortunately, many governments currently have no record of how much they have guaranteed; recording systems need to be developed to keep track of such commitments and to enable the commitments made by various branches of a government to be brought together for financial reporting purposes.

A unique type of liability is one that is related to solid waste landfill closure costs. PS 3270 requires "financial statements should recognize a liability for closure and post-closure care as the landfill site capacity is used."[42]

Other issues

A number of other government reporting issues also are of concern. One issue is the question of whether budgeted amounts should be disclosed in the statement of operations along with the actual results. Budget figures provide a basis of comparison and enable the user to see how effective the government was in controlling expenditures or in achieving anticipated revenue levels. Since the government can amend the budget during the year (thereby making the budget closer to actual), the budget figures should be "those originally forecast by the fiscal plan."[43] This is further supported in the "Senior Government Reporting Model" that states "an actual to budget comparison should be provided in the financial statements." [44]

39. PSAB 1500 ¶41 and PS 1800 ¶25.

40. PSAB 1500 ¶66 and PS 1700 ¶129.

41. PSAB 1500 ¶70 and PS 1700 ¶133.

42. PSAB 3270 "Solid Waste Landfill Closure and Post-Closure Liability," issued Feb. 1998, ¶13.

43. PSAB 1500 "General Standards of Financial Statement Presentation," issued Sept. 1997, ¶107.

44. CICA's "Senior Government Reporting Model," July 2000, p. 6.

Another issue is that of interfund transfers. Interfund transfers are sometimes reported as revenues to the receiving fund and expenditures to the transferring fund. In some cases, interfund transfers are used as a way of reducing surpluses or creating deficits in general or operating funds (or, conversely, eliminating a deficit). There are many legitimate reasons for interfund transfers, but such transfers should clearly be labelled and should appear on statements of operations. PS 1500 states that revenues should segregate transfers from other governments.[45] In consolidated statements, interfund transfers should be eliminated.[46]

Accounting for loans receivable is an issue because governments often grant forgivable loans or give grants that are repayable under certain circumstances. If a grant is accounted for as a loan receivable, it will not appear as an expenditure on the government's statement of operations; therefore the issue has real impact for measuring a government's surplus or deficit for the period. PS 3050 deals with this issue explicitly, and recommends criteria for determining whether a payment constitutes a loan or an expenditure. Another issue is loans that are provided with significant concessionary terms or where part of the loan is in substance a grant. There is also guidance in establishing when a write-off needs to be made for loan receivables.

Summary of Key Points

1. Governments have characteristics similar to those of non-profit organizations. The largest difference is that governments have a larger potential user group and a legal reporting requirement to legislatures or city councils.

2. The Public Sector Accounting Board sets the standards in accounting for the public sector. To date 22 public sector accounting recommendations have been issued in the *CICA Public Sector Accounting Handbook.*

3. The objectives of financial statements for local governments are different than for federal, provincial, and territorial governments due to their diverse set of potential users. Local governments often issue various financial reports in addition to financial statements to meet the specific needs of their user groups.

4. Four qualitative characteristics of good financial reports for governments are: comparability among governments, consistency between years, completeness, and timeliness.

5. Current recommendations issued in the "Senior Government Reporting Model" in 2000 propose four financial statements: statement of financial position; statement of operations; statement of changes in net debt; and statement of cash flow.

6. Governments have reporting issues that are similar to those of NPO: cash versus accrual accounting; expenditure versus expense; capital assets; consolidation; and restricted assets and revenues. The recommendations of the study group support a move towards full accrual accounting. In addition, they have many issues unique to the government—e.g., forgivable loans and liabilities related to solid waste landfill closure costs.

---

45. PSAB 1500, ¶75.

46. PSAB 2500 "Basic Principle of Consolidation," issued May 1999, ¶06.

Weblinks

Public Sector
www.cica.ca/cica/cicawebsite.nsf/public/SGPublicSector

The goal of the Public Sector Accounting Board (PSAcB) is to improve its financial and performance information for government decision making and accountability. PSAcB meets this goal by setting accounting standards for all levels of government—federal, provincial, territorial, and municipal. Standards are tailored to meet the unique information needs of the public sector.

Finance Canada Budget Info
www.fin.gc.ca/access/budinfoe.html

Read the Canadian annual budget and fiscal update for the past five years on this Web site. Also, consult the glossary of frequently used terms or access one of the many links to related sites.

Ontario Ministry of Municipal Affairs and Housing
www.mah.gov.on.ca

The Ministry of Municipal Affairs and Housing is concerned with local governments, land use planning, building regulations, and the housing market. Visit this detailed site to download documents about social housing reform, view recent press releases, or link to Ontario municipalities.

Review Questions

12-1 How does the primary user group for government financial statements differ from that for NPO financial statements?

12-2 What is the Public Sector Accounting Board? What is its role?

12-3 Are government auditors required to report in accordance with the PSAcB's recommendations?

12-4 Who controls municipal government reporting practices?

12-5 What types of financial statements do governments most commonly present in their public financial reports? How would this change if the proposals of the "Senior Government Reporting Model" are adopted?

12-6 What are the advantages of the government reporting on a modified accrual or accrual basis compared to a cash flow basis?

12-7 What problems are encountered by governments in capitalizing and depreciating capital assets?

12-8 How does the expenditure basis of accounting discourage reinvestment in long-lived assets?

12-9 Distinguish between fund *accounting* and fund *reporting*.

12-10 Why is it difficult to determine the governmental reporting entity?

12-11 How does the PSAcB recommend the reporting entity be defined?

12-12 Explain why liability measurement is so much more of a problem for governments than it is for NPOs and businesses.

12-13 How should interfund transfers be reported?

12-14 What is a forgivable loan?

Cases

Case 12-1

Comparison of Objectives

William Witherspoon III is executive vice-president of Marble Industries Ltd., a publicly held industrial company. Mr. Witherspoon III has just been elected to the city council of Turnwater, a major industrial city. Prior to assuming office as a city councillor, he asks you, as his accountant, to explain the major differences that exist in accounting and financial reporting for a large city when compared to a large industrial corporation.

Required:

Describe the major differences that exist in the purpose of accounting and financial reporting and in the types of reports of a large city when compared to a large industrial corporation.

[CGA–Canada]

Case 12-2

City of Echo Ridge

You are the controller for the City of Echo Ridge. You have just had a meeting with a new member of city council. The new councillor, who is also the owner/manager of a local automobile dealership, is confused by the different accounting terminology used by the city. "There is an operating fund, endowed fund, and a capital fund. There is also a capital asset group and a bonded debt group. Some funds have surpluses and others have deficits. What are these funds and groups and why can't they be combined? We don't have this mess at the dealership."

Required:

You have been asked to prepare a report for the next city council meeting to answer the councillor's specific concerns and to explain fund accounting to the council. Prepare a detailed report for the meeting.

[CGA–Canada]

Solutions to Self-Study Problems

SSP2-1

Worksheet Method
Archie Corp. Consolidation Worksheet

	Trial balances			Archie Corp.
	Archie Corp. Dr/(Cr)	Bunker Ltd. Dr/(Cr)	Adjustments Dr/(Cr)	consolidated trial balance*
Cash and current receivables	$ 200,000	$ 400,000	$ (80,000) **b** (200,000) **c**	$ 320,000
Inventories	900,000	500,000		1,400,000
Furniture, fixtures, and equipment (net)	2,000,000	1,700,000		3,700,000
Buildings under capital leases (net)	6,000,000	3,000,000		9,000,000
Investment in Bunker Ltd. (at cost)	1,000,000	—	(1,000,000) **a**	—
Accounts payable	(1,500,000)	(400,000)	80,000 **b** 200,000 **c**	(1,620,000)
Long-term liabilities	(4,000,000)	(2,000,000)		(6,000,000)
Common shares	(1,500,000)	(1,000,000)	1,000,000 **a**	(1,500,000)
Retained earnings, December 31, 2002	(2,100,000)	(1,600,000)		(3,700,000)
Dividends declared	2,000,000	500,000	(500,000) **d**	2,000,000
Sales revenue	(13,000,000)	(5,000,000)	4,000,000 **e**	(14,000,000)
Dividend income	(500,000)	—	500,000 **d**	—
Cost of sales	7,000,000	3,200,000	(4,000,000) **e**	6,200,000
Other expenses	3,500,000	700,000		4,200,000
	$ —	$ —	$ —	$ —

*The balance sheet and income statement must be prepared from the amounts in this column.
This worksheet does **not** constitute a set of financial statements!

Direct Method
Archie Corp. Consolidated Financial Statements

Balance Sheet
December 31, 2003

Assets

Current assets:

Cash and current receivables [200,000 + 400,000 – **80,000** – **200,000**]	$ 320,000
Inventories [900,000 + 500,000]	1,400,000
	1,720,000

Property, plant, and equipment:

Furniture, fixtures, and equipment, net of accumulated depreciation [2,000,000 + 1,700,000]	3,700,000
Buildings under capital lease, net of related amortization [6,000,000 + 3,000,000]	9,000,000
	12,700,000

Other assets:

Investment in Bunker Ltd. [1,000,000 – 1,000,000]	—
Total assets	$14,420,000

Liabilities and shareholders' equity

Liabilities:

Current payables [1,500,000 + 400,000 – **80,000** – **200,000**]	$ 1,620,000
Long-term liabilities [4,000,000 + 2,000,000]	6,000,000
	7,620,000

Shareholders' equity:

Common shares [1,500,000 + 1,000,000 – 1,000,000]	1,500,000
Retained earnings [3,100,000 + 2,200,000]	5,300,000
	6,800,000
Total liabilities and shareholders' equity	$14,420,000

Statement of Income and Retained Earnings
Year Ended December 31, 2003

Sales revenue [13,000,000 + 5,000,000 – **4,000,000**]	$14,000,000
Dividend income [500,000 – **500,000**]	—
	14,000,000

Operating expenses:

Cost of sales [7,000,000 + 3,200,000 – **4,000,000**]	6,200,000
Other operating expenses [3,500,000 + 700,000]	4,200,000
	10,400,000
Net income	$ 3,600,000
Retained earnings, December 31, 2002 [2,100,000 + 1,600,000]	3,700,000
Dividends declared [2,000,000 + 500,000 – **500,000**]	(2,000,0000)
Retained earnings, December 31, 2003	$ 5,300,000

SSP 3-1

Analysis of Fair Value of Net Assets Acquired:

	Book value	Fair value	Fair value increment		% share		FVI acquired
Cash and cash equivalents	$ 1,200,000	$ 1,200,000	$ —	×	100% =	$	—
Accounts receivable	1,800,000	1,800,000	—	×	100% =		—
Machinery and equipment, net	8,400,000	11,000,000	2,600,000	×	100% =		2,600,000
Deferred development costs	3,100,000	4,000,000	900,000	×	100% =		900,000
Accounts payable	(1,100,000)	(1,100,000)	—	×	100% =		—
Notes payable, long-term	(1,000,000)	(900,000)	100,000	×	100% =		100,000
	$12,400,000	$16,000,000	$3,600,000				$3,600,000

1. Direct Purchase of Blue's Net Assets for $20,000,000:

	Ace's book value	+ FV of Blue assets acq'd	+ Cost of purchase =	Ace assets after purchase
Cash and cash equivalents	$ 2,350,000	$ 1,200,000	$ (2,000,000)	$ 1,550,000
Accounts receivable	2,000,000	1,800,000		3,800,000
Land	5,000,000	—		5,000,000
Machinery and equipment, net	13,500,000	11,000,000		24,500,000
Deferred development costs	600,000	4,000,000		4,600,000
Goodwill*		4,000,000		4,000,000
				$43,450,000
Accounts payable	(650,000)	(1,100,000)		$ 1,750,000
Notes payable, long-term	(2,000,000)	(900,000)	(18,000,000)	20,900,000
Common shares	(15,000,000)			15,000,000
Retained earnings	(5,800,000)			5,800,000
	$ —	$20,000,000	$(20,000,000)	$43,450,000

* 20,000,000 purchase price - 16,000,000 fair value of net assets = 4,000,000 goodwill

2. Purchase of 100% of Blue's shares by issuance of Ace shares worth $20,000,000:

	Ace's book value	Blue's book value	Adjustments	Ace consolidated balance sheet
Cash and cash equivalents	$ 2,350,000	$ 1,200,000		$ 3,550,000
Accounts receivable	2,000,000	1,800,000		3,800,000
Land	5,000,000	—		5,000,000
Machinery and equipment, net	13,500,000	8,400,000	2,600,000	24,500,000
Investment in Blue*	20,000,000		(20,000,000)	—
Deferred development costs	600,000	3,100,000	900,000	4,600,000
Goodwill			4,000,000	4,000,000
				$45,450,000
Accounts payable	(650,000)	(1,100,000)		$ 1,750,000
Notes payable, long-term	(2,000,000)	(1,000,000)	100,000	2,900,000
Common shares*	(35,000,000)	(6,950,000)	6,950,000	35,000,000
Retained earnings	(5,800,000)	(5,450,000)	5,450,000	5,800,000
	$ —	$ —	$ —	$45,450,000

*These accounts are **after** recording the purchase of Blue's shares. The common shares account is increased by 400,000 × $50 = $20,000,000

3. Purchase of 100% of Blue's shares by shares and cash worth $14,500,000:

Note: in this scenario, the purchase price is less than the fair value of Blue's net assets.
Therefore, negative goodwill is $1,500,000.
Negative goodwill is offset against the intangible asset with no observable market value.

	Ace's book value*	Blue's book value	Adjustments	Ace consolidated balance sheet
Cash and cash equivalents*	$ 1,350,000	$ 1,200,000		$ 2,550,000
Accounts receivable	2,000,000	1,800,000		3,800,000
Land	5,000,000	—		5,000,000
Machinery and equipment, net	13,500,000	8,400,000	2,600,000	24,500,000
Investment in Blue*	14,500,000		(14,500,000)	—
Deferred development costs	600,000	3,100,000	{ 900,000	3,100,000
[Negative goodwill]			(1,500,000) }	
				$38,950,000
Accounts payable	(650,000)	(1,100,000)		$ 1,750,000
Notes payable, long-term	(2,000,000)	(1,000,000)	100,000	2,900,000
Common shares*	(28,500,000)	(6,950,000)	6,950,000	28,500,000
Retained earnings	(5,800,000)	(5,450,000)	5,450,000	5,800,000
	$ —	$ —	$ —	$38,950,000

*These accounts are **after** recording the purchase of Blue's shares. Cash is reduced by $1,000,000;
Common shares is increased by $270,000 x $50 = $13,500,000; Investment in Blue is increased by $14,500,000.

SSP4-1

Analysis of the purchase transaction:

Purchase price		$10,000,000
Net assets acquired:		
Book value of Subco's net assets	7,000,000	
Fair value increment on buildings	1,400,000	
		8,400,000
Goodwill		$ 1,600,000

a. Consolidated net income:

Separate-entity net incomes:		
Parco	$ 680,000	
Subco	350,000	
		$ 1,030,000
Adjustments:		
Eliminate dividend income from Subco	(150,000)	
Unrealized profit from upstream sales [200,000 × 20%]	(40,000)	
Amortization of fair value increment [1,400,000/14]	(100,000)	
Goodwill amortization [1,600,000/20]	(80,000)	
		(370,000)
Consolidated net income, year ended December 31, 2001		$ 660,000

b. Consolidated retained earnings:

	Parco	Subco	Consolidated
Separate-entity retained earnings, January 1, 2001	$3,450,000	$ 1,250,000	
Separate-entity net incomes for 2001	680,000	350,000	
Dividends declared in 2001	(200,000)	(150,000)	
Book value of retained earnings, December 31, 2001	$3,930,000	$ 1,450,000	$5,380,000
Consolidation adjustments:			
Eliminate dividend income from Subco			(150,000)
Unrealized profit from upstream sales [200,000 × 20%]			(40,000)
Amortization of fair value increment [1,400,000/14]			(100,000)
Goodwill amortization [1,600,000/20]			(80,000)
			(370,000)
Consolidated retained earnings, December 31, 2001			$5,010,000

c. Parco's equity-basis earnings in Subco

Subco's unadjusted separate-entity net income		$350,000
Equity-basis adjustments:		
Unrealized profit from upstream sales [200,000 x 20%]	$ (40,000)	
Amortization of fair value increment [1,400,000/14]	(100,000)	
Goodwill amortization [1,600,000/20]	(80,000)	
		(220,000)
Subco's adjusted equity-basis earnings		$ 130,000

SSP4-2

Analysis of the purchase transaction:

Purchase price   **$1,084,000**

	Book value	Fair value	Fair value increment	% share	FVI acquired	
Cash	$ 80,000	$ 80,000	—			
Accounts receivable	99,000	99,000	—			
Inventory	178,000	195,000	17,000 × 100% =		17,000	
Property, plant, and equipment	800,000	740,000	140,000 × 100% =		140,000	
Accumulated depreciation	(200,000)	—				
Accounts payable	(70,000)	(70,000)	—			
Long-term liabilities	(200,000)	(200,000)				
Total fair value increment			157,000 × 100% =		157,000	157,000
Net asset book value	$687,000		× 100% =			687,000
Fair value of assets acquired		$844,000				844,000
Goodwill						$ 240,000

Consolidated Financial Statements (direct method)

Statement of Income and Retained Earnings
Year Ended December 31, 2005

Sales revenue [1,200,000 + 987,000 – **390,000** – **150,000**]	$1,647,000
Cost of goods sold [800,000 + 650,000 – **390,000** – **150,000** –**12,000** + **(90,000 × 20%)** + **(50,000 × 40%)**]	936,000
Gross profit	711,000
Other operating expenses [235,000 + 147,000 **+ 210,000 + 14,000 + 12,000**]	618,000
Net income	93,000
Retained earnings, December 31, 2004 [1,153,000 + 330,000 – **437,000** –**17,000** – **12,000** – **(140,000/10 × 2)** – **(240,000/20 × 2)**]	965,000
Retained earnings, December 31, 2005	$1,058,000

Balance Sheet
December 31, 2005

Assets

Current assets:

Cash [120,000 + 110,000]	$ 230,000
Accounts receivable [150,000 + 135,000]	285,000
Inventory [240,000 + 195,000 – **(90,000 × 20%)** – **(50,000 × 40%)**]	397,000
	912,000
Property, plant, and equipment [1,400,000 + 910,000 – **60,000** – **210,000**]	2,040,000
Accumulated depreciation [510,000 + 320,000 – **200,000** + **(140,000/10 × 3)**]	(672,000)
	1,368,000
Goodwill [76,000 **+ 240,000** – **(240,000/20 × 3)**]	280,000
Total assets	$2,560,000

Liabilities and shareholders' equity

Liabilities:

Accounts payable (current) [142,000 + 60,000]	$ 202,000
Long-term notes payable [600,000 + 200,000]	800,000
	1,002,000

Shareholders' equity:

Common shares	500,000
Retained earnings [1,318,000 + 520,000 − **437,000** − **17,000** − **210,000**	
−(**90,000** × **20%**) − (**50,000** × **40%**) − (**140,000/10** × **3**) − (**240,000/20** × **3**)]	1,058,000
	1,558,000
Total liabilities and shareholders' equity	$2,560,000

Consolidation Worksheet

	Parent Ltd.	Sub. Inc.	Acquisition	Cumulative	Current	Purchase Ltd. consolidated trial balance
Cash	$120,000	$110,000				$230,000
Accounts receivable	150,000	135,000				285,000
Inventories	240,000	195,000			(18,000) **c2** / (20,000) **c4**	397,000
Property, plant & equipment	1,400,000	910,000	(60,000) **a**		(210,000) **c5**	2,040,000
Accumulated depreciation	(510,000)	(320,000)	200,000 **a**	(28,000) **b2**	(14,000) **c6**	(672,000)
Investments (at cost)	1,084,000		(1,084,000) **a**			—
Goodwill	76,000		240,000 **a**	(24,000) **b3**	(12,000) **c7**	280,000
Accounts payable	(142,000)	(60,000)				(202,000)
Long-term notes payable	(600,000)	(200,000)				(800,000)
Common shares	(500,000)	(250,000)	250,000 **a**			(500,000)
Retained earnings, December 31, 2004	(1,153,000)	(330,000)	437,000 **a** / 17,000 **a**	12,000 **b1** / 28,000 **b2** / 24,000 **b3**		(965,000)
Sales	(1,200,000)	(987,000)			390,000 **c1** / 150,000 **c3**	(1,647,000)
Cost of sales	800,000	650,000		(12,000) **b1**	(390,000) **c1** / (150,000) **c3** / 18,000 **c2** / 20,000 **c4**	936,000
Other operating expenses	235,000	147,000			210,000 **c5** / 14,000 **c6** / 12,000 **c7**	618,000
	$ —	$ —	$ —	$ —	$ —	$ —

Notes:

a1. The inventory on date of acquisition is assumed to have been sold. Therefore, the FVI on inventory has passed through cost of sales and is now in retained earnings.

a2. The $140,000 FVI on PP&E is recognized by eliminating Subsidiary's accumulated depreciation of $200,000 and by reducing the asset account by $60,000. The net effect is to increase net book value by $140,000.

b. The cumulative operations adjustments include two years' amortization of FVI and goodwill, and the unrealized profit in Parent's 2005 *beginning* inventory.

SSP5-1

Analysis of the purchase transaction:

Purchase price $150,000

	Book value	Fair value	Fair value increment (decrement)	% share	FVI acquired	
Cash	$ 10,000	$ 10,000	—			
Accounts receivable	20,000	20,000	—			
Inventory	30,000	30,000	—			
Land	45,000	80,000	$ 35,000 × 60% =		$21,000	
Buildings	150,000	130,000	(20,000) × 60% =		(12,000)	
Accumulated depreciation	(50,000)	—	50,000 × 60% =		30,000	
Equipment	130,000	10,000	(120,000) × 60% =		(72,000)	
Accumulated depreciation	(80,000)	—	80,000 × 60% =		48,000	
Accounts payable	(40,000)	(40,000)	—			
Long-term liabilities	(50,000)	(50,000)	—			
Total fair value increment			$ 25,000 × 60% =		$15,000	15,000
Net asset book value	$165,000		× 60% =			99,000
Fair value of net assets acquired		$190,000	× 60% =			114,000
Goodwill						$ 36,000

Notes:

1. The net fair value increment acquired for buildings works out to $18,000, as follows:

60% of buildings carrying value: $150,000 × 60%	$ 90,000
less 60% of accumulated depreciation: $50,000 × 60%	(30,000)
	60,000
60% of fair value: $130,000 × 60%	78,000
Net fair value increment of buildings acquired	$ 18,000

2. The net fair value decrement acquired for equipment is $24,000, as follows:

60% of equipment carrying value: $130,000 x 60%	$ 78,000
less 60% of accumulated depreciation: $80,000 x 60%	(48,000)
	30,000
60% of fair value: $10,000 × 60%	6,000
Net fair value (decrement) of equipment acquired	$(24,000)

These amounts are necessary for the solution, under both the direct approach and the worksheet approach.

Consolidated Balance Sheet (direct method)
January 10, 2003

Assets

Current assets:

Cash [10,000 + 50,000]	$ 60,000
Accounts receivable [70,000 + 20,000]	90,000
Inventory [80,000 + 30,000]	110,000
	260,000

Capital assets:

Land [0 + 45,000 **+ 21,000**]	66,000
Buildings [260,000 + 150,000 − **50,000** + **18,000**]	378,000
Accumulated depreciation [40,000 + 50,000 − **50,000**]	(40,000)
Equipment [175,000 + 130,000 − **80,000** − **24,000**]	201,000
Accumulated depreciation [70,000 + 80,000 − **80,000**]	(70,000)
	535,000
Goodwill [**150,000** − (**190,000** × **40%**)]	36,000
Total assets	$831,000

Liabilities and shareholders' equity

Liabilities:

Accounts payable (current) [80,000 + 40,000]	$120,000
Long-term liabilities [0 + 50,000]	50,000
	170,000
Non-controlling interest [**165,000** × **40%**]	66,000

Shareholders' equity:

Common shares [220,000 **+ 150,000**]	370,000
Retained earnings	225,000
	595,000
Total liabilities and shareholders' equity	$831,000

Consolidation Worksheet

| | Trial balances | | Acquisition | | Consolidated |
	Regina	Dakota	adjustment		trial balance
Cash	50,000	10,000			60,000
Accounts receivable	70,000	20,000			90,000
Inventories	80,000	30,000			110,000
Land	—	45,000	21,000	**a2**	66,000
Buildings	260,000	150,000	(32,000)	**a2**	378,000
Accumulated depreciation	(40,000)	(50,000)	50,000	**a2**	(40,000)
Equipment	175,000	130,000	(104,000)	**a2**	201,000
Accumulated depreciation	(70,000)	(80,000)	80,000	**a2**	(70,000)
Investments (at cost)	150,000		(99,000)	**a1**	51,000
			(51,000)	**a2**	(51,000)
Goodwill			36,000	**a2**	36,000
					—
Non-controlling interest			(66,000)	**a1**	(66,000)
					—
Accounts payable	(80,000)	(40,000)			(120,000)
Long-term liabilities	—	(50,000)			(50,000)
					—
Common shares	(370,000)	(100,000)	100,000	**a1**	(370,000)
Retained earnings	(225,000)	(65,000)	65,000	**a1**	(225,000)
	—	—	—		—

Solutions to

Self-Study

Problems

571

SSP5-2

Regina Ltd.

Consolidated Statement of Income and Retained Earnings (direct method)
Year Ended December 31, 2003

Sales [2,000,000 + 1,000,000 – **600,000**]	$2,400,000
Dividend income [24,000 + 0 – **24,000**]	—
Other income [7,000 + 0 – **2,500**]	4,500
	2,404,500
Cost of sales [1,000,000 + 600,000 – **600,000** + 40,000 + 20,000]	1,060,000
Other operating expenses [886,000 + 280,000 + **1,800** – **4,800**]	1,163,000
Interest expense [2,000 + 10,000 – **2,500**]	9,500
Goodwill amortization [**36,000** × **1/20**]	1,800
Non-controlling interest in earnings [(**110,000** – **40,000**) × **40%**]	28,000
	2,262,300
Net income	142,200
Retained earnings, December 31, 2002	225,000
Dividends declared [20,000 + 40,000 – **40,000**]	(20,000)
Retained earnings, December 31, 2003	$ 347,200

Consolidated Balance Sheet
December 31, 2003

Assets

Current assets:

Cash [28,000 + 10,000]	$ 38,000
Accounts receivable [110,000 + 30,000 – **50,000** – **2,500**]	87,500
Inventory [160,000 + 60,000 – **40,000** – **20,000**]	160,000
	285,500

Capital assets:

Land [0 + 135,000 + **21,000**]	156,000
Buildings [300,000 + 150,000 – **50,000** + **18,000**]	418,000
Accumulated depreciation [45,000 + 60,000 – **50,000** + **1,800**]	(56,800)
Equipment [200,000 + 130,000 – **80,000** – **24,000**]	226,000
Accumulated depreciation [80,000 + 90,000 – **80,000** – **4,800**]	(85,200)
	658,000
Goodwill [**36,000** × **19/20**]	34,200
Total assets	$ 977,700

Liabilities and shareholders' equity

Liabilities:

Accounts payable (current) [40,000 + 80,000 – **50,000** – **2,500**]	$ 67,500
Long-term liabilities [65,000 + 50,000]	115,000
	182,500
Non-controlling interest [(**235,000** – **40,000**) × **40%**]	78,000

Shareholders' equity:

Common shares	370,000
Retained earnings [348,000 + 135,000 – **65,000** – (**70,000** × **40%**) – (**40,000** × **60%**) – 20,000 – **1,800** + **4,800** – **1,800**]	347,200
	717,200
Total liabilities and shareholders' equity	$ 977,700

Consolidation Worksheet—Regina Ltd.

	Regina	Dakota	Adjustments Acquisition	Adjustments Operations	Consolidated trial balance
Cash	28,000	10,000			38,000
Accounts and other receivables	110,000	30,000		(52,500) **c4**	87,500
Inventories	160,000	60,000		(40,000) **c2** (20,000) **c3**	160,000
Land	—	135,000	21,000 **a2**		156,000
Buildings	300,000	150,000	(32,000) **a2**		418,000
Accumulated depreciation	(45,000)	(60,000)	50,000 **a2**	(1,800) **c6**	(56,800)
Equipment	200,000	130,000	(104,000) **a2**		226,000
Accumulated depreciation	(80,000)	(90,000)	80,000 **a2**	4,800 **c7**	(85,200)
Investments (at cost)	150,000		(99,000) **a1** (51,000) **a2**		—
Goodwill			36,000 **a2**	(1,800) **c8**	34,200
Accounts payable	(40,000)	(80,000)		52,500 **c4**	(67,500)
Long-term liabilities	(65,000)	(50,000)			(115,000)
Non-controlling interest			(66,000) **a1**	16,000 **c9** (28,000) **c10**	(78,000)
Common shares	(370,000)	(100,000)	100,000 **a1**		(370,000)
Retained earnings	(225,000)	(65,000)	65,000 **a1**		(225,000)
Dividends declared	20,000	40,000		(40,000) **c9**	20,000
Sales	(2,000,000)	(1,000,000)		600,000 **c1**	(2,400,000)
Dividend income	(24,000)			24,000 **c9**	—
Other income	(7,000)			2,500 **c5**	(4,500)
Cost of sales	1,000,000	600,000		(600,000) **c1** 40,000 **c2** 20,000 **c3**	1,060,000
Other operating expenses	886,000	280,000		1,800 **c6** (4,800) **c7**	1,163,000
Interest expense	2,000	10,000		(2,500) **c5**	9,500
Goodwill amortization				1,800 **c8**	1,800
Non-controlling interest in earnings				28,000 **c10**	28,000
	$ —	$ —	$ —	$ —	$ —

Operations adjustments:

c1 Eliminate intercompany sales, $400,000 upstream + $200,000 downstream

c2 Upstream unrealized profit, $100,000 × 40% gross margin = $40,000

c3 Downstream unrealized profit, $40,000 × 50% gross margin = $20,000

c4 Eliminate intercompany loan receivable and payable (1 year = current) + 1/2 year accrued interest

c5 Eliminate intercompany interest revenue and expense, $50,000 × 10% × 1/2 = $2,500

c6 Amortize FVI on building, $18,000/10 = $1,800

c7 Amortize FV *decrement* on equipment, $24,000/5 = $4,800

c8 Amortize goodwill, $36,000/20 = $1,800

c9 Eliminate Dakota's dividend payments

c10 Non-controlling interest's share of Dakota's earnings, ($110,000 − $40,000) × 40% = $28,000

SSP5-3

Analysis of the purchase transaction: see the solution to SSP5-1.

1. Non-controlling interest in earnings:

Dakota's separate-entity net income for 2004 (Exhibit 5-17)	$ 30,000
Plus unrealized upstream profit in opening inventory:	
$100,000 × 40% gross margin	40,000
Less unrealized upstream profit in ending inventory:	
$160,000 sales × 50% remaining in inventory × 40% gross margin	(32,000)
Adjusted Regina net income	38,000
Non-controlling interest share	× 40%
	$ 15,200

2. Non-controlling interest:

Dakota's shareholders' equity, December 31, 2004 (Exhibit 5-17)	$205,000
Less unrealized upstream profit at year-end:	
Ending inventory, $160,000 × 50% × 40%	(32,000)
	173,000
Non-controlling interest share	× 40%
	$ 69,200

3. Consolidated retained earnings:

Regina's separate-entity retained earnings,		
December 31, 2004 (Exhibit 5-17)		$348,000
Dakota's retained earnings, December 31, 2004	$105,000	
Less Dakota's retained earnings at date of acquisition	(65,000)	
Change in Dakota's retained earnings since acquisition	40,000	
Regina's ownership share	× 60%	
Regina's share of Dakota's cumulative earnings		24,000
Less unrealized profits at December 31, 2004:		
Upstream: $160,000 × 50% × 40% gross margin		(32,000)
Downstream: $40,000 × 50% gross margin		(20,000)
Regina consolidated retained earnings		$320,000

SSP6-1

Note: This is a *downstream* sale; minority interest is not affected, except by the gain from sale as scrap in 2016.

2003:

Sales	100,000	
Cost of sales		60,000
Equipment		40,000
Accumulated depreciation	2,000	
Depreciation expense (40,000 ÷ 10 × 1/2 year)		2,000

2004:

Retained earnings [40,000 − (40,000 ÷ 10 × 1/2 year)]	38,000	
Accumulated depreciation	2,000	
Equipment		40,000
Accumulated depreciation	4,000	
Depreciation expense (40,000 ÷ 10)		4,000

2008:

Retained earnings [40,000 − (40,000 ÷ 10 × 4.5 years)]	22,000	
Accumulated depreciation	18,000	
Equipment		40,000
Accumulated depreciation	4,000	
Depreciation expense		4,000

2015:

Accumulated depreciation	40,000	
Equipment		40,000

2016:

Non-controlling interest in earnings	200	
Non-controlling interest		200

SSP6-2

a. Consolidated income statement:

Power Corporation
Consolidated Income Statement
Year Ended December 31, 2005

Sales (2,000,000 + 900,000 − 400,000 − 250,000)	$2,250,000
Investment income (1,000,000 + 100,000 − 32,000)	1,068,000
Gain on sale of land (68,000 − 68,000)	—
Total revenues	3,318,000
Cost of goods sold (see below)	1,143,000
Other operating expenses (see below)	1,297,000
Non-controlling interest in earnings of Spencer Corporation	35,600
Total expenses	2,475,600
Net income	$ 842,400

Purchase transaction (January 1, 2001):

80% of net book value acquired ($3,000,000 × 80%)	$2,400,000
Fair value decrements:	
Building ($600,000 × 80%)	− 480,000
Long-term liabilities ($500,000 × 80%)	+ 400,000
Fair value of net assets acquired	2,320,000
Purchase price	2,500,000
Goodwill	$ 180,000

Cost of goods sold:

As reported:	
Power	$1,300,000
Spencer	+ 500,000
Less intercompany sales, 2005:	
Downstream	− 400,000
Upstream	− 250,000
Less realized profit, beginning inventories:	
Downstream (100,000 × 30%)	− 30,000
Upstream (70,000 × 40%)	− 28,000
Plus unrealized profit, ending inventories:	
Downstream (90,000 × 30%)	+ 27,000
Upstream (60,000 × 40%)	+ 24,000
Consolidated cost of sales	$1,143,000

Other operating expenses:

As reported:	
Power	$ 960,000
Spencer	320,000
Depreciation on unrealized loss on sale of machine	1,280,000
[210,000 − (15/20 × 400,000) ÷ 15]	+ 6,000
Additional amortization:	
FV decrement on building (480,000 ÷ 10)	− 48,000
FV decrement on long-term liabilities (400,000 ÷ 8)	+ 50,000
Goodwill (180,000 ÷ 20)	+ 9,000
Consolidated other operating expenses	$1,297,000

Non-controlling interest in earnings of Spencer:

Spencer's separate-entity net income, as reported (Exhibit 6-10)	$ 248,000
Adjustments for intercompany upstream profits:	
Unrealized profit from intercompany sale of land	− 68,000
Realized from beginning inventory (70,000 × 40%)	+ 28,000
Unrealized in ending inventory (60,000 × 40%)	− 24,000
Machine [210,000 − (15/20 × 400,000) ÷ 15]	− 6,000
Spencer net income adjusted for realized and unrealized profits	$ 178,000
Non-controlling interest's share	× 20%
Non-controlling interest in earnings of Spencer	$ 35,600

b. Check via equity-basis income:

Power Corporation separate-entity net income		$740,000
Equity in earnings of Spencer Corporation:		
Spencer separate-entity net income (248,000 × 80%)	$ 198,400	
Unrealized upstream profit from land sale (68,000 × 80%)	− 54,400	
Unrealized downstream profit, ending (90,000 × 30%)	− 27,000	
Unrealized upstream profit, ending (60,000 × 40% × 80%)	− 19,200	
Realized downstream profit, beginning (100,000 × 30%)	+ 30,000	
Realized upstream profit, beginning (70,000 × 40% × 80%)	+ 22,400	
Under-depreciation on intercompany sale of machine (6,000 × 80%)	− 4,800	
Amortization of FV decrement on building (480,000 ÷ 10)	+ 48,000	
Amortization of FVD on long-term liabilities (400,000 ÷ 8)	− 50,000	
Goodwill amortization (180,000 ÷ 20)	− 9,000	
Spencer adjusted net income		$134,400
Less dividends received from Spencer (40,000 × 80%)		− 32,000
		$842,400

SSP6-3 (Appendix)

The $500,000 face value bonds were purchased by Passion for $479,000, a discount of $21,000. The discount will be amortized by Passion over the six years remaining to maturity at $3,500 per year. On Sweetness's books, the original issue discount (which also is $21,000) will be amortized over 10 years at $2,100 per year. Over the life of the bonds, the book value of the $500,000 bonds on the issuing (Sweetness, the subsidiary) and investing (Passion, the parent) companies' books will be as follows:

	Sweetness	Passion
Original issue price, January 1, 2001	$479,000	
4 years' accumulated amortization	8,400	
Book value, December 31, 2004	487,400	
Purchase price, December 31, 2004		$479,000
2 years' amortization	4,200	7,000
Book value, December 31, 2006	491,600	486,000
4 years' amortization	8,400	14,000
Book value, December 31, 2010	$500,000	$500,000

The consolidation adjustments must dispose of the difference between the carrying values of the bonds on the two companies' books. Assuming that the bonds are carried *net* of the discount on each company's books, the adjustments under each method are as follows:

Agency method:

December 31, 2004

Bonds payable	487,400	
Bond investment		479,000
Gain on bond retirement		8,400
Non-controlling interest in earnings	2,520	
Non-controlling interest		2,520
[30% of the gain of $8,400]		

December 31, 2006

Bonds payable	491,600	
Bond investment		486,000
Non-controlling interest (5,600 × 30%)		1,680
Retained earnings		3,920
Interest income (including $3,500 amortization)	63,500	
Interest expense (including $2,100 amortization)		62,100
Minority interest [(3,500 − 2,100) × 30%]		420
Retained earnings		980

December 31, 2010

Bonds payable	500,000	
Bond investment		500,000
Interest income (including $3,500 amortization)	63,500	
Interest expense (including $2,100 amortization)		62,100
Minority interest [(3,500 − 2,100) × 30%]		420
Retained earnings		980

Par-value method:

December 31, 2004

Bonds payable	487,400	
Bond investment		479,000
Gain on bond retirement		8,400
Non-controlling interest in earnings	3,780	
Non-controlling interest [(500,000 − 487,400) × 30%]		3,780

December 31, 2006

Bonds payable	491,600	
Bond investment		486,000
Non-controlling interest (8,400 × 30%)		2,520
Retained earnings		3,080
Interest income (including $3,500 amortization)	63,500	
Interest expense (including $2,100 amortization)		62,100
Minority interest (2,100 × 30%)		630
Retained earnings		770

December 31, 2010

Bonds payable	500,000	
Bond investment		500,000
Interest income (including $3,500 amortization)	63,500	
Interest expense (including $2,100 amortization)		62,100
Minority interest (2,100 × 30%)		630
Retained earnings		770

SSP7-1

a. The total available votes and Numbers' share thereof are as follows:

	Total available votes			Numbers Inc.'s votes		
Class	Shares outstanding	Votes per share	Total votes	Shares held	Votes per share	Total votes
A	600,000	1	600,000	40,000	1	40,000
B	50,000	15	750,000	44,000	15	660,000
	650,000		1,350,000	84,000		700,000

Numbers Incorporated owns $700,000 \div 1,350,000 = 51.85\%$ of the votes, and therefore controls 212°F Corporation.

b. The ownership share for consolidation purposes (or for equity-basis earnings) is the proportion of residual earnings that accrues to Numbers. Preferred shares are a prior claim, and therefore do not participate in residual earnings. The two classes of common shareholders participate equally in earnings. Therefore, Numbers' ownership share is simply the investor's proportionate share of the total shares outstanding: $84,000 \div 650,000 = 12.923\%$.

c. The amount of the non-controlling interest is the sum of the preferred share redemption value (call price) plus 87.077% of the residual shareholders' equity after deducting the prior claim of the preferred shares:

Preferred shares:		
1,000,000 shares × $12 per share call price		$ 12,000,000
Residual common equity:		
Total 212°F shareholders' equity	$125,000,000	
Less preferred share redemption value	− 12,000,000	
Residual common equity	113,000,000	
Non-controlling interest percentage	× 87.077%	98,397,010
Non-controlling interest amount		$110,397,010

SSP7-2

Essentially, this problem requires that the balance of the investment account be determined at January 1, 2005, prior to the sale of part of the investment. The FVI and goodwill (if any) must be determined at each of the two purchase dates. The fact that the purchases are in midyear is not a problem; the year-to-date net income is simply included as part of the net book value (i.e., as retained earnings on acquisition). The two purchases can be analyzed as follows:

July 1, 2003 purchase (30%):

Purchase price	$312,500
Subco net fair value acquired: $875,000 × 30%	262,500
Subco net book value acquired: $875,000 × 30%	262,500

There is no *net* fair value increment, because the inventory FVI is offset completely by the capital asset fair value decrement:

Inventory fair value increment: $50,000 × 30%	$ 15,000
Capital asset fair value decrement: $(50,000) × 30%	(15,000)
Net fair value increment (decrement)	$ 0

The entire purchase price discrepancy of $50,000 is allocated to goodwill, to be amortized over 20 years at $2,500 per year. The FVI on inventory will flow through to earnings in two months (i.e., a "six times" inventory turnover rate) and the capital asset FVD will be amortized over 10 years at $1,500 per year (as a *reduction* in depreciation expense).

September 1, 2004 (15%):

Purchase price	$183,500
Subco net fair value acquired: $1,290,000 × 15%	193,500
Subco net book value acquired: $1,100,000 × 15%	165,000

Fair value increments total to $28,500:

Inventory fair value increment: $10,000 × 15%	$ 1,500
Capital asset fair value increment: $180,000 × 15%	27,000
Net fair value increment (decrement)	$ 28,500

However, the net fair value acquired is higher than the purchase price. Negative goodwill of $10,000 exists. The fair value increments must be reduced by $10,000 to fully absorb the negative goodwill. Any one of three approaches can be used:

1. Eliminate the FVI on inventory and reduce the FVI on capital assets to $18,500.

2. Reduce the FVI on both inventory and capital assets proportionately, to 185/285 of their full fair value.

3. Leave the inventory FVI at $1,500 and reduce the capital asset FVI by $10,000, to $17,000.

Each approach will yield a different result, but all will be "correct." In practice, the choice will depend on Parco's financial reporting objectives. We will use the third approach in the remainder of this solution.

After the two purchases have been analyzed, the balance in the equity-basis investment account can be determined as of the date of the sale, January 1, 2005. The balance is $558,433, as shown in Exhibit 7-10.

When Parco sells 4,000 of its 9,000 shares, the investment account must be reduced by 4/9. The difference between the sale proceeds and the proportionate carrying value of the investment is the gain or loss to Parco:

Proceeds from selling 4,000 Subco shares	$300,000
Carrying value of portion sold: $558,433 × 4/9	248,192
Gain on sale	$ 51,808

EXHIBIT 7-10

CALCULATION OF INVESTMENT ACCOUNT BALANCE, EQUITY METHOD

July 1, 2003 acquisition purchase price	$312,500
Subco earnings for remainder of 2003: $100,000 × 30%	30,000
FVI on inventory	– 15,000
1/2 year amortization on capital asset FV decrement	750
1/2 year amortization of goodwill	– 1,250
Balance, December 31, 2003	**$327,000**
September 1, 2004 acquisition purchase price	183,500
Subco earnings for 2004:	
$125,000 × 30% for first eight months	37,500
$30,000 × 45% for last four months	13,500
Amortizations:	
Inventory flow-through, second purchase	– 1,500
Capital assets, first purchase (FV decrement)	1,500
Capital assets, second purchase (FV increment)	– 567
Goodwill, first purchase	– 2,500
Balance, December 31, 2004	**$558,433**

SSP9-1

The *CICA Handbook* recommends that exchange gains and losses on long-term debt of fixed maturity be deferred and amortized over the remaining life of the debt. Amortization expense will flow into the income statement as shown in the table below:

Year	Exchange loss on €5,000,000	Annual amortization 2001	2002	2003
2001	$150,000	$ 50,000	$ 50,000	$ 50,000
2002	$200,000		100,000	100,000
2003	$ 50,000			50,000
Total	$400,000	$ 50,000	$150,000	$200,000

SSP9-2

a. Assuming the receivable is hedged

Note: The forward contract was established at $0.0520, a premium of $0.0020 per NTD over the spot rate at the date of the hedge. The total premium is NTD1,000,000 × $0.0020 = $2,000. The premium must be allocated over the periods for which the hedge is effective.

December 2, 2002:

Accounts receivable (NTD1,000,000 × $0.05)	50,000	
Sales revenue		50,000

[to record the sale at the spot rate of $0.0500]

December 31, 2002:

Accounts receivable [NTD1,000,000 × ($0.0500 − $0.0510)	1,000	
Deferred exchange gains and losses		1,000
[to adjust the receivable to the year-end spot rate of $0.0510]		

December 31, 2002:

Unrealized forward premium	1,000	
Exchange gains and losses		1,000
[recognition of one-half of the premium on the forward contract]		

February 1, 2003:

Cash (NTD1,000,000 × $0.0525)	52,500	
Deferred exchange gains and losses	1,000	
Exchange gains and losses		2,500
Accounts receivable		51,000
[receipt of NTD1,000,000 cash from the customer]		

February 1, 2003:

Cash (Cdn. dollars received on the forward contract)	52,000	
Exchange gains and losses	1,500	
Cash (NTD1,000,000 × $0.0525)		52,500
Unrealized forward premium		1,000
[settlement of the forward contract]		

b. Assuming the receivable is not hedged

December 2, 2002:

Accounts receivable (NTD1,000,000 × $0.0500)	50,000	
Sales revenue		50,000
[to record the sale at the spot rate of $0.0500]		

December 31, 2002:

Accounts receivable [NTD1,000,000 × ($0.0500 − $0.0510)	1,000	
Exchange gains and losses		1,000
[to adjust the receivable to the year-end spot rate of $0.0510]		

February 1, 2003:

Cash (NTD1,000,000 × $0.0525)	52,500	
Accounts receivable		51,000
Exchange gains and losses		1,500
[receipt of NTD1,000,000 cash from the customer]		

SSP9-3

October 14, 2003 (contract signed): no entries are necessary.

December 7, 2003 (delivery of equipment):

Equipment (US$200,000 × $1.22)	244,000	
Accounts payable (US$200,000 × $1.18)		236,000
Deferred exchange gains and losses		8,000

[to record the receipt of equipment, the related liability, and the premium on the forward contract]

December 31, 2003 (year end):

Deferred exchange gains and losses	2,000	
Accounts payable [US$200,000 × ($1.19 − $1.18)]		2,000

[to adjust the account payable to the year-end spot rate of $1.19]

January 30, 2004 (payment):

Accounts payable	238,000	
Deferred exchange gains and losses	10,000	
Cash (US$200,000 × $1.24)		248,000

[payment of US$200,000 by customer]

January 30, 2004 (settlement of forward contract):

Cash (US$200,000 × $1.24)	248,000	
Cash (received in Cdn. dollars)		244,000
Deferred exchange gains and loss		4,000

[payment of US$200,000 by customer]

SSP10-1

Income statements, translated at the average rate for the year.

	2002 @ $1.70	2001 @ $2.20
Revenue	$510,000	$484,000
Depreciation expense	102,000	132,000
Interest expense	68,000	88,000
Other expenses	204,000	176,000
	374,000	396,000
Net income	$136,000	$ 88,000

Balance sheets, translated at the year-end rate (except for shareholders' equity):

	2002 @1.50	2001 @2.00
Assets		
Cash	$ 45,000	$ 320,000
Accounts receivable	60,000	60,000
Temporary investments (at cost)	300,000	—
Tangible capital assets	900,000	1,200,000
Accumulated depreciation	(180,000)	(120,000)
	$1,125,000	$1,460,000
Liabilities and shareholders' equity		
Accounts payable, current	$ 15,000	$ 40,000
Notes payable, due January 1, 2004	300,000	400,000
	315,000	440,000
Common shares (Note 1)	1,250,000	1,250,000
Retained earnings (Note 2)	73,000	22,000
Translation loss (Note 3)	(513,000)	(252,000)
	810,000	1,020,000
	$1,125,000	$1,460,000

Notes:

1. The original investment is translated at the historical rate of $2.50.
2. The retained earnings is translated at the historical rate at which the subsidiary's earnings were included in the *parent's* net income:

	2002	2001
SF10,000 from 2001 @ $2.20	$22,000	$22,000
SF30,000 from 2002 @ $1.70	51,000	—
	$73,000	$22,000

3. The translation loss can be derived as a balancing amount in the balance sheet, but it also can be calculated independently, as follows:

Loss pertaining to 2001:

Loss on initial investment, SF500,000 × ($2.00 – $2.50)	$250,000
Loss on 2001 earnings retained, SF10,000 × ($2.00 – $2.20)	2,000
Balance, December 31, 2001	252,000

Loss pertaining to 2002:

Loss on beginning of year shareholders' equity, SF510,000 × ($1.50 – $2.00)	255,000
Loss on 2002 earnings retained, SF30,000 × ($1.50 – $1.70)	6,000
Balance, December 31, 2002	$513,000

SSP10-2

a. Translated 2001 financial statements (temporal method)

Income statement:

	Local currency	Exchange rate	Canadian dollars
Revenue	SF 220,000	2.20	$ 484,000
Depreciation expense	60,000	2.30	138,000
Interest expense	40,000	2.20	88,000
Other expenses	80,000	2.20	176,000
	180,000		402,000
Net income	SF 40,000		$ 82,000

Balance sheet:

	Local currency	Exchange rate	Canadian dollars
Assets			
Cash	SF 160,000	2.00	$ 320,000
Accounts receivable	30,000	2.00	60,000
Tangible capital assets	600,000	2.30	1,380,000
Accumulated depreciation	(60,000)	2.30	(138,000)
	SF 730,000		$1,622,000
Liabilities and shareholders' equity			
Accounts payable, current	SF 20,000	2.00	$ 40,000
Note payable, long term	200,000	2.00	400,000
	220,000		440,000
Common shares	500,000	2.50	1,250,000
Retained earnings	10,000	(Note 1)	22,000
Translation gain (loss)	—		(90,000)
	510,000		1,182,000
	SF 730,000		$1,622,000
Note 1			
Net income, per income statement	SF 40,000	(as above)	$ 82,000
Less dividends declared and paid at year-end 2001	(30,000)	2.00	(60,000)
Retained earnings	SF 10,000		$ 22,000

b. Translation loss

	Local currency	Exchange rate	Canadian dollars
(1) *Loss on current monetary items:*			
Current monetary balance, January 1, 2001	—		—
Additions:			
Investment by Irene Corporation	SF 500,000	2.50	$1,250,000
Funds from operations:			
Net income	40,000	(as above)	82,000
Depreciation	60,000	2.30	138,000
Cash provided by note payable	200,000	2.40	480,000
	800,000		1,950,000
Uses:			
Purchase of tangible capital assets	600,000	2.30	1,380,000
Dividends declared	30,000	2.00	60,000
	630,000		1,440,000
Computed balance, December 31, 2001			510,000
Actual balance, December 31, 2001	SF 170,000	2.00	340,000
Loss on current monetary items			170,000
(2) *Gain on long-term note payable:*			
SF200,000 × ($2.40 − $2.00)			(80,000)
Loss on current monetary items			$ 90,000

Presentation on consolidated statements:

(a) The loss on current monetary items of $170,000 will be shown as an exchange loss on Irene Corporation's 2001 income statement.

(b) The gain of $80,000 on the long-term note payable will be deferred and amortized over three years, 2001 through 2003, at 1/3 per year, or $26,667 per year.

c. Translated 2002 financial statements (temporal method)

Income statement:

	Local currency	Exchange rate	Canadian dollars
Revenue	SF 300,000	1.70	$ 510,000
Depreciation expense	60,000	2.30	138,000
Interest expense	40,000	1.70	68,000
Other expenses	120,000	1.70	204,000
	220,000		410,000
Net income	SF 80,000		$ 100,000

Balance sheet:

	Local currency	Exchange rate	Canadian dollars
A...			
...unts receivable	SF 30,000	1.50	$ 45,000
...orary investments	40,000	1.50	60,000
...gible capital assets	200,000	1.90	380,000
...cumulated depreciation	600,000	2.30	1,380,000
	(120,000)	2.30	(276,000)
	SF 750,000		$1,589,000
...iabilities and shareholders' equity			
Accounts payable, current	SF 10,000	1.50	$ 15,000
Note payable, long term	200,000	1.50	300,000
	210,000		315,000
Common shares	500,000	2.50	1,250,000
Retained earnings	40,000	(Note 1)	47,000
Translation gain (loss)	—		(23,000)
	540,000		1,274,000
	SF 750,000		$1,589,000

Solutions to Self-Study Problems

587

Note 1

	Local currency	Exchange rate	Canadian dollars
Balance, January 1, 2002	SF 10,000		$ 22,000
Net income, per income statement	80,000	(as above)	100,000
Less dividends declared and paid at year-end 2001	(50,000)	1.50	(75,000)
Retained earnings	SF 40,000		$ 47,000

d. Translation loss on current monetary items for 2002

	Local currency	Exchange rate	Canadian dollars
Current monetary balance, January 1, 2001	SF 170,000	2.00	$ 340,000
Additions:			
Funds from operations:			
Net income	80,000	(as above)	100,000
Depreciation	60,000	2.30	138,000
	310,000		578,000
Uses:			
Purchase of nonmonetary investments	200,000	1.90	380,000
Dividends declared	50,000	1.50	75,000
	250,000		455,000
Computed balance, December 31, 2001			123,000
Actual balance, December 31, 2001	SF 60,000	1.50	90,000
Loss on current monetary items			$ 33,000

Index

A

account groups, 527–528
accounting estimates, 3
accounting exposure
    to currency rate fluctuation, 433, 435, 439
    vs. economic exposure, 438–440
accounting policy
    choices, 2–3
    interim reporting, 369
Accounting Principles Board, 95
Accounting Standards Board, 546
acquisition adjustment, 137–139
adjustments, 48
affiliates
    reporting investments in, 42–45
    significantly influenced, 40–41
agency approach, 272
agency funds, 527
amortization
    capital assets, 498, 499
    direct, 243–245
    downstream sales, 240–242
    fair value increments, 131–132
    goodwill, 153–155
    long-term balances in foreign currency, 398–399
    long-term monetary items, 398
    upstream sales, 242–243
articulation, 250
Assurance Standards Board, 547
audited financial statements, waiver of, 6
average-rate approach, 448–450

B

balance sheet
    non-controlling interest, 198–199, 205–207
    one-year post-acquisition consolidation, 136–137
    post-acquisition consolidation, 253–255
    second subsequent year consolidation, 148–150
Beedle, A., 550
beneficial interest, 37
"big bath," 14–15

board-designated funds, 499, 506
bonds
    agency approach, 272
    indirect acquisitions, 269–271
    intercorporate investments, 34–35, 268–274
    long-term foreign currency, 397
    non-wholly-owned subsidiaries, 271–273
    par-value approach, 271–272
    subsidiary purchase of parent's bonds, 273
branch accounting, 33
Bretton Woods Agreement, 390, 391
British Columbia Company Act, 6
budgetary accounts, 516
business combination
    acquirer, identification of, 94
    alternative reporting approaches, 88–95
    carrying-value purchase method, 92
    vs. consolidation, 77
    consolidation procedures, 96–99
    contingent consideration, 79
    control, 77
    corporate restructuring, 94
    cost allocation, 80–81
    cost of purchase, measurement of, 78–79
    current cash equivalent, 90–91
    defined, 77–78
    direct approach, 96–97
    direct purchase of net assets, 81–82
    disclosure, 101–102
    earnings per share, post-combination, 93
    equity basis, 111
    exchange of shares, 85–88
    fair values, determination of, 79–80
    general approach, 78–81
    goodwill, 81, 84
    hostile takeover, 40, 83
    income tax allocation, 80, 108–111, 162
    international practices, 94–95
    negative goodwill, 81, 99–100
    net assets, 77
    new-entity method, 89, 91–92
    note disclosure, 155–156
    occurrence of, 39
    pooling-of-interests method, 89–91, 92–93
    purchase method, 89, 91, 92–94
    purchase price discrepancy, 89
    push-down accounting, 102–104
    reverse takeover, 86

share purchases, 83–88

statutory amalgamation, 86

substance of, 40, 87

temporary differences, 108–110

unrecognized tax loss carryforwards, 110–111

valuation of shares, 78–79

voting control, 94

worksheet approach, 97–99

Business Combinations Exposure Draft, 93

accumulated depreciation, 97

acquirer, defined, 86

business combination, defined, 77

common control, 94

contingent consideration, 79

fair value, 79–80

goodwill, 132

maximum amortization period, 131

negative goodwill, 100

valuation of shares, 78

voting control, 94

business organization, form of

partnerships, 8

private corporations, 5–7

public corporations, 5–7

C

Canada Business Corporations Act (CBCA)

current cash equivalent, 90–91

financial statements, submission of, 5, 6

Canadian Institute of Chartered Accountants (CICA), 546–547

capital asset group, 527–528

capital assets

amortization of, 498, 499

government organizations, 555–556

intercompany sale of long-term assets, 239

non-profit organizations, 498–499

tangible, 131

capital funds, 526

capital leases, 239

carrying-value purchase method, 92

cash flow

consolidated statement, 153

future flows, 10–11

measurement, 10

prediction objective, 9–11

cash vs. accrual debate, 496–497, 553

CICA Handbook

accounting alternatives, 3

allocation of costs, 328

capital assets, 131, 498, 499

and collections, 502

constructive obligation, 372

contingencies, 373

control, defined, 35, 36

current-rate method, 445

deferred exchange gains and losses, 399

departure from recommendations, 5

disaggregation of losses, 454

disclosed basis of accounting, 7

disclosure decisions, 3

discontinued operations of subsidiary, 144

donated goods and services, 500–501

expense-basis reporting, 554

extraordinary items of subsidiary, 144

fair values, determination of, 79–80

foreign currency transactions, 395

foundations, 502

future flows, 10–11

GAAP, defined, 4

general financial reporting objective, 9

goodwill amortization, 132, 154

government business organizations, 546

government compliance issues, 548

hedge accounting recommendations, 402, 410, 413

integrated operation, 443, 444, 446–447

intercorporate investments, 3

interim statements, 368–369, 372

joint ventures, 41

long-term investments, 43

long-term monetary items, 398

losses on intercompany sales, 239

minority interest, 40

non-controlling interest, 40, 199

non-profit organizations (NPOs), 495, 497, 498, 499, 503, 504, 505, 506–507

operating segment, 360, 361

parent, defined, 35

parent-company approach, 189

pledges, 501

pooling-of-interests method, 93

portfolio investments, 34

proportionate consolidation, 43

Public Sector Accounting

Recommendations, 547
Public Sector Assurance
    Recommendations, 547
    push-down accounting, 103–104
    representational faithfulness, 439
    restricted fund method, 509
    and securities acts, 548
    segmented reporting, 359–360, 362, 363
    segmented reporting disclosures, 363–364,
      366
    self-sustaining foreign operation, 443–444,
      445, 447
    step purchases, 325
    subsidiary, defined, 35
    subsidiary shares, issuance of, 331
    temporal method, 444, 446
    two-transaction theory, 392
    unconsolidated financial statements, 57–59
    valuation of shares, 78, 79
    write-down, 42
closed membership, 493
coattail provision, 321
collection, 501–502
collective goods and services, 494
commitments, 410–412, 558
consolidated statements, 129
    see also consolidation
consolidation, 33, 43–44
    accumulated depreciation, 97
    adjustments, 48
    articulation, 250
    business combination, 96–99
    vs. business combination, 77
    cash flow statement, 153
    CICA Handbook recommendation, 59
    cost method, example of, 46–52
    direct approach, 48–50, 96–97
    eliminations, 48
    and equity-basis recording, 55–56, 263–265
    equity pick-up, 55
    government organizations, 556–557
    group accounts, 96
    indirect holdings, 157
    limitations, 57
    non-controlling interest. *See* non-controlling
      interest
    non-profit organizations, 503–504
    note disclosure, 155–156
    one-year post-acquisition. *See* one-year
      post-acquisition consolidation
    parent-founded subsidiaries, 156–157
    pooling-of-interests method, 93
    post-acquisition. *See* post-acquisition
      consolidation
    preferred dividends, 320
    purchase method, 93
    second subsequent year. *See* second
      subsequent year consolidation
    separate-entity statement requirement,
      52–55
    subsequent years. *See* post-acquisition
      consolidation
    worksheet approach, 48, 50–52, 97–99
consolidation method of equity reporting, 144
contingencies, 373, 558
contingent consideration, 79
contract compliance objective, 11, 16
control
    business combination, 77
    common, 94
    indirect, 37
    joint, 42
    limitations on, 37–38
    meaning of, 35–36
    and non-profit organizations, 502
    restricted shares, 321
    shares, purchase of, 84
    voting, 94
controlled subsidiaries, 35–36
controlling interest. *See* ownership interest
corporate restructuring, 94
corporations without share capital, 492
cost allocation, 80–81
cost basis, 42
cost method, 42, 46–52, 58
cost recovery basis, 496
covenants, 11
Crown corporations, 492
currency swap, 401
current cash equivalent, 90–91
current/noncurrent method, 436–437
current rate, 430
current-rate method, 435–436, 445, 448–450
custodial funds, 527

D

deferral method, 507–509, 512–513, 515
denominated in foreign currency, 390
depreciation accounting, and NPOs, 498–499
derivative instruments, 401
direct approach
    accrual, 194–196
    business combination, 96–97
    consolidation, 48–50
    non-controlling interest, 190–192, 194–199, 204–207
    non-controlling interest in earnings, 194–196
    one-year post-acquisition consolidation, 133–137, 194–199
    post-acquisition consolidation, 250–255
    second subsequent year consolidation, 145–150, 204–207
direct purchase of net assets, 81–82
disaggregation, 442, 444–445, 454
disbursement basis, 496
disclosed basis of accounting (DBA), 5, 7–8
disclosure
    business combinations, 101–102
    decisions, and professional judgement, 3
    enterprise-wide, 363–364
    segmented reporting, 360, 363–364
discontinued operations, 144–145, 265
discount, 405
discrete approach, 370, 371
dividend income, and post-acquisition consolidation, 136–137
donated goods and services, 500–501
downstream sales, 132, 240–242

E

earnings management, "big bath," 14–15
economic exposure, 439–440
eliminations, 48
encumbrance system, 516–517
endowment contribution, 506, 509, 511–512
endowment funds, 527
enterprise funds, 526
enterprise-wide disclosures
    geographic areas, 364
    major customers, 364
    products, 363
    services, 363

entity method, 184, 185, 189–190
equity-basis investments, 327
equity-basis recording, 55–56, 263–265
equity-basis reporting
    consolidation method. *See* equity method
    and post-acquisition consolidation, 142–144, 261–263
equity method
    business combinations, 111
    income tax allocation, 111
    intercorporate investments, 42–43, 52–56
    non-consolidated subsidiaries, 140–144
    post-acquisition consolidation, 140–144
equity pick-up, 55
estimation errors, 370
exception reporting principle, 369
exchange of shares, 85–88
exchange rate changes, 390–391
executory contract, 406–407
expenditure, 497
expenditure reporting, 496–497, 554
expense recognition, and tax deferral, 13
expense reporting, 496–497, 554
Exposure Draft. *See* Business Combinations Exposure Draft
extraordinary items, 144–145, 265

F

fair values
    determination of, 79–80
    increments, amortization of, 131–132, 140, 162–164
    push-down accounting, 102–104
fiduciary funds, 527
Financial Accounting Standards Board (FASB)
    exchange gains/losses, 440–441
    pooling-of-interests method, 93
financial assets, 402
Financial Post listing of large corporations, 6
Financial Reporting by Governments, 549
financial reporting objectives
    cash flow prediction, 9–11
    conflict resolution among objectives, 17–18
    contract compliance objective, 11, 16
    contractual uses, 17
    defined, 9
    governmental reporting, 549–550
    hierarchy of objectives, 18

income smoothing, 15–16
income tax deferral, 13–14
matrix of objectives, 17
maximization of earnings, 14–15
minimization of earnings, 14
minimum compliance, 16
motivations, 13
non-profit organizations (NPOs), 495–496
other objectives, 16–17
performance evaluation objective, 11–12
predictive uses, 17
preparer objectives, 12–16
regulated companies, 16
retrospective uses, 17
user objectives, 6–12
wholly-owned foreign subsidiaries, 16–17
financial statements
articulation, 250
comparative statements, 153
consolidated. See consolidation
interim. See interim reporting
separate-entity, 32, 52–55, 128–129
unconsolidated, 57–59
Fisher Effect, 391, 437
fixed exchange rates, 390–391
foreign currency options, 401
foreign currency transactions
bonds, 397
current monetary balances, 393–394
debt without fixed maturity, 400
deferral and amortization, 398–399
deferral until realization, 397–398
denominated in foreign currency, 390
disaggregation, 444–445
exchange gains and losses, 392
exchange rate changes, 390–391
Fisher Effect, 391
historical rate approach, 394
immediate recognition, 398
impending changes, 399
inflation, 391
long-term debt, 396–400
lower-of-cost-or-market (LCM) approach, 394
mark-to-market, 399
nonmonetary balance, 396
one-transaction theory, 392
perpetual debt, 400
practical applications, 395

pre-determined standard rate, 395
prevalence of, 390
purchasing power parity (PPP), 391
vs. reporting currency, 390
settled amounts, 393
translation method, choice of, 391
two-transaction theory, 392
widely-used approach, 394–395
foreign operations
accounting exposure, 433, 435, 438–440
allocation of translation loss, 452–454
current/noncurrent method, 436–437
current rate, 430
current-rate method, 435–436, 445, 448–450
deferral, 442
disaggregation, 442, 444–445
economic exposure, 439–440
Fisher Effect, 437
functional currency, 444
hedging, 445, 446
historical rate, 431
hyper-inflationary economies, 446
immediate recognition, 440–441
integrated operation, 443, 444–445, 446–447
international practices, 443–444
monetary/nonmonetary method, 433
purchasing power parity (PPP), 437
self-sustaining, 443–444, 445–446, 447
temporal method, 430–433, 433–434, 444, 446, 450–454
transaction accounting, 433–434
translation gains/losses reporting alternatives, 440–442
translation methods, 429–438
foreign subsidiaries. See wholly-owned foreign subsidiaries
foreign transactions, 389
forward contracts. See hedging
forward rate, 405
foundations, 502
functional currency, 444
fund accounting, 499–500
account groups, 527–528
appropriations, 525
attributes of, 524
capital asset group, 527–528
capital funds, 526

defined, 525
development of, 524
endowment funds, 527
enterprise funds, 526
fiduciary funds, 527
and fund-basis reporting, 556
general funds, 525–526
interfund transfers, 528–529
long-term liability group, 528
operating funds, 525–526
purpose of, 525
recording *vs.* reporting, 525
reserve funds, 526
and segregation of funds, 528
self-sustaining funds, 526
special funds, 526
types of funds, 525–527
futures markets, 401

G

GAAP
applicability of, 4–5
deviation from, 5
and non-profit organizations, 504, 514–515
and partnerships, 8
public *vs.* private corporations, 5–7
U.S., 16
general funds, 525–526
geographic areas, 364
goods and services
collective, 494
donated, 500–501
private, 493
goodwill, 81, 84, 131–132, 140, 153–155
government business organizations, 546
government non-business organizations, 547
government organizations
budgeted amounts, disclosure of, 558
capital assets, 555–556
cash *vs.* accrual accounting, 553
commitments, 558
compliance issues, 548–549
consolidated statements, 556–557
contingencies, 558
current liabilities, 558
expenditure-basis reporting, 554
expense-basis reporting, 554

financial statements, types of, 551–552
fund accounting, 556
interfund transfers, 559
liability measurement, 558
loans receivable, 559
long-term debt, 558
modified accrual, 553, 554
municipalities, 548
vs. non-profit organizations, 545–546
"Objectives of Financial Statements"
PS1400, 549, 550
ownership, 557
public sector reporting standards, 546–549
qualitative characteristics, 550–551
reporting entity, 556–557
reporting issues, 553–559
reporting objectives, 549–550
restricted assets and revenues, 557
governmental accounting, 491
governmental units, 491–492
group accounts, 96

H

hedging
accounting recommendations, 402
alternative recording methods, 405–407
asset exposure, 407
commitment, 410–412
currency swap, 401
defined, 400
derivative instruments, 401
designated hedges, 413–414
discount, 405
foreign currency options, 401
foreign operations, 445
forward rate, 405
imperfect, 414–415
implicit, 412–414, 437
interest rate swaps, 401
intervening year-end, 408–410
journal entry, 405
monetary liabilities, 407
monetary position, 402–410
non-monetary assets, limitation on use of, 414
perfect, 414
premium, 405

revenue stream, 413
second method of accounting, 406
self-sustaining foreign operation, 446
spot rate, 402
third method of accounting, 406–407
ways of, 401
hierarchy of objectives, 18
high-quality earnings, 10
historical rate, 431
hostile takeover, 40, 83
hyper-inflationary economies, 446

I

IAS, 17
immediate recognition
foreign currency transactions, 398
foreign operations, 440–441
imperfect hedges, 414–415
implicit hedges, 412–414, 437
income and retained earnings, statement of.
See statement of income and retained
earnings
income smoothing, 15–16
income tax allocation
business combinations, 80, 162
equity basis, 111
fair value increments, 162–164
post-acquisition, 162–165
temporary differences in business
combinations, 108–110
unrealized profits, 164–165
unrecognized tax loss carryforwards,
110–111
income tax deferral objective, 13–14
income tax expense, 373
indirect control, 37
indirect holdings, 157
inflation, 391, 446
intangible capital assets, and fair value
increments, 131–132
integral approach, 370, 371–372
integrated operation, 443, 444–445, 446–447
intercompany sale of long-term assets
capital assets, 239
capital leases, 239
direct amortization, 243–245
discontinued operations, 265

downstream sales of amortizable assets,
240–242
extraordinary items, 265
general concept, 239–240
losses, 239
subsequent sale of, 245
subsequent-year consolidations. See post-
acquisition consolidation
unrealized profit, 240–241
upstream sales of amortizable assets,
242–243
intercompany transactions
bonds. See bonds
long-term assets. See intercompany sale of
long-term assets
one-year post-acquisition consolidation,
130, 139–140
intercorporate investments
accounting choices, 3
beneficial interest, 37
bonds. See bonds
business combination. See business
combination
carrying value, 34
consolidation, 43–44
control, limitations on, 37–38
controlled subsidiaries, 35–40
cost-basis reporting, 42, 46–52
cost method, 58
defined, 33–34
discount/premium amortization, 34
equity-basis investments, 327
equity-basis reporting, 42–43, 52–56
hostile takeover, 40
income from portfolio investments, 40
indirect control, 37
joint ventures, 41–42, 43, 44
ownership levels, changes in, 317
parent-founded subsidiaries, 38–39
portfolio investments, 33, 34–35
preferred shares. See preferred shares
recording methods, 44–45
reporting methods, 42–45
sale of part of investment, 328–330
shares. See shares
significant influence, 37, 40–41, 42–43
special resolutions, 37–38
strategic, 35–42
subsidiary, purchase of, 39–40

temporary investments, 33
unconsolidated financial statements, 57–59
interest rate swaps, 401
interest rates, and inflation, 391
interfund transfers, 528–529, 559
interim reporting
  accounting policies, 369
  allocation problems, 370
  annual basis costs, 372
  common uses of, 367–368
  constructive obligation, 372
  contingencies, 373
  defined, 367
  discrete approach, 370, 371
  estimation errors, 370
  example, 374–380
  exception reporting principle, 369
  general principles of application, 368–369
  income tax expense, 373
  insurance costs, 370
  integral approach, 370, 371–372
  inventory, 372
  note disclosure, 372
  periodicity problem, 366–367, 370
  practical application, 372–373
International Accounting Standards
  business combination, 95
  designated hedges, 414
  fair values, determination of, 80
  interim statements, 368
  liabilities, valuation of, 399
  non-controlling interests, 199
  proportionate consolidation, 43
  segmented reporting, 359
  wholly-owned foreign subsidiaries, 16–17
international practices
  business combination, 94–95
  foreign operations, 443–444
  minority interests, 199
  parent-company approach, 189
  segmented reporting, 359
inventory
  fair value increments, 131
  interim reporting, 372
inventory valuation
  accounting estimates, 3
  expense recognition, 13
investment reporting methods, 42
isomorphism, 439

J
joint control, 42
joint ventures, 41–42, 43, 44, 188

L
letters patent, 38
line of business reporting. *See* segmented
  reporting
loan agreement, 11
Local Government Financial Reporting, 550
long-term liability group, 528
low-quality earnings, 10

M
maintenance tests, 11
major customers, 364
mark-to-market, 399
materialicity threshold, 370
maximization of earnings, 14–15
minimization of earnings, 14
minimum compliance, 16
minority interest, 40
minority shareholders, 38
modified accrual, 553, 554
monetary balances, 393–394
monetary/nonmonetary method, 433
motivations, 13
municipalities, 548

N
negative goodwill, 81, 99–100
net assets, 77
new-entity method, 89, 91–92, 184, 189
non-business organization
  corporations without share capital, 492
  defined, 491
  fund accounting. *See* fund accounting
  governmental accounting, 491
  governmental units, 491–492
  vs. non-profit organizations, 491, 492
non-consolidated financial statements, 57–59,
  140–144
non-controlling interest, 40
  acquisition adjustments, 201, 207–208

balance sheet, 198–199, 205–207
classification of, 199
cumulative adjustments, 207–208
current operations, 201–202, 208
date of acquisition consolidation, 190–193
direct approach, 190–192, 204–207
in earnings, 194–196
entity method, 184, 185, 189–190
fair-value purchase method, 183
new-entity method, 184
as new variable, 190
one-year post-acquisition consolidation, 193–202
parent-company approach, 184, 185, 188–189
parent-company extension approach, 189
pooling-of-interests approach, 184
proportionate consolidation approach, 184, 185–188
second subsequent year consolidation, 202–209
statement of income and retained earnings, 196–197, 204–205
worksheet approach, 192–193, 200–202, 207–209
non-profit organizations (NPOs)
board-designated funds, 499, 506
budgetary control accounts, 516
Canadian Cancer Society example, 517–521
capital assets, 498–499
cash *vs.* accrual basis of reporting, 496–497
characteristics of, 492–493
CICA Handbook reporting methods, 506–507
closed membership, 493
collection, 501–502
collective goods and services, 494
combined statements, 503–504
commonality of interest, 496
consolidated statements, 503–504
controlled organizations, 502
cost recovery basis, 496
costs, 494–495
deferral method, 507–509, 512–513, 515
defined, 492
depreciation accounting, 498–499
different "bottom line" of, 493–494
donated goods and services, 500–501
dual reporting approach, 504

efficiency, evaluation of, 515
encumbrance system, 516–517
endowment contribution, 506, 509, 511–512
expenditure-based reporting, 505–506
expense *vs.* expenditure reporting, 496–497
financial reporting objectives, 495–496
financial statements, 505
foundations, 502
fund accounting. *See* fund accounting
and GAAP, 504, 514–515
with GAAP constraint, 497
vs. governments, 545–546
input basis of reporting, 495–496
vs. non-business organization, 491
non-ownership, 493
open membership, 493
output basis of reporting, 496
pledges, 501
primary reporting issues, 496
private goods and services, 493
public-beneficial organizations, 494
reporting entity defined, 502
reporting options, 505–512
restricted contributions, 506, 507, 511
restricted fund, 499, 504
restricted fund method, 507, 509–512, 513–514
revenue, 494–495
segregation of resources, 499–500
self-beneficial organizations, 494
social agency, 492
stewardship, 514–515
stewardship reporting, 495
traditional reporting method, 505–506
true residuals, 494
unrestricted contribution, 506, 507, 511
non-wholly-owned subsidiaries. *See* non-controlling interest
nonmonetary balance, 396
not-for-profit organizations. *See* non-profit organizations (NPOs)
note disclosure, 155–156, 372

O

"Objectives of Financial Statements" PS1400, 549, 550

one-line consolidation, 144

see also equity method

one-transaction theory, 392

one-year post-acquisition consolidation

see also post-acquisition consolidation

acquisition adjustment, 137–139

adjustments, 129–130

balance sheet, 136–137

basic information, 129–130, 193–194

direct approach, 133–137, 194–199

discontinued operations, 144–145

dividend income, 136–137

vs. equity reporting, 142–144

extraordinary items, 144–145

fair value increments, amortization of, 131–132, 140, 162–164

goodwill, 131–132, 140

income tax allocation, 162–165

intangible capital assets, 131–132

intercompany transactions, 130, 139–140

inventory, 131

non-controlling interest, 193–202

operations adjustments, 139–140

statement of income and retained earnings, 133–135

tangible capital assets, 131

unrealized profits, 132–133, 164–165

worksheet approach, 137–140, 200–202

Ontario Securities Act, 367

open membership, 493

operating funds, 525–526

operating segments

identification of, 360–361

reportable, 361–362

operations adjustments, 139–140

oppression of minority shareholders, 38

ownership interest

changes in, 317

decreases in, 328–332

equity-basis investments, 327

increase in, 323–327

parent-company approach, 331

reallocation of costs, 324–325

sale of part of investment, 328–330

significant influence, 327–328

step purchases, 322–327

subsidiary's shares, issuance of, 330–332

P

par-value approach, 271–272

parent-company approach, 184, 185, 188–189, 331

parent-company extension approach, 189

parent corporations, 35

see also subsidiaries

parent-founded subsidiaries, 38–39, 156–157

partnerships, 8

perfect hedges, 414

performance evaluation objective, 11–12

periodic earnings measurement, 10

periodicity, 366–367, 370

perpetual debt, 400

plant fund, 526

pledges, 501

pooling-of-interests method, 89–91, 92–93, 184

portfolio investments, 33, 34–35, 40

post-acquisition consolidation

see also one-year post-acquisition consolidation; second subsequent year consolidation

acquisition adjustments, 256–258

balance sheet, 253–255

basic information, 247–249

conceptual approach, 246–247

cumulative operations adjustment, 258–261

direct approach, 250–255

equity-basis reporting, 261–263

problematic adjustments, 247

statement of income and retained earnings, 250–253

tax allocation, 162–165

worksheet approach, 256–261

pre-determined standard rate, 395

preferred shares

dividends, treatment of, 320

investment in, 320

ownership interest, effect on, 318–320

premium, 405

preparers, 12

see also financial reporting objectives

private corporations, 5–7

private goods and services, 493

products, and enterprise-wide disclosures, 363

professional judgement, 2–3

accounting estimates, 3

accounting policy choices, 2–3

advanced accounting topics, 3–4

disclosure decisions, 3
  translation method, selection of, 444
  valuation of shares, 78, 79
profit, defined, 362
profit sharing, 42
proportionate consolidation, 43, 44, 184, 185–188
public-beneficial organizations, 494
public corporations, 5–7
Public Sector Accounting and Auditing Board, 546–547
Public Sector Accounting Board, 547
public sector reporting standards, 546–549
public service sector. *See* non-profit organizations (NPOs)
public utilities, 7
purchase method, 89, 91, 92–94
purchase price discrepancy, 89
purchasing power parity (PPP), 391, 437
push-down accounting, 102–104

Q

qualified audit opinion, 6

R

recording methods, 44–45
regulated companies, and financial reporting objectives, 16
regulatory accounting policies (RAP), 8
reportable segments, 361–362
reporting currency, 390
representational faithfulness, 439
reserve funds, 526
restricted contributions, 506, 507, 511
restricted fund, 499, 504
restricted fund method, 507, 509–512, 513–514
restricted shares
  coattail provision, 321
  control, 321
  defined, 320
  motivation for issuance of, 320, 321
  ownership, percentage of, 321–322
revenue requirements, 7
reverse takeover, 86
revolving funds, 526

S

second subsequent year consolidation
  see also post-acquisition consolidation
  acquisition adjustments, 150–152
  balance sheet, 148–150
  basic information, 145
  cost of sales, 147
  cumulative adjustments, 150–152
  current operations, 152–153
  direct approach, 145–150, 204–207
  fair value increments, amortization of, 162–164
  income tax allocation, 162–165
  non-controlling interest, 202–209
  unrealized profits, 164–165
  worksheet approach, 150–153, 207–209
secondary instruments, 401
Securities and Exchange Commission (SEC), and push-down accounting, 103
segmented reporting
  applicability, 359–360
  consistency requirement, 362
  defined, 359
  disclosure recommendations, 360
  enterprise-wide disclosures, 363–364
  examples of, 365–366
  information to be reported, 363
  international requirements, 359
  net operating income measure, 366
  operating segments, 360–363
  profit, defined, 362
  reportable, 361–362
  vertical integration, 361
segregation of funds, 528
segregation of resources, 499–500
self-beneficial organizations, 494
self-sustaining foreign operation, 443–444, 445–446, 447
self-sustaining funds, 526
"Senior Government Reporting Model," 551
separate-entity financial statements, 32, 52–55, 128–129
separate-period approach. *See* discrete approach
services, and enterprise-wide disclosures, 363
shareholders, minority, 38
shareholders' agreement, 11, 36, 42
shares
  and control, 84

current cash equivalent, 90–91
exchange of, 85–88
preferred. *See* preferred shares
purchase reasons, 83–85
restricted. *See* restricted shares
statutory amalgamation, 86
of subsidiary, 330–332
valuation of, 78–79
significant influence, 37, 40–41, 327–328
social agency, 492
special funds, 526
special purpose reports, 7
special resolutions, 37–38
spot rate, 402
spreadsheet approach. *See* worksheet
   approach
statement of income and retained earnings
   non-controlling interest, 196–197, 204–205
   one-year post-acquisition consolidation,
      133–135
   post-acquisition consolidation, 250–253
   second subsequent year consolidation,
      145–148
statutory amalgamation, 86
step acquisitions. *See* step purchases
step purchases, 317, 322–327
stewardship, 514–515
stewardship reporting, 495
subsidiaries
   bonds of parent, 273
   CICA definition, 35, 36
   consolidation, 43–44
   controlled, 35–36, 35–40
   corporate restructuring, 94
   discontinued operations, 144, 265
   downstream sales, 132
   equity pick-up, 55
   extraordinary items, 144, 265
   foreign. *See* wholly-owned foreign
      subsidiaries
   indirect holdings, 157
   non-consolidated, 140–144
   non-controlling interest. *See* non-controlling
      interest
   non-wholly-owned. *See* non-controlling
      interest
   oppression of minority shareholders, 38
   parent, defined, 35
   parent-founded, 38–39, 156–157

purchase of, 39–40, 88
reporting investments in, 42–45
shares, issuance of, 330–332
significantly influenced, 42–43
special resolutions, 37–38

T
tailored accounting policies (TAP), 8
tangible capital assets, 131
tax deferral. *See* income tax deferral objective
tax minimization. *See* income tax deferral
   objective
temporal method, 430–433, 433–434, 444, 446,
   450–454
temporary investments, 33
third sector organizations. *See* non-profit
   organizations (NPOs)
translation methods
   current/noncurrent method, 436–437
   current-rate method, 435–436
   monetary/nonmonetary method, 433
   and professional judgement, 444
   summary of, 437–438
   temporal method, 430–433, 433–434
trust funds, 527
two-transaction theory, 392

U
unconsolidated financial statements. *See* non-
   consolidated financial statements
unrealized profits, 132–133, 164–165
unremitted earnings, 53
unrestricted contribution, 506, 507, 511
upstream sales of amortizable assets, 242–243
U.S. GAAP, and wholly-owned foreign
   subsidiaries, 16
user objectives. *See* financial reporting
   objectives

V
vertical integration, 361
volunteer organizations. *See* non-profit
   organizations (NPOs)
voting control, 94

W

wholly-owned foreign subsidiaries
    financial reporting objectives, 16–17
    International Accounting Standards, 17
    U.S., 16
worksheet approach
    business combination, 97–99
    consolidation, 48, 50–52, 97–99

    non-controlling interest, 192–193, 200–202,
       207–209
one-year post-acquisition consolidation,
    137–140, 200–202
post-acquisition consolidation, 256–261
second subsequent year consolidation,
    150–153, 207–209